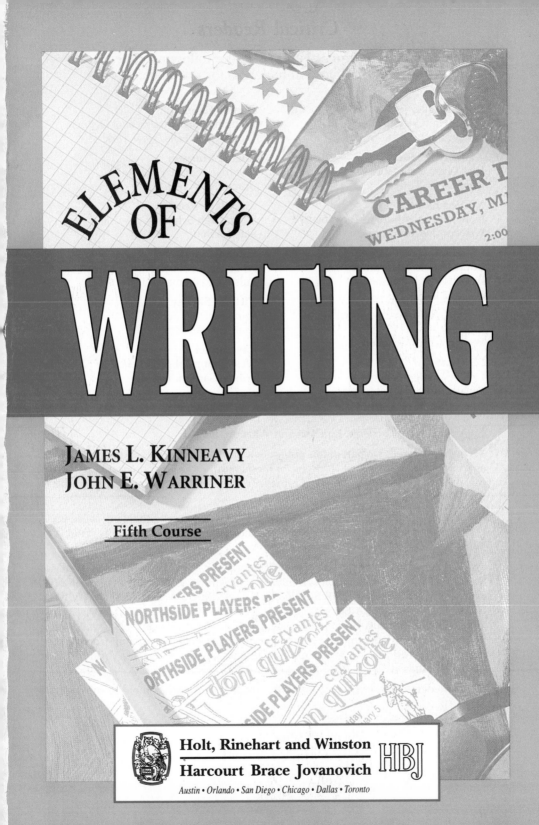

ELEMENTS OF
WRITING

JAMES L. KINNEAVY
JOHN E. WARRINER

Fifth Course

Holt, Rinehart and Winston

Harcourt Brace Jovanovich HBJ

Austin • Orlando • San Diego • Chicago • Dallas • Toronto

Critical Readers

Grateful acknowledgment is made to the following critical readers who reviewed pre-publication materials for this book:

Donald Baker
Peoria High School
Peoria, Illinois

Anthony Buckley
East Texas State University
Commerce, Texas

Norbert Elliot
New Jersey Institute of Technology
Newark, New Jersey

David England
Louisiana State University
Baton Rouge, Louisiana

Elaine A. Espindle
Peabody Veterans Memorial High
 School
Peabody, Massachusetts

Pat Graff
La Cueva High School
Albuquerque, New Mexico

Dennis Hannon
Wappingers Central School District
Wappingers Falls, New York

Ronald Murison
Riverdale Country School
Bronx, New York

Mary Jane Reed
Solon High School
Solon, Ohio

Linda E. Sanders
Jenks High School
Tulsa, Oklahoma

Victoria Skelley
Fairview High School
Cullman, Alabama

Kay Tanner
West Orange High School
Winter Garden, Florida

Printed in the United States of America

ISBN 0–03–047148–6

1 2 3 4 5 6 7 8 9 062 95 94 93 92

James L. Kinneavy, the Jane and Roland Blumberg Centennial Professor of English at The University of Texas at Austin, directed the development and writing of the composition strand in the program. He is the author of *A Theory of Discourse* and coauthor of *Writing in the Liberal Arts Tradition*. Professor Kinneavy is a leader in the field of rhetoric and composition and a respected educator whose teaching experience spans all levels—elementary, secondary, and college. He has continually been concerned with teaching writing to high school students.

John E. Warriner developed the organizational structure for the Handbook of Grammar, Usage, and Mechanics in the book. He coauthored the *English Workshop* series, was general editor of the *Composition: Models and Exercises* series, and editor of *Short Stories: Characters in Conflict*. He taught English for thirty-two years in junior and senior high school and college.

Writers and Editors

John Algeo is Professor of English at the University of Georgia. He is coauthor with Thomas Pyles of *The Origins and Development of the English Language.*

Ellen Ashdown has a Ph.D. in English from the University of Florida. She has taught composition and literature at the college level. She is a professional writer of educational materials and has published articles and reviews on education and art.

John Roberts has an M.A. in Education from the University of Kentucky. He has taught English in secondary school. He is an editor and a writer of educational materials in literature, grammar, and composition.

Alice M. Sohn has a Ph.D. in English Education from Florida State University. She has taught English in middle school, secondary school, and college. She has been a writer and editor of educational materials in language arts for twelve years.

Carolyn Calhoun Walter has an M.A.T. in English Education from the University of Chicago. She has taught English in grades nine through twelve. She is a professional writer and editor of educational materials in composition and literature.

Glenda A. Zumwalt has an Ed.D. in Teaching Composition and Rhetoric from East Texas State University. She teaches composition at Southeastern Oklahoma State University. She is a writer of educational materials in composition and literature.

Acknowledgments

We wish to thank the following teachers who participated in field testing of pre-publication materials for this series:

Susan Almand-Myers
Meadow Park Intermediate School
Beaverton, Oregon

Theresa L. Bagwell
Naylor Middle School
Tucson, Arizona

Ruth Bird
Freeport High School
Sarver, Pennsylvania

Joan M. Brooks
Central Junior High School
Guymon, Oklahoma

Candice C. Bush
J. D. Smith Junior High School
N. Las Vegas, Nevada

Mary Jane Childs
Moore West Junior High School
Oklahoma City, Oklahoma

Brian Christensen
Valley High School
West Des Moines, Iowa

Lenise Christopher
Western High School
Las Vegas, Nevada

Mary Ann Crawford
Ruskin Senior High School
Kansas City, Missouri

Linda Dancy
Greenwood Lakes Middle School
Lake Mary, Florida

Elaine A. Espindle
Peabody Veterans Memorial High
   School
Peabody, Massachusetts

Joan Justice
North Middle School
O'Fallon, Missouri

Beverly Kahwaty
Pueblo High School
Tucson, Arizona

Lamont Leon
Van Buren Junior High School
Tampa, Florida

Susan Lusch
Fort Zumwalt South High School
St. Peters, Missouri

Michele K. Lyall
Rhodes Junior High School
Mesa, Arizona

Belinda Manard
McKinley Senior High School
Canton, Ohio

Nathan Masterson
Peabody Veterans Memorial
   High School
Peabody, Massachusetts

Marianne Mayer
Swope Middle School
Reno, Nevada

Penne Parker
Greenwood Lakes Middle School
Lake Mary, Florida

Amy Ribble
Gretna Junior-Senior High School
Gretna, Nebraska

Kathleen R. St. Clair
Western High School
Las Vegas, Nevada

Carla Sankovich
Billinghurst Middle School
Reno, Nevada

Sheila Shaffer
Cholla Middle School
Phoenix, Arizona

Joann Smith
Lehman Junior High School
Canton, Ohio

Margie Stevens
Raytown Middle School
Raytown, Missouri

Mary Webster
Central Junior High School
Guymon, Oklahoma

Susan M. Yentz
Oviedo High School
Oviedo, Florida

Contents in Brief

Table of Contents

Montana Historical Society, Helena.

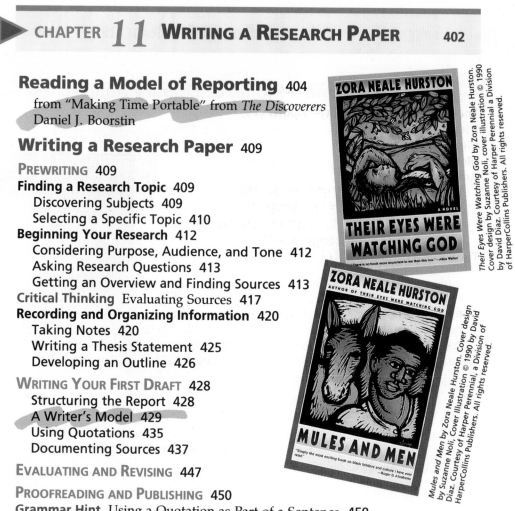

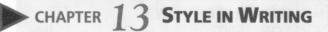

Montana Historical Society, Helena

CHAPTER **16** **IMPROVING SENTENCE STYLE**   541

Revising for Variety 541

Varying Sentence Beginnings 542
Varying Sentence Structure 545

Revising to Reduce Wordiness 546

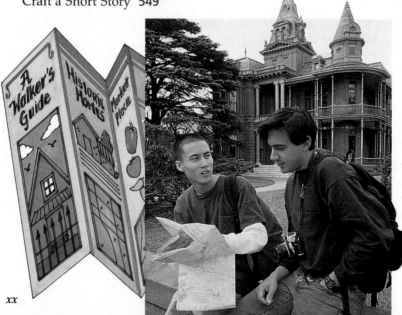

PART TWO HANDBOOK

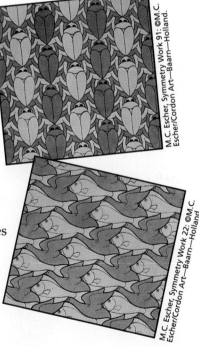

M. C. Escher, Symmetry Work 91: ©M.C.
Escher/Cordon Art—Baarn—Holland.

M. C. Escher, Symmetry Work 22: ©M. C.
Escher/Cordon Art—Baarn—Holland.

Kinds of Phrases and Their Functions

Carl Moon (1905)/From the Collection of Kurt Koegler

Subject and Verb, Pronoun and Antecedent

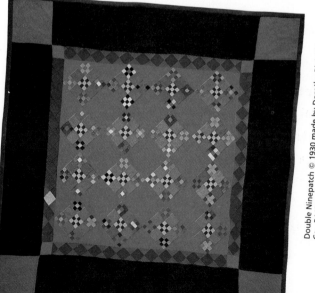

Double Ninepatch © 1930 made by Dorothy Bieler, Lancaster Co., PA/Courtesy Esprit Quilt Collection, San Francisco.

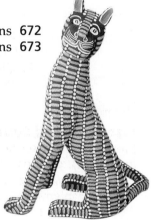

Other Marks of Punctuation

Improving Your Spelling

Fiction

Douglas Adams, *Life, The Universe and Everything*

Ray Bradbury, *The Toynbee Convector*

Lewis Carroll, *Through the Looking-Glass*

James Fenimore Cooper, *The Deerslayer*

Louis Dollarhide, "The Gift," *The Georgia Review*

Michael Dorris, *A Yellow Raft in Blue Water*

Shirley Ann Grau, "The Land and the Water," *The Wind Shifting West*

Zora Neale Hurston, *Jonah's Gourd Vine*

Cynthia Kadohata, *The Floating World*

Stanisław Lem, "The Sixth Sally," *The Cyberiad: Fables for the Cybernetic Age*

David Long, "Blue Spruce," *The New Yorker*

Ruthanne Lum McCunn, *Thousand Pieces of Gold*

Mike Montgomery, *It Was a Dark and Stormy Night: The Best(?) from the Bulwer-Lytton Contest*

Leslie Norris, "A Flight of Geese," *The Girl from Cardigan*

Katherine Anne Porter, "The Jilting of Granny Weatherall," *Flowering Judas and Other Stories*

V. S. Pritchett, "The Wheelbarrow," *Selected Stories*

John Steinbeck, "Flight," *The Long Valley*

Hyemeyohsts Storm, *Seven Arrows*

Amy Tan, *The Joy Luck Club*

Sabine Ulibarrí, "My Wonder Horse," *Tierra Amarilla: Stories of New Mexico*

Kurt Vonnegut, Jr., "Tom Edison's Shaggy Dog," *Welcome to the Monkey House*

Nonfiction

Tom and Jane D. Allen, *Dinosaur Days in Texas*

Maya Angelou, "Graduation," *I Know Why the Caged Bird Sings*

Isaac Asimov, "Learning Science," *The Tyrannosaurus Prescription and 100 Other Essays*

Francis Bacon, "Idols of the Mind," *Novum Organum*

Dave Barry, "Car-Buying: The Compleat Guide," *The Washington Post Magazine*

Joan Benoit with Sally Baker, *Running Tide*

"Black, Blue and Gray: The Other Civil War," *Ebony*

Mary Blocksma, "Pencils," *Reading the Numbers*

Daniel J. Boorstin, "Making Time Portable," *The Discoverers*

Mark Coleman, review of *Christgau's Record Guide: Rock Albums of the '80's*, *Rolling Stone*

Alistair Cooke, *Alistair Cooke's America*

Edward Corsi, "I Behold America," *In the Shadow of Liberty*

James West Davidson, "The Frontier Kitchen of the Plains," *Nation of Nations: A Narrative History of the American Republic*

Annie Dillard, *Pilgrim at Tinker Creek*

W.E.B. Du Bois, "Galileo Galilei," *The Education of Black People: Ten Critiques 1906–1960*

Roger Ebert, review "Star Wars," *Roger Ebert's Movie Home Companion*

Paul R. Ehrlich, David S. Dobkin, Darryl Wheye, "Visual Displays," *The Birder's Handbook*

"Eliot Porter," *Life*

Richard P. Feynmann, "The Making of a Scientist," *What Do You Care What Other People Think?*

Adrian Fisher & Georg Gerster, *Labyrinth: Solving the Riddle of the Maze*

Janet Frame, "You Are Now Entering the Human Heart," *The New Yorker*

Ernesto Galarza, *Barrio Boy*

Andrew García, *Tough Trip Through Paradise*

Mary Hager, et al., "'Dances With Garbage,'" *Newsweek*

Robert E. Hemenway, *Zora Neale Hurston: A Literary Biography*

Patrick Henry, "Speech in the Virginia Convention, 1775"

Alton Hornsby, *The Black Almanac*

Langston Hughes, *I Wonder as I Wander*

Jesse Jackson, *Jesse Jackson: Still Fighting for the Dream*

Andy Jacobs, Jr., "Replace 'The Star-Spangled Banner,'" *USA Today*

Chief Joseph, "An Indian's View of Indian Affairs," *Red & White: Indian Views of the White Man*

Linda Kanamine, "Wyoming Dinosaur Find May Be a Fossil First," *USA Today*

Jean Kerr, *Please Don't Eat the Daisies*

Henry Kisor, *What's That Pig Outdoors? A Memoir of Deafness*

James Kotsilibas-Davis, "Sands of Time," *Travel-Holiday*

John Lahr, "Introduction," *Baby, That Was Rock and Roll*

William Langewiesche, "The World In Its Extreme," *The Atlantic*

PART ONE

WRITING

WHERE'S THE ACTION?

James L. Kinneavy

The ocean seems to stretch forever. Whether a sheet of shimmering blue or a tangle of fierce waves, its surface gives no hint of what lies below. We don't see the treasures, the eerie life forms, the **action** lurking beneath the surface.

Away from the ocean, we are still mesmerized by surface features. We judge people by the way they look. We judge a house by its front door, a neighborhood by its streets, and the art of communication by what we see and hear via electronic media.

And the electronic media surround us. Politicians campaign and advertisers push their products on radio and television; CDs, audio and video cassettes, radio, and television entertain us; and telephones and computers satisfy our other information needs.

On the surface of our world, written words hardly seem a ripple; writing is a thing of the past. We get what we need by watching, listening, speaking, and pushing buttons. Isn't that where the action is? Hasn't writing lost its power?

The Action Below the Surface

You know that writing hasn't lost *all* of its power; after all, here you sit, reading a book about writing. But, you may well think that written words aren't very important in your life, at least your life outside of school. On the surface, the action seems to be elsewhere.

But peer through your diving mask and you'll see where the action is. On the surface, you see the actors, but behind the scenes scriptwriters write the dialogue and stage directions that the director, actors, and countless crew members work from. On television, you see the politicians, but they are supported by staffers who write and edit their speeches. TV anchors deliver news reports written by researchers and reporters; and those funny, powerful commercials are created from scripts hammered out by copywriters and art directors.

Even forms of communication that seem nonverbal are based on writing that lurks below the surface. Someone wrote a computer program for stock market reports and the year's most popular video game; someone wrote a playbook for the Super Bowl champions; and someone wrote a job training manual for workers in a factory.

Yes, much of the action is below the surface and much of it is dependent on writing. And if you don't have strong writing skills, you won't be part of the action.

To live life completely—not just as an observer but as an active participant—you need to be able to write effectively. Whether you are expressing your emotions and thoughts, sharing your ideas and knowledge, convincing others to share your opinions, or expressing your own creativity, writing is where the action is. Its power is yours to command.

The Writer's Power

It doesn't matter whether you are writing an opera, a business memo, or a letter to your brother, you are exercising a power that is common to all writers and speakers. That power, the power of communication, is basically very simple. Communication requires only the *writer*, a *subject,* (something to say), an *audience* (someone to say it to), and *language* (a way to say it). It helps to think of these elements in terms of a communications triangle with language—both written and spoken—at its very center.

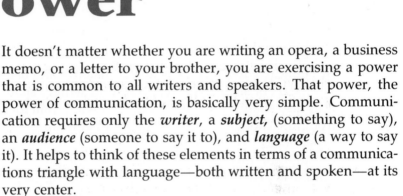

How Writers Communicate

The Writing Process

By being able to affect the action both above and below the surface, writers share a power. But if all writers share a power, they also share a *process:* a way of moving from idea to action; from first thought to first words to final writing. As your own experiences may show, there's no right or wrong way to go through the process. Each writer uses the process differently, but most writers work through the same basic steps.

Prewriting	Thinking and planning: thinking about your purpose and audience; deciding what to write about; developing ideas and gathering details; creating a plan for presenting ideas
Writing	Writing a first draft: expressing ideas and details in sentences and paragraphs; following a writing plan; incorporating new ideas
Evaluating and Revising	Reviewing the draft: deciding what works and what doesn't; changing the draft to improve it
Proofreading and Publishing	Finding and correcting mistakes: writing or printing out a final copy; sharing the writing with an audience

Why Writers Communicate

The Aims of Writing

Whether writing a fast-paced TV script, a powerful political speech, or a private diary, every writer has a reason for writing—a *purpose,* an *aim.* And when you look at all of those reasons and see how they're alike and different, you'll find that every piece of writing has one of four basic *aims,* or purposes.

Expository	**Informative:** Writers may want to give facts and information. **Explanatory:** They may want to explain something, using evidence. **Exploratory:** They may want to investigate complex ideas or find solutions to problems.
Persuasive	Sometimes writers want to convince people to accept an idea or take action.
Self-Expressive	Writers may want to express personal feelings and thoughts, for themselves alone or for others.
Literary	Sometimes writers want to create imaginative works, such as films, stories, poems, novels, and plays.

Next you'll read four pieces of writing, one for each aim. All four are on the same topic and illustrate how writers participate in the action. What does each writer want to accomplish?

EXPOSITORY WRITING

American Immigration:
Always Constant, Always Changing

Except for Native Americans, every person in the United States descends from an immigrant. Yet immigration has not been a single and unbroken stream since the first Europeans arrived. From only a brief overview, it's clear that immigration to the United States, while continuous, has constantly changed, with U.S. attitudes and policies toward immigrants also changing.

Before 1880, most immigrants came from western and northern Europe, followed by southern and eastern Europeans in the 1890s. By 1880, 75,000 Chinese immigrants lived in California, and by 1900, about 80,000 Mexicans lived in the Southwest. Between 1880 and 1920, over twenty-three million immigrants had arrived to begin new lives in America.

This wave ended in 1921 when Congress sharply limited annual immigration and established quotas by nationality, favoring northern Europeans. Asian immigrants were banned altogether, and Mexicans were admitted to work but not allowed to become citizens. Their labor was wanted, but as immigration after World War I rose to one million per year, opinion to restrict non-white groups mounted.

It was not until 1965 that a "Great Society" initiative abolished the national origins system, ended restrictions on Asian immigration, and enacted new provisions for accepting political refugees. . . .

READER'S RESPONSE

1. What do the words *immigrant* and *America* mean to you personally? Freewrite about one or both in your journal.
2. The excerpt from this report ends with 1965. What factual information about world events since 1965 and U.S. population today would you expect to find in the remainder of the report?

EXPRESSIVE WRITING

April 17, 1912

Today was the most exciting—and mos...
...of my life. We arrived

April 17, 1912—Today was the most exciting and frightening day of my life. We arrived in America! The boat trip over was a nightmare. So dirty, terrible food, many sick people crowded into so little space. The sun was just coming up when Mama woke me. She was very excited. We went up on deck and I saw the beautiful Statue of Liberty, her torch burning brightly, welcoming us majestically. And the "skyscrapers"! I could not believe my eyes.

Our first steps in America were onto Ellis Island. We had name tags pinned to our clothes. Papa clutched our ID papers. We awaited our turns to see the doctors, Papa very anxious. The worst thing that could happen was to have the doctor write a chalk letter on your clothes. That meant you had a disease, and you would be detained, maybe sent back home. We all made it through.

Then we were led to a huge three-stories-high hall— giant half-moon windows and globed chandeliers and a tiled ceiling. We joined many people on the long rows of wooden benches. Three hours later we were called to the inspector's desk. What's your name? age? Where will you live? Do you have work waiting for you? Do you have any money? Papa's answers must have been right—we were told we could stay in the United States. Then the train, New Jersey, Uncle Alfred's house (and bakery), my cousins. It is more than I can write tonight. I am bursting with—*everything*.

READER'S RESPONSE

1. Do you think an immigrant arriving in New York today would share these feelings? What might be the same or different? Why?
2. Is this writer writing only for himself or possibly for others? And *why* do you think he is writing? Explain.

PERSUASIVE WRITING

Dear Kim:

I hear your parents are trying to decide upon coming to the United States. At last! I am praying they will do it. How can we help to make up their minds?

Of course you know I like my new life very much--movies, pizza. There is <u>so much</u>. Stores are filled with food (our country's food, too), clothes, everything you'd want. Your parents won't have to search far for what they need.

And they will not feel alone. Many people from our homeland live nearby. My father knows the resettlement group that will help your father find work. You will first live with us. That way it will not be so shocking!

Your parents are probably scared too about not knowing the language and about your school. Yes, learning to speak is hard. But I take special classes, and in less than two years, I hear and read almost everything well and even speak English out of school.

I will not say it is easy to leave a country you have loved. I do not always feel welcome here, and I know my parents are more comfortable keeping to our group. But they do not regret their choice and do not want to give up freedoms after a life of war and fear. Truly, it is every day more our home.

Tell them! Tell them! May my words ease their fears and bring you to us soon.

Your friend,
Li

READER'S RESPONSE

1. What if Kim himself is not absolutely sure about coming to the United States? Do you think Li's letter would convince *him*? Do you think he might have other worries or questions? Explain.
2. Does Li's persuasion depend on logical reasoning and facts, appeals to emotion, or a combination of the two?

LITERARY WRITING

This poem is inscribed on the base of the Statue of Liberty.

THE NEW
COLOSSUS

BY EMMA LAZARUS

Not like the brazen giant of Greek fame,
　　With conquering limbs astride from land to land;
　　Here at our sea-washed, sunset gates shall stand
A mighty woman with a torch, whose flame
Is the imprisoned lightning, and her name
　　Mother of Exiles. From her beacon-hand
　　Glows world-wide welcome; her mild eyes command
The air-bridged harbor that twin cities frame.
"Keep, ancient lands, your storied pomp!" cries she
　　With silent lips. "Give me your tired, your poor,
Your huddled masses yearning to breathe free,
　　The wretched refuse of your teeming shore.
Send these, the homeless, tempest-tost to me,
　　I lift my lamp beside the golden door!"

READER'S RESPONSE

1. A few words from this poem are quoted frequently: " 'Give me your tired, your poor, / Your huddled masses yearning to breathe free. . . .' " How do these words make you feel? Why is it significant that these words greeted immigrants?
2. When a writer's aim is to create literature, the choice of words—language itself—is extremely important. What examples can you find in this poem that illustrate Emma Lazarus's concern for language—for example, a musical effect or an unusual image?

Writing and Thinking Activities

1. Look over the four models again, and then meet with two or three classmates to discuss these questions about the writers' aims.
   a. Which writer wants primarily to persuade?
   b. Which one uses facts and details to inform readers about something?
   c. Which one uses words in a way that is different from ordinary speech?
   d. Which one wrote for him- or herself, to express personal thoughts, feelings, and experiences?

2. What aims do you have when you write? Do you use some more than others? Keep track of how you communicate during a typical day. Jot down all your uses of language: writing, reading, speaking, and listening. Notice how much of your communication is informative, persuasive, self-expressive, or creative. Then get together with two or three classmates to discuss what you've learned about your own communication patterns.

3. What are the aims of people who try to communicate with you? For forty-eight hours, keep track of the reasons people are communicating with you. Include oral discussion and comments, telephone calls, television, radio, as well as anything you read for school or for pleasure. Keep a little notebook and jot down the type of communication and its purpose, for example, "TV ad, to persuade; phone call, to inform." At the end of the forty-eight hours, do a tally and allocate percentages to each of the four aims. Then share what you've learned with your classmates, attempting to discover whether you all experienced similar patterns.

4. Emma Lazarus's poem, "The New Colossus," is obviously creative writing. So are novels, short stories, and plays. But are these the only kinds of writing that can be called creative? Do you see creativity of language or thought in any of the other models? Think of any nonliterary writing you've done—a book report, science report, journal entry—that you consider creative in some way, and explain why.

1 WRITING AND THINKING

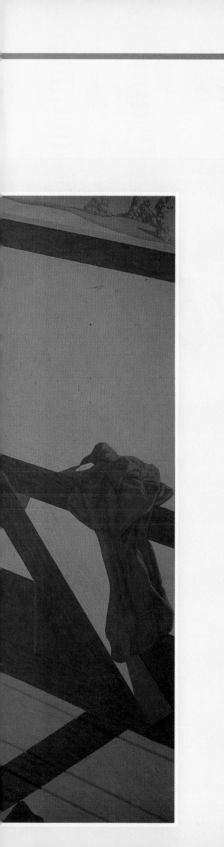

Looking at the Process

Consider this: Perhaps the title of this chapter should really be WRITINGANDTHINKING. When you write, what comes out on the paper just can't be separated from what goes on in your head. Analyzing, researching, sifting notes, even daydreaming: They're all part of the writing **process.**

Writing and You.   A good way to see how these two interact is to look at your personal writing and thinking process. Do you play with different ideas before settling on a topic? When you're drafting, do you mentally weigh each word? Or do you spit out sentences so that your thoughts keep flowing? Have you ever been *surprised* by what you actually write? Probably you have. Because writing is thinking, writing is discovery—for each writer in a different way.

As You Read.   A young girl once asked poet Pat Mora why she writes. As you read Mora's answer, notice what she believes that writing can both discover and *do*.

Jack Beal, *Drawing* (1974). Oil on canvas, 60" × 68". Courtesy of the Frumkin/Adams Gallery, New York.

Why I am a Writer

by Pat Mora

like people. I like long, slow lunches with my friends. I like to dance. I'm no hermit, and I'm not shy. So why do I sit with my tablet and pen and mutter to myself?

There are many answers. I write because I am a reader. I want to give to others what writers have given me, a chance to hear the voices of people I will never meet. Even if I met these authors, I wouldn't hear what I hear alone with the page—words carefully chosen, woven into a piece unlike any other, enjoyed by me in a way no other person will enjoy them. I love the privateness of writing and reading.

I write because I am curious. I am curious about me. Writing is a way of finding out how I feel about anything and everything. Now that I've left the desert where I grew up, for example, I'm discovering how it feels to walk on spongy autumn leaves and to watch snow drifting up on a strong wind. I notice what's around me in a special way because I am a writer. I notice my world more, and then I talk to myself about it on paper. Writing is a way of saving my feelings.

I write because I believe that Hispanics need to take their rightful place in American literature. We need to be published and to be studied in schools and colleges so that the stories and ideas of our people won't quietly disappear. Although I am happy when I finish the draft of a poem or story, I always wish that I wrote better, that I could bring more honor and attention to the *abuelitas*—grandmothers—I write about. That mix of sadness and pleasure frequently occurs in a writer's life.

> "I write because I am curious. I am curious about me."

Although we don't discuss it often because it is depressing, my people have been and sometimes still are viewed as inferior. We have all been hurt by someone who said, "You're not like us; you're not one of us. Speaking Spanish is odd; your family looks funny." Some of us decide we don't want to be different; we don't want to be part of a group that is often described as poor and uneducated. I spoke Spanish at home to my grandmother and aunt, but I didn't always want my friends at school to know that I spoke Spanish. And I didn't like myself for feeling that way. I sensed it was wrong, but I didn't know why. Now I know.

I know that the society we live in affects us. It is not easy to learn to disregard the unimportant things about people—the car they drive, the house they live in, the color of their skin, the language they speak at home. It takes courage to face the fact that we all have ten toes, get sleepy at night, get scared in the dark. Some families, some cities, some states, and even some countries foolishly convince themselves that they are better than others. Then they teach their children this ugly lie. It is like a weed with burrs and stickers that prick people.

How are young people who are Hispanic or members of an ethnic group supposed to feel about themselves? Some are proud of their cultural roots. But television commercials are busy trying to convince us that our cars, clothes, and even our families aren't good enough. It is so hard to be yourself, your many interesting selves, because billboards and magazine ads tell you that being beautiful is being thin, blond, and rich, rich, rich. No wonder we don't always like ourselves when we look in the mirror.

So I write to try to correct these images of worth. I take pride in being a Hispanic writer. I will continue to write and to struggle to say what no other writer can say in quite the same way.

"I write because I believe that Hispanics need to take their rightful place in American literature."

READER'S RESPONSE

1. Pat Mora says she writes because she loves the "privateness" of writing and reading, but another reason is a very public one: to "correct . . . images of worth" for Hispanics. Is this a contradiction? Can an extremely personal experience like reading have social consequences? Say what you think, and use examples from your own life if you can.

2. Mora also says writing is a way of "saving" new feelings—like her discovery of snow after a life in the desert. What things in your life surprised you when you first saw or experienced them? Recapture one of your surprising experiences in a brief journal entry.

3. Mora believes writers frequently feel a "mix of sadness and pleasure." What mix of feelings has a piece of writing caused you (delight and tear-out-your-hair? fear and then pride?), and why?

LOOKING AHEAD

This chapter will take you through a general approach to writing that you can apply to many different types of writing. You'll learn some specific writing techniques and explore how they can work for you. As you read and experiment, remember that

- writing and thinking are inseparable
- the writing process isn't an unchanging set of steps: it's both flexible and personal
- your topic, purpose, and audience are connected: they shape and influence each other

Aim—The "Why" of Writing

Consider the types of writing you see and hear about almost every day—ads, postcards, school essays, love letters, protest signs, movie scripts. With all the different writing everywhere around you, you would think the purposes for writing are limitless. Well, yes and no.

It's true that every writer writes for a very specific reason— for example, to say "I love you" to a heartthrob. But even though each writer has a particular intent for writing, each specific reason will fall within four basic purposes for all writing.

WHY PEOPLE WRITE	
To express themselves	To get to know themselves better; to find some kind of meaning in their own lives
To inform, to explain, or to explore	To give other people information that they need or want; to provide an explanation; to explore an idea or problem
To persuade	To convince other people either to do something or believe something they'd like
To create literary works	To be creative with language; to say something in a unique way

Probably everything written has one of these purposes, but it's also true that much writing has a combination of purposes. Someone may write about a strong opinion both to persuade others and to know her own values better. Someone may write a story both to be creative and to share special knowledge.

Your personal message will never be exactly the same as anyone else's, but you will share with all other writers the essential "why" of writing.

Process—The "How" of Writing

A *piece* of writing might be simply defined as words on some surface. But the *process* of writing always involves more than the typing, scratching, or crayoning of those words. Writing moves in stages (you don't go from idea to finished paper in one flash), and writing requires thinking (sometimes you may spend more time thinking than setting down the words).

In this chapter you'll have to think and write, because it's really impossible to separate the two. And you'll be working through the basic stages of the writing process, as shown in the diagram that follows. But note what the diagram shows: The process isn't a straight line. As a writer, you always have, and need, the freedom to jump forward, go back, or start over again.

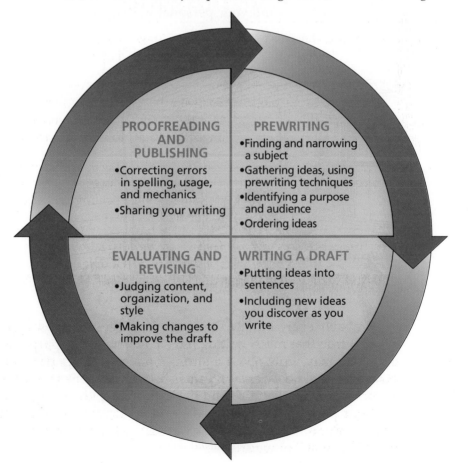

PROOFREADING AND PUBLISHING
- Correcting errors in spelling, usage, and mechanics
- Sharing your writing

PREWRITING
- Finding and narrowing a subject
- Gathering ideas, using prewriting techniques
- Identifying a purpose and audience
- Ordering ideas

EVALUATING AND REVISING
- Judging content, organization, and style
- Making changes to improve the draft

WRITING A DRAFT
- Putting ideas into sentences
- Including new ideas you discover as you write

Prewriting

Finding Ideas for Writing

Writing is built on ideas. The blank page is a terror to many writers, even professional writers, not because they lack the words but because they lack a workable idea. Writing starts with getting an idea and collecting information about it.

"Easily said," you may be thinking, "not so easily done." Well, there are practical helps: prewriting techniques for stirring up ideas. The following chart shows several. And these techniques aren't closed little boxes. You can use a combination of techniques for the same assignment. You may get an idea for a paper from your **writer's journal** and then use **imagining** to explore it and get started. You'll discover which techniques work for the task and your personal writing approach.

"Write about dogs!"

Drawing by Booth; © 1976 The New Yorker Magazine, Inc.

PREWRITING TECHNIQUES		
Writer's Journal	Recording personal experiences, perceptions, and ideas	Pages 23–24
Freewriting	Writing for a few minutes about whatever comes to mind	Pages 24–25
Brainstorming	Listing ideas (alone or with others) as quickly as they occur	Pages 25–26
Clustering	Drawing lines and circles to show connections between ideas	Page 26
Asking Questions	Using the news reporter's *5W-How?* questions: *Who? What? When? Where? Why?* and *How?*	Page 27
Reading with a Focus	Reading efficiently to locate and collect specific information	Page 28
Listening with a Focus	Listening attentively to locate and collect specific information	Page 28
Observing	Noticing details through the senses: sight, hearing, smell, taste, touch	Page 30
Imagining	Probing your imagination for ideas, often using a "What if?" approach	Pages 30–31

Keeping a Writer's Journal

Writers from antiquity to the present day have kept journals, and for a very good reason. A *journal*—a daily log of happenings—is a great way to keep a record of experiences, observations, feelings, opinions, original ideas, and unanswered questions. You can put anything you want into your journal: newspaper and magazine articles, interesting quotations, songs, poems, photos, dreams. Any of these bits and chunks may fit into some later piece of writing. On the following page are some suggestions for getting started.

1. Use a notebook, scrapbook, or file folder.
2. Try to add something to your journal every day, and date your entries. Consider writing at the same time every day, early in the morning or late at night perhaps. (But you can jot down notes any time on anything, and insert them later.)
3. Don't worry about punctuation, grammar, or usage.
4. Use your imagination. Be creative. Write original poems or song lyrics if you want. Jot down story ideas.
5. For paste-in entries, write notes beside them. Why did you like a particular poem, quotation, or cartoon?

Freewriting

When you're *freewriting,* you jot down whatever pops into your head.

1. Decide on a time limit of three to five minutes. Keep writing until your time is up.
2. Start with any topic or word, such as *photography* or *sports cars* or *honesty.*
3. Don't worry about complete sentences or proper punctuation. Your thoughts may be disorganized. You may repeat yourself. That's perfectly okay.
4. Occasionally, choose one key word or phrase from your freewriting and use it as a starting point for more writing. This *focused freewriting,* or *looping,* allows you to "loop" from what you've already written to something new.

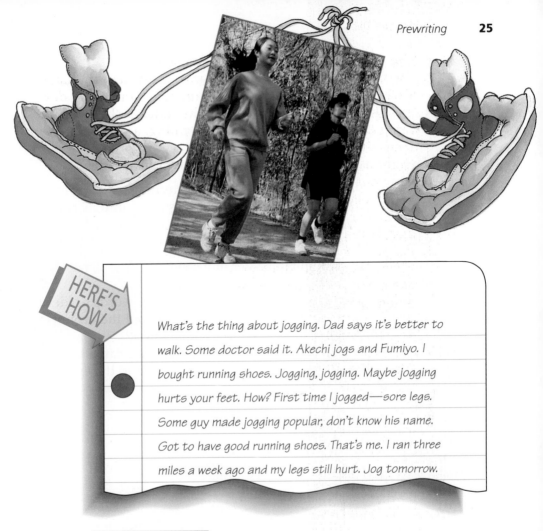

HERE'S
HOW

> What's the thing about jogging. Dad says it's better to
> walk. Some doctor said it. Akechi jogs and Fumiyo. I
> bought running shoes. Jogging, jogging. Maybe jogging
> hurts your feet. How? First time I jogged—sore legs.
> Some guy made jogging popular, don't know his name.
> Got to have good running shoes. That's me. I ran three
> miles a week ago and my legs still hurt. Jog tomorrow.

EXERCISE 1 ▶ **Freewriting in a Journal**

You can freewrite anywhere, but since you have started a journal, you can freewrite there. Start with this question: What's your favorite song? Write a couple of lines of the lyrics. Then give yourself exactly three minutes to write whatever comes into your head about the song.

Brainstorming

Another way to generate ideas is through *brainstorming,* or using free association. You can brainstorm alone or with others by using the following steps:

1. Write a word, phrase, or topic on your paper or on the board.

2. Without any careful thought, begin listing every related word or idea that enters your mind. One person can write for a group.
3. Don't stop to evaluate the ideas. Anything goes, even jokes and ideas that seem to be *off* the topic.

Clustering

Clustering is another free-association technique. Like brainstorming, it is used to break up a large subject into its smaller parts or to gather information, but it also shows connections. Clustering is sometimes called *webbing* or *making connections*.

1. Write a subject in the center of a sheet of paper. Draw a circle around it.
2. In the space around the circle, write all the words or ideas that come to mind. Circle each addition, and then connect it to the original circled subject with a line.
3. Create offshoots by adding and connecting related ideas. Then circle each related idea and connect it to the appropriate circle.

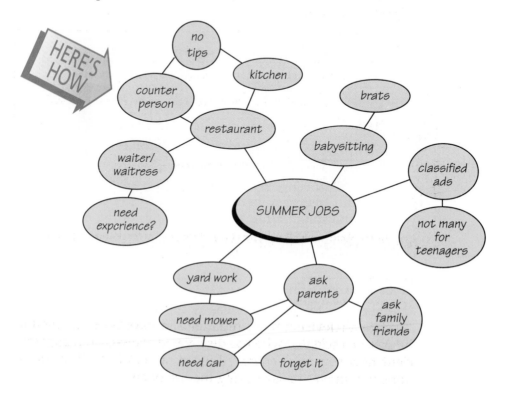

EXERCISE 2 ▶ **Practicing Brainstorming and Clustering**

Get together with another student, or form a small group, and choose one of the following subjects to brainstorm together. Keep going until you've exhausted every possible idea. Then, on your own, choose one of the other subjects and build a cluster diagram.

1. movies
2. the U.S. president
3. advertising
4. professional wrestling
5. vacations
6. automobiles

Asking Questions

The motto of the *New York Times* is "All the News That's Fit to Print." How do reporters for the *Times* go about finding "all the news"? Like reporters everywhere, they start with the *5W-How?* questions: *Who? What? Where? When? Why?* and *How?* Although not every question applies to every situation, the *5W-How?* questions are a good basic approach. You can also ask the same *5W-How?* question more than once, about various aspects of your topic.

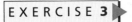

Topic: Today's Most Popular Recording Artist

Who?   Who is number one on the pop charts?

What?   What record or album won this year's Grammy Award?

Where?   Where do most people see or hear this artist's music performed?

When?   When did the artist first achieve stardom?

Why?   Why do so many people like this star?

How?   How did the star get his or her start in popular music?

EXERCISE 3 ▶ **Using the *5W-How?* Questions**

You are a television news reporter and have been assigned to interview a scientist who has discovered a low-cost, highly efficient new source of energy. Prepare a list of *5W-How?* questions you intend to ask during the interview.

Reading with a Focus

When you read a novel, you can sit back, relax, and enjoy the story. But when you read to gather information—for instance, for a paper on Dixieland music—you have to use a different approach. Here are some hints for finding and collecting information on a specific topic.

1. First, give the source of information a "once-over." Look for key words in the index (*jazz, Dixieland*), check the table of contents, and look through chapter headings and subheadings.
2. Skim passages until you find something about your topic; then slow down and take notes in your own words. Be sure to record publishing information for later use.

E X E R C I S E 4   **Reading for Specific Information**

Your task is to find material for a report on a famous African American in our nation's history. Some possibilities include Benjamin Banneker, Sojourner Truth, Rosa Parks, Frederick Douglass, Jackie Robinson, and Martin Luther King, Jr. Choose one. Next, find a source—perhaps your American history textbook or a biographical dictionary. Time yourself to see how long it takes to locate the material and to make notes answering the following questions.

1. When and where did the person live?
2. For what is he or she famous?
3. What was one major event in the person's life?

Then, using your notes, prepare a brief oral presentation in which you share some of the information you have discovered with your classmates.

Sojourner Truth   Jackie Robinson   Rosa Parks   Frederick Douglass

Listening with a Focus

Your ears are another powerful prewriting tool, but they can't do the work all by themselves. It pays to *prepare* to listen.

Listening for information may include listening to a tape recording, a radio or television program, a speech, or an expert during a personal or telephone interview.

1. Think ahead. Make an outline of information you need, or prepare questions to ask.
2. In an interview, concentrate on the question the person is answering. Don't allow your mind to wander to the next question.
3. Take notes even if you are also recording. However, don't try to write every word—use phrases and abbreviations and listen for main ideas and significant details.

☞ REFERENCE NOTE: For information on interviewing, see pages 950–952.

EXERCISE 5 ▶ **Listening for Specific Information**

Tune in to a local evening news broadcast on television. Listen for answers to these questions.

1. What is the lead news story—the event covered first? How much time does the station devote to the lead story?
2. What is the first feature story presented—that is, a story that isn't "hard" news?
3. How much air time is devoted to each kind of news: local, state, and national?

Observing

You can gather great writing material just by observing, but you need to remember that observation is purposeful and deliberate; it is not a passive activity. Here are some examples showing how one writer used his observation skills on a camping trip.

HERE'S HOW

SIGHT:	trout leaping high out of the water; campers struggling to win a tug of war; moonlit nights around the campfire
SOUND:	roar of the river water; chatter of crickets; crackling fire; campers' shouting and laughter
SMELL:	tangy odor of wet leaves and grass; musty smell of wet swimsuits drying; savory odor of fish frying
TASTE:	toasted marshmallows; tart lemonade from a bottle in an ice-filled tub
TOUCH:	rough, splintery firewood; shoulders aching from carrying backpacks; dry, crackling leaves underfoot

Imagining

Creative writers have active imaginations. How often have you heard about something that happened, then wondered, "Well, that's interesting, but what if . . . ?" You can put that same creative questioning into your search for writing ideas.

1. *What if I could change my circumstances?* (What if I were an only child or what if I were *not* an only child? What if I had lived during the Middle Ages?)

2. *What if a familiar thing in our world no longer existed?* (What if we had no music? What if we had no public schools?)

3. *What if major social changes were made overnight?* (What if racial prejudice no longer existed? What if everyone earned the same amount of money?)

You can take this "What if?" approach and apply it to any subject. Here are some "What if?" questions you might apply to the subject of environmental control.

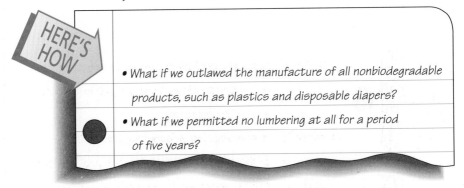

HERE'S HOW

• What if we outlawed the manufacture of all nonbiodegradable products, such as plastics and disposable diapers?

• What if we permitted no lumbering at all for a period of five years?

EXERCISE 6 ▶ Observing and Imagining

A good story can be about almost anything. Think about the four places listed below. Then choose one and observe it carefully. Write down some descriptive details about each event or place as you imagine it through your five senses. Finally, go one step further by writing a few "What if?" questions that might lead to good story plots.

1. a bus or subway train **3.** a shopping mall
2. a city park **4.** a river

EXAMPLE ***Inside an airplane: sensory perceptions***
blue sky; deep roar of the engines on takeoff; swaying sensation as the plane hits turbulence; inviting smell of the in-flight meal

Inside an airplane: "What if?"
What if hijackers with a time bomb were on the plane? What if the plane had to make a forced landing in a cornfield?

CRITICAL THINKING

Analyzing a Subject

An editor once asked a famous football coach if he'd like to write a how-to book for other coaches. "Sure," the coach replied. "I'd love to."

"Okay," the editor said. "On what?"

The coach looked puzzled. "On football. What else?"

Now, the coach was right in a way. The editor did want him to write a book on the broad subject of football. But the editor also expected the coach to *analyze* his subject a bit—to break it down, to select the various possibilities from among his best tricks of the trade—things other coaches might benefit from.

When you're preparing to write, you, too, should subdivide, or analyze. For example, you may be interested in transportation, but you can't begin writing on that broad subject. You need to find and explore a narrower, more manageable topic for the length of paper you plan.

Broad subject: transportation
More narrow subject:
  urban transportation
Topic: mass transit systems
More narrow topics:
  (1) history in U.S.
  (2) new and experimental
     systems

CRITICAL THINKING EXERCISE:
Analyzing Subjects and Topics

Answer each of the following questions. You might want to compare your answers with a classmate's.

1. Other subdivisions are possible at every level of the sample analysis. Under "mass transit systems," what subdivisions can you add to the two listed? Under "urban transportation," can you think of topics other than "mass transit systems"?
2. Take the analysis of "transportation" in another direction entirely. Instead of "urban transportation," choose another subdivision and analyze it through all the levels shown.

Prewriting

Considering Purpose, Audience, and Tone

Purpose.   You always have a reason, or *purpose,* for writing. Maybe you want to explain something to someone. You may want to persuade someone to come around to your way of thinking, or you may want to create a story or a poem. You may want to put your thoughts and feelings down on paper, just to see what you think. (You may even have a combination of purposes.) And just as you can have various reasons for writing, you can use various forms. The following chart shows some of the forms of writing in which you can achieve your purpose.

MAIN PURPOSE	FORMS OF WRITING
Self-Expressive	Journal, letter, personal essay
Literary works	Short story, poem, play
Expository: Informative, Explanatory, or Exploratory	Technical or scientific report, newspaper or magazine article, biography, autobiography, travel essay, brochure
Persuasive	Persuasive essay, letter to the editor, pamphlet, advertisement, political speech, poster

Audience.   You don't talk the same way to everyone, nor do you write the same way for everyone. You adjust your writing for your *audience.* Ask yourself the following questions to find out more about your audience.

- How much does my audience already know about the topic? Do I need to give background information or explain technical terms?
- What strong feelings might my audience have about the topic?

- What level of language should I use? Should the level be formal or informal? Should the writing be simple or complex?
- How can I make my message interesting and worthwhile to this particular audience?

Tone. When you are speaking to someone, your tone of voice usually contributes meaning to what you say. It tells your listener how you feel about your subject, as well as how you feel about the listener. Your writing also takes on a *tone*, whether you create it deliberately or not. But unlike your speech, in which tone is partly created by the way you control your voice (shouting or soothing, for example), tone in writing is created by choice of words, choice of details, and sentence structure.

- **Word Choice.** The choice of formal language (see pages 484–485) will convey a more serious tone than informal language. Generally, the use of contractions and colloquial language creates a more personal, friendly tone, while the use of polysyllabic words and impersonal language creates a less friendly, more serious tone. You also create a tone when you use objective, unemotional words or words with emotional connotations ("the old goat" or "the pleasant gentleman").
- **Choice of Details.** As you've seen in your reading, a list of facts creates a rather serious tone, while a set of personal examples or reminiscences creates a friendlier, perhaps even playful tone.
- **Sentence Length and Structure.** Long, involved sentences can produce a serious and weighty tone or even a lush tone. (Think of the kinds of sentences participants use on television news and public affairs programs.)

Whenever you write something, you should review and think about its tone. Will your readers object to it? Does it show how you feel and think about both the subject and your audience? The best approach is always to be honest and natural. When you feel anger, show it. When you feel that your subject and your audience should be taken seriously, show that. When you want to have fun and share that fun with your audience, be playful.

CRITICAL THINKING

Analyzing Purpose, Audience, and Tone

When you *analyze* something, you try to learn more about it by looking at its parts. You can learn more about writing by analyzing it, looking at purpose, audience, and tone.

You instinctively adjust your writing to your purpose and audience. Consider, for example, how a friendly letter to a favorite aunt differs from a chemistry lab report. The purpose, the audience, the tone—all are different. Let's look at how this adjustment works in practice. Read the following article about chameleons. Then read the newspaper advertisement on the next page for chameleons as pets.

> Chameleons live solitary lives. Males, in particular, guard their territory jealously. Any intruder merits vigorous countermeasures. For most, territorial battles consist of aggressive displays, not physical contests. When two rivals meet, they turn sideways to the threat, flatten their bodies, curl their tails and thrust out their throats. They puff themselves up, presenting a literally inflated image. They replace mundane colors and patterns with a vibrant combination intended to intimidate. Both contenders understand the symbolism.
>
> Finally they open their mouths, exposing the contrasting colors of their mucous membranes: this is often accompanied by a choreography of swaying and bobbing, punctuated by soft hisses. In most species, this signals the end of the conflict, as one of the antagonists will usually concede esthetic defeat and slink away. . . .
>
> James Martin, "The engaging habits of chameleons suggest mirth more than menace," *Smithsonian*

Why in the world would anyone want a *chameleon*?

You say you're satisfied with that old basset hound of yours? Fine. Dogs are wonderful pets. No one knows that better than the folks down at **The Pet Set**. Dogs are loyal, friendly, and lovable.

- But can they change their colors in the twinkling of an eye?
- Do they dance, hiss, and puff up like balloons?
- Do they make strangers say, "Boy, is that weird!"

If you answered "No" to any of these questions, perhaps the next question is: "Why don't you have a chameleon?"

Because, really and seriously, folks, chameleons are marvelous pets.

- They're neat, clean, and easy to care for.
- They don't bark, meow, chatter, or warble.
- Plus . . . They're the darndest conversation starters this side of a red turbo sports car.

The Pet Set
*Everything in Pets . . .
and Then Some*

Harborview Mall

You can see that there's a world of difference between the paragraphs on chameleons and the advertisement for them. The paragraphs are intended for adults with good reading skills. The writing is informative and precise, with a fairly difficult vocabulary and an objective but admiring tone. In contrast, the ad attempts to persuade a general audience to buy chameleons. Its tone is humorous but sincere.

CRITICAL THINKING EXERCISE:
Analyzing Purpose, Audience, and Tone

The following list identifies several different types of writing you see around you all the time. Choose any two from the list and find examples of them. For an ad, for example, look in a magazine. For a news article, look in the newspaper. After you have found the two examples, use the questions that follow to analyze them. When you've finished your analysis, get together with two or three classmates and discuss the differences you found between the two types of writing you examined.

Types of Writing

a news article	a newspaper editorial
an advertisement	an informative article
a lesson in a textbook	an autobiography (or excerpt)
a comic strip	a recipe or set of instructions
a short story	a poem

---

1. Who are the intended readers? What are their probable ages? interests? needs? concerns?
2. What is the writer's purpose? What is he or she trying to do? How can you tell?
3. What is the writer's tone? Is it serious, humorous, bitter, worried, light? What words or sentences show this tone?

Prewriting

Arranging Ideas

By the time you have gathered enough information to begin writing, you're likely to have your notes in various forms: on notepaper, on 3″ × 5″ cards, on photocopies. How do you bring order to this chaos? No, the answer isn't "Sleep on it."

When you step back and look, your information may be easier to arrange than you think. Much writing falls into clear patterns. For example, to explain how to enlarge a photograph, you'll put the explanation in step-by-step, or *chronological,* order. If you are describing the stage set for a play, you'll almost automatically arrange the description in *spatial* order— left to right, perhaps, or front to back.

If you're writing a campaign speech and want to make a strong impact, you may arrange points using *order of importance*—from the least important to the most important—to end on a rousing note. But if you want to emphasize the difference between yourself and another candidate, you may swing back and forth between points: "My opponent promises this; I promise that." This is *logical order*—the order that falls naturally out of your purpose for writing. The chart on the following page shows four common ways of arranging ideas.

Shoe, by Jeff MacNelly, reprinted by permission: Tribune Media Services.

ARRANGING IDEAS		
TYPE OF ORDER	DEFINITION	EXAMPLES
Chronological	Narration: Order that presents events as they happen in time	Story; narrative poem; explanation of a process; history; biography; drama
Spatial	Description: Order that describes objects according to location	Descriptions (near to far; left to right; top to bottom; and so on)
Importance	Evaluation: Order that gives details from least to most important or the reverse	Persuasive writing; descriptions; explanations (main idea and supporting details); evaluative writing
Logical	Classification: Order that relates items and groups	Definitions; classifications; comparisons and contrasts

REFERENCE NOTE: For more information on arranging ideas, see pages 75–77.

EXERCISE 7 ▶ **Arranging the Order of Details**

Do you remember the first time you tried to ride a bike, or attempted to roller skate, or boarded a roller coaster? First, brainstorm your memories of such an event for two different paragraphs: (1) a description of the skates, bike, roller coaster, or whatever, and (2) the story of what happened. Then arrange each set of details in a clear order, and discuss the order you used with some classmates.

Using Charts

Charts are a practical, graphic way to arrange your prewriting notes. They group related bits of information, allowing you to "see" the overall arrangement clearly. Sometimes charts are as simple as lists, but they can be more complex. Here's a chart for a student's paper on the inhabitants of Mexico before the Spanish conquest. Notice how the chart has both horizontal and vertical headings.

HERE'S HOW

MAJOR CULTURES OF MEXICO IN 1500		
PEOPLE	LOCATION	CHARACTERISTICS
Aztecs	Central Mexico	centralized government; large, efficient army; 365-day solar calendar; advanced engineering and architectural skills
Mayas	Yucatán peninsula	written language; base-20 mathematical system; 365-day calendar; sophisticated artistry, especially sculpture
Mixtecs	Southwest Mexico	fine stone and metal work; beautiful carvings in wood; painted polychrome pottery
Zapotecs	Southern Oaxaca and Isthmus of Tehuantepec	priestly hierarchy; ancestor worship; artistic heritage influenced by the early Maya

Another graphic way to organize notes is a *time line*—a chart showing information in chronological order. On the next page is a time line showing the periods of dominance of the four major cultural groups in Mexico.

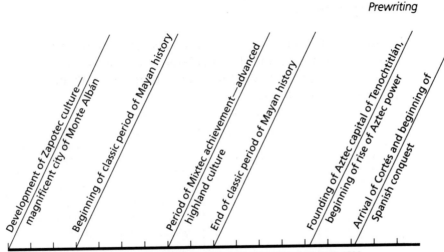

Stages of Pre-Columbian Cultures of Mexico

CRITICAL THINKING

Classifying Information

To make many kinds of charts, you're using the skill of *classifying:* grouping related information. When classifying information, ask yourself these questions:

- Which items are similar in some way? What heading will show what they have in common?
- Do some items *include* other items? Which ones?
- Do you have any items left over? Should you create another heading? Should you eliminate the leftovers?

 CRITICAL THINKING EXERCISE:
Classifying and Charting Information

Look at the following ideas for a paper on college football, and then answer the questions.

a. Teaches teamwork
b. Encourages school spirit
c. Many football players on scholarship not completing their degrees

    d. Scholarship program intended to offer a college education to economically disadvantaged students

    e. Competition encouraging colleges to violate recruiting rules

    f. Can give a college national recognition

    g. Colleges needing to emphasize academics more than sports

    h. Alumni fans donating money to alma maters with good football teams

    i. Prepares players for professional football careers

    j. Good football players often allowed to take easy courses; won't prepare them for life after college

    k. Star football players often given passing grades for poor academic work; some players actually illiterate

    l. Football very profitable for colleges; helps pay for academic courses and other sports programs

    m. Alumni pressure and money possibly corrupting to college football; alumni known to reward star players with money and cars

1. One natural way to classify the information is in two groups: favorable ideas about college football and unfavorable ones. Do this: List all the positive details under *Pro* and all the negative details under *Con*.

2. Another classification is items about players and items about schools. Make a chart that shows all four groupings: *Pro, Con, Players, Schools*. Does every item in the list fit in the chart?

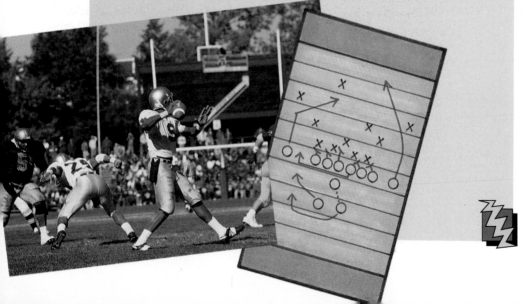

Writing a First Draft

W. Somerset Maugham, the English author, wrote a short story about a man who spent a lifetime gathering information for his *magnum opus*, or masterpiece. The man had stacks of information—but he died before getting a word of his book written. The moral is this: Prewriting is important, but at some point you've got to get a first draft on paper.

There is no magic formula, no one right way, to write a first draft. Your prewriting notes may be rough, or you may create a detailed outline. You may like to write *fast*, or you may slowly, carefully shape each sentence. Whatever feels right for your style of writing a draft, consider these suggestions:

- Use your prewriting notes or outline as a guide.
- Write freely. Concentrate on expressing your ideas.
- Include any new ideas that come to you as you write.
- Don't worry about making errors in grammar, usage, and mechanics. You can fix them later.

Here's a first draft of a paragraph on dogs and politics. Notice how the writer makes a few revisions and also writes some personal notes and questions right in the draft.

Dogs and politics go together like ham and eggs. Apparently there's something about a dog that makes its politician-owner more human, lovable, and electable. A first rule of politics would seem to be--own a dog. You've just got to own a dog. In 1944 the opponents of President Franklin D. Roosevelt claimed that Fala, FDR's Scottie [check breed], had been brought back from Alaska on a U.S. Navy destroyer sent especially for the purpose. The story was a lie, and Roosevelt's "Fala speech" of September [?] seriously hurt Thomas E. Dewey, his opponent. So a second rule is never to criticize someone else's dog. When Richard Nixon ran into trouble over the gift of a dog [was that all?] in his 1952 vice-presidential campaign, Nixon responded with his famous "Checkers speech"--Checkers being the dog in question. This speech, delivered eight years to the day after FDR's Fala speech, saved Nixon [how?]. Who can doubt that other dogs will arrive in the future to help other threatened politicians?

EXERCISE 8▶   **Writing a First Draft**

Have you ever daydreamed about being a famous performer like Hammer or Gloria Estefan? Here are some prewriting notes about the imagined life of a performer. Arrange or group the notes, and add to them if you like. Then use the details to write the first draft of a paragraph.

make millions of dollars
can't safely go out alone in
    public
own big house and expensive
    clothes
difficult to have personal
    relationships
people love you who don't even
    know you

travel a lot
sleep in strange hotels all
    over the country
followed by groupies every-
    where he or she goes
have to have bodyguards
    for personal protection
great satisfaction performing
    before crowds of people

Evaluating and Revising

Evaluating and revising go hand in hand. *Evaluating* means deciding what changes need to be made. *Revising* involves making the changes.

Evaluating

When you comb your hair in the morning, you look closely into a mirror. You decide what looks okay. You notice what's wrong. You use a similar process when you evaluate your first draft. What seems to be good about it? What changes will make it better?

Self-Evaluation.   Seeing what needs improvement in your writing can be difficult, but the following techniques will help.

TIPS FOR SELF-EVALUATION

1. **Reading Carefully.** Read your paper several times. First concentrate on *content* (what you say), next on *organization* (how you've arranged your ideas), and then on *style* (how you've used words and sentences).
2. **Listening Carefully.** Read your paper aloud, "listening" to what you've written. What looked all right on paper may sound awkward or unclear when read aloud.
3. **Taking Time.** If possible, put your paper aside for a while. A day or two (or even a few hours) will give you some mental distance from it and help you to see flaws you didn't notice before.

Peer Evaluation.   Every writer needs an editor—a person who can read critically and with a different viewpoint. You can get an editor (or editors) of your own through peer evaluation. Members of a peer-evaluation group read and comment on each other's papers. The group may consist of as few as two people or as many as four or five. Part of the time you'll be the writer whose work is being evaluated, and the rest of the time you'll be evaluating someone else's writing.

PEER-EVALUATION GUIDELINES

Guidelines for the Writer
1. Tell the evaluator what bothers you most about your own paper. Point out anything that has caused you difficulty.
2. Don't be defensive. Keep an open mind and make good use of the evaluator's comments.

Guidelines for the Peer Evaluator
1. Be sure to tell the writer what's right as well as what's wrong.
2. Make suggestions for improvement. If you see a weakness, give the writer some suggestions to correct it.
3. Concentrate on content and organization. Don't worry about mechanical errors such as spelling or punctuation.
4. Be sensitive to the writer's feelings. Make sure that your comments are constructive—that means offering solutions, not criticism.

Revising

Revision is one of the most important parts of writing—and one you may be tempted to skip because it's so difficult. Even if you identify some problems with your writing, you may have trouble deciding how to fix them. Take heart: Just as with prewriting, some directed practice makes this writing stage easier. The four basic ways to revise are to *add, cut, replace,* and *reorder.* The following chart shows how these techniques can be applied. In later chapters, you'll find similar charts that focus on specific types of writing.

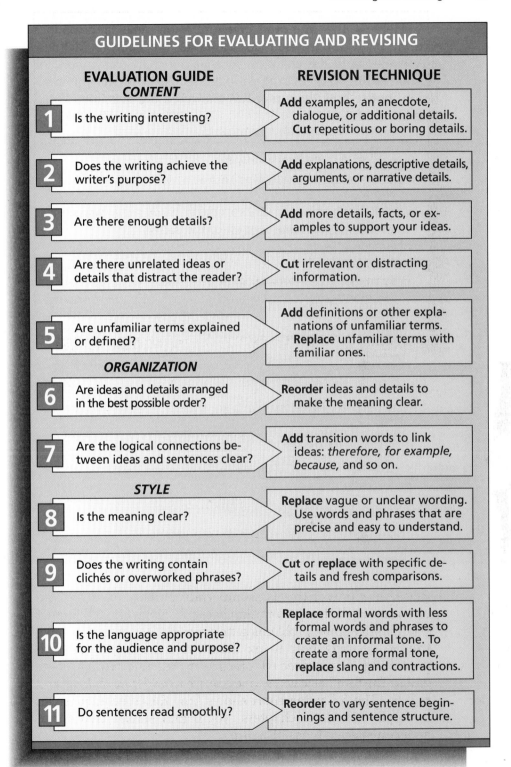

GUIDELINES FOR EVALUATING AND REVISING

EVALUATION GUIDE	REVISION TECHNIQUE
CONTENT	
1 Is the writing interesting?	**Add** examples, an anecdote, dialogue, or additional details. **Cut** repetitious or boring details.
2 Does the writing achieve the writer's purpose?	**Add** explanations, descriptive details, arguments, or narrative details.
3 Are there enough details?	**Add** more details, facts, or examples to support your ideas.
4 Are there unrelated ideas or details that distract the reader?	**Cut** irrelevant or distracting information.
5 Are unfamiliar terms explained or defined?	**Add** definitions or other explanations of unfamiliar terms. **Replace** unfamiliar terms with familiar ones.
ORGANIZATION	
6 Are ideas and details arranged in the best possible order?	**Reorder** ideas and details to make the meaning clear.
7 Are the logical connections between ideas and sentences clear?	**Add** transition words to link ideas: *therefore, for example, because,* and so on.
STYLE	
8 Is the meaning clear?	**Replace** vague or unclear wording. Use words and phrases that are precise and easy to understand.
9 Does the writing contain clichés or overworked phrases?	**Cut** or **replace** with specific details and fresh comparisons.
10 Is the language appropriate for the audience and purpose?	**Replace** formal words with less formal words and phrases to create an informal tone. To create a more formal tone, **replace** slang and contractions.
11 Do sentences read smoothly?	**Reorder** to vary sentence beginnings and sentence structure.

Here is the first-draft paragraph on dogs and politics (from page 43), revised according to the chart guidelines. To understand the changes, look at the chart of symbols for proofreading and revising on page 53. As you read this revision, notice how the writer has answered the questions noted on the draft.

Dogs and politics go together like ~~ham~~ **fireworks**   **replace**
~~and eggs.~~ **and the Fourth of July.** Apparently there's something

about a dog that makes its politician-owner

more human, lovable, and electable. A first

rule of politics would seem to be ^to own a dog.   **replace/reorder**

~~You've just got to own a dog.~~ In 1944 the   **cut**

opponents of President Franklin D. Roosevelt

claimed that Fala, FDR's Scottie ^sh **terrier** [check   **replace**

breed], had been brought back from Alaska   **cut**

on a U.S. Navy destroyer sent especially for

the purpose. The story was ~~a lie,~~ **untrue,** and   **replace**

Roosevelt's "Fala speech" of September [?] **23**   **replace**

seriously hurt **the chances of** Thomas E. Dewey, his   **add**

Other politicians learned from that incident. opponent. ~~So~~ a second rule **— discovered in the presidential election of 1944 —** is never to   **add/cut/add**

criticize someone else's dog. When Richard

Nixon ran into trouble over the gift of a dog
(among other things)
[was that all?] in his 1952 vice-presidential   **replace**

campaign, he responded with his famous
cuddly little
"Checkers speech"--Checkers being the ^dog   **add**

in question. This speech, delivered eight

years to the day after FDR's Fala speech,
^'s **nomination.**
saved Nixon [how?]. Who can doubt that   **replace**
wag into view
other dogs will ~~arrive~~ in the future to help   **replace**

other threatened politicians?

CRITICAL THINKING

Evaluating and Revising a Paragraph

The **Guidelines for Evaluating and Revising** (page 47) show you that *evaluating* is more than uttering a judgment: *This is OK. This is the pits. This is to die for.* A useful judgment is made by using clear criteria, or standards. When you evaluate your own writing or someone else's, you shouldn't simply react. You should have in mind concrete elements of strong writing—and to specify where you see them and where you don't.

CRITICAL THINKING EXERCISE:
Evaluating and Revising a Paragraph

Work with a partner to evaluate and revise the following first draft of a paragraph. Focus on organization, content, and style, using the guidelines on page 47. If you find mechanical and grammatical errors, you can correct them, but that's not your main task. When you've finished, check with another revision team to see if the problems and solutions they found match yours.

> Can you imagine being alive in world that does not have trees? You could say that trees are good to look at, and essential to our very lives. We use trees for paper, books, and the shelves and desks and tables and cabinets that we put them on to hold them. Some woods, such as ebony, mahogany, and rosewood, are gorgeous. As a matter of fact, just one ordinary average tree takes in a lot of carbon dioxide. About twenty-six pounds a year, much of it caused by automobile junk and other pollutants around. That same tree puts out enough oxygen to keep four persons breathing for about fifty-two weeks. Trees make shade. When they get planted around homes and other bildings, they lower the need for air conditioning plenty. Chairs, tables, picture frames, and pencils all started as plain, ordinary trees. So did boats, musical instruments, tennis rackets, etc.

Proofreading and Publishing

Proofreading. Once you're finished revising anything you've written, you may think it is perfect. Sometimes it may be—but you'll do well to take one last look. This final look is called *proofreading.* When you proofread, you catch and correct any remaining errors in grammar, usage, and mechanics (spelling, capitalization, punctuation). If you've been able to put aside your paper for a while, you'll find it easier to spot these mistakes. Here are some techniques for proofreading:

1. Focus on one line at a time. Use a sheet of paper to cover all the lines below the one you're proofreading. Or try beginning at the bottom line and working your way to the top. That way you'll be forced to concentrate on mechanics, not content.
2. Consider peer proofreading. Exchange papers with a classmate and proofread each other's papers.
3. When in doubt, look it up. For spelling, use a college dictionary. For grammar, usage, and punctuation, use a handbook like the one on pages 550–929.

Some kinds of errors occur again and again, so the following guidelines are designed to help you handle a few of them. By going over these guidelines before you begin to proofread, you'll have a head start on getting your paper exactly right.

GUIDELINES FOR PROOFREADING

1. Is each sentence a complete sentence? (See pages 515–519 and 582–583.)
2. Does every sentence end with the appropriate punctuation mark? (See pages 842–845.)
3. Does every sentence begin with a capital letter? Are all proper nouns and proper adjectives capitalized when necessary? (See pages 820–828.)
4. Does every verb agree in number with its subject? (See pages 649–662.)
5. Are verb forms and tenses used correctly? (See pages 715–747.)

(continued)

GUIDELINES FOR PROOFREADING *(continued)*

6. Are subject and object forms of personal pronouns used correctly? (See pages 675–681.)
7. Does every pronoun agree with its antecedent in number and gender? Are pronoun references clear? (See pages 664–666 and 701–707.)
8. Are frequently confused words (such as *slow* and *slowly*, *imply* and *infer*) used correctly? (See pages 792–809.)
9. Are all words spelled correctly? Are the plural forms of nouns correct? (See pages 902–929.)
10. Is the paper neat and in correct manuscript form? (See page 52.)

EXERCISE 9 ▶ **Proofreading**

The paragraph below has ten errors in grammar, usage, and mechanics. Use a college dictionary and the handbook at the back of the book to identify and correct each mistake.

Most people have strong feelings about there pets. Especially when it comes to dogs and cats. Both María and Fran said she preferred dogs because dogs are friendlier than cats. Chad disagreed, pointing out that he had never been chased or bite by a cat. Jennifer asked Chad if he had ever heard of a cat who had tried to save someone's life. After listening to what Jennifer had to say, Chad said that she had a good arguement. Just between you and I, I'm glad that each kind of pet are admired by somebody. The important thing is to love and take care of your pet, weather its a dog, a cat, or some other kind of animal.

Publishing. Your readers should always be on your mind, but the publishing stage is the time you can finally reach out to them. Here are a few suggestions for sharing your writing.

■ Submit your writing for publication in the school newspaper or magazine. Or, send it to your local newspaper. Most newspapers publish letters to the editors, and many accept feature stories.

- Look for writing contests. A few are specifically for high school students. Some offer prizes or certificates. Ask your teacher or counselor for information.
- Compile a class anthology of each student's favorite piece of writing. Donate it to your school library. If possible, make a copy for each contributor.

When someone else reads your paper—whether that person is your teacher, another student, or an adult outside of school—appearance is important. If you follow these guidelines for your final copy, your paper will look its best.

GUIDELINES FOR MANUSCRIPT FORM

1. Use only one side of a sheet of paper.
2. Use a typewriter or a word processor, or write in blue or black ink.
3. If you type, double-space the lines. If you write by hand, don't skip lines.
4. Leave margins of about one inch at the top, sides, and bottom of each page.
5. Indent the first line of each paragraph.
6. Number all pages (except the first page) in the upper right-hand corner.
7. Be sure all pages are neat and clean. You can make a few changes with correction fluid, but they should be barely noticeable.
8. Follow your teacher's instructions for placement of your name, the date, your class, and the title of your paper.

EXERCISE 10   **Publishing**

With your classmates, brainstorm ideas for publishing your writing. Anyone who has already been published should share his or her experiences. Work in smaller groups to gather specific information on each possibility—names and addresses of potential publishers, types of material each accepts, length and manuscript form required, and so on. Then compile the information from the different groups into a resource booklet.

SYMBOLS FOR REVISING AND PROOFREADING

SYMBOL	EXAMPLE	MEANING OF SYMBOL
ⒸⒶⓅ ≡	Spence college	Capitalize a lowercase letter.
ⓁⒸ /	our Best quarterback	Lowercase a capital letter.
∧	*the* on Fourth of July	Insert a missing word, letter, or punctuation mark.
/	*a* endurénce	Change a letter.
	Ohio the capital of Iowa	Change a word.
	hoped for to go	Leave out a word, letter, or punctuation mark.
	on that occassion	Leave out and close up.
	today's home work	Close up space.
∩∪	nieghbor	Change the order of the letters.
ⓣⓡ ∩∪	the counsel general of the corporation	Transpose words. (Write ⓣⓡ in nearby margin.)
¶	¶ "Wait!" I shouted.	Begin a new paragraph.
⊙	She was right⊙	Add a period.
⌄	Yes that's true.	Add a comma.
#	center#field	Add a space.
⊙	the following items⊙	Add a colon.
⌄	Evansville, Indiana⌄ Columbus, Ohio	Add a semicolon.
=	self=control	Add a hyphen.
⌄	Mrs. Ruiz's office	Add an apostrophe.
ⓢⓣⓔⓣ	a very tall building	Keep the crossed-out material. (Write ⓢⓣⓔⓣ in nearby margin.)

MAKING CONNECTIONS

Exploring the Creative Process

> In the writing process, the more a story cooks, the better.
>
> Doris Lessing

> I don't dawdle. I'm a surgeon. I make an incision, do what needs to be done and sew up the wound. There is a beginning, a middle and an end.
>
> Richard Selzer

Two writers, two very different writing approaches. Does one of those quotations hit home for you? Do you let your drafts "cook," or do you simply "get it over with"? Or do you alternate between the two approaches?

Write in your journal about whether, and when, writing flows for you or seems like a nightmare. (And you may have another metaphor for how writing feels.) Then, if it's comfortable, share your experience with others. You may get ideas for freeing up your writing.

Imitating a Writing Style

The annual Bulwer-Lytton Fiction Contest asks contestants to write "the worst possible opening sentence to a novel." (Edward Bulwer-Lytton wrote the infamous opening sentence "It was a dark and stormy night.") For example, the novel can be "mainstream," detective, espionage, science fiction, or romance. Here is a recent winner (loser?) in the science fiction category.

EDWARD BULWER-LYTTON

"Meteor storm!" Sparks cried, almost throwing the professor's frail body against the bulkhead in zero-grav haste, ignoring Zortran Threndoran's flailing purple tentacles in his fruitless effort to reach the null-space communicator as Bob Star slammed thruster levers into maximum and hoped against impossible odds that their shuddering, nearly fuelless Starcruiser would reach light-speed before the juggernautlike space rocks smashed them, along with the Federation's last hope for peace and Bob Star's only hope for real love, the professor's beautiful daughter Diana, into the cold oblivion of deep space.

Mike Montgomery

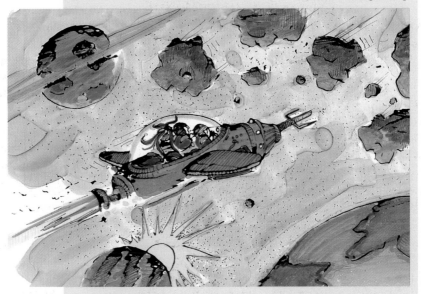

This paragraph is a ***parody*** of science fiction writing. A parody imitates the style of a writer or a type of writing, exaggerating its essential characteristics. The usually funny result is also "bad" writing because the quirks of the author or genre are pushed to an extreme.

What's bad about Mike Montgomery's parody of science fiction writing? Study this parody to see what makes it work. Is it the language? Is it exaggeration? Then use what you've discovered about Montgomery's parody to write a "Bulwer-Lytton" paragraph of your own, parodying any genre. For a double-bad paragraph, work with a partner.

2 UNDERSTANDING PARAGRAPH STRUCTURE

Looking at the Parts

You won't find paragraphs in poems or plays, but you'll find them in almost every other kind of writing—novels and short stories, articles, ads, business reports, petitions. They're the **parts** that make up the whole.

Writing and You.   In some ways, paragraphs are as elusive as they are essential. There is so much variety in their structure and use that it is difficult to pinpoint their common characteristics. They can be as short as one sentence or as long as many pages; they can show a transition from one idea to the next or develop a single idea; and they can break up long passages to make them easier to read. How have you used paragraphs in your own writing?

As You Read.   As you read the following selection from the autobiography of an Olympic runner, notice the different uses of paragraphs.

Richard Anuszkiewicz, *Trinity* (1970). Acrylic on canvas, 42" × 72". Collection of Alcoa Collection of Contemporary Art, Pittsburgh, PA. © 1993 Richard Anuszkiewicz/VAGA, New York.

57

from

RUNNINGTIDE

by Joan Benoit
with Sally Baker

Athletes who start young in their chosen sport can point to an early determination to excel in that sport alone. Tennis players, swimmers, and gymnasts begin intensive training when they are little more than babies; which is why, I believe, so many of them fall by the wayside so early. If you start working hard at seven, burnout is a real possibility by thirteen or fourteen. Long-distance runners shouldn't begin so early, as they could do permanent harm to developing bones and muscles, so they should experience a variety of sports and pursue other activities. I always knew I wanted to be an athlete because I loved to be active and to compete, but running wasn't a sport I gave much attention to as a child. So I can't look back and trace my primal devotions step by step, backing them up with training logs and competition results. There was no Little League for runners in my hometown and none was needed. A kindergarten teacher remembers that I used to hang on the fringes of the older kids' group in the playground and run away with their kickball when I got a chance. My childhood was filled with athletic endeavors, none of which would mean anything if I hadn't gone on to pursue a career in running.

But a career has to start somewhere, and, as nearly as I can tell, mine started at a gymkana in Norfolk, Connecticut.

It was the summer after my eighth birthday. My brother Peter and I were invited to drive to Norfolk with our aunt and uncle and several cousins. Peter and I would return home on a bus by ourselves. He was eleven and probably very reluctant to look after me, but it was a chance to travel and he grabbed it.

> "I used to hang on the fringes of the older kids' group in the playground and run away with their kickball when I got a chance."

On Saturday the Norfolk country club held its annual gymkana. My cousins were anxious to compete and I was eager to find out what a gymkana was (it sounded like an antelope), so their parents got us to the club early that morning. It slowly dawned on me that a gymkana was basically a track and field competition. Anyone could take part, so I signed up for everything appropriate for my age group.

One of the first events was an 880 for teenaged boys. Because I was small enough to wriggle to the front of the crowd without bothering anyone, I had a good view. Separated from Peter and my cousins, I was able to watch without distraction. I was fascinated. One young man took a quick lead in the race and maintained it to the end. He seemed confident; when he crossed the finish line he was winded, but I could tell he wasn't in as much pain as the other runners.

This race has stayed in my memory so long because I got my first good advice on running while watching it. I was trying to figure out what it was that made the lead runner look so good when a woman behind me said, "You can tell Jim runs for the high school team. Look at the way he carries his arms." Jim kept his arms close to his sides and ran with his elbows tucked in to his waist. His head and upper body hardly moved—he used his energy to power his legs. That was what made him look so good.

I remembered Jim's style when I ran my races later that day. I signed up for five running and two jumping events; holding my arms as the boy had, I won five blue ribbons.

No big deal, I thought, it was fun. My cousins, on the other hand, were none too pleased with my day's work; I couldn't understand why. The ride back to their house was silent. My aunt was mortified: her guest had turned out to be an eight-year-old ringer.

"Other people loved to win just as much as I did. Until that day I had not considered the costs of competition. Somebody had to lose."

After a time I couldn't stand the silence, so I made the mistake of admiring the red and white ribbons the others had won. I said I thought they were very nice. My cousins hissed at me. "Second place!" they screamed. "Third place! Hon-or-a-ble mention!"

Now I understood. Other people loved to win just as much as I did. Until that day I had not considered the costs of competition. Somebody had to lose. I didn't mind if I lost after doing my best, but I preferred to win and so did everyone else. I have my cousins to thank for an early lesson in the importance of winning with modesty.

READER'S RESPONSE

1. In her autobiography, Joan Benoit reveals some of her own thoughts about what makes a winning athlete. Based on your own experience, what do you think are some qualities or characteristics of an athlete who wins?
2. Benoit says that the fact that someone has to lose is one of the "costs of competition." In your journal, write about one of your own competitive experiences. What were the costs? the rewards?

WRITER'S CRAFT

3. Longer paragraphs are often used to develop a main idea. What idea does the writer develop in the first paragraph?
4. Shorter paragraphs often emphasize a point or provide a transition from one idea to the other. What's the function of the second paragraph in the selection?
5. Which paragraphs seem to be more effective, the shorter ones or the longer ones? What do you think makes a paragraph effective?

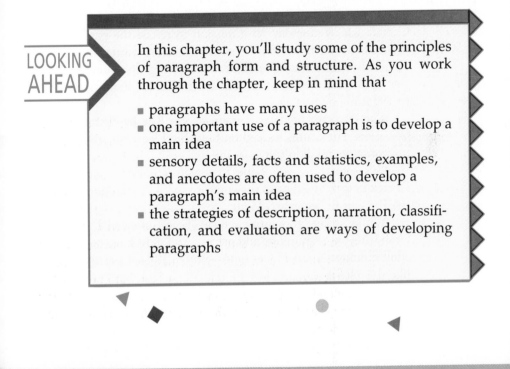

LOOKING AHEAD

In this chapter, you'll study some of the principles of paragraph form and structure. As you work through the chapter, keep in mind that

- paragraphs have many uses
- one important use of a paragraph is to develop a main idea
- sensory details, facts and statistics, examples, and anecdotes are often used to develop a paragraph's main idea
- the strategies of description, narration, classification, and evaluation are ways of developing paragraphs

The Uses of Paragraphs

In school assignments, you most often think of paragraphs as a group of sentences that work together to develop a main idea. But in many other kinds of writing, such as popular magazines and newspapers, ads, and "how-to" manuals, you often find short—even one-sentence—paragraphs that don't really develop a main idea. They're used for a different purpose. Here's a newspaper article that's made up of ten very short paragraphs. What purpose do these short paragraphs serve?

Wyoming dinosaur find may be a fossil first
by Linda Kanamine

No bones about it. Paleontologists are jumping for joy over the discovery of an intact dinosaur skeleton.

The recent find in northern Wyoming may be one of the oldest intact dinosaur skeletons ever found in the USA.

Paleontologists from Montana State University, the University of Wyoming and the Royal Tyrell Museum in Canada left Wednesday on a mission to rescue the partly exposed allosaurus, hoping to preserve it before winter hits.

Allosaurus—among earliest meat-eating dinosaurs— was a ferocious predator that roamed the Earth 136 million to 190 million years ago.

The dinosaur predates Tyrannosaurus Rex by 80 million years. Allosaurus walked on huge hind legs, but stood horizontally and didn't drag its tail.

"It's something you hope to see in a lifetime," says Patrick Leiggi, assistant to the curator at MSU's Museum of the Rockies in Bozeman, Mont.

While other allosauruses have been uncovered in Utah, they've been in bits and pieces. And most have been adult dinosaurs up to 35 feet long—not an 18-foot teenager like this rare find.

"It's really neat to look at," Leiggi says.

The fossil, Leiggi says, is another piece in the puzzle of the Jurassic period, when allosaurus roamed, and should give insights to the beast about which so little is known.

"People believe we know all about dinosaurs," Leiggi says. "But what we know is just a drop in the bucket."

USA TODAY

Three of the above short paragraphs (the longest have only two sentences) show that a person is speaking, but the rest make the article seem easy to read—they're visually appealing. Short paragraphs can also catch a reader's eye and make a point stand out or provide a transition from one idea to another. Reread the following paragraph from the opening selection.

I remembered Jim's style when I ran my races later that day. I signed up for five running and two jumping events; holding my arms as the boy had, I won five blue ribbons.

If you look back to see how this paragraph fits into the opening selection, you'll see that it marks the shift from the idea of studying a runner's techniques to Benoit's idea of becoming a winning runner herself.

EXERCISE 1 ▶ **Surveying the Uses of Paragraphs**

Get together with two or three classmates, and, as a group, make a survey of the way writers actually use paragraphs. Look at sources such as popular magazine and newspaper articles, ads, CD and album cover notes, "how-to" manuals, and movie, book, and restaurant reviews. Take notes about the different uses of paragraphs and the sources where you find them. You might find paragraphs that develop a main idea or that (1) emphasize a point, (2) show a transition from one idea to another, (3) indicate a change in speakers, or (4) create visual appeal.

Paragraphs That Develop a Main Idea

Paragraphs in thoughtful articles and other works of nonfiction, including essays that you write in school, usually develop one main idea. These main idea paragraphs are often—but not always—made up of a topic sentence and several supporting sentences that support, or prove, the main idea. The paragraphs that you'll read in this part of the chapter appeared originally as part of a longer piece of writing where they worked together to separate and to link ideas. They stand alone here so you can study their structure.

The Topic Sentence

Experienced writers have many options in writing paragraphs. One option is to put, somewhere in the paragraph, a single sentence that states the main idea of the paragraph. This *topic sentence* is a specific, limiting statement about the subject of the paragraph.

Location of a Topic Sentence.   You'll often find the topic sentence as the first or second sentence of a paragraph (sometimes following a catchy, inviting first sentence). But you can find a topic sentence any place in a paragraph. To create surprise or to summarize ideas, writers sometimes place topic sentences at or near the end of a paragraph.

Importance of a Topic Sentence.   Not all paragraphs have or need topic sentences. Paragraphs that relate sequences of events or actions in stories, for example, frequently don't contain topic sentences. In the writing that you do in school, however, you'll find that topic sentences are useful. They provide a focus for your reader, and they keep you from straying off the topic as you develop the rest of your paragraph.

EXERCISE 2 ▶ **Identifying Main Ideas and Topic Sentences**

By now you're probably an old hand at identifying main ideas and topic sentences, but you can refresh your skills by tackling the three paragraphs in this exercise. While all three of the paragraphs have a main idea, only two have topic sentences.

First, state the main idea in each paragraph, and then identify the topic sentences in the two paragraphs that have them. Make up a topic sentence for the other paragraph. [Hint: To state the main idea of a sequence of events or actions, give a one-sentence summary of what happens in the paragraph.]

1. English as the language of international pop music and mass entertainment is a worldwide phenomenon. In 1982, a Spanish punk rock group, called Asfalto (Asphalt), released a disc about learning English, which became a hit. The Swedish group Abba records all its numbers in English. Michael Luszynski is a Polish singer who performs almost entirely in English. There is no Polish translation for words like "Baby-baby" and "Yeah-yeah-yeah". Luszynski notes wryly that a phrase like "Słysze warkot pociągu nadjedzie na torze" does not roll as smoothly in a lyric as "I hear the train a-coming, it's rolling down the line . . ."

    Robert McCrum, William Cran, and
    Robert MacNeil, *The Story of English*

2. The captain was disgusted by the place. He said, "You let a sheet of paper fall and it takes forever to hit the ground. It's the heat." He tried to be polite. He asked me about the condition of the road. He asked me where I had

been and where I was going, and why. He knew I was a writer, and also a pilot, and this made him doubly distrustful. Why would a pilot travel so much by ground? And what was there to say about such emptiness? I tried to explain. He seemed worried about me.

William Langewiesche, "The World in Its Extreme"

3.   He became a learner and teacher of men and in this life career what did he accomplish three hundred years ago? The simple unexplained record is in itself wonderful: he found the law of falling bodies; he invented the telescope; he discovered the moons of Jupiter, he explained the reflected light of planets; he laid down the laws of cohesion; he studied the law of the pendulum and applied it to the clock; and above all he adduced irrefragable proof of the correctness of the Copernican doctrine that the sun and not the earth is the center of our universe. Simply and barely stated this accomplishment is tremendous. To few human beings has it been given, in a life of four-score years, to advance so momentously the sum of human knowledge.

W.E.B. Du Bois, "Galileo Galilei"

Supporting Sentences

Imagine what communication would be like if people wrote only in topic sentences.

> Some scientists believe that birds are the modern descendants of dinosaurs.
>
> When Abraham Lincoln first delivered his famous Gettysburg Address, many critics considered it a disgrace.
>
> We are selling the United States to the highest bidder.

These are surprising statements, and few readers would accept these generalizations without *supporting sentences* that give details to support, or prove, them. Even when topic sentences are not so surprising (*most Americans know little about geography; the planets revolve around the sun in elliptical orbits*), they still need support.

Supporting sentences often consist of sensory details, facts or statistics, examples, or an anecdote. A paragraph may be developed with one type of detail or with a combination of types.

Sensory Details

Sensory details are images of sight, sound, taste, smell, and texture that bring the subject to life for readers. In this paragraph, notice how sensory details help you see and hear the children, as well as smell the evening's refreshments.

> The weeks until graduation were filled with heady activities. A group of small children were to be presented in a play about buttercups and daisies and bunny rabbits. They could be heard throughout the building practicing their hops and their little songs that sounded like silver bells. The older girls (nongraduates, of course) were assigned the task of making refreshments for the night's festivities. A tangy scent of ginger, cinnamon, nutmeg and chocolate wafted around the home economics building as the budding cooks made samples for themselves and their teachers.
>
> Maya Angelou, *I know why the caged bird sings*

Facts and Statistics

Another way to support and clarify a main idea is to use facts and statistics. A *fact* is something that can be proven true by concrete information: *Archbishop Desmond Tutu, a South African civil rights leader, received the Nobel Prize for peace in 1984.* A *statistic* is a fact based on numbers: *The United States border with Mexico is 1,952 miles long.* To verify the accuracy of facts or statistics, you can cross-check them in reference materials. In the following paragraph, the writer uses statistics to illustrate the popularity of pencils.

> You'd think that the pencil would just fade away, what with pattering keyboards and ubiquitous ballpoint pens. Pencil popularity, however, seems here to stay—more than 2 1/2 billion pencils are produced in America every year. The U.S. government uses 45 million of them a year, and the New York Stock Exchange more than a million. Perhaps it's because the pencil's an old-fashioned hard worker—one standard pencil can leave a 35-mile trail, or about 45,000 words. At least forty materials from twenty-eight countries go into one.
>
> Mary Blocksma, *Reading the Numbers*

Examples

Many newspapers of the day called Abraham Lincoln's Gettysburg Address a disgrace; one example is the *Times* of London, which referred to the speech as "dull and commonplace." *Examples* are specific instances or illustrations of a general idea. The following paragraph (for example) uses specific examples to support the writer's main idea about the modern interest in mazes.

Since the 1970s, there has been a revolution in innovative puzzle mazes. Greg Bright's puzzle maze at Longleat had curving paths, wooden bridges, a complete lack of symmetry, and, above all, immense size. Stuart Landsborough's wooden mazes triggered off a maze craze in Japan, resulting in the construction of over two hundred three-dimensional wooden mazes during the 1980s. Our own puzzle innovations have encompassed traditional, interactive and color mazes, within a diverse range of landscape settings.

Adrian Fisher and Georg Gerster,
Labyrinth: Solving the Riddle of the Maze

Anecdotes

An *anecdote,* a little story that is usually biographical or autobiographical, can also be used to support, or prove, a main idea. In this paragraph, for example, the writer uses an anecdote to help support a point about General Stonewall Jackson's ability to ignore the suffering of his men.

He had a strange quality of overlooking suffering. He had a young courier, and during one of the battles Jackson looked around for him and he wasn't there. And he said, "Where is Lieutenant So-and-so?" And they said, "He was killed, General." Jackson said, "Very commendable, very commendable," and put him out of his mind. He would send men stumbling into battle where fury was and have no concern about casualties at the moment. He would march men until they were spitting cotton and white-faced and fell by the wayside. He wouldn't even stop to glance at one of them, but kept going.

Geoffrey C. Ward et al., "Men at War: An Interview with Shelby Foote," *The Civil War*

E X E R C I S E **3** ▶   **Collecting Supporting Details**

Now that you have looked at different kinds of supporting details, try creating your own. Here are four main ideas that you might use for paragraphs. Choose two of the ideas, and then list at least three details that support, or prove, the main idea. Use the type of detail—sensory details, facts and/or statistics, examples, or an anecdote—indicated after each main idea. You'll probably have to do a little research to supply most of the details.

EXAMPLE **1.** Roller coasters have an interesting history. (facts and statistics)

a. *Forerunner of roller coaster was Russian ice slide, built as early as the fifteenth century in Saint Petersburg*

b. *First roller coaster at Coney Island constructed in 1884*

c. *Before Depression of 1930s, 1,500 roller coasters existed; during Depression, number gradually declined*

d. *Roller coaster began to make a comeback, with numbers rising from 147 in 1979 to 164 in 1989*

1. Comic strips aren't just funny; sometimes, they teach important lessons about life. (examples)
2. A high school pep rally has a life of its own. (sensory details)
3. Planets revolve around the sun at different rates. (facts and statistics)
4. Good friends are there to share the good times and to help in the bad times. (anecdote)

The Clincher Sentence

A *clincher sentence,* a final sentence that emphasizes or summarizes the main idea, can help readers grasp the main idea of a paragraph, especially a longer paragraph. In the following paragraph, for example, the writer uses a clincher sentence to summarize and emphasize his main idea about Native American cultures. Notice that the topic sentence at the beginning of the paragraph also expresses the main idea.

In the past forty years, however, anthropologists have done some very thorough digging into the life of the North American Indians and have discovered a bewildering variety of cultures and societies beyond anything the schoolbooks have taught. There were Indian societies that dwelt in permanent settlements, and others that wandered; some were wholly democratic, others had very rigid class systems based on property. Some were ruled by gods carried around on litters, some had judicial systems, to some the only known punishment was torture. Some lived in caves, others in tepees of bison skins, others in cabins. There were tribes ruled by warriors or by women, by sacred elders or by councils. . . . There were tribes who worshiped the bison or a matriarch or the maize they lived by. There were tribes that had never heard of war, and there were tribes debauched by centuries of fighting. In short, there was a great diversity of Indian nations, speaking over five hundred languages.

Alistair Cooke, *Alistair Cooke's America*

Unity

Unity simply means that the paragraph "hangs together." In other words, all the supporting sentences work together to develop the main idea. A paragraph should have unity whether the main idea is stated in a topic sentence or is implied (suggested). In paragraphs that relate a series of actions or events, the main idea is often implied rather than stated. You can achieve unity in these kinds of paragraphs by the very sequence of the actions or events.

All Sentences Relate to the Main Idea Stated in the Topic Sentence.   In the following paragraph, the topic sentence states the main idea—that animals' eyes tell a lot about them. Each of the following sentences give some specific information about what you can see in their eyes.

> You can tell a lot about an animal's way of life by looking at its eyes. If it relies a lot on sight, its eyes will be relatively big. If it is a hunting animal, like the tiger, its eyes will be placed toward the front of its head, so that the fields of view of the two eyes overlap. This allows it to judge distance accurately for pouncing on prey. Animals with many predators, like the rabbit, usually have eyes at the sides of their heads. They can spot a predator coming from almost every angle, but they are not very good at judging distance.
>
> Tony Seddon and Jill Bailey, *The Living World*

All Sentences Relate to an Implied Main Idea.   The following paragraph doesn't have a topic sentence, but all the sentences support an implied main idea—American women began experimenting with shorter hairstyles during the early 1900s.

> One of the first women to commit the shocking act of cutting her hair was the famous American ballroom dancer Irene Castle. In 1913 she popularized a very short hairstyle called the Castle Clip, worn with a string of pearls around her forehead. It wasn't until after World War I, though, that most women found the courage to bob their hair and exchange their hairpins for the new spring-clip "bobby pin." The shortest cuts of the 1920s flapper age were the

"boyish bob" and the "shingle," for which the hair was actually shaved at the back of the neck. For women who wanted their short hair frizzy-curly rather than sleek, there was a new hair treatment called a permanent wave.

Lila Perl, *From Top Hats to Baseball Caps, From Bustles to Blue Jeans: Why We Dress the Way We Do*

All Sentences Relate to a Sequence of Events. The writer of the following paragraph achieves unity through the sequence of events and actions. You won't find a topic sentence in this paragraph, but you will find that all sentences relate to the experience of entering an emerald mine on a tire attached to a steel cable.

First came a drizzle. Then groundwater poured from the walls, and I was plunging through a waterfall. The darkest darkroom doesn't begin to compare to the pitch-black inside the mine shaft. I couldn't look upward at the patch of daylight above for fear of drowning. After about three minutes—an eternity—the unseen operator threw on the brake, jerking me to a stop two feet above the mud. To no one in particular, I sighed, "Welcome to the glamorous world of emeralds."

Fred Ward, "Emeralds"

© Fred Ward

EXERCISE 4 ▶ **Analyzing Notes for Unity**

Here are some notes, in the form of a cluster, for a paragraph on the infamous Trail of Tears. The writer's topic sentence is "Thousands of Native Americans, of several groups, died from hardships on the Trail of Tears." In a group of three or four classmates, try to determine which notes should be discarded because they would destroy the unity of the paragraph.

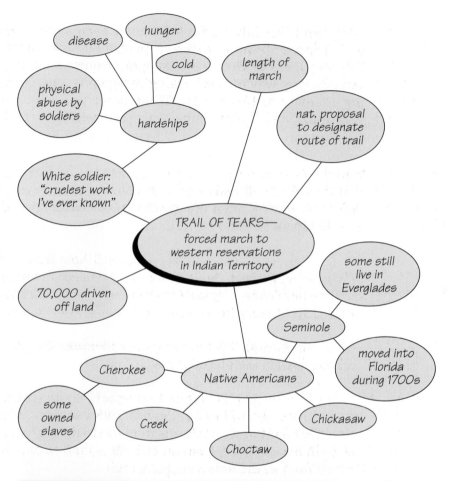

- disease
- hunger
- cold
- physical abuse by soldiers
- hardships
- length of march
- nat. proposal to designate route of trail
- White soldier: "cruelest work I've ever known"
- TRAIL OF TEARS— forced march to western reservations in Indian Territory
- 70,000 driven off land
- some still live in Everglades
- Seminole
- moved into Florida during 1700s
- Cherokee
- Native Americans
- Chickasaw
- some owned slaves
- Creek
- Choctaw

Jerome Tiger, *Trail of Tears* ($16\frac{1}{4}$" × $18\frac{7}{8}$"). Courtesy of The Five Civilized Tribes Museum, Muskogee, Oklahoma.

Coherence

Unity isn't the only quality of a good paragraph; *coherence* is also important. In a *coherent* paragraph, the relationship between ideas is clear—the paragraph flows smoothly. You can go a long way toward making paragraphs coherent by paying attention to two things: (1) the order you use to arrange your ideas, and (2) the connections you make between ideas.

Order of Ideas

When you create a paragraph, you need to arrange ideas so that the order will make sense to your readers. Four types of order that writers often use are *chronological order, spatial order, order of importance,* and *logical order.*

Chronological Order.   When you tell how things change over time, you usually give actions or events in the order they happen, or in *chronological* (time) *order.* You use chronological order to tell a story, to explain a process, and to explain cause and effect.

For an example of chronological order, see the paragraph on entering an emerald mine (page 73).

Spatial Order.   Description focuses on the subject itself and often calls for *spatial order,* the order of details by their location. You might describe details from left to right, from near to far, from front to back, from top to bottom, and so on. Note the spatial order in the following paragraph.

near	Laurel is up in the cool shadow on the porch roof, in dungarees and a sweatshirt, scraping off pine needles with a snow shovel.
farther away	Below, an old garden hose snakes across the knobby dirt, its pinhole leak shooting up a spray that fizzes in a slash of sunlight. There's a breath of wind, a commotion in the lilacs.
still farther away	Down the lane, stones are finally warming in their sockets. Between branches, she can see
farthest distance	the water tower on Buffalo Hill, the long gravel slide below the golf course, the blinding curlicues of the river.

David Long, "Blue Spruce"

Order of Importance.   When your purpose is to inform or to persuade, you'll often arrange ideas or details in *order of importance.* At times you may find it most effective to begin with the most important detail and move to the least important. Other times, you may want to reverse the order and start with the least important.

In this paragraph, the writer gives information about the help provided by black soldiers and sailors during the Civil War. The article begins with their least important contributions.

Long before Fort Pillow, and long before Sherman's dagger thrusts in Georgia, Black soldiers and sailors became indispensable elements in a war that could not have been won without their help. In the fall of 1862, they participated in minor actions at Island Mounds, Mo., and in skirmishes in Georgia and Florida. But their first major battles came in the summer of 1863 at Port Hudson, the last Confederate obstacle to the capture of Vicksburg, and in the famous "Glory" charge of the Fifty-fourth Massachusetts Volunteers at Fort Wagner in the Charleston, S.C., harbor.

"Black, Blue and Gray: The Other Civil War," *Ebony*

Logical Order.   When you use strategies of classification, including definition and comparison/contrast, you will usually find it makes sense to group related ideas together in *logical order.* The following paragraph, comparing two types of young adults during the 1950s, shows logical order.

Our world was divided into Tweeds and Greasers, both wanting to be "tough" and irresistible. The Tweeds were would-be Ivy Leaguers who bought Hollywood's Tab Hunter-Robert Wagner hard-sell—white bucks, khaki pants, button-down shirt, red-striped tie. We were shiny, formal, and eager. We trusted our façade to work for us as successfully as it had worked for our film heroes. They wore make-up; we had Clearasil. We wanted to be perfect. The Greasers swallowed James Dean and Marlon Brando whole. They were big on silence and scruffiness. They were losers in life, and, what's more, they didn't care; they gloried in it. That's why they were dangerous— they had nothing to lose. With their leather jackets, DA's, T-shirts with cigarette packs rolled in the turned-up sleeves, they wanted to be left alone. We wanted to be accepted.

John Lahr, "Introduction" to *Baby, That Was Rock and Roll,* by Robert Palmer

EXERCISE 5 ▶ **Arranging Paragraphs in Order**

The ideas in these three paragraphs aren't arranged in an order that makes sense. Identify the type of order that would work for each paragraph, and then revise each paragraph by re-arranging sentences into an appropriate order.

1.   Much evidence may be cited to show George Washington's enormous popularity immediately following his leadership and victories during the colonies' War of Independence. People generally thought of Washington as a genuine hero and model citizen. The most important testament of Washington's esteem came from Congress. Members of that body approved a bronze equestrian statue of Washington for the future capital in which the general was to be dressed in Roman clothes and wear a laurel wreath on his head. In addition, many cities, including Boston and Richmond, celebrated Washington's birthday, February 22.

2.   In the distance, the mountain towered above the landscape. Halfway down the mountain, the timberline began, the trees almost buried in deep snowdrifts. At the foot of the mountain, the boy made his camp. Near the camp, an icy stream rushed by, swollen with the slowly melting snow. The boy knew that deer foraged for food in those drifts and that some had already starved during that long, cold winter. Wreaths of heavy, smoky clouds hid the heavy rocks at the top that would make the ascent so dangerous. At night, curious animals came close on all sides of the camp—the boy often saw the fresh tracks in the snow the next morning.

3.   Chad sat on the sidewalk outside the grocery where he had just finished working and changed shoes. Chad met Coach and the other cross-country runners in front of the gym. He then tossed his good shoes into the car and drove the mile to school. They were ready when he got there, late from work as usual. They turned from Harrison onto Bell Street, which contained Killer Hill. The group of twelve runners warmed up with leg exercises before heading slowly down Harrison Street. Just as they started going up the hill, Chad heard Eric call to him, but he was busy thinking that working and running were getting too much for him, and didn't reply. "Chad," Eric yelled again. Chad was tempted, but shook his head. "No," he said. "We signed up to run, and we can't back out now." Chad finally turned toward Eric, who said, puffing, "Let's cut out."

Connections Between Ideas

Arranging ideas in an order that makes sense helps to make paragraphs coherent, but *direct references* and *transitional words and expressions* can also help. These words and phrases act as connectors between and among ideas so that the paragraph is clear to readers.

 REFERENCE NOTE: For help on using direct references and transitional words and expressions to connect ideas *between* paragraphs, see pages 117–118.

Direct References. Referring to a noun or pronoun that you've used earlier in the paragraph is a *direct reference.* You can make direct references by (1) using a noun or pronoun that refers to a noun or pronoun used earlier, (2) repeating a word used earlier, or (3) using a word or phrase that means the same thing as one used earlier.

In the following paragraph, the superscript numbers indicate the type of direct reference the writer is using.

Pepé drank from the water bag, and he[1] reached into the flour sack and brought out a black string of jerky. His[1] white teeth gnawed at the string[2] until the tough meat[3] parted. He[1] chewed[3] slowly and drank[2] occasionally from the water bag[2]. His[1] little eyes were slumberous and tired, but the muscles of his[1] face were hard-set. The earth of the trail was black now. It[1] gave up a hollow sound under the walking hoofbeats.

John Steinbeck, "Flight"

Transitional Expressions. Words and phrases that make a transition from one idea to another are called *transitional expressions.* These words and phrases include prepositions that indicate chronological or spatial order, as well as conjunctions, which connect and show relationships. The following chart includes some frequently used transitional expressions, grouped according to the relationships they indicate. The chart also indicates how the expressions are most often used.

TRANSITIONAL WORDS AND PHRASES		
Comparing Ideas/Classification and Definition		
also	another	similarly
and	moreover	too
Contrasting Ideas/Classification and Definition		
although	in spite of	on the other hand
but	instead	still
however	nevertheless	yet
Showing Cause and Effect/Narration		
as a result	consequently	so that
because	since	therefore
Showing Time/Narration		
after	eventually	next
at last	finally	then
at once	first	thereafter
before	meanwhile	when
Showing Place/Description		
above	down	next
across	here	over
around	in	there
before	inside	to
beyond	into	under
Showing Importance/Evaluation		
first	mainly	then
last	more important	to begin with

WRITING NOTE

Transitional expressions can help give your writing coherence. But don't overdo them. The result can be writing that sounds artificial and stilted.

Transitional words and phrases are underlined in the following paragraph about a woman who was paralyzed as a result of a diving accident. Notice how the words help to show relationships of time and space.

At first, when Marca Bristo was injured, she couldn't see what she could do beyond that time. Later, as she mastered coping with life in a wheelchair, she decided to fight for more opportunities for disabled people. Then she became executive director of Access Living, an organization that works to remove any barriers that prevent disabled people from becoming independent and taking part in society. Eventually, she co-founded the National Council on Independent Living and afterward prepared a report that resulted in the Americans with Disabilities Act.

EXERCISE 6 ▶ **Identifying Direct References and Transitional Expressions**

The following paragraph about volcanoes has both direct references and transitional expressions. Make one list of the direct references and another list of the transitional expressions. You may need to refer to the three kinds of direct references, discussed on page 79, as well as to the chart of transitional expressions.

The earth is full of volcanoes, which are named after Vulcan, the Roman god of fire. Some volcanoes are extinct and, therefore, pose no threat. Many of them, however, are dormant, and they could explode. Moreover, Mount St. Helens did erupt in Washington in 1980. Of course, you know that volcanoes are found mostly on land. But did you know that they are also on the ocean floor? Because most of the land volcanoes circle the Pacific Ocean, they are known as the Ring of Fire. An ancient Roman probably would have called the circle Vulcan's Ring.

Strategies of Development

Why are you writing your paragraph? What is its purpose? Who will read it? These are questions to consider when choosing a strategy, a method of development, for a paragraph. As you've seen, the type of strategy you select to develop an idea can influence the order you use to arrange ideas. It can also affect the kind of information with which you develop the paragraph.

Depending on your main purpose for writing the paragraph, you could choose from among the four strategies of development shown in the chart below. Remember that you can have more than one purpose (and more than one strategy of development) in a paragraph. For example, writers often combine description and narration in the same paragraph.

STRATEGIES OF DEVELOPMENT	
Description	Looking at individual features of a particular subject
Narration	Looking at changes in a subject over a period of time
Classification	Looking at a subject in relation to other subjects
Evaluation	Looking at the value of, or judging, a subject

Calvin & Hobbes, copyright 1992 Universal Press Syndicate. Reprinted with permission. All rights reserved.

Description

Have you already picked out the car that you hope to own someday? What does it look like? Is there a food that you especially dislike? What does it look, smell, or taste like?

When you need to focus on a subject, to tell what it's like, you have to examine its specific features. Then you select description as your strategy of development, using sensory details (details of sight, sound, taste, touch, and smell) for support. You'll often use spatial order to organize a description, but, depending on your subject or purpose, you might also use order of importance or chronological order. The writer of the following paragraph uses spatial order to describe a store in Nameless, Tennessee.

> The old store, lighted only by three fifty-watt bulbs, smelled of coal oil and baking bread. In the middle of the rectangular room, where the oak floor sagged a little, stood an iron stove. To the right was a wooden table with an unfinished game of checkers and a stool made from an apple-tree stump. On shelves around the walls sat earthen jugs with corncob stoppers, a few canned goods, and some of the two thousand old clocks and clockworks Thurmond Watts owned. Only one was ticking; the others he just looked at.
>
> William Least Heat-Moon, *Blue Highways*

EXERCISE 7 ▶ **Using Description as a Strategy**

Choose one of the following subjects and list five sensory details (details of sight, sound, taste, smell, and touch) that you could use to describe the specific features of the subject.

1. your yard—when you're faced with raking or mowing it
2. the kitchen—when you have to clean it up
3. a character from *Star Trek* or another science fiction book or movie
4. an old, abandoned house
5. a disgusting insect

Narration

What happened during the 1991 Communist coup against Mikhail Gorbachev? How do you replace a lost driver's license? What are the effects of peer pressure on teenagers?

Answering these questions requires the strategy of narration, of looking at changes over time. You may use narration *to tell a story or incident* (what happened during the coup), *to explain a process* (how to replace a driver's license), or *to explain causes and effects* (what the effects of peer pressure are). You usually use chronological order to present ideas and information in paragraphs of narration.

Telling a Story.   Writers use the strategy of narration to tell stories, either true or fictional, about incidents and events over time (what happened). In this paragraph, the writer tells part of a Native American story.

> The Youngman Started Out to Look for Wood. It was not long Before he Saw Wood that would Make a Beautiful Warm Fire, and he Began to Busy himself Gathering the Wood. Suddenly he Felt the Presence of the Owl. The Owl Reached Down and Put the Youngman in its Ear. The Youngman Strung his Bow and Fitted One of his Arrows, Letting it Fly from his Bow Deep Into the Ear of the Owl. And the Youngman was Free.
>
> Hyemeyohsts Storm, *Seven Arrows*

Explaining a Process.   Explaining a process—telling how something works or telling how to do something—is similar to telling a story. With each type of writing, you look at a subject as it changes over time. A writer explaining a process also uses the strategy of narration to tell what happens next or what is to be done next. In the following paragraph, for example, the writer explains how to perform the "Violin with Cord Elastic Strings" clown trick.

> You enter with a violin and prepare to play some lovely music. Taking out a pocket handkerchief, you fold it carefully and place it on your *right* shoulder as a violin rest. You then put the violin under your chin on your *left* shoulder (or vice versa if you are left-handed). Drawing the bow back on the [elastic-cord] strings, you suddenly send the bow flying offstage into the wings like an arrow! Dismayed, you produce a second bow and repeat the action, launching this bow offstage as well. You investigate the violin and discover the elastic strings, reacting with either embarrassment or delight (perhaps even leading into a full demonstration of target practice with "violin and arrow").
>
> Turk Pipkin, *Be a Clown!*

Explaining Causes and Effects. You also look at the way things change over time when you explain causes and effects. Here again, you use the strategy of narration to develop the paragraph. For example, the following writer explains the causes and effects of changes in free black and slave populations.

> The great increase in the free black population in America came after the Revolutionary War. In appreciation of the service of some 5,000 blacks in the War for Independence and as a result of the libertarian and egalitarian spirit that the Declaration of Independence and the war inspired, many masters, especially Northerners, freed their slaves. Soon individual states in the North decreed the gradual abolition of the institution, beginning with Vermont's action in 1777. In 1776 the population of the United States was about 2 1/2 million, more than 500,000 black slaves and approximately 40,000 free blacks. More than one half of these free blacks lived in the South. The Revolutionary leaders, including Washington and Jefferson, anticipated a continuation of the trend toward emancipation until eventually slavery would disappear from the

land. This expectation was to be drowned, almost literally, by the whirring noise of Eli Whitney's cotton gin. The invention of this native of Massachusetts made cotton production increasingly profitable and caused rapid and substantial increases in the slave population, so that on the eve of the Civil War there were 4 million black slaves in the South.

Alton Hornsby, *The Black Almanac*

EXERCISE 8 ▶ Using Narration as a Strategy

You have probably used the strategy of narration many times, perhaps without even being aware that you were doing so. Now practice the strategy by following the three sets of instructions given below.

1. Give the major actions that preceded and followed the assassination of President John F. Kennedy. (If you don't remember, go to your library and research the subject.)
2. Imagine that you are telling a fourteen-year-old the basics of how to drive. List the major steps involved in starting up a car, moving forward, and coming to a smooth stop.
3. Give at least three causes for the popularity of credit cards, and then identify three potentially harmful effects.

Classification

What are the different departments of the CIA? The word *glasnost* became popular during the late 1980s—what does it mean? How is the appearance of poisonous snakes different from that of nonpoisonous snakes?

When you answer questions like these, you're using the strategy of *classification.* You can classify a subject by dividing it into its parts (the departments of the CIA), defining it (the term *glasnost*), or comparing and contrasting it with something else (poisonous snakes/nonpoisonous snakes).

Dividing.   Classifying by *dividing* means looking at the parts of a subject in order to understand the subject as a whole. For example, to explain what woodwind instruments are, you could discuss the different kinds of woodwind instruments, such as clarinet, flute, and recorder. In the following paragraph, the writers divide dinosaurs into two groups in order to explain their characteristics.

> To begin with, dinosaurs fell into two groups: the bird-hipped ones, or *ornithischians*, and the reptile-hipped ones, or *saurischians*. (*Ornith–* is Greek for "bird," and *saur–* is Greek for "reptile.") The bird-hipped dinosaurs were almost all herbivores, or plant-eaters, while the reptile-hipped group contained both meat eaters (carnivores) and plant-eaters.
>
> Tom and Jane D. Allen with Savannah Waring Walker,
> *Dinosaur Days in Texas*

Defining.　To *define,* you first identify a subject as a part of a larger group or class (a *pediatrician* is a doctor). Then you discuss some features that make the subject different from other members of the class (who specializes in the treatment of children). In the following paragraph, the writer defines pikas.

> Pikas are mountain-dwelling mammals that are tiny relatives of rabbits and hares. Pikas are only about six inches long and have short, rounded ears. They live in colonies in rocky areas. They prepare for winter by gathering grass and spreading it out to dry in the sun. Then they make little haystacks near their dens, and eat the dried grass throughout the winter.

Comparing and Contrasting.　You also use the strategy of classification when *comparing* subjects (telling how they're alike), *contrasting* them (telling how they're different), or when both comparing and contrasting. The following paragraph compares and contrasts the heads of dogs and wolves.

> A dog's skull is generally somewhat smaller and rounder than a wolf's and its brain is about twenty percent smaller. Wolves and all the other kinds of wild dogs have upstanding ears, which act as sound funnels. Like antennas, they

gather sound waves from the air and direct them down the ear canals into the inner ear. Most domestic dogs have lop ears: at rest their ears hang limply down, although they can be pricked up to listen to interesting sounds. . . . For all of the dogs, both wild and domestic, the ears are not only organs of hearing but also organs of expression. The position of a dog's ears can communicate a great deal about its mood.

Alvin and Virginia Silverstein, *Dogs: All About Them*

EXERCISE 9 ▶ Using Classification as a Strategy

What parts does it have? What is it? How is it like or different from something else? The same subject may be handled using different ways of classification. For practice, try classifying an animal of your choice according to the following directions. Use the library or your textbooks to find information.

1. Divide the animal group by listing three different types of animals within the group. (What are three kinds of sharks, giant snakes, bats?)
2. Define the animal group. Put it into a larger group (is it a reptile, a mammal, what?) and then list three details about it that make it different from other members of the group.
3. Compare and contrast the animal with another animal. List three major ways the animals are alike and three major ways they are different. (Both humpbacks and blue whales are types of whales. How are they similar? different?)

THREE KINDS OF SHARKS

Evaluation

Is spanking a good punishment for children? Was the movie *Robin Hood: Prince of Thieves* worth the cost of renting the tape?

Evaluation means judging the value of something. You often evaluate a subject in order to inform readers or to persuade them to think or act differently. An evaluation should be supported with reasons showing *why* you made the judgment about the subject.

The following paragraph is part of a review of recent movies. Notice the reasons the writer gives for the evaluation of the three movies.

> "Movies are better then ever" can usually be regarded as nothing more than a slogan to sell tickets, but now there are some movies that may make it a slogan to believe. After several years of movies of doubtful mentality, the early 1990s gave us some surprisingly intelligent, beautifully filmed, thought-provoking films, such as *Dances With Wolves*, *Fried Green Tomatoes*, and *Cinema Paradiso*. These go back to the artistry of the best movies of the past and go against the tendency to film everything in closeup, with the eventual (or immediate) transfer to videotape in mind. Movies should be movies, made as these are for large screens, and should give audiences something to admire and think about as these do. Not all movies are better than ever, but some are. Let's hope it's a trend.

EXERCISE 10 ▶ Using Evaluation as a Strategy

It's your turn to be an entertainment critic. Start by identifying three subjects from the following list.

1. a movie you've seen (at the theater or on videotape)
2. a television special or series you have watched
3. a book or story you've read
4. a recording (tape or CD) you have listened to

For each subject, state your overall opinion (good, bad, somewhere in between), and then list three reasons why you hold this opinion. Share your evaluations with a classmate.

MAKING CONNECTIONS

WRITING PARAGRAPHS FOR DIFFERENT PURPOSES

In this chapter, you have studied the form and structure of paragraphs. As a result of this study, you have knowledge that you can apply by writing paragraphs for different purposes. Remember, the four basic aims or purposes of writing are to express yourself; to inform, explain, or explore; to persuade others; and to create literary works.

Writing a Self-Expressive Paragraph

If you have ever written about your thoughts and feelings in a journal, in a letter to a friend, or even in a song lyric, you've written to express yourself. Self-expressive writing is a good way to get feelings out that you might not be able to vent in any other way; and, sometimes, it can help you develop a better understanding of yourself. Self-expressive writing is often intended to be private, but not always—people write books and even movie or TV scripts about personal experiences, thoughts, and feelings.

Using one of the following "starters" or an idea of your own, write a paragraph expressing your thoughts and feelings about a subject.

A person, place, or object that's important to me is ____.
I've learned a great deal in my life about ____.
I've got to learn more about ____.
A big disappointment has been ____.
I'm very happy about ____.

Prewriting. If you're having trouble getting started, try freewriting with the starter sentence as a beginning. Don't worry about getting your ideas into any special form—just let them flow. Then use the ideas you have jotted down as the basis for a paragraph. Imagine that you're "talking" to a good friend or a special relative.

Writing, Evaluating, and Revising. If your writing is private and you don't want to share it, write a draft of your paragraph and then leave it. Or, imagine that someone might read your paragraph many years from now, as you might read the autobiography of a movie star or famous athlete. How might you revise the paragraph so that this wider audience will understand it? What do you need to explain or clarify?

Proofreading and Publishing. If you plan to share your paragraph, proofread it carefully—you wouldn't want mistakes to prevent readers from knowing the real you. "Publish" your paragraph by sharing it with a trusted adult or friend or by putting it in your own version of a time capsule. Tuck it in the back of a drawer or closet; you might enjoy reading it a year from now.

Writing an Expository Paragraph

The purpose of many paragraphs that you write, especially those for school, is expository: You are informing, explaining, or exploring a subject. You might, for example, share information about the next Spanish Club party, explain the effects of drinking and driving, or explore possible solutions to the problems of hazardous waste disposal.

The next diagram contains some information about radio signals. Using the explanations and drawings in the diagram, write an informative paragraph. (Try the strategy of dividing to develop your paragraph; see pages 86–87.) If you need more information about radio signals, do some research in your library. In writing your paragraph, assume that your readers (classmates) know nothing about radio signals and that it is your job to give them a concise, clear, simple explanation.

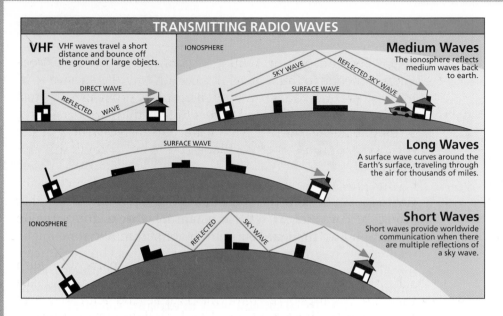

TRANSMITTING RADIO WAVES

VHF VHF waves travel a short distance and bounce off the ground or large objects.

DIRECT WAVE
REFLECTED WAVE

IONOSPHERE

Medium Waves
The ionosphere reflects medium waves back to earth.

SKY WAVE
REFLECTED SKY WAVE
SURFACE WAVE

SURFACE WAVE

Long Waves
A surface wave curves around the Earth's surface, traveling through the air for thousands of miles.

IONOSPHERE

REFLECTED
SKY WAVE

Short Waves
Short waves provide worldwide communication when there are multiple reflections of a sky wave.

Prewriting. Study the diagram carefully to understand the different types of radio signals. Formulate your topic sentence based on the purpose of the paragraph (to inform your readers about radio signals) and the strategy of development (dividing). To divide the concept of radio signals, look at the different kinds of waves in the preceding diagram. Your supporting sentences should explain the divisions. You might try a topic sentence like this one: "Radio signals consist of VHF, medium, long, and short waves."

Writing, Evaluating, and Revising. Start with your topic sentence and then add at least three or four sentences that present information from the diagram. Remember that each supporting sentence should prove your main idea. After you've finished a first draft, take time to evaluate it. Does your topic sentence give the main idea of your paragraph and state the divisions of radio signals? Do your supporting sentences explain the divisions? Revise and rearrange any sentences that aren't clear or that break the unity of the paragraph.

Proofreading and Publishing. Review your paragraph to find and correct any errors in grammar, usage, and mechanics. (Check carefully the spellings of technical words.) Use your paragraph to inform someone, perhaps a friend or relative, about radio signals.

Writing a Persuasive Paragraph

When your purpose in writing is persuasive, you try to convince someone to think or act in a certain way. Persuasive writing is all around you, even though you may not realize it. Most ads, solicitation letters, and letters to the editor are persuasive writing. Entertainment reviews are persuasive writing if the reviewer's purpose is to persuade you to act or think in a certain way.

Imagine that you're trying to persuade a friend to move (or not to move) back to your area or city. What could you say that would be convincing? Write a paragraph that might persuade your friend to do what you think he or she should do.

Prewriting. Start your planning for this paragraph with what you believe about life in your area or city. You could make one list of things you think are positive and another list of things you think are negative. The list might include schools, the environment, recreational facilities, shopping, and the friendliness (or lack of it) of the residents. Then choose a position and draw your reasons and supporting information from the list.

Writing, Evaluating, and Revising. To begin your draft, write down your position statement. The remainder of your paragraph should contain the reasons and supporting information for your position. After you have written your draft, examine the reasons you've given to determine whether they sound convincing. Revise your paragraph to make it more persuasive.

Proofreading and Publishing. Correct any errors in grammar, usage, and mechanics. Then try your paragraph out by sharing it with a small group of classmates. Are they convinced?

Writing a Literary Paragraph

What is it that makes a short story different from a news story on the front page of the newspaper? Is a description of the Empire State Building in a novel different from the description of the same building in an encyclopedia article? Part of the difference is a result of imagination and creativity—the writer's urge to make a new and original statement. When you create literature, you work with language—words and groups of words—in the same way the artist uses watercolors and the composer uses musical notes.

The following poem is an example of literature; in it the poet has used his imagination and language to look at a common thing—a fire truck—in a new and unique way.

The Great Figure
by William Carlos Williams

Among the rain
and lights
I saw the figure 5
in gold
on a red
fire truck
moving
tense
unheeded
to gong clangs
siren howls
and wheels rumbling
through the dark city.

Think about the originality in the preceding poem. What words does the writer use to create images in our minds—sights and sounds? The writer creates a new impression of the fire truck; it almost seems that the truck has become a human being. How does he create this impression? Could this poem be rewritten in paragraph form and still be creative? How would you have to change it?

Paragraphs can be literary, just like poems; think of the individual paragraphs in your favorite short story or novel. To use what you know about paragraph form in a literary paragraph, borrow an idea from William Carlos Williams: Write about an ordinary object in a new and different way. Along with your imagination and language, you will use the strategy of description to point out the features or characteristics of the object you are writing about.

Prewriting. Begin by observing what is around you or brainstorming to think of an ordinary object that you find interesting, perhaps the telephone, a running shoe, a car. William Carlos Williams found the fire truck and the number on its side interesting; otherwise he wouldn't have been able to create such a delightful poem. Once you've decided what object you'll describe, think about how you might describe it in a new and different way. What could you compare it to? What features would you stress? Jot down your ideas on a piece of paper, and think about how you might organize your paragraph.

Writing, Evaluating, and Revising. Using your prewriting notes, write a draft of your descriptive paragraph. Remember that your purpose is to create literature; you want to use words imaginatively to create a new and different picture of an ordinary object. Do you want to call attention to sounds, textures, visual patterns? Let your imagination drive your ideas. After you've finished your draft, exchange paragraphs with a classmate. Does your paragraph cause your classmate to see the object you are describing in a new way? When you've decided what to add or remove, revise your paragraph.

Proofreading and Publishing. Review your paragraph to look for problems with usage and mechanics and then share it with your classmates. Are your paragraphs as imaginative as Williams' poem?

3 UNDERSTANDING COMPOSITION STRUCTURE

Looking at the Whole

What do you see when you look at a jazzy sports car? Do you notice the **parts**—the wheels, the sleek shape, the leather seats? Or do you notice the **whole** car—that gorgeous machine? A composition is a little like that car; taken as a whole, it's a fantastic machine.

Writing and You.   What do a movie review in *People Weekly*, an article about the Buffalo Bills in *Sports Illustrated*, and an article in *PC World* have in common? They all use a standard form, the structure of a composition. You use this structure, too. Haven't you written reports in science class and essays in English class?

As You Read.   As you read the following essay from a book by Isaac Asimov, think about its form. How do the words and sentences come together as a whole piece of writing?

Jasper Johns. *Map* (1961). Oil on canvas, 6'6" × 10'3 $\frac{1}{8}$".
Collection, The Museum of Modern Art, New York. Gift of Mr. and Mrs. Robert C. Scull. © Jasper Johns/VAGA, New York 1993.

learning science

by Isaac Asimov

I imagine that many a young scholar has asked him- or herself, rebelliously, why on Earth s/he must learn science when s/he has no intention of being a scientist.

Someone who feels that may feel that s/he need know no more than the minimum that will allow him or her to just barely get through life. Why should one know history if one is not going to be a historian? Or geography or languages if one isn't going to travel much?

But surely there is more to life than what one "does." Even if one lives quietly at home and works at some simple, routine job, there must nevertheless be *some* value to understanding the world about us, to understanding events in the light of the past, to having an appreciation of other places and other cultures.

In fact, it is surely *fun* to know things. It brightens one's life, sharpens one's wits, reduces one's boredom, broadens one's horizon, makes one more interesting and more pleasurable to be with.

This is true of any sort of knowledge or skill, actually, even of those that are not strictly "school subjects." Someone who knows how to carve wood into clever little devices, or who knows all about stamp collecting, is surely more fun to be with and to watch and to listen to than someone who knows nothing at all.

"...it is surely *fun* to know things. It brightens one's life, sharpens one's wits, reduces one's boredom, broadens one's horizon, makes one more interesting and more pleasurable to be with."

If, then, you know these other things, do you have to know science, *too?* Is there something special about science? Actually, there is.

Our modern world is founded on science —and on technology, which is the application of science to everyday affairs. Almost everything we do depends on our modern devices, such as automobiles, record players, and television sets, and these in turn depend on scientific principles. Our future will depend on computers, robots, nuclear power, rocket ships, all of which only make sense if we understand science.

If a person does not understand what makes these things work, they might as well be magic. People without science live in a mystery world that makes no sense to them. Even if they say, "So what? All I want to do is make a living, have a family, and look at the scenery," they may find that is not so easy. In an increasingly scientific world, the good jobs, the money-making jobs, will go to those who understand science.

" Our future will depend on computers, robots, nuclear power, rocket ships, all of which only make sense if we understand science."

"In an increasingly scientific world, the good jobs, the money-making jobs, will go to those who understand science."

Then, too, science has its dangers and its benefits. Used improperly, science can flood the Earth with pollution, with dangerous chemicals, with radiation, with devices that destroy our privacy and our freedom. Used wisely, however, science can increase our energy and food supply, improve our health, expand our joy, extend our lives, and broaden our sense of security.

Who decides how best to use science, however? In a democracy, it should be the people generally. But how can the people come to an intelligent decision if hardly any of them know much about science to begin with?

Surely it will be increasingly important, as the years pass, for people to understand science if they are going to be expected to help make intelligent decisions about how to use science to save the world, and not destroy it.

That is why it is important to study science, even if one is not going to be a professional scientist.

"Surely it will be increasingly important, as the years pass, for people to understand science if they are going to be expected to help make intelligent decisions about how to use science to save the world, and not destroy it."

READER'S RESPONSE

1. What do you think of Asimov's arguments for studying science? Are they convincing?
2. Do you believe that everyone should study science? Why or why not?

WRITER'S CRAFT

3. What is the thesis—the main idea—of this essay? What details does the author use to support the thesis?
4. How do the last two paragraphs, the conclusion, help make this essay a "whole" piece of writing?

LOOKING AHEAD

In this chapter, you'll study the structure of a composition. You'll learn that

- most compositions have a thesis statement
- most have an introduction that catches the reader's attention
- compositions usually have a body made up of paragraphs that are unified and coherent
- most compositions have a conclusion that ties ideas together and brings the composition to a satisfying close

What Makes a Composition

You've been writing compositions for years, but you may have called them essays or reports. You've written them for different classes as assignments and on tests, and you'll continue to write them in school and for job, college, and scholarship applications.

In other chapters in this book, you'll use the composition form when you compare and contrast subjects, write about causes and their effects, and explore problems and their solutions. You'll also use it to write about literature and to write a research paper. In this chapter, you focus on aspects of composition form itself.

The Thesis Statement

When you write a composition, you have something specific to say about your topic. This is your *thesis,* and the sentence that you write to express this main idea is the *thesis statement.* The thesis statement helps you control the direction of your composition: The entire composition will support the ideas in this statement. In the writing you do now, you might want to make the thesis statement a part of the introduction. However, experienced writers often use the thesis statement later in the composition. You'll even find compositions (articles and essays) in which the thesis statement is implied, not directly stated.

There are different kinds of thesis statements. One kind simply states the topic, as in this example: "Gotham City collects tons of garbage daily." Other thesis statements go further—they state what the writer will prove in the composition.

For example, "Unless some innovative solutions are found quickly, there will be no place to put the millions of tons of garbage that Gotham City collects daily."

HINTS FOR WRITING AND USING A THESIS STATEMENT

1. **Use your prewriting notes.** Before you begin to write, you'll gather a great deal of information about your topic. Look over this information carefully. What one idea is most important? What one idea unifies the facts and details you have? Answering these questions will help you to focus your thinking—an important step in developing a thesis statement.

2. **State both your topic and your main idea.** Your thesis statement needs to make clear two things: your topic and your main idea. Remember that your topic will be a limited one, and you will have a specific, unifying idea to express about it. When you first write out your thesis statement, underline your limited topic and circle your main idea to make sure you've included both.

   For example, think about this thesis statement: "If you want to be among the nearly eight million teens who are employed part time, the following tips on finding and landing a job may boost your chances of success." You can tell from this that the topic is the teen part-time job market and that the main idea is how to improve your chances of finding a part-time job.

3. **Change your thesis statement if you need to.** To begin with, reword your thesis statement until it says clearly what you want it to say. Then remember that it isn't written in concrete. If you get a different idea or decide to change the focus of your composition, just write a new thesis statement.

4. **Use your thesis statement to guide your writing.** Keep your thesis statement in front of you as you write, and be sure that all your ideas and details support it. Throw out any that don't, so that your composition will focus on your main idea.

The first draft of your thesis statement will probably be very plain and direct. However, an indirect statement of your thesis may be more interesting to your readers. Remember that one purpose of an introduction is to capture your reader's interest, and a catchy thesis statement can help. Try rewriting your thesis statement until it sounds interesting or exciting. Notice the difference in the following preliminary thesis statement after revision.

PRELIMINARY   The total solar eclipse over Hawaii on July 11, 1991, occurred under nearly ideal conditions, which resulted in some new knowledge for scientists.

REVISED   When the morning sun grew dark over Hawaii on July 11, 1991, the eclipse shed light on mysteries that have baffled astronomers for centuries.

EXERCISE 1 ▶ Analyzing Thesis Statements

In the list below, find the four effective thesis statements: They each have a specific topic and a clear main idea. The remaining thesis statement is weak: It is missing a specific topic or a clear main idea. Rewrite it as needed to make it more effective.

1. Exciting new technology has made it possible for millions of Americans to work at home.
2. Alaska is a rugged land that is exemplified by the resourcefulness and independent spirit of its people.
3. Japanese Americans have made many important contributions to art and music in the United States.
4. Shopping malls are important to American families.
5. The citizens of Massachusetts are taking positive actions to preserve their state's natural resources.

> E X E R C I S E **2** ▶ **Writing a Thesis Statement**

The limited topic of the following list of details is the famous 369th Infantry Regiment. What is a specific main idea you can form from the details? Write a thesis statement for the following topic and list of details. Express both the topic and the main idea clearly and specifically in the statement.

Limited Topic: the 369th Infantry Regiment

Details
- famous African American regiment in World War I
  went from United States to France in 1918
  attended training school in France
- bravery
  received eleven citations for bravery
  entire regiment received the French *Croix de Guerre*
  not one soldier from regiment was ever captured
  never showed fear of danger
- service
  served in France more than a year
  "Battle of Henry Johnson" named for member of
    regiment who showed great bravery in battle
  first troop to march through Washington Square
    Arch in New York City after returning home

Early Plans and Formal Outlines

You may be a super-organized person, a super-scattered one, or sort of in-between. No matter what your organizational skills, you'll benefit from planning your writing. Before you write your composition, *group* and *order* your details. *Early plans* and *formal outlines* can help you do this.

The Early Plan

The *early plan*—sometimes called a *rough,* or *informal, outline*—gives you a rough idea of the kinds of information you want to include in your composition. It also helps you see how to group details without the complication of arranging them into outline form with numerals and letters.

Grouping.   Well-organized people often group related items in their closets. Winter clothes go in one place, summer clothes in another. School clothes have their own spot, as do clothes for after school. When you *group* details for a composition, you can follow these steps to put related items in one spot.

- Sort related ideas and details into separate groups.
- Make a separate list of details that don't fit into any group. (At some later stage you may find a use for them.)
- Give each group of details a separate label.

Here's an early plan for a composition on teens finding part-time jobs.

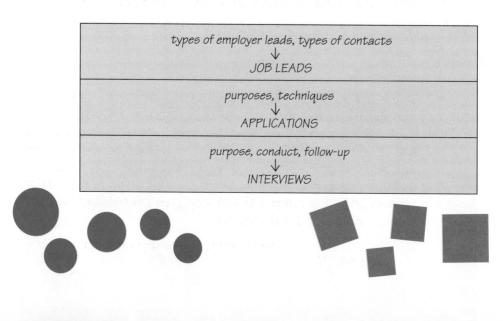

types of employer leads, types of contacts
↓
JOB LEADS

purposes, techniques
↓
APPLICATIONS

purpose, conduct, follow-up
↓
INTERVIEWS

Ordering.   *Ordering* involves arranging the details within each group and the groups themselves. Your topic may suggest the best arrangement to use. For example, if you're writing about events that happen over time, you will probably use *chronological* (time) *order.* When you describe something, you often use *spatial* (space) *order,* arranging details according to their location in space. In persuasive writing, you'll probably use *order of importance.* If you're comparing and contrasting items, you will use *logical order* and group related ideas together. Often you might use a combination of two or more of these orders.

 REFERENCE NOTE: For more help in arranging details, see pages 75–77.

The Formal Outline

Structured outlines sometimes grow out of early plans. A *formal outline* has numerals and letters to identify headings and subheadings and indentations to show levels of subordination. It may be a *topic outline,* which uses single words and phrases, or a *sentence outline,* which uses only complete sentences. Formal outlines may be used for planning, but they are more often written after the composition is complete, providing an overview or summary for the reader.

 REFERENCE NOTE: For more information on formal outlines, see pages 426–427.

Here's a formal topic outline for the composition on pages 110–111 about teens finding part-time jobs. (Notice how this formal outline fleshes out the basic ideas developed in the early plan on page 106. Also notice how it follows a particular structure to show the relationships among ideas.)

Title: It Takes Work to Get Work

Thesis Statement: If you want to be among the nearly eight million teens who are employed part time, the following tips on finding and landing a job may boost your chances of success.

I. Job leads
   A. Employer leads
      1. Signs
      2. Newspaper ads
      3. Employment agencies
   B. Contacts
      1. Potential employers
      2. Friends
      3. Family members
      4. Business acquaintances
      5. School counselor

II. Job applications
   A. Purpose
   B. Techniques
      1. First impression
      2. Skills and accomplishments

III. Job interviews
   A. Purpose
   B. Conduct
      1. Grooming/dress
      2. Preparation
      3. Directness/honesty
   C. Follow-up

DATA ENTRY– Market research firm needs experienced data entry operators. Approx 15 hours per week, $5/hour. Call Mon-Wed 10 am-2 pm 555-7390

Mario's Pizza
needs reliable drivers for pizza delivery. Must have own car and good driving record. Wed - Sun, 5pm to 9 pm. Call 555-6120

DENTAL ASSISTANT– North suburban dental office seeks person for part-time chairside asst. Min 16 hrs/wk. Call Cheryl–555-4700.

RECEPTIONIST
Temporary
Pleasant real estate office seeki... dependable receptionist for S... days during the summer mon... Responsibilities include ans... ing phones, light typing, s... projects. Send resume to: ...time Receptionist, Home-ers, Inc., 2958 Northwest... way, Suite 16, Johnson City

...ESTAURANT– Friendly, ...le counter help needed ...od restaurant. After sc... ...eekend hours availab... ...y. Apply in person, M... ...pm to 6 pm or Sat ... Buddy's Burgers, ...Springville.

...ALES: Par... ...d for cl... ...wee... ...st...

EXERCISE 3 ▶ **Making an Early Plan or Formal Outline**

Do you have more week than money left at the end of a pay period? The following notes about managing money might help. Working with a partner, organize these notes into either an early plan or a formal outline. [Hint: Your main headings can be Income, Expenses, Money Management, and Savings.]

income
money management
insurance
savings bonds
investments
savings account
certificates of deposit
publications
loans
cash
options
savings
expenses
wages
college savings
living expenses
big purchases
car expenses
interest
credit cards
adult advice
unexpected expenses
charge accounts
spending
purpose
taxes
allowance
bank personnel

Income
Expenses
Money Management
Savings

A WRITER'S MODEL

The following composition on teens getting part-time jobs includes the thesis statement on page 108 and follows the formal outline on page 108. You might want to use this composition as a model as you write your own composition.

It Takes Work to Get Work

INTRODUCTION

Thesis statement

    "You're hired!" These are exciting words to any anxious teen entering the job market for the very first time. If you want to be among the nearly eight million teens who are employed part time, the following tips on finding and landing a job may boost your chances of success.

BODY
Major point: Job leads

    The first step is to find out what part-time jobs are available in your area. Some job leads come directly from employers: signs in store and restaurant windows, help wanted ads in the newspaper, listings at employment agencies. Other leads can be developed by contacting potential employers yourself or by making use of contacts, such as friends, family members, business acquaintances, and your school counselor. The more leads you have, the more likely you are to find the job you want.

Major point: Job applications

    Once you have a list of job leads, start applying for some jobs. In most cases, the first thing you'll be asked to do is fill out a job application. This is the way an employer decides who to interview. It's your first chance to show that you are qualified for the job.

    Here are some ways to use the job application to make a good first impression. First of all, neatness counts; use a pen and write clearly. Make sure you use standard English and use no slang words. Spell words correctly and use good grammar. Finally, answer all questions honestly and clearly.

    Above all, don't sell yourself short. Most job applications have a space to list special skills and accomplishments. Be honest, but don't be shy. Does the job involve selling? Maybe you've sold ads for your school annual. Do you speak a second language?

Many businesses need bilingual employees. Are you on the honor roll? Many employers know that people who work hard at school will also work hard at a job. Do you have job skills from completing courses in typing, computers, bookkeeping, shop? Let your potential employer know.

Major point: Job interviews

After reviewing all the job applications, employers will choose some candidates to interview. An interview is the employer's chance to find out more about you, and your chance to find out more about the job.

Arrive for the interview well-rested, clean, well-groomed, neatly dressed, and about five minutes early. Have your Social Security card and a pen and pad of paper with you. During the interview, look the interviewer in the eye, smile, and remember to use the interviewer's name (always Ms., Mrs., or Mr.--never first names). Be direct and honest, and be ready to answer questions. (Prepare yourself in advance by consulting employment booklets at the library that list some of the most commonly asked interview questions.) When the interview is over, express your interest in the job and thank the interviewer for his or her time.

Finally, that evening, type or neatly write a brief letter expressing your interest in the job and reminding the interviewer of the attributes that make you the perfect person for the job. Thank the interviewer for considering you. Address the envelope to the interviewer and mail the letter the next day.

CONCLUSION

It may take a little time to prepare for and follow through with your job search, but it's worth the effort. You'll be glad you did it right when you finally hear the words "You're hired!"

The Introduction

Many writers think the *introduction* of an article or composition is the hardest part to write; it is the critical time to get the audience's attention and let them know what the topic is. The length of an introduction may vary a great deal—from one sentence to several paragraphs. However, there are three things an introduction needs to accomplish:

- catch the audience's attention (otherwise they may not read on)
- set the tone, or show the writer's attitude, toward the topic (humorous, serious, critical, and so forth)
- present the thesis (sometimes at the beginning, but often at the end, of the introduction)

Techniques for Writing Introductions

The following techniques represent some of the options experienced writers have for getting the reader's attention. When you're trying to decide how to start a composition, try one or two of them.

1. **Begin by addressing the reader directly.** In the writer's model on pages 110–111, the writer addresses the reader directly with "You're hired!" This also sets an informal, friendly tone and involves the reader.

2. **Begin with an interesting or dramatic quote.** A writer used this technique in a biographical sketch of American photographer Eliot Porter.

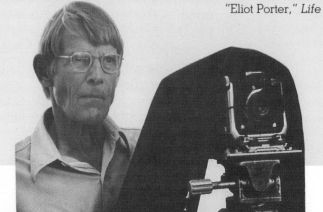

"Color," Eliot Porter used to say when asked to reveal the secret behind his photographs. "Color is the only thing I'm really concerned about. Color and patterns. That's all."

"Eliot Porter," *Life*

3. **Begin with an anecdote or example.** Starting with an anecdote, or little story, or giving an example of something can immediately involve your reader, especially if the anecdote is humorous or mysterious. This first sentence of the following introduction begins an anecdote about a discovery in an attic.

> One stifling summer afternoon last August, in the attic of a tiny stone house in Pennsylvania, I made a most interesting discovery: the shortest, cheapest method of inducing a nervous breakdown ever perfected.
>
> S. J. Perelman, "Insert Flap 'A' and Throw Away"

4. **Begin with an unusual or enlightening fact.** Some new or unusual fact will often entice your audience to read on and learn more about your topic. For example, an article about a most unusual bird begins this way:

> The hoatzin is an odd bird. Not only does it eat leaves—far more than any other bird—but it digests them like a cow or a sheep, grinding the leaves up in its specialized, muscular crop. Up close the hoatzin smells bad, and it flies poorly.
>
> "Geographica," *National Geographic*

5. **Begin with a question or a challenge.** When you start with a question or a challenge, you immediately involve your readers. Even if they know the answer, they'll want to know what you have to say about the subject.

> What do the following people have in common: Lewis Temple, inventor of a harpoon that revolutionized whaling; James Beckwourth, Western trailblazer; Benjamin Banneker, surveyor and mathematician; and Henry Blair, inventor of a corn seed planter?

6. **Take a stand on some issue.** When you are writing persuasion, you can begin with a statement that expresses a strong, even controversial, opinion. This will make your readers want to read on to see how you will support your opinion.

> Bad times don't kill banks—bad bankers do.
> When the system works, regulators protect bad bankers from their worst instincts. But the system hasn't been working.
>
> Mitchell Zuckoff, "Lax regulation, inadequate laws promote insider-lending abuse," *The Boston Globe*

7. **Begin with an outrageous or comical statement.** An outrageous or comical statement will let your readers know to expect a humorous or satirical composition. Most readers are attracted to humor and will want to keep reading.

> The first rule of car-buying is one that I learned long ago from my father, namely: Never buy any car that my father would buy.
>
> Dave Barry, "Car-Buying: The Compleat Guide," *The Washington Post Magazine*

8. **Begin with a simple statement of your thesis.** Often a well-written thesis statement is all you need to catch your reader's attention.

The decision of Justice Thurgood Marshall to step down from the Supreme Court left President Bush with an unusually significant vacancy to fill.

"The Talk of the Town,"
The New Yorker

EXERCISE 4 ▶ **Analyzing Introductions**

What do the movie *Dances with Wolves* and a boy with an overactive imagination have in common? Nothing—but they help to make the following two introductions by professional writers appealing to readers. Read the introductions, and then answer the following questions about each one.

- Which of the eight techniques (on pages 112–115) does the writer use in the introduction?
- Does the technique work well enough to make you want to read the article?
- What is the tone of the introduction? What words or phrases reveal the author's attitude toward the topic?

1.   *Unci Maka.* The language is Lakota, spoken by the Sioux, and the words, used in prayer, mean Grandmother Earth. Historically, Native Americans revered and defended their land, especially from the ravages of white men—a tradition portrayed in the hit movie, "Dances with Wolves." But just miles from the film's location, a civil-engineering firm is developing plans for a solid-waste landfill. Why are engineers from Connecticut on a South Dakota reservation? Leaders of the Rosebud Sioux tribe

invited them. South Dakota Sen. Tom Daschle, an outspoken opponent, calls the plan "Dances With Garbage."

Mary Hager *et al*, "'Dances With Garbage'" *Newsweek*

2.   This is my brother's fault.

As a young boy, I was plagued with an overactive imagination—compounded by the fact that we lived in a house with your standard, monster-infested basement. Occasionally, I would hear my father's command that never failed to horrify me: "Go down to the basement, Gary, and bring up some firewood." Death.

Gary Larson, *The Far Side Gallery*

"Uh-oh, Donny. Sounds like the monster in the basement has heard you crying again. ... Let's be reaaaal quiet and hope he goes away."

EXERCISE 5 ▶ Writing an Introduction

Get together with two or three classmates, and try writing a new introduction for "Learning Science," pages 98–100. Experiment with any of the techniques for capturing readers' interest that you've just read about, but be sure to include the thesis statement and to set the tone. When you finish, compare your introductions with those of other groups.

The Body

The *body* of a composition is the part where you develop the main idea of your thesis statement. Each paragraph expresses a major point of your thesis and supports, or proves, it with details. These paragraphs should connect with one another and relate directly to your thesis statement. You can achieve these goals if the body has *emphasis, unity,* and *coherence.*

Emphasis

To *emphasize* is to stress, and in most compositions you have some ideas that you want to stress because you think they are more important. The primary method for emphasizing ideas is to give them more attention, to devote more time and space to them. However, you can also emphasize an idea by discussing it first or last—the two positions that are most likely to draw the attention of the reader. The model composition on pages 110–111 places more emphasis on applications and interviews, by giving them more space and attention, than it does on leads.

Unity

Unity means "oneness." In a composition unity means that every paragraph and every detail supports a single main idea. Each topic sentence for each paragraph should relate to the thesis statement of the composition. And each sentence in a paragraph should relate to the topic sentence of the paragraph.

Coherence

Coherence means "logical connection." A composition has coherence if all the ideas are connected in a sequence that readers find easy to follow. Sentences flow smoothly, and paragraphs connect sensibly. The best way to achieve coherence is to use *direct references* and *transitional expressions.*

Direct References.   One way to link ideas is to refer directly to something that came immediately before. You can achieve coherence by using the following techniques.

1. Repeat key words or phrases from the preceding paragraph, or repeat or rephrase the last idea in that paragraph.
2. Use pronouns to refer to nouns already used.
3. Use synonyms or rewordings of ideas and key words.

Transitional Expressions.   *Transitional expressions,* words
and phrases such as *for example, of course, therefore, meanwhile,*
and *later,* lead your readers from one sentence or paragraph to
another. They help make relationships clear and create smooth
connections among ideas.

👉 REFERENCE NOTE: For more about using direct references and
transitional words and phrases, see pages 79–81.

WRITING NOTE
In a long composition or article, a short paragraph
can be used to create a transition. Often such a
paragraph is a single sentence acting as a bridge
between the ideas in one paragraph and those in another.

EXERCISE 6 ▶   **Analyzing the Use of Transitions**

Most writers really do use the techniques you've been reading
about. Identify the nouns, their direct-reference pronouns, and
any transitional expressions in the following paragraph.

David Farragut, son of a Spanish naval officer who
fought on the side of the American colonists during the
Revolutionary War, is one of the greatest naval heroes of
the United States. He made an early start on his career by
joining the U.S. Navy when he was only nine years old.
Not long after, when he was twelve, he became a prize master, commanding a ship captured from the
British during the War of 1812. Later, he
fought pirates in the Caribbean and then
served in the Mexican War (1846–48).
Although he was over sixty years old
when the Civil War began, he took
command of a Union fleet. Because
of his great bravery and ability, he
became the first American to be
given the rank of full admiral in
the U.S. Navy.

The Conclusion

When you read a book or see a movie, you expect it to have a definite *conclusion,* or ending. Compositions also need satisfying endings; readers need to feel that the ideas are tied together and are complete. The following techniques are some options that experienced writers choose from to create effective conclusions.

1. **Refer to the introduction.** The model composition on page 111 neatly wraps up ideas in the conclusion by referring to the introduction.

   > You'll be glad you did it right when you finally hear the words "You're hired!"

2. **Offer a solution or make a recommendation.** When you've taken a stand on an issue, you can stress your point by offering a solution or recommending a course of action in the conclusion.

   > People do get the government they deserve, and our low voter turnout shows that we deserve no better than what we have. We need a grassroots campaign nationwide to educate and convince people that voting is not only a right and a privilege but also a serious responsibility. Complaining to each other about the mess the country's in is no answer. Putting the responsibility where it belongs, on all of us, is.

Vote

REGISTER TO VOTE

REGISTER TO VOTE FULTON COUNTY RESIDENTS ONLY

REGISTER TO VOTE FULTON COUNTY RESIDENTS ONLY

3. **Restate your thesis.** Another good way to wind up your composition is to restate your thesis. Use different words to say the same thing, bringing your composition to an end that echoes the beginning. For example, look at the conclusion of Isaac Asimov's essay "Learning Science" (pages 98–100).

4. **Summarize your major points.** Another satisfying ending is a summary of the major points of a composition. For instance, the main points of an article on emeralds are briefly included in this conclusion.

> Gems satisfy primal needs—the lure of instant wealth, some sort of desire, perhaps, to join with the secrets of the earth. They fulfill our longing for beauty. They are our link to mysteries we can appreciate but cannot explain. Gems are as near the eternal as anything we can ever own.
>
> Fred Ward, "Emeralds," *National Geographic*

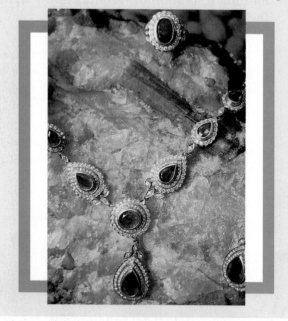

Other ways to conclude a paragraph include closing with an example of your main idea, personally commenting on your topic, or posing a dramatic question or challenge. The important thing is that you tie your ideas together and leave your readers with the emotion you intended.

EXERCISE 7 ▶ **Writing a Conclusion**

Try out some of your options for writing conclusions. Get together with two or three classmates. With your group members, try writing a new conclusion for "Learning Science," the essay that ends on page 100, or the Writer's Model that ends on page 111. Don't be afraid to experiment with different kinds of conclusions. When you finish, share your work with other groups.

WRITING NOTE   Often writers wait until they finish their compositions before deciding on a title. After you write your composition, try to think of a title that lets readers know what to expect in subject and tone. (Don't put a catchy, funny title on a serious essay, or vice-versa!)

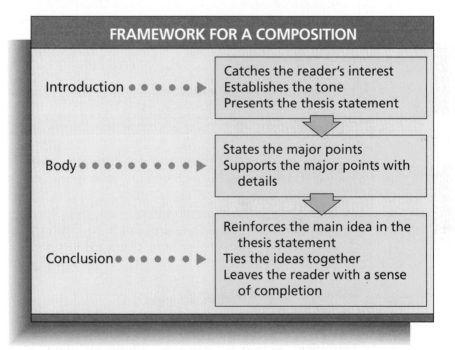

FRAMEWORK FOR A COMPOSITION

Introduction ● ● ● ● ● ▶	Catches the reader's interest Establishes the tone Presents the thesis statement
Body ● ● ● ● ● ● ● ● ● ▶	States the major points Supports the major points with details
Conclusion ● ● ● ● ● ● ▶	Reinforces the main idea in the thesis statement Ties the ideas together Leaves the reader with a sense of completion

MAKING CONNECTIONS

Writing an Informative Composition

In this chapter you have reviewed the basic elements of composition form, and now you have a chance to use what you've learned in a complete piece of writing. You will be writing a composition to inform your readers about swimming as a competitive sport. The following information has already been gathered for you. Although a title is suggested, you are welcome to create a different one.

Swimming for the Gold

1. Swimming an Olympic event since 1896
2. Swimming contests believed held in Japan as early as the 1st century B.C.
3. Organized competitive swimming, beginning in England, in 1840s
4. To ancient Greeks and Romans, swimming a major part of military training programs
5. Crawl stroke often used in competition freestyle events
   —chest down, one arm extended forward out of water, arm below surface making pulling movement
   —flutter kick
6. Backstroke used in competition
   —swimmer on back, one arm out of the water to complete stroke, other arm in water for forward-pulling motion
   —flutter kick
7. Breast stroke used in competition
   —chest down in water, hands carried together forward from under the chest to full extension, then swept back in lateral plane, parallel to body
   —both legs drawn up, knees bent, each turned outward, then thrust back parallel to line of body
   —frog kick

8. Winners of competitions determined by best elapsed time
9. Predetermined distance
10. 7 gold medals in swimming won by Mark Spitz at 1972 Olympics
11. Olympic events for both individual and team swimming, including the medley and relay

 Prewriting. You may not use all the information supplied, but be sure you have enough to write a brief informative composition. If you want to add other information from personal knowledge or research, do so, but limit your topic so that it can be covered in a short paper. Then decide on a thesis statement that expresses your main idea, and create an early plan.

Writing, Evaluating, and Revising. Use your early plan to guide your writing. Start writing by using one of the introduction techniques (pages 112–115). When you write the body, be sure to emphasize the most important ideas. Keep your thesis in mind, but don't let it become a straitjacket. Write a conclusion that ties your information together (see pages 119–120). Set your paper aside and then compare it to the framework on page 121 in order to evaluate and revise it, working to achieve unity and coherence.

 Proofreading and Publishing. When you've revised your paper, read it again to look for errors in grammar, usage, and mechanics. Exchange papers with a classmate and proofread each other's compositions, using the proofreading guidelines on pages 50–51. Make a clean, final copy of your paper and share it with someone interested in competitive swimming.

Discovering Yourself

Some discoveries, like that of a planet beyond this solar system, make world news. What you **discover about yourself** through expressive writing probably won't make headlines. But it's important in its own way.

Writing and You. A man drafts a document that reflects the feelings of his fellow citizens two hundred years later. A woman, calling for the freedom of all people, writes her story. Both people expressed their thoughts and feelings in writing. When have you written to express yourself?

As You Read. In the following letter, written in 1861, a major in the Union Army during the Civil War expresses his thoughts and feelings. What are they?

Vincent van Gogh, *Irises*, (1889), Dutch, 1853–1890. Oil on canvas. 28″ × 36 ⅝″. Collection of the J. Paul Getty Museum, Malibu, CA.

A letter

written by
Major Sullivan Ballou
to his wife

July 14, 1861
Camp Clark, Washington

My very dear Sarah:

The indications are very strong that we shall move in a few days—perhaps tomorrow. Lest I should not be able to write again, I feel impelled to write a few lines that may fall under your eye when I shall be no more. . . .

I have no misgivings about, or lack of confidence in the cause in which I am engaged, and my courage does not halt or falter. I know how strongly American Civilization now leans on the triumph of the Government, and how great a debt we owe to those who went before us through the blood and sufferings of the Revolution. And I am willing—perfectly willing—to lay down all my joys in this life, to help maintain this Government, and to pay that debt. . . .

Sarah my love for you is deathless, it seems to bind me with mighty cables that nothing but Omnipotence could break; and yet my love of Country comes over me like a strong wind and bears me unresistibly on with all these chains to the battle field.

The memories of the blissful moments I have spent with you come creeping over me, and I feel most gratified to God and to you that I have enjoyed them so long. And hard it is for me to give them up and burn to ashes the hopes of future years, when, God willing, we might still have lived and loved together, and seen our sons grown up to honorable manhood, around us. I have, I know, but few and small claims upon Divine Providence, but something whispers to me—perhaps it is the wafted prayer of my little Edgar, that I shall return to my loved ones unharmed. If I do not my dear Sarah, never forget how much I love you, and when my last breath escapes me on the battle field, it will whisper your name. Forgive my many faults, and the many pains I have caused you. How thoughtless and foolish I have often times been! How gladly would I wash out with my tears every little spot upon your happiness. . . .

But, O Sarah! if the dead can come back to this earth and flit unseen around those they loved, I shall always be near you; in the gladdest days and in the darkest nights . . . <u>always, always,</u> and if there be a soft breeze upon your cheek, it shall be my breath, as the cool air fans your throbbing temple, it shall be my spirit passing by. Sarah do not mourn me dead; think I am gone and wait for thee, for we shall meet again. . . .

". . . I feel impelled to write a few lines that may fall under your eye when I shall be no more. . . ."

"I shall always be near you; in the gladdest days and in the darkest nights. . . always, always. . ."

READER'S RESPONSE

1. Major Ballou was killed at the first battle of Bull Run shortly after he wrote this letter. How does this knowledge affect the way you feel about the letter?
2. After reading the letter, what thoughts and feelings do you have about war? Write a short entry in your journal about Major Ballou's words.

WRITER'S CRAFT

3. Writers of personal expression may reveal their thoughts directly, or they may suggest them indirectly. How does Ballou feel about the cause for which he is fighting?
4. How does Ballou feel about his chances for survival? What direct statements does he make that reveal this feeling? What does he say that suggests the feeling?

Ways to Express Yourself

Personal expression is all around you—in letters (like the one written by Major Ballou), poems, articles, books, and even greeting cards. There are many ways to express your thoughts and feelings in writing. Here are four ways you can express yourself.

▶ **Narration:**   telling a friend about a humorous incident that happened on a family trip; in your journal, recounting a disappointing experience at school.

Description: describing the unsettling chaos and unfriendliness of your new room after your family moves to a different house; in a song lyric, describing your most cherished possession and its importance to you.

Classification: in a journal entry, comparing your thoughts on starting school this year with your thoughts on starting school last year; in an informal discussion, exploring your thoughts about the advantages and disadvantages of teenagers' working part time.

▶ **Evaluation:**   in your journal, noting what you have learned by being on the debate team; in an essay, exploring the benefits you feel you have gained from being an only child.

LOOKING AHEAD

In the main assignment in this chapter, you'll use the strategies of evaluation and narration to develop a personal essay. As you work through the writing assignment, keep in mind that a personal essay

- tells about an important experience in your life
- uses specific narrative and descriptive details to make the experience seem real
- gradually reveals the full significance of the experience

Writing a Personal Essay

Prewriting

Choosing a Personal Experience

Time changes you physically; experience changes you mentally and emotionally. Taking a look back over past experiences can give you fresh insights on how you've changed and developed over time. A journal or diary can be an excellent source for reviewing your important life experiences. If you don't keep a journal, use your powers of memory to call up your past. Then you can settle on an experience to explore further through your writing by asking yourself

- *What "feels important"? What experiences have played a part in forming or revealing the "real me"?* Some experiences come to mind immediately when you start reviewing what's been important in making you who you are.
- *What do I remember vividly?* If you can remember an event "like it happened yesterday," chances are it's important, even if you don't realize it—yet!
- *What's not too private to share?* Some experiences need to remain just with you, their significance explored only within your diary or journal entries. Others, however, may bloom with meaning when exposed to "the light of day."

WRITING NOTE To qualify as "important," an experience need not be a dramatic life-and-death situation. Henry David Thoreau, for example, hoed a field of beans and discovered something about the importance of work. As Thoreau reflected on this discovery, he was able to craft some memorable writing about his experience. So don't discount your experience in art class or in sports as trivial or unimportant. Any experience—as long as it feels significant to you—can be the starting point for your personal essay. And if the experience was important to you, chances are it will be for others, too.

EXERCISE 1 ► Drawing on Personal Experience

What were you like last week, last month, last year, five years ago? Call up a variety of past experiences by completing each of the following sentence beginnings one or more times. How would you have finished the sentence when you were ten? Would you finish it differently today? Share your responses with a small group of classmates.

1. I never felt prouder than when . . .
2. A person who has really influenced me is . . .
3. Looking back, I wish I had . . .
4. Somehow I felt different after . . .

WRITING ASSIGNMENT

PART 1:
Choosing an Experience for a Personal Essay

What experiences made you the person you are today? Look over your collection of experiences from Exercise 1 (above) and select one to write about in your personal essay. Use the questions on page 130 as a guide in making your choice.

Prewriting

Planning Your Personal Essay

After reading or hearing about your classmates' experiences, you may have thought *I've been in a similar situation* or *I know exactly what she means*. You'll be aiming for this type of response from your readers. However, achieving it requires careful thought and planning.

Thinking About Purpose, Audience, and Tone

Your main *purpose* for writing a personal essay is to express and explore your thoughts and feelings. You may also feel that it's important to share your experience and its meaning with others or to leave a record of your experience behind you.

Because writing a personal essay is a discovery process—you often discover the meaning of the experience as you write—your first *audience* will be yourself. Keep in mind, though, the wider audience who will read your essay. What information will they need to understand the experience? How will you reveal its importance to them?

A personal essay includes *your* thoughts and feelings, so you should write in your own natural *voice*. Write in the first person, using *I, me, our,* and *we,* and use everyday vocabulary and sentence structure to create a natural, conversational *tone*.

 **Speaking and Listening: Surveying Reader Response**

An ancient Chinese poet put his exquisite verses into a stream and watched them float away, never to be read by others. Your personal essay, however, will be read by others; and their response is important. This exercise will help you get an early response to the experience you chose to write about.

Get together with two or three classmates and take turns presenting and responding. As a "presenter," briefly review the events of your experience and your feelings about it. Then listen closely to your classmates' responses. As a "responder," listen carefully to each classmate's presentation, and ask your-self the following questions. Share your answers with each pre-senter in your group.

1. Have I ever had a similar experience? If so, how were my feelings similar or different?
2. What specific question(s) do I have about events in this particular experience?
3. After hearing a brief summary of the experience, what else do I want to know?

Recalling Details

By the time you have thought about purpose, audience, and tone, you probably will have remembered many things about your experience. At this point in the process, you can use your memory to "travel back in time" to recall and record details that will show readers your experience. As you do, you may gain fresh insights for yourself as well. To take yourself back in time, try these strategies:

- Close your eyes and visualize the scene, replaying the events in your mind.
- Talk with others who shared the experience with you.
- Return to the place where the experience happened.
- Use a memory prompt. You may have a particular reminder of the experience—perhaps a photograph, a ribbon, a ticket stub, or a song.

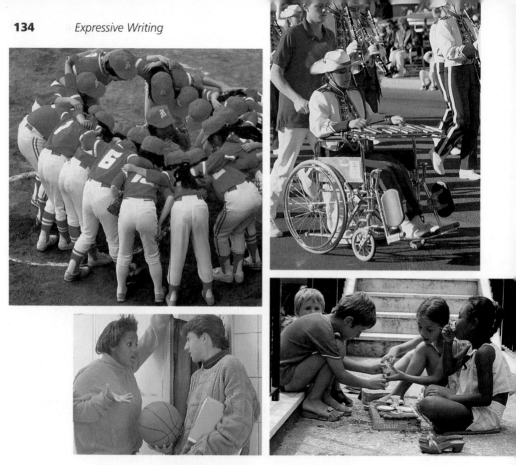

Once you're back in time, you need to record details that will help your readers understand the experience and its meaning. *Narrative details* tell about specific events and actions: *I stumbled clumsily into the room. There, in the glare of the spotlight, I stood on stage, absolutely alone and absolutely speechless.* They may suggest or reveal thoughts and feelings: *I stared blankly into the air, uncomfortably aware that three hundred pairs of eyes were riveted on me.* Narrative details often include *dialogue,* the exact words of the speaker. *Descriptive,* or *sensory, details* appeal to the five senses and describe important people, places, and objects.

☞ REFERENCE NOTE: For more help with narrative and descriptive details, see pages 67 and 175.

Arranging Details

Details in a personal essay are often arranged in *chronological,* or time, *order.* Sometimes, in order to heighten interest, writers begin with a particularly dramatic event and then relate earlier events that led up to it, but you may need to arrange details in other ways as well. If you're describing a place or a person, for example, you may need to arrange details *spatially* or in *order of importance*.

The following chart shows how one writer recorded some of the details she recalled about a summer experience. Notice that the events are arranged in chronological order.

Events	Narrative/Descriptive Details
Event 1— Susan asks me to work for her—I say OK	Wiping tables and filling salt shakers; Susan, "Joe's coming. Will you work for me?"; auditions in 30 minutes; neck tightens—hate to miss auditions, but don't have nerve to say no; lie on lumpy bed; wisps of fog on trees; pretending sleep when Susan comes home
Event 2— Susan asks me to work for her again—I say No!	Next Friday Susan asks again; almost say yes, but look at Susan, so excited; No!; stomach in knots, hard to breathe; Me, "Susan, you'll have to do something else."

REFERENCE NOTE: For more help on arranging ideas, see pages 75–77.

WRITING ASSIGNMENT

PART 2:
Recalling and Arranging Details

In a chart like the one above, jot down the narrative and descriptive details you remember and arrange the events in the order you plan to present them. Then use at least one of the ideas on page 133 to "go back in time," reliving your experience in your memory. Add to your chart any other details you recall.

Reflecting on the Meaning of the Experience

A successful personal essay requires both the short and the long view. Recalling details has already given you the short view: an up-close examination of what happened and of the people, places, and objects that were a part of the experience.

Now it's time to take the long view, to take a step back from the experience in order to understand its importance. Look at this experience as you are today and ask

- *What have I learned about myself or others from the experience?*
- *How did the experience cause me to change or to think differently about things?*
- *How have my goals changed as a result of this experience?*

At first, you may not fully understand what the experience has meant to you. As you plan and draft your essay, however, you will need to reflect on its meaning. Answering questions like the ones you have just read can help you do this.

CRITICAL THINKING
Evaluating Details

When you *evaluate,* you judge the value of something against a set of criteria. When your teacher evaluates your research paper, for example, he or she uses criteria like documentation of sources and clarity of thesis. When you're trying to decide which details to include in a personal essay, you must also use the critical-thinking skill of evaluation. You need to judge, using the following criteria, whether the details

- help to make the experience clear to the reader
- help make the experience seem real to the reader
- contribute to the experience's overall meaning

CRITICAL THINKING EXERCISE:
Evaluating Details for a Personal Essay

The following paragraph is part of a personal essay that tells how the writer learned to overcome his fears and trust his own instincts. As you read it, pay special attention to the four sets of underlined details. Then use the three criteria above to determine whether the underlined details are important. Identify the details that should be cut from the paragraph and those which should be kept. Share your comments with your classmates.

I had never told anyone about my secret dream to be another track and field star like Carl Lewis, not even my mom and dad. [1] I thought they'd laugh at me. [2] My dad is a big tease and he laughs at everything I do. I could hardly believe I had the nerve to think about going out for the varsity track team. But that Monday, just as I was trying to figure out what to take home out of my locker, my best friend, José, came running down the hall. [3] I remember he almost ran into our science teacher. It was 2:20; the team tryouts started in ten minutes, [4] just time for me to change my shoes and run to the field.

Writing Your First Draft

Have you ever watched a photograph slowly develop? Outlines, shapes, and highlights appear first, and then, as the process continues, images become sharper and clearer and shadows fill up until the picture is complete. Your personal essay should develop just like a photo.

The Structure of Your Personal Essay

Like other compositions, a personal essay includes an introduction, a body, and a conclusion. Unlike some other types of essays, however, its main idea—the meaning of the experience—is not directly stated in the *introduction*. Instead, the introduction only hints at the meaning. Most of these introductions do, however, give background information that readers need to understand the experience.

Each part of the *body* develops a related event and contributes to the reader's understanding of the essay's unfolding meaning. The *conclusion* may reveal the final outcome of the events, or it may include a few reflective comments. Even at the end, the essay's main idea or meaning may be implied rather than directly stated. But, whether stated or implied, it should be clearly understood.

In the following personal essay, the writer witnesses the conflicting emotions of immigrants coming to this country. As you read, notice how each event reveals feelings of wonder and hope or fear and loss. What final realization does the writer come to about these opposite feelings?

A PASSAGE FROM AN AUTOBIOGRAPHY

from I Behold America
by Edward Corsi

INTRODUCTION
Hint about meaning

My first impressions of the new world will always remain etched in my memory, particularly that hazy October morning when I first

Background information

Feelings

saw Ellis Island. The steamer *Florida*, fourteen days out of Naples, filled to capacity with sixteen hundred natives of Italy, had weathered one of the worst storms in our captain's memory; and glad we were, both children and grown-ups, to leave the open sea and come at last through the Narrows into the Bay.

Background information

Feelings

BODY
Event 1

Descriptive details

My mother, my stepfather, my brother Giuseppe, and my two sisters, Liberta and Helvetia, all of us together, happy that we had come through the storm safely, clustered on the fore-deck for fear of separation and looked with wonder on this miraculous land of our dreams.

Giuseppe and I held tightly to stepfather's hands, while Liberta and Helvetia clung to mother. Passengers all about us were crowding against the rail. Jabbered conversation, sharp cries, laughs and cheers—a steadily rising din filled the air. Mothers and fathers lifted up the babies so that they too could see, off to the left, the Statue of Liberty.

Narrative
details—
Feelings

Unfolding
meaning

I looked at that statue with a sense of bewilderment, half doubting its reality. Looming shadowy through the mist, it brought silence to the decks of the *Florida*. This symbol of America — this enormous expression of what we had all been taught was the inner meaning of this new country we were coming to — inspired awe in the hopeful immigrants. Many older persons among us, burdened with a thousand memories of what they were leaving behind, had been openly weeping ever since we entered the narrower waters on our final approach toward the unknown. Now somehow steadied, I suppose, by the concreteness of the symbol of America's freedom, they dried their tears.

Event 2
Descriptive
details

Dialogue

Directly in front of the *Florida*, half visible in the faintly-colored haze, rose a second and even greater challenge to the imagination.

"Mountains!" I cried to Giuseppe. "Look at them!"

"They're strange," he said, "why don't they have snow on them?" He was craning his neck and standing on tiptoe to stare at the New York skyline.

Stepfather looked toward the skyscrapers, and, smiling, assured us that they were not mountains but buildings — "the highest buildings in the world."

On every side the harbor offered its marvels: tugs, barges, sloops, lighters, sluggish freighters and giant ocean liners — all moving in different directions, managing, by what seemed to us a miracle, to dart in and out and up and down without colliding with one another. They spoke to us through the varied sounds of their whistles, and the *Florida* replied with a deep echoing voice. Bells clanged through our ship, precipitating a new flurry among our fellow-passengers. Many of these people had come from provinces far distant from ours, and were shouting to one another in dialects strange to me. Everything combined to increase our excitement, and we rushed from deck to deck, fearful lest we miss the smallest detail of the spectacle.

Finally the *Florida* veered to the left, turning northward into the Hudson River, and now the incredible buildings of lower Manhattan came very close to us.

The officers of the ship, mighty and unapproachable beings they seemed to me, went striding up and down the decks shouting orders and directions and driving the immigrants before them. Scowling and gesturing, they pushed and pulled the passengers, herding us into separate groups as though we were animals. A few moments later we came to our dock, and the long journey was over.

A small boat, the *General Putnam* of the Immigration Service, carried us from the pier to Ellis Island. Luckily for us, we were among the first to be transferred to the tiny vessel, and so were spared the long ordeal of waiting that occasionally stretched, for some immigrants, into several days and nights.

Narrative details

Descriptive details

Narrative details— Feelings

Event 3

Narrative details

**Thoughts—
Unfolding
meaning**

During this ride across the bay, as I watched the faces of the people milling about me, I realized that Ellis Island could inspire both hope and fear. Some of the passengers were afraid and obviously dreading the events of the next few hours; others were impatient, anxious to get through the inspection and be off to their destinations. . . .

CONCLUSION

So they had shuffled aboard at the Italian port, forsaking the arduous security of their villages among the vineyards, leaving behind the friends of their youth, of their maturity, or their old age. The young accepted the challenge with the daring of youth; the old pressed forward without a hope of return. But both saw in the future, through their shadowy dreams, what they believed was an earthly paradise. They did not weigh the price of their coming against the benefits of the New World. They were convinced, long before they left Italy, that America had enough and more for all who wished to come. It was only a question of being desired by the strong and wealthy country, of being worthy to be admitted.

**Full meaning
of experience**

from *In the Shadow of Liberty*

EXERCISE 3▶ **Analyzing a Personal Essay**

After you have finished reading the excerpt from Edward Corsi's autobiography (pages 138–142), meet with two or three classmates to discuss these questions.

1. In what order does Corsi present the events in his essay?
2. What are some examples of specific sensory details, other than sight details, that Corsi includes?
3. The descriptive details in the third paragraph are arranged spatially and in order of importance. What is the effect of ending the paragraph with *the Statue of Liberty*?
4. Why do you think Corsi includes the incident in which he and Giuseppe mistake the skyscrapers for mountains?
5. What details in the body of the essay reveal or suggest the immigrants' feelings of hope or wonder? What details reveal feelings of fear or loss?
6. In your own words, explain the meaning of Corsi's experience as he explains it in the conclusion. How does this paragraph explain the immigrants' mixed feelings of hope and wonder?

A Basic Framework for a Personal Essay

In *I Behold America* Edward Corsi shows readers an experience that involves complex thoughts and feelings. The experience related in the following essay is less complex, but it has the same basic structure and purpose as Corsi's essay. As you read, notice that this writer's model includes several hints about the meaning of the experience.

A WRITER'S MODEL

An Actor Is Born

INTRODUCTION
Hint of meaning

I wish I could say that I was planning my debut on Broadway next season--or even that the experience was mildly successful. But I can't. I don't even know how I became involved in the first place. I've always known all the techniques for avoiding attention. I'm never late for class. I always sit in the back row. I keep my head down at the right times. But last year my family got involved, and life hasn't been the same since.

Background information

The yearly drama production is always a big event around school. Last year, posters with strange objects that were supposed to be wind-mills, but looked more like clock hands run amock, went up everywhere. They decorated every available space--over the doors, on lock-ers, even hanging from ceiling fixtures. One of the newspaper reporters, a real go-getter, even managed to get a write-up in the local paper: "NORTHSIDE PLAYERS PRESENT A DRAMA-TIZATION OF SCENES FROM <u>DON QUIXOTE</u>. This fall, the Northside High School drama group has scheduled a production of scenes from Cervantes' classic novel <u>Don Quixote</u>. . . ."

BODY
Event 1

Not long after the article appeared, my par-ents began one of those dinner table conversa-tions about "Susan's Shyness and What Can Be Done About It."

Narrative details— Dialogue

"Why don't you sign up?" my father urged. "There are lots of things you can do offstage-- lights, costumes, prompting. And it'll be good for you. You'll meet people and get out of your-self a little."

Sentence fragment for emphasis

Silence from me.

For some reason, this particular play really caught on at school. Maybe it was just the nuttiness--the strange, wonderful man who thought he was a knight and went off fighting windmills and showed people what it was like

Sensory details

to have a dream. We had seen pictures of him in our world lit books, dressed up in his great-grandfather's old, rusty armor. Anyway, my one true friend signed up and, in a moment of misguided fervor, so did I.

Event 2
Narrative details

After that, it was all a chain of circum-stances. Halfway through rehearsal, the actress playing Camilla got sick. I was learning

to work the lights, enjoying my place in the half-darkness of the back of the theater, when Mr. Guedez called my name. I don't know why he ever chose me as an understudy in the first place--probably because it was a minor role and he had to have somebody, after all. It certainly wasn't my stage presence. Anyway, no one thought for a moment that Elizabeth wouldn't be there. I don't think she'd missed a day of school since kindergarten--until opening night, that is. That's when she came down with the flu.

Event 3
Narrative
details

Everything happened awfully fast that night. I was rushed into Elizabeth's costume and pushed out onstage. It took a moment for me to adjust to the bright lights (the ones I was supposed to work). Then I saw John dressed up in that crazy armor and staring at me with a

Thoughts and
feelings

strained look on his face. "Oh," I thought confusedly. "I'm supposed to say something." But

Event 4
Narrative
details

nothing came out. There, in the glare of the spotlight, I stood onstage, absolutely alone and absolutely speechless.

Later, they told me that I seemed to be saying my lines but that nobody could hear them. It didn't get easier as the longest play in history went on. I remember stumbling onto the stage each time in a kind of merciful daze. I discovered if I didn't look at the audience, I could retrieve most of my lines from my dim memory. No one mentioned afterward that Camilla seemed fixated on the empty space above the stage.

**CONCLUSION
Meaning of
experience**

I didn't suddenly blossom into Katharine Hepburn, but the world didn't come to an end, either. You still won't find me leaping up to answer questions in class. But it was fun to go to the party with the rest of the cast, to laugh at some of the funny bloopers, and to feel good because everyone liked the play so much. For once in my life, I'd been in the limelight a little. And it didn't feel so bad, after all.

The essay you have just read is based on the following framework, which you might find helpful in developing your own personal essay.

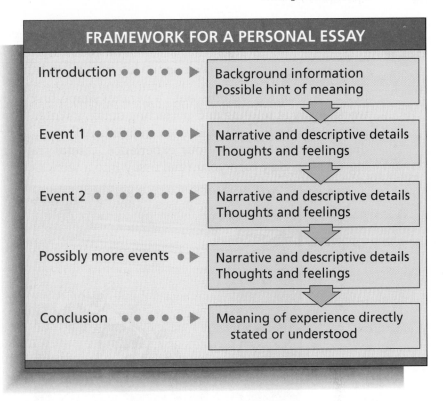

FRAMEWORK FOR A PERSONAL ESSAY

Introduction ● ● ● ● ● ▶ Background information
Possible hint of meaning

Event 1 ● ● ● ● ● ● ● ▶ Narrative and descriptive details
Thoughts and feelings

Event 2 ● ● ● ● ● ● ● ▶ Narrative and descriptive details
Thoughts and feelings

Possibly more events ● ▶ Narrative and descriptive details
Thoughts and feelings

Conclusion ● ● ● ● ● ▶ Meaning of experience directly
stated or understood

Reminder

When writing a draft of your personal essay

■ introduce background information and a hint of the experience's meaning early
■ use specific narrative and descriptive details
■ gradually reveal more of the experience's significance
■ conclude with a full recognition of significance

WRITING
ASSIGNMENT

PART 3:
Writing a Draft of Your Personal Essay

Now that you've gathered details and reflected on the meaning of your experience (Writing Assignment, Part 2), it's time to shape your notes and ideas into essay form. Using your prewriting notes, write a draft of your personal essay.

Evaluating and Revising

Just as a sculptor "roughs out" a general shape first and then works away at refining and perfecting detail, a writer "drafts" a general shape that must later be refined. Although your first draft gives first form to your experience, careful crafting during revision may turn your final essay into a work of art!

Illustrator: Dan Krovatin

The chart on the following page can help you evaluate and revise your own work. If you find a problem indicated in the left-hand column, try the revision technique suggested in the right-hand column.

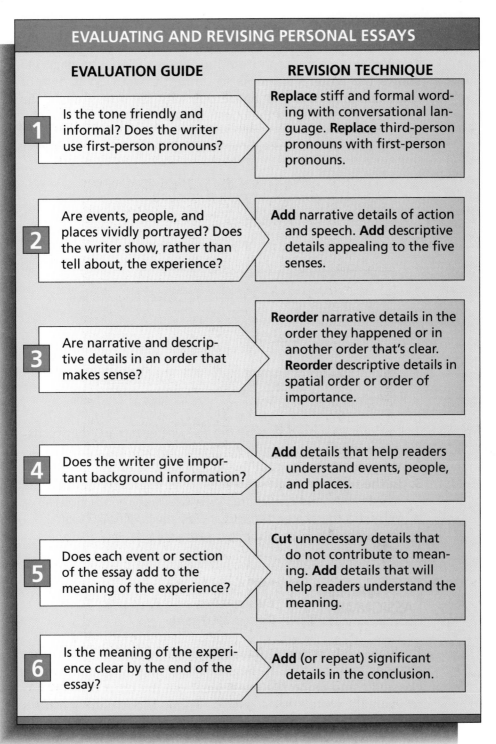

EVALUATING AND REVISING PERSONAL ESSAYS

EVALUATION GUIDE	REVISION TECHNIQUE
1 Is the tone friendly and informal? Does the writer use first-person pronouns?	**Replace** stiff and formal wording with conversational language. **Replace** third-person pronouns with first-person pronouns.
2 Are events, people, and places vividly portrayed? Does the writer show, rather than tell about, the experience?	**Add** narrative details of action and speech. **Add** descriptive details appealing to the five senses.
3 Are narrative and descriptive details in an order that makes sense?	**Reorder** narrative details in the order they happened or in another order that's clear. **Reorder** descriptive details in spatial order or order of importance.
4 Does the writer give important background information?	**Add** details that help readers understand events, people, and places.
5 Does each event or section of the essay add to the meaning of the experience?	**Cut** unnecessary details that do not contribute to meaning. **Add** details that will help readers understand the meaning.
6 Is the meaning of the experience clear by the end of the essay?	**Add** (or repeat) significant details in the conclusion.

E X E R C I S E 4 ▶   **Analyzing a Writer's Revisions**

The following paragraph from the Writer's Model on page 145 shows the writer's attempts to refine the draft. With two or three classmates, try to figure out why the writer made the changes. Then answer the questions that follow.

Everything happened awfully fast

~~Events went on at a rapid rate~~ that night.   **replace**

I was rushed into Elizabeth's costume and

pushed out onstage. It took a moment for me

to adjust to the bright lights (the ones I

was supposed to work). ~~Mr. Guedez drafted~~   **cut**

~~Jennifer to work them in my place.~~ Then I

crazy

saw John dressed up in that armor and   **add**

staring at me with a strained look on his

confusedly

face. "Oh," I thought, "I'm supposed to say   **add**

something." But nothing came out. There, in   **add**

absolutely alone and absolutely speechless

the glare of the spotlight, I stood onstage.   **add**

1. In the first sentence, why did the writer replace the words *events went on at a rapid rate*? [Hint: Review page 132.]
2. Why did the writer cut the fourth sentence?
3. In the fifth and sixth sentences, why did the writer add the words *crazy* and *confusedly*? Why are these good choices?
4. Why did the writer add the words *absolutely alone and absolutely speechless* to the last sentence?

WRITING ASSIGNMENT

PART 4:

Evaluating and Revising Your Personal Essay

Evaluate your finished draft overall to determine what other changes will improve it. Begin by exchanging papers with a classmate and using the questions from the chart on page 149 to evaluate each other's essays. Think about your partner's comments, and then use the chart to evaluate your own essay. Finally, make revisions to improve your essay.

Proofreading and Publishing

Give your personal essay your personal best, including careful *proofreading* for mistakes in spelling, capitalization, punctuation, and usage. Then share your final copy with a larger audience. Here are two suggestions for *publishing* your essay.

- Send a copy (or copies) of your essay to those who shared the experience with you.
- Share your essay with a trusted adult.

MECHANICS HINT

Punctuating Dialogue

Dialogue adds a sense of immediacy to events and expresses thoughts and feelings effectively. To write dialogue, enclose a person's exact words or thoughts in quotation marks and begin a new paragraph if you switch speakers within a conversational exchange. If a dialogue tag (*he said, Joan muttered*) interrupts a sentence, the first word after the tag usually isn't capitalized.

EXAMPLE   "I hate to tell you this, but you've got the measles," Dr. James observed.
"Oh, no," I groaned to myself, "a kid's disease."

☞ REFERENCE NOTE: For more information on punctuating dialogue, see pages 878–881.

WRITING ASSIGNMENT

PART 5:

Proofreading and Publishing Your Essay

Don't let all the work you've put into your essay go unnoticed. Proofread your final draft and correct any errors. Then use one of the ideas above or one of your own to publish your essay.

Writing an Anecdote

Prewriting. Have you ever acted with the best of intentions but had something go wrong? Or, like Langston Hughes, have you ever been on the receiving end of a good-intention-gone-bad? If you haven't, brainstorm for another entertaining experience that you'd like to relate. Select one that's relatively short and amusing. Then, to recall the experience, use the techniques that you read about in this chapter.

Writing, Evaluating, and Revising. Try to follow Langston Hughes's framework in writing your anecdote:

- Introduce your anecdote with a general comment or phrase whose meaning will be completely understood at the end.
- Present your story's narrative details in chronological order and add descriptive details that reinforce your story's humor.

You may want to repeat your introductory comment or a slight variation of it at the end. Revise your draft to make the action clearer and the humor stronger.

Proofreading and Publishing. After checking for and correcting any errors, you might submit your anecdote to your school newspaper or magazine for publication. If the publication doesn't already have a humor section, you could suggest one.

"The best way to cheer yourself up is to try to cheer somebody else up"

Mark Twain

MAKING CONNECTIONS

WRITING ACROSS THE CURRICULUM

Group Self-Expression in History

In a personal essay, one person shares his or her experience with others. But groups of people can also express their shared feelings about a common experience. Group self-expression may be a public announcement, or declaration, like the Declaration of Independence, or it may take other forms, such as a myth, a creed, or a law.

With a small group of your classmates, choose one instance of group self-expression in history, such as the ones listed below and on the next page. Then do some research to find out the background and purpose of the item you select. How and why did it develop? What thoughts and feelings about the group does it express? Report to your classmates on your research.

1. the Boy Scout Oath or Girl Scout Promise
2. the Bill of Rights
3. the Equal Rights Amendment
4. the Greek myth of Persephone
5. the preamble to the charter of the United Nations

6. a Native American myth about the origin or harvesting of crops
7. your school song
8. the code of the Japanese samurai warrior
9. the Emancipation Proclamation
10. your state's laws regarding public access for people who are disabled

SELF-EXPRESSION AND THE FUTURE

Setting Goals

Do you make New Year's resolutions? Do you know other people who do? New Year's resolutions are a kind of joke because most people don't take them seriously. But resolutions in the form of goals for your future are extremely important. Without goals you don't know where you want to go or how to get there. Realistic goals are hard to set, though; to plan for the future, you have to understand your past and your present. That's where expressive writing comes in; it allows you to develop a better understanding of yourself.

Since your high school years are almost over, this is a good time to think about goals. What are you going to do with your life after high school? Are you going to a trade school or college? Are you going to look for a job right away or perhaps join the military? Where do you want to be five years from now—or even ten years from now? To begin to set goals for yourself, think through your answers to the following questions.

1. Start by looking at the expressive essay you wrote in this chapter. What did you learn about yourself? Did you discover anything that is especially important to you?

2. Think about goals you've had before. Have you achieved any of them? What have you accomplished that you set out to accomplish? How did you manage to do it?

3. Where do you want to be when you are twenty-five years old? Think about where you want to be living, what kind of work you want to be doing, whether you want to be single or married. (Your answers here are your long-range goals.)

4. What do you have to do right after you graduate from high school to ensure you can be where you want to be at the age of twenty-five? (Your answers here are your medium-range goals.)

5. What do you have to do during the next year and a half to make sure you can do what you want right after high school? (Your answers here are your immediate goals.)

After you've thought about these questions, begin to write some goals in your diary or journal. These goals aren't set in stone; you'll probably revise them from time to time. However, they will help you plan your future. If you want, share your goals with a good friend or an adult you trust. Otherwise, keep them in your journal and look back at them every few months to see if you're on your way to meeting them.

PEANUTS reprinted by permission of UFS, Inc.

5 CREATIVE WRITING

Imagining Other Worlds

A classroom is a natural place to talk about **imagining other worlds.** Be honest: Can't you daydream yourself right out the window?

Writing and You.   When you daydream, you're just exercising your imagination, as writers do when they create places and people, settings and characters that let us—for a while—leave our ordinary worlds. Sometimes the imagined place *is* ordinary, like the hot, dusty Texas in S. E. Hinton's novels. Sometimes it's the out-of-this-world world of a science fiction movie, like *Star Wars*. Always, though, in stories, plays, and films, words and imagination create fictional worlds that seem so real we actually believe in them. Could your daydreams hold realities waiting for words?

As You Read.   The poet Ishmael Reed dares you to read the following poem. What does that say about his imagination? Will you dare? What does that say about your imagination?

James Doolin, *Last Painter on Earth* (1983). Oil on canvas, 72" × 120". Courtesy of Koplin Gallery, Santa Monica, CA.

BEWARE: DO NOT READ THIS POEM

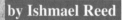
by Ishmael Reed

tonite, *thriller* was
abt an ol woman, so vain she
surrounded herself w/
   many mirrors

It got so bad that finally she
locked herself indoors & her
whole life became the
   mirrors

one day the villagers broke
into her house, but she was too
swift for them, she disappeared
   into a mirror
each tenant who bought the house
after that, lost a loved one to
   the ol woman in the mirror:
   first a little girl
   then a young woman
   then the young woman/s husband

the hunger of this poem is legendary
it has taken in many victims
back off from this poem
it has drawn in yr feet
back off from this poem
it has drawn in yr legs
back off from this poem
it is a greedy mirror
you are into this poem, from
    the waist down
nobody can hear you can they?
this poem has had you up to here
        belch
this poem aint got no manners
you cant call out frm this poem
relax now & go w/ this poem
move & roll on to this poem

    do not resist this poem
    this poem has yr eyes
    this poem has his head
    this poem has his arms
    this poem has his fingers
    this poem has his fingertips

this poem is the reader & the
    reader this poem

statistic: the us bureau of missing persons reports
        that in 1968 over 100,000 people disappeared
        leaving no solid clues
            nor trace   only
a space   in the lives of their friends

READER'S RESPONSE

1. Being swallowed by a poem may seem like an unusual idea, but maybe Reed has just chosen an unusual way to put it. What poem, story, movie, childhood puppet show, or campfire ghost tale held your attention so completely that you were "lost"?
2. What's your reaction to this poem? Do you think it's funny? Did you have trouble following it? Any other thoughts about the poem?
3. In your opinion, what is this poem *about*? Why do you think the poet wanted to write it?

WRITER'S CRAFT

4. Poems don't have to tell stories, but this one contains several stories, or at least hints of problems or conflicts that could be stories. What are the stories or conflicts?
5. This poem gives you a series of dramatic images by appealing not just to your sense of sight, but to your other senses, too. Find lines that appeal to the senses of sound, taste, and touch.
6. Read this poem out loud if you haven't. What is the rhythm like? What does it remind you of? How does the sound of the poem relate to what it supposedly *does*?

Strategies for Writing Creatively

Writers of poems, short stories, and plays all have the same purpose—to create literary works, to use language creatively.

When people write creatively, they start with their imagination and use their craft with words to make something that has never existed before. They create not just poems and stories but novels, song lyrics, movie and television scripts—even comic strips. Here are examples of different ways in which people write creatively.

▶ **Narration:** writing a science fiction story about creatures from another galaxy who land in a huge automobile junkyard on Earth; in a mystery novel, telling about a girl detective who saves a rock star from being killed by an insane fan.

▶ **Description:** in a poem, describing a baseball field at midnight; in a story about the Civil War, describing the sounds, sights, and smells of a battlefield.

Classification: in a song, comparing the rainbow to a trail; in a poem, comparing a bird's feathers to a musical instrument.

Evaluation: in a movie script, showing how one person's honesty can teach a lesson to an entire town; in a comic strip, telling a funny story to show that men and women should share housework.

LOOKING AHEAD

In the main assignment in this chapter, you'll use the strategies of narration and description to write a story. As you work through the assignment, keep in mind that a short story

- uses imagination to entertain the reader
- has a plot built on a problem or conflict
- develops characters and settings in believable and vivid ways

Writing a Short Story

Prewriting

Exploring Story Ideas

Any person, situation, or place can become a story, with imagination. Some of you may be thinking, "But I'm not the creative type." You're mistaken. Remember all the play stories you invented as a child—in your head or in a backyard fort with friends? One way to revive that inventiveness is by asking "What if?" questions, a technique many professional writers use.

- What if the commander of an isolated army outpost becomes a friend of the Sioux he's expected to fight?
- What if two teenagers from warring families fall in love?
- What if a race of humans is completely and totally logical—never ruled by emotions?

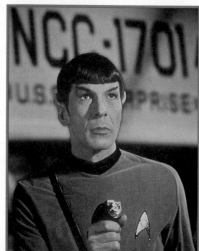

The familiar story ideas on the previous page were once just glimmers of ideas in the writers' minds, perhaps sparked by something simple—a picture of a dusty, abandoned cabin, for example. So when you're looking for story ideas, pay attention to everything—from conversations you overhear on the bus to an article in a newspaper, to your own daydreams, nightmares, and memories—and ask "What if?" Unleash your imagination and see where it goes.

EXERCISE 1 ▶ **Exploring Story Ideas**

To see where your imagination leads you, start with "What if?" and freewrite about any two of the following ideas.

1. the first time you were left alone in the house
2. a dream or a nightmare
3. a stranger who made you nervous
4. a news item you couldn't believe
5. a time you were disappointed, angry, scared, happily surprised, or too excited to sleep

WRITING ASSIGNMENT

PART 1:
Finding Your Story Ideas

Did your freewriting for Exercise 1 spark a story idea? If not, keep your eyes, ears, and mind open. You could transform the familiar: *What if at breakfast your mother announces she's decided to become a country-western singer?* Or you could explore the familiar: *What if a teenager wants to drop out of school?* When you find a story idea, write it in a sentence or two.

Prewriting

Planning Your Story

Now you're going to build on your idea, bringing your glimpse of a good story into full view. And you can do it. Even though there's always a touch of mystery in every creation, story writing—like any kind of writing—has basic elements that you can learn about, focus on, and make work for you.

Developing Conflict and Plot

A *plot* is what happens in a story, but it's not just any series of events. You may have noticed that all the examples of story ideas so far contained a problem, or at least a germ of one. That's crucial: At the heart of every plot is a *conflict,* a problem that the main character faces. Without conflict there's no story; and with it, there's every kind of story under the sun.

TYPES OF CONFLICT		
External Conflict	The main character is in conflict with another character, a group, or society's rules.	Alfonso's parents want him to stay in school, but he's failing computer class and English.
	The main character is in conflict with a force of nature.	A woman must survive the flood that's sweeping away her house.
Internal Conflict	The main character struggles with his or her own feelings, values, or needs.	Justine's obsession with earning money is taking over her life.

A plot also has a definite shape. It isn't as random as real life can be: The main conflict makes the characters act. Events connect to each other in a chain of cause and effect. The writer pulls readers steadily along.

To heighten interest, *complications* may arise: a setback for the main character or a new conflict (perhaps a wild animal threatens the flood-bound woman).

But eventually comes a tense moment, the *climax*, when the conflict is decided, one way or another. The climax (sometimes called the "turning point") isn't always a fireworks scene; it may be a quiet decision. But it's the point in your story where your main character comes to terms with the conflict.

The complications and climax of the story eventually lead to the *resolution:* the aftermath, the final details that show how the conflict is resolved. The resolution should leave the reader feeling satisfied that, whether it is happy or sad, the ending is appropriate.

When you're planning your plot, keep this rising and falling shape in mind: conflict, complications, CLIMAX, resolution. Here is one writer's plan for the plot of his story.

Conflict:	<u>External</u>—Alfonso vs. computers, English, etc. He may fail. <u>Internal</u>—pride vs. feeling defeated—also wanting to succeed for parents
Plot Events:	Alfonso struggles with his computer assignment. Getting <u>mad</u>. Thinks about parents, past. Elvira comes in, offers to teach Alfonso. He tries, it's worse, gets madder, pops off at Elvira. She starts to leave.
Climax:	Alfonso swallows his pride and apologizes. Elvira stays.
Resolution:	Alfonso's doing better in school. He's dating Elvira.

WRITING ASSIGNMENT

PART 2:
Developing Your Conflict and Plot

Now, start to shape your story idea from Writing Assignment, Part 1. What conflict will be the heart of your plot? How will it be solved? What events will lead to the climactic moment? What complications could create suspense? After you know what's going to happen in your story, summarize the plot in a few sentences. You might follow the format in the Here's How.

Exploring Characters and Setting

Characters.   *Characters* are fun to dream up. You can make them be anything and do anything, but you can also borrow bits and pieces from real-life people. You might, for instance, create a woman space explorer who looks a little like your cousin Deanna but has the brains of your math teacher. Even if your main character is a horse (why not?), that horse has to be a solid, distinctive individual. Here are some questions to help you create your characters.

- What's the character's name?
- How does the character look, dress, and talk?
- What does the character like to do and think about?
- What words best describe the character's personality?
- What do other characters think about this character?

Setting.   If the time or place of your story, its *setting,* is unusual—frontier days, for example, or another galaxy— you've probably already imagined some details. Remember, though, that any setting—a mall, a car—can tell readers about your characters and their world.

Setting can even be central to a conflict, like a flood, and it can definitely set a mood (create a general feeling). Just think of stories set in a scorching, breathless desert or at a sad, cheap carnival. Use the following questions to explore how setting can work for your story.

- Exactly when and where does the story take place?
- What objects, weather, buildings, or details of everyday life could be important?
- Could setting add to mood? Could it convey a particular emotion or atmosphere?
- What sounds, smells, sights, tastes, and textures should be described?
- What details of setting could convey information about the plot or the characters in your story?

WRITING NOTE You will probably come up with many more details about characters and setting than you'll actually use when you write your story, but the details you jot down now will make your characters and their background more real to you. It's like putting money into savings. Once it is there, you can take out what you need when you need it. So feel free to explore your characters and setting fully.

WRITING ASSIGNMENT

PART 3:
Imagining Your Characters and Setting

Can you imagine your setting and characters so vividly that you can see yourself standing there with them? To make your readers see your characters and setting, you must first be able to see them clearly yourself. Use the questions on page 168 and above to give flesh to your creations. You may want to use freewriting or brainstorming to keep ideas flowing. Save your notes to use later.

Choosing a Point of View

When you choose a *point of view* for your story, you are deciding the vantage point from which readers will see events. Remember, though, it is not your personal viewpoint; it is the viewpoint of the narrator. As the following chart shows, you have three basic points of view to choose from: first-person, third-person omniscient, and third-person limited. Each point of view has its own set of advantages and disadvantages.

POINT OF VIEW	
NARRATOR	EFFECTS
First-person: The narrator is a character in the story and uses the first-person pronouns *I, me, our,* and so on.	This point of view is personal and immediate but can only tell what one person sees, hears, feels, and believes.
Third-person omniscient: The narrator is outside of the story and can enter any character's mind. (*Omniscient* means "all-knowing." *Third-person* means using the pronouns *he, them,* and so on.)	This narration is more impersonal but has unlimited freedom—showing the past or future, speaking to the reader, telling (or withholding) any detail.
Third-person limited: The narrator is outside the story but enters the mind of *one* character.	This point of view gives one character's perspective without being restricted to that person's actions or location. It combines the personal with a storyteller's distance.

Once you have decided on the point of view you want to use, you must stick to it. Shifts in point of view can be very confusing to your readers.

IN OR OUT (DEPENDING ON YOUR POINT OF VIEW)

THAVES 9-6

FRANK & ERNEST reprinted by permission of NE

CRITICAL THINKING

Analyzing Point of View

When you use the critical thinking skill of *analysis*, you examine something closely, studying its parts in order to understand how they function or how they relate to each other. To understand point of view, it is essential to analyze, or examine closely, its effects on the telling of a story. Here are some questions you can use to analyze point of view:

- What is the effect if the narrator stands back in the distance, knowing everything that is going on, including what all of the characters are thinking?
- What is the effect if the narrator is a minor character in the story—perhaps the friend or younger brother of the hero or heroine? What can this narrator know about what the main character thinks and feels?
- What is the effect if the narrator is the main character in the story? How objective is this narrator?

CRITICAL THINKING EXERCISE:
Analyzing Point of View

The following passage uses third-person limited point of view. Working with two or three classmates, read it and use the questions for discussion and analysis.

> Lalu felt herself shoved in front of the customs officer. She had never been close to a white man before and she stared amazed at the one that towered above her. His skin was chalk white, like the face of an actor painted to play a villain, only it was not smooth but covered with wiry golden hair, and when his mouth opened and closed, there were no words to make an audience shake with anger or fear, only a senseless roaring. Beside him, a Chinese man spoke.
>
> Ruthanne Lum McCunn, *Thousand Pieces of Gold*

1. Which character's mind is "entered" in the narration? What are you told about the character? What are some of the character's personal perceptions?
2. How would the narration change if the central character were telling about this incident? To explore, rewrite the passage in the first person. Be sure to use *I* and *me* and to think about the character's personality.
3. Choose one of the other characters (there are two others: did you find both?), and rewrite the passage, using *either* first-person or third-person omniscient point of view. You may add details, but don't change events.

Thinking About Purpose, Audience, and Tone

Purpose and Audience.   Your main *purpose* in writing your story is to be creative and to entertain your *audience,* which will probably be your classmates. That's why it is important to think ahead about the effect you want to have on your readers. Do you want to scare them or give them the creeps? Would you love for them to cry buckets of tears? Remember that entertaining people doesn't always mean making them laugh, but it does mean keeping them interested and involved.

Sometimes you may want to plant in your readers' minds the seed of an idea—about pride or gangs or even dieting. A message like this is called a ***theme,*** and although you don't usually state messages outright in a story (*our society's obsession with thinness often hurts people*), you can often show them through characters and plot.

Tone.   *Tone,* of course, is tied up with purpose because it's the attitude you take toward the characters and events. Your story's tone may be mysterious, affectionate, joking, angry, matter-of-fact—you name it. It's any feeling that fits your tale.

The point of view you choose contributes to tone. A depressed character, for instance, won't make a cheerful first-person narrator. You also create tone through descriptive details (perhaps flying clouds and warm sun), type of language (perhaps blunt words and slang), and rhythm of sentences (perhaps short, simple ones). In a story, everything adds up.

Reminder

To plan your story

- start with a main character facing a definite conflict, and decide how you'll solve it
- give the plot a shape—a chain of events with complications, climax, and resolution
- imagine characters and setting in solid detail
- choose a point of view and stick with it
- think ahead about the effects and ideas you want to create for readers

WRITING ASSIGNMENT

PART 4:
Planning Your Story

Now it's time to gather together the notes you have made about plot, character, and setting (from Parts 2 and 3 of your Writing Assignment). Also decide on your point of view. Remember that you are drawing a blueprint, not building a final house with solid walls and locked doors. You're very likely to make some changes—dropping events, even adding a character—when you draft, but put your plan on paper first.

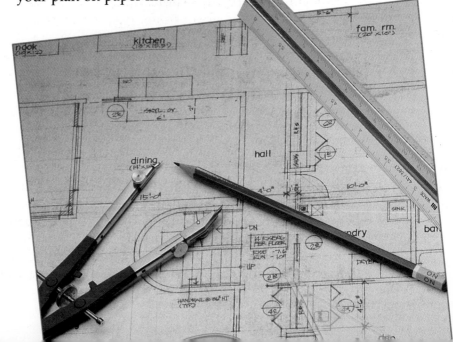

Writing Your First Draft

You know what it's like to lose yourself in a story. You are so drawn into the story that you seem to be living alongside the characters. That's the kind of reality you need to aim for in your first draft, and here are some tips that will help.

Combining the Basic Elements of Stories

Believable Characters. It's tempting to tell your readers about a character: *Aisha was a vain girl who spent a lot of time working on how she looked.* However, it is better to stand back and let your characters create themselves.

- **Show the character in action.** *Aisha stepped in front of the mirror to check her hair for the third time.*
- **Let readers hear the character's thoughts.** *Aisha thought her new lipstick looked extremely cool with her golden skin.*
- **Show how other characters react.** *"Aisha," Kim said, "like, you're the fairest, OK? Give me my compact and let's go."*

Notice that *dialogue* really adds to believability. It must sound natural, though, so give each speaker words that fit the character's age, personality, and background. You can use contractions, slang, fragments—whatever sounds right.

EXERCISE 2 ▶	**Speaking and Listening:** **Creating Dialogue**

Get together with a partner to make up a dialogue for the characters in one of the following situations. First, spend some time imagining details of character and setting. When you're happy with your dialogue, set the scene for the class and present the dialogue. Ask for some feedback on why you sounded natural—or why you didn't quite make it.

1. A teenager tells a parent that he or she wants to get married right after graduation from high school.
2. A police officer talks to a young boy he has found out on the street after midnight.
3. A woman tells her boss she has won the lottery and is quitting her job.

Vivid Descriptions.   A good story is a sensory experience. You can create such a story by using *images*—sensory details that let readers see, hear, smell, taste, and touch what's happening. This doesn't mean describing every object, person, and event in microscopic detail, but it does mean using imagery to bring important elements into sharp focus. Notice how every descriptive detail in the following passage makes the setting concrete, moves the action forward, reveals character, or creates mood.

> We hurried along. The white daytime moon showed on a patch of turquoise sky between clouds. The rain was fine, like sifted flour. My mother was in a good mood but seemed aware this could easily pass. She looked at the rain and the sky as if they were possessions someone might take from her at any moment. The clouds suddenly seemed to be turning over themselves, and in a second they broke. We got drenched.
>
> Cynthia Kadohata, *The Floating World*

The passage also shows how *figurative language* such as *metaphors* and *similes*—comparisons of two unlike things—can enrich description. Rain "like sifted flour" is a swift, clear word picture far more vivid than "fine rain."

 REFERENCE NOTE: For more about figurative language, see pages 373 and 495–497.

A Tight Plot.   If an action or a detail doesn't advance your story, don't let it in. In other words, keep your plot lean and mean. The best way to hook your readers is to get to the conflict and main character as soon as possible. And remember the "chain-link" plot: One event clearly leads to another. Keep readers guessing about what a scene will hold, not how they got there!

Another way to make events clear for your readers is to maintain chronological order (see page 75), except when you must give a *flashback,* a passage that supplies important past events. Use a flashback only if it is really needed—to help readers understand a conflict, for example.

Looking at a Short Story

Although the following story, by a professional writer, is a real knuckle-whitener, it has a simple plot, just one human character, and almost no dialogue. As you read, notice how the writer gets your attention and keeps it. What makes the characters believable and the plot a tight chain?

A SHORT STORY

The Gift
by Louis Dollarhide

Setting/Suspense

Flashback

Setting/Mood

How many days, she wondered, had she sat like this, watching the cold brown water inch up the dissolving bluff. She could just faintly remember the beginning of the rain, driving in across the swamp from the south and beating against the shell of her house. Then the river itself started rising, slowly at first until at last it paused as if to turn back. From hour to hour it slithered up creeks and ditches and poured over low places. In the night, while she slept, it claimed the road and surrounded her so that she sat alone, her boat gone, the house like a piece of drift lodged on its bluff. Now even against the tarred planks of the supports the waters touched. And still they rose.

Third-person
limited point of
view

Conflict
established

Character
developed

Mood heightened/
Sight and sound
images

Figurative
language and
sensory images

As far as she could see, to the treetops where the opposite banks had been, the swamp was an empty sea, awash with sheets of rain, the river lost somewhere in its vastness. Her house with its boat bottom had been built to ride just such a flood, if one ever came, but now it was old. Maybe the boards underneath were partly rotted away. Maybe the cable mooring the house to the great live oak would snap loose and let her go turning downstream, the way her boat had gone.

No one could come now. She could cry out but it would be no use, no one would hear. Down the length and breadth of the swamp others were fighting to save what little they could, maybe even their lives. She had seen a whole house go floating by, so quiet she was reminded of sitting at a funeral. She thought when she saw it she knew whose house it was. It had been bad seeing it drift by, but the owners must have escaped to higher ground. Later, with the rain and darkness pressing in, she had heard a panther scream upriver.

Now the house seemed to shudder around her like something alive. She reached out to catch a lamp as it tilted off the table by her bed and put it between her feet to hold it steady. Then creaking and groaning with effort the house struggled up from the clay, floated free, bobbing like a cork, and

swung out slowly with the pull of the river. She gripped the edge of the bed. Swaying from side to side, the house moved to the length of its mooring. There was a jolt and a complaining of old timbers and then a pause. Slowly the current released it and let it swing back, rasping across its resting place. She caught her breath and sat for a long time feeling the slow pendulous sweeps. The dark sifted down through the incessant rain, and, head on arm, she slept holding on to the bed.

Sometime in the night the cry awoke her, a sound so anguished she was on her feet before she was awake. In the dark she stumbled against the bed. It came from out there, from the river. She could hear something moving, something large that made a dredging, sweeping sound. It could be another house. Then it hit, not head on but glancing and sliding down the length of her house. It was a tree. She listened as the branches and leaves cleared themselves and went on downstream, leaving only the rain and the lappings of the flood, sounds so constant now that they seemed a part of the silence. Huddled on the bed, she was almost asleep again when another cry sounded, this time

so close it could have been in the room. Staring into the dark, she eased back on the bed until her hand caught the cold shape of the rifle. Then crouched on the pillow, she cradled the gun across her knees. "Who's there?" she called.

The answer was a repeated cry, but less shrill, tired sounding, then the empty silence closing in. She drew back against the bed. Whatever was there she could hear it moving about on the porch. Planks creaked and she could distinguish the sounds of objects being knocked over. There was a scratching on the wall as if it would tear its way in. She knew now what it was, a big cat, deposited by the uprooted tree that had passed her. It had come with the flood, a gift.

Unconsciously she pressed her hand against her face and along her tightened throat. The rifle rocked across her knees. She had never seen a panther in her life. She had heard about them from others and had heard their cries, like suffering, in the distance. The cat was scratching on the wall again, rattling the window by the door. As long as she guarded the window and kept the cat hemmed in by the wall and water, caged, she would be all right. Outside, the animal paused to rake his claws across the rusted outer screen. Now and then, it whined and growled.

When the light filtered down through the rain at last, coming like another kind of dark, she was still sitting on the bed, stiff and cold. Her arms, used to rowing on the river, ached from the stillness of holding the rifle. She had hardly allowed herself to move for fear any sound might give strength to the cat. Rigid, she swayed with the movement of the house. The rain still fell as if it would never stop. Through the gray light, finally, she could see the rain-pitted flood and far away the cloudy shape of drowned treetops. The cat was not moving now. Maybe he had gone away. Laying the gun aside she slipped off the bed and moved without out a sound to the window. It was still there, crouched at the edge of the porch, staring up at the

Dialogue

Suspense

Character developed/ Actions

Setting and plot details

Character developed

Character
developed/
Thoughts

live oak, the mooring of her house, as if gauging its chances of leaping to an overhanging branch. It did not seem so frightening now that she could see it, its coarse fur napped into twigs, its sides pinched and ribs showing. It would be easy to shoot it where it sat, its long tail whipping back and forth. She was moving back to get the gun when it turned around. With no warning, no

Conflict

crouch or tensing of muscles, it sprang at the window, shattering a pane of glass. She fell back, stifling a scream, and taking up the rifle, she fired through the window. She could not see the panther now, but she had missed. It began to pace again. She could glimpse its head and the arch of its back as it passed the window.

Setting/Sensory
images/Mood

Shivering, she pulled back on the bed and lay down. The lulling constant sound of the river and the rain, the penetrating chill, drained away her purpose. She watched the window and kept the gun ready. After waiting a long while she moved again to look. The panther had fallen asleep, its head on its paws, like a housecat. For the first time

Character
developed/
Thoughts and
actions

since the rains began she wanted to cry, for herself, for all the people, for everything in the flood. Sliding down on the bed, she pulled the quilt around her shoulders. She should have got out when she could, while the roads were still open or before her boat was washed away. As she rocked back and forth with the sway of the house a deep ache in her stomach reminded her she hadn't eaten. She couldn't remember for how long. Like the cat, she was starving. Easing into the kitchen, she made a fire with the few remaining sticks of wood. If the flood lasted she would have to burn the chair, maybe even the table itself. Taking down the remains of a smoked ham from the ceiling, she cut thick slices of the brownish red meat and placed

Sensory images

them in a skillet. The smell of the frying meat made her dizzy. There were stale biscuits from the last time she had cooked and she could make some coffee. There was plenty of water.

While she was cooking her food, she almost

Character and
suspense
developed/
Dialogue and
actions

forgot about the cat until it whined. It was hungry too. "Let me eat," she called to it, "and then I'll see to *you*." And she laughed under her breath. As she hung the rest of the ham back on its nail the cat growled a deep throaty rumble that made her hand shake.

After she had eaten, she went to the bed again and took up the rifle. The house had risen so high now it no longer scraped across the bluff when it swung back from the river. The food had warmed her. She could get rid of the cat while light still hung in the rain. She crept slowly to the window. It was still there, mewing, beginning again to move about the porch. She stared at it a long time, unafraid. Then without thinking what she was doing, she laid the gun aside and started around the edge of the bed to the kitchen. Behind her the cat was moving, fretting. She took down what was

Climax

left of the ham and making her way back across the swaying floor to the window she shoved it through the broken pane. On the other side there was a hungry snarl and something like a shock passed from the animal to her. Stunned by what she had done, she drew back to the bed. She heard the sounds of the panther tearing at the meat. The house rocked around her.

Resolution

The next time she awoke she knew at once that everything had changed. The rain had stopped. She felt for the movement of the house but it no longer swayed on the flood. Drawing her door

Setting

open, she saw through the torn screen a different world. The house was resting on the bluff where it always had. A few feet down, the river still raced on in a torrent, but it no longer covered the few feet between the house and the live oak. And the

Descriptive details

cat was gone. Leading from the porch to the live oak and doubtless on into the swamp were tracks, indistinct and already disappearing in the soft mud. And there on the porch, gnawed to whiteness, was what was left of the ham.

EXERCISE 3 ▶ **Analyzing a Short Story**

After you read "The Gift," meet with a small group of classmates to discuss the story. See if you can agree on the answers to the following questions.

1. The main conflict in this story is external: a character versus nature. Survival is at stake. What conflict sets the story in motion? What second conflict arises in a complication?
2. What kind of person is the main character? What details reveal her character and personality? Do you see any internal conflicts in her? Explain.
3. The big cat is also a character. How does the writer give it "personality"?
4. What role does setting play in this story? Point out passages to show what you mean.
5. The climax of this story is a decision and an action. What is it? How is it related to the character's main conflict?

Using a Framework for a Short Story

"The Gift" is a very successful story, but in a way the writer set himself quite a task: using a single human character, closed up in a house, with two "opponents" who can't talk (the flood and the cat). Most writers, like the one whose story follows, are easier on themselves and use a more common pattern. You may want to follow this pattern when you write your own story.

A WRITER'S MODEL

A Little Help

Character introduced
Dialogue and action

Alfonso Moreno stared at the computer screen and wished he had a shovel to hit it with.

"Don't go blinking BAD COMMAND at me," he ordered. "Just tell me what to do!" Like a caged animal he glared around the lab but saw no one who could free him from the machine. Row after row of bright blue monitors shone coldly back at him.

Hint of conflict

Desperate to finish his computer assignment, Alfonso began to press buttons. He hit escape and enter, then help, end, and exit, pausing to groan at questions the computer demanded answers to--like SAVE DOCUMENT?

Character developed/ Dialogue and action

Setting/ Background

Conflict

Character's thoughts (third-person)

Background

Flashback

Sensory images
Figurative language

Dialogue

Character developed/ Actions

"What document?" he demanded in a fury. "There isn't any document, dummy. You won't let me make a document!"

Alfonso smacked the side of his computer terminal with the flat of his hand and jumped out of his seat. At the window he stared out at the empty tennis courts and the deserted baseball field behind them. He had never been to a school like this. A lawn and covered walks. A sports program. He still felt like a stranger.

"I'll never make it," he muttered to himself. "I'm failing English. I'm failing this stupid computer class. I'm already seventeen and still in tenth grade. What's the use?"

Education had never been his dream, anyway, he thought angrily. It was his parents' dream for him, and it wasn't coming true. His father had made it as far as the sixth grade. His mother had an eighth-grade education. They were traveling south now, looking for work. Alfonso had traveled with them and worked in the fields for much of each school year until this past September. When he thought of the fields, he remembered how the odor of garlic never left his hands. He remembered the ache in his knees and back, like the bite of a snake, the sweat streaming down his face and neck. His parents had taken him to stay with his godfather, a mechanic who had steady work in a garage.

"You stay in school, now," his father said. "You can do better than us. We want you to make something of yourself."

Alfonso turned quickly as the door to the computer lab opened, and Elvira Valdez walked in. "Hi," she said. "¿Qué pasa?"

Alfonso just stared.

She spoke again. "I'm Elvira Valdez."

Alfonso glanced around to make sure no one else was in the lab. Was Elvira talking to him?

"Oh. Sure. ¿Qué pasa?" Well, that was a cool response. He turned back to his computer, feeling like an idiot. He tried not to look at her, but it wasn't easy. She didn't have to introduce herself. He knew who she was. One of just a handful of Hispanic girls in the school, Elvira was beautiful, with long, dark brown hair, and deep eyes that had never looked at him before. At least not on purpose. Elvira was a senior, and Alfonso had heard that next year she was going to a big-name college on a full scholarship.

Descriptive details

Sensory images

Alfonso began punching keys again. A clean, flowery smell, right at his elbow, suddenly awakened all of his senses. She was right there beside him! "Isn't your name Alfonso Moreno?" she asked.

Characters developed/ Dialogue

"Yeah, that's me," Alfonso mumbled. She must think he was stupid!

"You're working late," Elvira said. "You like computers?"

"Oh, yes," he answered, starting to get worked up again, Elvira beside him or not. "I love computers, but they hate my guts. The truth is I never saw a computer before this year, and I wish it'd stayed that way." He pulled out his last test paper. "See, I don't even know what the words mean. What's scroll? What's default? What kind of crazy English is this anyway?"

"Oh, that's just word-processing stuff. Let's see." Elvira tapped a couple of keys. "Computers are easy when you know what the commands mean. You want me to show you?"

Character's thoughts

Plot developed

Alfonso started to say, "Yeah, help the dumb kid," but he hesitated. She seemed OK.

He pulled a chair over for her. She told him to do this and that, he did it. So far so good. He tried something on his own, he got lost. Every time. As he grew more and more nervous, he slouched farther and farther in his seat. He couldn't look at her.

They both turned sharply when the lab door opened and three girls stepped in, looking surprised.

Complication/Suspense

"Elvira," said the little blond one, "we thought you were coming." They stared at Alfonso.

"I am. This won't take long. I'll see you at Shelley's." And she waved them off.

Character's thoughts

Alfonso wanted to be invisible. The dumb garlic picker. He won't take long.

"OK," said Elvira. "Let's try that part again. You remember the symbols for 'all files'?"

He touched * *.

"No, but almost--"

Conflict heightened

Alfonso shoved his chair back so hard it almost tipped. "Well, hey. I'm real sorry I didn't get it <u>all</u> right so you could leave faster. Go on. Catch up with your friends. I didn't ask you anyway and this is getting boring, man."

Elvira gathered her books in a very dignified way and stood up. "All right," she said. "Hasta la vista."

Alfonso reached back to the computer and hit exit. Hard. Then he turned away, pretending to look out the window, but a very small voice struggled out: "Sorry."

Climax

Elvira paused with her hand on the door.

"It's my problem, not yours," he said. "Computers are too complicated for me. A lot of things are complicated."

Characters developed/ Dialogue and action

"Yeah," said Elvira. "Yeah. But not computers."

To his surprise she was sitting back down beside him.

"Do you want to get simple?" she asked.

He had to laugh. "As simple as you can get."

"All right," said Elvira, "get some paper. When I wanted to kill my computer, I once made a list of Computer Steps for Any Idiot. Number one . . ."

Resolution

That afternoon Alfonso learned enough to get a C on Friday's quiz. By the end of the month he had the top grade in his computer class. And somehow figuring out crazy computer English made regular English not so scary. He wasn't failing any more.

"How did you do it?" his bewildered computer instructor, Mr. Washington, asked when Alfonso first aced a computer quiz. He shook his gray head. "You were the worst student I ever had--not because you were dumb, but because you had such a bad attitude. I knew you could make it, but you didn't know. Now you're acting like college material. What happened?"

"Oh, a lot of long hours in the lab. Dedication." Alfonso could have stopped, but he didn't. "Really, I had a tutor, a very patient one. She's waiting for me now."

"In the lab?" Mr. Washington asked. He held up the quiz. "But you have a perfect score."

"No," said Alfonso, "she's not in the lab. Uh, it's complicated, Mr. Washington. Hasta la vista."

The Writer's Model follows the framework below, which you may also want to use for your story. As you can see, the framework includes the basic parts of the plot identified on pages 166–167.

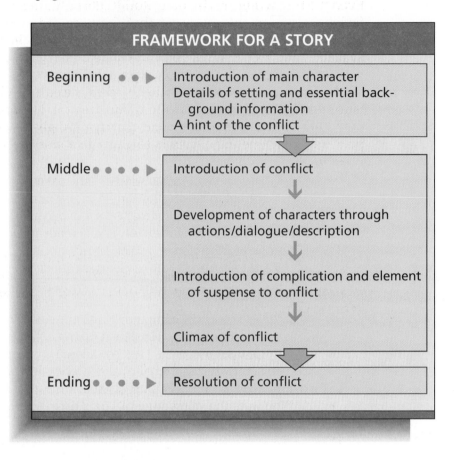

FRAMEWORK FOR A STORY

Beginning
- Introduction of main character
- Details of setting and essential background information
- A hint of the conflict

Middle
- Introduction of conflict
- Development of characters through actions/dialogue/description
- Introduction of complication and element of suspense to conflict
- Climax of conflict

Ending
- Resolution of conflict

WRITING ASSIGNMENT

PART 5:
Writing a Draft of Your Story

By now you have done so much thinking about your story that it is ready to take on a life of its own. Let your story write itself: *Record* what your characters say and do, the events they cause and confront. And if you do get stuck, use your prewriting notes to get your creative juices flowing again.

Evaluating and Revising

Even the best writers revise their stories. It's only after getting a fictional world down on paper that they can judge whether words have made their imaginings real. And with all the words available, and all the ways you can connect them, it would be very surprising if a first creation were a final one.

Trying your world out on other readers is also a good idea. Since it will be completely new to them, they can tell you how they find "living" there. The chart on page 190 gives you and peer reviewers specific elements to check in a story as well as ways to attack problems.

EXERCISE 4 ▶ **Analyzing a Writer's Revisions**

The writer of "A Little Help" made the following changes in one paragraph of his story (page 183). Use the evaluation and revising chart on page 190 to help you answer the questions after the paragraph.

> "Don't go blinking BAD COMMAND at me," he
> ~~He didn't know why the computer was~~   **replace**
> ordered.
> ~~blinking BAD COMMAND and said,~~ "Just tell
>
> me what to do!" Like a caged animal he
> glared   the lab
> ~~looked~~ around but saw no one who could   **replace/add**
>
> free him from the machine. ~~And he dreaded~~   **cut**
>
> ~~the rest of the day. He still had to help Juan~~
>   Row after
> ~~with a transmission and write a paper.~~ He   **replace**
> row of bright blue monitors shone coldly back at him.
> ~~hated looking at all these computers.~~

1. Why did the writer make the replacement in the first sentence? What's its effect?
2. How do the words *glared* and *the lab* help the paragraph?
3. Why did the writer cut two sentences?
4. What do you think the writer was aiming for by replacing the last sentence?

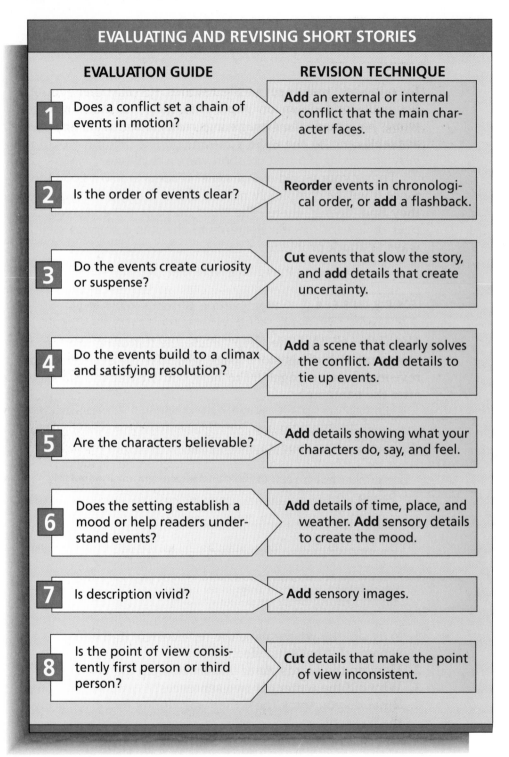

EVALUATING AND REVISING SHORT STORIES

EVALUATION GUIDE	REVISION TECHNIQUE
1 Does a conflict set a chain of events in motion?	**Add** an external or internal conflict that the main character faces.
2 Is the order of events clear?	**Reorder** events in chronological order, or **add** a flashback.
3 Do the events create curiosity or suspense?	**Cut** events that slow the story, and **add** details that create uncertainty.
4 Do the events build to a climax and satisfying resolution?	**Add** a scene that clearly solves the conflict. **Add** details to tie up events.
5 Are the characters believable?	**Add** details showing what your characters do, say, and feel.
6 Does the setting establish a mood or help readers understand events?	**Add** details of time, place, and weather. **Add** sensory details to create the mood.
7 Is description vivid?	**Add** sensory images.
8 Is the point of view consistently first person or third person?	**Cut** details that make the point of view inconsistent.

WRITING
ASSIGNMENT

PART 6:
**Evaluating and Revising
Your Story**

Use feedback from your classmates and the chart on page 190 as a guide to revising your story. Don't be afraid to change things. As a "world-maker," you have a chance to get one particular slice of life just right. Go for it.

GRAMMAR HINT

Using Precise Verbs

Many beginning story writers pile up adverbs to be descriptive about actions. Here's a hint from professional writers: The right verb can often paint a word picture more vividly than a vague verb plus an adverb. Look for action verbs that will create precise, accurate pictures in your reader's mind.

EXAMPLES

Vague Verbs with Adverbs	**Precise Verbs**
She **entered** the room **happily.**	She **bounced** into the room.
She **took** his hand **fearfully.**	She **gripped** his hand.
The smoke trail **blew lightly** toward them.	The smoke trail **floated** toward them.

☞ REFERENCE NOTE: For more information on verbs and adverbs, see pages 565–569.

Proofreading and Publishing

Proofreading.   You are probably prone to making certain errors in writing (everyone is), and you probably know to look carefully for them—perhaps misspelling words or confusing pronouns like *I* and *me*. In addition to looking for these kinds of problems, you can proofread your story for errors that are common in stories.

For example, be sure you have included both beginning and ending quotation marks for dialogue and have begun a new paragraph when speakers change. Pronoun antecedents are another checkpoint. When you say "she" jumped out of the car, do readers know who "she" is? It can make quite a difference.

Publishing.   Besides turning your story in to your teacher or sending it to magazines (see your library's copy of *Writer's Digest* for markets), you could try these publishing ideas:

- Divide your story into parts and serialize it in the school newspaper (you might revise a bit to create cliffhanger scenes).
- Give your story to an art class for practice in illustration.

| WRITING ASSIGNMENT | PART 7: **Proofreading and Publishing Your Story** |

It is time to give your story one final polish before letting your audience read it. Proofread your work carefully before sharing it with others. People like stories, so don't just hide yours in a folder. Why not read it to your younger brother or sister at bedtime or use one of the publishing choices listed above?

WRITING WORKSHOP

A Scene in a Play

In many ways plays are like short stories. Both are written for the purpose of creating literature; and both have characters, settings, and a central conflict.

Stories and plays, though, have one major difference. A story is written to be read, but a play is written to be acted out in front of a live audience or a movie camera. This means that the writer of a play can show character and conflict only through dialogue, action, and a kind of description called stage directions that appears only in the written script. *Stage directions* tell how the actors should move and speak and can also describe setting, mood, costumes, props, and lighting. A *scene* is a portion of a play. Most scenes have a continuous action, with no break in time and no change of place.

As you read the following scene from an award-winning stage play, think about how you find out about the characters. What do you learn about them from what they say and do? What do the stage directions tell you about them?

from A Raisin in the Sun
by Lorraine Hansberry

RUTH	Sit down and have your breakfast, Travis.
TRAVIS	Mama, this is Friday. (*Gleefully*) Check coming tomorrow, huh?
RUTH	You get your mind off money and eat your breakfast.
TRAVIS	(*Eating*) This is the morning we supposed to bring the fifty cents to school.
RUTH	Well, I ain't got no fifty cents this morning.
TRAVIS	Teacher say we have to.
RUTH	I don't care what teacher say. I ain't got it. Eat your breakfast, Travis.
TRAVIS	I *am* eating.
RUTH	Hush up now and just eat!

(*The boy gives her an exasperated look for her lack of understanding, and eats grudgingly.*)

TRAVIS	You think Grandmama would have it?
RUTH	No! And I want you to stop asking your grand-mother for money, you hear me?
TRAVIS	(*Outraged*) Gaaaleee! I don't ask her, she just gimme it sometimes!
RUTH	Travis Willard Younger— I got too much on me this morning to be—
TRAVIS	Maybe Daddy—
RUTH	*Travis!*

(*The boy hushes abruptly. They are both quiet and tense for several seconds.*)

Lorraine Hansberry

TRAVIS	(*Presently*) Could I maybe go carry some groceries in front of the supermarket for a little while after school then?
RUTH	Just hush, I said. (*Travis jabs his spoon into his cereal bowl viciously, and rests his head in anger upon his fists.*) If you through eating, you can get over there and make up your bed. (*The boy obeys stiffly and crosses the room, almost mechanically, to the bed and more or less carefully folds the covering. He carries the bedding into his mother's room and returns with his books and cap.*)
TRAVIS	(*Sulking and standing apart from her unnaturally*) I'm gone.
RUTH	(*Looking up from the stove to inspect him automatically*) Come here. (*He crosses to her and she studies his head.*) If you don't take this comb and fix this here head, you better! (TRAVIS *puts down his books with a great sigh of oppression, and crosses to the mirror. His mother mutters under her breath about his "slubbornness."*) 'Bout to march out of here with that head looking just like chickens slept in it! I just don't know where you get your slubborn ways . . . And get your jacket, too. Looks chilly out this morning.
TRAVIS	(*With conspicuously brushed hair and jacket*) I'm gone.
RUTH	Get carfare and milk money—(*Waving one finger*)— and not a single penny for no caps, you hear me?
TRAVIS	(*With sullen politeness*) Yes'm. (*He turns in outrage to leave. His mother watches after him as in his frustration he approaches the door almost comically. When she speaks to him, her voice has become a very gentle tease.*)
RUTH	(*Mocking; as she thinks he would say it*) Oh, Mama makes me so mad sometimes, I don't know what to do! (*She waits and continues to his back as he stands stock-still in front of the door.*) I wouldn't kiss that woman good-bye for nothing in this world this morning! (*The boy finally turns around and rolls his eyes at her, knowing the mood has changed and he is vindicated; he does not, however, move toward her yet.*) Not for nothing in this world! (*She finally laughs aloud at him and holds out her arms to him and we see that it is a way between them, very old and*

practiced. He crosses to her and allows her to embrace him warmly but keeps his face fixed with masculine rigidity. She holds him back from her presently and looks at him and runs her fingers over the features of his face. With utter gentleness—) Now—whose little old angry man are you?

TRAVIS   *(The masculinity and gruffness start to fade at last.)* Aw gaalee—Mama . . .

RUTH   *(Mimicking)* Aw—gaaaaalleeeee, Mama! *(She pushes him, with rough playfulness and finality, toward the door.)* Get on out of here or you going to be late.

1. Most scenes center on a minor conflict within the larger conflict of the play. What is the conflict between Travis and Ruth? How is it resolved?
2. What kind of person is Ruth? How do you know?

3. What words would you use to describe Travis? What dialogue and actions cause you to describe him in this way?

4. What role do stage directions play in the scene? Give examples to support your ideas.

Writing a Scene

 Prewriting.   To find an idea for your scene, you might think about conflicts that come up in a family, at school, or in a community. By asking "What if?" you can imagine your way to specific characters and conflict details. Since you won't have much time to develop actions in a single scene, keep the conflict simple. Flesh out your characters' attitudes and personalities, as well as their physical characteristics. And don't forget that you're writing for a stage—keep your setting simple.

 Writing, Evaluating, and Revising.   As you write, remember that you have two means to reveal your characters to the audience: dialogue and action. Make sure the language you use in the dialogue reflects the characters' personalities and backgrounds. And in your stage directions be as thorough and clear as possible. If you "see" a character constantly cracking his knuckles, write it down so the actor will know. Describe what the characters will be wearing as well as where and how they will move.

After drafting, get some friends to read your scene aloud as actors. Are they—in the flesh—accomplishing what you intended? Ask them, too, to make suggestions and to point out places where they weren't sure what to do or felt uncomfortable with dialogue. Then revise.

Proofreading and Publishing.   Notice the way the script from *A Raisin in the Sun* is set up, and use the same form for your scene. After you've proofread your script, you can make copies and hold an audition or ask particular people to take parts. You'll need a director (maybe not yourself) and possibly someone in charge of props. Be sure to allow time for at least three rehearsals before a performance. How about videotaping the performance so both you and the actors can see it?

WRITING WORKSHOP

Poetry

Poems are another form of literary, or creative, writing. Like fiction (the story and play you wrote earlier in this chapter), poems are ways for you to create something new from your imagination; and also like fiction, poems can tell stories. But not all, or even most, poems do that. Instead of capturing a period of time, they capture a moment. Like a flash camera, the poet's imagination illuminates an experience, emotion, object, or person and holds it still for you.

Description is a large part of the poet's magic, just as it is in stories; but poems are also musical. They use the sounds and rhythm of language very deliberately to communicate emotion and meaning. Here are some specific techniques that you can use in writing poetry.

WRITING POETRY	
TECHNIQUE	EXAMPLE
Imagery: Concrete details that appeal to the senses of sight, sound, touch, taste, or smell.	"water lilies as they float / in the cooling air" (Anita Endrezze)
Simile: A comparison of unlike things using *like* or *as*.	"And eyes, like sparks of frost" (Walter de la Mare)
Metaphor: A comparison that equates two unlike things.	"Juliet is the sun!" (Shakespeare)
Personification: Human qualities given to something nonhuman.	"belch / this poem aint got no manners" (Ishmael Reed)
Rhyme: Repetition of words in which accented vowel sounds and all following sounds are the same.	"No time to see, in broad daylight, / Streams full of stars, like skies at night." (W. H. Davies)
Alliteration: Repetition of the same consonant sounds in words close together.	"still seeking / the last light" (Anita Endrezze)
Rhythm: The beat made by accented and unaccented syllables. **Metrical verse** has meter: a regular, recurring pattern of beats. **Free verse** has no pattern. Language's natural beats, repetition, and pauses create rhythm.	Metrical: "The Grass divides as with a Comb— /A spotted shaft is seen—" (Emily Dickinson) Free: "one day the villagers broke / into her house, but she was too / swift for them, she disappeared" (Ishmael Reed)

Read the following poem, aloud if you can, listening to its music and letting its images unfold. What experience does the poet want to give to you?

Sunset at Twin Lake
by Anita Endrezze

Colville Indian Reservation

The heron stalks
the webbed water,
its feathers made of mirrors.

We hear the white breath
of water lilies as they float
in the cooling air.

The heron is a bringer
of reed music:
legs, beak, feathers—
all are godly instruments
in the evening wind.

Even the mountains
have a distant message
although we are more concerned
with things closer:
our hands still seeking
the last light
as we cast our lines
and the trout jumping
into the net
of the low-rising moon.

1. How would you describe the mood of this poem? Point out one line or phrase that you think helps create the mood.
2. Often a poem is called a "word picture," but many senses, not just sight, can be involved. Find images of sound, touch, and sight.
3. What examples of figurative language do you see in the poem?
4. Is this poem metrical, or is it free verse? Where has the poet used alliteration or onomatopoeia to create musical effects?
5. What if the poet had used this experience to create a short story? Discuss how the story would be different from the poem.

Writing a Poem

Prewriting. Does the model poem remind you of an experience you have had? Think about something that's important to you, something you love, hate, or will always remember. You could write about a food, an animal, a person, a place (mall, cafeteria); a time (an early memory, vacation); an object (clothing, camera, car). Write your subject on a sheet of paper and cluster phrases, images, and comparisons around it, or try freewriting about it.

Writing, Evaluating, and Revising. If you write free verse, the form of your poem is up to you. You can arrange the lines any way that makes sense to you. However, if you would rather try another form, you can experiment with regular meter and rhyming lines. After you've written a draft, evaluate your use of sound effects and sensory images. Be a stern judge: Have you used rhyme, alliteration, or rhythm to heighten the effect you want to create? Are your visual images concrete? Ask a classmate for reactions and then revise.

Proofreading and Publishing. After you have checked your poem carefully to make sure it looks the way you want, recopy it. You may want to give your poem to someone you care about. Do keep it for yourself: It will be a record of something you felt strongly about at an important time in your life.

MAKING CONNECTIONS

Imagining a Historical Dialogue

Have you ever thought about what might happen if historical figures from different times could meet? For example, what might Abraham Lincoln and Martin Luther King, Jr., say to each other? With a partner, create a scene in which two historical figures talk about a social or political topic. Do you want to use people whose lives had common aspects or people from wildly different backgrounds—say St. Francis and Albert Einstein? Try to come up with a pair whose lives are important to you or who will generate an unusual exchange.

Do some basic research if you need to about the people and their times, and then brainstorm for comments each historical figure might say about the topic. Write the dialogue, at least in rough form, decide which role each of you will assume, and practice the conversation before presenting it to your class. You might even take questions and improvise answers. Here are some suggestions of figures to start your thinking: Eleanor Roosevelt and Harriet Tubman; Hernando Cortés and Adolf Hitler; Cleopatra and Queen Victoria.

DESCRIPTION IN FICTION

Sensory words and figurative language are as basic to fiction as to poetry, especially as writers try to create living pictures of people and places. In the following portrait of "Aunt Ida," notice not only the wealth of detail but its wonderful sharpness. Read it once—as a whole piece—and then read it again, taking time with each word. Which part of the description (even a word) do you wish you had thought of? Which of your senses does the description tap? Where is metaphor or simile used?

> I heard a swishing sound like knives being sharpened on stones, and Aunt Ida appeared from where the building had concealed her. Her size amazed me, the breadth of her brown shoulders, the columns of her arms as they stretched before her, pushing a lawnmower, plowing through the grass. At first I thought she had dyed her hair, but then I saw it was a wig, the kind of thing advertised on the back pages of comic books, "$11.95 and natural-looking." She wore overalls and sunglasses and had false teeth. She sang like Stevie Wonder, tilting her neck as she moved, bellowing a Johnny Lee song in English to an invisible audience. . . .
>
> Michael Dorris, *A Yellow Raft in Blue Water*

Now, bring your own character to life in a description for a short story. You can start with an image of someone real, but transform the person imaginatively into a new character. If you would like, you may rewrite a description from the story you wrote earlier. Perhaps you'll be able to improve your story. Let Michael Dorris's description be your inspiration:

- use details that appeal to all senses, not just sight
- create swift, surprising pictures with figurative language like "the columns of her arms"

Seeing Patterns and Relationships

What's the most economical car on the road today? Which had the more advanced civilization—the Aztecs or the Incas? It is natural to want information and to want to share what you know with others. One common way of gaining and sharing information is by looking at **patterns and relationships.**

Writing and You.   People share information by showing patterns or relationships in several ways. For example, a movie critic gives information about a movie by comparing the sequel to the original. A politician defines *liberty* by saying what it is and what it is not. When you're deciding which sound system to buy, you might put them in categories—by price or speaker size. When was the last time you noticed patterns or relationships in something?

As You Read.   In the following passage, a character sees a relationship between two things. What are they? What is the relationship?

Andy Warhol, *Ethel Scull Thirty-six Times* (1963). Silkscreen ink on synthetic polymer paint on canvas. 36 Panels, each 19 7/8 ″ × 15 7/8 ″; overall, 6′7 3/4 ″ × 11′11″. © 1993 The Andy Warhol Foundation for the Visual Arts, Inc./ARS, N.Y.

205

from

THE JOY LUCK CLUB

**by
Amy Tan**

"Let me! Let me!" I begged between games when one brother or the other would sit back with a deep sigh of relief and victory, the other annoyed, unable to let go of the outcome. Vincent at first refused to let me play, but when I offered my Life Savers as replacements for the buttons that filled in for the missing pieces, he relented. He chose the flavors: wild cherry for the black pawn and peppermint for the white knight. Winner could eat both.

As our mother sprinkled flour and rolled out small doughy circles for the steamed dumplings that would be our dinner that night, Vin-

cent explained the rules, pointing to each piece. "You have sixteen pieces and so do I. One king and queen, two bishops, two knights, two castles, and eight pawns. The pawns can only move forward one step, except on the first move. Then they can move two. But they can only take men by moving crossways like this, except in the beginning, when you can move ahead and take another pawn."

"Why?" I asked as I moved my pawn. "Why can't they move more steps?"

"Because they're pawns," he said.

"But why do they go crossways to take other men. Why aren't there any women and children?"

"Why is the sky blue? Why must you always ask stupid questions?" asked Vincent. "This is a game. These are the rules. I didn't make them up. See. Here. In the book." He jabbed a page with a pawn in his hand. "Pawn. P-A-W-N. Pawn. Read it yourself."

My mother patted the flour off her hands. "Let me see book," she said quietly. She scanned the pages quickly, not read-ing the foreign English symbols, seeming to search deliberately for nothing in particular.

"This American rules," she con-cluded at last. "Every time people come out from foreign country, must know rules. You not know, judge say, Too bad, go back. They not telling you why so you can use their way go forward. They say, Don't know why, you find out yourself. But they knowing all the time. Better you take it, find out why yourself." She tossed her head back with a satisfied smile.

I found out about all the whys later. I read the rules and looked up all the big words in a dictionary. I borrowed books from the Chinatown library. I studied each chess piece, trying to absorb the power each contained.

> "I studied each chess piece, trying to absorb the power each contained."

READER'S RESPONSE

1. Think of a time you had to follow rules you didn't understand, perhaps at school, in your driving, or at a part-time job. Tell your classmates about the experience. How did it make you feel?
2. Perhaps your forebears came to this country from another country, or perhaps you know someone from another country. If so, explain what problems immigrants to this country face with "rules." Are there problems getting jobs, succeeding in schools, finding a place to live? Explain.

WRITER'S CRAFT

3. *The Joy Luck Club* is a work of fiction; Amy Tan's primary purpose is to create a literary work, not to inform. Yet, there is information in this passage. What information does she share?
4. Writers often explain an unfamiliar subject by showing how it relates to a more familiar subject; they *compare* the two subjects. If the chess game is the more familiar subject, what is the less familiar one it is compared with?

Author
Amy Tan

Strategies for Writing to Inform

Looking at patterns and relationships is one strategy writers use to inform; it's the strategy of *classification*. Following are examples of how you might use the four basic strategies of writing—narration, description, classification, and evaluation—to inform.

Narration: writing a biographical sketch of a famous movie star or sports figure; reporting what happened at a four-alarm fire in your neighborhood.

Description: in a travel essay, describing the view from the Sears Tower in Chicago; in a report for your art appreciation class, describing one of the paintings of Winslow Homer.

▶ **Classification:** in an essay for history class, comparing Presidents George Bush and Ronald Reagan; explaining *loyalty* to your younger brother.

Evaluation: explaining to your best friend why you don't want to go back to the new sandwich shop on the corner; in English class, writing a review of a movie you saw last weekend.

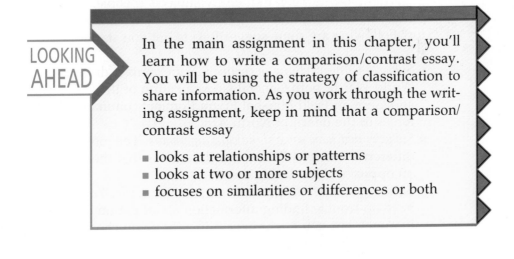

LOOKING AHEAD

In the main assignment in this chapter, you'll learn how to write a comparison/contrast essay. You will be using the strategy of classification to share information. As you work through the writing assignment, keep in mind that a comparison/contrast essay

- looks at relationships or patterns
- looks at two or more subjects
- focuses on similarities or differences or both

Writing a Comparison/Contrast Essay

Prewriting

Considering Subjects, Purpose, and Audience

You're starving for a taco. Which fast-food joint will you visit to satisfy your craving? You quickly narrow it to two choices: Tons of Tacos and Tacos R Us. Tons of Tacos is closer and cheaper, while Tacos R Us is farther and more expensive. That thought process is an example of how you apply the strategy of comparison/contrast to common decisions in your everyday life, but comparison/contrast is equally important as a writing strategy you can use to develop many kinds of topics.

Subjects.   In school, you have probably found that many test questions and essay writing assignments ask you to compare and contrast—two short stories, two countries, two animals. Later in your life, you may find yourself writing to compare and contrast on your job—perhaps you need to compare two possible locations for a new shoe store or two candidates for a clerk in your office. In many of these situations, you don't have to decide what two *subjects* to compare or contrast. The pairing of the two subjects is a natural part of the writing situation.

When you do need to identify subjects (people, places, or things) to compare and contrast, however, what do you look for? Following are some suggestions to get you started.

- *Subjects with something in common.* For example, during World War II, both General George Patton of the U.S. Army and German Field Marshal Erwin Rommel commanded tank forces in the desert of North Africa.
- *Subjects that have some significant differences.* The most obvious difference between Patton and Rommel is that they fought on opposite sides during the war.
- *Subjects about which information is fairly accessible.* You would have no trouble finding information about Patton and Rommel, but you might have difficulty if you chose lesser known military leaders.

GEORGE PATTON

ERWIN ROMMEL

Purpose and Audience. The strategy of comparison/contrast can be used for all of the basic *purposes* of writing—to express yourself, to inform, to persuade, or to create literary works. In the main part of this chapter, however, you're going to concentrate on using comparison/contrast to inform. Within the overall purpose of informing, you may have a more specific purpose:

- to show similarities between the subjects
- to show differences between the subjects
- to show both similarities and differences between the subjects

Since you are attempting to inform (part of the expository aim), you will be concerned about your *audience's* knowledge. What do they already know? What information will be new to them? Informative writing is interesting only if it presents new information, or old information in a new way. Perhaps by comparing two subjects no one else has compared, you can help your audience see one or both of them in a new way.

WRITING NOTE

Comparison points out the similarities between things, people, or ideas, while contrast points out the differences. However, the word *comparison* is often used to mean both comparing and contrasting. For example, when your United States history teacher asks you to "compare" Abraham Lincoln and Robert E. Lee, you probably need to point out differences as well as similarities.

PART 1:
Choosing Subjects to Compare/Contrast

For this assignment, you have a chance to choose your own subjects, so think about what interests you. Is it pro basketball, music of the 1960s, or Chinese food? Start with that area of interest, and then choose two subjects to explain through the strategy of comparison/contrast. Just be sure your subjects have some basic similarity and enough differences to be interesting. Also, remember that explanations aren't interesting unless they give readers some new information.

EXERCISE 1 ▶ Speaking and Listening: Listening for Subjects

If you're stuck for subjects, try listening to radio or TV with paper and pencil in hand. What do you see or hear that bothers you or makes you curious? Are you upset that your favorite team is in the doldrums? Maybe you can explain its losing streak by comparing and contrasting this season's coaching staff and players with last year's coaching staff and players. Are you puzzled when the announcer says that a typhoon has hit Japan? Perhaps you can explain the storm by comparing and contrasting it with a more familiar storm, the tornado.

Prewriting

Planning a Comparison/Contrast Essay

Here's a comparison for you. Your comparison/contrast essay is like a building, and you have just laid the foundation by choosing two subjects. The next step is to gather the main building blocks—information about the two subjects—and start to arrange them as you'll need them later.

Gathering Information

Sources of Information.   When you are writing to inform, you need to share accurate information. If you're writing about two subjects you know well, you may be able to pull most of the information out of your own memory and knowledge. For example, if you're a great baseball fan and you want to compare the Cincinnati Reds and the Boston Red Sox, you may know enough to write the essay. However, if you're writing about Patton and Rommel, you will probably have to do some research. In your research, remember that you're not just looking for *enough* information; you need *all* the important information. For example, you would not want to leave out the fact that Patton was American and Rommel was German. Refer to Chapter 11 (pages 413–417 and 437–446), if you need help with identifying and documenting sources.

Relevance of Information.   As you are gathering information, you may come up with all kinds of similarities and differences; but they aren't all equally useful. The Cincinnati Reds and the Boston Red Sox are both located in cities that are north of the Mason-Dixon line, but that's of no importance when you are comparing and contrasting their World Series records. What you're looking for are *relevant* (related and important) *features* or points that both subjects have in common.

The following example shows how one writer gathered information on the relevant features of schools in Colonial America and schools in the year 2150. Notice that this writer used a Venn diagram to sort differences and similarities. In a Venn diagram, you place any points the subjects have in common in the overlapping segments of the circles.

School in
Colonial America

School in
year 2150

HERE'S
HOW

One-room school-
house with few
books, no
chalkboards;
students learn
3 R's and pen-
manship; school
for 1/3 of year

Places of learning
with some set
curriculum; teach
"communication";
emphasize writing

Learning room
with government-
supplied computers;
curriculum designed
for special needs;
core curriculum
in A.M.; year-
round school

CRITICAL THINKING
Analyzing Subjects for Their Relevant Features

When you *analyze* something, you try to understand it by looking at its parts. Before you can compare or contrast two subjects, you have to analyze them to find their relevant (related
and important) features or points.

To identify relevant features, think about the basis for comparison—the common groups your subjects belong to. Red
Cloud and Sitting Bull, for example, were two great Sioux leaders. Features that would help you show this basic similarity
include their leadership in war, spiritual matters ("medicine"),
and politics.

CRITICAL THINKING EXERCISE:
Analyzing Subjects for Their Relevant Features

Working with a partner or small group, try out your analyzing
skills. For each set of subjects in the list on the next page, first

decide what group both subjects belong to. (You may need to do some research on subjects you're not familiar with.) Then, for each set of subjects, identify at least three or four relevant features. Remember that the relevant features are the important characteristics the two subjects have in common.

EXAMPLE

> *Subjects:* pyramids in Mexico, pyramids in Egypt
> *Common group:* huge structures with similar shapes
> *Relevant features:* size, religious uses, astronomical uses

1. tepees and igloos
2. tornadoes and hurricanes
3. jazz and blues
4. Hank Aaron and Willie Mays
5. TV situation comedies in the 1970s and TV situation comedies today

Developing a Thesis Statement

At some point during the planning of your essay, you have to think about your *thesis*, the main idea you will be sharing. You have two subjects. Are you going to stress how much they are alike, or are you going to stress how different they are? Perhaps you don't want to do either; you just want to share information about their similarities as well as their differences. Once you have made that decision, you know the main idea of your essay. Then you can write a thesis statement to guide your planning and writing. (For more information about developing thesis statements, see pages 102–104.) Here are some examples of thesis statements for comparison/contrast essays.

EXAMPLES   The Sioux chiefs Red Cloud and Sitting Bull differed in their attitudes toward the government but were similar in their approaches to war, spiritual matters ("medicine"), and politics. [This essay will look at both differences and similarities.]

The effects of migrating west during the nineteenth century were much different for American women than for American men. [This essay will stress the differences, even though the two subjects obviously had the migration itself in common.]

General George Patton of the U.S. Army and German Field Marshal Erwin Rommel had similar leadership styles. [This essay will stress similarities, even though there are many differences between the two men.]

WRITING NOTE   The fact that you are comparing two subjects does not mean you should ignore their differences. Essays that explore similarities often begin with one or two differences and then focus primarily on the similarities. And the reverse is true with essays that contrast two subjects. You might begin with a similarity or two and then devote the rest of the essay to information related to the differences between the subjects. In fact, by acknowledging both similarities and differences, you show your audience that you are aware of various aspects of your topic. This can make your readers more likely to take your ideas seriously.

Relevant
feature 1:
Ved Mehta

Relevant
feature 2:
Ved Mehta

Relevant
feature 2:
Henry Kisor

Background
about
interview

Likewise, Mehta sharpened his "facial vision," a kind of blind person's radar. Its precise nature is elusive, but it helps those lucky enough to have it to detect the presence of obstacles without needing artificial aids, such as canes and seeing-eye dogs.

Most important, however, we both learned to be independent. As a young student at an impecunious state school, Mehta may not have received much of an academic education—that would come later, at Pomona College, Oxford and Harvard—but he shunned canes and did everything he could to get rid of "blindisms," physical idiosyncrasies that signaled sightlessness.

So, also, did I avoid "deafisms" such as sign language. Whether it was by chance or my parents' design, I grew up entirely among hearing people, speaking and lipreading well enough, however imperfectly, to consider myself a normal person. Sign language was for those unlucky enough to be born deaf or lose their hearing before they had developed speech. Those who needed sign, I thought, were condemned to a narrow, limited world, and I felt sorry for them.

When I met Mehta early one morning in New York, I half-expected an intense fellow, perhaps one constantly on edge, always out to prove himself. But the slim 51-year-old man who greeted me gravely in his living room was relaxed and dignified, with a gentle smile. He gave a fatherly

Ved Mehta

Development
through
interview

Details—
Relevant
feature 1:
Ved Mehta

peck and a pat to his 14-month-old daughter, Sage, before sending her off with his wife of three years, Linn.

He hesitated before passing through the doorway to the library where we would talk, as if he knew he was off center, then adjusted his step to enter straight through the middle. "Were you using facial vision for that?" I asked. "What is facial vision, anyway?"

"Sometimes my mind isn't on what I'm doing," he said with a chuckle. "I tend to be a dreamy person, like most writers. If I'm not concentrating, it's quite likely that I'd go off center. Also, you got me in the morning before I had my first cup of coffee.

"As for facial vision, it's not clear that scientists know what it is. There's much misunderstanding about it. I go by sound, echoes, the air pressure around the ears. When I'm in a familiar place, I know where the door is and, as I poetically call it, 'where the sound-shadows change.' That's an open, more airy place."

"Can you always depend on facial vision?" I asked, thinking about how my knack for lip-reading can desert me at the worst possible moments. The compensations handicapped people can make are remarkable, but they're by no means foolproof.

"It lets me down when there's a pneumatic drill or terrific wind, or at the airport with a lot of planes," he said. "If there are a lot of blanketing sounds, then my facial vision suffers. A jackhammer almost completely paralyzes me; I can't tell where I am or what I'm doing."

Ironically, another situation in which Mehta's facial vision falters is in "an absolutely open field without trees. For facial vision to be most effective, there has to be an object to which I can establish some kind of relationship—and also there has to be a fair degree of quiet so that I can discriminate between different kinds of sound-shadows."

Facial vision serves Mehta well enough so that he can stand at a busy Manhattan intersection, listening for changes in the thrum of traffic and for the click of crossing signals, and make his way across the street as agilely as any other New Yorker—and without a cane or a guide dog. Facial vision does not, however, guard him from such hazards as two-foot-long standpipes jutting at waist level from the side of a building.

"Do you think a seeing-eye dog could be of some help?" I asked.

"Not to me," he replied. "As with people who have all their faculties, the abilities of the blind and perhaps the deaf vary a lot. Certain blind people, especially those who lose their eyesight late in life, find a seeing-eye dog very useful. But when I was growing up I didn't even know there was such a thing."

"Do you use any kind of device to aid you?" I asked. "Not at the moment," Mehta said, "but as I grow older and injuries take longer to heal, I might well start using a cane. There's a real shift in the way I think about some of these problems. When I was younger, perhaps I had contempt for people who had to rely on the cane. But now I will use whatever helps me to function. If a time should come that I lose my hearing as well, I might use a seeing-eye dog, too.

CONCLUSION

"But there are so many ways in which you can be independent. Independence is a matter of the spirit."

EXERCISE 2 ▶ **Analyzing a Comparison/Contrast Article**

What was your reaction to this article? Meet with two or three classmates to discuss these questions about the Kisor piece.

1. What does the writer do to grab the reader's attention in the introduction?
2. Kisor briefly compares several features of his and Ved Mehta's lives. What is the feature that he devotes most of the article to?
3. At one point, Kisor contrasts his expectations of Ved Mehta with his experience on meeting him. How does the expectation differ from the reality?
4. Kisor's main purpose is to share information about Ved Mehta and his book. How does his comparison of his own life to Mehta's help him accomplish that purpose?
5. What new information did you learn about people with disabilities from this article?

A Framework for a Comparison/Contrast Essay

Kisor uses comparison/contrast as a part of a longer article focused on one of his two subjects, Ved Mehta. You might find it easier to organize your essay like the following writer's model. See if you think the block method of organization makes the essay easy to follow.

A WRITER'S MODEL

INTRODUCTION
Attention grabber

     Imagine you could travel back in time to Colonial America and then zip forward to the year 2150. Probably the last place you'd choose to be is in school, but imagine that's where you find yourself. What was school like then, and what will it be like in the future? You would probably find some amazing differences in classroom equipment,

Thesis statement

curriculum, and length of school year.

BODY
SUBJECT 1:
School in 1720

     In 1720 in a small Connecticut town, you would find yourself in a one-room schoolhouse made of logs. The dozen or so girls and boys--with no slates,

Feature 1: classroom equipment

chalkboards, or maps--sit on benches. You use a goose-quill pen and homemade ink to write in a copybook you've made by carefully sewing together several sheets of folded coarse, dark paper. The few books in your classroom are filled with proverbs, fables, and stories to improve your character.

Feature 2: curriculum

Feature 3: length of school year

Reading, writing, penmanship, and ciphering (that's arithmetic) are what you study. To learn arithmetic, you listen to your teacher read from a sum book. Then you copy the rules and problems he reads aloud into your own sum book. You're in a "moving school"--one that sets up in three different parts of a region during a year. You only go to school a third of the year, but you like seeing your friends every day. Your neighbor has written in his copybook: "School is better than doing chores sunup to sundown, everyday, everyday, everyday. School has friends and recess."

SUBJECT 2: School of 2150

Feature 1: classroom equipment

Zapped into the future, in 2150 in the very same Connecticut town, you can't find a school anywhere. You've landed inside a dwelling unit (home) inside a housing unit next to a girl your age. She explains that students are instructed by government-supplied computers in the Learning Room inside each dwelling unit. There are no pencils, pens, or text-books. Everything is done by a voice-activated computer. From the beginning, the curriculum is specially designed to meet each student's special

Feature 2:
curriculum

Feature 3:
length of
school year

abilities and interests. Three morning hours cover
required curriculum: earth science, communication
(including foreign languages), and social sciences.
The three afternoon hours are reserved for exploring
any subject that interests the students, with heavy
emphasis on writing. Every student has a Visiting
Tutor, who checks progress once a week and
suggests creative projects. From age one, children
learn to use their computers. And the school year
runs year-round, six hours a day. It's lonesome, you
complain--you miss your friends.

CONCLUSION
Final
comment

Your journey is finished. Which school did you
enjoy more--the primitive school in a one-room log
cabin or the high-tech, but lonely, school of the
future? Maybe you prefer your familiar school of the
present. After looking back and ahead, it might
seem like a good choice.

WRITING
ASSIGNMENT

PART 3:
Writing a First Draft

You have focused your creativity on planning your essay; now
it's time to unleash it! Using your prewriting diagrams and
notes and your thesis statement, write a first draft of your
essay. Remember to develop your comparison/contrast with
specific examples and details that the reader can understand.

Evaluating and Revising

Sometimes, years after they've published books, writers become dissatisfied with the books—and revise and publish them again. The evaluation and revision process won't take that long for you. In fact, you may have to begin shortly after completing your first draft. However, the following chart can help you to get the objective view of your paper that time might otherwise give you. Begin by asking yourself each question in the left-hand column, and if your answer reveals a weakness, use the revision technique in the right-hand column.

"I like to tinker. Every sentence is potentially revisable in 30 directions, and it's tough to stop doing that, to know when you've ended."

Jay McInerney

EVALUATING AND REVISING COMPARISON/CONTRAST ESSAYS

EVALUATION GUIDE	REVISION TECHNIQUE
1 Does the introduction grab the reader's attention?	**Add** an anecdote, quotation, question, or specific detail.
2 Is the main idea clear?	**Add** a thesis statement that identifies the subjects and states the main idea of the essay.
3 Is the essay organized clearly?	**Reorder** the essay by moving sentences to follow the block or the point-by-point organization.
4 Are the relevant features handled in the same order for both topics?	**Reorder** sentences so the relevant features are discussed in the same order for both subjects.
5 Does the essay contain information that will interest the reader?	**Add** details or information that will be new to your readers. **Add** details that show your subjects in a new way.
6 Does the essay include all important information?	**Add** facts or details that are essential to an understanding of the significant similarities and differences.
7 Is the essay brought to a satisfying end?	**Cut** the ineffective sentences. **Add** statements that summarize or restate the main idea.

EXERCISE 3 ▶ **Analyzing a Writer's Revisions**

Before you begin to attempt to evaluate and revise your own essay, it's helpful to study some other writer's work. The following paragraphs show a writer's work in progress—a portion of the first draft of the model on pages 224–226. This sample shows some revisions the writer made after evaluating the essay. To analyze the writer's revisions, get together with two or three other students and discuss the questions on the next page. Were the writer's revisions effective?

you could travel back in time to *then zip forward to*

Imagine Colonial America and the year
add

2150. Probably the last place you'd choose to

be is in school, but imagine that's where you

find yourself. What was school like then, and

what will it be like in the future? You would
in classroom equipment, curriculum, and length of school year.
probably find some amazing differences
add

In 1720 in a small Connecticut town, you

would find yourself in a one-room school-

house made of logs. The dozen or so girls

and boys--with no slates, chalkboards, or

maps--sit on benches. Reading, writing,
reorder

penmanship, and ciphering (that's

arithmetic) are what you study. You use a

goose-quill pen and homemade ink to write *coarse, dark paper.*
you've made by carefully sewing together several sheets of folded
in a copybook. The few books in your class-
add

room are filled with proverbs, fables, and

stories to improve your character. To learn

arithmetic, you listen to your teacher read

from a sum book. Then you copy the rules

and problems he reads aloud into your own

sum book.

1. Why did the writer add the words *you could travel back in time to* and *then zip forward to* to the first sentence? How do these changes improve the essay?
2. Why did the writer add *in classroom equipment, curriculum, and length of school year* to the last sentence of the first paragraph?
3. Why did the writer move the third sentence of the second paragraph? [Hint: Review pages 217–218.]
4. Why did the writer add the information about hand-sewn sheets of dark paper? Is this information new to you?

WRITING ASSIGNMENT

PART 4:
Evaluating and Revising Your Comparison/Contrast Paper

Now you be the judge—of both your essay and a partner's essay. First, use the chart on page 228 to evaluate your own essay, and then exchange papers with a classmate and evaluate each other's papers. Try to be as objective as a real judge (or literary critic) might be. Finally, use your partner's comments and your own evaluations to revise your essay.

Proofreading and Publishing

Proofreading. Once you have evaluated and revised your essay, it is ready for its final inspection, a search for any mistakes in spelling, capitalization, punctuation, and usage. (See pages 50–51 for **Guidelines for Proofreading.**)

USAGE HINT

Degrees of Comparison

When you compare and contrast, you often use adjectives and adverbs, the forms of which change according to the number of subjects being compared. Most adjectives and adverbs have three degrees of comparison. You add *–er* and *–est* to words of one syllable and *more* and *most* to words of two or more syllables. A few words, like *good*, have irregular forms to show comparison.

POSITIVE	COMPARATIVE	SUPERLATIVE
thin	thinner	thinnest
carefully	more carefully	most carefully
good	better	best

When comparing two subjects, use the comparative degree.

> Going to school is **easier** than doing chores from sunup to sundown.

When comparing three or more subjects, use the superlative degree.

> Of all the things I can think of doing, lying in front of the TV is the **easiest**.

☞ REFERENCE NOTE: For more information about degrees of comparison, see pages 770–774.

Publishing. Try one of these ideas for publishing your finished paper.

- Use your comparison/contrast essay as the basis for a game. Choose three items of information about each subject, and read them to a partner or small group of classmates. Jot down pieces of information that are new to listeners. When everyone has finished, determine the total amount of new information in your group.
- Compile your essays into a booklet and send it to your local middle school. Younger students might find your information very interesting.

WRITING ASSIGNMENT

PART 5:
Proofreading and Publishing Your Essay

Is your essay ready for final inspection? Proofread it carefully to correct all errors. Write your final version, and then decide how you will publish or share it with others.

A STUDENT MODEL

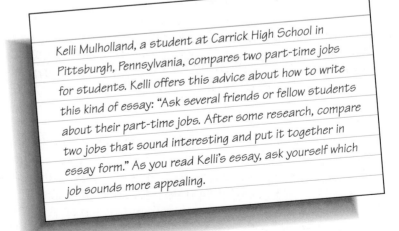

Kelli Mulholland, a student at Carrick High School in Pittsburgh, Pennsylvania, compares two part-time jobs for students. Kelli offers this advice about how to write this kind of essay: "Ask several friends or fellow students about their part-time jobs. After some research, compare two jobs that sound interesting and put it together in essay form." As you read Kelli's essay, ask yourself which job sounds more appealing.

Choosing a Part-Time Job
by Kelli Mulholland

Working a part-time job after school can be a fun and educating experience. By working after school, a young person can gain knowledge in the working field and make some extra money. There are many jobs out there for high school students. Two of the most popular jobs are telemarketing and working at fast-food restaurants. These two fields are worlds apart, but they also have a great deal in common.

Telemarketing, selling goods or services over the telephone, has been around for many years. Telemarketing offices are always looking for outgoing, enthusiastic people to fill telemarketing positions. It doesn't take much experience to be a telemarketer, just a good disposition. There are many advantages to telemarketing. You only have to work about four hours a day. Most telemarketing places pay their employees an hourly wage, although some places pay both an hourly wage and a commission. Another advantage is that some telemarketing places let employees work out of their homes. Imagine not even leaving the house and getting paid for it. Telemarketing is also good experience in sales. Unlike delivering papers or baby-sitting, telemarketing is a very pleasant and easy part-time job for those who enjoy talking with other people.

Another very popular and exciting job is working at a fast-food place. Fast-food places are always hiring high school students. The benefits of this kind of job are great. Meeting people and making money while doing it is one advantage. An employee will learn how to cook and how to use a cash register and may even become manager of the whole store. Also, when young people apply for a job after high school, employers want to see that prospective workers have worked with other people and are able to be productive under a little pressure. Working at a fast-food restaurant will show that.

Both jobs are very appealing in many ways. They will both look good on a résumé after high school and show that you do have some work experience. Baby-sitting and delivering papers show responsibility, but they don't show punctuality and compatibility. Consider your options in choosing a part-time job. Find a job that fits your personality, and one that interests you most.

WRITING WORKSHOP

An Extended Definition

When you organized and wrote your comparison/contrast essay for this chapter, you were using the strategy of *classification*. You had to be sure that the two subjects you chose to write about belonged to the same class or group of things before you examined them in terms of their relationship to each other. You also use the strategy of classification when you define a subject. First, you identify the general category your subject belongs to. Then, you describe the characteristics that distinguish it from (show its relationship to) other items in its category. Here's a one-sentence definition of *independence*.

> Independence is a character trait that enables an individual to make decisions and act upon them without placing too much emphasis on the opinions of others.

The first part of the definition shows that *independence* belongs to the general category "character traits." The second part distinguishes *independence* from other character traits.

An **extended definition** also puts the subject into a category and shows how it is different from other subjects in the category. But then it goes further: It extends the basic definition with details such as examples, descriptions, explanations, and opinions. For example, following is an extended definition of *independence*. As you read, notice the many techniques the writer uses to extend the definition of this character trait.

> When teenagers think about what independence means, we often think of it as something someone else gives us. But independence is not something that comes from outside ourselves. We may also think of independence as the freedom to do anything we want. But that is probably not the real meaning of the word. Independence is a character trait that enables an individual to make decisions and act upon them

without placing too much emphasis on the opinions of others.

A very young girl may think of herself as achieving independence the first time her parents let her go to the mall unsupervised. That, of course, can be a step toward independence. But if the girl is concerned the whole time she's there with doing what other kids consider cool, then she's really not independent at all. She is only trading dependence on her parents for dependence on her friends. Her parents

have given her the opportunity to be independent. She is the one who has to become independent, who has to develop the character trait.

Some kids say that they are really independent because they don't care what anyone else says or thinks. But that attitude stretches or distorts the meaning of independence. There's a difference between refusing to slavishly follow what other people do and being absolutely indifferent to what others think. Total indifference to others is selfishness, not independence. And even the founding fathers who declared this nation independent were concerned with having "a decent respect to the opinions of mankind."

To develop into independent people, we have to learn to think for ourselves, but we don't have to act as if we are the only ones who can think or the only ones whose opinions matter. Only then can we learn to act independently in the best interests of ourselves and others.

1. **What techniques does the writer use to extend the definition?**
2. **Do you think the writer clearly explains the meaning of *independence*? What other examples or descriptions could you add to this definition?**

Writing an Extended Definition

 Prewriting. Think of a subject that interests you and that can't be adequately defined in just one or two sentences. Here are some possibilities:

longtime friend   dream car
country music   bad date
loyalty   bravery

Think of examples, details, comparisons, contrasts, facts, or quotes to extend your definition. Consult a dictionary, encyclopedias, magazines, or friends for ideas. List any background information your audience will need.

Writing, Evaluating, and Revising. As you begin your extended definition, try to sum up your subject in one or two sentences. Start by identifying the class to which it belongs, and then extend your definition by showing how it is similar to or different from others in its class. Let another student read your definition and make suggestions for improving it. Does your definition have enough specific details? Would your definition help someone unfamiliar with your subject to understand it fully? Keep revising until you're satisfied with your definition.

Proofreading and Publishing. Be sure to proofread your definition carefully before sharing it with others. (For help with proofreading, see pages 50–51.) Then read your definition to a small group of classmates or to the whole class. See if they can guess the subject.

MAKING CONNECTIONS

WRITING ACROSS THE CURRICULUM

Comparison/Contrast in Literature

Situational irony is a literary device that relies on indirect comparison/contrast; the writer shows a discrepancy between the outcome of a situation and what was expected. When it is humorous, irony creates a delicious pleasure for the reader. It's fun to have expectations turned upside down in fiction—as they often are in real life. For example, the poet Dorothy Parker creates situational irony in the following poem about a rose.

One Perfect Rose
by Dorothy Parker

A single flow'r he sent me, since we met.
　　All tenderly his messenger he chose;
Deep-hearted, pure, with scented dew still wet—
　　One perfect rose.

I knew the language of the floweret;
　　"My fragile leaves," it said, "his heart enclose."
Love long has taken for his amulet
　　One perfect rose.

Why is it no one ever sent me yet
　　One perfect limousine, do you suppose?
Ah no, it's always just my luck to get
　　One perfect rose.

Think about the irony in "One Perfect Rose." How does the ending of the poem contrast with what you expected? Find another poem that contains situational irony (or you may write your own). Bring the poem to class and read it aloud, asking everyone to describe the irony. Discuss how the situation leads you to expect one thing and then how the poet creates a different (contrasting) outcome.

WRITING ACROSS THE CURRICULUM

Classification in Science

Classifying, looking at subjects in terms of their relationships to other subjects, is an extremely useful tool for making sense of the world. A large part of science consists of attempts to classify things. Plants, animals, clouds, rocks, bodies of water, and weather systems are just a few examples of things that are classified into categories.

On science tests or reports, you are often asked to classify items. The first step is to identify the principle of classification. For example, if you are to classify viruses, you must decide how. Will it be by genetic material (RNA or DNA) or by disease (like influenza, hepatitis, or rhinovirus)? Next, be sure to divide the whole subject. For example, if you are classifying burns, you don't want to leave out any of the three degrees of burns: first degree, second degree, and third degree. As you describe each category, use enough details to show the reader the differences among the categories. You might even decide which main characteristics you will describe for each category. As in your comparison/contrast essay, you'll want to present the same characteristics in the same order for each category.

Following is a jumbled list of facts about the three types of blood cells. First, identify the three categories (for help you might consult an encyclopedia or science text). Then organize the facts for each category in the same general order. Write a paragraph that classifies and describes the blood cells.

Red blood cells carry oxygen to body tissues.
Platelets measure 150,000–500,000 per microliter of blood ($\frac{1}{30,000}$ of an ounce).

Red blood cells live approximately 120 days.

Life span of a platelet is 8–10 days.

White blood cells fight disease and invading substances.

Platelets formed in the bone marrow.

5,000–10,000 white blood cells per microliter of blood.

Platelets essential for clotting blood.

Four to six million red blood cells per microliter.

Most white blood cells formed in the bone marrow; some formed in tissues like lymph nodes and spleen.

Red blood cells formed in the bone marrow.

Life span of white blood cell varies from a few hours to a lifetime.

White Blood Cells

Red Blood Cells

Platelets

7 WRITING TO EXPLAIN

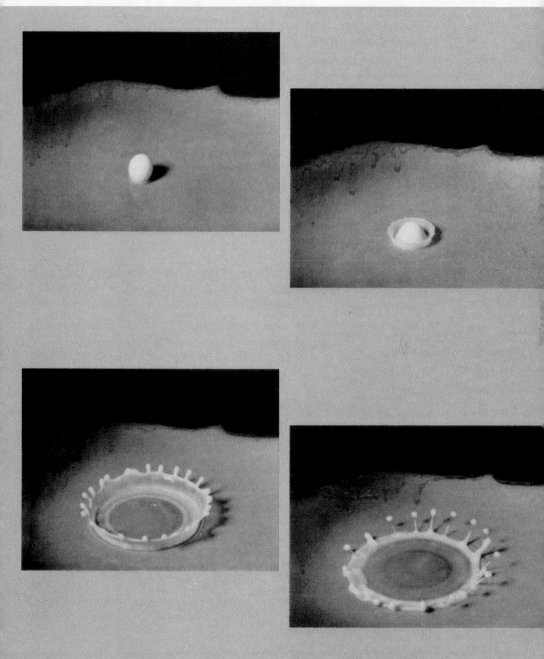

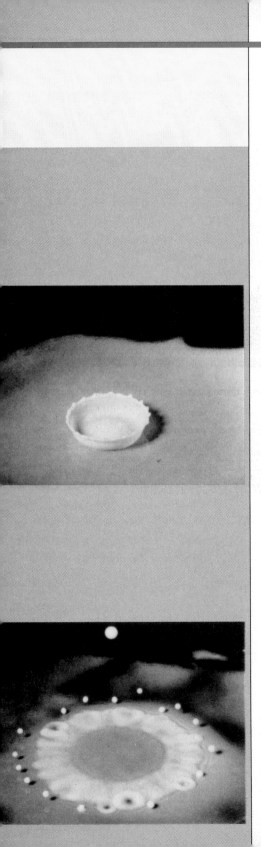

Making Things Clear

What causes recessions? What are the effects of the loss of the ozone layer? How will I have time to finish my homework if I get a job after school? These questions show that we live in a world in which we are constantly looking for explanations, explanations that will **make things clear.**

Writing and You. Writers often attempt to explain something in the world around them. A scientist tells how a new medication combats a form of cancer. A biographer examines the effects of a backwoods childhood on Abraham Lincoln. A reporter for a school newspaper writes about the causes of the football team's winning season. What explanations could you give that would help make the world a little clearer to other people?

As You Read. In the following selection, Mark Mathabane tells how he explained the benefits of knowledge and education to the young people of Harlem. How did he make the benefits clear?

Dr. Harold E. Edgerton, *Milk-Drop Splash Series* (1935). Photograph. © The Harold E. Edgerton 1992 Trust. Courtesy of Palm Press, Inc., Concord, MA.

241

from Kaffir Boy in America

by Mark Mathabane

I was at this time writing more commentary articles for the *St. Petersburg Times* on events in South Africa than learning the basics of objective journalism. I poured my time into completing *Kaffir Boy*; wandered about Harlem comparing the black experience there with that in South Africa's ghettos; read the speeches of Malcolm X, the essays of James Baldwin, and the poetry of Langston Hughes; and taught tennis to black youngsters who were part of the I-House tutorial program. I shared with them my experiences growing up in Alexandra, and the important role education had played in my life. I encouraged them never to give up the fight to escape from the ghetto; it could be done, I said, provided they believed in themselves, kept away from drugs and gangs, and never allowed villains to become their role models and peer pressure to force them to do bad things.

I was able to reach many of these youngsters because they trusted me, and considered me a celebrity because I was friends with Stan Smith and Arthur Ashe. It wrung my heart to realize that most of these kids were as impressionable and talented as kids anywhere, but that in their case the lack of positive role models and support systems, the deadly influence and lure of street life, the disintegration of black fam-

Arthur Ashe

"These men and women have more power than most of your athletes and entertainers and all of the drug dealers you know."

ily life and the attendant loss of positive values, and the inhumanity of life in New York City for the powerless and the have-nots would eventually derail them into the dead-end life of crime and drugs and teenage motherhood.

The only way I could fight their struggle, I clearly saw, was to become a role model to them, in much the same way as Arthur Ashe had been one to me. But I was quick to warn them that they could not all hope to become professional athletes; that they could not all be Diana Ross or Michael Jackson; but that they could all become proud and productive human beings by becoming educated. Many wondered why I made such a big deal about an education, and challenged me to show them blacks who, because of an education, were as famous or as rich as the athletes and entertainers or the drug dealers with the fancy cars, expensive jewelry, flashy clothes, and Rolex watches.

I brought up the names of famous black achievers, including Jesse Jackson, A. Philip Randolph, Harriet Tubman, Paul Robeson, Ralph Bunche, Marian Anderson, Maya Angelou, and George Washington Carver. Except for Jackson, they hardly recognized any of the names.

"These men and women have more power than most of your athletes and entertainers and all of the drug dealers you know."

"What you mean? Do they have a lot of money?" asked a thirteen-year-old boy.

"Many don't. But they have something more valuable than money."

"What could be more valuable than money?" asked a twelve-year-old boy.

"An educated mind."

"What's that?" a fifteen-year-old girl asked facetiously.

"You see, money, fancy clothes, Rolexes, chains, all that can be lost, can be taken away from you. But the treasures in your mind, those no one can ever take away from you. And by the treasures of the mind I mean knowledge. Knowledge of what freedom means. Knowledge of what you can do despite what others may say. Knowledge of what your rights and responsibilities are as an American citizen. Knowledge of how computers work. Knowledge of how to read and write. Knowledge of your true heritage as a black person. And through knowledge one can overcome the greatest oppression of all: mental slavery. Any of you heard of Bob Marley?"

A few had heard the legend's music.

"Well, Bob Marley once wrote a song called 'Redemption Song,' in which he said that to be truly free black people must liberate themselves from mental slavery, and that none but ourselves can free our minds. So instead of getting high on drugs why don't we get high on knowledge? You know, a free mind is a most powerful weapon. Armed with it you'll be able to fight for what is yours, to define who you are, rather than have others do things for you, set limits to your aspirations, and end up running your life."

Bob Marley

Some of the youngsters seemed unable to grasp the full meaning of my words; but there was no doubt that I had made some impression on all of them. I hoped that in time, whatever seeds I had planted in their young minds would blossom into a determination to be educated, to realize their potential as human beings, no matter what the obstacles.

Mark Mathabane

READER'S RESPONSE

1. Mark Mathabane writes about the importance of role models. Do you have a role model or a hero? What do you think are the characteristics of a good role model?
2. By explaining the effects of an education, Mathabane attempted to inspire the young people he worked with in Harlem. Do you think this kind of explanation can change people's lives? Can you think of a time when learning about the possible effects of something made you think or act differently?

WRITER'S CRAFT

3. In this passage from his book, Mathabane explains some of the causes for lives of "crime and drugs and teenage motherhood." What causes does he identify?
4. According to Mathabane, what are the effects of an educated mind?

Strategies for Writing to Explain

In explaining the effects of an education, Mathabane used the strategy of narration. Narration always involves things happening, or changing, over the course of time; an effect is always a change, and it always happens later than the cause. Darkness (the effect) occurs *after* the sun goes down (the cause). Of course, writers can use other strategies to explain. Here are some examples that show how the four basic writing strategies can be used to explain.

▶ **Narration:** in a history paper, looking at the causes of the War of 1812; explaining to the principal how the elimination of a third level of Spanish would affect students in your school.

Description: describing a rock cliff and giving evidence to illustrate the different strata (layers) of rock; describing the structure of your city's government and showing that your description is accurate.

Classification: explaining and giving evidence to show the differences between the rock music of today and of the 1950s; defining the word *brave* and supporting your definition.

Evaluation: taking a stand on the value of a poem and attempting to prove to your English teacher that your evaluation is sound; evaluating a new hair dryer on the basis of performance and identifying evidence to support your evaluation.

LOOKING AHEAD

In the main assignment in this chapter, you'll use the strategy of narration to explain causes and/or effects. As you work through the chapter, keep in mind that a cause-and-effect explanation

- identifies a situation or condition
- answers one or both of these questions: Why did it happen (what caused it)? What were the effects?
- attempts to prove that the explanation is sound

Writing a Cause-and-Effect Explanation

 *Prewriting*

Considering Topic, Purpose, and Audience

An Appropriate Topic. A topic for a cause-and-effect explanation starts with a situation or condition. Then it asks *Why?* or *What's the result?*

EXAMPLE

Situation:	A new law
Why?	Why was this law passed?
What's the result?	What will be the effects of this new law?

As with all writing, a good topic is one that you find interesting. If you couldn't care less about the reasons for the soccer team's recent loss, don't write about it. If you're worried about what will happen if car insurance rates are raised in your state, you may have found yourself a topic.

How do you begin finding a topic? One good way is to call to mind any recent changes that have affected your life. They could be problems, trends, or inventions.

Problem: Our high school band is losing members. What are the causes?

Trend: Some teenagers are spending $100 for athletic shoes. What are the causes? the effects?

Invention: More and more people are getting telephone answering machines. What are the effects, good and bad?

Another approach is to focus on a particular subject that interests you—science, law, history, sports—and look for interesting situations. What will be the effects of artificial blood on medicine? Why did the Chicago Cubs break a 72-year tradition and finally install lights for night games at Wrigley Field?

Of course, there are many times when you don't have to look for a topic for a cause-and-effect essay. The topic "comes to you." Your history teacher may ask you to write an essay explaining the causes of the decline of communism in the Soviet Union. Or perhaps you have a job in the mayor's office in your town. Someone has proposed adding a stoplight at an intersection near the high school, and the mayor asks you to investigate and explain the possible effects. The ability to look at and explain causes and effects will be useful throughout your school and work life.

Purpose and Audience.   Although you could look at causes and effects in order to persuade, to express yourself, or to create a literary work, in this chapter your basic *purpose* is to explain. That purpose will affect how you present the causes or effects.

In an explanation, you are attempting to clarify something, to make it clear. You want your *audience* to understand your explanation and to accept it as reasonable and thoughtful. For that reason, you can't just say one thing caused another and be done with it. You have to give some evidence that will lead your audience to accept your explanation. For example, you might want to explain to your audience that the band doesn't play well because the members don't take the band seriously. What if your audience says, "How do you know that?" Then you need to provide evidence. "Our band comes in last in the county band contest every year." "Attendance at band practice is lower than it has been in the past ten years."

WRITING NOTE

The expository purpose (or aim) for writing includes three categories: informing, explaining, and exploring. When you inform (see Chapter 6), you share facts. When you explain, you use facts to prove that your explanation is accurate or sound. When you explore (see Chapter 9), you attempt to discover facts and/or other evidence.

Reminder

To find a topic for a cause-and-effect essay

- brainstorm, read, or observe to find a situation that intrigues you
- look for situations created by problems, trends, or inventions
- be sure you can ask *Why?* or *What's the result?* about your topic

---

EXERCISE 1

Speaking and Listening: Exploring Causes and Effects

Increase your awareness of causes and effects by reviewing your local newspaper, watching a television news program, or looking through a current issue of a news magazine such as *Time* or *Newsweek*. Look for stories or issues that interest you, and then select one for which the reporter or writer identifies some causes and/or effects. In a brief oral report to your class, identify the story or issue, the causes and/or effects mentioned by the reporter or writer, and any additional causes or effects you may think of.

WRITING ASSIGNMENT

PART 1:
Choosing a Topic

Select a topic that interests you. You might use one you discovered in your research for Exercise 1 or you might brainstorm alone or in a small group for other ideas. Be careful that your topic is not too broad. In a brief essay, you can't cover all the effects of the Civil War, but you can discuss the military equipment invented as a result of that conflict.

Prewriting

Planning a Cause-and-Effect Explanation

Remember that your purpose is to explain clearly the causes and/or effects of a situation. To do this, you'll need to identify your main idea and gather information about your topic, including facts, statistics, and examples to back up your statements.

Identifying Your Thesis

Between the time you identify the situation, or topic, and the time you begin to organize your ideas, you need to identify your main idea, or *thesis.* There's nothing wrong with identifying your thesis before you gather information, but you may find you change your mind as you look into the situation. For example, you may be concerned about the effects of "increased student activity fees." While you're gathering your information, however, you decide that you also need to look at the causes—low funding from the state, an economic recession, and so forth.

The focus of a cause-and-effect explanation may be the causes of a situation, the effects, or both causes and effects. That focus will determine your main idea, or thesis. Here are examples of thesis statements with the three different focuses.

Causes: There are three basic reasons most teenagers feel they need to buy a car.

Effects: While buying a car seems like a liberation, it may bring consequences that are not so pleasant.

Causes and Effects: Many teenagers have good reasons for buying a car, but some effects may be negative.

Gathering Information

Sources of Information.   For some topics, you will be able to analyze both causes and effects from your own knowledge. For example, if you're writing about a local school issue, like the effects of starting school an hour earlier, you can probably rely on your own experience and understanding of the situation. However, for many topics your critical thinking will have to include some research. If you were writing about the causes and effects of brain injuries, for example, you might need to consult a number of different sources—magazine or newspaper articles, books, experts on the subject, and so forth. (For more help with research, see Chapter 11.)

Types of Information.   A cause-and-effect explanation has two types of information: (1) the causes and/or effects of the situation and (2) the evidence to show that the causes and/or effects are accurate. Here are some questions you can use to guide your search for causes, effects, and evidence:

QUESTIONS FOR GATHERING INFORMATION

Causes
- What are the obvious causes?
- Are there any hidden causes? What are they?
- Is there a main, or most important, cause? What is it?
- What is the most recent cause?
- Did any of the causes occur in the distant past?

Effects
- What are the obvious effects?
- Are there any hidden effects? What are they?
- What was (or will be) the first effect?
- What effect(s) might occur in the distant future?

Evidence
- What facts or statistics show that this cause (or effect) exists?
- What expert(s) acknowledges that this cause (or effect) exists?
- What is enough evidence?

PART 2:

Identifying a Thesis and Gathering Information

Ask the two big questions about your topic: *Why?* and *What's the effect?* Brainstorm for as many causes and effects as you can think of; then research others in books or tapes, or do on-site observation and interviewing. Write down all the causes and effects you come up with, as well as evidence to back them up. Stop at some point to identify your focus and write your thesis statement.

Organizing Information

Occasionally a single cause produces a single effect, but not often: Most interesting situations or trends have multiple causes and/or effects. Depending upon the focus of your essay—causes only, effects only, or both causes and effects—the organization may vary a great deal. One helpful way to organize your information is to "map" it. The following example shows how one writer mapped an essay that focused on the effects of buying a car.

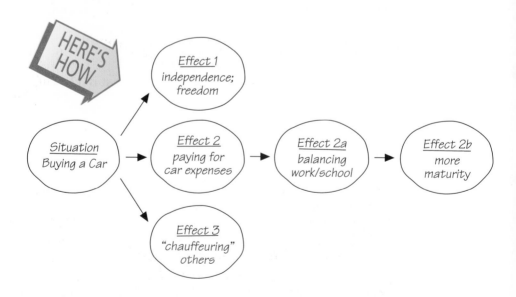

The following examples illustrate how mapping works with other focuses.

Focusing on Causes

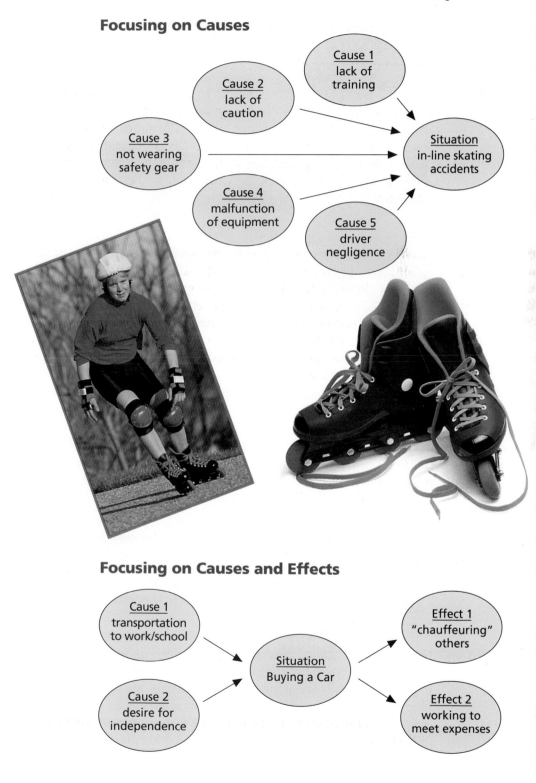

Focusing on Causes and Effects

Focusing on a Chain of Causes and Effects

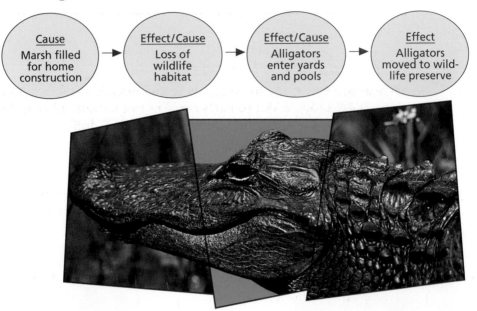

You'll notice that in the Here's How section and in two of the other maps, the causes and effects are numbered. That means the writer will discuss the first cause and related evidence, then the second cause and related evidence, and so forth. But how do you know which cause or effect to list first or last? Most of the time you would use *order of importance* and list the most important cause or effect last, where it will have the most impact. However, with some topics it would make sense to list the causes and effects in *chronological order*.

☞ **REFERENCE NOTE:** See pages 38–39 and 75–76 for more information on order of importance and chronological order.

PART 3:
Organizing Your Information

Now that you have ideas and information, as well as a focus and a thesis statement, you need to think about how to put this material together for your audience. Create an organizational map of your information that you can use later as a guide for writing. Remember that the shape of your map (see pages 252–254) is determined by your focus and your thesis statement.

Writing Your First Draft

The Structure of a Cause-and-Effect Explanation

When you are ready to write, the usual question is *Where do I begin?* Actually, it doesn't matter. The important thing is to start. This is the structure you will use in your draft.

1. In your *introduction*

   ▪ grab the readers' attention
   ▪ identify the situation or condition you are explaining
   ▪ let your reader know what your main idea (thesis) is

2. In the *body*

   ▪ explain the causes and/or the effects of the situation
   ▪ use facts, statistics, and examples to illustrate and clarify each cause or effect

3. In your *conclusion*

   ▪ sum up the explanation
   ▪ possibly, predict future changes or effects

In the following essay about frontier life, the writers explain *effects*. As you read, notice how the authors establish an interesting situation in the introduction. In the body of the essay they lead you into a discussion of several effects, each one supported with specific, colorful details. In the conclusion the writers provide a historical perspective by summarizing how the overall situation changed over the course of time.

Courtesy Museum of New Mexico, 14659

A PASSAGE FROM A BOOK

from Nation of Nations
by James West Davidson et al.

The Frontier Kitchen of the Plains

INTRODUCTION
Attention grabber
Background
information

Out on the treeless plains the Indians had adjusted to scarcity of food, water, and other necessities by adopting a nomadic way of life. Their small kinship groups moved each season to wherever nature supplied the food they needed. Such mobility discouraged families from acquiring extensive material possessions. Tools and housing had to be light and portable. Even tribes that raised crops as part of their subsistence cycle often moved with the seasons.

Situation

White settlement was different. Farmers, ranchers, and townspeople rooted themselves to a single place. What the surrounding countryside could not supply had to be brought from afar, generally at great effort and expense. In areas distant from the railroad or other transportation links, families generally had to learn either to do without or to improvise from materials at hand.

Thesis statement

Effect 1
Evidence for
effect 1

Keeping food on the table was nearly impossible some seasons of the year. Coffee and sugar were staples in such short supply that resourceful women invented a variety of substitutes. "Take a gallon of bran, two tablespoonsful of molasses, scald and parch in an oven until it is somewhat browned and charred," one woman suggested. Something as simple as finding water suitable for drinking or cooking became a problem in many western areas, where the choice might be between "the strong alkaline water of the Rio Grande or the purchase of melted manufactured ice (shipped by rail) at its great cost." To prepare for the lean winter months, women stocked their cellars and made wild fruits into leathery cakes, eaten to ward off the scurvy that resulted from vitamin deficiency.

Effect 2

Evidence for effect 2

Gardening, generally a woman's responsibility, brought variety to the diet and color to the yard. The legume family of peas and beans, in particular, provided needed protein. Superstition had it that plants which grew above ground, like peas, beans, and squash, should be planted in the new moon, whereas root plants such as carrots, potatoes, radishes, and turnips went in as the moon waned. As the moon rose, the theory went, plants rose; as it dropped, so did the root plants. Flowers were much prized but seldom survived the winds, heat, and dry periods. Dishwater and laundry water helped keep them alive. One woman was so excited by the discovery of a hardy dandelion that she cultivated it with care and planted its seeds each spring.

Montana Historical Society, Helena

Effect 3
Evidence for effect 3

Until rail lines made shipment of goods cheap and Sears, Roebuck "wishbooks" brought mail order to the frontier, a woman's kitchen was fairly modest. A cast iron stove, which sold for $25 in the East, was in such demand and so expensive to ship that it fetched $200 in some areas of the West.

One miner's wife in Montana during the 1870s considered her kitchen "well-furnished" with two kettles, a cast iron skillet, and a coffeepot. A kitchen cupboard might be little more than a box nailed to a log. In sod houses cooking could be difficult after a cloudburst. One "soddie" recalled that her kitchen remained snug and dry during a rainstorm, but she discovered that the downpour had taken its toll as the water seeped slowly through the thick roof. After the sun came out, the still-waterlogged roof began to leak. She ended up frying pancakes on her stove under the protection of an umbrella while the sun shone brightly outside.

Montana Historical Society, Helena

Effect 4
Evidence for
effect 4

Without doctors, circumstances forced women to learn the rudiments of caring for the hurt and sick. Most folk remedies did little more than ease pain. Whiskey and patent medicines, often more dangerous than the disease, were used to treat a range of ills from frostbite to snake bite and from sore throats to burns and rheumatism. Settlers believed that onions and gunpowder had valuable medicinal properties. Cobwebs could bandage small wounds; turpentine served as a disinfectant. Mosquitoes were repelled with a paste of vinegar and salt. One woman in Wyoming prevented winter snow blindness by burning pitch pine until it was black and smudging the skin below the eyes with it to cut glare.

Most parents thought the laxative castor oil could cure any childhood malady. And if a family member had a fever, one treatment was to bind the head with a cold rag, wrap the feet in cabbage leaves, and then force down large doses of sage tea, rhubarb, and soda. Some women adapted remedies used on their farm animals. Sarah Olds, a Nevada homesteader whose family was plagued by fleas and lice, recalled that "we all took baths with plenty of sheep dip in the water. . . . I had no disinfectant . . . so I boiled all our clothing in sheep dip and kerosene."

CONCLUSION
Statement about later changes

Gradually, as the market system penetrated the West, families had less need to improvise in matters of diet and medicine. Through catalogs one might order spices like white pepper or poultry seasoning and appliances such as grinders for real coffee. If a local stagecoach passed by the house, a woman might send her eggs and butter to town to be exchanged for needed store-bought goods like threads and needles. It took a complex commercial network to bring all that the good life required to a land that produced few foods and necessities in abundance.

EXERCISE 2 ▶ **Analyzing a Cause-and-Effect Essay**

Now that you have read the essay on the frontier kitchen (pages 256–259), meet with two or three classmates to discuss the following questions.

1. The authors' subject is white settlers, yet they begin with the Plains Indians. Why do you think they do this?
2. The essay focuses on the *effects* of this situation: frontier families had to improvise or do without. Some *causes* of this situation are briefly presented as background in the introduction. What are the causes?
3. A map of this essay would show four main effects. What are they? Can you think of others to add to the essay—anything you're curious about when you think of frontier survival?
4. The authors use evidence to back up their main points. Find examples of the types of support they use—such as quotations, examples, or anecdotes.
5. Do you find details that don't strictly illustrate the essay's main idea about improvising on the frontier? If so, discuss them, and explain why you would keep them or cut them.

A Basic Framework for a Cause-and-Effect Essay

The following essay on buying a car gives you another example of cause-and-effect writing. Like "The Frontier Kitchen of the Plains," it presents a series of effects. However, you'll notice that the writing here is not as detailed, and its organizational structure is more straightforward. You may wish to follow this model when you write your own essay.

A WRITER'S MODEL

Owning a Car: The Pros and Cons

INTRODUCTION
Attention grabber

What one object do most teenagers want to own? A car. Why? Freedom. Buying a car seems like liberation: You can go where you want when you

Thesis statement

want. And that's true--up to a point. Putting your-self in the driver's seat can also have consequences that aren't so cool. I am speaking from experience.

Effect 1
Evidence for
effect 1

One benefit of buying a car is definitely inde-pendence. You don't have to count on parents, friends, bus schedules, or good weather (water-logged biking is no fun). You are not always asking favors, making last-minute arrangements, and fol-lowing other people's schedules. You can accept a good job that's on the other side of town, and you won't miss parties because you're stranded at home without a ride.

Effect 2
Evidence for
effect 2

But an unexpected part of not needing a chauf-feur is that you can become one. With another car in the household, I'm now the one who takes my sister to Little League and goes to the store for milk. And I'm now the one who gives rides to my carless friends. Because I know what they're up against, I don't want to refuse them, but after a while I need money for expenses, and having to ask for it is no fun.

Effect 3
Evidence for
effect 3

Owning a car costs money--in ways you don't appreciate as a passenger. Gasoline isn't free, in-surance for teenagers is expensive, and mainte-nance (not to mention repairs) drains finances. To meet car expenses, I had to work more hours, which meant less free time. Unfortunately, I re-sponded to that situation by studying less, which caused one term of very bad grades, which in turn put my car keys in my parents' pockets for six weeks.

Effect 4
Evidence for effect 4

Summary of effects

CONCLUSION

So, a final effect of car ownership can be growing up. You have to balance freedom with responsibility, learn how to afford your dream of driving without shortchanging something else. Car keys really are the key to a lot of fun and to being on your own, but you have to be ready to pay the price.

This essay follows a standard, easy-to-follow framework for any cause-and-effect essay. Basically, it follows this pattern.

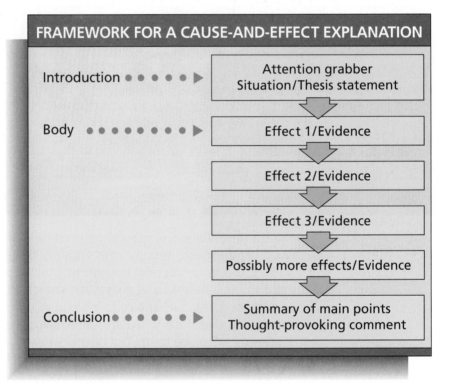

FRAMEWORK FOR A CAUSE-AND-EFFECT EXPLANATION

Introduction • • • • • ▶ Attention grabber
Situation/Thesis statement

Body • • • • • • • • ▶ Effect 1/Evidence

Effect 2/Evidence

Effect 3/Evidence

Possibly more effects/Evidence

Conclusion • • • • • • ▶ Summary of main points
Thought-provoking comment

If your essay focuses on causes only, you can follow this same framework, simply substituting causes for effects. Or, you might describe both causes and effects—for example, in an essay that treats the causes and effects of the Vietnam War. And, if your essay focuses on both causes and effects, you can still use this framework: First you treat the causes, and then the effects.

CRITICAL THINKING

Using Induction

As you plan and write, you're in a continual process of drawing conclusions and making judgments about causes and effects. How can you tell if the conclusions you reach are *valid,* or grounded in evidence? One good way is to think about how you think! Examine your reasoning process.

Induction is one basic and sound reasoning process. When you use induction, you begin with a set of specific facts or observations. By studying this evidence, you reach a general conclusion, or generalization. Induction always goes from the *specific* to the *general.* Here's an example.

> The first time I went to Bessy's room, it was a mess.
> The second time, her room was a disaster.
> I've never been to Bessy's room when it was neat.
> *Generalization:* Bessy is not a tidy housekeeper.

Calvin & Hobbes, copyright 1990 Universal Press Syndicate. Reprinted with permission of Universal Press Syndicate. All rights reserved.

Chances are, you'll find yourself using induction in your cause-and-effect essay, especially if you're examining a new trend or a social situation. Suppose, for example, you want to explore how high school students' studies are affected when they take outside jobs with long hours. You might begin by interviewing students who have held jobs for at least twenty hours or more per week. The data you gather and your subsequent generalization could look something like this.

> Marna's grade average dropped from A– to B–.
> Joe's grade average dropped in everything but math.
> Lucy's grade average went from B to C; her grades rose again when she quit the job.
> *Generalization:* Students' taking jobs of twenty hours or more per week causes grades to drop.

How can you tell if the generalization you make (your conclusion) is valid? The validity depends partly on the population you are generalizing about. If you're generalizing about everyone in the United States, you obviously need to do more research than interview a few friends. A *mixture* of research is usually best: personal observations, published statistics, and opinions of authorities. To reach a sound conclusion for the example you've just read, you would need to interview a large sampling of students, interview teachers and counselors, and read magazine articles about national trends.

Here are three key questions to ask yourself when you want to test the validity of your conclusion.

How much evidence supports my generalization?
Is the source of the evidence trustworthy?
Does all the evidence lead to the same generalization?

CRITICAL THINKING EXERCISE:
Analyzing the Validity of a Generalization

Read the inductions below with two or three classmates. Determine together what kind of research is needed to make each generalization valid. Suggest sources for gathering the necessary data.

1. *Topic: The effects of a high-sugar breakfast*
   When I have only a doughnut for breakfast, I feel a "letdown" by 10 A.M. It's hard for me to concentrate on my school work. Tina says she feels the same way.
   Generalization: A sugary breakfast interferes with learning.

2. *Topic: The effects of dropping out of high school on a person's earning ability*
   David dropped out of high school and got a low-paying job. Margie dropped out and went on welfare.
   Generalization: Dropping out of high school lessens the chance of making a good income.

REFERENCE NOTE: For information about deduction, see page 401.

WRITING ASSIGNMENT

PART 4:
Writing a Draft of Your Explanation

Finally, with much good work behind you, it's time to write a rough draft of your cause-and-effect explanation. Start wherever you want; but before you finish your draft, write an introduction, the body, and a conclusion. Then put your draft aside so you can come back to it later.

Evaluating and Revising

After you finish drafting your essay, push it from your mind for a while. Then when you've cleared your mind a bit, you can use the chart on the following page to pinpoint the strengths and weaknesses in your first draft. Ask yourself each question in the left-hand column, and use the revision techniques in the right-hand column to solve any problems you discover.

EXERCISE 3 ▶ **Analyzing a Writer's Revisions**

Before you revise your own essay, take time to study another writer's revision efforts. Here's the revision of the fourth paragraph in the essay on pages 260–262. Use the questions that follow to help you analyze the changes that were made.

Owning a car costs money — in ways

~~There are things~~ you don't appreciate as   **replace**

(↑ *insurance for teenagers is expensive* ↑)

a passenger. Gasoline isn't free and   **add**

maintenance (not to mention repairs)

drains finances. To meet car expenses, I had

to work more hours, which meant less free

time. Unfortunately, I responded to that

situation by studying less, which in turn put

my car keys in my parents' pockets for six

weeks. ~~I had~~ *which caused* one term of very bad grades. ~~No~~   **replace/reorder**

~~teenager can afford a car.~~   **cut**

1. Why did the writer replace *There are things* with *Owning a car costs money—in ways* in the first sentence?
2. Why did the writer add the additional information to the second sentence? What does it tell the reader?
3. Why did the writer move the information about bad grades to the previous sentence?
4. Why did the writer delete the last sentence? [Hint: See the information on inductive thinking, pages 263–265.]

EVALUATING AND REVISING CAUSE-AND-EFFECT EXPLANATIONS

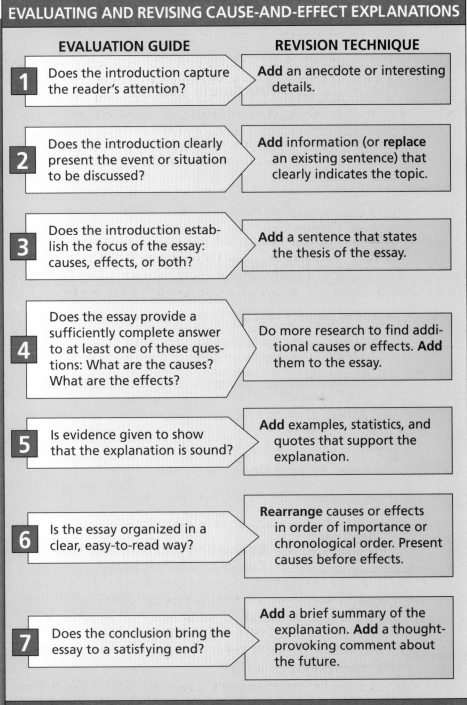

EVALUATION GUIDE	REVISION TECHNIQUE
1 Does the introduction capture the reader's attention?	**Add** an anecdote or interesting details.
2 Does the introduction clearly present the event or situation to be discussed?	**Add** information (or **replace** an existing sentence) that clearly indicates the topic.
3 Does the introduction establish the focus of the essay: causes, effects, or both?	**Add** a sentence that states the thesis of the essay.
4 Does the essay provide a sufficiently complete answer to at least one of these questions: What are the causes? What are the effects?	Do more research to find additional causes or effects. **Add** them to the essay.
5 Is evidence given to show that the explanation is sound?	**Add** examples, statistics, and quotes that support the explanation.
6 Is the essay organized in a clear, easy-to-read way?	**Rearrange** causes or effects in order of importance or chronological order. Present causes before effects.
7 Does the conclusion bring the essay to a satisfying end?	**Add** a brief summary of the explanation. **Add** a thought-provoking comment about the future.

GRAMMAR HINT

Subordinate Clauses

In a cause-and-effect essay, you want to show clearly the relationships between ideas. What's the cause? What's the effect? Subordinate conjunctions, which introduce subordinate clauses, can help you do this if you are careful to choose conjunctions that make relationships clear. Examples of conjunctions that show *cause* are *because, as, since, whereas.* Conjunctions that show *effects*, or results, include *that, in order that, so that.*

You may find yourself using the word *and* to connect clauses, when more specific conjunctions would work better. If so, replace *and* (or other unclear conjunctions) with words or phrases that clarify the causes and effects.

CONFUSING   The crop failed and there was a drought.
CLEAR   The crop failed **because** there was a drought.

CONFUSING   Owning a car costs so much money, and I had to work.
CLEAR   Owning a car costs so much money **that** I had to work.

👉 REFERENCE NOTE: For more information about subordinate clauses, see pages 629–637.

WRITING ASSIGNMENT

PART 5:
Evaluating and Revising Your Cause-and-Effect Essay

Put your essay aside for at least a day. Next, reread your paper and use the evaluating and revising chart on page 267 to decide what changes will improve it. Mark passages that seem thin, and jot down ideas you would like to add. Then, exchange papers with another student and use the chart to evaluate each other's essays. Carefully consider your partner's comments as well as your own evaluation. Finally, make the changes on either your hard copy or your word processor.

Proofreading and Publishing

Proofreading. Most cause-and-effect essays have technical or difficult words you don't often use. Check your sources again to make sure you spelled all these words correctly, including the names of people you have quoted. Then proofread your entire essay once again, making a final check for spelling, grammar, and punctuation. Use any proofing method that works for you—one that helps you slow down and concentrate in order to find errors. Some writers proofread one line at a time, keeping other lines covered.

Publishing. You wrote with real readers in mind, and now is the time to send your work out to them. Try to share your essay with at least two people other than your teacher, perhaps using one of the following suggestions.

- Send your essay to people who are personally involved or interested in your topic. If your essay deals with a community event, send it to the newspaper as a letter to the editor. If it deals with a school event, submit it as an article for your school newspaper. If you wrote about a subject such as history or science, share it with a teacher who specializes in that subject.

- Have a class-wide essay swap. Post a sheet in the classroom that lists the titles of all the essays. Each classmate can find the topic that interests him or her most and sign up to read it.

WRITING ASSIGNMENT

PART 6:
Proofreading and Publishing Your Essay

Proofread your paper with care, and correct any errors you find. Then let others read your work.

WRITING WORKSHOP

A Process Explanation

While the cause-and-effect essay that you wrote earlier in this chapter explains *why*, writing that examines a process explains *how* or *how to*. You don't have to look far to find examples of process explanations. Just take a glance at any magazine stand and you'll see titles like these: "How Your VCR Works," "How Ad Agents Find New Talent," "How to Lose Weight Quickly and Forever," "What to Do When Your Friends Give You the Silent Treatment," and "How to Be Your Own Car Mechanic."

Each of these articles is an example of a process analysis. As the term implies, this type of writing breaks down a process and explains each step. Process analyses fall into two basic types: the "how," which simply tells how the process works or happens; and the "how-to," which tells how *you* can make the process work or happen.

This essay explains the process of one special effect used in the movies. To most people it's a "how-it-works" essay, but if you are an amateur filmmaker, it could be a "how-to" guide.

Once Is Not Enough
by Jane O'Connor and Katy Hall

Late-night TV movies abound with ghosts—those semitransparent figures that may appear out of nowhere (thanks to stop-motion photography), walk through a few closed doors, and then, just as suddenly, disappear. Often these spirits are the result of an optical trick called *double exposure.*

To make a ghost walk right through a cemetery wall, from one side to the other, a camera is set up so that both sides of the wall are visible. The cameraman then exposes, say, twenty feet of film of just this wall. (Film is talked about in *feet* rather than frames when so much film is used that it would be awkward to talk about a huge number of frames. There are 16 frames to one foot of movie film.)

Bob Hope in *The Ghost Breaker.* (1940)

Now the cameraman winds the twenty feet of film *backward* in the camera. There is a footage counter on the camera so that he knows just how far to rewind the film. The same twenty feet of film are now ready to be exposed *again.* The camera is taken to another set at this point and the actor playing the ghost is filmed—on the same twenty feet of film—simply walking across the set. Now the twenty feet of film has been exposed to light two different times. It has been *double exposed.*

The scene that was filmed first—the cemetery wall—"burned" its image onto the film and, on screen, it will appear as a solid image. The scene that was filmed second—the walking ghost—was photographed with the camera's iris closed down, letting less light into the camera, and so the image is fainter, and appears translucent on the screen—just the way a ghost should look.

from *Magic in the Movies*

1. What optical trick are the authors explaining? How do they catch your interest and make you curious to read on?
2. The basic organization for a process essay is chronological order, giving the steps in the order of occurrence. Why do you suppose the "closing the iris" event is explained at the end of the essay, not when it happens?
3. Could you now explain this special effect to someone else, or do you still have questions? "Grade" this essay on its clarity, giving specific examples.

Writing a Process Analysis

Prewriting. What process are you curious about or expert in? Would you like to know how to copyright a song or how a facsimile (fax) machine works? Can you explain how to format columns on a computer (better than your badly written manual) or how a bill becomes a law? Choose a process that you can explain with enthusiasm, and start analyzing it. Make notes on terms, equipment, or materials that readers will need to know or have; and then list the steps of the process.

Writing, Evaluating, and Revising. As always, draft an attention-grabbing opening, and then be sure to give readers any "advance" information they need—ingredients, tools, technical definitions, scientific principles—before launching into steps. Generally, a process essay is organized chronologically. Use transitional expressions to keep order clear: *first, now, next, at the same time,* and so on.

When you've finished, have others read your essay and mark any passage that "lost" them or seemed out of place. You or others can test a "how-to" essay by performing the process (or pretending to). Make any revisions that will make the process clearer.

Proofreading and Publishing. It's important to proofread carefully because errors in punctuation or grammar can confuse or frustrate readers who are trying to understand the process you are explaining. After you have finished proofreading and correcting errors, you should be able to find a real audience—a receptive one—for your essay. Practical how-to explanations and clear breakdowns of intriguing processes attract readers. For example, you might send instructions for making tortillas to the newspaper's food editor or give a speech to a local nature club explaining how certain species of hummingbirds "hibernate."

MAKING CONNECTIONS

TEST TAKING

Cause-and-Effect Essay Questions

When taking history or social studies tests, you will often face essay questions that ask you to explain causes and effects. The skills you have learned in this chapter will help you when that kind of question appears. Just write a shorter version of what you did in your essay—a clear, logical explanation of causes, effects, or both. Back up your main ideas with evidence—specific facts or examples.

Below is a typical essay question that might appear on a social studies test. Answer it in a paragraph or two by using the information that's provided. Simply describe the causes, and provide any backup data that you think is necessary.

Question: How were only 1,000 Spanish troops able to over-throw millions of Aztecs in Mexico in 1521? Describe the causes.

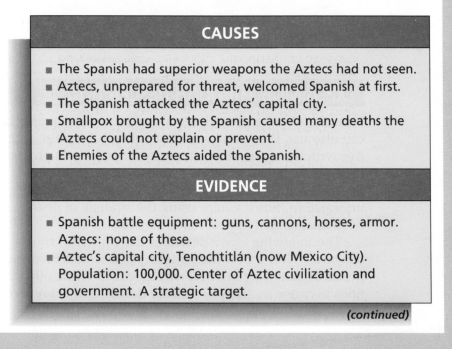

CAUSES

- The Spanish had superior weapons the Aztecs had not seen.
- Aztecs, unprepared for threat, welcomed Spanish at first.
- The Spanish attacked the Aztecs' capital city.
- Smallpox brought by the Spanish caused many deaths the Aztecs could not explain or prevent.
- Enemies of the Aztecs aided the Spanish.

EVIDENCE

- Spanish battle equipment: guns, cannons, horses, armor. Aztecs: none of these.
- Aztec's capital city, Tenochtitlán (now Mexico City). Population: 100,000. Center of Aztec civilization and government. A strategic target.

(continued)

EVIDENCE *(continued)*

- After Montezuma II, supreme ruler of Aztecs, was killed, his replacement died of smallpox.
- Thousands of people whom the Aztecs had previously conquered joined the Spanish and actually saved their lives in an important battle, *la noche triste* (the sad night).

The Bettmann Archive

EXPLAINING THROUGH DESCRIPTION

Causal and process analyses are narrative strategies, but you can also use the strategy of description to explain. In descriptive writing, you explain a topic by describing its physical qualities—how it looks, feels, sounds, moves, smells, or tastes. Because your purpose is *to explain*, you need to supply accurate information. Since you're using the strategy of *description*, you need images that appeal to the senses.

The following essay describes the courtship rituals of various birds. Notice how the writer *explains* what's involved in the rituals by *describing* in detail what goes on. While other descriptions may use a variety of sensory details, this essay focuses on visual and sound details.

from The Birder's Handbook
by Paul R. Ehrlich, David S. Dobkin, and Darryl Wheye

Often courtship displays accent a striking feature of the bird's plumage. The conspicuous, labored flight displays of the male Red-winged Blackbird exaggerate its red shoulder patches. The display flight of the male Yellow-headed Blackbird is performed with the body cocked upward so that its prominent yellow head is held high.

On the other hand, some male birds do not advertise with physical attributes; they demonstrate skills. Male terns court females by displaying a fresh-caught fish. Courting male European Gray Herons perform ritualized hunting movements, erecting head feathers, pointing their bills downward and clashing their mandibles together. Many male passerines [birds that perch], when courting, also lower their bills as if pecking at something below them. Perhaps, next to singing, the most common component of courtship displays in male songbirds is vibration of the wings; other components include fluffing of the body feathers, bill raising, thrusting the head forward, and running using short steps.

Calvin & Hobbes, copyright 1987 Universal Press Syndicate. Reprinted with permission of Universal Press Syndicate. All rights reserved.

Write one or two paragraphs of your own that explain something by describing it in accurate detail. Pick any topic that you know well. You could explain the characteristics of a kind of flower or fish, the features of an electric guitar, the movements of an aerobics class, a performance you've seen of your favorite musician, or a custom or lifestyle difference you noticed while traveling. Remember that your purpose is to explain through the use of description.

8 WRITING TO PERSUADE

Taking a Stand

Wouldn't life be boring if everybody agreed on everything all the time? Where would new ideas come from? What incentive would we have to take risks? How would we ever make progress if everyone was afraid to **take a stand**?

Writing and You.   When we want to change someone's mind about something or convince others to take action, we have to take a stand. Advertisers take a stand when they persuade you to buy CDs, jeans, and cereal. You take a stand for your own qualifications when you apply for a job. Politicians take a stand when they want a new law passed or defeated. Have you ever admired someone who took a stand—and won?

As You Read.   Two years after the 1877 surrender of the Nez Percés to the United States Army, Chief Joseph's views of Native American life were published in a magazine. As you read the following selection, notice how he combines reason with emotional appeal to persuade whites to view Native Americans differently.

FROM "An Indian's View of Indian Affairs"

BY CHIEF JOSEPH (IN-MUT-TOO-YAH-LAT-LAT) OF THE NEZ PERCÉS

. . . I have heard talk and talk, but nothing is done. Good words do not last long unless they amount to something. Words do not pay for my dead people. They do not pay for my country, now overrun by white men. They do not protect my father's grave. They do not pay for all my horses and cattle. Good words will not give me back my children. Good words will not make good the promise of your War chief General Miles. Good words will not give my people good health and stop them from dying. Good words will not get my people a home where they can live in peace and take care of themselves.

I am tired of talk that comes to nothing. It makes my heart sick when I remember all the good words and all the broken promises. There has been too much talking by men who had no right to talk. Too many misrepresentations have been made, too many misunderstandings have come up between the white men about the Indians.

If the white man wants to live in peace with the Indian he can live in peace. There need be no trouble. Treat all men alike. Give them the same law. Give them an even chance to live and grow. All men were made by the same Great Spirit Chief. They are all brothers. The earth is the mother of all people, and all people should have equal rights upon it.

Montana Historical Society, Helena.

You might as well expect the rivers to run backward as that any man who was born a free man should be contented when penned up and denied liberty to go where he pleases. If you tie a horse to a stake, do you expect he will grow fat? If you pen an Indian up on a small spot of earth, and compel him to stay there, he will not be contented, nor

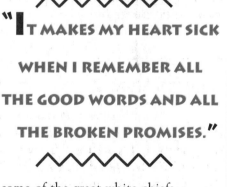

"**IT MAKES MY HEART SICK WHEN I REMEMBER ALL THE GOOD WORDS AND ALL THE BROKEN PROMISES.**"

will he grow and prosper. I have asked some of the great white chiefs where they get their authority to say to the Indian that he shall stay in one place, while he sees white men going where they please. They cannot tell me.

I only ask of the government to be treated as all other men are treated. If I cannot go to my own home, let me have a home in some country where my people will not die so fast. . . .

When I think of our condition my heart is heavy. I see men of my race treated as outlaws and driven from country to country or shot down like animals.

I know that my race must change. We cannot hold our own with white men as we are. We ask only an even chance to live as other men live. We ask to be recognized as men. We ask that the same law shall work alike on all men. If the Indian breaks the law, punish him by the law. If the white man breaks the law, punish him also.

Let me be a free man—free to travel, free to stop, free to work, free to trade where I choose, free to choose my own teachers, free to follow the religion of my fathers, free to think and talk and act for myself—and I will obey every law, or submit to the penalty.

Whenever the white man treats an Indian as they treat each other, then we will have no more wars. We shall all be alike—brothers of one father and one mother, with one mother, with one sky above us and one country around us, and one government for all. Then the Great Spirit Chief who rules above will smile upon this land, and send rain to wash out the bloody spots made by brothers' hands from the face of the earth.

For this time the Indian race are waiting and praying. I hope that no more groans of wounded men and women will ever go to the ear of the Great Spirit Chief above, and that all people may be one people.

"YOU MIGHT AS WELL EXPECT THE RIVERS TO RUN BACKWARD AS THAT ANY MAN WHO WAS BORN A FREE MAN SHOULD BE CONTENTED WHEN PENNED UP AND DENIED LIBERTY TO GO WHERE HE PLEASES."

READER'S RESPONSE

1. Does Chief Joseph convince you that the government had treated the Nez Percés unfairly? If you were a government official listening to this speech, how would you answer Chief Joseph?
2. What values do you share with Chief Joseph? Which of his ideas do you think are still important today?

WRITER'S CRAFT

3. What specific support—reasons, facts, and examples—does Chief Joseph give for the idea that his people should be free to go wherever they choose?
4. Find some words and phrases that carry a definite emotional charge. Contrast them with more neutral words that would carry the same basic meaning.
5. Which groups might most strongly object to what Chief Joseph says? What might be their reasons? Has Chief Joseph considered and answered these reasons? Explain.

Ways to Persuade

Like Chief Joseph, writers who persuade want people to change their minds or take action about something. Persuasive writing shows up in speeches, of course, but you also see it in advice columns, advertisements, editorials, sermons, magazine and newspaper articles, and business proposals. Here are some examples showing the basic ways you can develop a persuasive message.

Narration: telling about a narrow escape from a hurricane to convince others to follow evacuation directions; telling about having to help your uncle fix his car to persuade your teacher to let you take the exam later.

Description: describing the dance competitions at a pow-wow to get some friends to go with you; describing your old watch to persuade a friend to buy it from you.

Classification: comparing two used cars to convince your parents that one of them is a better buy; defining the word *democracy* to convince your audience to vote in the student council election.

▶ **Evaluation:**   evaluating a rap group you heard on the radio to convince your friends that their concert ticket is worth the price; forming an opinion about gun control and writing to the head of the National Rifle Association attacking or supporting its position on the subject.

LOOKING AHEAD

In this chapter, your main writing assignment will be to develop a persuasive essay. Your primary writing and thinking strategy will be evaluation. Keep in mind that persuasive essays

- state the writer's point of view, or opinion, about an important issue
- provide convincing support for the writer's stand, or position
- answer the main opposing positions

Writing a Persuasive Essay

Prewriting

Focusing on an Issue

You have strong feelings about many *issues*, topics about which people have opposing opinions. Many of these issues would make good topics for a persuasive essay.

Choosing a Specific Issue

Should the same amount of money be spent for boys' and girls' athletic teams in high school? Does the government have the right to censor artists that it helps support? If you ask around, you'll find people who will say yes, as well as people who will say no, to both of these questions. Clearly, these issues spark disagreement; but if they don't spark your interest, they aren't the best choice for you to write about. To find a good topic for your own essay, use these criteria:

- The issue is important to you. You have an opinion about it, or at least a strong interest and curiosity.
- It is a real issue, not just a matter of personal taste. (You may be a football fanatic, but you'll never be able to persuade die-hard baseball fans that football is a better sport.)
- The issue is arguable. People have different opinions about it, and it matters to them.
- There is an audience out there that you would really like to convince.

When you find an issue that meets all of these criteria, you've got a winner.

WRITING NOTE   It's possible to choose an issue because you feel it is important and you want to know more about it. Sometimes you have an opinion that leans to one side of an issue, but you don't yet feel qualified to draw a final conclusion. Gathering information and writing the essay will help you explore your own opinion. By the time you finish, you may have strengthened your original belief or even have changed your opinion. (For more on writing to explore, see Chapter 9, pages 318–357.)

Calvin & Hobbes, copyright 1990 Universal Press Syndicate. Reprinted wit permission of Universal Press Syndicate. All rights reserved.

Developing a Position Statement

When you select an issue to write about, you usually know your opinion, or position, on it. For example, you have chosen the issue of the amount of money spent on girls' and boys' sports, and you know which side you are on: You think the amount spent should be equal. In a persuasive essay, this is your position on the issue. As you begin to plan your essay, it's good to state your position, or opinion, in a sentence. This statement of position, often called a *proposition,* will help you focus your ideas as you gather support and draft your paper.

EXAMPLE POSITION STATEMENTS

> Girls should pay their own expenses when they're out with boys on dates.

> Serving in the armed forces builds character.

> Children up to age ten and pregnant women should receive free medical care.

> Foreign language classes in high school should be abolished.

EXERCISE 1 ▶ **Exploring Issues**

With a group, use the following idea starters to generate a list of possible issues for a persuasive essay. Don't be shy about expressing opinions when good ideas surface: That's part of your exploration.

- Brainstorm about any of these subjects: dating, schools, taxes, violence, rip-offs, discrimination, food, imports, pollution.
- Complete each of these sentences:
  If I could get rid of anything, I'd abolish ____.
  There ought to be a law against ____.
  We should have the right to ____.
- Skim the articles, pictures, and advertisements in a school, local, or national newspaper. What issues do they raise or suggest?

EXERCISE 2 ▶ **Evaluating Position Statements**

Working with a small group, use the criteria for choosing an issue (page 283) to decide which of the following positions is suitable for a persuasive essay. Explain why any statement isn't appropriate, and try to rework it so it could be used.

EXAMPLE Cars with front-wheel drive are better than cars with rear-wheel drive.
Unsuitable: Personal taste, not an issue
Suitable rewrite: Smaller cars are better for the environment.

1. U.S. consumers should buy only products made in the United States.
2. Children must be protected from abuse.
3. Disabled people can perform well in many jobs.
4. Smoking should be banned in all restaurants.

WRITING ASSIGNMENT

PART 1:
Choosing an Issue to Write About

Did you find your issue in Exercise 1? If not, listen to yourself carefully for a day or so. When do you say (or *want* to say), "Well, I think . . ."? You could also do some brainstorming or look in your writer's journal for issues you think are important. When you have an issue you care about, write your position statement. Check it carefully. Is it an arguable opinion—not a matter of personal taste or a belief that most people share?

Thinking About Purpose, Audience, and Tone

Your *purpose* in writing a persuasive essay is (1) to make your readers think as you do about an issue and sometimes (2) to move them to do what you suggest.

It isn't easy to get people to change their minds, adopt a new idea, or act on their beliefs. That's why in a persuasive essay you pay very close attention to *audience*. And as you think about your audience, don't be surprised if you find that it's made up of different groups. To target each group, you need to explore their interests and concerns by looking for answers to crucial questions. How much do they know about this issue?

What points do you and your audience agree on? Why is their opinion different from yours? What arguments will they use to oppose you?

Purpose and audience are also linked to the *tone* and *style* of persuasion. General persuasion is often informal and may use everyday speech. When the purpose is purely to convince the audience, a direct, personal—sometimes even humorous—tone can be very persuasive. Most speeches, letters to the editor, and advertising fall into this category.

However, the persuasive essay is sometimes more formal and serious. In school, for example, you may be asked to develop a logical, reasoned argument. In that case, your tone and language should be formal and serious. For more information on formal and informal language, see pages 484–488.

WRITING ASSIGNMENT	PART 2: **Identifying the Audience for Your Essay**

There is little point in aiming persuasion at people who already agree with you. In school you're often writing for your teacher and class, but a persuasive paper is a real chance to target an audience. Look closely at the issue you identified in Writing Assignment, Part 1 (page 286). Exactly who is it that needs to be convinced on the issue? Who actively disagrees with your opinion? Who is neutral but important to sway? Make a chart listing real readers for your essay, and identify which ones are neutral, which ones actively disagree, and which ones already agree with you.

Prewriting

Supporting Your Opinion

To win others to your opinion, you could try shouting louder than your opponents, but why waste your time and lungs on something that won't work? To be successful at persuading, you need to develop support that will convince your readers that your opinion is right.

Using Logical Appeals

Logical appeals are appeals to reason, not emotion. Because most people like to think that they are rational, thoughtful citizens, you need to show that your opinions are based on clear thinking and solid evidence.

Reasons. *Reasons* are the main points you use to support your opinion. They are often the answer to the audience's question "Why should I accept your opinion?"

Position Statement: A class in multicultural history and literature should be required for graduation from our high school.

Reasons: An understanding of cultures other than European and Anglo-Saxon will benefit all of our students.
A narrow cultural focus is unfair to our diverse student body.

Evidence. Most audiences, however, aren't satisfied if you just give them reasons. They also want *evidence*, that is, proof that your reasons are sound. Two basic kinds of evidence are

- **facts**—statements that can be checked by testing, by reading a reliable reference source, or by observing firsthand. Facts may be statistics, examples, and anecdotes (brief stories, often based on personal experiences).

    The student body is now 25 percent Hispanic, 25 percent African American, 7 percent Native American, and 9 percent Asian American.

    Our school offers only one year of U.S. history and one year of European history.

For the past two years, groups of students taking U.S. history have asked to give special reports to their classes on African American and Native American roles in the nation's history.

■ **expert opinions**—statements by people who are considered authorities on the subject.

Patricia Ann Romero and Don Zancanella, who teach Hispanic American literature in Albuquerque, New Mexico, recently wrote in the *English Journal* that American students are lucky to have so many cultures around them and should explore different literatures to "better understand the diversity of American society."

For some issues, your own knowledge and experience will provide all the support any audience could ask for. For other issues, you will need to do some research. Although a persuasive essay is not a research paper, you might refer to Chapter 11 for help with identifying sources. As you collect information, make sure it's objective and reliable. Inconsistent sources—or just one biased source—can wreck your audience's trust in you.

Using Emotional Appeals

When you take a stand on something important to you, you often want to appeal to readers' hearts as well as their minds. In analyzing your audience and collecting evidence, you may already have seen ways to use emotional appeals in your essay.

Examples and Details. Suppose that you want to persuade your audience to contribute money for the homeless. To show that the homeless need help, you present the evidence that many have no jobs or are unable to work and therefore cannot pay for housing. But then you add an emotional appeal by telling the story of how one woman froze to death on a cold night. Numerical facts may be impressive, but they're impersonal. The specific example and vivid details make the suffering real.

Language.   You also use emotional appeals when you pick words with strong connotative meanings. *Denotative* meanings are the ones that the dictionary gives you, but *connotative* meanings are the feelings or attitudes that a word suggests. For example, Chief Joseph (pages 278–280) chose strongly connotative words. Some of the words with negative connotations he used are *bloody, wounded, outlaws, die,* and *punish.* But he repeated words with positive connotations more often: *smile, earth, mother, brothers, peace, law,* and *free.*

Choose emotional appeals carefully, and recognize their power. They're best used to focus attention on important arguments because using them too often may make your audience feel that you are exaggerating the situation and misleading them.

Using Ethical Appeals

Do you know someone whom you think is intelligent, responsible, and sincere? Would you accept that person's opinion more quickly than the opinion of someone you think is unintelligent, irresponsible, and insincere? That's the way *ethical appeals* work. They suggest to the audience that the writer is of good character—someone sincere who speaks with some knowledge and authority.

When you write your essay, you can show that you can be trusted (that you are fair) by showing both sides of the issue. If you have experience with the issue, you can also discuss it in personal terms, as Chief Joseph did in "An Indian's View of Indian Affairs."

Identifying Opposing Positions

Effective persuasion doesn't *ignore* strong opposing positions: It counters them. Your audience analysis may yield some good reasons against your position, and you should also be on the alert for opposing reasons and evidence while doing research. Plan your answer to these objections— your *rebuttal.*

In collecting support, you may come across an opposing position you should mention but can't answer. Don't worry. Admitting this, called *conceding a point,* shows your audience that you've considered all sides of the issue and are fair. The chart below shows how one writer organized her support.

HERE'S HOW

<u>Position statement:</u> Drivers younger than twenty-one who have a blood alcohol content over the legal limit should lose their licenses for two years.
<u>Audience:</u> Teenagers and adults who read the local newspaper

<u>Logical Appeal:</u>

Reasons	Evidence
• will save lives of both drivers and victims	quotation from Cohens—more accidents than other age groups
	quotation from Golden—25,000 killed each year by drunk drivers
• stop dangerous behavior before it happens	teens not addicted, respond to peer pressure

<u>Emotional Appeal:</u> loss of freedom

<u>Ethical Appeal:</u>

Opposing Positions	Rebuttals
• unfair to treat teens differently	teens don't know limits; judgment clouded by alcohol
• teens are better drivers than older people	teens have less experience and are less cautious

WRITING NOTE

Sometimes your purpose may be to develop a *formal argument,* a line of reasoning that proves your proposition (opinion) is true. A formal argument relies strictly on logic and looks at all available evidence, both favorable *(pro)* and unfavorable *(con)*. Some school essays and business proposals require formal arguments, but if your purpose is to persuade (not prove), you don't have to follow this strict procedure. To convince your audience, you can select the evidence that is favorable and appeal to your audience's emotions and biases. Most of the examples of persuasion you find in magazines, newspapers, and popular books do not present formal arguments.

Reminder

In planning your support

- identify logical appeals (reasons and evidence) to support your position statement
- identify emotional and ethical appeals appropriate for your audience
- plan your rebuttal by considering audience objections, looking for opposing reasons and evidence in your research, and deciding how to answer the objections

WRITING ASSIGNMENT

PART 3:
Supporting Your Opinion

You are now ready to gather support for your position statement (Writing Assignment, Part 1, page 286). Start by listing the information you already have about the issue or by brainstorming ideas—alone or with someone else. Then decide whether you need to refer to outside sources. Remember to look for logical appeals and to consider possible emotional and ethical appeals. After you take notes, organize your information in a chart like the one in the Here's How on page 291.

EXERCISE 3 ▶ **Speaking and Listening: Refining Your Rebuttal**

Work with a partner or small group to find out if the rebuttal you plan is strong and realistic. Begin by identifying your audience and asking your listeners to play their role. Using your chart of support, read your position statement and your supporting reasons and evidence (*not* your rebuttal). Your classmates should listen carefully, take notes, and then get together to propose objections. As they present opposing arguments, you must think on your feet—draw on your planning to answer as persuasively as possible. Afterward, discuss how your written plan compared to the actual exchange, and make revision notes. Then change roles.

Writing Your First Draft

The Basic Elements of Persuasion

The basic elements of persuasion fit clearly into composition form (pages 112–121). In the *introduction* you present your opinion, or position, and give any background readers will need to understand the issue. It is especially important in persuasion to get the audience's attention right away and make them care about your issue.

In the *body* you develop all of the support for your position—logical and emotional appeals—and present opposing positions with your rebuttal.

In the *conclusion* you return with force to your position and possibly give a **call to action,** something you want readers to do.

The Organization of a Persuasive Essay

Persuasive essays can be organized in varied ways, but a simple, effective plan is to present your logical and emotional appeals first, followed by opposing positions and rebuttals.

- **Order of Importance.** You may want to arrange your appeals by *order of importance,* beginning or ending with your most irresistible appeal. Remember to think about their importance *to your audience.*
- **Chronological Order.** For other topics, though, *chronological order* may be natural. For example, if you were attempting to persuade your readers to stop smoking, you might present the effects in the order they would occur.
- **Logical Order.** A comparison and contrast strategy works well in presenting opposing positions and rebuttals. You may present all the objections at once, followed by all your answers, or you may go back and forth from each objection to its answer (a good plan if you're covering several opposing positions).

The writers of the following persuasive essays combine the elements of persuasion in two different ways. As you read, notice the kinds of evidence and appeals each uses.

TWO NEWSPAPER EDITORIALS

Opinion

Keep "The Star-Spangled Banner"
by Vicki Williams

Attention
grabber

I've never been able to sing *The Star-Spangled Banner*. But, then, there are lots of songs I've never been able to sing.

I have a musical range of exactly one octave.

Ethical appeal

When a song rises above or falls below it, I simply drop out and resume when my personal octave returns.

Opposing
position

Most people are more capable musically than I am, but they still can't pull off the entire *Star-Spangled Banner*. In any audience of 10,000, there will generally be only 1,000 or so who can stretch their lungs to the full capacity demanded by the most difficult parts of this song.

Rebuttal

Facts

But still, we've been struggling to sing *The Star-Spangled Banner* since Congress adopted it in 1931 as our national anthem. In fact, Americans have been working at singing it since 1814, when Francis Scott Key wrote the words and set them to the music of an old English tune.

Reason

Emotional
appeal

And perhaps there should be some effort to singing our national anthem, just as there must be effort in keeping the United States the kind of country it is.

Opposing
position

America the Beautiful is a lovely song, but it is too easy, with its pleasant talk of purple mountain majesties and amber waves of grain. There is

Rebuttal

Emotional
appeal

no sense of struggle here. It just flows along as if freedom and brotherhood came naturally, without hardship.

Emotional
appeal

By contrast, in *The Star-Spangled Banner,* we can almost feel the imprisoned patriot's anguish as he wondered during that long night in Baltimore Harbor if the flag would continue to wave. And his heartfelt gratitude when the rockets' red glare and the bombs bursting in air revealed that it was still proudly flying over Fort McHenry.

There are many songs about America, and we should sing them wholeheartedly, for they all illustrate elements of what this country represents.

It is "America the beautiful" and "this land is your land and my land." And it is "a sweet land of liberty."

Reason

Emotional appeal

But I don't believe our national song should change with the passing whim of popularity.

Restatement: main reason

The Star-Spangled Banner deserves to be our anthem because it reminds us that patriotism sometimes requires sacrifice, and that, in order to continue to be the land of the free, we must also remain the home of the brave.

Emotional appeal

USA TODAY

Replace "The Star-Spangled Banner"
by Andy Jacobs, Jr.

Attention grabber

"I have two favorite songs. One of them is *Yankee Doodle* and the other one ain't." The words are those of our 18th president, Ulysses Grant.

Background

On March 4, 1931, when he signed it into law, *The Star-Spangled Banner* was one of the favorite songs of our 31st president, Herbert Hoover.

Reason

Emotional
appeal

As time becomes history, what we favor musically to express our love of country may change. The love itself, like the love of family, remains pretty much the same.

Facts

But listen: *Their blood has washed out their/ foul footsteps' pollution . . .* The third verse of *The Star-Spangled Banner* does not speak well of our friends, the British.

Reason

Opposing
position/
Ethical appeal

Emotional
appeal

America the Beautiful is not about hatred for long-ago enemies. It is not about a war nor about the flag. It is about America. Yes, an instrumental presentation of *The Star-Spangled Banner* does wondrously chilling things to our feelings. As a former Marine, I snap to attention and present arms. *The land of the free and the home of the brave.* I love that line, even if I can't sing it.

Reason
repeated

Emotional
appeal/
Fact

But the thrust of our anthem is war. Martial matters do not measure the length and breadth of our national being. *America the Beautiful* sends a more positive message at a time when enlightenment seems to be showering peaceful and liberating dividends around the globe.

Facts

The Star-Spangled Banner would endure as a suitable and stirring sound for military occasions. But not all of them. At the memorial for our Challenger astronauts, *The Star-Spangled Banner* was not heard. It was *America the Beautiful* which splendidly stated our pride and sorrow. At the Statue of Liberty rededication, *The Star-Spangled Banner* was initially and perfunctorily played. But the ceremony itself was laced and graced by *America the Beautiful,* which suggests the inner strength of a self-confident people.

Emotional
appeal

Reason

Fact

This all-American song does not lack suitable tribute to those who have given their lives in uniform: *Oh beautiful for heroes proved/in liberating strife. Who more/than self their country loved/and mercy more than life.*

Emotional
appeal

Those words are calm yet strong, like heroism itself, which is *proved* not so much by politically histrionic demands for inflicting pain as by enduring it.

Summarizing statement/ Emotional appeals

America the Beautiful is not boisterous; neither is true patriotism—an abiding thing, calm and steady in storm as well as in the safety of the harbor. Vicarious violence may fire the passions of some, but, as in marriage, passion isn't much upon which to build a lifetime of loyalty.

USA TODAY

EXERCISE 4 ▶ **Analyzing the Elements of Persuasive Essays**

You can't agree with both of the writers taking a stand on the national anthem, but you can learn something about persuasion from both of them. After you've read the essays, meet with two or three classmates to discuss the answers to the following questions.

1. The opinions of both writers are in their titles, but their positions are actually more specific than just "keeping" or "replacing" the current national anthem. Give a full position statement for each.
2. Which reason do you think is strongest in each essay? Where in the essay does it appear? Why do you think it was placed there?

3. In your opinion, which essay has stronger reasons and evidence? Explain your judgment.
4. Both essays employ many emotional appeals. In each one, point out effective details and connotative language.
5. Find an opposing position in each essay. Exactly how does the writer rebut it? Brainstorm to think of any opposing positions each writer may have missed.

A Basic Framework for a Persuasive Essay

The two essays you've just read are by professional writers, tackling an issue that is inescapably emotional. Your essay will be more heavily based on logic and facts and will use a more conventional organization. You may want to follow the basic framework in the following writer's model.

A WRITER'S MODEL

A Chance for Life

INTRODUCTION
Attention grabber

Last week eight teenagers on their way home from a party were killed when their truck crashed into a tree. The autopsy on the seventeen-year-old driver showed that his blood alcohol level was more than twice the legal limit.

Background

The leading cause of death for youths sixteen to nineteen years old is not cancer or heart disease or any other illness that may strike without warning.

Emotional appeal

Position statement

It is driving while under the influence of alcohol. We must do something to stop this slaughter, and we can: Drivers under the age of twenty-one who have a blood alcohol level over the legal limit should immediately lose their licenses, and they should not be allowed to drive again for at least two years.

BODY
Reason
Evidence/ Expert opinion and facts

The most important reason for my proposal is that it will save lives of both drivers and innocent victims. Drunk driving is a tragic mistake at any age, but as Susan and Daniel Cohen write in their book A Six-Pack and a Fake I.D., "Drivers under twenty-one are involved in much more than their share of serious traffic accidents." According to Sandy Golden, author of <u>Driving the Drunk off the Road</u>, of the 25,000 people who are killed every year in drunk driving accidents, one fifth are teenagers.

Reason
Explanation
Evidence/Fact

Another reason is that the penalty can stop dangerous behavior <u>before</u> it happens. Teenagers are not like adults, who may have hardened, hard-to-change habits. Most teens drink, not because they're addicted to alcohol, but because of peer pressure. With the freedom that a driver's license brings, they can go to unchaperoned parties where they drink to prove their new adult status. But if teens knew they could lose this glorious freedom, they would be less likely to take the risk.

Emotional appeal

Opposing position/ Ethical appeal

Some people claim that it's unfair to treat teens differently from others. If eighteen-year-olds are old enough to vote and fight in a war, they argue, then eighteen-year-olds are adults and should have the same rights as adults.

Rebuttal Evidence/Facts

I believe teenagers <u>should</u> be treated differently. As new drinkers, teens don't fully understand the effects of alcohol. They don't know their limits, and they don't realize how alcohol clouds their judgment. To make this shaky condition worse, teens have curfews. Often they rush home, without giving themselves time to sober up.

Emotional appeal

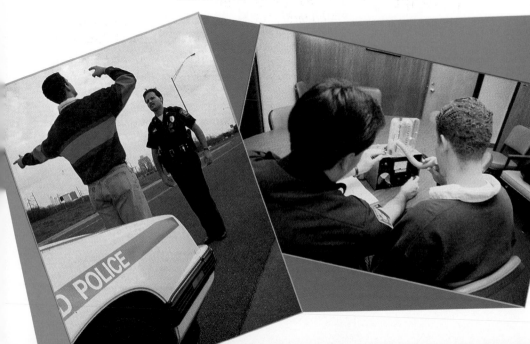

Fact

Moreover, teenagers are breaking the law just by buying and drinking alcohol. They are already different from adults under the law, and they compound their crime when they drink and drive.

Opposing position

Some people argue that teenagers are better drivers than older people. It's generally true that young people have faster reflexes than middle-aged and elderly drivers, but they also have less

Rebuttal

Facts

experience on the road. Some older drivers who are under the influence of alcohol drive slowly; but teenagers, confident in their abilities, tend to be less cautious even when sober. In fact, most alcohol-related collisions involving teens are caused by reckless driving and speeding.

CONCLUSION

Repeat of opinion and call to action

Emotional appeal

We must keep all drunk drivers off the road, and tough penalties for teenagers are a firm step toward that goal. Support a law that gives teenagers a clear message: If you drink, your license is gone. Give them this chance to learn. It may be their last chance at life.

You may have noticed that both of the professional models and the writer's model use contractions. In persuasion, the language of everyday communication helps create a personal appeal. If you were writing a formal argument in school or at work, you might need to use formal language, avoiding contractions and colloquial words.

☞ REFERENCE NOTE: For more information on colloquial language, see pages 486–487.

The author of "A Chance for Life" presented two main reasons and rebutted two opposing positions, but your essay may be different. The issue you've picked will shape your line of reasoning, rebuttal, and organization: Persuasion (like deeply felt opinions) takes many forms. You can, though, use a basic framework like the one below to put your thoughts in order.

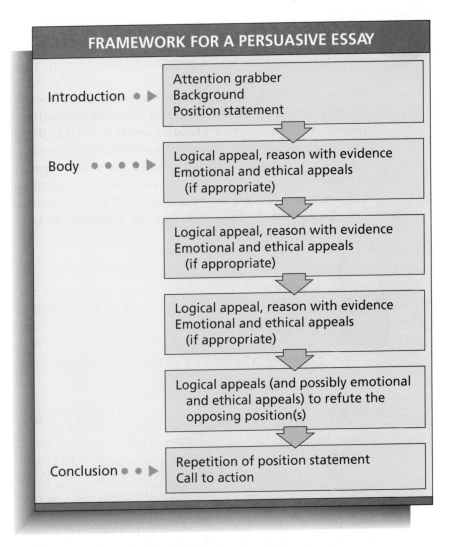

FRAMEWORK FOR A PERSUASIVE ESSAY

Introduction
- Attention grabber
- Background
- Position statement

Body
- Logical appeal, reason with evidence
- Emotional and ethical appeals (if appropriate)

- Logical appeal, reason with evidence
- Emotional and ethical appeals (if appropriate)

- Logical appeal, reason with evidence
- Emotional and ethical appeals (if appropriate)

- Logical appeals (and possibly emotional and ethical appeals) to refute the opposing position(s)

Conclusion
- Repetition of position statement
- Call to action

WRITING ASSIGNMENT

PART 4:
Writing a Draft of Your Persuasive Essay

Now's the time to go back to your chart of support and put your ideas in order. What details can you add to create emotional appeals? How will you order your logical appeals and rebuttal? Make a final plan now. Then, before you write, think of your audience one more time. Picture them. Step into their shoes. What will get them walking in the direction of your ideas? Keep these readers vividly in your mind as you draft.

Evaluating and Revising

When you evaluate a persuasive essay, you check to see whether you have laid out a potent line of reasoning. Is your persuasion foolproof? It probably isn't: A draft is the place to get something *said* so you can then concentrate on the *saying*. Even though your persuasion really can't be foolproof (there are no "true" opinions), an important part of evaluating a persuasive essay is checking your logic and your persuasive powers. You need to take this step in addition to your usual evaluation and revision.

CRITICAL THINKING

Evaluating Your Reasoning

An extremely important part of your persuasive essay is the logical support for your position statement. But here's something to watch out for: *fallacies.* They look like reasons; they sound like reasons. But they're fakes: They're not logical.

These fallacies sometimes work, of course. People who aren't thinking clearly may be convinced, but at least some members of your audience will be reading your essay critically. If critical readers find any of these fallacies, they may decide that you are a sloppy thinker—or a sneaky one. And neither idea will help your case. In your review, be tough on your reasoning, and watch for these fallacies.

1. **Begging the Question.** When you beg a question, you assume something is true that you really need to prove.

Begging the Question:	Our local newspaper's bias against nuclear energy is responsible for public opposition to the proposed plant.
Assumption to Be Proved:	Local newspaper coverage is biased against nuclear energy.

1960 debate between presidential candidates John F. Kennedy and Richard M. Nixon.

2. **Attacking the Person.** The formal name of this fallacy is the *ad hominem* fallacy (literally, "to the person"); informally, it's known as name-calling. You may notice examples of this type of illogical argument during political campaigns when candidates attack their opponents instead of facing issues.

Attacking the Person: People who oppose capital punishment are soft on crime.

Facing the Issue: Some people oppose capital punishment because they think it's an act of vengeance, not punishment.

3. **Hasty Generalization.** A hasty generalization is a conclusion based on insufficient evidence or one that ignores exceptions. Sometimes broad generalizations can be made acceptable by using qualifying words like *most, generally,* and *some.*

Hasty Generalization: Network television focuses on violence, crime, and abnormality.

Acceptable Generalization: Many prime-time network programs focus on violence, crime, and abnormality.

4. **Either-Or Reasoning.** This fallacy assumes that only two extreme alternatives exist for a question or course of action. In most situations, several choices or positions are possible between the extremes.

> **Either-Or Reasoning:** If funding for the space program is cut, the United States will destroy its own future.
>
> **Realistic Reasoning:** If funding for the space program is cut, it will eliminate research now dedicated to solving problems Earth will face in the future.

5. **False Analogy.** Comparing two things that are alike in important ways is an analogy, and it's a good way to make a point swiftly and vividly. A false analogy makes an illogical and misleading link: The similarities are false or trivial.

> **False Analogy:** Putting Native Americans on reservations is like sentencing them to death row.
>
> **Effective Analogy:** A Native American confined to a reservation is like a free horse suddenly tied to a stake.

CRITICAL THINKING EXERCISE:
Evaluating Reasons

See how good you are at catching sloppy, or sneaky, thinking. First, identify which of the five kinds of fallacies each statement is. Then, write a logical reason to replace each fallacy. Write your reasons either in favor of the opinion or against it.

Opinion: Tipping in restaurants should be prohibited.

1. Tipping is so established that all waiters and waitresses expect tips, no matter what service they provide.
2. If tipping continues, employers will never pay waiters and waitresses decent salaries.
3. People who tip simply like to show off how much money they have.
4. We should follow the example of the thrifty people who don't tip.
5. Tipping is like giving a handout to a beggar.

Shoe, by Jeff MacNelly, reprinted by permission: Tribune Media Services.

The following chart will help you evaluate and revise other elements in your essay. Begin by asking yourself a question in the left-hand column. If you find that weakness in your essay, strengthen your paper by using the revision technique suggested in the right-hand column.

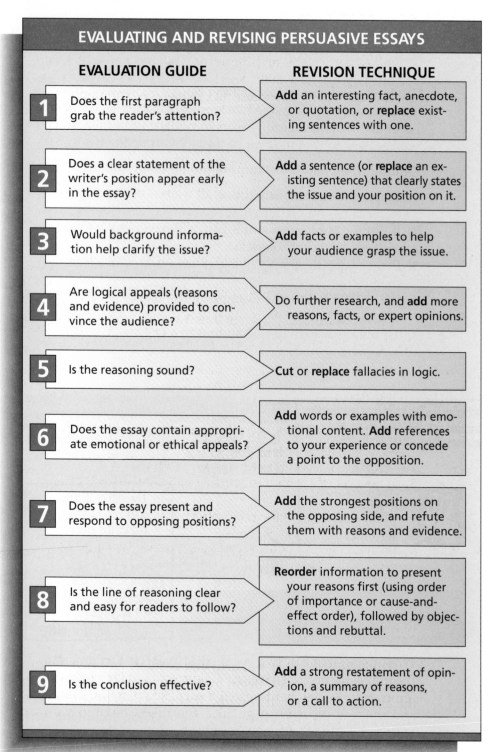

EVALUATING AND REVISING PERSUASIVE ESSAYS

EVALUATION GUIDE	REVISION TECHNIQUE
1 Does the first paragraph grab the reader's attention?	**Add** an interesting fact, anecdote, or quotation, or **replace** existing sentences with one.
2 Does a clear statement of the writer's position appear early in the essay?	**Add** a sentence (or **replace** an existing sentence) that clearly states the issue and your position on it.
3 Would background information help clarify the issue?	**Add** facts or examples to help your audience grasp the issue.
4 Are logical appeals (reasons and evidence) provided to convince the audience?	Do further research, and **add** more reasons, facts, or expert opinions.
5 Is the reasoning sound?	**Cut** or **replace** fallacies in logic.
6 Does the essay contain appropriate emotional or ethical appeals?	**Add** words or examples with emotional content. **Add** references to your experience or concede a point to the opposition.
7 Does the essay present and respond to opposing positions?	**Add** the strongest positions on the opposing side, and refute them with reasons and evidence.
8 Is the line of reasoning clear and easy for readers to follow?	**Reorder** information to present your reasons first (using order of importance or cause-and-effect order), followed by objections and rebuttal.
9 Is the conclusion effective?	**Add** a strong restatement of opinion, a summary of reasons, or a call to action.

EXERCISE 5 ▶ **Analyzing a Writer's Revisions**

Examine the writer's revision of one paragraph of "A Chance for Life" (pages 298–300). Working with a partner or a small group, answer the questions that follow the paragraph to analyze the writer's changes.

> Another reason is that the penalty can
>
> stop dangerous behavior <u>before</u> it happens.
> *(may have hardened, hard-to-change habits.)*
> Teenagers are not like adults, who just can't ⟶ **replace**
>
> ~~change. But some people say punishment~~ ⟶ **cut**
>
> ~~has to be the same for teens and adults.~~ ⟶ **cut**
> *(drink, not because they're) (but because of peer pressure)*
> Most teens aren't addicted to alcohol. With ⟶ **replace/add**
>
> the freedom that a driver's license brings,
> *(can go to unchaperoned parties where they drink)*
> they start drinking to prove their new adult ⟶ **replace**
> *(knew they could lose this glorious freedom,)*
> status. But if teens stand to lose their ⟶ **replace**
>
> ~~licenses~~, they would be less likely to take
>
> the risk.

1. What logical fallacy does the writer avoid by replacing *just can't change* in the second sentence?
2. Why did the writer cut the entire third sentence?
3. Where has the writer strengthened evidence in the paragraph?
4. What's the reason for the replacement in the final sentence?
5. Who do you think is one audience for this writer's essay? Why do you think so?

EXERCISE 6 ▶ **Evaluating and Revising a Persuasive Essay**

Working with one or two classmates, evaluate the beginning of the following persuasive essay. Figure out what changes might improve it. Remember to use the suggestions in the evaluating and revising chart on page 306. You might enjoy discussing your suggestions with another group.

Three minutes between classes isn't enough. If you're not a winner of the 100-yard dash, you're late to class all the time. I know I am. We don't even have time to get to our lockers between classes. I'm tired of dragging all my stuff from one class to the next. We just sprint from one class to the next like jet planes. It's little wonder we sometimes crash in the halls. But don't worry. Your friendly hall supervisor is sure to be sympathetic and give you a nice restful detention-- after school. Stressed-out students, we need to revolt.

GRAMMAR HINT

Varying Sentence Structure

In persuasive writing, the last thing you want to do is bore your readers. But even with an enticing issue and convincing logical, emotional, and ethical appeals, you risk that effect if your sentences are monotonous. The standard English sentence begins with a subject that is closely followed by a verb. To avoid being monotonous, use the following techniques to vary sentence structure.

- Start with a prepositional phrase.

  As new drinkers, teens don't fully understand the effects of alcohol.

- Start with a verbal phrase.

  To make this shaky condition worse, teens have curfews.

- Start with a dependent clause.

  If eighteen-year-olds are old enough to vote and fight in a war, they argue, eighteen-year-olds are adults and should have the same rights as adults.

 REFERENCE NOTE: For more on prepositional phrases, verbal phrases, and dependent clauses, see pages 605–620 and 629–637; for more on improving sentence style, see pages 541–548.

| WRITING ASSIGNMENT | PART 5: **Evaluating and Revising Your Persuasive Essay** |

You are no doubt thoroughly convinced by your paper, but then you're a pushover audience! Try out your logic and emotional appeals on someone else. Exchange essays with a classmate, and use the chart on page 306 to evaluate each other's essays and suggest improvements. After hearing what your partner says, evaluate and revise your own writing.

Proofreading and Publishing

Proofreading.   Evidence of thoroughness and care is important in persuasion, because an error-free paper may make your readers accept your ideas more easily. People who don't agree with your opinion will be looking for all kinds of mistakes in your paper, so don't let them find mistakes in usage, punctuation, and spelling.

Publishing.   Because you can't convince someone who hasn't heard or read what you have to say, publishing is an essential step in persuasive writing. If you didn't have a specific publishing plan as you developed your essay, you need to think of one, perhaps with your teacher's help or the help of an expert you consulted. Also consider these ideas:

- Send a copy of your essay to a national magazine that covers the kind of issue you wrote about.
- Get permission to set up a table outside a supermarket or mall, and hand out copies of your class's essays.
- Present or mail your paper to a local group concerned with the issue.

WRITING ASSIGNMENT

PART 6:
Proofreading and Publishing Your Essay

Don't let all your exploration and thinking remain a private accomplishment. Now is the time to share with others the essay you have created: They'll admire your effort even if you make them mad! Proofread, correct, and publish.

WRITING WORKSHOP

A Persuasive Speech

Another way to take a stand on an issue is to give a speech about it: to persuade both with words and voice. Exactly the same elements occur in a persuasive essay and a persuasive speech, but in a speech you must make a swift connection with your audience—command their interest in some way and make your argument clear on one hearing.

Jesse Jackson, an outstanding speaker of our time, gave the following persuasive speech to a group of young people in 1978. As you read, imagine how Jackson delivered this speech, and notice how he combines logical and emotional appeals.

Keep Your Eyes on the Prize
by Jesse Jackson

Every now and then I hear young people brag about the new generation. It's not really anything to brag about because you didn't do anything to become the new generation. Your parents did something to make the new generation. You are the new generation without effort. So why brag about being *new* when it's not the result of your work? Why brag about being black or white? It's not the result of your work. Your challenge is to become a greater generation. And you become a greater generation because you serve. If you feed more hungry people, you are a greater generation. If more people of this generation are educated, it's a greater generation. If the racial lines that separate us are overcome, you are a greater generation. And so our challenge is to be not just a new generation, based on birth, but to be a greater generation based upon work and effort.

There's always the challenge of concentration. We used to have a saying some years ago in the freedom struggle, "Keep your eyes on the prize." If your prize is to develop your mind; if your prize is to develop your body; if your prize is to develop spiritual depth; if your prize is to grow up healthy, marry, and develop a family — if that is your prize, then don't let any activity divert you from your prize. When we are traveling, sometimes there are bumps in the road. Sometimes there are potholes in the road. Sometimes nails and broken glass may puncture our tire and delay us and divert us from the prize. Keep your eyes on the prize.

from *Jesse Jackson: Still Fighting for the Dream*

1. To what opinion is Jesse Jackson reacting in this speech? Put his position statement into one sentence.
2. Jackson admits that what he is arguing for isn't easy. Where and how does he express the difficulties that his audience may face?
3. What words and phrases have the strongest connotations, positive or negative, for you? What other emotional appeals does Jackson use?
4. Jackson skillfully uses both repetition and subtle variety to emphasize important points. Find some examples of each technique in his speech.

Writing a Speech

 Prewriting. What issue can automatically put energy or an edge into your voice? What worries you or makes you angry? Try to find something that stirs your feelings. You may want to look through your writing journal or think about the last time you had an argument. You can also use a current magazine or newspaper for ideas.

After you have your topic, write a sentence that states your position on it. Do some research if you need to find reasons and evidence to back up your opinion. To get an expert opinion, you may want to talk to a teacher or to another person who is knowledgeable about this issue.

Writing, Evaluating, and Revising. People usually speak from notes. But you need to write out your speech first. Seeing your ideas on paper will help you build a sound argument. When you do your first draft, don't worry about choosing each word carefully. Just get your reasons and evidence down on paper.

When you are ready to evaluate and revise your speech, say it aloud. Listen not just to the ideas, but to how they sound. Vary your sentence structure and use repetition to emphasize important ideas.

Proofreading and Publishing. To get permission to give a speech, you sometimes have to show a group what you're going to say. Proofread your speech carefully, looking for errors in spelling, capitalization, and usage, before you show it to anyone. Since TV and radio stations often provide free time for speeches and announcements in the public interest, consider sending a copy of your speech to the closest television or radio station. If your topic is related to school, you might want to deliver your speech before the student council, school board, or parents and teachers association.

"IF MY MIND CAN CONCEIVE IT, AND MY HEART CAN BELIEVE IT, I KNOW I CAN ACHIEVE IT."

JESSE JACKSON

MAKING CONNECTIONS

PERSUASION ACROSS THE CURRICULUM

Political Cartoons

No one in modern America could doubt the power of visual images to sway our feelings and ideas: We're practically under attack through our eyeballs. But getting a message across with pictures is nothing new. As just one example, political cartoons (or *editorial cartoons*) go back to colonial times. They're still a prominent feature of editorial pages and give us the artists' concise, witty, pointed opinions about breaking events.

Here is a political cartoon by Ben Sargent. What is his opinion about the status of free speech in 1991 America?

Sargent, Copyright 1991. Austin American Statesman. Reprinted

To create your own political cartoon, first find some examples in newspapers or magazines. Study them carefully to see how they create their effects. The cartoons with most impact tend to be simple and direct. Notice that there's a reason for every single detail in a cartoon. Especially notice how the cartoonist draws people. Features are exaggerated to create the personality or feeling that the cartoonist wants to convey. You may find some cartoons with no words at all. Bring your cartoons to class and discuss which ones are most effective. How do the artists make an *idea* clear?

Next, watch or listen to the news for a day or two to find an issue about which you have strong feelings. Write a sentence that expresses your opinion about the issue, and then draw a political cartoon that puts your opinion into pictures.

SPEAKING AND LISTENING

Persuasion in the Media

If there were competitions in the art of persuading, advertisers would probably walk off with most of the prizes. That's because millions of dollars depend on their ability to convince you that you won't be happy until you buy whatever they are selling. Unfortunately for the consumer, advertisers rely more on emotional appeals than on logical appeals. Here are some of the emotional appeals they use:

- The **bandwagon appeal** tries to make you think that you should "jump on the bandwagon," that is, not be left out of what everybody else is doing. Advertisers know that most people don't want to be oddballs. What is an example? *Put on Sound Barrier Blades for your next roll down the street. You don't want to be out of formation when everybody else takes off.*

- *Snob appeal* uses words that appeal to your desire to be famous, wealthy, brainy, witty, and, *especially*, better than other people: *Elegante Inn is the perfect setting for a magnificent vacation. The only kind you deserve.* The opposite of snob appeal is called *plain folks,* and it reinforces down-to-earth values: *For value, versatility, and comfort you can't beat a Bumpo flannel shirt. The design hasn't changed for fifty years, because if it was good enough for our grandfathers, it's best for us.*

- A *veiled threat* cleverly suggests that something bad may happen if you don't buy the product: *If you use Denta-well, you'll know you've done as much as you can to make your teeth last as long as you do.*

Form a "Media Watchers" group, and look for radio, television, and print ads that use one or more of these emotional appeals. Find examples in each medium, and take notes on them or cut them out. Analyze the ads, paying attention to the roles of words, sounds, and images, and rating each ad's persuasiveness. Then give a talk about their logical and emotional appeals.

PERSUASION IN ACTION

Letters to the Editor

Letters to the editor are a form of persuasion that countless people use every day. In fact, many readers turn immediately to the editorial page of a newspaper or the "sound off" page of a magazine: Gripes, outrages, and passions make for lively reading.

Usually, the audience for letters to the editor isn't really the editor; it is the publication's readers, some of whom are bound to care about the same issue that the writer cares about. The writer may be responding to an article or an earlier letter or introducing a totally new issue. Letters to the editor are a great way to express your opinions.

To see what these letters are like, read the ones printed in a local newspaper for several days, or read the ones in several recent issues of a favorite magazine. What ideas do you want to challenge? What issue do you want to bring into the forum?

In writing your letter, apply everything you've learned about persuasion in this chapter, but *be brief.* Publications usually reserve the right to edit, so be your own editor first. Also be sure to read any requirements about form and submission. Mail your letter, and look for it in print. If it's published, bring a copy to class. Check, too, for responses. Other readers may give you a pat on the back or an argument.

Just say no to spending requests

RENOVATION COULD ALTER SITE'S HISTORICAL LEGACY

Council Members Stall Progress With Bitter Debate

PERCEPTIONS OF CANDIDATES FAR FROM REALITY

Asking Questions, Seeking Answers

Out in the dark, silent expanse of outer space, the U.S. spaceship *Voyager 2* travels, sending messages back to earth, shedding light on mysteries of the universe. Human beings have always **asked questions** and **sought answers** for mysteries or problems. As they do, they constantly develop new ideas.

Writing and You. Explorations may start in the mind, but often they turn into an article, an essay, or a book. Thor Heyerdahl asked questions about the seafaring abilities of ancient people and wrote *Kon-Tiki*. A reporter explores problems in education and writes an editorial outlining possible solutions. What about your own explorations—questions you've asked, answers you've found?

As You Read. In the following selection, Annie Dillard wonders about the weather and its effects. Does her exploration lead to answers, or just to more questions?

Isadore Seltzer, *Inner Outer Space* (1984). Acrylic on canvas. 20″ × 30″.

from Pilgrim at Tinker Creek
by Annie Dillard

There are seven or eight
categories of phenomena in the world
that are worth talking about, and one of
them is the weather. Any time you care
to get in your car and drive across the country
and over the mountains, come into our valley, cross
Tinker Creek, drive up the road to the house, walk across the
yard, knock on the door and ask to come in and talk about
the weather, you'd be welcome. If you came tonight from up
north, you'd have a terrific tailwind; between Tinker and Dead
Man you'd chute through the orchardy pass like an iceboat.
When I let you in, we might not be able to close the door. The
wind shrieks and hisses down the valley, sonant and surd, drying
the puddles and dismantling the nests from the trees.

Inside the house, my single goldfish, Ellery Channing, whips around and around the sides of his bowl. Can he feel a glassy vibration, a ripple out of the north that urges him to swim for deeper, warmer waters? Saint-Exupéry says that when flocks of wild geese migrate high over a barnyard, the cocks and even the dim, fatted chickens fling themselves a foot or so into the air and flap for the south. Eskimo sled dogs feed all summer on famished salmon flung to them from creeks. I have often wondered if those dogs feel a wistful downhill drift in the fall, or an upstream yank, an urge to leap ladders, in the spring. To what hail do you hark, Ellery?—what sunny bottom under chill waters, what Chinese emperor's petaled pond? Even the spiders are restless under this wind, roving about alert-eyed over their fluff in every corner.

READER'S RESPONSE

1. Have you ever noticed how often people talk about the weather? Why is it so important to people? Can you remember a time when the weather created a problem, or perhaps solved one, in your life? Explain.
2. Many people like to read Annie Dillard's observations of nature because of her curiosity and her sense of wonder. Did you enjoy reading this piece? Why or why not?
3. Why do you think the goldfish "whips around and around the side of his bowl"? What unexplained animal, bird, or fish behavior have you noted and wondered about?

WRITER'S CRAFT

4. When you write to explore, you may do it to raise questions or to find a new answer. What kind of exploration does Annie Dillard write about?
5. Part of exploring a subject is noticing anomalies, things that are unusual or different. What anomalies does Dillard think might be caused by the wind?

Ways to Explore

Annie Dillard's writing is an example of open-ended exploration: She lets her own curiosity and wonder take over and explores for the sake of exploring. Other writers are often more focused and deliberate; they want to solve a problem or discover a new idea. The explorations may be in writing, or they may take place entirely in the writers' minds. Once the writers find solutions or new ideas, however, they want to inform other people and sometimes even to convince others to do something. Exploratory writing, combined with informative or persuasive writing, may appear in newspapers, magazines, speeches and sermons, business proposals, and books.

There is more than one way that exploratory writing can be developed. Here are some examples of how you might use the four strategies to develop your own explorations.

▶ **Narration:**   tracing the history of your family to discover and explain where your favorite family heirloom came from; studying the events that preceded the Persian Gulf Conflict of 1990–1991 to discover how future international conflicts might be avoided.

Description: describing the symptoms of a sick person over the phone so that a doctor can make a diagnosis; describing the sound your car transmission makes to help your mechanic identify the problem.

▶ **Classification:**   comparing and contrasting two possible solutions to school overcrowding; looking at three classes of cafeteria lunches—salad bar, hot-food bar, and sandwich bar— as you explore solutions to the problem of low student interest in cafeteria food.

Evaluation: asking questions about three recent presidents of the United States and identifying what personal and professional characteristics to look for in our next president; explaining why your football team did so poorly (or so well) last season and explaining how the team might improve (or maintain excellence).

LOOKING
AHEAD

In this chapter, you'll learn the process of exploration and discovery. The main writing assignment takes the form of a problem-solution essay. You'll use the strategies of narration and classification to explore the problem. Later, as you discuss possible solutions to the problem, you'll use mostly the strategy of narration. As you work through the main writing assignment, keep in mind that in a problem-solution essay, the writer

- identifies and explores a problem
- proposes and evaluates solutions to the problem
- explains (and proves) the best solution to the problem

"Problems are only opportunities in work clothes."

Henry J. Kaiser

Writing a Problem-Solution Essay

Prewriting

Exploring Problems

When you use writing to explore, you often do so for personal reasons. Maybe you've used your diary or journal to explore the solutions to a personal problem—a disagreement with a friend, for example. You probably don't share that kind of personal exploration with an audience. Instead, you consider what you've learned and act on it.

At times, however, you may be called upon to explore a problem and present your findings to an audience. When that happens, you're usually expected to think through the problem and its possible solutions carefully. And you are expected to explain clearly to your audience why the solution you propose is an effective one. In school, this kind of audience-directed exploratory writing is often called a *problem-solution essay.* It has two basic aims. The first aim is to explore the problem and all its possible solutions in order to identify the best one. Then, as you write the essay, your aim shifts to one of explaining, and proving, the advantages of the solution (or solutions) you decide is best.

Identifying a Problem

The personal problems you explore may have meaning only to you: *How am I ever going to get money together for gas this week?* The problem you write about for an audience, however, should be significant not only to you but to others. "My split ends and what to do about them" is not an appropriate topic for a serious problem-solution essay, except, perhaps, for a hairstylist. On the other hand, you don't want to choose a problem that even the best minds have been unable to solve satisfactorily. "Achieving world peace in our time" is probably too tough to handle.

If you're concerned about a national or international issue, you may want to follow the advice "Think globally; act locally." For example, if you're concerned about world hunger, focus your attention on the problem of hunger in your community. Many writers find it rewarding to work with problems that directly affect them or people they know well.

> *Perhaps you're concerned about something at school:* Does the band need new uniforms? Are there too many students in classes at your school?
>
> *You may be concerned about something that's happening in your community:* Do the parks need cleaning up? Are there enough street lights?

As you brainstorm for problems, consider the significance of each one by asking

- Does it affect a number of people?
- Is it important to the people that it affects?

EXERCISE 1 ▶ **Speaking and Listening: Identifying Problems**

One way to learn about problems of local concern is to tune in to local news and commentary on radio and TV. If a local station has a listener or viewer call-in show, you may want to make a point to watch or listen during those hours—perhaps even call in with your own views. Follow the news for an evening or two to identify problems in your community. Make a list of three or four problems and share them in class discussion. Which ones are important to a number of people?

Investigating a Problem

You can't begin to solve a problem that you don't understand. The following questions will help you investigate the problem you've chosen.

- Who or what is directly affected by this problem?
- How does this problem affect them?
- What causes the problem? Is there more than one cause?
- Is this problem like any other problem? Is it related to another problem?

Usually you won't have the answers to all of these questions—you'll need to do some research. You can use the library to find out how widespread the problem is or do some personal or telephone interviewing with people who have expert knowledge about the problem. For example, if you think there aren't enough street lights in your neighborhood, check out other neighborhoods. Or, ask a local police officer if poor lighting contributes to the crime or accident rate in the community.

WRITING ASSIGNMENT

PART 1:

Identifying and Investigating a Problem

What's bothering you? Start with your list from Exercise 1, and brainstorm a list of problems that affect your school and community, as well as some national and international problems. Then evaluate the problems to decide which one would make the best topic and find out as much as you can about it. Use the list of questions above to guide your search for information.

Prewriting

Exploring Solutions

How much information do you have about your problem? Could you talk about it for ten or fifteen minutes? Would you be able to answer someone's questions about the background to the problem? If you've thoroughly investigated your problem, you're ready to move on to the answers.

Identifying Possible Solutions

Most problems have more than one possible solution, and many of these solutions may have already been tried. Still, it is always possible to devise creative solutions to problems that seem to defy solution. Continue your exploration by finding out how others have tried to solve the problem and how effective these solutions have been. To find information, you may again have to do some interviewing, viewing, listening, or reading. A questioning strategy can help you analyze possible solutions.

STRATEGIES FOR ANALYZING POSSIBLE SOLUTIONS

Ideas of Others
1. What solutions to the problem have already been tried?
2. How effective have these solutions been?
3. What solutions are currently being proposed?

Your Own Ideas
1. Can some of the problem's causes be eliminated? How?
2. What can be done about the effects of the problem?
3. Is there any part of the problem that seems especially difficult to solve?
4. Which part of the problem is easiest to solve? Why?
5. What is the most unusual way you can think of to solve the problem? the easiest way? the most popular way?

As you answer some of these questions, you may discover your own solutions. For example, one writer used two of the questions as prompts for focused freewriting about the problem of homelessness. Notice that the writer isn't evaluating the solutions yet, just trying to come up with ideas.

HERE'S HOW

<u>Can some of the causes of homelessness be eliminated? How?</u>

One cause of homelessness is a lack of low-cost housing. We could eliminate this lack by building more low-cost housing, but where would the money come from? Maybe there could be a special tax on every real estate transaction. Maybe we wouldn't even need to build more low-cost housing if we just fixed up what we already have. Maybe a program like Habitat for Humanity to help rehab existing properties as well as build new ones?

<u>What is the strangest way you can think of to solve the problem?</u>

Maybe the local government could pay people to take homeless families into their homes. This might help some marginal families earn more money so they wouldn't become homeless, too. This could provide a role model for the homeless, too. But could complete strangers get along?

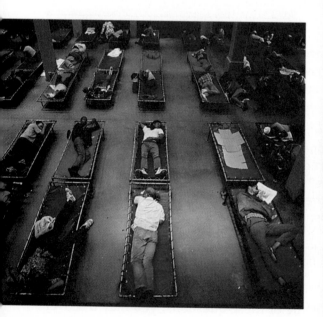

PART 2:
Identifying Possible Solutions

Find out how many minds have tried to solve your problem and how effective they have been. Using the strategies on page 327, analyze the solutions other people have proposed—and remember that this process of analysis may require some further research on your part. Then search for your own solutions, using brainstorming or freewriting to come up with as many solutions as possible. Save your list for later use.

Finding the Best Solution

In the search for possible solutions to a problem, you may find several. But all solutions (just like all apples in the barrel) are not created equal. Which is the best one? How do you begin to decide which solutions to discard when there is no single solution that is CLEARLY THE BEST? Following are three questions you can ask yourself to try to sort through the solutions you are considering:

1. **What are the strengths and weaknesses (or advantages and disadvantages) of each solution?** To find the answer to this question, list all the possible solutions you've identified. Then create a chart in which you list the strengths and weaknesses of each solution. Which solutions start to look better than others?
2. **Which solution is the most practical?** Often, the best solution is the most practical one: It can be put into effect easily, and it doesn't create more problems than it solves. If you have several solutions that look equally strong or equally weak, look to see which one is the most practical.
3. **Does any solution have a comparative advantage?** Sometimes one solution appears to be the fairest one: It will actually do the most good for the most people. In that case it has a comparative advantage. If an analysis of strengths and weaknesses and practicality doesn't identify a single "best" solution, look at the solution that does the most good for the most people.

The following chart shows how one writer found the best solution to the pet overpopulation problem.

HERE'S HOW

Problem: Many animals are killed at the local animal shelter every week because nobody wants them.

Possible Solutions	Strengths	Weaknesses
educate public	increases public awareness	doesn't target pet owners; facts impersonal and abstract
encourage adoption from animal shelters	fewer animals must be killed	too many animals; each family of four would need to adopt 28 dogs and cats
encourage pet owners to spay and neuter animals	gets at pet owners; works in communities with active Humane Society programs—they report 30–60% fewer euthanized animals	cost of operation; 6 to 7 million animals still put to death each year
provide low-cost spay/neuter programs	lower cost $50–$100; 15 yrs. after first spay/neuter clinic in Los Angeles, shelter animals decrease from 150,000 to 80,000	some people still don't spay and neuter pets; still 60,000 animals killed per yr. in Los Angeles
pass a law requiring pet owners to spay/neuter pets	covers all pets; makes owners responsible; makes noncompliance more costly than compliance; San Mateo, Calif., passed a similar law	drastic action that infringes on personal freedom

Practicality

The solution of only encouraging adoptions from the shelters is not practical; number of abandoned animals too high. That eliminates that solution.

Comparative Advantage

Law requiring pet owners to spay and neuter their pets seems to be the fairest solution; also seems to do the most good for the most animals—seems to be the best solution, because it's the only way to counteract irresponsible behavior of some pet owners.

Notice that the strengths and weaknesses listed by the chart's writer include solid facts and sound reasons that are as specific as possible. Because two solutions may be inexpensive, listing *it won't cost much* as an advantage for each won't help you to decide between the two. But listing *the cost to the average taxpayer would be only about fifty-five cents per year* for one and *the cost to the average taxpayer would be only about a dollar per year* for the other would help. Again, finding this information may require that you do outside research.

EXERCISE 2 ▶ **Evaluating Possible Solutions**

You are the director of youth services in your community, and this problem has come to your attention: Teenagers don't have very many places to go at night.

In the following chart, several possible solutions and some of their strengths and weaknesses are listed. Think of at least one other possible solution and add it to the list. And, if you see strengths or weaknesses in addition to those already listed, make a note of these as well. Use the criteria of *practicality* and *most good for the most people* to evaluate all possible solutions and then select the one that you feel is best. Be prepared to explain your decision to others in your class.

Possible Solutions	Strengths	Weaknesses
open the community center in the evening	programs and facilities already in place	additional staff and operating expenses for extended hours; not just for teens
recruit teen-oriented businesses like a "juice bar" for the community	new, different types of activities; might increase commercial revenues	recruiting may take a long time; costs may keep some teens from using
encourage existing programs (Scouts; church, synagogue, and school groups; YMCA; Rec. Dept.) to offer more teen programming	programs already in existence; variety of groups meets a variety of needs	need added commitment from adult volunteers; limited outreach to those not already involved

Listing Necessary Steps

Don't put away your thinking cap just because you've identified the best solution. You still have to think through the steps that will be needed to put your idea into action. Think in specific, practical terms. "First, get a million dollars" is not very helpful advice. You must decide exactly what has to be done, how it is to be done, and in what order it is to be done. For example, getting a spay/neuter law passed might involve these steps:

1. Propose a law that (a) requires all pet owners to have their dogs and cats spayed or neutered, (b) makes an exception for professional breeders but requires them to purchase a special breeding license, and (c) imposes stiff fines for those who break the law.
2. Make people aware of the need for spaying and neutering, and gather support for such a law.
3. Convince officials that most citizens support such a law.

To explore a problem and find a solution

- choose a problem that is significant but solvable
- investigate the problem to see what its causes and effects are
- identify a number of possible solutions, including both your own ideas and the ideas of others
- identify the best solution by looking at strengths and weaknesses, practicality, and comparative advantages

---

WRITING ASSIGNMENT

PART 3:

Identifying Your Best Solution and Listing Necessary Steps

So, what's your answer? Take time to evaluate all your possible solutions carefully and identify the best solution to your problem. Use a chart like the one in the Here's How on page 330 to identify strengths and weaknesses, practicality, and comparative value. Then make a list of the steps necessary to carry out this solution. Try to arrange these steps in the order they'll need to be done.

Prewriting

Planning Your Problem-Solution Essay

Up to this point you have been exploring the problem and its possible solutions. Now your attention will shift to the planning of your paper.

Considering Your Purpose, Audience, and Tone

Purpose.   You have gone through the stages in which your purpose is to explore the problem. Now, as you get ready to write your essay, your purpose shifts to explaining the problem and its solution(s) to your readers. You've been asking *What is the solution to this problem?* Now your question is *How can I prove to my audience that this solution is the best?*

Audience.   Your audience becomes really important at this point, and answering these questions will help you address their concerns:

- *Who is the audience?* It may be your teacher and other students in your class, but there are other possible audiences as well. Who would have a vested interest in solving this problem? Who would have the power to solve this problem?
- *What do your readers already know about this problem? How do they react to it?* If your audience isn't personally affected by the problem, you may have to spend more time showing them that the problem really exists and that it's important to solve it.
- *What solutions might your audience favor?* Some readers may favor a solution you've rejected. In this case, you'll need to explain the disadvantages of your rejected solutions carefully.
- *What objections might your audience have to your solution?* Some readers may be quick to point out the flaws in your solution, so you'll need to explain its value thoroughly and attempt to answer their objections.

Tone. Your exploration has been thorough and objective, and you want your essay to reflect that attitude, so use objective language as you write. Stay away from words that carry emotional overtones. But since you're recounting a personal exploration (your own investigation), put yourself into your writing by using the first person pronoun *I*. This will make your exploration and explanation seem credible to your audience. It will also make your problem-solution essay sound more informal than some other types of expository essays.

"Will the reader turn the page?"

Catherine Drinker Bowen

Providing Support

When you present the problem you have identified and the solution you think is best in your essay, you have two tasks:

- explain the problem and solution to your audience
- prove to your audience that the problem is serious and that your solution will work

Your audience won't automatically accept the seriousness of the problem or the solution you propose. They may say, "Why should I worry about how to solve this problem? How do you know this is the best solution?" To convince your audience, you need to provide reasons and evidence, or proof, that you are right. Reasons, facts, statistics, and examples will help you build a solid case for the seriousness of the problem and the desirability of your solution.

Where do you find reasons and evidence to support the solution you have chosen? When you are investigating the problem and exploring possible solutions—looking at strengths and weaknesses, practicality, and comparative advantage—you are (whether you realize it or not) identifying bits and pieces of evidence. As you plan your essay, you can go back and look at those reasons and pieces of evidence and write down the ones that would be convincing to your audience. You may also need to do some research to identify additional reasons, examples, or facts and statistics that show the seriousness of the problem and that support the solution you have identified.

CRITICAL THINKING

Evaluating Evidence

When you *evaluate* something, you judge whether it measures up to a set of criteria or standards. For example, to evaluate a TV, you might measure it against these criteria: price, length of warranty, quality of color, and repair record. When you are looking for support for a problem-solution essay, you may also need to evaluate your evidence (your facts, statistics, and examples). To be acceptable, your evidence must meet these criteria:

1. The evidence should be **trustworthy.** It should be from sources that are reliable, sources with reputations for integrity such as *The New York Times, Time, Newsweek*, the Gallup Poll, and many individual "experts."
2. The evidence should be **accurate.** Even the best sources sometimes make errors, so learn to question the information you find. If a fact or statistic seems unlikely, check its accuracy in a second source. Also, be certain that you copy facts and statistics correctly.
3. The evidence should be **useful,** or relevant. Evidence that is both trustworthy and accurate may not be useful. Useful evidence has a logical connection to your problem or solution. It helps to prove your point.

CRITICAL THINKING EXERCISE:
Evaluating Evidence

A writer is exploring the problem of teachers' lack of time for class preparation. The solution that has been proposed is "Use parent volunteers to serve as class sponsors, reading tutors, and library aides, thus freeing teachers from these responsibilities." Following is the evidence gathered by the writer to support this solution. Based on the information you've just read, how acceptable is the evidence? Get together with a partner and weigh each piece of evidence against the three criteria—trustworthiness, accuracy, and usefulness.

1. Parent volunteers would save teachers more than forty-four hours per week.
2. An article in *The Washington Post* says that volunteerism is up all over the country.
3. One parent has donated money for an informational mailing to all parents.
4. A federally funded study of education says that teachers have too many nonclassroom duties to perform.
5. A survey of teachers in the school indicates that 88 percent of them support the plan.

WRITING ASSIGNMENT

PART 4:

Planning Your Problem-Solution Essay

Now take the time to pull together the results of your own exploration and create a plan for your essay. First, list the problem, your solution, and the steps needed to implement it. Then, look at your evaluation of possible solutions (Writing Assignment, Part 3) and list any evidence that would support your solution. If necessary, do some additional research to identify more reasons, examples, facts, and statistics. Add those to your list of support. Don't forget to include information that will help you respond to any objections your audience might have. Finally, list the possible solutions you have rejected and the major disadvantage of each.

Writing Your First Draft

The Basic Elements of a Problem-Solution Essay

Like many other essays, a problem-solution paper can follow several different patterns. However, most problem-solution essays contain the following elements:

- an explanation of the problem
- evidence of the problem's seriousness
- a description of the proposed solution
- a list of steps to implement the solution
- evidence to support the solution and counter possible objections
- discussion of the advantages and disadvantages of other solutions

Like other types of essays, the problem-solution essay often begins with some sort of attention grabber. This may be especially important to do if your audience isn't really convinced that a problem even exists. The problem-solution essay may end with a call to action—telling readers what they can do to help—or it may end with a simple restatement of the proposed solution and its advantages.

In the following essay, Shannon Long discusses the problem that she and other students faced on her college campus. The problem is not a unique one. It is faced by many students and workers on campuses and in office buildings across the country. What solution to the problem does Long propose?

A PROBLEM-SOLUTION ESSAY

Wheelchair Hell: A Look at Campus Accessibility
by Shannon Long

INTRODUCTION
Personal anecdote

Attention grabber

It was my first week of college, and I was going to the library to meet someone on the third floor and study. After entering the library, I went to the elevator and hit the button calling it. A few seconds later the doors opened, I rolled inside, and the doors closed behind me. Expecting the buttons to be down in front, I suddenly noticed that they were behind me — and too high to reach. There I was stuck in the elevator with no way to get help. Finally, someone got on at the fourth floor. I'd been waiting fifteen minutes.

BODY
Statement of problem

I'm not the only one who has been a victim of inaccessibility. The University of Kentucky currently has twelve buildings that are inaccessible to students in wheelchairs (Karnes). Many other buildings, like the library, are accessible, but have elevators that are inoperable by handicapped students. Yet, Section 504 of the Rehabilitation Act of 1973 states that

> No qualified handicap person shall, because a recipient's facilities are inaccessible to or unusable by handicapped persons, be denied the benefits of, be excluded from participation in, or otherwise be subjected to discrimination under any program or activity receiving Federal financial assistance (Federal 22681).

When this law went into effect in 1977, the University of Kentucky started a renovation process in which close to a million dollars was spent on handicap modifications (Karnes). But even though that much money has been spent, there are still

Examples/
seriousness of
problem

many more modifications needed. Buildings still inaccessible to wheelchair students are the Administration Building, Alumni House, Barker Hall, Bowman Hall, Bradley Hall, Engineering Quadrangle, Gillis Building, Kinkead Hall, Miller Hall, Safety and Security Building, and Scovell Hall (Transition).

So many inaccessible buildings creates many unnecessary problems. For example, if a handicapped student wants to meet an administrator, he or she must make an appointment to meet somewhere more accessible than the Administration Building. Making appointments is usually not a problem, but there is still the fact that able-bodied students have no problem entering the Administration Building while handicapped students cannot. Though handicapped students can enter the Gillis Building, they cannot go above the ground floor and even have to push a button to get someone to come downstairs to help them. Finally, for handicapped students to get counseling from the Career Planning Center, they must set up an appointment to meet with someone at another place. In this case, some students might not use the Center's services because of the extra effort involved (Croucher).

Examples/Extent
of problem

Even many of the accessible buildings have elevators, water fountains, and door handles that are inoperable by handicapped students (Karnes).

Elevators in the Library and Whitehall Classroom Building, for instance, have buttons too high for wheelchair students, forcing them to ask somebody else to hit the button. If there is nobody around to ask, the handicapped person simply has to wait. In the Chemistry and Physics Building, a key is needed to operate the elevator, forcing wheelchair students to ride up and down the hall to find somebody to help. Many water fountains are inaccessible to people in wheelchairs. Some buildings have only *one* accessible water fountain. Finally, hardly any buildings have doorknobs that students with hand and arm impairments can operate.

Many residence halls, such as Boyd Hall, Donovan Hall, Patterson Hall, and Keenland Hall, are also completely inaccessible. If a handicapped student wanted to drop by and see a friend or attend a party in one of these dorms, he or she would have to be carried up steps. Kirivan and Blanding Towers have bathrooms that are inaccessible. Also, in Kirivan Tower the elevator is so small that someone has to lift the back of the chair into the elevator. The complex lowrises—Shawneetown, Commonwealth Village, and Cooperstown Apartments—are also inaccessible. Cooperstown has some first floor apartments that are accessible, but a handicapped student couldn't very well live there because the bathrooms are inaccessible. All eleven sororities are inaccessible, and only five of the sixteen fraternities are accessible. Since the land sororities and fraternities are on is owned by U.K., Section 504 does require that houses be accessible (Transition 14, 15).

With so many U.K. places still inaccessible, it is obvious that hundreds of modifications need to be done. According to Jake Karnes, the Assistant Dean of Students and the Director of handicap Student Services, "It will probably take close to a million dollars to make U.K. totally accessible." U.K.'s current budget allows for just $10,000 per year to go toward handicap modification (Karnes).

Current solution

Disadvantage

Proposed solution
Advantage

Steps necessary
for implementation

Answer to possible
objections

If no other money source is sought, the renovation process could be strung out for many years.

A possible solution could be the use of the tuition. If only $2 could be taken from each student's tuition, there would be almost $50,000 extra per semester for handicap modification. Tuition is already used to pay for things ranging from teacher salaries to the funding of the campus radio station. This plan could be started with the beginning of the 1990 Fall semester. The money could be taken from each of the existing programs the tuition now pays for, so there would be no need for an increase in tuition. Also, this would not be a permanent expense because with an extra $50,000 a semester, all of the needed modifications could be finished in ten years. After that, the amount taken from the tuition could be lowered to fifty cents to help cover upkeep of campus accessibility. This plan is practical — but more important, it is ethical. Surely if part of our tuition goes to fund a radio station, some of it can be used to make U.K. a more accessible place. Which is more important, having a radio station to play alternative music or having a campus that is accessible to all students?

CONCLUSION

June 1980 was the deadline for meeting the requirements of Section 504 (Robinson 28). In compliance with the law, the University of Kentucky has spent close to a million dollars making

Restatement of proposed solution

its campus more accessible. But there are still many more changes needed. These changes will take a lot of money, but if two dollars could be used out of each student's tuition, the money would be there. Handicapped students often work to overachieve to prove their abilities. All they ask for is a chance, and that chance should not be blocked by high buttons, heavy doors, or steps.

Works Cited

Croucher, Lisa. "Accessibility at U.K. for Handicapped Still Can Be Better." *Kentucky Kernal.* Date unknown.

Federal Register. Volume 42 (4 May 1977):22681.

Karnes, Jake. Personal Interview. 17 Oct. 1989.

Robinson, Rita. "For the Handicapped: Renovation Report Card." *American School & University* (Apr. 1980):28.

University of Kentucky — Transition Plan. [report]. Date unknown.

EXERCISE 3 ▶ **Analyzing a Problem-Solution Essay**

Read and review Shannon Long's essay (pages 338–342) before meeting with two or three classmates to discuss these questions.

1. Who is the intended audience for the essay? Explain your answer.
2. What technique does Long use to get her readers' attention and to increase their awareness of the problem?
3. How does Long establish that the problem is a serious one?
4. What comparative advantage does Long's proposed solution have over the current solution? What other strengths does Long's proposed solution have?
5. What are the disadvantages of Long's solution? How does she address possible objections on the basis of those disadvantages?

A Basic Framework for a Problem-Solution Essay

Although the problem-solution essay can follow several different patterns, the following Writer's Model illustrates one basic pattern. You might want to follow this pattern when you write your own essay.

A WRITER'S MODEL

Pet Overpopulation in Cranford County

INTRODUCTION
Attention-grabbing facts

I had heard the statistics. I knew, for example, that only one out of four puppies born in the United States actually finds a home. I knew that about fifteen million pet animals are brought to municipal and private animal shelters each year. I knew it, but these statistics didn't really make an impact on me until I went to the county animal shelter last Thursday to adopt a cat. There I was faced with how serious the pet overpopulation problem really is.

Statement of the problem

Anecdote illustrating problem

In the shelter that day, there were eighteen adult dogs, twenty-seven puppies, thirteen adult cats, and twenty-nine kittens. By Saturday morning, most of them would be gone, but they would not be missing because someone adopted them. They would be gassed because no one wanted them. By the next Friday, the shelter would be full again. On Saturday, the gas chamber would be full again, too.

I was horrified. I had always assumed that animals taken to the local shelter were adopted. I think most people assume that. But that's not the case. According to its director, Madge Simmons, our local shelter takes in from fifty to eighty animals in any given week. A small percentage of those animals--on the average three or four per week--turn out to be lost, and their owners claim them. Sometimes as many as five animals are adopted in a week. The rest are kept from seven to ten days and then destroyed.

**BODY
Evidence of
seriousness and
extent of problem**

But this is just one of the awful consequences of the pet overpopulation problem. Many unwanted animals never make it to the relatively humane conditions in the shelter. They are dumped along the highways in rural areas and left to starve. The people who dump them may believe they are giving the dogs or cats a chance at survival. But the animals' chances may be much better at the shelter. Local veterinarian Dr. Kanzer estimates that fewer than one in fifty abandoned dogs survives longer than six months. The odds are not much better for cats. And death for an abandoned animal is often prolonged and painful.

Possible solution

In the past, various solutions have been tried to solve the pet overpopulation problem. Groups such as the American Humane Association have tried to educate the public about pet overpopulation through pamphlets and news releases. Unfortunately, many people, like me, hear the numbers but the problem remains abstract to them. These groups have also promoted adoption programs for abandoned animals. But according to a pamphlet from our local shelter, to give every cat and dog alive in our country at this moment a home, every individual in the United States would have to adopt at least seven animals. That's twenty-eight animals for a typical family of four. Clearly, this is not a practical solution.

**Disadvantage
Possible solution**

Disadvantage

Possible solution

Encouraging the voluntary spaying and neutering of pets is another possible solution. Educating pet owners targets those with the ability and responsibility to act. If pet owners understand that unrestricted breeding is a kind of animal murder, then they will see the importance of spaying and neutering their pets. Many people, however, who intend to have their cats or dogs spayed will put off the operation when they discover the cost at the local veterinarian's office. For these people, programs such as our own shelter's low-cost spay and neuter program are a solution. But in cities with low-cost spay and neuter programs such as Los Angeles, even this solution doesn't go far enough. Some people simply refuse to cooperate. They think of their animals as property that they have a right to control. Or they want their pets to experience the "miracle of birth." Or they just procrastinate.

Disadvantage

Possible solution

Disadvantage

Only one solution can meet the magnitude of the pet overpopulation problem and counteract the irresponsible behavior of some pet owners. The solution is a law that takes the good, but inadequate, voluntary solutions of the past a step further by making them mandatory. Under this law, owners, except licensed breeders, must have their pets spayed or neutered or face a stiff fine if they do not. A recent survey by the Cranford County Gazette indicates that almost 65 percent of the county's pet owners support such a law. And the current participation of veterinarians in our low-cost spay/neuter clinics suggests that they, too, are in favor of the law. Also, the mechanism for carrying it out--the clinics--is already in place.

Explanation of comparative advantage

Evidence/ Statistic

Evidence/Fact

CONCLUSION
Answers possible objections

Necessary steps

Restatement of proposed solution

Although this solution may seem a bit drastic, it is not as drastic as sending hundreds of unwanted animals to the gas chamber each year. The major hurdle is convincing our local officials to pass such a law. First, we have to propose the law in a public forum and convince the general public that it will help solve our pet overpopulation problem. Once we can demonstrate public support for the law, our local officials will also see the benefits and move ahead to pass the ordinance. The animals who suffer and die daily can't speak for themselves. A spay and neuter ordinance would let the law speak for them.

"Pet Overpopulation in Cranford County" uses the following framework. You might follow it as you write your first draft.

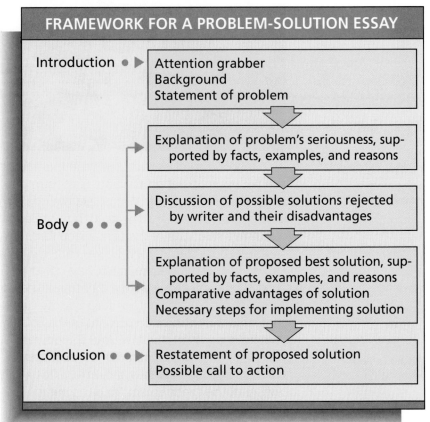

FRAMEWORK FOR A PROBLEM-SOLUTION ESSAY

Introduction ● ▶ | Attention grabber
Background
Statement of problem

Explanation of problem's seriousness, supported by facts, examples, and reasons

Discussion of possible solutions rejected by writer and their disadvantages

Body ● ● ● ●

Explanation of proposed best solution, supported by facts, examples, and reasons
Comparative advantages of solution
Necessary steps for implementing solution

Conclusion ● ● ▶ | Restatement of proposed solution
Possible call to action

WRITING
NOTE In "Wheelchair Hell," Shannon Long uses parenthetical citations and a list of Works Cited to tell
readers where she got her information. The
Writer's Model, "Pet Overpopulation in Cranford County," credits
its information sources more informally by naming the sources
within the paper. Either form is acceptable as long as you acknowledge your sources. (For more help with crediting sources,
see Chapter 11, Writing a Research Paper.)

**WRITING
ASSIGNMENT**

PART 5:
Writing a Draft of Your Essay

Now you can put your exploration to good use as you attempt
to explain why your solution is a good one. As you write your
first draft, remember to use solid evidence to back up your
explanation. Also, think about how you can best show that the
problem is serious and that your proposed solution is both
good and workable.

PEANUTS reprinted by permission of UFS, Inc.

Evaluating and Revising

Any first draft is just a starting point. You always need to evaluate the strengths and weaknesses in what you've written. Even if you do find problems, however, your revision solutions needn't be as drastic as those suggested in the following cartoon. Consider *adding, cutting, replacing,* and *reordering* before exploding. (And remember: It's usually very helpful to have someone else read your writing and offer suggestions for improvement. Many professional writers would be lost without their editors!)

© John Caldwell 1991.

The following chart can be used to evaluate and revise problem-solution essays. Start by asking yourself the question in the left-hand column. If the answer is no, you can use the revision technique suggested in the right-hand column.

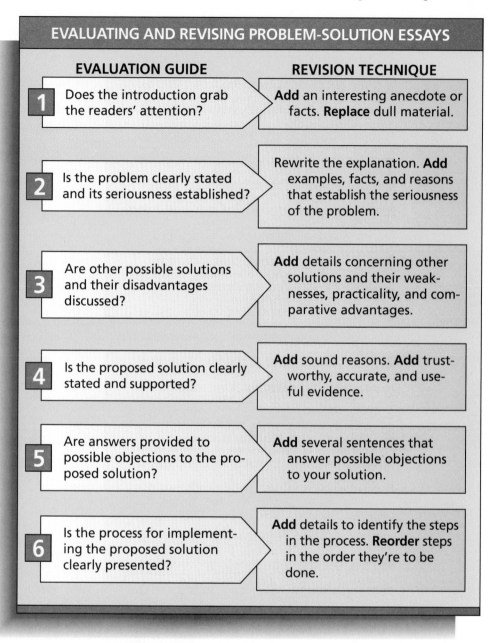

EVALUATING AND REVISING PROBLEM-SOLUTION ESSAYS

EVALUATION GUIDE	REVISION TECHNIQUE
1 Does the introduction grab the readers' attention?	**Add** an interesting anecdote or facts. **Replace** dull material.
2 Is the problem clearly stated and its seriousness established?	Rewrite the explanation. **Add** examples, facts, and reasons that establish the seriousness of the problem.
3 Are other possible solutions and their disadvantages discussed?	**Add** details concerning other solutions and their weaknesses, practicality, and comparative advantages.
4 Is the proposed solution clearly stated and supported?	**Add** sound reasons. **Add** trustworthy, accurate, and useful evidence.
5 Are answers provided to possible objections to the proposed solution?	**Add** several sentences that answer possible objections to your solution.
6 Is the process for implementing the proposed solution clearly presented?	**Add** details to identify the steps in the process. **Reorder** steps in the order they're to be done.

E X E R C I S E **4** ▶ **Analyzing a Writer's Revisions**

Following is a revised draft of the last two paragraphs of "Pet Overpopulation in Cranford County" (pages 345–346). Working with some classmates, figure out how the revisions improve the paragraphs. Then answer the questions that follow.

*Only one solution can meet the magnitude
of the pet overpopulation problem and*

~~To~~ counteract the irresponsible behavior   **replace**

The solution is

of some pet owners, ~~we need~~ a law that takes   **add/replace**

the good, but inadequate, voluntary solutions

of the past a step further by making them

mandatory. Under this law, owners, except

licensed breeders, must have their pets

spayed or neutered or face a stiff fine if they

do not. A recent survey by the Cranford

65

County <u>Gazette</u> indicates that almost ~~90~~   **replace**

the county's pet owners support such a law.

percent of ~~registered voters own pets~~. And   **replace**

the current participation of veterinarians in

our low-cost spay/neuter clinics suggests that

they, too, are in favor of the law. Also, the

mechanism for carrying it out--the clinics--

is already in place.

        Although this solution may seem a bit

⌃ *it is not as drastic as sending hundreds of unwanted animals to the gas chamber*

drastic ~~to some people, it is not~~. The major *each year*   **replace**

hurdle is convincing our local officials to

pass such a law. Once we can demonstrate

public support for the law, our local officials

will also see the benefits and move ahead to

First,

pass the ordinance. We have to propose the   **add/reorder**

law in a public forum and convince the

general public that it will help solve our pet

overpopulation problem. The animals who

suffer and die daily can't speak for them-

selves. A spay and neuter ordinance would

let the law speak for them.

1. Why did the writer add the new information and create a new sentence at the beginning of the first paragraph? How does this sentence make a connection to other possible solutions?
2. In the third sentence, why did the writer replace the words *90 percent of registered voters own pets* with the words *65 percent of the county's pet owners support such a law*? (How did the change strengthen the evidence?)
3. Why did the writer revise the sentence at the beginning of the second paragraph? How is this a better answer to possible objections?
4. Why did the writer reorder the two sentences in the second paragraph?

PART 6:
Evaluating and Revising Your Essay

You may, of course, use the Evaluating and Revising Chart (page 349) as a guide to revise the draft of your essay. However, after you have made those changes, you might still benefit from feedback. Why not ask at least one classmate who is interested in the problem you've explored to read your draft and make suggestions? Based on your reader's responses, make any changes that you feel are necessary.

Proofreading and Publishing

Proofreading. By now you know the importance of proof-reading your final draft to find and correct careless mistakes in grammar, usage, or mechanics. Most writers feel about their manuscripts the way parents do about their children. They don't want to send them out into the world without their hair combed and their teeth brushed.

Publishing. But where can you send your essay? You might want to consider how you can best reach the people with the power to solve the problem. Perhaps you can do that in one of these ways:

- ask the editor of the school newspaper or the local news-paper to publish your essay as a column on the Op-Ed page
- rewrite your essay in the form of a business letter and mail it to the chairperson of an organization that can work to solve the problem
- send a copy of your essay to a local TV or radio talk show host and volunteer to talk with the host and answer questions about the problem and your proposed solution

GRAMMAR HINT

Affect and *Effect*

When you explored your problem, you asked yourself about the causes and effects of the problem. When you write your essay, you'll be using the words *affect* and *effect* to explain the causes and effects to readers. If you're like most people, you probably find these words confusing. One way to keep them straight is to remember that *affect* is almost always used as a verb:

> How did that decision *affect* the people of Detroit?
> Charissa was *affected* by her parents' decision to move.

Effect, on the other hand, is almost always a noun.

> The *effect* of the decision was a decline in population.
> The move had a good *effect* on Charissa.

Of course, just to complicate things, *effect* can also be a verb that means "to bring about."

> How will we ever *effect* change in that policy?

You can test to see whether your are using *effect* correctly as a verb by substituting "bring about." If "bring about" sounds awkward or wrong, use *affect*.

REFERENCE NOTE: For more help with *affect* and *effect*, see page 793.

WRITING ASSIGNMENT

PART 7:
Proofreading and Publishing Your Essay

You've done a great deal of thinking, planning, rethinking, and rewriting for your essay—and one last push will help ensure that your efforts will be noticed. Proofread your essay and make any necessary corrections. Then share it with an audience.

WRITING WORKSHOP

Group Problem Solving

You've probably heard the old saying "Two heads are better than one." That's often the case when it comes to exploring problems and their solutions. In that case, three—four— even five or six heads are usually better than one.

To be most effective, group exploration needs to be a bit more systematic than many typical brainstorming sessions. One way to begin is by assigning specific roles to the members of the group.

ROLE	DUTY
Facilitator	Keeps discussion focused on the subject. Monitors the noise level of the group. Watches the time.
Questioner	Attempts to keep the group open to possibilities. Asks the questions necessary to keep ideas flowing. Asks group members to explain or elaborate upon answers. Asks members who haven't spoken for their ideas.
Clarifier	Paraphrases and sums up what others have said. Often acts as the recorder.

For the group to function well, it's important that everyone speak. But it's equally important that everyone *listen* carefully. The group can arrive at the best solution only if members really hear one another.

Why not put these ideas into practice? With four or five classmates, select a problem to explore. You can explore the problem of homelessness in your community by beginning with some of the ideas you read about in the Here's How (page 328), or you can explore a problem from the list you developed in Writing Assignment, Part 1 (page 326).

Exploring a Problem and Writing a Group Presentation

Prewriting. Even though one person will be acting as a recorder for the group, it's a good idea for each group member to have a pencil and paper to jot down notes, questions, and flashes of insight as the group discusses the problem. In the prewriting state, your purpose is to explore the problem and possible solutions. The questioner will need to make sure that the group covers these questions: What are the causes of the problem? What are the effects of the problem? What solutions have already been tried? What new solutions are possible? What are the strengths and weaknesses of each suggested solution? What is the best overall solution to the problem?

Writing, Evaluating, and Revising. For this project, you'll prepare a report to present orally to the rest of the class. The report need not be as carefully structured as an essay—it should, however, serve as a guide to the presenters. If your group couldn't agree on a proposed solution, your report should explain the solutions you considered and the reasons that you couldn't agree. Your purpose in making the presentation is to explain the problem and solutions to your audience, so be certain that you have evidence—facts, examples, and reasons—to support your explanation.

Proofreading and Publishing. Although you can't literally proofread it, an oral report can still be polished. Before presenting the group's analysis of the problem and its solutions, ask the person who will be speaking for the group to practice before the group. Listen carefully and offer positive suggestions for improvements.

MAKING CONNECTIONS

WRITING TO EXPLORE AND TO EXPRESS YOURSELF

A Journal Entry

In the main writing assignment of this chapter, you combined the aim of writing to explore with writing to explain. It's also useful to combine writing to explore with writing to express yourself—especially when you're faced with a personal problem. One way to sort out the thoughts and issues that sometimes bombard your brain is to put them down on paper. Following is a sample journal entry in which one writer explores her need to convince her parents to allow her to get a job.

> I'm supposed to be studying for my chemistry test, but all I can think about is that job at Peterson's that my parents won't even let me apply for. They say it'll hurt my studying, but their refusal to listen is hurting it right now! I want a job! I don't want to ask them for money for everything. Since they won't discuss it, maybe I should write them a letter. Maybe I should make it a formal proposal. Maybe even a contract—"I'll work and keep my grades up, or at the end of the semester, I'll quit my job."

If you've had a falling out with your best friend or you're thinking about dropping out of school or you're bothered by something else, you might try exploring the causes of your problem or possible solutions to it in a journal entry. Although you'll be writing for an audience of one (yourself), don't skimp on details. You may be surprised at the understandings you uncover with a little exploration.

EXPLORATORY WRITING ACROSS THE CURRICULUM

History

One way to think of history is as a study of problems faced by people, both collectively and individually, and their solutions to them. In this light, you can think of the Declaration of Independence as a problem-solution essay.

Find a copy of the Declaration of Independence and read it over carefully. Then get together with several classmates and answer these questions:

1. What problem did the colonists face?
2. What part of the Declaration discusses the extent and seriousness of the colonists' problem? Name three specific examples from the Declaration that illustrate the extent and seriousness of the problem.
3. What solution does the Declaration propose?
4. What other solutions are mentioned within the Declaration? What are their disadvantages?

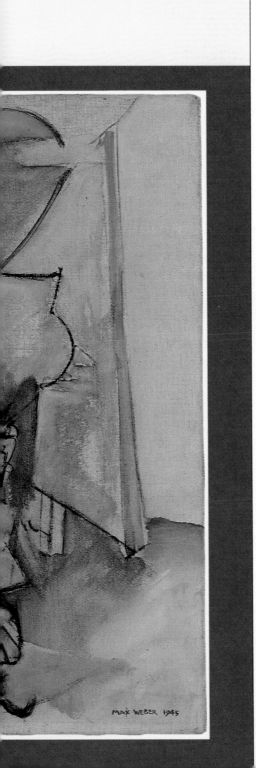

Reading and Responding

Have you ever read a story that was so exciting you passed it on to a friend as soon as you finished it? We all **respond to literature as we read** it, just as we respond to movies we see or music we listen to.

Writing and You.   Sometimes our responses are as simple as "It's terrible!" or "It's terrific!" At other times we look at the book (or movie or concert) more critically and write about it. In English class, you write an essay about a story you just read. A book reviewer reads a book that has just been published and writes a review that is printed in a national magazine. Have you ever decided whether or not to read a book (or see a movie or concert) on the basis of a review you read?

As You Read.   In the following essay, one writer, Mark Twain, takes a critical look at the work of another writer, James Fenimore Cooper. On the basis of Twain's comments, would you want to read Cooper's novel *The Deerslayer*?

Max Weber, U.S., 1881–1961. *Three Literary Gentlemen* (1945). Oil on canvas, 29 1/4" × 36".Gift of the William H. Lane Foundation. Courtesy of Museum of Fine Arts, Boston.

The Deerslayer

by James Fenimore Cooper

CHAPTER I.

On the human imagination, events produce the effects of time. Thus, he who has travelled far and seen much, is apt to fancy that he has lived long; and the history that most abounds in important incidents, soonest assumes the aspect of antiquity. In no other way can we account for the venerable air that is already gathering around American annals. When the mind reverts to the earliest days of colonial history, the period seems remote and obscure, the thousand changes that thicken along the links of recollections, throwing back the origin of the nation to a day so distant as seemingly to reach the mists of time; and yet four lives of ordinary duration would suffice to transmit, from mouth to mouth, in the form of tradition, all that civilized man has achieved within the limits of the republic. Although New York, alone, possesses a population materially exceeding that of either of the four smallest kingdoms of Europe, or materially exceeding that of the entire Swiss Confederation, it is little more than two centuries since the Dutch commenced their settlement, rescuing the region from the savage state. Thus, what seems venerable by an accumulation of changes, is reduced to familiarity when we come seriously to consider it solely in connection with time.

This glance into the perspective of the past, will prepare the reader to look at the pictures we are about to sketch, with less surprise than he might otherwise feel; and a few additional explanations may carry him back in imagination, to the precise condition of society that we desire to delineate. It is matter of history that the settlements on the eastern shores of the Hudson, such as Claverack, Kinderhook, and even Poughkeepsie, were not regarded as safe from Indian incursions a century since; and there is still standing on the banks of the same river, and within musket-shot of the wharves of Albany, a residence of a younger branch of the Van Rensselaers, that has loop-holes constructed for defence against the same crafty enemy, although it dates from a period scarcely so distant.

Fenimore Cooper's Literary Offences

by Mark Twain

The *Pathfinder* and *The Deerslayer* stand at the head of Cooper's novels as artistic creations. There are others of his works which contain parts as perfect as are to be found in these, and scenes even more thrilling. Not one can be compared with either of them as a finished whole.

The defects in both of these tales are comparatively slight. They were pure works of art.—*Prof. Lounsbury.*

The five tales reveal an extraordinary fulness of invention.

. . . One of the very greatest characters in fiction, Natty Bumppo. . . .

The craft of the woodsman, the tricks of the trapper, all the delicate art of the forest, were familiar to Cooper from his youth up.—*Prof. Brander Matthews.*

Cooper is the greatest artist in the domain of romantic fiction yet produced by America.—*Wilkie Collins.*

It seems to me that it was far from right for the Professor of English Literature in Yale, the Professor of English Literature in Columbia, and Wilkie Collins to deliver opinions on Cooper's literature without having read some of it. It would have been much more decorous to keep silent and let persons talk who have read Cooper.

Cooper's art has some defects. In one place in *Deerslayer,* and in the restricted space of two-thirds of a page, Cooper has scored 114 offences against literary art out of a possible 115. It breaks the record.

There are nineteen rules governing literary art in the domain of romantic fiction—some say twenty-two. In *Deerslayer* Cooper violated eighteen of them. These eighteen require:

"There are nineteen rules governing literary art in the domain of romantic fiction—some say twenty-two. In *Deerslayer* Cooper violated eighteen of them."

— Mark Twain

1. That a tale shall accomplish something and arrive somewhere. But the *Deerslayer* tale accomplishes nothing and arrives in the air.

2. They require that the episodes of a tale shall be necessary parts of the tale, and shall help to develop it. But as the *Deerslayer* tale is not a tale, and accomplishes nothing and arrives nowhere, the episodes have no rightful place in the work, since there was nothing for them to develop.

3. They require that the personages in a tale shall be alive, except in the case of corpses, and that always the reader shall be able to tell the corpses from the others. But this detail has often been overlooked in the *Deerslayer* tale.

4. They require that the personages in a tale, both dead and alive, shall exhibit a sufficient excuse for being there. But this detail also has been overlooked in the *Deerslayer* tale.

5. They require that when the personages of a tale deal in conversation, the talk shall sound like human talk, and be talk such as human beings would be likely to talk in the given circumstances, and have a discoverable meaning, also a discoverable purpose, and a show of relevancy, and remain in the neighborhood of the subject in hand, and be interesting to the reader, and help out the tale, and stop when the people cannot think of anything more to say. But this requirement has been ignored from the beginning of the *Deerslayer* tale to the end of it.

6. They require that when the author describes the character of a personage in his tale, the conduct and conversation of that personage shall justify said description. But this law gets little or no attention in the *Deerslayer* tale, as Natty Bumppo's case will amply prove.

7. They require that when a personage talks like an illustrated, gilt-edged, tree-calf, hand-tooled, seven-dollar Friendship's Offering in the beginning of a paragraph, he shall not talk like a negro minstrel in the end of it. But this rule is flung down and danced upon in the *Deerslayer* tale.

8. They require that crass stupidities shall not be played upon the reader as "the craft of the woodsman, the delicate art of the forest," by either the author or the people in the tale. But this rule is persistently violated in the *Deerslayer* tale.

9. They require that the personages of a tale shall confine themselves to possibilities and let miracles alone; or, if they venture a miracle, the author must so plausibly set it forth as to make it look possible and reasonable. But these rules are not respected in the *Deerslayer* tale.

10. They require that the author shall make the reader feel a deep interest in the personages of his tale and in their fate; and that he shall make the reader love the good people in the tale and hate the bad ones. But the reader of the *Deerslayer* tale dislikes the good people in it, is indifferent to the others, and wishes they would all get drowned together.

11. They require that the characters in a tale shall be so clearly defined that the reader can tell beforehand what each will do in a given emergency. But in the *Deerslayer* tale this rule is vacated.

In addition to these large rules there are some little ones. These require that the author shall

12. *Say* what he is proposing to say, not merely come near it.

13. Use the right word, not its second cousin.

14. Eschew surplusage.

15. Not omit necessary details.

16. Avoid slovenliness of form.

17. Use good grammar.

18. Employ a simple and straightforward style.

Even these seven are coldly and persistently violated in the *Deerslayer* tale.

Cooper's gift in the way of invention was not a rich endowment; but such as it was he liked to work it, he was pleased with the effects, and indeed he did some quite sweet things with it. In his little box of stage properties he kept six or eight cunning devices, tricks, artifices for his savages and woodsmen to deceive and circumvent each other with, and he was never so happy as when he was working these innocent things and seeing them go. A favorite one was to make a moccasined person tread in the tracks of the moccasined enemy, and thus hide his own trail. Cooper wore out barrels and barrels of moccasins in working that trick. Another stage-property that he pulled out of his box pretty frequently was his broken twig. He prized his broken twig above all the rest of his effects, and worked it the hardest. It is a restful chapter in any book of his when somebody doesn't step on a dry twig and alarm all the reds and whites for two hundred yards around. Every time a Cooper person is in peril, and absolute silence is worth four dol-

James Fenimore Cooper

lars a minute, he is sure to step on a dry twig.

There may be a hundred handier things to step on, but that wouldn't satisfy Cooper. Cooper requires him to turn out and find a dry twig; and if he can't do it, go and borrow one. In fact, the Leather Stocking Series ought to have been called the Broken Twig Series.

READER'S RESPONSE

1. Did you enjoy this review of *The Deerslayer*? What did you like or dislike about Twain's style?
2. It's fairly obvious that Twain thinks Cooper's novels are not very good. If you haven't read any of Cooper's novels, how can you tell if Twain's criticisms are valid? Try reading the first paragraph from *The Deerslayer*, printed on page 360; or see if you can find a copy of the book and sample a few pages. What do you think?

WRITER'S CRAFT

3. You've probably read some other things written by Mark Twain and know that much of his writing is humorous. How does Twain create humor with his third point—the point about corpses? What other examples of humor can you find?
4. Twain begins his essay by quoting three people who think highly of Cooper's work. Why do you think he includes these quotes? How does he counteract their comments?
5. Twain says there are at least nineteen rules governing the literary art of "romantic fiction," and he claims that Cooper broke eighteen of those rules. Which of these rules do you think you could apply to writing today? Why?
6. How does Twain use details and examples to support his opinions? Why do you suppose he doesn't develop rules 12–18 at all?

Purposes for Writing About Literature

Even though he's funny about it, Mark Twain despises *The Deerslayer* and Cooper's fiction in general, and he gives eighteen reasons why. His purpose is to persuade his audience to accept his opinion about Cooper's novels. (His essay, by the way, became quite famous—or infamous.)

But there are other purposes for writing about literature (or for writing about any of the other arts—music, dance, film, photography, painting, sculpture). In school your purpose for writing about literature may be to show your teacher that you understand the poem or the story you've read in class. Another purpose might be just to share information—what you've learned by looking closely at the poem or story—with your teacher and your classmates. Here are some examples of the purposes you might have when you write about literature.

Self-Expressive: writing an entry in your response journal about a novel, a story, or a poem that has special meaning for you; starting a reading list—with comments—of your favorite novels (perhaps in your response journal).

Persuasive: for a column in your school newspaper, writing a review of the drama club's production of Cole Porter's *Anything Goes* to encourage readers to buy tickets and see the play; writing a letter to the editor of your local newspaper explaining why a particular novel shouldn't be banned from the library.

▶ **Expository:**   in your school literary magazine, writing about the latest winner of the Nobel Prize for literature and discussing some of the writer's works that are in your school library; writing a critical analysis explaining the use of symbolism in a poem you read for English class.

Literary: writing a poem in which you respond to a poem that is one of your favorites; writing a skit that is a *parody* (a "mocking imitation") of a television soap opera.

In this chapter, you'll explore several purposes and ways of writing about literature, but you'll concentrate most of your attention on the critical analysis. In the critical analysis you write, your purpose will be to inform and explain. As you work through the assignments in this chapter, keep in mind that an effective critical analysis

- starts with a careful reading of the work
- identifies the writer's main idea, or thesis, about the work
- provides examples from the work that support, or prove, the main idea

"Some books are to be tasted, others to

be swallowed, and some few to be chewed

and digested."

Sir Francis Bacon

Writing a Literary Analysis

Prewriting

Reading and Responding to Literature

When you read a poem or story, your first thought may be *I like this* or *I don't like this*. But to really enjoy or understand what you read, you need to go beyond this first thought. You start with the poem or story itself and your personal responses to it, but then you look at it critically to understand it more fully.

Starting with Personal Response

Trace a writer's words. They go from the writer's brain onto the printed page, then from the printed page into the reader's brain—an amazing journey. But once in the reader's brain another amazing thing happens. Each reader responds—feels and reacts—differently.

Twenty different readers respond to a poem or story in twenty different ways because every reader is unique. Since there is no one exactly like you, no one who's led your life and thought your thoughts, your responses to a poem or any work of literature may be different from those of your friends, your classmates, and your teacher.

Calvin & Hobbes, copyright 1987 Universal Press Syndicate. Reprinted with permission of Universal Press Syndicate. All rights reserved.

STRATEGIES FOR RESPONDING TO LITERATURE

1. **Listen to your inner voice.** Let yourself respond without worrying about what other people would think.
2. **Write your responses in your journal.** Allow the poem or story to trigger your thoughts and then freewrite in any direction. Does a character in the story remind you of anyone you know? Have you had a similar experience? How did you feel when you finished reading?
3. **Get together with a friend or a group of classmates and share your responses.** Remember that your responses will be different but equally valid.
4. **Respond creatively.** Write another poem or story based on something you felt or thought when you were reading. Write a new ending or beginning to a story. Convert the ideas in a poem to a play or story.

The following poem is about a man who lived his greatest moments in his youth. What would that be like?

A POEM

Ex-Basketball Player
by John Updike

Pearl Avenue runs past the high-school lot,
Bends with the trolley tracks, and stops, cut off
Before it has a chance to go two blocks,
At Colonel McComsky Plaza. Berth's Garage
Is on the corner facing west, and there,   5
Most days, you'll find Flick Webb, who helps Berth out.

Flick stands tall among the idiot pumps—
Five on a side, the old bubble-head style,
Their rubber elbows hanging loose and low.
One's nostrils are two S's, and his eyes   10
An E and O. And one is squat, without
A head at all—more of a football type.

Once Flick played for the high-school team, the Wizards.
He was good: in fact, the best. In '46
He bucketed three hundred ninety points,   15
A county record still. The ball loved Flick.
I saw him rack up thirty-eight or forty
In one home game. His hands were like wild birds.

He never learned a trade, he just sells gas,
Checks oil, and changes flats. Once in a while,   20
As a gag, he dribbles an inner tube,
But most of us remember anyway.
His hands are fine and nervous on the lug wrench.
It makes no difference to the lug wrench, though.

Off work, he hangs around Mae's Luncheonette,   25
Grease-grey and kind of coiled, he plays pinball,
Sips lemon cokes, and smokes those thin cigars;
Flick seldom speaks to Mae, just sits and nods
Beyond her face towards bright applauding tiers
Of Necco Wafers, Nibs, and Juju Beads.   30

EXERCISE 1    **Responding to a Poem**

What did your inner voice tell you about this poem? Respond in writing in one of the following ways.

1. Write your response in your journal. Start with the title of the poem or the line or image that you reacted to most strongly. Follow where your own thoughts and feelings lead you. Or start with what you think Updike means by the poem and your own reaction to that meaning.
2. Write another poem, one that reflects the feelings or thoughts "Ex-Basketball Player" triggered in your mind.
3. Write a short story with Flick as the main character. Set the story in the past, when he played basketball, or in his future.

EXERCISE 2   **Speaking and Listening: Giving an Oral Response**

With a partner, develop one of the following ideas in response to "Ex-Basketball Player." Write a script, decide which role each of you will take, and present the scene to your class.

A local news reporter is interviewing the ex-basketball player on the occasion of the twentieth anniversary of the state championship game.

The ex-class nerd and the ex-basketball player meet at their twenty-year class reunion.

Reading Literature Critically

Think about your personal response to a car. It's fun to drive; the seats are comfortable; you'd like to drive it again. But what if you had to prepare an analysis of that car for a consumer-awareness report? You would certainly have to look at the car more closely and more critically. You might have to know something about different types of brakes or transmissions, as well as how well they work on this particular car. And just as you would need to look more critically at a car to write a consumer report, you have to look more closely at a poem or story to write a literary analysis. An analysis of literature, unlike a personal response, uses objective standards that many people agree upon to examine a piece of writing.

Using Critical Reading Strategies. You may read many things carefully—the instruction manual for a new camera, a chapter in your history book, and so on. But reading carefully is not quite the same thing as reading critically. Here are some strategies that will help you read literature critically.

STRATEGIES FOR READING CRITICALLY

1. **Read the work again.** Once isn't enough. Each time you reread a poem or a story, you'll discover something new. Read a poem aloud to hear the sound effects.
2. **Look for the elements.** Find examples of the elements (see this page and pages 373–374), and take notes. If you can, make a copy of the work so you can underline, circle, and write marginal notes.
3. **Be prepared for puzzles.** Don't give up if you don't understand something. Do what you can (reread, use context clues, try a dictionary, ask someone) and go on.
4. **Compare your findings.** Talk about the work with classmates who have read it, too.

Examining Literary Elements. An automobile expert talks about transmissions and disc brakes and mph; a critical reader of literature talks about imagery and plot and symbols. To analyze and describe a work of literature, you need a special vocabulary, as well as an understanding of what the terms mean. The following charts define some of the basic terms, or elements, and provide some questions for use in analyzing a poem or story.

THE ELEMENTS OF POETRY

Speaker—the voice that talks to the reader, that tells the poem	Who is the speaker? How does the speaker affect the mood and theme of the poem?
Imagery—words or phrases that appeal to the senses	What images are contained in the poem? How do they affect the poem's meaning?

(continued)

THE ELEMENTS OF POETRY *(continued)*

Diction—the writer's choice of words	What kind of language does the poet use—formal or informal? concrete or abstract? unusual words or phrases?
Figurative Language—a word or phrase that is not meant to be taken literally	Does the poet use personification—giving human qualities to an object or animal? Does the poet use similes or metaphors to compare two unlike things? What feelings or ideas does this language suggest?
Symbol—a person, place, thing, or event that stands for something else	Does any person, place, thing, or event seem to have symbolic value? If so, what?
Sound Effects—use of sounds of words to create certain effects	What sound effects are used? How do they contribute to meaning or suggest images?
Rhyme—repetition of vowel sounds in accented syllables and all succeeding syllables	Does the poem contain rhyme? If so, what is the pattern, and how does it affect the meaning of the poem?
Rhythm—pattern of stressed and unstressed syllables	Is the rhythm regular or like the natural pattern of speech? How does it reflect the mood and theme of the poem?
Repetition—repeated consonant sounds, vowel sounds, words, or phrases	What words, phrases, or sounds are repeated? What impression do they create? What effect do they have on the meaning of the poem?
Theme—the meaning, or main idea, the poem reveals or suggests	Does the poem examine any common problem or life experience? What message or theme does it suggest?

THE ELEMENTS OF FICTION

Setting—the time and place of the story	Does the setting suggest a tone or a mood? How does the setting affect the development of the plot?
Character—a person (sometimes an animal or thing) in a story or novel	What is the role of the characters in the development of the plot? Are any meanings suggested by their names or their physical descriptions? How do they talk? act? think?
Plot—the events that follow each other and cause other events to happen	Are the events predictable? What is the central problem or conflict in the story? How does the outcome of the story relate to theme or meaning?
Point of View—the perspective or vantage point from which a story is told	Is the story told by a first-person or a third-person narrator? How much does the narrator know? How does the narrator seem to feel about the characters and events in the story?
Theme—an underlying idea or insight that the work reveals about life and people	Does this work reveal any underlying idea or insight about human experiences and problems? Does it attempt to teach any lessons about human nature or relationships? What details and passages reflect the theme?

Some people make notes as they are reading critically. Here is an example of one person's critical comments as she read Lucille Clifton's poem "an ordinary woman."

HERE'S HOW

an ordinary woman
by Lucille Clifton

Speaker

the thirty eighth year
of my life,

Simile

plain as bread
round as a cake

Repetition for emphasis
and sound

an ordinary woman.   5

an ordinary woman.

Difference in expectation
and reality

i had expected to be
smaller than this,
more beautiful,
wiser in Afrikan ways,   10
more confident,

Meaning?

i had expected
more than this.

i will be forty soon.
my mother once was forty.   15
my mother died at forty four,

Diction—only hard word

a woman of sad countenance
leaving behind a girl

Simile

awkward as a stork.
my mother was thick,   20

Metaphor

her hair was a jungle and
she was very wise
and beautiful
and sad.

Repetition of consonant sounds	i have dreamed dreams	25
	for you mama	
	more than once.	
Meaning?	i have wrapped me	
	in your skin	
	and made you live again	30
Repetition	more than once.	
	i have taken the bones you hardened	
	and built daughters	
Symbol	and they blossom and promise fruit	
Simile	like Afrikan trees.	35
	i am a woman now.	
Repetition of phrase	an ordinary woman.	
	in the thirty eighth	
	year of my life,	
	surrounded by life,	40
Repetition of consonant sounds	a perfect picture of	
	blackness blessed,	
Why isn't she happy?	i had not expected this	
Emphasizes loneliness	loneliness.	
Metaphor	if it is western,	45
Repetition of long "i" sounds	if it is the final	
	Europe in my mind,	
	if in the middle of my life	
	i am turning the final turn	
Symbol of death?	into the shining dark	50
Diction—pun on "whole" and "holy"	let me come to it whole	
	and holy	
Wish to end her life	not afraid	
unafraid, no longer lonely	not lonely	
	out of my mother's life	55
Theme—acceptance of her own identity	into my own.	
	into my own.	
Repetition of earlier lines	i had expected more than this.	
	i had not expected to be	
	an ordinary woman.	60

E X E R C I S E 3 ▶ Reading Critically

You had a chance to respond personally to "Ex-Basketball Player" (pages 369–370); now take another look at it. Use the strategies for critical reading (page 372) and what you know about the elements of poetry to study the poem and answer these questions.

1. Who is the speaker in the poem? How does the speaker feel about the subject of the poem?
2. What sensory images occur in the poem? How do they affect the poem's meaning?
3. What figures of speech are used in the poem? What feelings do they suggest?
4. What kind of language does the poet use? How does it affect the meaning of the poem?
5. What is the central theme or meaning of the poem?

WRITING ASSIGNMENT

PART 1:

Responding and Reading Critically

In this chapter, you'll write an analysis of a poem. Choose a poem, either one you would like to read or one your teacher recommends. You can always skim through your literature book or a book of poetry until you find something you like.

First, read the poem and respond to it naturally. How do you feel about it? Then, read it critically, using the strategies on page 372. It might also help to refer to the definitions of the elements and related questions on pages 372–374.

 *Prewriting*

Planning a Literary Analysis

It is possible to read a poem or story critically and stop there. You have developed a better understanding of the work, and that's enough. But when you are going to write a literary analysis, you need to think about what you want to accomplish in the paper. Then you need to plan how you will bring your information and ideas together.

Thinking About Purpose, Audience, and Tone

The *purpose* of a literary analysis is expository. The writer wants to share information, explain how the piece of literature works, and convince readers that his or her information and explanation are sound.

When you write a literary analysis for your English class, you have two *audiences*—your classmates and your teacher. You need to explain the poem or story in a way that will be clear and interesting to your classmates, and you need to demonstrate to your teacher that you have a clear understanding of the poem or story and its elements.

Most literary analyses are formal papers with a formal, businesslike *tone*. Unlike the book and movie reviews you may read, the typical literary analysis avoids the first-person point of view, contractions, and colloquial language.

Finding a Focus for Your Analysis

What part of the poem do you think is the most interesting? the most challenging? You probably can't write an analysis of all the elements in any poem; you have to focus on some aspect of the poem or the writer's style. For example, you might

- analyze the images and figures of speech and explain why they're unusual or particularly effective
- analyze the use of sound effects (rhyme, rhythm, and so on) and explain how sound contributes to meaning
- explain the poem's theme and show how the poet develops it through images and figures of speech

Developing a Thesis Statement

Once you have identified the focus for your analysis, you are very close to having a preliminary *thesis statement*. The **thesis statement** identifies the thesis, or main idea, that you will attempt to explain and prove in your paper. You can use a prelimi- nary thesis statement as a guide for your planning and writing, but you should feel free to revise it at any time. As you collect evidence and start to write, you may find that your thesis is too broad or too narrow and needs to be revised. Thesis statements may be more than one sentence, as the fol- lowing example shows.

> In "an ordinary woman," Lucille Clifton uses figurative language, diction, and sound patterns to reveal her theme. This theme is a woman's discovery that, although she is a simple woman, she has an important identity of her own.

WRITING ASSIGNMENT

PART 2:
Identifying a Focus and a Thesis

Trying to analyze all of the literary elements in a poem would be overwhelming to both you and your audience. Target the two or three elements you've decided to focus on and ignore the others. Then think about what thesis, or main idea, you want to try to prove in your analysis and write a thesis statement.

Gathering Evidence to Support Your Thesis

In a literary analysis you can't just state your thesis and forget it. For example, someone who read the thesis statement given above might ask, "How do you know Lucille Clifton uses figu- rative language to reveal her theme?" You need to back up your statements with specific evidence.

Where does the evidence come from? Most evidence comes from the *primary source,* the work itself. However, a *secondary source* such as an encyclopedia or literary reference work can provide helpful information about the writer and his or her work. (See pages 416–417 for more information on secondary sources.)

STRATEGIES FOR GATHERING EVIDENCE

1. Review the work of literature, looking for details and quotations you can use to support your thesis.
2. As you read, make notes on note cards or sheets of paper.
3. Identify the line (for poetry) or page (for fiction) where you found the detail or quotation.
4. Avoid plagiarism by giving credit to your sources for ideas as well as quoted material.

The following example shows how one writer used a chart to compile her notes for an analysis of "an ordinary woman."

HERE'S HOW

ELEMENT	EXAMPLES	SUPPORT FOR THESIS
SIMILES	"plain as bread," l. 3 "round as cake," l. 4	Very plain household images show ordinary woman—not glamorous
	"awkward as a stork," l. 19	awkward, ungraceful woman—like ugly duckling
	"promise fruit/like Afrikan trees," ll. 34–35	trees of Africa (woman) bring life
METAPHORS	the speaker's mother had hair that was "a jungle," l. 21	jungle—something that grows wild—not shaped
REPETITION	"an ordinary woman," ll. 5, 6, 37, 60—used 4 times	ll. 5, 6, speaker "ordinary woman" at 38 l. 37, speaker "ordinary woman" has "dreamed dreams" and has daughters l. 60, speaker "ordinary woman" but "into my own"
DICTION	ll. 51–52, "whole"/"holy" mostly small words	"whole" suggests whole person, not lonely "holy" suggests sacred quality of identity
	"countenance," l. 17, only big word	small, everyday words fit theme of "ordinary"

CRITICAL THINKING

Evaluating Supporting Evidence

When you *evaluate,* you judge the value or worth of something. This thinking skill comes into play when you are gathering evidence for a literary analysis. During that process you need to evaluate the evidence to determine whether or not it will help you prove your thesis. For example, the person writing an essay about "an ordinary woman" wrote the thesis statement you read on page 379:

> In "an ordinary woman," Lucille Clifton uses figurative language, diction, and sound patterns to reveal her theme. This theme is a woman's discovery that, although she is a simple woman, she has an important identity of her own.

How will the person evaluate the evidence she gathers to determine whether it is valid? She can judge it by applying two standards or criteria: (1) Is it specific information that goes beyond the thesis statement and does not merely repeat it? and (2) Is it relevant to the main idea in the thesis?

EXAMPLES

■ Specific information rather than a restatement of the thesis.

UNACCEPTABLE   In "an ordinary woman," Lucille Clifton uses language and sound to show how a simple woman discovers she has an identity of her own. [Repeats the thesis statement.]

ACCEPTABLE   Clifton's simple vocabulary (the only difficult word is *countenance* in line 17) highlights the "ordinary" quality of the speaker.

■ Information that is relevant (related) to the main idea.

UNACCEPTABLE   Many women feel that their lives are ordinary. [This has nothing to do with the thesis statement.]

ACCEPTABLE   The simple words "an ordinary woman" used four times in the poem indicate that the speaker accepts her identity as an ordinary woman.

CRITICAL THINKING EXERCISE:
Evaluating Supporting Evidence

Before you attempt to evaluate the evidence you are using for your own literary analysis, take this opportunity to practice the skill. Get together with two or three of your classmates and review the following thesis statement and list of supporting evidence from Updike's poem "Ex-Basketball Player" (pages 369–370). Decide which evidence is valid support for the thesis and which is not. Apply these criteria as you evaluate: (1) The evidence provides new information and does not merely repeat the thesis. (2) The evidence is relevant to the main idea.

Thesis Statement: The imagery in John Updike's poem "Ex-Basketball Player" depicts the meaningless life of an athlete when the days of glory are past.

Evidence:
1. In John Updike's poem "Ex-Basketball Player," an ex-athlete's life has little meaning.
2. Images such as "He bucketed three hundred ninety points" (line 15) and "His hands were like wild birds" (line 18) show the glory of Flick's basketball days.
3. Many basketball players don't do as well as Flick, who is the subject of John Updike's poem "Ex-Basketball Player."
4. The fact that Flick looks "towards bright applauding tiers/Of Necco Wafers, Nibs, and Juju Beads" (lines 29–30) is an ironic reminder of the days when he faced cheering crowds.

5. Today, Flick's hands "are fine and nervous on the lug wrench" (line 23), but "It makes no difference to the lug wrench" (line 24).

Deciding on an Order of Ideas

How you organize your ideas depends partly on the direction you are taking in your analysis. If you're analyzing the imagery and figures of speech in "Ex-Basketball Player" (pages 369–370), for instance, you might arrange your ideas in the *order of importance.* That is, if you decided the most important element is imagery, you would discuss it first and then go on to discuss figures of speech. If you intended to focus your essay on imagery alone, you'd probably arrange your details (including quotations and line references) in *chronological order,* the order in which the images occur in the poem.

As you gather and organize your evidence

- remember your focus and stick to it
- find examples of each element you plan to discuss
- if necessary, consult secondary sources for background information on the poet and/or the poem
- evaluate your evidence to make sure it's specific and relevant
- arrange your ideas in an order that will make sense to your reader

WRITING ASSIGNMENT

PART 3:
Gathering and Organizing Your Ideas

It's time to pick up where you left off in Writing Assignment, Part 2 (page 379). Collect evidence to support your thesis and then make an early plan for your essay. Jot down each main idea and its supporting evidence, perhaps using a chart like the one on page 380. Then decide on an order for presenting your ideas.

Writing Your First Draft

You have decided on a focus and a main idea for your literary analysis, turned your main idea into a thesis statement, and gathered supporting evidence. Now it's time to turn your plan into a first draft. When you are writing your draft, remember that an essay of literary analysis is objective. The word *I*, referring to your personal thoughts and feelings, is not appropriate.

The Structure of a Literary Analysis

Like other expository compositions (see pages 112–120, 204–275, and 318–357), a literary analysis often has three parts.

- The *introduction* states the poem's title and author and may give some background information. The thesis statement expresses the main idea of your paper and mentions the literary elements of the poem in the order you will discuss them.
- The *body* presents a major point about each of the elements (one element at a time) in a separate paragraph. Specific examples from the poem support each major point.
- The *conclusion* brings the essay to an end, summarizing its major points.

"When you consider that there are a thousand ways to express even the simplest idea, it is no wonder writers are under a great strain."

E. B. White

MECHANICS HINT

Incorporating Supporting Evidence

As you write your draft, you'll use supporting evidence—direct quotations and paraphrases—from the literary work to support your main ideas. Follow these conventions for using direct quotations and paraphrases:

1. Incorporate the quotation into your own sentence structure (it shouldn't sound as though it has just been plunked down into your paper).

2. Enclose the direct quotation in quotation marks. Double-check to be sure you've copied the quote exactly as it appears in the original work.
3. Use a slash (/), with a space before and after it, to indicate the end of a line of poetry.
4. Use ellipsis points (. . .) to indicate an omission.
5. For both direct quotations and paraphrases, cite the line numbers (page numbers, for fiction) or secondary source in parentheses at the end of a sentence.

QUOTATION The speaker in "an ordinary woman" wants to be different from her mother: "not afraid / not lonely / out of my mother's life / into my own. / into my own." (lines 53–57).

PARAPHRASE The speaker in "an ordinary woman" expresses a wish to be different from her mother, to be unafraid, and to live her own life (lines 53–57).

👉 REFERENCE NOTE: For more help with using quotation marks and ellipses, see pages 878–883 and 885–886.

A Basic Framework for a Literary Analysis

Here's an essay of literary analysis based on Lucille Clifton's poem "an ordinary woman" (pages 375–376). As you read, notice the writer's use of evidence from the poem to support the thesis statement.

A WRITER'S MODEL

No "Ordinary Woman"

INTRODUCTION
Poet/Title
Background

In contrast to the title of her poem, Lucille Clifton is no "ordinary woman." She is an award-winning African American poet whose memoirs and four volumes of poetry are widely read. All these works celebrate African American men and women who have a strong sense of their own identities.

Thesis
statement
Theme of poem

In "an ordinary woman," Clifton uses figurative language, diction, and sound effects to reveal her theme. This theme is a woman's discovery that, although she is a simple woman, she has an important identity of her own.

BODY
Major point:
Figures of speech

Clifton carefully chooses figures of speech that support the image of an "ordinary" woman. For example, the speaker uses two similes to compare herself to common foods. She says that she is "plain as bread" and "round as a cake" (lines 3-4). She also

Quotations from work

uses metaphors, saying her daughters are her "fruit," who "blossom and promise fruit / like Afrikan

Quotations from work

trees" (lines 34-35). These metaphors show that the woman has also given the gift of life that promises to grow and develop.

Major point:
Diction

Diction--the choice of words--also contributes to the poem's meaning. Clifton's simple vocabulary

Examples of diction

(the only difficult word is <u>countenance</u> in line 17) highlights the "ordinary" quality of the speaker. A play on the words <u>whole</u> and <u>holy</u> (lines 51-52) shows the speaker's growing awareness of her identity as she prepares to die. She is no longer lonely because she knows herself as a "whole" woman. The simple words "an ordinary woman" used four times in the poem indicate that the speaker accepts her identity as an ordinary woman.

Major point: Sound effects

Examples of repetition

Repetition of vowel sounds

The poem has no regular rhythm or rhyme, but there are many sound effects. Repetition is important. The repetition of "not afraid" and "not lonely" (lines 53-54) suggests a new spirit of life. Moreover, the repetition of "into my own. / into my own." (lines 56-57) shows that the speaker accepts her identity as an African American woman. Assonance (repetition of the long i sound in final, mind, life, shining, my, i) is also important. Here the speaker emphasizes her growing sense of I--her own identity.

CONCLUSION Restatement of theme

Restatement of thesis

The speaker "had not expected to be / an ordinary woman" (lines 59-60), but she has come to realize that being an ordinary woman is a triumph. It is ordinary women, after all, who care for their families and help their children to a more promising future than their own. Throughout the poem, Clifton effectively develops this theme through figures of speech, diction, and sound effects.

You may find it helpful to model your own composition on the preceding literary analysis. It follows this framework.

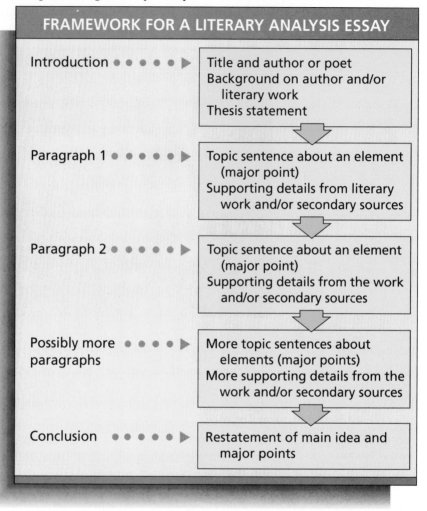

FRAMEWORK FOR A LITERARY ANALYSIS ESSAY

Introduction ● ● ● ● ● ▶
Title and author or poet
Background on author and/or
   literary work
Thesis statement

Paragraph 1 ● ● ● ● ● ▶
Topic sentence about an element
   (major point)
Supporting details from literary
   work and/or secondary sources

Paragraph 2 ● ● ● ● ● ▶
Topic sentence about an element
   (major point)
Supporting details from the work
   and/or secondary sources

Possibly more ● ● ● ● ▶
paragraphs
More topic sentences about
   elements (major points)
More supporting details from the
   work and/or secondary sources

Conclusion ● ● ● ● ● ▶
Restatement of main idea and
   major points

WRITING ASSIGNMENT

PART 4:
Writing a Draft of Your Essay of Literary Analysis

Michelangelo wrote this note to his young assistant: "Draw, Antonio, draw, Antonio, draw and do not waste time." So follow the advice of Michelangelo. Gather what you need: paper, pen, or pencil (or even a word processor), your prewriting notes, the poem itself, and the framework. Now write. Unless there's a fire or other emergency, don't stop until you've finished your draft.

WRITING NOTE

When you draft your essay, use the *literary* (or *historical*) *present* tense. This means that you refer to most events in the poem in the present tense.

> The speaker **uses** two similes to compare herself with common foods.
> She **is** no longer lonely because she **knows** herself as a "whole" woman.

Use other tenses, such as past or past perfect, when characters themselves speak in those tenses.

> The speaker says that her mother **died** at age forty-four.
> The speaker says that she **had thought** she **would be** different.

☞ REFERENCE NOTE: For more help on verb tenses, see pages 736–747.

Evaluating and Revising

The following chart can help you step back and take an objective look at your paper. Ask yourself the questions in the left-hand column. If you find a problem, use the revision technique suggested in the right-hand column.

EVALUATING AND REVISING ESSAYS OF LITERARY ANALYSIS

EVALUATION GUIDE	REVISION TECHNIQUE
1 Does the introduction give the title and author and provide necessary background information?	**Add** the title and author; **add** interesting, relevant information about the author and the work.
2 Does the thesis statement appear in the introduction? Does it clearly state the main idea and the elements to be discussed in the essay?	**Add** a thesis statement or **replace** the existing one. In your statement, identify the elements you will discuss in the same order you will cover them in the essay.
3 Does the essay include enough supporting evidence? Is the evidence relevant and specific?	**Add** additional evidence from the work or from secondary sources. **Cut** irrelevant, general, or repetitious evidence.
4 Is the essay's organization clear and consistent?	**Reorder** the ideas and evidence in an order that makes sense, such as chronological order or order of importance.
5 Does the conclusion bring the essay to a definite close?	**Add** a sentence that restates your thesis and/or summarizes the major points.

EXERCISE 4 ▶ **Analyzing a Writer's Revisions**

Here's the writer's draft of the third paragraph on pages 386–387. (As you can see, it wasn't perfect the first time.) See if you can figure out why the writer made these changes.

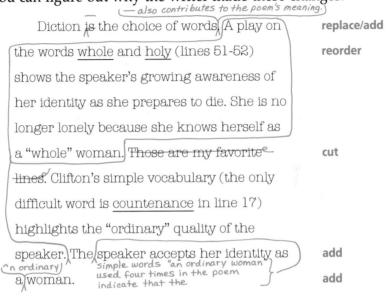

— also contributes to the poem's meaning.

Diction ~~is~~ the choice of words. [A play on   replace/add

the words <u>whole</u> and <u>holy</u> (lines 51-52)   reorder

shows the speaker's growing awareness of

her identity as she prepares to die. She is no

longer lonely because she knows herself as

a "whole" woman. ~~These are my favorite~~   cut

~~lines.~~ Clifton's simple vocabulary (the only

difficult word is <u>countenance</u> in line 17)

highlights the "ordinary" quality of the

speaker. The speaker accepts her identity as   add

an ordinary   *simple words "an ordinary woman"*
a woman.   *used four times in the poem*   add
               indicate that the

1. Why did the writer add the information about diction contributing to the poem's meaning? What is the function of this sentence in the paragraph?
2. Why did the writer change the order of the second and third sentences? By moving these sentences, what order does the writer follow?
3. Why did the writer delete the fourth sentence?
4. Why did the writer add the information in the last sentence? [Hint: What does the reader need in order to accept the writer's thesis?]

WRITING ASSIGNMENT

PART 5:

Evaluating and Revising Your Literary Analysis

Work with some classmates in a small group to evaluate each other's first drafts. Then, read over your own essay, deciding for yourself what changes need to be made. Finally, evaluate your own and your classmates' suggestions and make changes that will improve your essay.

Proofreading and Publishing

Proofreading. Your final draft should be as free as possible from any errors. If you suspect a mistake, look up the appropriate section in the grammar, usage, and mechanics chapters of this textbook. Use a college dictionary to check spellings. Also, check carefully to see that you've spelled the author's name and the title of the work correctly.

Publishing. With your teacher's help, plan some special class time for sharing papers. Here are two ways to find an audience beyond your classroom:

■ Start a literary magazine or journal, if one doesn't exist already. Encourage everyone in school to submit original poems and stories, as well as essays of literary analysis.
■ Organize a literary conference. Volunteers should read their papers to a group of teachers and students from other classes. Plan a question-and-answer period after each reading.

Shoe, by Jeff MacNelly, reprinted by

WRITING ASSIGNMENT

PART 6:
Proofreading and Publishing

This is the time to catch and correct every error. Read your essay aloud—or have someone read it to you—to spot mistakes. When you're sure your essay is the best you can make it, use the suggestions you've just read—or use some ideas of your own—to share it with a wider audience.

A STUDENT MODEL

In her essay of literary analysis, Niaima Turner writes about L. Woiwode's short story "The Beginning of Grief." Niaima, who attends Woodrow Wilson High School in Camden, New Jersey, analyzes how the author uses point of view to reveal the father's character to the reader. As you read her essay, notice how Niaima uses evidence from the story to support her ideas.

A Father's Trial by Grief and Parenthood
by Niaima Turner

In his short story "The Beginning of Grief," L. Woiwode uses the limited third-person point of view to help the reader understand the main character's responses to his sorrows and difficulties. William Stanion is a bereaved husband who lost his wife one year earlier. Now in his role as a single parent he undergoes additional stress as he attempts to raise his five children alone.

At home Stanion thinks constantly about his performance as a responsible father while he tries to keep his sanity. He is tormented by his memories of his wife who was "the periphery of everything" (84). At one point Stanion even thinks he might take "his life just to end the torment, just to be at peace, and maybe to be with her" (84). Yet, he doesn't commit suicide because he loves his children and recognizes his obligations to them. Bothered by feelings of helplessness, he worries about disciplining his children and rearing them properly.

Stanion is very conscious of what is going on with his children. At supper time, he travels through the events of their day, "prying his way into them, find out what the trouble was, find out who had caused it, and set right the one who was at fault, or, if there had been fighting, punish him" (83). A gentle man, he hates to punish the children. Stanion had left the discipline up to his wife which she had done prudently and judiciously. Now "it was difficult for him to pass judgment on anyone, much less his own children, and even harder for him to see them hurt" (83).

A turning point for Stanion comes during an incident with Kevin, his ten-year-old son. A practiced liar with a strong temper, Kevin is difficult to handle. Stanion resents the fact that Kevin is always in trouble. After discovering that Kevin has kicked a child in his most recent encounter, Stanion realizes punishment is in order. But when he becomes angry, he accidentally slaps his youngest daughter and out of frustration he kicks Kevin in the rump. Following the chaos, Stanion "realized what he had done" (87) and he knows he must bring calm to the family.

As Stanion works through the crisis with Kevin, he examines himself and achieves a greater understanding of his role as a single parent. He realizes his behavior must change. He needs to alter the way he communicates. After their conversation, Stanion and Kevin start to understand each other's point of view. Stanion has begun to question Kevin's behavior in his mind: "what led the boy to do this? what did this hark back to?" (88-89). Both want to be closer to each other and they start to reach out to one another. Though he still feels helpless, Stanion has begun to seek solutions.

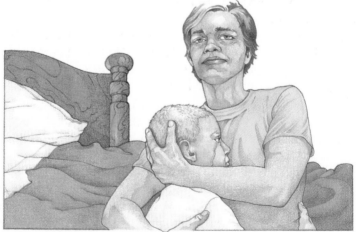

WRITING WORKSHOP

A Movie Review

In Shakespeare's day, audiences went to the theater for a rollicking good time; today, you go to the movies. As expensive as movies are today, you can be sure you're getting your money's worth by checking out the review first. In many ways, a movie review is similar to the essay of literary analysis you wrote about a poem. A movie review analyzes the elements of a movie—script, acting, special effects, and so on. However, a review combines analysis with evaluation; the writer judges the worth of the work. As you read this excerpt from Roger Ebert's review of the classic film *Star Wars*, think about its content and its tone. Notice that the tone is less formal than that of a literary analysis.

Star Wars
by Roger Ebert

Star Wars is a fairy tale, a fantasy, a legend, finding its roots in some of our most popular fictions. The golden robot, lion-faced space pilot, and insecure little computer on wheels must have been suggested by the Tin Man, the Cowardly Lion, and the Scarecrow in *The Wizard of Oz.* The journey from one end of the galaxy to another is out of countless thousands of space operas. The hardware is from *Flash Gordon* out of *2001,* the chivalry is from *Robin Hood,* the heroes are from Westerns and the villains are a cross between Nazis and sorcerers. *Star Wars* taps the pulp fantasies buried in our memories, and because it's done so brilliantly, it reactivates old thrills, fears, and exhilarations we thought we'd abandoned when we read our last copy of *Amazing Stories.*

The movie works so well for several reasons, and they don't all have to do with the spectacular special effects. The effects *are* good, yes, but great effects have been used in such movies as *Silent Running* and *Logan's Run* without setting all-time box-office records. No, I think the key to *Star Wars* is more basic than that.

The movie relies on the strength of pure narrative, in the most basic storytelling form known to man, the Journey. All of the best tales we remember from our childhoods had to do with heroes setting out to travel down roads filled with danger, and hoping to find treasure or heroism at the journey's end. In *Star Wars,* George Lucas takes this simple and powerful framework into outer space, and that is an inspired thing to do, because we no longer have maps on Earth that warn, "Here there be dragons." We can't fall off the edge of the map, as Columbus could, and we can't hope to find new continents of prehistoric monsters or lost tribes ruled by immortal goddesses. Not on Earth, anyway, but anything is possible in space, and Lucas goes right ahead and shows us very nearly everything. We get involved quickly, because the characters in *Star Wars* are so strongly and simply drawn and have so many small foibles and large, futile hopes for us to identify with. And then Lucas does an interesting thing. As he sends his heroes off to cross the universe and do battle with the Forces of Darth Vader, the evil Empire, and the awesome Death Star, he gives us lots of special effects, yes—ships passing into hyperspace, alien planets, an infinity of stars—but we also get a wealth of strange living creatures, and Lucas correctly guesses that they'll be more interesting for us than all the intergalactic hardware.

1. How much does the writer tell you about the plot of *Star Wars*? What *doesn't* he tell you?
2. Describe the review's tone. What makes it fun to read?

3. This is only part of Ebert's review of *Star Wars*. What do you think is Ebert's overall evaluation of the film?
4. Have you seen *Star Wars*, either in a theater or on videotape? Do you agree with Ebert's evaluation?

Writing a Movie Review

 Prewriting. Make a list of movies you've seen recently, and decide which movie you'd like to review for an audience of your friends and classmates. You may want to choose one that's available on videotape so you can see it again.

These features are usually found in movie reviews.

1. The title and genre (horror, comedy, romance, science fiction, adventure, and so on).
2. Some background information about the movie's subject.
3. The purpose and/or theme. Is the purpose of the work simply to entertain (a scary adventure thriller), or does it reveal some truth about life and people?
4. A very short summary of the plot. (Don't give away any surprises, including the movie's ending.)
5. An evaluation of the main characters' performances.
6. An overall evaluation, backed up with solid reasons.

Writing, Evaluating, and Revising. Keep your tone light, and find a way to capture your reader's interest. The introduction might cover features 1–3 on the list above. Features 4 and 5 and whatever else you would like to say about the movie could be discussed in the body of the review. Your conclusion should cover feature 6, your overall evaluation.

In a group of three or four classmates, comment on each other's first drafts. Does the review give the reader enough information to decide whether to see the movie? Is the review concise? Is it fun to read?

 Proofreading and Publishing. If you are writing about a first-run movie or a video available at local stores, submit your review to your school newspaper. Consider compiling a special edition of movie reviews to share with friends and other classes. (It's especially interesting to compare several students' reviews of the same movie.) Before you publish, proofread the final draft carefully.

MAKING CONNECTIONS

A Musical Performance Review

Literary performances share certain elements with musical performances: Both communicate feelings about events and people. Likewise, a critical evaluation of a musical performance resembles a critical review of a movie in many ways.

Think of a musical performance that you've heard or seen lately, or think of one you would like to hear or see in the next few days. The performance could be a live or taped musical drama; a video performance of a single rock, pop, or country song; or an audiotape, record, or compact disc recording of a song. After you have selected the performance, use the following questions to evaluate it.

1. What kind of music is being performed, and who are the performers?
2. What type of musical performance (for example, musical drama, video recording, or audio recording) is it? What style (rock, pop, country, classical, dramatic) is it?
3. What is the quality of the performance? How good is the music itself? How good are the lyrics?

4. How effective are individual performers? How good is the lead singer or musician? How good is the backup?

5. If the performance is visual, how effective are the costumes, props, and lighting?

As you read the following review of a performance, identify the elements the reviewer has chosen to evaluate.

Típica Sound of Cuba
by Peter Watrous

The band was playing the típica style of Cuban music, a form that mixes strings with flute and heavy percussion and that is rarely heard anymore.

Formed four months ago by Rene Lorente, who arrived in the United States from Cuba some eight months ago, the group is meant to be an American version of Cuba's great Orquesta Aragon, in which Mr. Lorente played the flute.

The flute in the típica style plays the role of the lead singer, and Mr. Lorente didn't fool around: he's an exciting improviser, almost vicious with his use of rhythms. When the band moved into the improvisatory montuno section of a piece, he kept an endless flow of ideas rolling, starting a solo with a short riff or two, playing some long and gently floating lines, then jumping back into a sharp riff.

The rhythms, meant to give dancers accents to play with, snapped and exploded and made themselves feel inevitable.

The singers, Pepe Mora and Jorge Castillo, offered words of advice to the audience on how to enjoy themselves, throwing up a choir of voices to counter Mr. Lorente's improvising. The audience, taking the verbal and rhythmic suggestions, did just that.

Write a brief critical review of a musical performance, and share it with your classmates. Follow the three-part format (introduction, body, conclusion) of your movie review (page 397). Your musical performance review should cover some—though not necessarily all—of the questions above and on page 398. If you write about tapes or compact discs, you might play an excerpt before you read your review aloud to the class.

LITERATURE AND PERSUASION

A Book Advertisement

Books, like movies, are often advertised in newspapers, magazines, and book club flyers, and on the covers of the books themselves. A book advertisement has a different purpose than a literary analysis. The purpose of the advertisement is to persuade the reader to buy a particular book; the purpose of a literary analysis is to inform and explain.

Book advertisements differ greatly, but most ads have these basic features:

- title and author
- an interest-catching opening
- information about the type of book and its content that will be appealing to the reader

The following advertisement is the back-cover text of Paul Theroux's *Riding the Iron Rooster*, the author's account of train travel through China. Does reading the ad make you want to read the book?

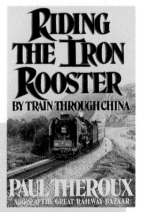

The world seems to grow smaller every day. Travelers cross oceans and continents in the blink of an eye. But the world is not so small that there is no room left for adventure and discovery. In RIDING THE IRON ROOSTER, Paul Theroux invites you to join him on the journey of a lifetime—a journey in the grand romantic tradition. Vowing to reach the other side of the world without jet lag, Theroux began his odyssey in London. He traveled by train across Europe, through the vast underbelly of Asia, and into the heart of Russia. But the crown jewel of his journey was China itself. Here is a magnificent land and an extraordinary people as you have never before known them: China by rail, as seen and heard through the eyes and ears of one of the most intrepid and insightful travel writers of our time.

Try writing an advertisement for a book you have read recently or for one of your all-time favorites. Do you own some books—perhaps paperbacks—that you would like to sell or swap? Your class might start a Book Swap Shop. You can "publish" ads on the bulletin board, or you can start a small weekly or monthly flyer advertising books you and your classmates would like to sell or swap. You can even illustrate your ads. The final step is to enjoy your ads and the new books you'll get from the Swap Shop.

LITERATURE AND EVALUATION

Understanding Deductive Reasoning

When you reason *inductively* (Chapter 7, pages 263–265), you observe a number of particulars or specific instances and draw a conclusion about them. The opposite kind of reasoning is called *deductive:* You start with a general rule or general knowledge and apply it to a specific instance in order to draw a conclusion about that instance.

You use deductive reasoning when you evaluate something, whether it is a movie, a pair of shoes, or a poem. If you wrote a movie or music review earlier in this chapter, part of your task was to evaluate. For example, the *Star Wars* review (page 395) uses deductive reasoning to evaluate the movie.

> **General rule (Major premise):** A strong narrative, strongly drawn characters, and good special effects create a good movie.
> **Specific instance (Minor premise):** *Star Wars* has a strong narrative, strongly drawn characters, and good special effects.
> **Conclusion:** *Star Wars* is a good movie.

Get together with a partner and reread the reviews you wrote earlier in this chapter as well as four or five movie, book, or music reviews in newspapers or magazines. Look for deductive reasoning. What general rule does the writer state? How is it applied to the work being reviewed? What is the writer's conclusion?

Exploring Your World

When you think of someone exploring the world, you may think of expeditions to the South Pole or to the top of Mount Everest. But there are other ways to **explore your world:** you can listen, observe, experiment, and read.

Writing and You.   Reports of research and explorations come in many forms. A corporate executive puts her findings about a new management technique in a memo; a football scout takes notes on a rival team's strategies and presents the coach with a written or oral report; and a reporter researches the state's court system and prepares a documentary for a local television station. How do you think these people found their information?

As You Read.   The following selection explains how the young Galileo discovered a principle that changed timekeeping significantly. What way did Galileo use to explore his world?

from

MAKING TIME PORTABLE

from

" ...Galileo's own way of learning, from observing and measuring what he saw, expressed the science of the future."

❖

In 1583 Galileo Galilei (1564–1642), a youth of nineteen attending prayers in the baptistery of the Cathedral of Pisa, was, according to tradition, distracted by the swinging of the altar lamp. No matter how wide the swing of the lamp, it seemed that the time it took the lamp to move from one end to the other was the same. Of course Galileo had no watch, but he checked the intervals of the swing by his own pulse. This curious everyday puzzle, he said, enticed him away from the study of medicine, to which his father had committed him, to the study of mathematics and physics. In the baptistery he had discovered what physicists would call the isochronism, or equal time of the pendulum—that the time of a pendulum's swing varies not with the width of the swing but with the length of the pendulum.

This simple discovery symbolized the new age. Astronomy and physics at the University of Pisa, where Galileo was enrolled, had consisted of lectures on the texts of Aristotle. But Galileo's own way of learning, from observing and measuring what he saw, expressed the science of the future. His discovery, although never fully exploited by Galileo himself, opened a new era in timekeeping. Within three decades after Galileo's death the average error of the best timepieces was reduced from fifteen minutes to only ten seconds per day.

A clock that kept perfect step with countless other clocks elsewhere made time a measure transcending space. Citizens of Pisa could know what time it was in Florence or in Rome at that very moment. Once such clocks were synchronized they would stay synchronized. No longer a mere local convenience for measuring the craftsman's hours or fixing the time for worship or the town council's meeting, henceforth the clock was a universal yardstick. Just as the equal hour standardized the units of day and night, summer and winter, in any particular town, so now the precision clock standardized the units of time all over the planet.

Certain peculiarities of our planet made this magic possible. Because the earth turns on its axis, every place on earth experiences a 24-hour day with each full 360-degree turn. The meridians of longitude mark off these degrees. As the earth turns, it brings noon successively to different places. When it is noon in Istanbul, it is still only 10 A.M. westward at London. In one hour the earth turns 15 degrees. Therefore we can say that London is 30 degrees longitude, or two hours, west of Istanbul, which makes those degrees of longitude measures of both space and time. If

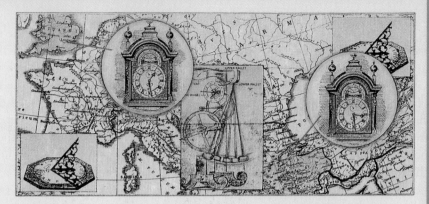

you have an accurate clock set to the time at London and carry it to Istanbul, by comparing the time on the clock you have carried with the local time in Istanbul, you will also know precisely how far you have traveled eastward, or how far east Istanbul is from London.

The Discoverers

READER'S RESPONSE

1. Few people make the world-shaking discoveries that Galileo did. Yet most people, at one time or another, notice some of the oddities of the physical world—a chameleon changing colors, water disappearing into steam, the optical illusion of a mirage. In a brief journal entry, explore one such oddity that made an impression on you.
2. Some people argue that we would be better off *without* timepieces accurate to the microsecond and life geared to the clock. What do you think? What would it be like if every town in America just kept time for itself? More personally, what do you notice about your life when you don't wear a watch?

WRITER'S CRAFT

3. Daniel Boorstin gives no source notes for his information because it has been known and handed down for centuries. In what books or reference works might you find information about Galileo or timekeeping?
4. Boorstin explains some potentially difficult concepts—isochronism, meridians of longitude, degrees of rotation as measures of space and time—clearly and simply. How does he do it? Point out some good explanatory details and illustrations.

Ways to Develop Research

In our age, every day seems to bring an amazing advance in the communication of information: encyclopedias on diskettes, research data and pictures from spacecraft, computer networks for everything from disease control to sports statistics. You have available to you a multitude of research reports from a multitude of sources: businesses, government, "think tanks," and marketers.

Some of these reports are *informal;* that is, they don't contain footnotes or a detailed list of the sources of the report's information. The preceding selection by Daniel J. Boorstin is an example of this kind of informal report. A *formal report,* on the other hand, like the one you'll be writing in this chapter or the ones in scholarly journals, always documents the sources used. Formal reports not only cover a topic in depth, but also tell readers where the writer obtained the information, so that readers can consult the writer's sources if they wish.

Reports on research, whether they give information informally or formally, can be developed in various ways. Here are some examples.

▶ **Narration:** producing a documentary videotape about how volunteers in your community helped citizens build new houses; reporting on events leading up to the Persian Gulf Conflict (1990–1991) in the Middle East.

Description: describing the camouflage markings of rain forest moths; describing the Mayan artifacts discovered in an archaeological dig in Yucatán.

▶ **Classification:** reporting on specific genes that produce hereditary diseases; comparing and contrasting the military achievements of American Civil War generals Ulysses S. Grant and Robert E. Lee.

Evaluation: reporting scientific findings about the effects of pollutants dispersed from a paper mill into a local river; reporting the results of tests to determine which brand of television set has the best performance record.

In this chapter, you will work step by step in planning, organizing, gathering data for, and writing a formal research report. You'll also work on informal reports about travel and about a newsmaker in your community. In your formal report, you will use the strategy of either narration or classification. As you work, keep in mind that a formal report

- presents factual information about a specific topic
- presents information from a number of sources
- documents its sources of information

"RESEARCH

is formalized curiosity.
It is poking and prying
with purpose."

Zora Neale Hurston

Writing a Research Paper

Prewriting

Finding a Research Topic

When the Library of Congress purchased the six thousand books in Thomas Jefferson's library, those books formed the basis of its entire collection. The world was a simpler place then. Today if you walk into a public library in any city, you are likely to find many times that number of books. Some are fiction, of course, but many represent a whole world of research: results of research, reports on research studies, and springboards for additional research.

Discovering Subjects

Any library, bookstore, or video store provides evidence of the inexhaustible list of subjects people find fascinating. But what fascinates *you*? To write an effective research report, investigate your own interests first. Here are some ways to get started.

SOURCES FOR RESEARCH SUBJECTS

- **Family and friends:** Does someone you know have an interesting job or hobby—a legislator? a spelunker?

- **Heroes:** Whom do you admire and wish you knew more about—an inventor? a film director? a president?

- **Places near and far:** What trip was a highlight of your life? What place have you always wanted to see—a city? a landmark? a landform? a country?

- **Current events:** When you turn on television news or open a newspaper, which events and subjects grab your attention—environmental disasters? civil rights?

- **Library and media:** What subjects arouse your curiosity if you browse through books, magazines, and the card catalog; turn the pages of the *Readers' Guide to Periodical Literature;* or check out television listings and videotapes—modern warfare? opera? American pioneers?

Selecting a Specific Topic

Your first idea may be a very broad subject, such as "great scientists" or "the American Civil War" or "African American literature." However, you have to narrow the focus of that broad idea: to find a specific aspect of the subject that intrigues you and that can be covered in a composition. (Your teacher may specify a length for the paper; a usual range is five to ten pages.)

One way to narrow the focus is to look for subtopics in the card catalog, the *Readers' Guide*, encyclopedias, and specialized dictionaries. And sometimes you can narrow a topic just by closer scrutiny. Whatever your process, your constant challenge to yourself is this: *Be more specific.*

HERE'S HOW

Subject:	I'm interested in African American literature.
Be more specific:	Zora Neale Hurston is great.
Be more specific:	She was an anthropologist <u>and</u> a novelist.
Be more specific:	I could research her work as an anthropologist and her fiction.
Limited topic:	How Zora Neale Hurston's study of anthropology and her fiction are related

Finally, your choice of topic must be suitable for a research paper. Besides personal interest and scope, keep the following requirements in mind.

CHECKLIST FOR A SUITABLE TOPIC

1. **Available sources of information.** Since your purpose is to report information, be sure you can *find* five or six good sources. You may not be able to find enough sources for very new or technical topics.

2. **Objectivity and facts.** Your interest leads to a topic, but your experience isn't the basis of a report. You could write about how sonar detection of fish works, but not about your fishing trips using the equipment.

3. **Audience interest.** Almost any topic can be interesting, but think ahead. If your topic isn't automatically appealing ("the Smoot-Hawley Tariff Act of 1930") or is so appealing it's widely known ("the disappearance of dinosaurs"), what unusual approach can you take? What could intrigue your readers?

EXERCISE 1 **Evaluating Topics for Research**

Which of the following topics are suitable for a seven- to ten-page research report? Some may be too broad, too narrow, or too personal. For each topic that seems unsuitable, first tell what's wrong with it; then suggest a more workable topic.

1. how the War of Jenkins' Ear got its name
2. a television program worth watching
3. daily life of women in the Iroquois Nation
4. John Bardeen's contributions to developing the transistor
5. the American space-exploration program

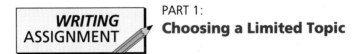

WRITING ASSIGNMENT

PART 1:
Choosing a Limited Topic

What topic can hold your attention? What do you wish you knew more about? Use the idea starters on page 409; if your idea is too broad, *be more specific*. Narrow your topic, and make sure it meets checklist requirements given above.

Prewriting

Beginning Your Research

In a real way, you're a hunter on the eve of a wide-open hunt. You don't know exactly what you are going to find or where you will find it. A hunter in this position could be excited, apprehensive—or both, although a research hunt doesn't have to be aimless or its trail filled with obstacles. There's a well-established method that will help you in your search.

Considering Purpose, Audience, and Tone

Start with first things first: Why are you setting out, and what are you supposed to bring back?

Purpose.   Your *purpose* is to inform readers through research; but you're not just compiling a list of facts and expert opinions, and you're not writing only for others. Your research paper will be an original **synthesis** (combination) of information, and it will widen your own experience and knowledge. To write, you'll have to *think about* what you discover, and you'll pass on your insights.

Audience.   Usually you are writing for your classmates and teacher and have a good idea of what background explanations you must give and how technical you can be. Don't lose readers by being either too elementary or too complex. If you plan your report for another specific *audience,* then tailor your approach and content to them.

Tone.   Anyone who bothers to thoroughly investigate a topic takes that topic seriously; but the *tone* of the report, although a serious one, may vary from somewhat informal to very formal. Research reports that are included in popular periodicals or in mass market nonfiction may be relatively informal. However, the typical academic report, like the ones that are required in school, and the typical professional report, like the ones you may do on your job someday, are formal in tone. In this chapter, you are writing an academic report, and your audience will probably expect a formal tone. A formal tone usually has the following characteristics:

- *Third-person point of view.* You do not use the word *I*.
- *Relatively formal language.* You don't want to sound stuffy, but you should not be too casual and colloquial. Formal language usually does not include slang, colloquial expressions, or contractions.

☞ REFERENCE NOTE: To review the use of formal and informal language, see pages 484–488.

Asking Research Questions

A first step toward your research is posing general questions that you want to answer. At this early stage, you can't come up with *all* the important questions about your topic, but you can establish guides for exploration. The following example shows how one writer developed questions to focus the research about Zora Neale Hurston's anthropology and fiction.

Did Zora Neale Hurston write any fiction before becoming an anthropologist? If so, did it differ from her fiction written afterward?

What did Hurston focus on as an anthropologist?

Do elements of her studies appear in her fiction, and how? folk tales? characters?

Did Hurston herself ever suggest links between her academic studies and her fiction?

Getting an Overview and Finding Sources

You can use general reference works like encyclopedias and biographical dictionaries to get an overview of your topic. In the process, you may get ideas for other research questions, and you may find helpful references to other information sources.

If your topic is narrowly focused ("weather forecasting by supercomputer"), you may not find an encyclopedia entry for it, but you can look for related or larger topics ("meteorology," "supercomputers"). If you already have a solid background in your topic, you can eliminate general reference works and go directly to the types of sources listed in the chart on the next page. As you look for information, remember both print and nonprint sources, library and community resources.

INFORMATION RESOURCES	
LIBRARY	
SOURCES	**TYPES OF INFORMATION**
Card catalog or on-line catalog	Books, audiovisuals (separate catalogs in some libraries)
Readers' Guide to Periodical Literature or on-line periodical indexes	Magazines and some journal articles
Newspaper indexes, specialized reference books	Newspapers (often on micro-film); dictionaries, encyclo-pedias, bibliographies on particular topics
Microfilm or microfiche	Indexes to major newspapers; back issues of some news-papers and magazines
COMMUNITY	
SOURCES	**TYPES OF INFORMATION**
Museums, historical societies, government offices	Exhibits, records, experts
Schools and colleges	Libraries, experts
Television and radio, video stores	Documentary and instruc-tional programs and video-tapes

☞ REFERENCE NOTE: For more help on using the library, see pages 959–965.

Making Source Cards.   When you find possible sources, it's important to keep accurate and complete information on them. Your *Works Cited list*—the list of sources at the end of your report—must contain specific information because some of your readers may want to consult your sources.

The best method of collecting accurate information is to put each source on a 3″ x 5″ card. Sample *source cards* (sometimes called *bibliography cards*) are shown on page 415. In the long run you'll save time by doing your source cards in final format, pre-pared in the exact style required for the Works Cited list. (Many more examples of proper style are shown in **Sample Entries for the List of Works Cited,** pages 442–446.)

GUIDELINES FOR SOURCE CARDS

1. **Assign each source a number.** Later, when you're taking notes, it will save time to write a number instead of the author and title.
2. **Record full publishing information.** Record everything you might need: subtitles, translators, and volume and edition numbers. It's better to have too much than to be missing information for your Works Cited list and have to backtrack. (For examples of the types of information you will need, see the sample Works Cited entries on pages 442–446.)
3. **Note the call number or location.** This information will help you relocate the source quickly if you need to.

Sample Source Cards

Book

> 5
>
> Hurston, Zora Neale. <u>Mules and Men</u>. Philadelphia:
>   Lippincott, 1935.
>
>   School Library
>   398.3
>   Hur

HERE'S HOW

Magazine

> 6
>
> Pinckney, Darryl. "In Sorrow's Kitchen." <u>New York</u>
>   <u>Review of Books</u> 21 Dec. 1978: 55–57.
>
>   Northside Library

Although the style for documenting sources shown in this chapter is the one recommended by the Modern Language Association of America (MLA), an organization of language scholars, your teacher may ask you to use a different style. Whatever style you use, it is important to be consistent and to include all the information required.

Evaluating Sources.   Just as you can't judge a book by its cover, you can't always judge your sources by their titles. Before using a source, you need to evaluate its usefulness to you. A good way is to see if it meets the "4R" test.

1. *Relevant.* Does the source's information relate directly to your limited topic? For a book, check the table of contents and index. Skim magazine articles. Some nonprint sources include summaries and you may also find reviews.
2. *Reliable.* Can you trust it? A respected scholar, or a respected magazine such as *The Atlantic* or *Scientific American,* can usually be relied on for accuracy. Look for authors who are quoted frequently or appear in most bibliographies on your topic.
3. *Recent.* Be sure you aren't using outdated information, especially for rapidly changing topics. For any topic, look for the most recent work about it. If the author is thorough, you'll learn which older sources of information are still being consulted.
4. *Representative.* If you are working on a controversial topic, you'll need to show different points of view. You don't want a list of sources that are all pro or all con. Your task as a researcher is to study, balance, and interpret the views on all sides.

Using Primary and Secondary Sources.   A *primary source* is firsthand, original information: a letter, an autobiography, an interview with a person who participated in the experience being researched, a work of literature, historical documents. A *secondary source* is information derived from, or about, primary sources and even from other secondary sources: an encyclopedia, a documentary film, a biography, history books, or an interview with a historian.

For example, if you are writing about post-Revolutionary America, the Articles of Confederation and Thomas Jefferson's letters are primary sources. A biography of Jefferson is a secondary source (as your completed paper will be).

Although secondary sources are plentiful and essential to your paper and usually provide excerpts from primary sources, don't use them exclusively when primary sources are available. At the same time, don't assume that all primary sources are exempt from evaluation. Memory may be faulty or selective in an autobiography, and emotions may override facts in a letter. Read and research as widely as possible, so that you have a good basis for deciding what's accurate and what's slanted or biased.

CRITICAL THINKING

Evaluating Sources

Sometimes it isn't possible to know whether a book, an article, or a tape contains material useful to your research until you examine it. But you can evaluate, or judge, some sources even during your initial search by taking careful note of authors, titles, the reputation of magazines and journals, and dates. Remember *relevant, reliable, recent,* and *representative,* the "4R" test (discussed on page 416) that gives you particular qualities to look for in your sources.

CRITICAL THINKING EXERCISE:
Evaluating Sources

Assume that you are working on this topic: "how Zora Neale Hurston's study of anthropology relates to her fiction." From your overview, you know that Hurston lived from either 1891 or 1901 (her birth records aren't certain) to 1960. She studied in the 1930s with Franz Boas, a distinguished anthropologist at Columbia University, and her best novel is generally considered *Their Eyes Were Watching God*, published in 1937.

Discuss the following possible sources in class or in smaller groups. Which ones would probably be helpful? Which ones would not? Why? If you feel uncertain about a source, explain what further information you would like to have about it.

1. Wilson, Margaret F. "Zora Neale Hurston: Author and Folklorist." Negro History Bulletin Oct.-Nov.-Dec. 1982: 109-10.
2. Walker, Alice. "In Search of Zora Neale Hurston." Ms. Mar. 1975: 74+.
3. Fisher, Maxine. Recent Revolutions in Anthropology. New York: Franklin Watts, 1986.
4. Hemenway, Robert E. Zora Neale Hurston: A Literary Biography. Urbana: U of Illinois P, 1977.
5. Boas, Franz. Anthropology and Modern Life. Rev. ed. [revised edition]. New York: Norton, 1932.
6. Hurston, Zora Neale. Jonah's Gourd Vine [a novel]. Philadelphia: Lippincott, 1934, 1971.
7. Bone, Robert. The Negro Novel in America. New Haven: Yale UP, 1958.

Reminder

To begin your research

- identify preliminary research questions
- using general reference works, develop an overview of your topic
- use library and community resources to find possible sources, recording full publishing information for each one on a source card
- evaluate each source according to the "4R" test (page 416)

WRITING ASSIGNMENT

PART 2:
Beginning Your Research

Follow the steps in the Reminder above to start your research, but remember that every research project is unique. Perhaps an instructional videotape, rather than an encyclopedia, could provide an overview of your topic. You may find all the sources you need in a library, or your topic may lead you first to a museum. Whatever path you follow, find at least five or six sources for your paper, each one carefully evaluated and then accurately recorded on a source card.

Calvin & Hobbes, copyright 1987 Universal Press Syndicate. Reprinted with permission of Universal Press Syndicate. All rights reserved.

Prewriting

Recording and Organizing Information

Your source cards list promising sources of information. Your preliminary questions show some of the specific paths your research will take. Now it's time to collect the information you'll need and to find a way of organizing it.

Taking Notes

Before you begin to take notes, read through the material and think about its full meaning. Then go back over the material, using 4" x 6" cards to record your notes. Later, when you're organizing your report, cards make it easy to arrange and rearrange information. Here are more specific tips about note cards. A sample note card is shown on page 421.

GUIDELINES FOR NOTE CARDS

1. **Use a separate card or a half-sheet of paper for each source and item of information.** Again, this will pay off in ease of organizing.
2. **Record the source number.** In the upper right-hand corner of each note card, write the number you have assigned each source. This is important; it's a shorthand system to show exactly where you got the information.
3. **Write a label, or heading.** In the upper left-hand corner of the card, identify the main idea of your note so that you don't later have to reread each note card to discover its basic content.
4. **Write the page number(s).** At the end of your note, write the page numbers from which the information comes. Page references are required for the documentation in your paper.

There are two main kinds of notes you'll take: *direct quotations* and *summaries or paraphrases.*

Direct Quotations.   Resist the urge to quote too much. Quote an author directly only when you want to be sure of technical accuracy or when the author's words are interesting or especially well phrased. Copy the statement exactly (including punctuation, capitalization, and spelling) and enclose it in quotation marks.

Summaries and Paraphrases.
In most of your notes, you will record the author's ideas and facts *in your own words*. A *summary* is highly condensed—typically one fourth to one third the length of the original. A *paraphrase* is a restatement in your own words that allows for more detail.

Whether you summarize or paraphrase, you must use your own words and sentence struc-ture. Try setting the passage aside and writing ideas from memory. Also, use lists and phrases—not complete sen-tences. (See pages 1018–1024 for information on more formal uses of summaries and paraphrases.)

Mules and Men by Zora Neale Hurston. Cover design by Suzanne Noli, Cover Illustration © 1990 by David Diaz. Courtesy of Harper Perennial, a Division of HarperCollins Publishers. All rights reserved.

SAMPLE NOTE CARD

early use of folk tales   5

Arna Bontemps (a black writer and Hurston's friend)
says many of folk tales in <u>Mules and Men</u> were part
of Hurston's storytelling before anthropology at Barnard.
Some early short stories confirm his memory of hearing
the tales when she first came to NY.

pp. 166–67

WRITING NOTE Remember that you must give the writer credit when you use an author's *words or ideas* in your paper. Not to do so is *plagiarism,* an extremely serious offense. Even a summary or paraphrase—if it is someone else's original idea—must be credited.

☞ **REFERENCE NOTE:** For more help with summarizing and paraphrasing, see pages 1018–1024.

EXERCISE 2 ▶ **Taking Notes**

The following excerpt is from an article about the Yanomama Indians that appeared in *Newsweek,* December 3, 1990, on page 48. Assume that you're researching a paper on the world's ancient peoples (those most untouched by civilization) who are threatened by modern life. You've given the article the source number 9. Working with a partner, develop a list of questions using the *5W-How?* questions (page 27). Then prepare a source card and take notes on note cards to answer the questions you have written.

from The Last Days of Eden
by Spencer Reiss

Doshamosha-teri sits on a little hill near a bend in the clear black Siapa River, just north of the equator, in one of the least traveled regions of the Amazonian rain forest. Two dozen extended families of Yanomama Indians—149 broad-chested men, painted women and their children—live there, in one roughly circular thatch-roofed dwelling furnished only with bark hammocks. They cultivate small plots of plantains, gourds and bananas on the hillside. Beyond that the great wall of the emerald rain forest rises, enclosing a dazzling bazaar of wild pigs, monkeys and plumed birds. Most people in Doshamosha-teri ("Maggot-of-the-Gumba-Tree Place") have never heard of Venezuela, though they happen to live there. They have yet to invent the wheel. Their entire number system consists of "one," "two" and "many." Ask about abstractions such as work and leisure, poverty or wealth, and you get a blank stare. Life consists of survival. . . .

Until recently, the Yanomama had the good fortune to live their Stone Age lives on land that no one else wanted. Today their world, 60,000 square miles of rain forest straddling the Venezuelan-Brazilian border, sits in the path of the onrushing juggernaut of development. The 9,000 Yanomama in Brazil have dwindled by one sixth since the gold rush began three years ago, luring tens of thousands of prospectors—and the malaria and other diseases they carry. The dazed survivors are scattered among 19 reserves, gold-hungry miners pressing in from all sides. "The dangers to the Yanomama 20 years ago were minuscule compared to what they are now," anthropologist Napoleon Chagnon said during a recent three-day visit to Doshamosha-teri and other Yanomama settlements in Venezuela's remote Siapa River Valley. "The best we can hope for is a respite, long enough for them to consider their choices."

As the world's largest remaining group of unacculturated tribal people, the Yanomama represent a last chance for the modern world to atone for the savage obliteration of so many of the original Americans, North and South alike. Without fast action, the Yanomama will suffer the same fate—or, perhaps worse, give up their independent ways and join the modern world's long list of pathetic misfits. Governments, Indian activists and scientists agree on the need to save them. The question is, how?

| EXERCISE 3 ▶ | **Speaking and Listening: Conducting an Interview** |

It's one thing to take notes from a written passage; it's quite another to take notes while you are interviewing someone. To practice your interviewing techniques, get together with a partner and identify someone in your community who is knowledgeable about one of the following subjects or another subject of your choice:

emerging technologies
a local historical figure or building
high school or college athletics
domestic animals or wildlife

After you've chosen a subject and identified a person you could interview, contact that person and request an interview. Then, follow these steps:

- Using the *5W-How?* questioning strategy (page 27), prepare a list of eight to ten questions to ask. You may have to do a little background reading to prepare the questions.
- Limit the interview to twenty or thirty minutes, even if you don't finish all your questions. During the interview, one of you should ask the first four or five questions, and the other should ask the remaining four or five questions. Both of you should take notes related to all questions. Be sure to thank the interviewee orally.
- After you've finished the interview, write a follow-up note thanking the interviewee for his or her time. Then compare your interview notes with those of your partner. What are the differences? What do you think caused those differences?

| **WRITING** ASSIGNMENT | PART 3: **Taking Notes** |

Look back at your preliminary research questions (from Writing Assignment, Part 2, page 419) to identify ideas you intend to explore further. Then start reading or viewing your sources and taking notes. Really think about which information you'll need to remember and use when you write. If you aren't selective in your note taking, you will soon be buried in 4″ × 6″ note cards.

Writing a Thesis Statement

You may sit at your desk staring at a stack of notes without knowing what to do next. Read them—again. While you are recording information, you can't see your information as a whole. Once you have gathered your information, you need to review and reflect.

After rereading your notes, you should have a fairly clear picture of your report's main ideas, and you should be able to write a preliminary, or working, thesis statement. The *thesis statement* is a sentence or two stating both your topic and what you will say about it. It's an aid that will help keep you on track as you write your report. Still, your thesis may change as your writing progresses, and often you'll word it differently when drafting. Consider the thesis statement to be a guidepost, not a one-way road. Following are some examples of thesis statements for research papers.

SAMPLE THESIS STATEMENTS

Zora Neale Hurston's work in anthropology affected her fiction--its events, characters, and language.

In the 1950s, Senator Margaret Chase Smith of Maine had the qualifications to be president, but a woman was considered unelectable at the time.

The great Apache chief Cochise was quite different in real life from the Cochise shown in the movies.

Zora Neale Hurston

Margaret Chase Smith

Cochise

☞ REFERENCE NOTE: See pages 102–104 for more help with writing thesis statements.

Developing an Outline

After you have identified your thesis, you are ready to give order to your wealth of information. Start by sorting your note cards into stacks according to their labels. These stacks may immediately suggest the main sections or ideas of your report, as well as the ideas you will emphasize (the larger the stack of note cards, the more attention you will probably give to the idea in your report). Then you can decide how best to order the ideas and which supporting details to use, in which sequence.

Your working outline can be rough or more formal—whatever will give shape and direction to your drafting. But for your completed paper, your teacher may request a final, *formal outline.* This serves basically as a table of contents and is prepared *after* you've finished the report. Following is a portion of a final outline that a writer prepared for a report on Zora Neale Hurston. (Formal outlines often omit the introduction and conclusion.)

Folklore into Fiction:
The Writings of Zora Neale Hurston

I. Childhood in Eatonville
   A. Incorporated black town
   B. Early exposure to folklore
II. College years
   A. Morgan College and Howard University
   B. Early stories using folk tales and Eatonville
   C. Study of anthropology
      1. Ruth Benedict at Barnard College
      2. Franz Boas at Columbia University
         a. Decision to become social scientist
         b. Grant to collect southern folklore
III. Connections between anthropology and fiction
   A. Plots and characters
   B. Dialect and idiom
   C. Portrayal of black life

 **REFERENCE NOTE:** See pages 107–108, 1018 for more on outlining.

WRITING ASSIGNMENT

PART 4:
Organizing Your Information

Doing a research paper doesn't have to be like entering a maze. To start organizing your information, remember your research questions and thesis statement as well as the labels on your note cards. Develop a sense of your main ideas first. Then group your note cards and arrange them in a sensible order, and write a working outline for your draft.

Writing Your First Draft

Structuring the Report

The research report is longer than most papers you write, with several special elements. Use the chart below to get an overview of a report's main parts.

ELEMENTS OF A RESEARCH REPORT	
Formal outline (optional)	Your teacher may ask you to include a final outline of the content of your report.
Title	Your title, often on a separate title page, should be both attention-catching and informative. Ask your teacher about format.
Introduction	Your introduction should draw readers into your report with interesting details or a striking quotation.
Thesis statement	The statement of your thesis should appear early, usually in or at the end of the intro-duction. It might be more than one sentence.
Body	Paragraphs in the body of your report should develop the main ideas that support the thesis statement.
Conclusion	The conclusion should briefly restate your thesis in different words, summarize your main points, or both.
Citations	Throughout the paper, you should include brief references in parentheses (or foot-notes if your teacher recommends them) to credit sources for specific information.
Works Cited list	In a list at the end of the report, you should include all the sources you have cited.

The following writer's model, which shows how one writer used research findings to develop an original paper, can be a guide for writing your first draft. Notice how facts, quotations, and summaries of ideas are worked in. You will see source information in parentheses throughout the paper; these *cita-tions* are fully explained on pages 438–441.

A WRITER'S MODEL

Folklore into Fiction:
The Writings of Zora Neale Hurston

INTRODUCTION
Interesting anecdote/ Summary of article, author named

In 1973, Alice Walker, the author of The Color Purple, made a sentimental visit to the all-black city of Eatonville, Florida. Her goal was to find the grave of a writer she greatly admired, Zora Neale Hurston. Hurston, a major figure of the Harlem Renaissance, died in poverty in 1960. Walker found no grave or marker in Eatonville, Hurston's hometown. Instead, she learned that her literary idol had been buried in an unmarked grave in a segregated cemetery in Fort Pierce, Florida. She commissioned a headstone, which now stands at the site:

ZORA NEALE HURSTON
"A GENIUS OF THE SOUTH"

NOVELIST   FOLKLORIST
ANTHROPOLOGIST
1901   1960

Background information

It is significant that Alice Walker, poet, novelist, and winner of the Pulitzer Prize for fiction, would add "folklorist" and "anthropologist" to her description of the neglected author. For Zora Neale Hurston was more than a gifted novelist. She was also a perceptive student of her own culture, an author of two notable books of folklore, a member of the American FolkLore Society, the American Ethnological Society, and the American Anthropological Society (Hurston, Dust Tracks 171).

Thesis statement

Hurston's work as an anthropologist is, in fact, directly related to her creative writing. The connection is clear in many elements of her fiction.

BODY
Eatonville childhood

Hurston's life story begins in Eatonville, Florida, not far from Orlando. Eatonville was originally incorporated as an all-black town--a unique situation that had an impact throughout Hurston's life. Her

Important details

hometown was also her earliest training ground

Direct quotation

(although she could hardly have realized it at the time) in black southern folklore, the place where she heard the local storytellers tell their big "lies" (Hurston, Dust Tracks 197).

Young Zora, whose father was a Baptist preacher, received little formal education and worked at menial jobs. However, she read whenever and whatever she could, and her great goal was education.

College years

Paying her own way, Hurston was able to study at Morgan College and Howard University. By that time she was already a writer, using folk tales and her hometown in her fiction. At Howard she wrote

Specific examples

"John Redding Goes to Sea," which had "black folk beliefs" about witches' curses and screech owls

Authors and pages cited

(Ikonné 185-186). Another early short story, "Spunk," was set in "an unnamed village that is obviously Eatonville" (Hemenway 41, 77-78).

Then came a turning point in her life. In 1925 she was admitted to prestigious Barnard College in New York City--its first black student (Howard, "Being Herself" 101-02). At Barnard, Hurston

Study of anthropology

studied anthropology under Ruth Benedict. Just before she graduated, Franz Boas of Columbia University, another eminent anthropologist, read one of her term papers. Boas invited Hurston to study with him and gave her another way to look at the Eatonville tales she loved to tell. According to

Author named in text, more than one title in Works Cited

Lillie Howard, "She learned to view the good old lies and racy, sidesplitting anecdotes . . . as invaluable folklore, creative material that continued the African oral tradition . . ." ("Hurston" 135). Hurston decided then to become a serious social scientist. In 1927 Boas recommended her for the first of several grants she was to receive, and she headed south to gather folklore.

Writer's conclusion/ transitional statement

Clearly, Hurston's attraction to her culture's stories and to writing fiction were always intertwined. Anthropology simply made her natural attention to black folklore and culture more systematic and

Direct quotation within a sentence

intensive; as she said, "research is formalized curiosity" (qtd. in Chamberlain).

Connections between anthropology and fiction

After she began doing fieldwork, she alternated between anthropological and creative writing. Her study of Eatonville folk tales and New Orleans hoodoo (voodoo) in 1927 and 1928 resulted in the book of folk tales <u>Mules and Men</u>, and she wrote her first novel, <u>Jonah's Gourd Vine</u>, soon after. Many critics have noted that all of Hurston's novels showed the effects of her study of anthropology, and one of the most obvious connections between the two appears in her fiction's plots and characters.

Plots and characters

Examples

Just one example of how Hurston's research worked into the plot of <u>Jonah's Gourd Vine</u> is the "bitter bone" that An' Dangie uses in a ritual to make Hattie invisible (200). In <u>Mules and Men</u>, Hurston reported how she underwent a whole ceremony to get the "Black Cat Bone," or bitter bone, of invisibility (272).

In later books, too, these connections occur. A field trip to Haiti and Jamaica in 1936 produced <u>Tell My Horse</u>, another study of voodoo. A year after its appearance she published the novel <u>Moses, Man of the Mountain</u>, which has been described as a blend of "fiction, folklore, religion, and comedy" (Howard, "Hurston" 140). In it, Moses is a "hoodoo man," an idea that also appears in <u>Jonah's Gourd Vine</u> (231).

Dialect and black idiom

Dialect and black idiom are also important parts of both Hurston's scientific work and her creative writing. She worked into her fiction the words she heard and researched in the field. According to her biographer, Robert Hemenway, the long sermon that is the climax of <u>Jonah's Gourd Vine</u> "was taken almost verbatim from Hurston's field notes" (197). The novel, in fact, contains so many folk sayings that Robert Bone has claimed ". . . they are too non-functional, too anthropological . . ." (127).

Most critics have agreed with Darryl Pinckney that Hurston's "ear for the vernacular of folk speech is impeccable" (56). Even a critic in 1937 who found Hurston's dialect "less convincing" than another writer's suggested that Hurston's dialect might be more realistic (Thompson). Her excellent

ear and her "skill at transcribing" (Young 220) made the language in her first novel something new and therefore somewhat hard to read:

Long quotation, indented; quotation marks for dialogue

> "Iss uh shame, Sister. Ah'd cut down dat Jonah's gourd vine in uh minute, if Ah had all de say-so. You know Ah would, but de majority of 'em don't keer whut he do, some uh dese people stands in wid it. De man mus' is got roots uh got piece uh dey tails buried by his door-step. . . ." (230)

However, some black writers of Hurston's time disapproved of her "playing the minstrel" in her fiction's use of southern black dialect--and in other ways as well. Zora Neale Hurston was in fact a controversial figure within the Harlem Renaissance. She was attacked for her novels' picture of black life, and this portrayal is another connection between her anthropology and her fiction (Howard, "Being Herself" 156).

Portrayal of black life

Hurston came to New York when the Harlem Renaissance was in full bloom. This literary movement of the 1920s included such noted writers as Langston Hughes, Countee Cullen, Jean Toomer, and Arna Bontemps. They, too, were celebrating blackness and bringing it to the public, but they saw their mission as "a guiding elite" for other blacks who were not as liberated (Pinckney 55). They didn't want to support a stereotyped image in art. Sterling Brown even attacked Hurston's nonfiction. He said that "Mules and Men should be more bitter" (qtd. in Howard, "Hurston" 139).

Background: *Harlem Renaissance*

Paraphrase

Hurston, on the other hand, believed she was serving an unmet need. Negro folklore had always fascinated the American public; but it had been presented mostly by white writers (such as Joel Chandler Harris), and to her it seemed either patronizing or inadequate (Wilson 109). She wanted to put it in its true social context.

Moreover, Hurston felt her picture of blacks in Jonah's Gourd Vine and in Their Eyes Were Watching God, generally regarded as her finest

novel, was thoroughly realistic. She felt that the Harlem Renaissance writers were unfairly criticizing her fiction because it didn't have a political message. She said they believed ". . . Negroes were supposed to write about the Race Problem," while her intent in Jonah's Gourd Vine was "to tell . . . a story about a man" (Dust Tracks 214).

Hurston did not intend to be a reformer if it meant falsifying what she saw as a scientist and wanted to achieve as an artist. Through her field-work she knew intimately the everyday, "normal life of Negroes in the South," and that's what she focused on in much of her fiction (Thompson). Also, her study of many cultures showed her that folk tales functioned, in part, the same way all over the world, as "communal tradition in which distinctive ways of behaving and coping with life were orally trans-mitted" (Pinckney 56). Hurston thought the tales were sophisticated and important and should be shown as they were. Margaret Wilson sums up Hurston's anthropological and fictional beliefs this way: "She saw people as people" (110).

Several sources used as support

So even though critics like Richard Wright, Alain Locke, and Sterling Brown objected to the "minstrel image" of blacks in a novel such as Their Eyes Were Watching God, other critics saw both a realistic, vibrant main character (Janie) and Hurston's "fullest description of the mores [customs and values] in Eatonville" (Hemenway 241-42; Pinckney 56). Perhaps Hurston would have been more "race conscious" if she had not grown up in and studied Eatonville, a wholly self-governing black town; but that does not negate the reality of what she observed and transformed into fiction (Wilson 109; Pinckney 56).

Writer's addition in brackets

Two sources cited at once

CONCLUSION

Restatement of thesis

For better or worse, Hurston's fictional world-- its plots, characters, language, and picture of life-- grew out of the folklore she had heard as a child and then studied as a professional. Like the fine anthropologist she was, Zora Neale Hurston intended to get that world down on paper, and to get it down right.

Clincher statement

Works Cited

Bone, Robert. The Negro Novel in America. New Haven: Yale UP, 1958.

Chamberlain, John. "Books of the Times." New York Times 7 Nov. 1942: 13.

Hemenway, Robert E. Zora Neale Hurston: A Literary Biography. Urbana: U of Illinois P, 1977.

Howard, Lillie P. "Zora Neale Hurston." Dictionary of Literary Biography. 1987 ed.

---. "Zora Neale Hurston: Just Being Herself." Essence Nov. 1980: 100+.

Hurston, Zora Neale. Dust Tracks on a Road: An Autobiography. Philadelphia: Lippincott, 1942.

---. Jonah's Gourd Vine. Philadelphia: Lippincott, 1934, 1971.

---. Moses, Man of the Mountain. Philadelphia: Lippincott, 1939.

---. Mules and Men. Philadelphia: Lippincott, 1935.

---. Tell My Horse: Voodoo and Life in Haiti and Jamaica. Philadelphia: Lippincott, 1938.

Ikonné, Chidi. From Du Bois to Van Vechten: The Early New Negro Literature, 1903-1926. Westport: Greenwood, 1981.

Pinckney, Darryl. "In Sorrow's Kitchen." New York Review of Books 21 Dec. 1978: 55-57.

Thompson, Ralph. "Books of the Times." New York Times 6 Oct. 1937: 23.

Walker, Alice. "In Search of Zora Neale Hurston." Ms. Mar. 1975: 74+.

Wilson, Margaret F. "Zora Neale Hurston: Author and Folklorist." Negro History Bulletin Oct.-Nov.-Dec. 1982: 109-10.

Young, James O. Black Writers of the Thirties. Baton Rouge: Louisiana State UP, 1973.

Using Quotations

Even though much of what you put in your report will be summarized or paraphrased, you'll find that good quotations, especially short ones, can add interest and authority to your writing. You can work quotations smoothly into your paper in several ways.

GUIDELINES FOR USING QUOTATIONS

1. *Quote a whole sentence, introducing it in your own words.*

   EXAMPLE Margaret Wilson sums up Hurston's belief this way: "She saw people as people" (110).

2. *Quote part of a sentence within a sentence of your own.*

   EXAMPLE The long sermon "was taken almost verbatim from Hurston's field notes" (Hemenway 197).

3. *Quote just one or a few words within a sentence of your own.*

   EXAMPLE Eatonville was where she heard the local story-tellers tell their "lies" (Hurston, Dust Tracks 197).

4. *Use ellipses (three spaced dots) to indicate omissions from quotations.* Sometimes you need only a part of a quotation to make your point. Use ellipses to indicate words deleted within a quotation or any deletion that leaves a quotation that appears to be a complete sentence but is only part of the original.

   EXAMPLE According to Lillie Howard, "She learned to view the good old lies . . . as invaluable folk-lore . . . " ("Hurston" 136).

5. *Set off longer quotations as "blocks."* If a quotation will be more than four typed lines, start a new line, indent the entire quotation ten spaces from the left, and do not use quotation marks. Double-space a long quotation just like the rest of your report. For an example, see the blocked quotation on page 432. [Note: The example uses quotation marks because it is *dialogue* in the source.]

EXERCISE 4 ▶   **Creating Tables, Charts, and Graphs**

Sometimes neither summary nor quotation is the best method of presenting source information to readers. For numerical data or other detailed facts, a table, chart, or graph can show a great deal of information clearly and compactly. You can use a chart you find during research or create your own. (For more information on creating charts, see pages 39–41 and 1017.)

Suppose you're writing a paper about the role teenagers play in the national economy. To practice putting research findings into graphic form, work with others to conduct a survey of students about finances and spending habits. Use an anonymous questionnaire, and survey representative groups, perhaps all members of one homeroom at each grade level. Find out the facts indicated in the sample table, and follow its form to display your findings. [Note: *Discretionary spending* is spending for personal, nonessential purposes—a student's "free" money.] The sample table follows the MLA style.

Table 1

Average Weekly Income and Discretionary Spending of Students at [High School Name, Year][a]

	Allowance	Earnings	Discretionary Spending	% of Total Income
Seniors	$ —	$ —	$ —	—
Juniors	$ —	$ —	$ —	—
Sophomores	$ —	$ —	$ —	—
Freshmen	$ —	$ —	$ —	—

[a] Figures based on a survey of [Report the number of students surveyed and the groups they represent]

Documenting Sources

Deciding which information you must *document,* or give credit for, in a research paper sometimes requires thought. That thought process can start with noticing what is or is not documented when you read reports of research. The following guidelines will also help you stay clear of documentation pitfalls.

WHAT TO DOCUMENT

1. In general, don't document information that appears in several sources or facts that appear in standard reference books. For example, a statement like *"Their Eyes Were Watching God* is generally considered Hurston's finest novel" needs no documentation because it clearly relies on several sources. The main facts of her life that are available in encyclopedias and other standard references also do not need to be credited.
2. Document the source of each direct quotation (unless it's very widely known, such as Patrick Henry's "Give me liberty or give me death!").
3. Document any original theory or opinion other than your own. Since ideas belong to their authors, you must not present the ideas of other people as your own.
4. Document the source of data or other information from surveys, scientific experiments, and research studies.
5. Document unusual, little known, or questionable facts and statistics.

EXERCISE 5 ▶ **Judging What to Document**

If each of the following items were to appear in a research paper on the baseball player Christy Mathewson, which ones would you need to document? Discuss your responses in class.

1. Christy Mathewson, a right-handed pitcher, played for the New York Giants from 1900 to 1916.
2. A little-known Chicago Cub first baseman, Vic Saier, hit five career home runs off Mathewson—more than any other player.

3. About Mathewson's early death, Kenesaw Mountain Landis said, "Why should God wish to take a thoroughbred like Matty so soon, and leave some others down here that could well be spared?"

4. The grave of Christy Mathewson is in City Cemetery, Lewisburg, Pennsylvania.

5. Luke Salisbury, commenting on Eric Rolfe Greenberg's novel *The Celebrant*, said that Mathewson embodied baseball.

Parenthetical Citations. A *parenthetical citation* gives source information in parentheses in the body of a research paper. There are two main issues concerning the handling of these citations: (1) Exactly where does the citation go? (2) What are the content and correct form of the citation?

To determine where to place a citation, you can follow the general rules given below. You'll also find it helpful to look at the Writer's Model to see how citations appear there.

PLACEMENT OF CITATIONS

1. Place the citation as close as possible to the material it documents, if possible at the end of a sentence or at another point of punctuation.

2. Place the citation *before* the punctuation mark of the sentence, clause, or phrase you are documenting.

EXAMPLE   Her best work appeared after she had abandoned the narrow academic approach (Hemenway 215).

(continued)

PLACEMENT OF CITATIONS *(continued)*

3. For a quotation that ends a sentence, put the citation *after* the quotation mark but *before* the end punctuation mark.

   EXAMPLE   As Lillie P. Howard points out, "She wasn't but had sense enough to say that she was" ("Being Herself" 160).

4. For an indented quotation, put the citation *two spaces after* the final punctuation mark.

   EXAMPLE   (See page 432.)

The content and form of parenthetical citations are fairly easy once you understand the basic principle, which is this: *The citation should provide just enough information to lead the reader to the full source listing in Works Cited.*

Since the Works Cited list is alphabetized by authors' last names, an author's last name and the page numbers are usually enough. There are some exceptions of course; information about some of them is given below.

- A nonprint source such as an interview or audiotape will not have a page number.
- A print source of fewer than two pages (such as a one-page letter) will not require a page number.
- If you name the author in your sentence, you need give only the page number (for print sources of more than one page) in parentheses:

  According to her biographer, Robert Hemenway, the long sermon that is the climax of <u>Jonah's Gourd Vine</u> "was taken almost verbatim from Hurston's field notes" (197).

- If the author has more than one work in the Works Cited list, you will also have to give a short form of the title so readers will know which work you are citing:

  (Hurston, <u>Dust Tracks</u> 171).

Sources do vary, of course, and you'll sometimes have to refer to guidelines for correct form. The chart that follows shows the form for seven kinds of sources.

BASIC CONTENT AND FORM FOR PARENTHETICAL CITATIONS

These examples assume that the author or work has not already been named in a sentence introducing the source's information.

Works by One Author

Author's last name and a page reference

(Hemenway 197)

Separate Passages in a Single Work

Author's last name and multiple page references

(Hemenway 41, 77-78)

Works by More than One Author

All authors' last names or *et al.* ("and others") if over three

(Brooks and Warren 24)
(Anderson et al. 313)

Multivolume Works

Author's last name plus volume and page

(Cattell 2: 214-15)

Works with a Title Only

Full title (if short) or a shortened version

("Old Eatonville" 2)
(World Almanac 809)

Literary Works Published in Many Editions

As above, but with other identifying information after a semicolon (for example, act and scene numbers)

(Shakespeare, Hamlet III. 4. 107–08)

Indirect Sources

Abbreviation *qtd. in* [quoted in] before the source

(qtd. in Howard 161)

More than One Work in the Same Citation

Citations separated with semicolons

(Bone 127; Pinckney 56)

[Note: One-page articles do not require a page number.]

WRITING NOTE
Your teacher may want you to use a documentation style different from the parenthetical citation system just discussed. The other common system uses footnotes or endnotes. Footnotes and endnotes are identical except that a footnote is placed at the bottom of the page where you use the source information, while endnotes are listed all together at the end of the report.

Each note is numbered, and a number also appears in the body of your report. The first note for a source gives full information; following notes are shortened. You will need guidelines to prepare notes. One example follows.

EXAMPLE

Note number in body of report   The long sermon "was taken almost verbatim from Hurston's field notes."[3]

Note (full form)   [3] Robert E. Hemenway, <u>Zora Neale Hurston: A Literary Biography</u> (Urbana: U of Illinois P, 1977) 197.

"Writing is the only thing that, when I do it, I don't feel I should be doing something else."

Gloria Steinem

List of Works Cited.   As its name tells you, the Works Cited list contains all the sources, print and nonprint, that you credit in your report. (The term *Works Cited* is a broader title than *Bibliography*, which refers to print sources only.) You may have used other sources, such as general reference works, but if you didn't need to name them, you don't include them in a Works Cited list. (However, some teachers want a list of Works Consulted—all the sources you examined, whether cited or not, instead of, or in addition to, the Works Cited list. Ask to be sure.)

GUIDELINES FOR PREPARING THE LIST OF WORKS CITED

1. Center the words *Works Cited* on a new sheet of paper.
2. Begin each entry on a separate line. Position the first line of the entry even with the left margin and indent the second and all other lines five spaces. Double-space all entries.
3. Alphabetize the sources by the author's last name. If there is no author, alphabetize by title, ignoring *A, An,* and *The* and using the first letter of the next word.
4. If you use two or more sources by the same author, include the author's name only in the first entry. For all other entries, write three hyphens where the author's name would normally be, followed by a period (---.).

You can use the following sample entries, which use MLA style, as a reference for preparing your Works Cited list. All of the information you need to prepare your list is already on your source cards. Notice that you supply page numbers only for articles or other works that are one part of a whole work, such as one essay in a collection of essays.

SAMPLE ENTRIES FOR THE LIST OF WORKS CITED

Standard Reference Works
When an author of an entry is given in a standard reference work, that person's name is written first. Otherwise, the title of the book or article appears first. Page and volume numbers aren't needed if the work alphabetizes entries. For common reference works, only the edition year is needed.

ENCYCLOPEDIA ARTICLE
"Hurston, Zora Neale." Encyclopedia Americana. 1991 ed.

ARTICLE IN A BIOGRAPHICAL REFERENCE BOOK
Howard, Lillie P. "Zora Neale Hurston." Dictionary of Literary Biography. 1987 ed.

(continued)

SAMPLE ENTRIES FOR THE LIST OF WORKS CITED *(continued)*

Books

ONE AUTHOR

Huggins, Nathan Irvin. Harlem Renaissance. New York: Oxford UP, 1971.

TWO AUTHORS

Logan, Rayford W., and Irving S. Cohen. The American Negro: Old World Background and New World Experience. Boston: Houghton, 1970.

THREE AUTHORS

Bell, Roseann, Bettye Parker, and Beverly Gwy-Sheftall. Sturdy Black Bridges: Visions of Black Women in Literature. Garden City: Anchor, 1979.

FOUR OR MORE AUTHORS

Anderson, Robert, et al. Elements of Literature: Fifth Course. Austin: Holt, 1989.

NO AUTHOR SHOWN

American Statistics Index. Washington: Congressional Information Service, 1992.

EDITOR OF A COLLECTION OF WRITINGS

Locke, Alain, ed. The New Negro: An Interpretation. New York: Boni, 1925.

TWO OR THREE EDITORS

Meier, August, and Elliott Rudwick, eds. The Making of Black America: Essays in Negro Life and History. New York: Atheneum, 1969.

TRANSLATION

Niane, D. T. Sundiata: An Epic of Old Mali. Trans. G. D. Pickett. London: Longman, 1965.

Selections Within Books

FROM A BOOK OF WORKS BY ONE AUTHOR

Hughes, Langston. "April Rain Song." The Dream Keeper and Other Poems. New York: Knopf, 1932. 8.

(continued)

SAMPLE ENTRIES FOR THE LIST OF WORKS CITED *(continued)*

FROM A BOOK OF WORKS BY SEVERAL AUTHORS
Hemenway, Robert. "Zora Neale Hurston and the Eatonville Anthropology." The Harlem Renaissance Remembered: Essays Edited with a Memoir. Ed. Arna Bontemps. New York: Dodd, 1972. 190-214.

FROM A COLLECTION OF LONGER WORKS (NOVELS, PLAYS)
Edmonds, Randolph. Bad Man. The Negro Caravan. Ed. Sterling A. Brown, Arthur P. Davis, and Ulysses Lee. New York: Arno, 1969. 507-34. [Bad Man is a play. The Negro Caravan is a collection.]

Articles from Magazines, Newspapers, and Journals

FROM A WEEKLY MAGAZINE
Huggins, Nathan Irvin. "The Negro Artist and the Racial Mountain." Nation 23 June 1926: 692-94.

FROM A MONTHLY OR QUARTERLY MAGAZINE
Howard, Lillie P. "Zora Neale Hurston: Just Being Herself." Essence Nov. 1980: 100+. [The + sign indicates that the article isn't printed on consecutive pages.]

WITH NO AUTHOR SHOWN
"The Battle for Malcolm X." Newsweek 26 Aug. 1991: 52-54.

FROM A DAILY NEWSPAPER, WITH A BYLINE
Chamberlain, John. "Books of the Times." New York Times 7 Nov. 1942: 13.

FROM A DAILY NEWSPAPER, WITHOUT A BYLINE
"Zora Hurston, 57, Writer, Is Dead." New York Times 5 Feb. 1960: 27.

UNSIGNED EDITORIAL FROM A DAILY NEWSPAPER, NO CITY IN TITLE
"The Last Hurrah." Editorial. Star-Ledger [Newark, NJ] 29 Aug. 1991: 30.

(continued)

SAMPLE ENTRIES FOR THE LIST OF WORKS CITED *(continued)*

FROM A SCHOLARLY JOURNAL

Beal, Frances. "Slave of a Slave No More." <u>Black
Scholar</u> 6 (1975): 2-10.

Other Sources

PERSONAL INTERVIEW

Wilson, August. Personal interview. 27 Aug. 1990.

TELEPHONE INTERVIEW

Brooks, Gwendolyn. Telephone interview. 3 Nov. 1991.

PUBLISHED INTERVIEW

Walker, Alice. Interview. <u>Interviews with Black Writers</u>.
Ed. John O'Brien. New York: Liveright, 1973.
185-211.

RADIO OR TELEVISION INTERVIEW

Morrison, Toni. <u>All Things Considered</u>. Natl. Public
Radio. WNYC, New York. 16 Feb. 1986.

UNPUBLISHED LETTER

Hurston, Zora Neale. Letter to Mary Holland. 13 June
1955. Historical Collection. U of Florida,
Gainesville.

UNPUBLISHED THESIS OR DISSERTATION

Ward, Hazel Mae. "The Black Woman as Character:
Images in the American Novel, 1852-1953."
Diss. U of Texas, Austin, 1977.

CARTOON

Frascino, Edward. Cartoon. <u>New Yorker</u> 2 Sep. 1991: 46.

SPEECH OR LECTURE

King, Rev. Martin Luther, Jr. "I Have A Dream."
Lincoln Memorial. Washington, 28 Aug. 1963.

RECORDING

Robeson, Paul. "Going Home." Rec. 9 May 1958. <u>Paul
Robeson at Carnegie Hall</u>. Vanguard, VCD-72020,
1986.

(continued)

> ### SAMPLE ENTRIES FOR THE LIST OF WORKS CITED *(continued)*
>
> FILM, FILMSTRIP, OR VIDEOTAPE
> The Color Purple.   Dir. Steven Spielberg.   With Danny
>   Glover, Whoopi Goldberg, Margaret Avery, and Oprah
>   Winfrey.   Warner Bros., 1985. [The title, director,
>   distributor, and year are standard information.
>   You may add other information, such as performers.]

Shoe, by Jeff MacNelly, reprinted by permission: Tribune Media Services.

PART 5:
Writing Your First Draft

Using your outline, note cards, and any other prewriting notes, write the first draft of your research report. As with any draft, focus on getting your ideas down, not writing with a final polish. Also, don't worry unnecessarily about the mechanics of your parenthetical documentation. While drafting, just insert a citation with basic information wherever you *think* one may be needed; you can check and correct the form later (see pages 439–440) and delete any unnecessary citations. When you have finished writing, prepare your list of Works Cited from your source cards, using the sample entries as guides (pages 442–446). Include only the sources you credited in the text.

Evaluating and Revising

You've put a great deal of work into your paper so far. Take some time to assess the content, organization, and presentation of your material, using the chart on page 448.

EXERCISE 6 ▶ **Analyzing a Writer's Revisions**

In a small group, discuss the following revised paragraph from the Writer's Model (page 431). Use the questions below and the guidelines on page 448 to explore the writer's changes.

> In later books, too, these connections
> occur. ~~"By 14 April 1936 she was in the~~ *A field trip to Haiti and Jamaica in 1936 produced Tell My Horse, another story*
> ~~Caribbean, collecting material for her~~ *of voodoo.*
> ~~second book of folklore, Tell My Horse~~
>
> ~~(1938)" (Howard, Hurston 139). Hurston~~
>
> ~~had been working for the WPA Federal~~
>
> ~~Theater Project before that.~~ A year after *its* ~~Tell~~
> ~~My Horse~~ *appearance* she published the novel Moses,
>
> Man of the Mountain, which has been
>
> described as a blend of "fiction, folklore,
> religion, and comedy" (Howard *, Hurston* 140). In it,
> Moses is a "hoodoo man," *an* ~~a pretty wild~~ idea
> *that also appears in* Jonah's Gourd Vine *(231)*.

replace

cut

replace

add

replace
add

1. Why did the writer replace the second sentence, which is a direct quotation?
2. Why was the third sentence deleted? How is the change in the following sentence related to this deletion?
3. Why did the writer add a shortened title to the parenthetical citation? [Hint: See the Works Cited list.]
4. Why did the writer replace *pretty wild* in the final sentence?
5. Why did the writer add information to the last sentence? How does it help the paper?

EVALUATING AND REVISING RESEARCH REPORTS

EVALUATION GUIDE	REVISION TECHNIQUE
1 Is the report developed with sufficient primary and secondary sources that meet the "4R" test (page 416)?	**Add** facts, examples, opinions of experts, and primary sources if possible. **Cut** outdated or questionable information.
2 Is a thesis statement included early in the report?	**Add** a sentence or two stating your main idea to the introduction of your report.
3 Is the report suitable for and appealing to its audience?	**Add** needed definitions, background information, and explanations. **Add** interesting, unusual, or surprising details.
4 Is the tone of the report appropriate?	**Replace** words or phrases that are too informal for a research report.
5 Are facts and ideas stated mostly in the writer's own words?	**Cut** unnecessary quotations. **Replace** words, phrases, and sentences that do not use your own wording.
6 Is all information in the report related directly to the topic and thesis?	**Cut** unnecessary material.
7 Is every source of information credited when necessary?	**Add** documentation for any direct quotations and facts or ideas that aren't common knowledge.
8 Does all documentation follow the format recommended by your teacher?	**Replace** as necessary to follow the MLA format or another format recommended by your teacher.

Reminder

When you evaluate and revise your report, remember to

- include every element of the report that your teacher has specified
- develop ideas with enough details to make them clear and convincing
- indicate differing viewpoints when they exist and are important to the topic

PART 6:
**Evaluating and Revising
Your Report**

Exchange reports with a classmate. Read each other's reports and, using the guidelines on page 448, offer advice and criticism. Think about your classmate's suggestions carefully, and accept any recommended changes that seem valid. Then evaluate your own report and make any additional changes you think will make it more effective.

"I had written a few short stories, but the idea of attempting a book seemed so big, that I gazed at it in the quiet of the night, but hid it away from even myself in the daylight."

*Zora Neale Hurston,
on writing Jonah's Gourd Vine*

Proofreading and Publishing

Proofreading. Checking the mechanics of your documentation (parenthetical citations and list of Works Cited) is a very important part of proofreading a research paper. Remember that your documentation is there for readers' use and accuracy is required because they may want to find one of your sources. Also be sure to check capitalization, spelling, punctuation, grammar, and usage—your accomplishment is significant and you don't want errors to detract from your efforts.

GRAMMAR HINT

Using a Quotation as Part of a Sentence

When you use a direct quotation within your own sentence, you must incorporate the quote so that the entire sentence is grammatically correct. Always check the sentence to be sure the quotation serves properly as a grammatical part and is not merely "hanging" within the sentence or stuck onto it.

EXAMPLES

Quotation as part of a subordinate clause	The novel was even criticized because the "folk sayings may become the main point of the novel" (Bone 127).
Quotation as a subject	Her "skill at transcribing" made the language in <u>Jonah's Gourd Vine</u> somewhat hard to read (Young 220).
Quotation as a direct object of the verb	She knew intimately the everyday, "normal life of Negroes in the South" (Thompson).

☞ REFERENCE NOTE: For more information on using quotations within sentences, see page 879.

Publishing.   A research report is a substantial piece of work, a paper to be proud of and *use*. Since using implies sharing your research with others, you might try one of the following suggestions for publishing your paper.

■ During your research, you may have discovered persons or groups that are especially interested in your subject. For example, the researcher who did the Zora Neale Hurston report learned of an organization called Preserve Eatonville Community, Inc., which might appreciate a copy of the Hurston report for its files. If you came across anyone or any group similarly involved with your subject, consider sending them a copy of your report.

■ Make an audiotape of your report, adding sound effects or background music, if appropriate. Play the tape for your family, for your class, or for a club or other organization. You might also use your report for a videotape documentary.

■ Since schools and employers frequently request writing samples, save your report as an example of your writing and research skills for a college or job application.

PART 7:
**Proofreading and Publishing
Your Report**

Proofread your research paper, paying special attention to documentation in the body of the paper and in your list of Works Cited. Be sure to refer to the chart on pages 442–446 for help with the correct format for various kinds of sources. Then use one of the suggestions given above for publishing your paper.

A STUDENT MODEL

Bill Langhofer, a student at Washington High School in South Bend, Indiana, readily acknowledges that a well-written research paper results from good writing skills, research, and hard work. As you read each of the following excerpts from Bill's research paper, notice how he develops his thesis: from the introduction, to a paragraph in the body, to his paper's conclusion.

from Barry Holstun Lopez--The Naturalist
by Bill Langhofer

Barry Lopez began his life as the Modern Age drew to a close, making way for contemporary writing. The change from modern to contemporary literature resulted in little variety from the previous period. One of the few fluctuations was that authors expanded the ideas from the past. Unlike previous authors, who gave wild animals the appearance of being ravenous beasts, Barry Lopez shows us animals' lives from a scientific and naturalistic point of view. He broadens the insight of the reader by producing a realistic concept of nature. . . .

Barry Lopez's greatest books are Of Wolves and Men and Arctic Dreams. In Of Wolves and Men he appeals to the reader's senses and gets him to think about the future of animals by showing how badly the wolf has been treated in the past. Lopez says

> . . . if I focused on this one animal, I might be able to say something sharp and clear about the way we treat all animals, and about how we relate to the natural world in the latter part of the twentieth century. (Goldsworthy 250)

In discussing Arctic Dreams, Lopez tells about two incidents that inspired him to write this book:

> One was the sight, in the midnight light of the northern summer, of a flight of birds and a small herd of

caribou crossing a river. The other took place not in the Arctic but in rural Michigan, where he came across the grave of a sailor who had died in an Arctic expedition in 1884. (Goldsworthy 250)

From these inspirations Lopez produced a book that contained many different themes, including Arctic exploration, geography, weather, and animal migration and behavior. . . .

Barry Lopez uses powerful imagery to show us our fore-fathers' mistakes. As the settlers fought for a living in this rugged wilderness, they ruined the natives' lifestyles, wreaked havoc on the environment, and eliminated many animal populations. His book Of Wolves and Men centers on one animal, the wolf. He hopes that people will see the destruction they have brought on themselves in their desire to overcome the forces of nature, and he hopes that they will change their ways. "What is in my gut as a writer is a concern with the fate of the country I live in and the dignity and morality of the people I live with" (Colby 550). In his other book, Arctic Dreams, Lopez covers the geography, the history, and the bird and animal life in the Arctic. He realizes that technology has radically altered the landscape and the animals living on the land. As a superb naturalist, he has helped all of us realize that we have squandered valuable resources. It is now our choice to make a difference.

WINNER OF THE AMERICAN BOOK AWARD
THE NEW YORK TIMES BESTSELLER

ARCTIC DREAMS
IMAGINATION AND DESIRE IN A NORTHERN LANDSCAPE
BARRY LOPEZ
author of Of Wolves and Men

Barry Holstun Lopez
author of ARCTIC DREAMS
OF WOLVES AND MEN

WRITING WORKSHOP

An Informative Research Article

The articles that you read in newspapers and magazines almost always involve research, frequently a personal interview. These articles cover all types of topics, but some of the more interesting ones focus on one person's unique experiences or interests. From the smallest hamlet to the largest city, creative people can be found doing interesting things, and reporters make a point of finding them. For this workshop, you'll identify one such person in your community and write a 200-word report on what he or she is doing. Before you do your interview, use the guidelines that follow to plan what you'll ask and record. (See also the steps listed in Exercise 3, page 424.)

GUIDELINES FOR A REPORT OF AN INTERVIEW

1. Identify clearly the person you're writing about: Give his or her name and position or job title. Make absolutely certain that the spelling and wording in your identifications are correct.
2. Show what is especially intriguing about the person you've chosen—what it is that sets him or her apart.
3. Include enough details so that the reader gets a good idea of what the person does.
4. Use at least one quotation from the person you've interviewed plus any other quotes that add substance and appeal to your report.

Following is a brief report that appeared in *New Jersey Monthly* magazine. Study it to determine whether the writer's published article, based in part on an interview, adheres to the guidelines given above.

Education: A Sit-Down Tour
by Matt Tomlinson

For high school students who are eyeing Stanford University instead of Stockton State College, the all-important trip to visit the campus can carry a steep price tag.

Cliff Kramon has a solution. As vice president of Tenafly's Collegiate Choice Inc.—professional guidance counselors for college-bound kids—Kramon spent the last three and a half years videotaping more than 300 U.S. colleges. Students interested in faraway schools can now pop one of Kramon's tapes into the VCR and evaluate their choices.

Collegiate Choice counsels mostly Bergen County and New York City students, but orders for the videotapes come from all over the country. Twelve New Jersey schools are in the catalog, and the videotapes are more helpful than any sanitized pamphlet. While a Drew University brochure says that the school offers "an impressive array of unusual opportunities in the context of an education rooted in the liberal arts," the onscreen guide covers everything from graduation to the university's resident ghosts. The Rutgers video is wonderfully cacophonous, full of the trains and traffic that provide the school's urban background music.

Still, Kramon has the heart of a guidance counselor, not a salesman: He tries to convince students to skip the video tours when campuses are close by. The tapes are the second best way to see a school, he says: "The best way is going yourself."

1. What kinds of research evidently went into the writing of this report? How can you tell?
2. The first paragraph shows that the focus of the article is local, not national. In what way? How might the writer have changed the first sentence if the article were aimed at a national audience?
3. What two purposes do you think the second paragraph accomplishes?
4. What kinds of specific details are used in the third paragraph to illustrate the nature of the videotapes?
5. Where and why does the writer use quotations?

Writing an Article Based on an Interview

 Prewriting. For your interview, you might consider people you already know—a friend who's won a prize, a relative with an intriguing job, a neighbor who's gained community attention. Or check the local newspaper for people in the news. When you've found your person, set up a personal or a telephone interview. Do some background research in the library or by talking to other people to learn whatever else you can about the person and his or her featured activity, and plan questions in advance. Take careful notes—even if you use a tape recorder. (For more information on interviewing, see pages 424 and 950–952.)

Writing, Evaluating, and Revising. Since this is a brief report, you can easily plan its paragraphing. You may want to follow the four-paragraph "Sit-Down Tour" model—introduction, identification, support, conclusion—or you may prefer a plan of your own. In evaluating and revising your first draft, use the guidelines on page 448. Also compare your article with others in the newspaper. Does yours have a similar lively, nonscholarly tone and style?

 Proofreading and Publishing. Go over your final draft, correcting any errors in spelling, capitalization, punctuation, and usage. Then see if the local paper or a city magazine will publish your report. Your school paper could also run a "Newsmaker" series to publish all the class articles. Finally, be *sure* to give a copy to the person you interviewed.

MAKING CONNECTIONS

TRAVEL WRITING

From one-line postcards to full-length books, records of travel are being written and read by millions every day. People seem to have as great a need to tell and read about new places and events as they do to experience them. And all writing about travel involves research in some way, from firsthand observation to reading a map to browsing through a brochure. What research might have gone into this introduction to an article on the Painted Desert?

from Sands of Time
by James Kotsilibas-Davis

They resemble sailing frigates and fairytale castles, gigantic mushrooms or abstract forms that might be found in a Soho art gallery. But these random sculptures, such as the geological flukes in Blue Canyon, are not man-made. They were shaped by the erosional action of the Little Colorado River as it wound its prehistoric way through what is now the American West. The color-stroked mounds that form the Painted Desert were deposited some 225 million years ago, toward the end of the Triassic Period of the Mesozoic Era. Protected in Petrified Forest National Park, this sequence of rocks is part of the meandering Chinle Formation, which sweeps majestically across Arizona, Utah and New Mexico like a land-bound rainbow.

Petrified logs in the Blue Mesa section of the Petrified Forest fell like fragments of ancient pillars after their 150-million-year-old coating eroded. The once-verdant forest, which flourished here 200 million years ago, was buried, then preserved, when rainwater seeped through deep layers of volcanic ash, dissolving silica from it. As the water penetrated, silica replaced the logs' organic materials with glasslike deposits of silicon dioxide. Paiutes believed these gleaming formations were the arrow shafts of their thunder god. To Navajos, they were bones of a mythic giant.

Travel-Holiday

Where have you been that you'd like to tell other people about? You may not live in—or have visited—a landscape as spectacular as the Painted Desert, but the places you have traveled to or your own community are sure to contain some attraction for armchair travelers. Do some research, and write a few paragraphs to entice someone to visit a new place. It could be a park, a local museum, an old farmers' market, a turn-of-the-century house, or a modern factory.

Your information may come from interviews, visits, newspaper clippings, books, videotapes, or brochures. Just be sure to provide important and interesting facts about the place and to arouse curiosity with vivid description. And since the rules against plagiarism apply in travel writing, too, be sure to use your own words and give credit for ideas you have borrowed from someone else.

RESEARCH ACROSS THE CURRICULUM

Science

Richard P. Feynman, one of the most accomplished physicists of this century, worked on the Manhattan Project, won the Nobel Prize, and played in a samba band. When the nation mourned the explosion of the space shuttle *Challenger* in 1986, he was asked to sit on the president's commission to determine the cause of the disaster. It was he who uncovered the problem with the faulty O-rings. What produces a creative scientist like

Feynman? In his autobiography, *What Do You Care What Other People Think?*, he explains how his father taught him to think. In the passage below, Feynman's father is speaking to his son.

"See that bird?" he says. "It's a Spencer's warbler." (I knew he didn't know the real name.) "Well, in Italian, it's a *Chutto Lapittida*. In Portuguese, it's a *Bom da Peida*. In Chinese, it's a *Chung-long-tah*, and in Japanese, it's a *Katano Tekeda*. You can know the name of that bird in all the languages of the world, but when you're finished, you'll know absolutely nothing whatever about the bird. You'll only know about humans in different places, and what they call the bird. So let's look at the bird and see what it's *doing*—that's what counts." (I learned very early the difference between knowing the name of something and knowing something.)

Richard Feynman, *What Do You Care What Other People Think?*

1. What research technique was Feynman's father teaching him?
2. How do you think Feynman might have applied this technique in his later life?

You might want to read more about this unusual scientist or about one of these other remarkable scientists: Albert Einstein, Robert H. Goddard, Irene Joliot-Curie, George Washington Carver, Nikola Tesla, Maria Mitchell. Check your library's card catalog, on-line catalog, or *Readers' Guide to Periodical Literature* for information on these scientists; then report back to your classmates on your findings.

12 ENGLISH: HISTORY AND DEVELOPMENT

LOOKING AHEAD

The English language is as lively and varied as the people who use it. Over thousands of years, it's grown and changed to become the most expressive and the most widely used language in the world. In this chapter, you will learn

- where English comes from
- how English has grown and developed
- what varieties of English are used in the United States and throughout the world

A Various Language

What would you think if someone came up to you and said, "Hæl, god freond! Hwæt destu?" Among other things, you would probably think you were hearing a foreign language. That, however, is the way an English speaker a thousand years ago might have said, "Hey, good buddy, what's up?" (or, more literally, "Hail, good friend! What dost thou?").

The English of today has come to us from ancient times. During the past seven thousand years, our language has changed so much that now we cannot easily recognize its earlier forms. Even the English of one thousand years ago is so different from the language we speak that it seems like a foreign tongue. Yet there is continuity across the ages.

A language changes gradually as it is passed on from one generation to the next. New words are added, and old ones are lost. The way we pronounce and spell words changes, and so does the way we put them together to make sentences. We imitate speakers of other languages and change our own language in the process. The result is a wonderfully various language, containing within itself the fruits of its long and varied past.

The history of our language can be divided into four main periods: *Pre-English, Old English, Middle English,* and *Modern English.* The following time line shows approximately when English moved from one period to the next. It also shows which languages had the most influence on the early development of English.

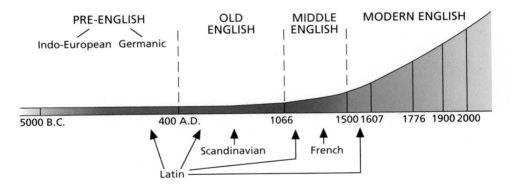

The Origins of English: Pre-English

Seven thousand or more years ago, a language that was the ancestor of English (and of many other languages, too) was spoken in Asia Minor or southeast Europe—we are not sure exactly where. We call that language ***Proto-Indo-European*** because most of the languages of Europe and many of those of north India and Iran developed from it. (*Proto–* means "first or earliest.")

The people who spoke Proto-Indo-European migrated all around Europe and south central Asia. One group of those migrants settled in what is today northern Germany and along the coast of the North Sea. They were organized into several tribes—the Angles, the Saxons, and the Jutes. Their version of the Indo-European language, called **Germanic,** is the ancestor of present-day English.

While living in northern Europe, the Anglo-Saxons (as the tribes are collectively called) got to know another Indo-European people to their south, the Romans. They learned from the Romans—among other things—about streets, dishes, miles, and walls. At the same time, the Anglo-Saxons learned the Latin words for these things. *Street* is from the Latin words *strata via,* "paved road." *Dish* is from *discus* (which later was also borrowed in that form, as well as the shorter *disk* and *disc*). *Mile* is from *milia passuum,* "a thousand paces." And *wall* is from *vallum,* "a rampart."

Words that people borrow from other languages are called **loanwords.** Early English speakers certainly borrowed from other languages before they came into contact with the Romans. But the Latin words borrowed on the continent of Europe nearly two thousand years ago are the first loanwords we can be sure about.

Old English

Eventually, the Romans hired some of the Angles and Saxons to serve in the Roman army and shipped them off to the British Isles. The Romans had made Britain and its native population of Celts into a province of the Roman Empire. The Romans needed help in defending the southern part of the main island and the Celts who lived there against some fierce northern neighbors called Picts.

Although the Romans eventually gave up ruling Britain, the Anglo-Saxons stayed on after their job was done. Soon kin of theirs from the Continent arrived to join them. Eventually these Germanic peoples took over the south of the main island from the native Celts. The Anglo-Saxons called the island after themselves, *Engla land*—the land of the Angles—or, as we know it today, England. They called their language *Englisc;* we call it *Old English.*

The English the Anglo-Saxons spoke was very different from the English we know today. They had sounds we have lost, as in their word *hnutu*, which became our *nut*. At first they wrote with an angular-looking alphabet called runes—when they wrote at all, which wasn't often.

The Anglo-Saxons had some words we don't, such as *guma* for "man" or *boda* for "messenger," and they lacked a great many words we have, such as *message*. Some words have changed meaning. For example, *wif* meant "woman" rather than "wife," as it now does; and *gift* referred to a kind of wedding present rather than to any sort of gift.

Their words also had endings or alternative forms to show how they fit together in a sentence. The order of most words in the sentence could stay the same, while the form of the words changed to express different meanings.

MODERN ENGLISH	The man gave the messenger an answer. The messenger gave the man an answer.
OLD ENGLISH	**Se** guma geaf **thæm** bodan andsware **Thæm** guman geaf **se** boda andsware

Although English has changed over the centuries, many of our most familiar, everyday words are still native English. That is, they have been used by English speakers as far back in the past as we can see or imagine. Most of these words have changed their pronunciation and spelling, and many have changed their meanings, too. Yet the old forms of the words are still recognizable from the modern ones. The following lists show the Old English and Modern English forms of several everyday words.

OLD ENGLISH	MODERN ENGLISH
cnif	knife
hus	house
modor	mother
æppel, "fruit"	apple
wyrm, "serpent"	worm

EXERCISE 1 ▶ Identifying Original Forms of Words

Look up each of the following words in a dictionary that gives *etymologies* (word origins). What did the word look like in Old English? What did it mean in Old English?

1. earth   **3.** strut   **5.** wade
2. love   **4.** mildew

After they had settled in the British Isles, the English were converted to Christianity and borrowed many more Latin words. Many of these words were for religious matters, such as *church* and *bishop*, but some were for other subjects, such as *school* and *butter*.

In a series of raids during the ninth to eleventh centuries, the Norse from Scandinavia invaded England and settled there, introducing Scandinavian words such as *sky*, *skirt*, and the pronouns *they*, *them*, and *their*. The corresponding Anglo-Saxon forms were *heofon* (which survives as *heaven*), *scyrte* (which survives as *shirt*), and the pronouns *hie*, *hem*, *heora*.

Middle English

In 1066, another group of Norse conquered England. Called the Normans (or "north men"), these people had earlier settled in France and learned French. The Normans began the process of introducing French words into the English language. *Castle, chair, table, pen, judge,* and *library* are a few of those words.

During much of the **Middle English** period, English was displaced by French and Latin as the important language of the country. Government, education, religion, law, and literature were in those foreign languages rather than in English.

English wasn't used for important purposes again until around the fourteenth century. By that time, English speakers had forgotten the native English words for many technical and specialized subjects. They found it easiest to borrow large numbers of French and Latin words to use in talking about these matters. For example, the native English word *leorningcild* ("learning-child") was replaced by a word from Latin, *studiante,* which became our word *student.*

Following are some more examples of French and Latin loanwords from the Middle English period:

FRENCH	armee	lettre	palais	preiere
MODERN ENGLISH	army	letter	palace	prayer

LATIN	alphabetum	ecclesiasticus
MODERN ENGLISH	alphabet	ecclesiastical

Modern English

After moving to Britain, the Anglo-Saxons lived there fairly comfortably and as quietly as they could, considering that their neighbors in Scandinavia and France kept moving in with them without waiting for an invitation. Despite the Scandinavian and Norman French invasions of England, the English were relatively isolated and protected for nearly 1,200 years. Most of them were illiterate, with no need to write or read because handwritten manuscripts were too expensive for ordinary people. When the English did write, they spelled (and used) words in many different ways.

Near the end of the fifteenth century, however, William Caxton introduced the printing press to England, and cheap books soon became readily available. Mass publication and the resulting increase in literacy helped to standardize the English language.

Around the sixteenth century, some English people got the itch to travel and see whether they could make their fortunes in foreign lands. A little more than one hundred years after Columbus had stumbled upon the Western Hemisphere, the English decided they would try to plant some colonies there, too. The first successful English settlement in the New World was at Jamestown, Virginia, in 1607; the next was at Plymouth, Massachusetts, in 1620. Later, English settlers and traders ventured to Canada, the Caribbean, India, Australia, New Zealand, South Africa, and many other places, taking the English language with them wherever they went.

"Look! Look, gentlemen! . . . Purple mountains! Spacious skies! Fruited plains! . . . Is someone writing this down?"

The Far Side cartoon by Gary Larson is reprinted by permission of Chronicle Features, San Francisco, CA.

Meanwhile, back in England, the Industrial Revolution of the late eighteenth and early nineteenth centuries introduced more efficient methods of manufacturing. The combination of abundant goods and worldwide commerce helped spread the English language all over the globe and make it into an important international tongue. At the same time, English people's interaction with other cultures brought many new loanwords into English.

EXERCISE 2 ▶	Discovering the Origins of Borrowed Words

What language was each of the following words borrowed from? Make a guess first, and then check the etymology of each word in the dictionary.

1. anchovy
2. bluff ("to mislead")
3. cosmonaut
4. kimono
5. kindergarten

6. lacrosse
7. luau
8. moccasin
9. piano
10. tamale

EXERCISE 3 ▶	Researching Words from Names

Many words in English come from the names of people. Who was the person commemorated in each of the following words? To find the answers, look up the etymology of each word in a dictionary.

1. Braille
2. levis

3. maverick
4. sequoia

5. cardigan

American English

When people are in close contact with one another and talk together often, their language will change in the same way for all of them. For example, most people will talk alike in a small town where everybody knows everybody else. But if half the townspeople move to the other side of a mountain and lose touch with their old neighbors, within a few generations the two groups will be talking very differently from each other. They will have developed two distinct varieties of the language.

That is what happened to the English settlers in the New World and the English who stayed home. The language went on changing on both sides of the Atlantic Ocean, but it changed in different ways on the two sides. In time, *American English* and *British English* drifted apart and became two recognizably different varieties.

The history of American English is divided into three periods: *Colonial, National,* and *International.*

The Colonial Period (1607–1776)

When the first English speakers set foot in the New World, they talked just the way the people back home did. But they had to start adapting their language to new conditions almost as soon as they arrived.

The early settlers had to borrow and invent words for some animals they had never known before. For example, they encountered a bushy-tailed, black animal that had a white streak down its back and that sprayed a foul-smelling liquid when it was frightened. They imitated the Algonquian name for this creature as best they could, calling it a *skunk*. Another unfamiliar animal they met lived in the water and had a long tail and webbed hind feet. Because it was a rodent and because it had a musky smell about it, the settlers called it a *muskrat.*

In other cases, the settlers adapted old words to new uses. In England the streams that flowed through the countryside were for the most part nearly level with the surrounding land. In America, however, many of the rivers had worn a deep channel down through the earth. To get to those streams, the settlers had to climb down an incline. The settlers needed a name for these inclines for which there was no distinctive English term. They took the English word for a mound or ridge or slope of a hill—*bank*—and applied it to the slope leading down to a stream. And so a new use was born, which became the normal American meaning of the word.

The early English colonists in the New World had some language changes forced on them almost immediately because of the new conditions under which they lived. However, all languages are constantly changing from one generation to the next. If a language is alive, it changes.

The National Period (1776–1898)

At first, English was spoken in the New World only in the colonies along the eastern seaboard of the continent. But as settlers moved westward, English gradually began to spread. More and more new words entered the language, and American English became increasingly different from British.

The year 1776, when the thirteen original colonies declared their independence from England, was the beginning of *American English* as a separate national standard. A number of the nation's founders—including Thomas Jefferson, John Adams, and Benjamin Franklin—recognized that the new nation had to be independent not only in government but also in literature, language, and thought. The person who did the most toward establishing American English as a separate national standard was Noah Webster.

Webster wrote a spelling book, popularly known as the "Blue-Backed Speller," that was very widely used in the United States. It popularized certain spellings in this country that still distinguish American English from British English. In the eighteenth century, many words were spelled in more than one way: *center* or *centre, humor* or *humour, realize* or *realise.* Webster settled in each case on one spelling that he thought was simpler, better historically, or more like other English spellings.

The spellings Webster chose were learned by generations of schoolchildren and were used in the dictionaries he wrote. Thus they became the normal American forms of the words. However, Webster also proposed some simplified reform spellings, like *tung* for *tongue* and *fether* for *feather.* Though these spellings were sensible, they never caught on and so did not survive.

Today, many dictionaries put the name "Webster" in their titles, but no present-day dictionary has anything left in it of Webster's old books. The name "Webster" has simply become associated with dictionaries the way "Shakespeare" has with great literature or "Washington" has with honesty.

By the end of the nineteenth century, American English was a distinct national variety, with its own words, pronunciations, spellings, and grammar. The American variety of the language was recorded in its own dictionaries and grammars, with its own literature and outlook on life.

LOOKING AT *Language*

I'm OK—You're OK

The most successful of all American words is *OK*, now used by speakers of languages all over the globe. Its origin was a puzzle until solved by the linguist Allen Walker Read. He discovered that *OK* stands for "oll korrect," a comic misspelling (among others like *OW* for "oll wright" and *KG* for "know go") used in Boston newspapers of 1838–1839.

In 1840, a political organization called the "O.K. Club" was formed to support Martin Van Buren's reelection as President of the United States. Van Buren was nicknamed "Old Kinderhook" after his hometown of Kinderhook, New York. The O.K. Club's name referred to that nickname but also punned on the humorous misspelling: Old Kinderhook was "oll korrect." During the election campaign of 1840, the expression *OK* was spread all over the country. Van Buren lost the election, but *OK* went on to win a permanent place in American English—and in other languages all over the world.

EXERCISE 4 ▶ Identifying Americanisms

Which of the following words are Americanisms—words that entered the English language in the United States? To find out, look up each word in a dictionary that identifies Americanisms.

(A good one is *Webster's New World Dictionary*, which labels each Americanism with a star.)

1. A-OK	6. foxhole
2. clipboard	7. hologram
3. cocoa	8. kerosene
4. dogfight	9. locker room
5. electrician	10. sloppy

The International Period (1898 to the Present)

Near the end of the nineteenth century, America became increasingly involved with foreign affairs. As a result of the Spanish-American War in 1898, the United States brought Puerto Rico and the Philippines within its sphere of influence. Nineteen years later (in 1917), America entered World War I; and twenty-three years after the conclusion of that war, our country entered World War II (in 1941).

The continued presence of U.S. military bases in Europe, the location of the United Nations headquarters in New York, and our embroilments in Korea, Vietnam, and Kuwait have kept the United States involved in international matters. Those wars and political affairs, as well as commercial activities around the globe, have helped spread the influence of American English to other lands. They have also promoted the influence of other languages on English.

Following are some of the words English has borrowed from other languages in the twentieth century.

Afrikaans: apartheid	Latin: spelunking
Arabic: falafel	Mexican Spanish: bronco
Chinese: chow mein	Norwegian: slalom
Czech: robot	Pennsylvania German: spritz
French: discothèque	Portuguese: bossa nova
German: moped	Russian: sputnik
Greek (Classical): cybernetics	Spanish: rumba
Greek (Modern): pita (bread)	Swedish: smorgasbord
Hawaiian: ukulele	Swiss German: muesli
Italian: pepperoni	Tagalog: boondocks
Japanese: honcho	Yiddish: schmaltz

In turn, English has been influencing other languages around the world. Nowadays the French may *golfer* on *le weekend* (play golf on the weekend), while the Dutch who are not worried about their *fitness* spend the time watching a *videofilm*. When Danes decide not to *zappe* from one television channel to another, they may go for a real *workout* in a *triatlon* (triathlon). The well-dressed German may wear a *Pullover* (nicknamed a *Pulli*) at a *Fussball* (football) game. And a Japanese person may eat a *hotto doggu* (hot dog) while watching *futtobooru* (football) on *terebi* (television).

American and British English

In some respects, American English has changed less than British English. Those who traveled to the new land were more conservative in the way they talked than the homebodies were. For example, most Americans pronounce *r* where it is spelled, as in *roar* and *card.* But many English people do not pronounce *r* unless it is immediately followed by a vowel, so their *roar* sounds like *raw*, and their *card* sounds like *cod.* The American pronunciation is older, as the spelling suggests.

So, too, Americans say both "She's got an idea" and "She's gotten an idea" but mean different things by them. "She's got an idea" is equivalent to "She has an idea," whereas "She's gotten an idea" means "An idea has occurred to her" or "She's thought up an idea." *Got* and *gotten* are both past participles of the verb *get*, but *gotten* is the older form. In England today, people do not generally use *gotten* anymore. They have lost one of the forms of the verb, while Americans have kept it.

On the other hand, Americans have added many words to the English language, perhaps more than the British have. Here is a sample of words—both older and newer ones—that Americans have contributed to English.

avocado	jampacked	shack
belittle	kerosene	T-shirt
cedar chest	lipstick	upside-down cake
day-glo	mileage	volleyball
eggbeater	nifty	waffle
finger painting	ouch!	xerox
glitzy	parking lot	yo-yo
hamburger	quarterback	zipper
inchworm	road hog	

EXERCISE 5 ▶ **Translating British Expressions**

Look up each of the following expressions in a dictionary to find out what meaning it has in British English. What word or words do you use to mean the same thing?

1. bed-sitting room   3. convenience   5. tube
2. biscuit   4. pram

The Future of English

Today the English language is spread all over the world. It is the world's most important language for international communication in business, diplomacy, science, technology, and entertainment. Several countries, such as India, that have more than one native language use English as a second language for government and education. Some people in most nations of the world use English at least occasionally for a number of special purposes.

For a long while, the British variety of English was the one most widely studied and used by speakers of other languages. But movies, television, popular music, and technology have helped to spread American English outside the United States. Now both major national varieties—those of the United States and of the United Kingdom—are widely used, and some newer ones, such as Australian English, are also becoming influential.

On a popular level, English is becoming more diversified around the world as it is being used by many peoples for their own purposes. Japanese conducting business with Arabs are likely to do so in English—but an English rather different from what a native English speaker would use. International use exposes standard English to increased influence from many other languages.

Some people fear that as English is used in different regions around the world, it will break up into many local languages—just as Latin developed into Italian, French, Spanish, Portuguese, and Romanian at the end of the Roman Empire. Local varieties of English are developing, but so is an international standard of English usage. Airplane travel, television, movies, computers, and other forms of mass communication promote uniformity in our language.

Today we are well on the way toward an international variety of English combining American, British, and many other influences. It will still be a various language, but following the motto of the United States, *e pluribus unum*, the English of the future will be one language joining many varieties.

LOOKING AT

What's Your Body Language?

The language we speak is accompanied by hundreds of gestures that reinforce what we are saying—or sometimes contradict it. Many gestures are universal—that is, people all over the world, whatever language they speak, use similar gestures in similar ways. For example, when people are puzzled and want an answer to some question, they tend to lift their eyebrows and open their eyes wide. That gesture seems to say, "I need to see more, so I am looking with wide-open eyes."

Other gestures are language-specific—that is, different cultures and languages may use quite different gestures for the same thing, just as they use different words for the same thing (like English *goodbye*, Spanish *adiós*, and Hebrew *shalom*). When English speakers want to say goodbye with a gesture, they raise a hand with the palm away from them and hold the fingers together while moving them repeatedly down to a horizontal position and back up to a vertical one. We call that "waving goodbye." In some other countries the corresponding gesture is made by holding the hand with the palm facing the gesturer. The result is similar to the gesture we use to signal "Come here," just the opposite of "Goodbye."

Varieties of American English

From the time when English speakers first came to America, they have varied in the way they spoke and wrote the language. The most widely used variety of English is *standard English*. In addition, American English includes many subvarieties called *dialects*.

Dialect

The language we use tells much about us—our home locality, ethnic background, education, gender, and age. Language variation that tells such things about us, thus helping to identify who we are and where we come from, is called *dialect.* The two main types of dialect used in the United States are *regional dialects* and *ethnic dialects.*

Regional Dialects

The earliest settlement of America by English colonists set a pattern for geographical differences, or *regional dialects,* in the United States. The colonists settled in four main cultural areas: (1) New England, (2) the Middle Atlantic area centered on Philadelphia, (3) the Southern Mountains, and (4) the Coastal South. From those areas, the early population moved westward, taking their dialects with them.

Today there are four main regional dialects spoken in the eastern and midwestern United States. However, it's important to remember that not everyone in a region speaks that region's dialect.

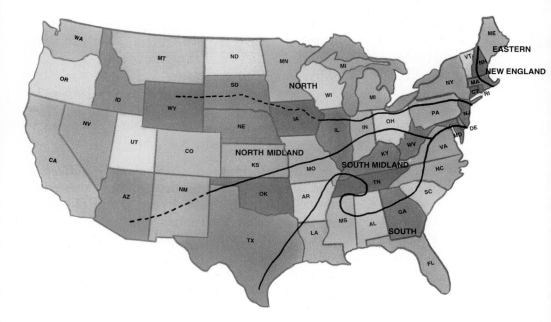

This chart shows some of the features of pronunciation, vocabulary, and grammar that distinguish one regional dialect from another.

FEATURES OF REGIONAL DIALECTS				
	NORTHERN	NORTH MIDLAND	SOUTH MIDLAND	SOUTHERN
PRONUN-CIATION	"greassy"	"greassy"	"greazy"	"greazy"
	"hahg"	"hahg" or hog	hog	"hawg"
	"pahked cah"	parked car	parked car	"pawked caw"
WORD CHOICE	burlap bag or gunny sack	burlap bag	burlap bag	burlap bag or croker sack
	pail	bucket	bucket	bucket
	devil's darning needle	snake feeder	snake doctor	skeeter hawk
GRAMMAR	quarter of/to	quarter to	quarter till	quarter till/to
	you, youse	you	you, you'uns	you, y'all

Ethnic Dialects

In addition to regional dialects, there are also *ethnic dialects*— the speech patterns of special communities that have preserved some of their heritage from the past. Every group of people that has come to the United States has brought something characteristic of its original homeland and culture. For example, English, Scottish, Irish, Welsh, French, Spanish, Dutch, Scandinavian, German, Yiddish, Polish, Czech, Italian, Greek, Armenian, Indic, Chinese, Japanese, Korean, and Vietnamese people have all influenced American English.

The most prominent ethnic dialect in the United States is that of African Americans. It unites some features of West

African languages with some features of early Southern speech and yet other usages developed by the African American community itself. Some features are *aunt* pronounced "ahnt," *He be sick* meaning a continuing rather than temporary illness, and *tote* meaning "carry" (of African origin but now common in all Southern use).

The boundaries of ethnic dialects, like those of regional dialects, are fluid. For example, not all African Americans use the ethnic dialect associated with their group, and some features of African American dialect turn up in other speech communities, too.

The second most prominent ethnic dialect is Hispanic English, which has three subvarieties: Mexican-influenced English in the Southwest, Cuban-influenced English in Florida, and Puerto-Rican-influenced English in New York City and, of course, in Puerto Rico.

Early Hispanic influence in the West introduced such words as *vamoose* (from Spanish *vamos*, "let's go"), *hoosegow* (from *juzgado*, "courtroom"), *lariat* (from *la reata*, "the lasso"), and *mesa* ("table"). Today, Spanish-influenced English uses English words with the meanings of similar Spanish words. For example, *apple* is often used with the meaning of *manzana*, "city block" (*manzana* also means "apple"); *conference* with the meaning of *conferencia*, "lecture"; and *direction* with the meaning of *dirección*, "address." The number of speakers of Hispanic English has been growing in recent years and so, consequently, has the importance of their dialect.

| EXERCISE 6 ▶ | **Identifying Dialect Differences** |

What word do you use for each of the following items? Do you know any other words for the same thing? Read each description to a friend, relative, or neighbor who grew up in a different region (or a different country) than you did. Note any differences between that person's word choices and your own.

1. a thin, circular band of elastic material put around things to hold them together
2. a flavored, sweet, carbonated beverage sold in capped bottles or in cans
3. a fixture over a sink for turning the water on and off
4. a sandwich made on a long roll sliced lengthwise and filled with meats, cheeses, and vegetables
5. a round, flat piece of fried batter, usually eaten with syrup

Standard English

Standard English is a variety of language that is not limited to a particular place or ethnic group. It is used all over the country (and even all over the world) by people of all backgrounds without indicating what place or group they belong to. It is the one variety of English that belongs to everybody.

Standard English is more a matter of writing than of speech, especially in the United States. It is used for treating important matters seriously, and it is especially appropriate for talking with or writing to people we don't know well. It is the language of public affairs and education, of publications and television, of science and technology, of business and government. It is the variety of English recorded in dictionaries and grammar books.

You can find some of the rules and guidelines for using standard English in the **Handbook** in this textbook. To identify the differences between standard English and other varieties of English, the **Handbook** uses the labels *standard* and *nonstandard*. *Nonstandard* doesn't mean wrong language. It means language that is inappropriate where standard English is expected.

Standard English is the most useful and the most widely used of all functional varieties. Nobody needs to use it all the time, but everybody should be able to use it when it is the right variety to use.

MAKING CONNECTIONS

The Foreign Gourmet

An area that is especially productive of words borrowed from other languages is food and cooking. Many terms come from abroad along with the items of food or the style of cooking that they name. Here are two activities to make you a gourmet linguist.

1. Make a list of ten foods you particularly like. Look up the names of those foods in a dictionary to find out where the words come from. How many of these names came into English from other languages?

2. Do you ever eat in ethnic restaurants? Many communities have Italian, Chinese, Mexican, Indian, Greek, Japanese,

and other ethnic restaurants. Do some fieldwork by going to an ethnic restaurant and reading its menu. Jot down any food terms that seem to be special to the ethnic style of cooking of that restaurant.

Then, using an unabridged dictionary, look up the terms you have gathered from the menu to see what they mean and where they come from. If any of the words are not in the dictionary, they may be new words for English. See whether you can find out what they mean.

As a group project, join with four or five other members of your class to arrange a "word-meal." Plan an imaginary dinner consisting of international foods from the menus people in your group have read. Write your own menu of various dishes. For each item on the menu, give its name, describe the dish, and identify the ethnic origin of both the dish and the name.

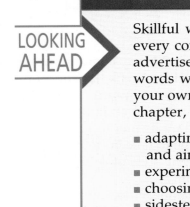

13 STYLE IN WRITING

LOOKING AHEAD

Skillful writing can seem like magic. But behind every compelling story, article, poem, letter, and advertisement is a real-life writer who chose words with care. With practice, you can develop your own style to bring life to your writing. In this chapter, you will work on your style by

- adapting your writing to audience, situation, and aim
- experimenting with voice and tone
- choosing livelier, clearer words
- sidestepping some common obstacles to style

What Is Style?

How many ways can you think of to explain how to ride a bike? to thank someone for a gift? to describe a rainy day? The English language offers you many different ways to express your thoughts and ideas. Every time you talk and write, you make your own choices about what words to use and how to use them. The kinds of choices you make add up to your *style.*

Style is your unique way of adapting your language to suit different occasions. When you develop a style, you make your words your own. You craft your writing to put something of yourself—your own personality—into it.

Adapting Your Style

Having a style doesn't mean writing in the same way all the time. When you speak and write, your language changes depending on

- your *audience*—who you are writing for
- your *situation*—when and where you are writing
- your *aim*—why you are writing

Audience and situation are the circumstances of your writing. They help determine whether your language should be formal or informal, serious or playful. Aim is what gives your words a purpose. Your aim may be to persuade, to give information, to express your thoughts and feelings, or to create literature. Each of these four aims of writing has distinctive features of style.

Read the following four sentences about the same event. Notice how in each case, a change in aim brings a change in language.

INFORMATIVE   At a banquet held in her honor on Saturday evening, ten-year-old Raven Carmichael was named Hero of the Year for her rescue of a four-year-old child trapped in a drainage pipe.

PERSUASIVE   I urge you to name Raven Carmichael Hero of the Year because of her bravery, her quick thinking, her composure in the face of danger, and her disregard for her personal safety during the rescue of a child not much younger than she.

EXPRESSIVE   When I saw Tommy's head go under, I figured he was stuck, so I jumped in and kept feeling around until I could tear him loose from the branches and stuff that were washing down the ditch.

LITERARY   Scurrying down the muddy embankment into the flooding ditch, Raven groped for the child's head and arms, yanking him above water and then tearing at the sodden debris that entangled his legs.

Voice and Tone

People have distinctive voices in writing just as they do in speaking. *Voice* in writing is the unique sound and rhythm of the writer's language. You can recognize voice by the ring of authenticity it brings to writing. When you read a letter from a friend and can imagine the person standing right there talking to you, you know your friend has written in a true voice.

Voice is an important part of your style. It gives your writing a sound of honesty and authority. Your voice can shine through in any kind of writing—not just in letters and journal entries but also in research papers and poems. Most often, you will want to write in a voice that sounds like you. Sometimes, though, you will want to write in a voice that sounds like someone else—for example, when you imitate another writer's style or when you write dialogue for a character in a story.

Like your speaking voice, your writing voice has a wide range. When you speak, your tone of voice helps express how you feel—happy, sad, angry, afraid, serious, offhand, sarcastic. It even tells people how you want *them* to feel about your subject. But when you write, your words have to do all the work, putting across feelings as well as meanings.

Tone in writing is the attitude or feeling that the writer's words express. If you're writing a newspaper editorial to protest the killing of dolphins in commercial fishing nets, your tone might be angry. But if you're writing a report on marine mammals for biology class, your tone will probably be neutral and objective.

Sometimes you can create a tone with just a few words. If you describe rain on a window as looking "like a string of diamonds," your tone is positive, even romantic. If you describe the rain as looking "like tears streaking a face," your tone is sad and mournful.

As you read the following passages, listen to each writer's voice. How do each writer's words and sentences help create the sound and rhythm of the writing? How do they help set the tone?

> He was white. White as memories lost. He was free. Free as happiness is. He was fantasy, liberty, and excitement. He filled and dominated the mountain valleys and surrounding plains. He was a white horse that flooded my youth with dreams and poetry.
>
> Around the campfires of the country and in the sunny patios of the town, the ranch hands talked about him with enthusiasm and admiration. But gradually their eyes would become hazy and blurred with dreaming. The lively talk would die down. All thoughts fixed on the vision evoked by the horse. Myth of the animal kingdom. Poem of the world of men.
>
> Sabine Ulibarrí, "My Wonder Horse"

> The coyote is a long, slim, sick, and sorry-looking skeleton, with a gray wolf-skin stretched over it, a tolerably bushy tail that forever sags down with a despairing expression of forsakenness and misery, a furtive and evil eye, and a long, sharp face, with slightly lifted lip and exposed teeth. He has a general slinking expression all over. The coyote is a living, breathing allegory of Want. He is *always* hungry. He is always poor, out of luck, and friendless. The meanest creatures despise him, and even the fleas would desert him for a velocipede. He is so spiritless and cowardly that even while his exposed teeth are pretending a threat, the rest of his face is apologizing for it.
>
> Mark Twain, *Roughing It*

> ## EXERCISE 1 ▶ Experimenting with Tone

Write two descriptions of an animal, a place, or a thing that's familiar to you. In the first version, give a neutral, objective description of your subject. In the second version, use words that reveal your attitude toward your subject—affection, disgust, fear, humor, or whatever.

Compare your paragraphs with those of a classmate. How are your word choices different from one another's? What distinguishes your voice from your classmate's?

Formal to Informal

Audience, situation, and aim help determine whether your language is *formal* or *informal*. In many cases, you change the formality of your language automatically. For example, your language is naturally more formal in a graduation speech or a research paper than it is in a journal entry or a note to a friend.

The kinds of language you use in different situations are called **levels of usage.** The levels of usage in standard English range from very formal to very informal. Most usage falls somewhere in between. Following are some of the appropriate uses of **formal English** and **informal English.**

WRITING	
Formal	**Informal**
serious essays, official reports, research papers, some literary criticism, and speeches on serious or solemn occasions	personal letters, journal entries, newspaper and magazine articles, nonfiction books, novels, short stories, and plays
SPEAKING	
Formal	**Informal**
formal occasions, banquets, dedication ceremonies, addresses, presentation ceremonies	everyday conversation at home, school, work, and recreation

The following chart lists some of the features of formal and informal English in both speaking and writing.

FEATURES OF FORMAL AND INFORMAL ENGLISH			
WORDS			
FORMAL	EXAMPLE	INFORMAL	EXAMPLE
longer	*angry*	**shorter**	*mad*
technical	*accelerate*	**everyday**	*speed up*
rare	*funambulist*	**common**	*tightrope walker*
precise	*helpful, friendly*	**fuzzy**	*nice*
specialized	*allegro*	**general**	*lively*
serious	*distasteful*	**offhand**	*icky*
restrained	*very enjoyable*	**exaggerated**	*absolutely incredible*
PRONUNCIATION			
FORMAL	EXAMPLE	INFORMAL	EXAMPLE
slower	*Stand up quickly.*	**faster**	*Standupquick!*
precise	*What do you say?*	**relaxed**	*Whatcha say?*
SPELLING			
FORMAL	EXAMPLE	INFORMAL	EXAMPLE
in full	*will not*	**contractions**	*won't*
conventional	*through*	**unconventional**	*thru*
GRAMMAR			
FORMAL	EXAMPLE	INFORMAL	EXAMPLE
complex	*The band that played today was from Milwaukee.*	**compound**	*The band was from Milwaukee, and it played today.*
complete	*It is hot today.*	**fragmentary**	*Hot today.*
explicit	*What you just said is surprising.*	**implied**	*Wow!*

| EXERCISE 2 ▶ | **Classifying Language as Formal or Informal** |

How would you classify the following passage—formal or informal? Give specific examples to support your answer.

> I never meant to say anything about this, but the fact is that I have never met a dog that didn't have it in for me. You take Kelly, for instance. He's a wire-haired fox terrier and he's had us for three years now. I wouldn't say that he was terribly handsome but he does have a very nice smile. What he *doesn't* have is any sense of fitness. All the other dogs in the neighborhood spend their afternoons yapping at each other's heels or chasing cats. Kelly spends his whole day, every day, chasing swans on the millpond. I don't actually worry because he will never catch one. For one thing, he can't swim. Instead of settling for a simple paddle like everybody else, he has to show off and try some complicated overhand stroke, with the result that he always sinks and has to be fished out. Naturally, people talk, and I never take him for a walk that somebody doesn't point him out and say, "There's that crazy dog that chases swans."
>
> Jean Kerr, *Please Don't Eat the Daisies*

Informal English Usage

Because informal English is flexible, its style is loose and free. Out of this freedom come two types of expressions: *colloquialisms* and *slang*.

Colloquialisms are words and phrases of conversational language. In fact, the word *colloquial* derives from a Latin word meaning "conversation." Used appropriately, colloquialisms can give your writing a lively, personal tone.

EXAMPLES   Gene **took a notion** to wash the car in the rain.
I think I'll **put in for** that delivery job.
Colloquialisms can **put across** a point **pretty** fast.
We're all **pulling** for Ramona to win the race tonight.

Many colloquialisms are *idioms*. **Idioms** are words and phrases that mean something different from the literal meanings of the words. For example, if a friend says it's time to "hit the road," that doesn't mean you should run outside and slap the pavement. It means it's time to leave. Always use idioms with care. In many idioms, the change of a word or two can alter the whole meaning of the expression.

CLEAR **We're up a creek.** [The idiom *up a creek* means "in deep trouble."]

UNCLEAR **We're down a creek.** [The use of *down* makes the reader unsure whether the writer misused the expression *up a creek* or intended a completely different meaning.]

Slang is highly informal language that consists of made-up words or of words used in new ways. It is often lively, imaginative, and entertaining. Almost any group of closely associated people creates slang. Teenagers, musicians, sailors, cooks, truck drivers, and fashion models all build a slang vocabulary that's unique to each group.

The following words and phrases are considered slang when used with the given meanings.

bad: good, excellent	*stupid fresh:* very good
dudette: woman or girl	*yup yup:* yes
par: good	*gear:* clothing
rad or *radical:* good	*frontin':* not being honest

Don't be surprised if many of these slang words seem outdated. Most slang rides a crest of popularity and then dies out quickly. For instance, for some young people in the 1950s, the slang word *shoe* briefly replaced the slang words *neat* and *cool.*

Other slang words have been around for centuries. The word *duds,* meaning "clothing," dates back to the sixteenth century. Occasionally, slang words are used so widely that they stop being slang and become part of general English usage. The words *nice, pants,* and *nickel* were once slang.

STYLE NOTE

A few slang words can instantly set a story in time and make characters seem real. For example, if a character uses the expression "the cat's pajamas," a slang expression from the 1920s, this tells you that the story probably isn't set in the present day.

When you write a story, make sure that any slang expressions you use are from the right time period. Otherwise your characters' dialogue may sound inauthentic.

EXERCISE 3 ▶ **Writing an Informal Dialogue**

Write an informal dialogue in which two teenagers talk about an adventure movie they've just seen. One character is very impressed with the movie; the other thinks it is awful. Have each character talk in the informal, everyday language that you and your friends use. Give "translations" for any slang words that readers from another generation may not understand.

Levels of Meaning

In the following passage, Lewis Carroll's Humpty Dumpty presents his solution to the task of choosing the right word.

> "When *I* use a word," Humpty Dumpty said, in rather a scornful tone, "it means just what I choose it to mean—neither more nor less."
>
> "The question is," said Alice, "whether you *can* make words mean so many different things."
>
> "The question is," said Humpty Dumpty, "which is to be master—that's all."
>
> Lewis Carroll, *Through the Looking-Glass*

Humpty Dumpty may think he is "master" of his words, but he really isn't. Having mastery of language doesn't mean using words any way you want. It means being able to express your ideas with clarity and style. To make words work for you, you need to know what meanings they will communicate to your readers.

Dictionaries help you choose words that have the right literal meanings. But words are much more than their dictionary definitions. A word can mean different things depending on how, when, why, and even by whom it is used. And two words that mean basically the same thing can have very different effects on people.

Synonyms

Using *synonyms*—different words with similar meanings—is an excellent way to add zest to your writing. Instead of using the word *said* over and over, why not opt for some livelier, more specific words—*blurted, growled, muttered, shrieked?* Instead of writing that someone *laughed,* why not have the person *giggle, hoot, snicker,* or *snort?*

You can use a *thesaurus,* a book of synonyms, to find different ways of saying the same thing. But remember that no two words have exactly the same meaning. Be sure to look up an unfamiliar synonym in a dictionary before you use it as a replacement. Otherwise you may write something you did not intend. Notice how the replacement of one word changes the meaning in the following sentences.

> The young man **walked** toward the crowd in the street.
> The young man **strolled** toward the crowd in the street.
> The young man **strutted** toward the crowd in the street.

Strolled and *strutted* are both synonyms for *walked.* But while *walked* is a general word, *strolled* and *strutted* describe specific ways of walking. *Strolled* suggests the man is casual and relaxed, while *strutted* suggests he is proud and swaggering.

LOOKING AT
Language

Malapropisms

When Richard Sheridan wrote his play *The Rivals,* he created the now-famous character Mrs. Malaprop. Mrs. Malaprop is the sort of person who pretends to know more than she does. Her misuse of words is so strikingly humorous that similar blunders are now called *malapropisms.* (*Malaprop* comes from the French phrase *mal à propos,* meaning "not appropriate.")

Mistaking the word *pineapple* for *pinnacle,* Mrs. Malaprop exclaims, "He is the very pineapple of politeness!" When her niece becomes interested in a man Mrs. Malaprop finds unsuitable, she advises the girl to "Illiterate him, I say, quite from your memory." Of course, the word Mrs. Malaprop was looking for was *obliterate,* not *illiterate.*

Seen from afar, Mrs. Malaprop's bloopers are humorous. However, mistakes like hers are all too easy to make because many words sound alike or have similar meanings. For example, which of the following sentences is correct?

The perfect anecdote for a broken heart is a new romance.
The perfect antidote for a broken heart is a new romance.

The second sentence uses the correct word. An *antidote* counteracts poison or relieves pain. An *anecdote* is something else entirely—a very brief story. Familiarize yourself with the precise meanings of easily confused words, such as *effect* and *affect,* *imply* and *infer.* With careful word choice, you'll be a *prodigy* of learning rather than, as Mrs. Malaprop would say, "A *progeny* of learning."

Nonsexist Language

Nonsexist language is language that applies to people in general, both male and female. For example, *humanity* and *humankind* are nonsexist replacements for the gender-specific word *mankind.* If you are referring to humanity as a whole, it's preferable to replace gender-specific expressions with nonsexist synonyms. Otherwise, your words may distract your audience and interfere with your aim.

In the past, many occupations were open only to men or only to women. Job titles such as *policeman* and *stewardess* reflect those limitations. Now that most jobs are held by both men and women, our language is adjusting to reflect this change in our society.

Following are some widely used nonsexist terms that you can use to replace the older, gender-specific ones.

Gender-specific	Nonsexist
chairman	chairperson
deliveryman	delivery person
fireman	firefighter
mailman	mail carrier
manmade	synthetic
may the best man win	may the best person win
policeman	police officer
salesman	salesperson
steward, stewardess	flight attendant
watchman	security guard

EXERCISE 4 ▶ Using Synonyms

Use a thesaurus and your imagination to rewrite the following paragraph. Replace the underlined general words with specific synonyms. To create clear, vivid images, you may need to replace one word with several words. You may also replace or rearrange other words and add details. Make sure your synonyms are appropriate in the context of the paragraph.

We <u>went</u> up the mountain path early on a Saturday morning. Everywhere we looked, <u>colorful</u> leaves were <u>falling</u> from tree branches and <u>moving</u> in the air. As we struggled up the steep trail, the cold October wind <u>went</u> through our jackets as if they were paper. We climbed steadily for almost an hour. By the time we reached the top of the ridge, we were all <u>tired</u> and sore. But the <u>difficult</u> climb was worth it. As we rested against a rock, the first light of the sun began to <u>show</u> above the trees. <u>Colors</u> fanned out across the sky. It was the <u>nicest</u> sunrise I had ever seen.

Denotation and Connotation

Before you use a word, you need to know both its *denotation* and its *connotations*. **Denotation** is the literal meaning given in a dictionary's definition of a word. **Connotations** are the emotional meanings and associations that people may connect with the word.

Some words tend to evoke positive emotions in the people who hear or read the words. For instance, people often have positive responses to the words *new, vacation,* and *victory* because they connect these words with pleasant experiences. Other words bring out negative emotions. For example, the words *pollute, exploitation,* and *defeat* have negative connotations for almost everyone. Many words, such as *paper, cloth,* and *table,* are emotionally neutral because they don't have strong associations for most people.

Be aware of connotations when you write. Keep in mind that emotionally charged words affect the tone of writing. If you use a word without considering its connotations, you may send an emotional message you do not intend.

Loaded Words

A word that has very strong connotations, either positive or negative, is said to be a **loaded word.** Loaded words affect the tone of your writing because they appeal to your readers' emotions. For example, in the following sentence pairs, notice how the tone changes when a neutral word is replaced with a loaded one.

EXAMPLES   She is an **easygoing** person who rarely argues.
She is a **wishy-washy** person who rarely argues.

Advertisers want to **influence** your opinion.
Advertisers want to **prejudice** your opinion.

Politicians, advertisers, lobbyists, and writers of newspaper editorials know and use the power of loaded words. You might use loaded words in persuasive writing to influence your audience. However, keep in mind that loaded language can't take the place of clear reasons and evidence in a persuasive essay. Support your opinions with facts and examples, not with appeals to emotion.

EXERCISE 5 ▶ **Responding to Connotations**

What feelings do you associate with each of the following words? Which words remind you of pleasant experiences? Which words have negative associations? Which words don't stir any feeling at all? Compare your reactions with those of your classmates.

1. sit
2. sunny
3. worn-out
4. compete
5. free
6. flow
7. musical
8. gossip
9. genuine
10. arrogant

EXERCISE 6 ▶ **Analyzing Connotations**

The words in each of the following pairs have similar meanings but different connotations. For each word pair, write a sentence using the first word to describe an imaginary person. Then rewrite the sentence using the second word in place of the first. (You may have to rearrange the sentence slightly.) How is the tone of the second version different? Which description is more flattering?

EXAMPLE **1. fastidious, fussy**
> **1.** *Nathan is a fastidious dresser; his shirts never have a wrinkle.*
> *Nathan is a fussy dresser; his shirts never have a wrinkle.*

1. determined, stubborn
2. sly, cunning
3. blunt, frank
4. slender, skinny
5. weak, delicate

Jargon

People who share the same profession, occupation, hobby, or field of study often use a specialized or technical vocabulary called *jargon*. **Jargon** is language that has a special meaning for a particular group of people.

Informative writing or speaking often employs jargon. Used appropriately, jargon is a practical way of compressing technical information into a precise word or two. For example, when a doctor writes in a medical report that a patient has a "circumorbital hematoma," he or she is using medical jargon in a perfectly acceptable way. But if the doctor writes about that patient for a magazine of general interest, the ordinary, less precise term *black eye* is a more appropriate choice.

Similarly, if you write a sports article with the headline "Islanders Snap Sabers' Winning Streak," you are using sports jargon appropriately. But you would be misusing jargon if you wrote in an English essay that Edgar Allan Poe "had a short winning streak and then struck out."

EXERCISE 7 ▶	**Replacing Jargon with Everyday Language**

Each of the following five sentences contains jargon. First, decide which word or words are being used in a technical sense. Then, rewrite the sentence and replace the jargon with plain, ordinary words. Use a dictionary if necessary.

1. The lawyer consulted his briefs before answering the question.
2. Printed in bold letters, the newspaper headline practically jumped off the page.
3. The entire staff worked all night to get the bugs out of the new computer program.

4. In the opening scene of the film, the camera panned the corral and then zoomed in on the cowhand.
5. The relief pitchers warmed up in the bullpen before the game.

Don't Cramp Your Style

Some kinds of words and expressions get in the way of style. They weaken your writing by boring or confusing your reader. When you eliminate these stumbling blocks to style, you bring clarity and interest to your writing.

Tired Words

A *tired word* is one that has been used so much that it has become worn out and weak. Most tired words were clear and forceful when they were first used. For example, the word *fabulous* originally referred to something so striking that it might be legendary—worthy of a position in a fable. But today, *fabulous* is used to refer to anything very pleasant. When we say that a book or a film or a meal is "fabulous," we aren't saying much at all. The adjectives *good, nice, great,* and *wonderful* are also tired words.

Tired words most often appear in everyday conversation. They may be acceptable when you talk to friends or family, but they are not precise enough to be effective in writing. Each tired word is a lost opportunity to develop an exact, vivid description of your subject.

Clichés

A tired expression is called a *cliché.* Some clichés began as apt quotations that became fashionable sayings. For instance, vivid phrases like "Footprints on the sands of time" helped make Henry Wadsworth Longfellow a popular poet. But overuse has killed the freshness of the expression and made it trite.

Many clichés are figurative comparisons, such as *quick as a flash, hungry as a horse,* and *light as a feather.* Other clichés are simply common phrases like *last but not least, I for one,* and *with all due respect.*

STYLE
NOTE

Clichés are so familiar to us that we rarely think about what they really mean or whether they're actually true. Oscar Wilde, who was famous for his wit, liked to contradict the stock expressions that were popular in his time. Through humor, he helped readers see such expressions in a new light.

On what clichés did Wilde base the following statements?

Truth is rarely pure, and never simple.

The Importance of Being Earnest

A man cannot be too careful in the choice of his enemies.

The Picture of Dorian Gray

Experiment with rearranging clichés to create lively, meaningful expressions. For example, instead of saying someone is *busy as a bee,* why not say the person is *busy as the freeway at rush hour* or *busy as the hallway between classes?* Instead of offering *a word to the wise,* why not offer *a word to the* un*wise* (those who could use the advice!)?

EXERCISE 8 ▶

Revising to Eliminate Tired Words and Clichés

A student has drafted the following review for publication in the school newspaper. Because tired words and clichés distract from the writer's message, the review isn't as convincing as it could be. Help the writer out by suggesting changes to improve the style. First, identify any tired words and clichés in the review. (You should be able to find at least five.) Then, write down livelier, more specific words and phrases to replace the dull, vague ones. You may also see other ways to improve the style of the review.

Star Trek: The Next Generation is a far cry from the original Star Trek series, but it's good in its own way. Viewers notice the change as soon as they hear the voice-over at the opening of each episode. The Enterprise is still on its "continuing mission," but its captain, Jean-Luc Picard, has learned about nonsexist language: the crew now ventures "where no one has gone before."

On the Enterprise of the '90s, women play more important roles: navigating the ship, running Sick Bay, and counseling the crew. In addition, the next-generation crew is more diverse than the old one. Not all of the main characters are human or humanlike. There's even a Klingon security officer--a fact that might cause Captain James T. Kirk to turn over in his grave.

The Klingon crew member Worf represents another nice thing about the series: a generation later, the Federation has made peace with some of its fiercest enemies, including the Klingons. In fact, the new Enterprise crew engages in more peacekeeping than fighting--though when they do launch into battle, the special effects are great.

Some viewers may complain that the new show isn't as good as the old one because it has more dialogue and less action. But if the characters do tend to beat around the bush sometimes, that's just because they're confronting real-life moral dilemmas--a rare thing in this day and age of prime-time television. When all is said and done, Star Trek: The Next Generation is worth taking a chance on.

Mixed Figures of Speech

A *figure of speech* is an expression that describes one thing by comparing it to something else. Figures of speech aren't meant to be taken literally. For example, the expression "it's a jungle out there" doesn't mean that lions and tigers actually prowl the streets. It means that, like a jungle, the world can be a savage and dangerous place.

When you use figurative language, be sure to stay consistent. If you begin by comparing a man's voice to a horn and then compare his eyes to a dog's, you create a *mixed figure of speech*.

MIXED   **The burning question of how to rescue those still at sea drowned all other discussion.** ["Burning question" suggests fire, which would hardly have "drowned" anything.]

BETTER   **The burning question of how to rescue those still at sea swept away all other discussion.**

> **EXERCISE 9** ▶ **Revising Mixed Figures of Speech**

Each of the following sentences contains a mixed figure of speech. Revise each sentence to make the figure of speech consistent throughout.

1. Like a mother hen, the young woman shepherded her child through the park.
2. In the heat of anger, he froze us with his stare.
3. Our inflated hopes were dampened by the sad news.
4. Like summer dew, tears of joy crept from her eyes.
5. A flock of reporters pounced on the woman as she emerged from the courthouse.

Shoe, by Jeff MacNelly, reprinted by permission: Tribune Media Services.

Euphemisms

Euphemisms are indirect, agreeable words and phrases that replace more direct, less appealing ones. We often use euphemisms to avoid offending people or hurting their feelings. For instance, few people would tell a woman that her child is a *brat;* instead, they might say the child is *high-spirited.* Similarly, you might call someone *cautious* rather than labeling him or her a *coward.*

Euphemisms help eliminate negative connotations that could interfere with a writer's aim. For example, a writer's job may be to persuade people to accept a garbage dump in their neighborhood. Very likely, the writer will avoid the negative connotations associated with the word *garbage*. Instead, he or she may say *waste disposal plant* or *refuse management facility*.

Some of the euphemisms you might hear or read on almost any day are included in the following chart.

EUPHEMISM	MORE DIRECT TERM
casualties	dead
correctional institution	prison
offender	criminal
faux	imitation
memorial garden	cemetery
misrepresentation	lie
additional revenues	higher taxes
socially maladjusted	rude

Euphemisms are appropriate when they are used as a courtesy. However, too many euphemisms can weaken your writing and obscure your meaning. Use direct language whenever possible. When you must use euphemisms, use them sparingly and purposefully.

Gobbledygook

Gobbledygook is wordy, puffed-up language. You can recognize gobbledygook by its long, confusing sentences filled with long, difficult words. For example, read the following sentence:

> Experience indicates that timely measures of effective implementation may consequently result in a ninefold savings in labor expenditures.

If the same statement were written in clear and simple language, it might read like the following proverb:

> A stitch in time saves nine.

Don't bury your own natural voice in gobbledygook. Few readers are impressed by confusing, empty language. In fact, gobbledygook leaves most people wondering what the writer is trying to hide. Show that you respect the intelligence of your readers by writing in a clear, straightforward manner.

EXERCISE 10 ▶	**Revising to Eliminate Euphemisms and Gobbledygook**

The following paragraph is written in wordy, indirect, confusing language. First, figure out what the writer is really saying. (You may need to look up some words in a dictionary.) Then, rewrite the paragraph in simple, straightforward language.

In the event that a conflagration is being experienced, personnel are advised to modify their deportment in accord with the implementation of the following prescribed series of actions. All personnel within ambulatory distance of a nonelectric device for descent to lower levels shall avail themselves of the opportunity to vacate the area. In order to ensure an orderly procession to a secure area, personnel deployed in lower levels shall have priority in evasion of any possible exposure to unacceptable levels of heat. All personnel are summarily advised to maintain a cautious deportment as well as to practice courtesy as they proceed at minimum speed to an area not less than one thousand yards from the site of the problematic situation. Additionally, due to the fact that communication between members of staffing pools is sometimes counterproductive, supervisors are advised to direct subordinates to limit verbalization at all times during any circumstances that may tend to warrant such a precautionary measure.

MAKING CONNECTIONS

Write with Different Aims

You're glancing through the newspaper one morning when you see the following article.

Teenagers Find and Return Stolen Money

On Friday evening, local police were surprised to see two juveniles carrying a large, battered suitcase into the 5th Street station house. Dwight E. Jones, 16, and Yolanda Mae McClaren, 17, reported that they spotted the suitcase in an alley near the Hollendale-Branchwater Bank on their way home from school. The suitcase contained over $100,000 in unmarked currency. Detectives have confirmed that the same amount of money was stolen from the bank in an armed robbery Friday afternoon. The alleged perpetrators, who were apprehended minutes after the robbery occurred, apparently abandoned the heavy suitcase as they fled the scene. Bank officials expressed their thanks to the teenagers but said that they have no plans for issuing a reward.

Writing to Persuade

Do you think that Dwight and Yolanda should receive a reward for returning the money? Write a letter to the editor expressing your opinion. If you think a reward is due, try to persuade readers that they should write letters of protest asking the bank officials to reconsider. If you think the bank officials made the right decision, give reasons to support your opinion.

Remember that your aim is to persuade readers to think or act in a certain way. Choose your words carefully to make your letter convincing. The following checklist will help you revise your letter for style.

Revision Checklist

- Is your tone appropriate for your aim and your audience?
- Have you used any highly informal expressions, such as slang, that may distract readers from your message?
- Are your words clear and straightforward?
- Have you avoided tired words and clichés?
- Have you weighed words for their connotations— their likely effect on readers?

Writing to Express Yourself

How would it feel to be a hero for the day? Put yourself in the place of Dwight or Yolanda, and write a letter to a friend describing your experience. Explain how it felt to discover the money, to turn it over to the authorities, and to read about yourself in the newspaper the next day.

You want to share your experience with your friend in every detail. The following checklist will help you make your letter more expressive.

Revision Checklist

- Does your letter have an authentic voice? That is, does it sound like a real person talking?
- Have you used lively, vivid words to describe your experience?
- Have you used figures of speech in a consistent way?

14 WRITING CLEAR SENTENCES

LOOKING
AHEAD

Clarity is important for the style as well as the sense of what you write. In this chapter, you will learn how to make your sentences clearer and smoother by

- structuring sentences to show the relationships between ideas
- checking sentences for completeness and correct punctuation

Ways to Achieve Clarity

Have you ever adjusted a camera lens to bring an image into focus? Just as you can sharpen the focus of a camera to take a clearer picture, you can sharpen the focus of your writing to better express your meaning. One of the best ways to achieve clarity is to write sentences that show the appropriate relationships between ideas. You show these relationships by adapting the structure of your sentences.

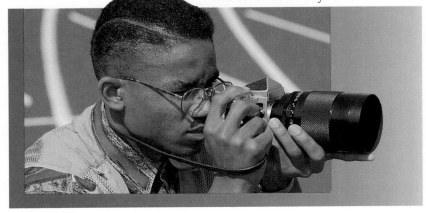

Coordinating Ideas

Equally important ideas in a sentence are called *coordinate* ideas. To show that ideas are coordinate, you join them with a coordinating conjunction (*and, but, or, for, nor, so, yet*) or another connective. The connective tells your reader how the ideas are related. For example, *and* links equal and similar ideas, while *but* links equal and contrasting ideas.

In each of the following sentences, notice how the writer uses a coordinating conjunction to join two complete thoughts, or *independent clauses*. When you use coordination to link two independent clauses, the result is a *compound sentence*.

EXAMPLES   The watch was ended at last, **and** we took our supper and went to bed.

Mark Twain, *Life on the Mississippi*

In the fall the war was always there, **but** we did not go to it any more.

Ernest Hemingway, "In Another Country"

You can also form a compound sentence with a semicolon and a conjunctive adverb or just a semicolon.

EXAMPLE   But that L-shaped rip on the left sleeve got bigger; bits of stuffing coughed out from its wound after a hard day of play.

Gary Soto, "The Jacket"

MECHANICS HINT

Punctuating Compound Sentences

When you join two independent clauses with a coordinating conjunction, you usually put a comma before the conjunction.

> We walked along the shore for a while, and then we dove into the ice-cold water.

However, a comma isn't necessary if the clauses are very short and clear.

> Shawna swam and I sunbathed.

☞ REFERENCE NOTE: For more about using commas with coordinating conjunctions, see pages 848–849.

Sometimes you may have several equal, related ideas within a single independent clause. In addition to linking coordinate independent clauses, you can also link coordinate words and phrases in a sentence.

EXAMPLES   Some **distant lamp or lighted window** gleamed below me. [compound subject]

James Joyce, "Araby"

I cleared my throat and coughed tentatively. [compound predicate]

Robert Cormier, "The Moustache"

Anyone who had passed the day with **him and his dog** refused to share a bench with them again. [compound object of a preposition]

Kurt Vonnegut, "Tom Edison's Shaggy Dog"

For three days the fire had been burning and Evans, **red-armed in his shirt sleeves and sweating along the seams of his brow,** was prodding it with a garden fork. [coordinate verbal phrases]

V. S. Pritchett, "The Wheelbarrow"

Subordinating Ideas

Look at the money in this picture.

Just as some of this money has greater value than the rest, some of your ideas in writing are more important than others. However, the importance of an idea isn't always as obvious as the worth of a coin. To make the main ideas stand out in your writing, you need to downplay, or *subordinate,* the less important ones.

You can subordinate an idea in a sentence by putting the idea in a subordinate clause. The subordinate clause elaborates on the thought expressed in the independent clause.

EXAMPLES   Maria, **who likes Kevin Costner,** saw the movie
            Dances with Wolves three times.
            Dances with Wolves is a rare moviegoing experience
            **because it uses Native American dialogue with
            English subtitles.**

Adverb Clauses

An *adverb clause* modifies a verb, an adjective, or an adverb in a sentence. You introduce an adverb clause with a subordinating conjunction (*although, after, because, if, since, when, whenever, where, while*).

EXAMPLES **Whenever the memory of those marigolds flashes across my mind,** a strange nostalgia comes with it and remains long after the picture has faded.
> Eugenia Collier, "Marigolds"

This confession he spoke harshly **because its unexpectedness shook him.**
> Bernard Malamud, "The Magic Barrel"

She held back her skirts and turned her feet one way and her head another **as she glanced down at the polished, pointed-tipped boots.**
> Kate Chopin, "A Pair of Silk Stockings"

"If there'd been any farther west to go, he'd have gone."
> John Steinbeck, *The Red Pony*

The subordinating conjunction you use is important. It shows your reader the relationship between the ideas in the adverb clause and the independent clause. This chart lists the subordinating conjunctions you can use to express the following relationships of *time or place, cause or reason, purpose or result, or condition.*

SUBORDINATING CONJUNCTIONS				
TIME OR PLACE				
after as	before since	until when	whenever where	wherever while
CAUSE OR REASON				
as	because		since	whereas
PURPOSE OR RESULT				
that		in order that		so that
CONDITION				
although if		even though provided that		unless while

WRITING NOTE   As you can see from the examples on page 507, an adverb clause can make sense at either the beginning or the end of a sentence. Try a clause in both positions to see which sounds better to you. When you place an adverb clause at the beginning of a sentence, remember to separate it from the independent clause with a comma. Otherwise, you may confuse your reader.

EXAMPLE   A space shuttle must have a foolproof thermal protection system **because friction with the earth's atmosphere creates intense heat.**

or

Because friction with the earth's atmosphere creates intense heat, a space shuttle must have a foolproof thermal protection system.

EXERCISE 1   **Selecting Appropriate Subordinating Conjunctions**

For each of the following sentences, choose an appropriate subordinating conjunction to fill in the blank. The hint in parentheses tells you what kind of relationship the conjunction should express.

1. _____ it is called a lake, Moraine is really a three-acre pond located beneath a high majestic ridge on Grapetree Mountain. (condition)
2. _____ we visited Lake Moraine, we heard wild geese and saw beavers building dams. (time)
3. _____ we were sitting by the tent one summer evening, a snowshoe hare crept from behind the pine trees to eat lettuce from our hands. (time)
4. Lake Moraine, a wonderful, peaceful place, is now threatened _____ acid rains are destroying the brook trout that swim in its waters. (cause or reason)
5. _____ acid pollutants from factory fumes enter the atmosphere, they fall to the earth in rain and snow. (time)
6. High-altitude ponds such as Lake Moraine get a heavy dose of acid rains _____ the mountains trap moisture-bearing air masses. (cause or reason)

7. ____ the acid pollutants end up in the mountain ponds, fish, especially trout, suffer and die in great numbers. (time)

8. Many remote trout ponds are encased in granite ____ little soil or organic matter exists to trap or buffer the acid rain. (purpose or result)

9. ____ it is possible to develop acid-tolerant strains of trout, such a program of selective breeding will likely take many years. (condition)

10. More and more isolated ponds like Lake Moraine will become trout graveyards ____ we don't find a way to combat the effects of acid rain. (condition)

Adjective Clauses

An *adjective clause* modifies a noun or pronoun in a sentence. It usually begins with *who, whom, whose, which, that,* or *where.*

EXAMPLES   Stashed somewhere in the larder there was always a jar of raisins and some vanilla pods **which appeared in the kitchen only on special occasions.**

Ernesto Galarza, *Barrio Boy*

Chicago seemed an unreal city **whose mythical houses were built of slabs of black coal wreathed in palls of gray smoke,** houses **whose foundations were sinking slowly into the dank prairie.**

Richard Wright, *American Hunger*

Before you use an adjective clause in a sentence, you need to decide which idea you want to emphasize and which you want to subordinate. For example, suppose you want to combine these two ideas in one sentence:

Award-winning novelist Rolando Hinojosa-Smith writes in both Spanish and English. He was raised in a bilingual family.

If you want to emphasize that Hinojosa-Smith writes in Spanish and English, put the information in the second sentence into an adjective clause.

Award-winning novelist Rolando Hinojosa-Smith, **who was raised in a bilingual family,** writes in both Spanish and English.

But if you want to emphasize that Hinojosa-Smith was raised in a bilingual family, put that information in an independent clause and the other information in an adjective clause. You may need to change the word order to make the sentence work. For clarity, be sure that you place the adjective clause next to the word it modifies.

Award-winning novelist Rolando Hinojosa-Smith, **who writes in both Spanish and English,** was raised in a bilingual family.

 REFERENCE NOTE: For more about combining sentences by subordinating ideas, see pages 536–538.

EXERCISE 2 ▶ **Subordinating Ideas by Using Adjective Clauses**

Change the emphasis in each of the following sentences. Emphasize the idea that is now in the subordinate clause, and subordinate the idea that is now in the independent clause. You may have to delete some words, change the word order, or use a different word to begin the new subordinate clause. Which version of the sentence sounds better to you? Why?

1. N. Scott Momaday, who writes eloquently about Native American culture, won a Pulitzer Prize for the novel *House Made of Dawn.*
2. *House Made of Dawn,* which was published in 1968, focuses on a Native American man's struggle to reconcile traditional tribal values with modern-day American life.

3. Momaday spent his boyhood on several different reservations, where he acquired extensive knowledge of Native American history and culture.
4. Momaday's book *The Way to Rainy Mountain*, which gives a perceptive account of Native American life, focuses on the history and culture of the Kiowa tribe.
5. Momaday, who has also published two collections of poems, considers himself primarily a poet.

Correcting Faulty Coordination

Before you join ideas with a coordinating conjunction, it's important to make sure the ideas are of equal importance. Otherwise you may end up with *faulty coordination,* unequal ideas presented as if they were coordinate. Faulty coordination blurs the focus of your writing because it doesn't show the relationships between ideas. You can correct faulty subordination by putting the less-important ideas into phrases or subordinate clauses.

FAULTY   My aunt is one of the performers in the musical, and she was able to get us tickets, and the tickets were for opening night.

REVISED   **Because she is one of the performers in the musical,** my aunt was able to get us tickets **for opening night.**

or

My aunt, **who is one of the performers in the musical,** was able to get us tickets **for opening night.**

Using Parallel Structure

If you've ever ridden a bicycle on a rocky road, you know the difference between the smooth feel of gliding over concrete and the jolting sensations of a bumpy ride on gravel. Like a comfortable bicycle ride, writing should have smooth movement and not be a journey over mental potholes and gravel.

You can make your writing smoother and clearer by checking your sentences for *parallel structure.* You create parallel structure in a sentence by using the same grammatical form to express equal, or parallel, ideas. For example, you pair a noun with a noun, a phrase with a phrase, a clause with a clause, and an infinitive with an infinitive.

Use parallel structure when you link coordinate ideas.

NOT PARALLEL   **In winter I usually like skiing and to skate.**
                [gerund paired with infinitive]
PARALLEL   **In winter I usually like to ski and to skate.**
                [infinitive paired with infinitive]

NOT PARALLEL   **The company guaranteed that salaries would be increased and shorter working days.** [noun clause paired with a noun]
PARALLEL   **The company guaranteed that salaries would be increased and that working days would be shorter.** [noun clause paired with noun clause]

Use parallel structure when you compare or contrast ideas.

NOT PARALLEL   To think logically is as important as calculating accurately. [infinitive compared with a gerund]

PARALLEL   **Thinking** logically is as important as **calculating** accurately. [gerund compared with a gerund]

NOT PARALLEL   Einstein liked mathematical research more than to supervise a large laboratory. [noun contrasted with an infinitive]

PARALLEL   Einstein liked mathematical **research** more than **supervision** of a large laboratory. [noun contrasted with a noun]

Use parallel structure when you link ideas with the conjunctions *both . . . and, either . . . or, neither . . . nor,* or *not only . . . but also.* These pairs are called *correlative conjunctions.*

NOT PARALLEL   With *Ship of Fools,* Katherine Anne Porter proved she was talented not only as a short-story writer but also in writing novels.

PARALLEL   With *Ship of Fools,* Katherine Anne Porter proved she was talented not only **as a short-story writer** but also **as a novelist.**

When you use correlative conjunctions, be sure to place the conjunctions directly before the parallel terms. Otherwise the relationship between the ideas won't be clear.

UNCLEAR   A President of the United States must not only represent his own political party but also the entire American people.

CLEAR   A President of the United States must represent **not only** his own political party **but also** the entire American people.

EXERCISE 3 ▶ **Revising Sentences by Using Parallel Structure**

Some of the following sentences are out of balance. Bring balance to them by putting the ideas in parallel form. You may need to delete, add, or move some words. If a sentence is already correct, write C.

1. Sports fans may disagree over whether going to baseball games or to watch football is more fun, but few people can ignore the importance of sports in America.

2. Sports has always been a topic for friendly and not-so-friendly arguments.
3. Some sports fans argue endlessly and with anger about whether football or baseball is truly the American pastime.
4. Baseball backers may insist that baseball is the more important game because it requires skill, dexterity, and to be fast.
5. On the other hand, football fans may praise a quarter-back's speed, skill, and how agile he is.

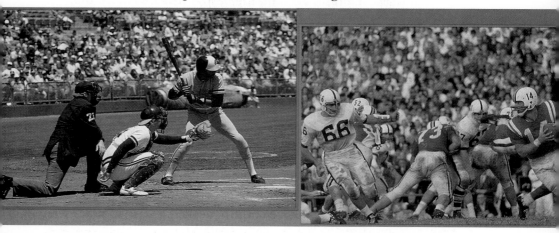

R E V I E W   A ▶ Revising a Paragraph for Clarity

Faulty coordination and faulty parallelism make the following paragraphs confusing. Using the methods you've learned in this chapter, revise each faulty sentence to make it clear and smooth. You may need to add, delete, or rearrange some words in the sentences. Remember to check the placement of correlative conjunctions.

For most writers, the road to fame is long and with difficulty. But Amy Tan published The Joy Luck Club in 1989, and she became an instant celebrity. The Joy Luck Club topped the bestseller list soon after its publication, and it was Tan's first novel.

Tan is a Chinese American writer, and she writes skillfully about the lives of second-generation Chinese Americans. In The Joy Luck Club and her second novel, The Kitchen God's Wife, she also portrays family relationships both with humor and insightful.

Tan seems like a natural-born storyteller, but she didn't always plan to write fiction. In fact, her parents hoped she would become a neurosurgeon. Tan was working as a freelance business writer, and she decided to try her hand at writing short stories. She joined a writing workshop and submitted her first story. She was revising it, and the story grew, changed, and eventually to become the basis for The Joy Luck Club.

Obstacles to Clarity

In the first part of this chapter, you had some practice at putting your ideas in proper relationship to one another. The next important step toward clarity is to check your sentences for completeness. As you revise, you need to be on the alert for two obstacles to clarity, *sentence fragments* and *run-on sentences.*

Sentence Fragments

A sentence should express a complete thought. If you punctuate a part of a sentence as if it were a complete sentence, you create a *sentence fragment.*

FRAGMENT **Has large horns shaped like corkscrews.** [The subject is missing. *What* has large horns shaped like corkscrews?]

SENTENCE **A male kudu has large horns shaped like corkscrews.**

FRAGMENT **The kudu, a type of antelope, in Africa.** [The verb is missing.]

SENTENCE **The kudu, a type of antelope, lives in Africa.**

FRAGMENT **The kudu, a type of antelope, found in Africa.** [The helping verb is missing.]

SENTENCE **The kudu, a type of antelope, is found in Africa.**

FRAGMENT **While the kudu stands 5 feet high at the shoulder.** [This has a subject and a verb, but it doesn't express a complete thought.]

SENTENCE **While the kudu stands 5 feet high at the shoulder, with its long horns its total height can reach past 11 feet.**

The meaning of a fragment you have written may seem clear to you because you know the information you have left out. Try looking at what you have written as though the information is all new to you. Ask what else a reader might need to know.

STYLE
NOTE

Experienced writers sometimes use fragments deliberately for effect. For example, in the following excerpt, Leslie Norris uses fragments to imitate the sounds of natural speech. Notice that the meaning of the fragments is made clear by the sentences that come before and after them.

> "This was an unusual goose," my uncle said. "Called at the back door every morning for its food, answered to its name. An intelligent creature. Eddie's sisters tied a blue silk ribbon around its neck and made a pet of it. It displayed more personality and understanding than you'd believe possible in a bird. Came Christmas, of course, and they couldn't kill it."
>
> Leslie Norris, "A Flight of Geese"

Fragments can be effective when they are used as a stylistic technique. You may want to experiment with using them in expressive and creative writing such as journals, poems, and short stories. You can also use fragments when an informal, shorthand style is appropriate—for example, in classified ads.

However, don't use fragments if they might interfere with your aim or confuse your audience. For example, you wouldn't use fragments in a research paper or a book report, since your readers expect formal, straightforward language in these kinds of informative writing.

EXERCISE 4 ▶ **Revising to Eliminate Sentence Fragments**

Decide which of these word groups are sentences and which are fragments. If an item contains only complete sentences, write *C*. If it contains a fragment, revise the fragment.

Susan B. Anthony

Willa Cather

Booker T. Washington

1. Many great Americans had little or no formal education. Among these are political leaders, writers, artists, scientists, and business executives.

2. Eleanor Roosevelt had little formal education. Susan B. Anthony the equivalent of a high-school education.

3. When Abraham Lincoln was a young man, he worked in a general store. And at the same time studied books on law.

4. Although Carl Sandburg left school when he was thirteen years old. He later went on to Lombard College after serving in the army during the Spanish-American War.

5. Andrew Carnegie, who gave away many millions to charity, started to work at the age of thirteen. He did not go to high school.

6. Gordon Parks, who had a high-school education, named photographer of the year by a major magazine.

7. Booker T. Washington walked five hundred miles to attend school at Hampton Institute. Later founded Tuskegee Institute.

8. One of the great letter writers of all time, Abigail Adams, had no formal schooling.

9. Our first president, George Washington, was a slow reader and a poor speller. Who struggled in later life to overcome his educational deficiencies.

10. On the other hand, many famous Americans had excellent educations. As a child, Willa Cather, for instance, was taught Greek and Latin by a Nebraska shopkeeper.

Phrase Fragments

One type of sentence fragment is a phrase fragment. A *phrase* is a group of related words that doesn't contain a subject and a verb. Because a phrase doesn't express a complete thought, it can't stand on its own as a sentence.

☞ REFERENCE NOTE: The types of phrases include prepositional, appositive, and verbal phrases. For explanations of these types of phrases, see pages 605–621.

Often, you can correct a phrase fragment by attaching it to the sentence that comes before or after it.

FRAGMENT **During her long and productive life.** Nina Otero excelled as an educator, writer, and public official. [prepositional phrase]

SENTENCE During her long and productive life, Nina Otero excelled as an educator, writer, and public official.

FRAGMENT **Descended from a long line of political leaders.** Otero became active in politics soon after she graduated from college. [verbal phrase—participial]

SENTENCE Descended from a long line of political leaders, Otero became active in politics soon after she graduated from college.

FRAGMENT She was one of the first Mexican American women. **To hold important public posts in New Mexico.** [verbal phrase—infinitive]

SENTENCE She was one of the first Mexican American women to hold important public posts in New Mexico.

FRAGMENT In 1917, she became superintendent of schools in Santa Fe County. **An unusual position for a woman at that time.** [appositive phrase]

SENTENCE In 1917, she became superintendent of schools in Santa Fe County, an unusual position for a woman at that time.

Subordinate Clause Fragments

A *clause* is a group of words that contains a subject and a verb. An *independent clause* expresses a complete thought and can stand alone as a sentence. But a *subordinate clause* doesn't express a complete thought and can't stand alone as a sentence. It is another type of sentence fragment.

FRAGMENT   Michael Jackson made his film debut as the Scarecrow in *The Wiz*. **Which was based on *The Wizard of Oz*.**
CORRECT   Michael Jackson made his film debut as the Scarecrow in *The Wiz*, which was based on *The Wizard of Oz*.

FRAGMENT   Jackson topped his earlier popularity. **When he performed in his first music video.**
CORRECT   Jackson topped his earlier popularity when he performed in his first music video.

☞ REFERENCE NOTE: If you have any questions about the difference between independent clauses and subordinate clauses, see pages 628–637.

While checking over your work, you may find that two other constructions cause you trouble. They are items in a series and compound verbs.

FRAGMENT   I packed only casual clothes. **A pair of jeans, two T-shirts, and a sweater.** [items in a series]
CORRECT   I packed only casual clothes. **I packed** a pair of jeans, two T-shirts, and a sweater.

or

I packed only casual clothes: a pair of jeans, two T-shirts, and a sweater.

FRAGMENT   Jay went sightseeing on his own. **But caught up with the group later.** [compound verb]
CORRECT   Jay went sightseeing on his own but caught up with the group later.

E X E R C I S E 5 ▶   **Revising to Eliminate Fragments**

Some of the following items are sets of complete sentences, while others contain fragments. If an item has only complete sentences, write *C*. If it contains a fragment, revise it to include the fragment in a complete sentence.

1. Nat Love, who was born a slave in Tennessee, became a cowboy. When he was just fifteen years old.
2. An expert horseman, Love traveled throughout the West. Driving cattle on the open range.
3. After taking first prize in a riding, roping, and shooting contest in Deadwood, South Dakota, became known as "Deadwood Dick."

4. In 1907, Love published his autobiography, *The Life and Adventures of Nat Love, Better Known in Cattle Country as Deadwood Dick.*

5. The book both true stories and "tall tales" about Love and other famous characters of the Old West. Because Love did have many real-life adventures, it's difficult to tell which stories are fact and which are fiction.

Montana Historical Society, Helen

6. Another figure of the Old West. Andrew García, tells of similar exploits in his autobiography *Tough Trip Through Paradise.*

7. García describes some of the tough characters he met when he traveled with an outlaw band. One of the most notorious characters was the horse thief George Reynolds, better known as "Big Nose George."

8. Like many of the outlaws García knew. Reynolds died a violent death.

9. Although tempted to become an outlaw himself. García eventually settled down. And began writing his exciting account of his life.

10. García didn't live to see his memoirs published. The manuscripts, which he had packed away in dynamite boxes. Were discovered years after his death.

Run-on Sentences

When you're writing a draft, you may like to race full-speed ahead to get your thoughts down on paper. But when you revise, it's important to know when to put on the brakes. Each complete thought should come to a full stop or be linked correctly to the next thought. If you run together two sentences as if they were a single thought, you create a *run-on sentence.*

There are two kinds of run-on sentences. A *fused sentence* has no punctuation at all between the two complete thoughts. A *comma splice* has just a comma between them.

> FUSED   Lightning speeds to our eyes at 186,000 miles per second thunder creeps to our ears at 1,087 feet per second.
>
> COMMA SPLICE   We can't hear and see the event at the same time, we sense it twice in different ways.

There are many different ways to correct a run-on sentence. Depending on the relationship you want to show between the two ideas, one method may be better than another.

1. You can make two sentences.

   Lightning speeds to our eyes at 186,000 miles per second. Thunder creeps to our ears at 1,087 feet per second.

2. You can use a comma and a coordinating conjunction.

   Lightning speeds to our eyes at 186,000 miles per second, **but** thunder creeps to our ears at 1,087 feet per second.

3. You can change one of the independent clauses to a subordinate clause.

   While lightning speeds to our eyes at 186,000 miles per second, thunder creeps to our ears at 1,087 feet per second.

4. You can use a semicolon.

   Lightning speeds to our eyes at 186,000 miles per second; thunder creeps to our ears at 1,087 feet per second.

5. You can use a semicolon and a conjunctive adverb.

   Lightning speeds to our eyes at 186,000 miles per second; **however,** thunder creeps to our ears at 1,087 feet per second.

STYLE NOTE You've probably noticed that well-known writers sometimes use run-ons in their works. You might wonder: If an expert writer uses run-ons, why can't I use them, too?

You *can* use run-ons occasionally in short stories, journal entries, and other kinds of expressive and creative writing. Run-ons can be especially effective in *stream of consciousness* writing, a style that imitates the natural flow of a character's thoughts, feelings, and perceptions. What is the effect of the run-on sentence below?

> The blue light from Cornelia's lampshade drew into a tiny point at the center of her brain, it flickered and winked like an eye, quietly it fluttered and dwindled.
>
> Katherine Anne Porter,
> "The Jilting of Granny Weatherall"

Always check your writing for unintentional run-ons. If you use run-ons for effect, make sure that your meaning will be clear to your reader.

E X E R C I S E 6 ▶ Revising Run-on Sentences

The following items are confusing because they're run-on sentences. Revise each run-on by using the method given in parentheses. (The examples on page 521 will help you.) If you have to choose a connecting word or subordinate an idea, make sure your revised version shows the appropriate relationship between the ideas.

1. The Victorian Era was a time of extreme delicacy and tact in language, direct references to the body were considered offensive in polite society. (two sentences)
2. The word *limb* had to be used instead of *leg* or *arm* even a reference to the "leg" of a chair was considered impolite. (semicolon)
3. In reference to poultry, the thigh was called the second joint the leg was called the first joint or the drumstick. (comma and coordinating conjunction)

4. Delicate language was carried to an even greater extreme by some people, they referred to a bull as a "gentleman cow." (subordinate clause)
5. This kind of prissy language seems funny to us now, even today we use indirect language to replace words and phrases that might be considered offensive. (semicolon and conjunctive adverb)

REVIEW B ▶ **Revising Paragraphs to Eliminate Fragments and Run-Ons**

Revise the following paragraphs to eliminate the fragments and run-ons. Add or delete words wherever necessary. Be sure to check your revised version for correct capitalization and punctuation.

War reports--both fact and fiction--have fascinated people since the first warriors and bards sat around campfires. Not all war literature is based on firsthand experience some comes out of imagination. One of America's most prominent war novelists, Stephen Crane, wrote about war before he ever saw a battle, Crane's short novel The Red Badge of Courage about a young soldier's reactions to fear during a major Civil War battle. Was written almost thirty years after the battle took place.

On the other hand, many of Ernest Hemingway's novels and stories were based on his own experiences during World War I. Before the United States entered the war. Hemingway worked as an ambulance driver for the Italian army. His novel A Farewell to Arms. Which is often called the most important novel about World War I, follows the experiences of a young ambulance driver.

After World War II. Writer John Hersey introduced a journalistic technique to war fiction. His book Hiroshima. Which describes the effect of the dropping of the A-bomb. Combines the literary techniques of fiction with the factual style of journalism. The Vietnam era produced several notable works of nonfiction. Including Ron Kovic's Born on the Fourth of July, which became an Academy-Award-winning movie. A Vietnam veteran. Kovic describes how his feelings about war changed after he lost the use of his legs.

MAKING CONNECTIONS

Use Parallel Structure for Rhythm and Emphasis

Parallel structure can add more than clarity to language. It can also add rhythm and emphasis. The best way to appreciate the effect of parallelism is to hear it. Read aloud the following passage, listening to the rhythm and emphasis that parallel structure creates. How does parallel structure affect the tone of the passage? How does it help you hear the similarities between the parallel ideas?

from "The Toynbee Convector"
by Ray Bradbury

"We made it!" he said. "We did it! The future is ours. We rebuilt the cities, freshened the small towns, cleaned the lakes and rivers, washed the air, saved the dolphins, increased the whales, stopped the wars, tossed solar stations across space to light the world, colonized the moon, moved on to Mars, then Alpha Centauri. We cured cancer and stopped death. We did it—Oh Lord, much thanks—we did it. Oh, future's bright and beauteous spires, arise!"

Write a paragraph about a familiar object—something that you see every day at home or at school. Use parallel structure to create rhythm in your paragraph and to show similarities between ideas.

Before you start writing, jot down words and phrases that come to mind when you think of the object. List as many details as you can think of. Then, read through your list to see which details express similar, equal ideas. Write a second list in which you pair the equal ideas and put them in parallel form.

Finally, draw on these parallel ideas to write your paragraph. As you write, you may want to add, discard, or rearrange some details. When you've finished your paragraph, check to make sure you've presented each set of parallel ideas in the same grammatical form.

Here are one writer's sample lists and final paragraph.

old	oldest, most comfortable
most comfortable	many washings, many wearings
many washings	faded, threadbare
worn often	tears along the pockets, paint
faded	stains on the sleeve
threadbare	
torn along pockets	
paint stains on the sleeve	

My oldest, most comfortable shirt is a sorry-looking blue button-down that I've had since I was twelve. It's faded and threadbare from many washings and wearings. With tears along the pockets and paint stains on the sleeve, it looks like a perfect candidate for someone's rag collection. But it's still my favorite shirt for mowing the lawn, washing the dog, or just hanging around the house.

15 COMBINING SENTENCES

LOOKING AHEAD

Sentence-combining techniques are handy tools for improving your style. They can help you add detail to your sentences and variety to your writing. In this chapter, you will learn how to combine sentences by

- inserting words and phrases
- coordinating ideas
- subordinating ideas

Combining Sentences for Style

Revising isn't just a matter of checking your writing for completeness and correctness. When you revise, you also look at your writing with an eye for style. It's important to notice how your sentences work together to shape each of your paragraphs. A short sentence may be fine by itself, but a long series of short sentences can make writing sound choppy and dull.

Read the following sentences. Does the writing style help hold your interest, or does it distract you from the meaning of the paragraph?

> He was stranded. He was on prehistoric Earth. He was stranded as the result of a sequence of events. The sequence was complex. It involved his being blown up. It involved his being insulted. These things had happened in bizarre regions of the galaxy. There were more of these bizarre regions than he had ever dreamed existed. Life had now turned quiet. It was very, very, very quiet. He was still feeling jumpy.
>
> He hadn't been blown up now for a while. It had been five years.

The choppy sentences you just read are based on the following well-crafted sentences by science fiction writer Douglas Adams. Notice how much better Adams's sentences sound. Also notice how his smooth, lively style helps create a humorous tone.

> He was stranded on prehistoric Earth as the result of a complex sequence of events that had involved his being alternately blown up and insulted in more bizarre regions of the Galaxy than he had ever dreamed existed, and though life had now turned very, very, very quiet, he was still feeling jumpy.
>
> He hadn't been blown up now for five years.
>
> Douglas Adams,
> *Life, the Universe and Everything*

Perhaps you have your own sentence style, one that's unique to your writing. But no matter what your style, you can add a smooth rhythm to your writing by balancing short sentences with longer, more detailed ones. Sentence combining helps you create this balance. It also helps make your sentences more precise by eliminating repeated words and ideas. In this chapter, you'll learn several different ways to combine sentences for style.

Combining by Inserting Words and Phrases

Often, you can combine related sentences by taking a key word or phrase from one sentence and inserting it into another sentence. The word or phrase adds detail to the other sentence, and repeated words are eliminated.

THREE SENTENCES — This flight simulator gives a realistic experience of flight. It uses computer graphics to do this. The experience is so real it's amazing.

ONE SENTENCE — Using computer graphics, this flight simulator gives an amazingly realistic experience of flight.

or

With computer graphics, this flight simulator gives an amazingly realistic experience of flight.

Usually you will have some choice in where you insert a word or phrase. Just watch out for awkward-sounding combinations and ones that confuse the meaning of the original sentences. For example, avoid combinations like this one: *Amazingly, using computer graphics, this flight simulator gives a realistic experience of flight.*

Single-Word Modifiers

Sometimes you can take a word from one sentence and insert it directly into another sentence as a modifier. Other times you will need to change the word into an adjective or adverb before you can insert it.

USING THE SAME FORM

ORIGINAL   Timing is essential for performing magic tricks. The magician's timing must be excellent.

COMBINED   **Excellent** timing is essential for performing magic tricks.

ORIGINAL   Magicians guard the secrets of their tricks. They guard them carefully.

COMBINED   Magicians **carefully** guard the secrets of their tricks.

CHANGING THE FORM

ORIGINAL   The famous magician Harry Houdini performed impossible escapes. The escapes only seemed impossible.

COMBINED   The famous magician Harry Houdini performed **seemingly** impossible escapes.

ORIGINAL   He escaped from a sealed crate that had been lowered into a river. He had handcuffs on.

COMBINED   **Handcuffed,** he escaped from a sealed crate that had been lowered into a river.

Prepositional Phrases

You can usually take a prepositional phrase from one sentence and insert it into another without any change in form.

ORIGINAL   Our English class is reading "Everyday Use." It is by Alice Walker.

COMBINED   Our English class is reading "Everyday Use" **by Alice Walker.**

You can also combine sentences by changing part of a sentence into a prepositional phrase.

ORIGINAL   A female narrator tells the story. Her tone is conversational.

COMBINED   A female narrator tells the story **in a conversational tone.**

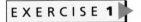 **E X E R C I S E 1**   **Combining by Inserting Single-Word Modifiers and Prepositional Phrases**

Combine each group of short, related sentences by inserting adjectives, adverbs, or prepositional phrases into the first sentence. You may need to change the forms of some words before you insert them. Add commas where they are necessary.

EXAMPLE   **1.** The Iroquois moved to the Northeast. They moved during the thirteenth century. They moved from the Mississippi region.
   1. *During the thirteenth century, the Iroquois moved from the Mississippi region to the Northeast.*

1. The Iroquois formed a confederation. The confederation was powerful. The Iroquois formed the confederation in the Northeast region.

2. A central council of the confederation made decisions. The council made decisions unanimously.

3. Women nominated delegates. They were women from the confederation. They nominated delegates to the central council.

4. The Iroquois confederation subdued other groups of people. These people were Native American. Their subduing of the groups was systematic.

5. The groups exchanged belts to ratify treaties. Their belts were of wampum. The treaties were important.

6. The Iroquois developed trade routes. The trade routes were extensive. The trade routes were along waterways and trails.

7. Hunting was an important element. It was an element in Iroquois society. It was always an important element.

8. The Iroquois also depended on farming. They depended heavily on farming. They depended on farming for food.

9. Entire villages moved in search of soil. They were searching for soil that was richer. They needed the rich soil for farming.
10. The structure of Iroquoian life changed. The structure was complex. The change was considerable. The structure changed during the late seventeenth century.

Participial Phrases

A *participial phrase* contains a participle and words related to it. The whole phrase acts as an adjective. Like other modifiers, participial phrases add concrete details to sentences.

EXAMPLE   Da-duh, **holding fast to my hand,** became my anchor as they circled around us like a nervous sea, exclaiming, **touching us with calloused hands, embracing us shyly.**

> Paule Marshall, "To Da-duh, in Memoriam"

👉 REFERENCE NOTE: For more about participles and participial phrases, see pages 611–612.

Sometimes you can lift a participial phrase directly from one sentence and insert it into another sentence. Other times you will need to change a verb into a participle before you can insert the idea into another sentence.

ORIGINAL   Ants smell, taste, touch, and hear with antennae. The antennae are attached to their heads.
COMBINED   Ants smell, taste, touch, and hear with antennae **attached to their heads.**

ORIGINAL   Weaver ants bind leaves together to make nests. They use the silk from their silk-spinning larvae.
COMBINED   **Using the silk from their silk-spinning larvae,** weaver ants bind leaves together to make nests.

WRITING NOTE

Be sure to place a participial phrase close to the noun or pronoun you want it to modify. Otherwise, your sentence may end up with a meaning you did not intend.

MISPLACED   Hidden under the bench, we found the kitten.
IMPROVED   We found the kitten **hidden under the bench.**

EXERCISE 2 ▶   **Combining by Inserting
Participial Phrases**

Combine each of the following sentence pairs. First, reduce the second sentence to a participial phrase, changing the form of the verb if necessary. Then, insert the phrase into the first sentence. Be sure to place the participial phrase next to the noun or pronoun it modifies.

EXAMPLE   **1.** Recycling helps reduce pollution. It transforms useless trash into new materials.
    1. *Transforming useless trash into new materials, recyling helps reduce pollution.*

1. Waste paper becomes wet, soft pulp. It becomes pulp when it is processed through a container called a pulper.
2. Next, a spinning cylinder helps clean the pulp. The cylinder removes paper clips, staples, and other trash.
3. A water removal machine further processes the pulp. It squeezes out chemicals, ink, and other liquid.
4. The pulp forms a thick substance. It becomes thick as it is mixed with clean water.
5. The material dries to form clean, white sheets of paper. It dries as it is rolled in layers.

Appositive Phrases

Appositive phrases can also add detail to your sentences. An *appositive phrase* is made up of an appositive and its modifiers. (An appositive identifies or explains a noun or pronoun in a sentence.) Like a participial phrase, an appositive phrase should be placed directly before or after the noun or pronoun it modifies. It should be set off by a comma (or two commas if you place the phrase in the middle of the sentence).

EXAMPLE   In Gainesboro, **a hill town with a square of businesses around the Jackson County Courthouse,** I stopped for directions and breakfast.

William Least Heat-Moon, *Blue Highways*

You can also combine two sentences by placing one of the ideas in an appositive phrase.

TWO SENTENCES   Arna Bontemps wrote for the magazine *Opportunity.* Arna Bontemps was a major figure in the Harlem Renaissance.

ONE SENTENCE   Arna Bontemps, **a major figure in the Harlem Renaissance,** wrote for the magazine *Opportunity.*

or

A major figure in the Harlem Renaissance, Arna Bontemps wrote for the magazine *Opportunity.*

or

Arna Bontemps, **a writer for the magazine *Opportunity*,** was a major figure in the Harlem Renaissance.

Notice that the last combination emphasizes Bontemps' role in the Harlem Renaissance, while the first two combinations emphasize his work for *Opportunity*. In the last example, the ideas have been rearranged to change the emphasis, and the verb *wrote* has been changed to a noun, *writer*, to form the appositive.

EXERCISE 3 ▶ Combining by Inserting Appositive Phrases

Combine each pair of sentences by turning one of the sentences into an appositive phrase. You may see several ways to create the appositive; choose the combination that sounds best to you. Be sure to set off the appositive phrase with commas.

EXAMPLE   **1.** Calligraphy is an elegant form of handwriting. It requires a special pen or brush.
1. *Calligraphy, an elegant form of handwriting, requires a special pen or brush.*

筆

Brush

1. Calligraphy has been used for over two thousand years to decorate books and paintings. It is an ancient art form.
2. Chinese calligraphy is done with a paint brush. Chinese calligraphy is the oldest form of calligraphy.
3. In the 600s, Japanese artists learned calligraphy from the Chinese. The Chinese were the first masters of the art.

Pen

4. Islamic artists developed Kufic writing. Kufic writing is one of the most graceful styles of calligraphy.
5. In Islamic countries, you can see sentences from the Koran inscribed in beautiful calligraphy on buildings. The Koran is the Islamic holy book.

Combining by Coordinating Ideas

Sometimes you will want to combine sentences that contain *coordinate*, or equally important, ideas. You can join coordinate words, phrases, or clauses with coordinating conjunctions (*and, but, or, for, yet*) or correlative conjunctions (*both—and, either—or, neither—nor*). The relationship of the ideas determines which connective works best. When they are joined in one sentence, the coordinate ideas form compound elements.

ORIGINAL   Richard will lend you the album. Mark will lend you the album.

COMBINED   **Either Richard or Mark** will lend you the album.
[compound subject]

ORIGINAL   We could drive across country. We could take the train.

COMBINED   We could **drive across country or take the train.**
[compound predicate]

ORIGINAL   The baseball player argued forcefully. The umpire refused to listen.

COMBINED   The baseball player argued forcefully, **but** the umpire refused to listen. [compound sentence]

You can also form a compound sentence by linking independent clauses with a semicolon and a conjunctive adverb (*however, likewise, therefore*) or just a semicolon.

EXAMPLE   You accept risk as part of every new challenge; it comes with the territory.

Chuck Yeager, *Yeager: An Autobiography*

☞ REFERENCE NOTE: For more about coordination, see pages 504–505.

EXERCISE 4 ▶ **Combining by Coordinating Ideas**

Combine each of the following sets of sentences by forming a compound element. Be sure to choose a connective that expresses the correct relationship between the ideas. You may need to add punctuation, too.

EXAMPLE **1.** William Least Heat-Moon traveled across America. He wrote about his trip.
1. *William Least Heat-Moon traveled across America and wrote about his trip.*

1. William Least Heat-Moon's first name comes from an English ancestor. His last name was given to him by his Sioux father.
2. In 1977, Least Heat-Moon left his Missouri home. He began traveling across the country on back roads.
3. The title of his book *Blue Highways* doesn't refer to the actual color of roads. It refers to the blue lines that marked the back roads on his highway map.
4. Least Heat-Moon's trip began in the middle of the nation. His route was shaped like a jagged sideways heart.
5. Small, oddly named towns made his journey memorable. Friendly, helpful people made his journey memorable.

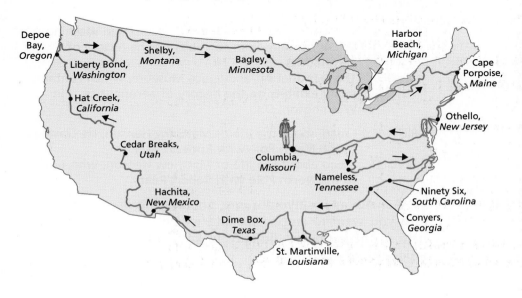

Combining by Subordinating Ideas

If two sentences are unequal in importance, you can combine them by placing the less-important idea in a subordinate clause.

EXAMPLES   He had a habit of pausing to fix his gaze on part of the congregation as he read, and that Sunday he seemed to be talking to a small group of strangers **who sat in the front row.** [adjective clause]

Andrea Lee, "New African"

My aunt Giorgiana regarded them **as though they had been so many daubs of tube-paint on a palette.** [adverb clause]

Willa Cather, "A Wagner Matinée"

What he had the most of was time. [noun clause]

Juan Sedillo, "Gentleman of Río en Medio"

☞ **REFERENCE NOTE:** For more about subordinating ideas, see pages 506–510. For more about the different types of subordinate clauses, see pages 629–637.

Adjective Clauses

You can change a sentence into an adjective clause by replacing its subject with *who, whose, which,* or *that.* Then you can use the adjective clause to give information about a noun or pronoun in another sentence.

ORIGINAL   The National Air and Space Museum is in Washington, D.C. It contains many exhibits on the history of aeronautics.

REVISED   The National Air and Space Museum, **which contains many exhibits on the history of aeronautics,** is in Washington, D.C.

ORIGINAL   I read about the life of Matthew Henson. He traveled to the North Pole with Robert Peary.

REVISED   I read about the life of Matthew Henson, **who traveled to the North Pole with Robert Peary.**

As with appositive phrases, you need to decide first which idea you want to emphasize and which you want to subordinate in the sentence. Be sure to keep your main idea in the independent clause.

Punctuating Adjective Clauses

How you punctuate an adjective clause depends on whether the clause is essential to the meaning of the sentence. If the clause is not essential, you need to set it off from the rest of the sentence with a comma or commas. If the clause is essential, no commas are necessary.

NONESSENTIAL The baseball game, **which was the first of the season,** was played in the park on Saturday.

ESSENTIAL The coach postponed the game **that was scheduled for Saturday.**

☞ REFERENCE NOTE: For more information on punctuating adjective clauses, see page 632.

Adverb Clauses

An adverb clause modifies a verb, an adjective, or another adverb in the sentence it is attached to. To make a sentence into an adverb clause, add a subordinating conjunction like *although, after, because, if, when, where,* or *while* at the beginning. The conjunction shows the relationship between the ideas in the adverb clause and the independent clause. It can show a relationship of time, place, cause or reason, purpose or result, or condition.

ORIGINAL The British general Burgoyne attacked a second time. The Americans won a decisive victory.

REVISED **When the British general Burgoyne attacked a second time,** the Americans won a decisive victory. [time]

ORIGINAL Yukio and Julia both receive high grades. They work hard.

REVISED Yukio and Julia both receive high grades **because they work hard.** [cause]

☞ REFERENCE NOTE: For more about using adverb clauses to subordinate ideas, see pages 506–508.

MECHANICS HINT

Punctuating Adverb Clauses

When you place an adverb clause at the beginning of a sentence, separate it from the independent clause with a comma.

EXAMPLE **Although the shar-pei was first bred as a guard dog,** it was later used for fighting.

☞ REFERENCE NOTE: For more about the use of commas with subordinate clauses, see pages 632, 851–852, and 854.

Noun Clauses

You can make a sentence into a noun clause by adding a word like *that, how, what, whatever, who,* or *whoever* at the beginning. You may also have to delete or move some words. Then, insert the clause into another sentence just like an ordinary noun.

ORIGINAL   Ramón is going to the carnival tonight. Eliza told me this.

REVISED   Eliza told me **that Ramón is going to the carnival tonight.**

EXERCISE 5 ▶ **Combining by Subordinating Ideas**

Combine each of the following pairs of sentences by turning one sentence into a subordinate clause. [Hint: You may have to add, delete, or change some words in the sentences. Add commas where necessary.]

1. Space medicine is one of the most important areas of space study. Space medicine deals with the physical effects of space travel.
2. Doctors learned more about the human body's reactions to space travel. They collected medical data during early space missions.

3. Engineers must consider the effects of acceleration. They must consider how the spacecraft's acceleration will affect the astronauts' bodies.
4. A space shuttle is designed to protect the astronauts against the high-intensity radiation. They encounter this radiation in space.
5. Astronauts must exercise regularly in space. A person's heart and muscles weaken in a weightless condition.

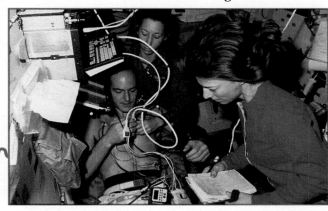

REVIEW ▶ **Revising a Paragraph by Combining Sentences**

Using all the sentence-combining skills you have learned, revise the following paragraph for style. Use your judgment about which sentences to combine and how to combine them. Don't change the meaning of the original paragraph.

Mildred ("Babe") Didrikson Zaharias was born in Beaumont, Texas, in 1914. She was considered one of the finest track-and-field performers of all time. Babe gained national attention in 1930. She competed in a track-and-field meet in Dallas. She won two events. She broke the world record in a third event. The event was the long jump. Babe competed in the Olympic games in 1932. She entered the high jump, the long jump, and the hurdles. She set records in all of these events. They were world records. Only two of these records were made official. Babe's high-jump performance was disqualified. It was disqualified over a technicality. Babe was a champion in women's track and field for more than a decade. She was a world champion in track and field. Babe later became a world champion golfer.

MAKING CONNECTIONS

Write the Opening of a Mystery Story

By day, you're an ordinary teenager. But by night, you're the Masked Mystery Writer, penning thrillers under a pseudonym. You're hard at work on your next gripping story. To help set the mood for the opening, you've jotted down these details.

lurking below the FIRE ESCAPE
SINISTER
hooded
CLENCHING A SMall, WRAPPED box
as the RAIN MISTED MY WINDOW
SILENTLY
IN the dARKNESS
CREEPING
REACHING FOR A FLASHLIGHT
when I SAW the FACE beNEATH the hood

Write the first paragraph or two of your story, using at least five of the words, phrases, and clauses in your list. To hook your reader's attention, you'll want to craft interesting, varied sentences that work together smoothly.

After you've written your paragraph, check to see if you can improve any of your sentences by combining them.

16 IMPROVING SENTENCE STYLE

LOOKING AHEAD

Chapter 15 explained some methods of combining short sentences into longer ones. Now you can use these and other revision techniques to improve your style. As you work through this chapter, you will learn how to

- vary the beginnings of your sentences
- vary the structure of your sentences
- pare down wordy sentences

Revising for Variety

Look closely at this woven tapestry. What makes it interesting?

Just as artists can use a variety of colors and textures to enrich their art, you can use a variety of sentence patterns to enrich your writing.

As you read the following passage, notice how the sentences work together to form a smooth, effective paragraph.

> Grace advanced her hand toward the nearest cobra. The snake swayed like a reed in the wind, feinting for the strike. Grace raised her hand above the snake's head, the reptile twisting around to watch her. As the woman slowly lowered her hand, the snake gave that most terrible of all animal noises—the unearthly hiss of a deadly snake. I have seen children laugh with excitement at the roar of a lion, but I have never seen anyone who did not cringe at that cold, uncanny sound. Grace deliberately tried to touch the rigid, quivering hood. The cobra struck at her hand. He missed. Quietly, Grace presented her open palm. The cobra hesitated a split second, his reared body quivering like a plucked banjo string. Then he struck.
>
> Daniel Mannix, *All Creatures Great and Small*

Mannix's carefully crafted sentences add syle and interest to his writing. You can improve your own writing style by revising your sentences for variety.

Varying Sentence Beginnings

Have you ever heard or read a story that kept you on the edge of your seat? Chances are the sentence openings helped hold your attention. Instead of beginning every sentence with a subject and a verb, the storyteller probably began some sentences with attention-grabbing words, phrases, and clauses: "Suddenly . . ."; "At the bottom of the cliff . . ."; "When she opened the door . . .".

Varied sentence beginnings do more than hold a reader's attention. They also improve the overall style of writing. The following examples show how you can revise your sentences to open them with introductory words, phrases, and clauses. Note that when you vary sentence beginnings, you sometimes must reword the sentences for clarity. Be sure to place phrase modifiers close to the words they modify.

SENTENCE CONNECTIVES	
SUBJECT FIRST	The seal has a few natural enemies, including sharks, polar bears, and killer whales. The seal's most dangerous enemies are human beings, though.
COORDINATING CONJUNCTION FIRST	The seal has a few natural enemies, including sharks, polar bears, and killer whales. **But** the seal's most dangerous enemies are humans.
SUBJECT FIRST	Animal protection laws forbid commercial harvesting of seals in the United States. Seals are still hunted in many parts of the world.
CONJUNCTIVE ADVERB FIRST	Animal protection laws forbid commercial harvesting of seals in the United States. **However,** seals are still hunted in many parts of the world.
SINGLE-WORD MODIFIERS	
SUBJECT FIRST	The octopus is shy and intelligent and rarely harms people.
SINGLE-WORD MODIFIERS FIRST	**Shy and intelligent,** the octopus rarely harms people.
SUBJECT FIRST	Octopi usually keep their distance from humans.
SINGLE-WORD MODIFIER FIRST	**Usually,** octopi keep their distance from humans.
SUBJECT FIRST	An octopus may bite a person with its sharp beak if provoked.
SINGLE-WORD MODIFIER FIRST	**Provoked,** an octopus may bite a person with its sharp beak.
PHRASE MODIFIERS	
SUBJECT FIRST	A team of determined Norwegian skiers began a 413-mile trek to the North Pole in March 1990.
PREPOSITIONAL PHRASE FIRST	**In March 1990,** a team of determined Norwegian skiers began a 413-mile trek to the North Pole.
SUBJECT FIRST	They used only skis and manually drawn sledges and set a record for reaching the Pole unassisted.
PARTICIPIAL PHRASE FIRST	**Using only skis and manually drawn sledges,** they set a record for reaching the Pole unassisted.

(continued)

PHRASE MODIFIERS *(continued)*	
SUBJECT FIRST	They wanted to keep their sledges light, so they brought only enough fuel to melt ice for water.
INFINITIVE PHRASE FIRST	**To keep their sledges light,** they brought only enough fuel to melt ice for water.
CLAUSE MODIFIERS	
SUBJECT FIRST	Over one million species of plants, animals, and insects may be wiped out if burning of the Brazilian rain forest continues.
ADVERB CLAUSE FIRST	**If burning of the Brazilian rain forest continues,** over one million species of plants, animals, and insects may be wiped out.
SUBJECT FIRST	Parts of the rain forest are now protected, but about 20 percent of the forest has already been destroyed.
ADVERB CLAUSE FIRST	**Although parts of the rain forest are now protected,** about 20 percent of the forest has already been destroyed.

E X E R C I S E 1 ▶ **Varying Sentence Beginnings**

Revise each of the following sentences by varying their beginnings. The hint in parentheses will tell you which type of beginning to use.

1. People have used signs and gestures to communicate their thoughts since prehistoric times. (phrase)
2. A system of commonly understood gestures often helped Native American nations communicate with each other. (single-word modifier)
3. Nations in the Plains area spoke many different languages, so a well-developed sign language was essential for trading. (clause)
4. The scope of the sign language grew as more groups settled on the Plains. (clause)
5. The gesture shown at right was used to mean "peace" and was known by many nations. (phrase)

Varying Sentence Structure

You can also improve your style by varying the structure of your sentences. That means using a mix of simple, compound, and complex (and sometimes even compound-complex) sentences in your writing.

☞ REFERENCE NOTE: For information about the four types of sentence structure, see pages 640–641.

Read the following short paragraph, which is made up of only simple sentences.

> San Francisco is famous for its scenic views. The city sprawls over forty-two hills. Driving through San Francisco is like riding a roller coaster. Atop one of San Francisco's hills is Chinatown, a thriving ethnic neighborhood. Atop another is Coit Tower, a great lookout point. The most popular place to visit is the San Francisco Bay area. There the stately Golden Gate Bridge and the picturesque Fisherman's Wharf attract a steady stream of tourists.

Now read the revised version of the paragraph. Notice how the writer has used sentence-combining techniques to vary the structure of the sentences.

> San Francisco is famous for its scenic views. Because the city sprawls over forty-two hills, driving through San Francisco is like riding a roller coaster. Atop one of San Francisco's hills is Chinatown, a thriving ethnic neighborhood; and atop another is Coit Tower, a great lookout point. The most popular place to visit is the San Francisco Bay area, where the stately Golden Gate Bridge and the picturesque Fisherman's Wharf attract a steady stream of tourists.

WRITING NOTE You may find that simple sentences work best in some of your paragraphs. Don't try to force sentences into compound or complex structures if a simple structure sounds better. But if a paragraph sounds flat and dull, varied sentence structure may help improve it.

EXERCISE 2 ▶ **Revising a Paragraph to Vary Sentence Structures**

Decide which sentences in the following paragraph will sound better with compound, complex, or compound-complex structures. Then use sentence-combining techniques to vary the sentence structures. Work for clear sentences that fit together smoothly.

> These people may look like villains from a science fiction movie. They're actually kendo players. Kendo is an ancient Japanese martial art. It requires skill, concentration, and agility. The contestants fight with long bamboo swords called <u>shinai</u>. Kendo can be dangerous. The players must wear protective gear that includes a mask, a breastplate, and thick gloves. Each match lasts three to five minutes. The first contestant to score two points wins. Kendo is a graceful, dignified sport. Respectfulness toward one's opponent is important. A contestant can even be disqualified for rudeness.

Revising to Reduce Wordiness

Read the following sentence. Could you remove a single word from it without changing its meaning or lessening its impact?

> At last I knelt on the island's winter-killed grass, lost, dumb-struck, staring at the frog in the creek just four feet away.
> Annie Dillard, *Pilgrim at Tinker Creek*

Skilled writers make every word count. They know that conciseness is essential for style. You can make your own writing more concise by eliminating the clutter of extra words.

To avoid wordiness in your writing, keep these three points in mind:

- Use only as many words as you need to make your point.
- Choose simple, clear words and expressions over pretentious, complicated ones.
- Don't repeat words or ideas unless it's absolutely necessary.

The following examples show some ways to revise wordy sentences.

1. Take out a whole group of unnecessary words.

WORDY   After descending to the edge of the river, we boarded a small boat that was floating there on the surface of the water.

BETTER After descending to the edge of the river, we boarded a small boat.

2. Replace pretentious words and expressions with straight-forward ones.

WORDY   The young woman, who was at an indeterminate point in her teenage years, wore in her hair a streak of pink dye that could be considered garish.

BETTER The **teenager** wore a streak of **bright** pink dye in her hair.

3. Reduce a clause to a phrase.

WORDY   Su Li, who lives in Washington, D.C., can conveniently visit the Smithsonian.

BETTER **Living in Washington, D.C.,** Su Li can conveniently visit the Smithsonian.

WORDY   George, who is my childhood friend, lives in Baltimore.

BETTER George, **my childhood friend,** lives in Baltimore.

Shoe, by Jeff MacNelly, reprinted by permission: Tribune Media Services.

4. Reduce a phrase or a clause to one word.

WORDY   Angelo likes cooking from the South.
 BETTER   Angelo likes **Southern** cooking.

WORDY   The dance class that has been canceled will be
           rescheduled.
 BETTER   The **canceled** dance class will be rescheduled.

Here is a list of wordy phrases and their simpler replacements. Watch out for these wordy phrases in your writing.

Wordy	Simpler
at this point in time	now
at which time	when
by means of	by
due to the fact that	because, since
in spite of the fact that	although
in the event that	if
the fact is that	actually

E X E R C I S E 3   **Reducing Wordiness**

Some of the following sentences are wordy. Revise each wordy sentence to make it straightforward and concise. If a sentence doesn't need improving, write C.

1. Good writing is precise and straightforward.
2. Have you ever read sentences that seem to ramble on and keep going forever?
3. Annie Dillard, who is a careful writer, revises heavily.
4. Redundant sentences are boring and repetitive.
5. Sentences that are longer than it is necessary for them to be may confuse your reader.
6. A sentence with too many clauses that are subordinate becomes a mental maze for the unsuspecting reader.
7. Think of the sounds and rhythms of the writing you like best.
8. Sentences stuffed with extra, unneeded words resemble Saint Bernards squeezed into Chihuahua-size sweaters.
9. Carefully crafted sentences are like well-tailored suits.
10. William Strunk, Jr., said "Vigorous writing is concise."

MAKING CONNECTIONS

Craft a Short Story

Walking down the street, you catch sight of the people in this picture. You wonder: *Who are they? Where are they going? What's their story?* Use your imagination to come up with some answers to these questions. Then write a short story (two or three paragraphs) about the people. Invent as many details as you wish.

After you've completed a draft or two, read your story slowly, sentence by sentence. Are the sentences lively and varied? Are they concise? Do they fit together smoothly? Using the methods you've learned, revise your sentences for style.

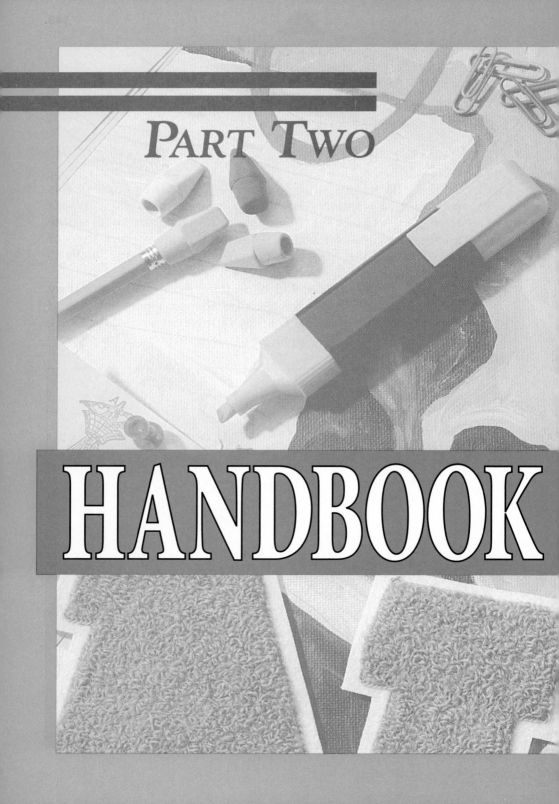

PART TWO

HANDBOOK

17 THE PARTS OF SPEECH

Their Identification and Function

Identifying Parts of Speech

Identify the part of speech of each italicized word in the following paragraph.

Thursday, April 4, 1974, **[1]** *was* a day that will **[2]** *always* be remembered in the history of **[3]** *baseball*. At 2:40 P.M. in Riverfront Stadium in Cincinnati, Henry Aaron **[4]** *of* the Atlanta Braves tied Babe Ruth's **[5]** *unbroken* record of 714 home runs during a major league baseball career. Aaron was at bat for the first time in the **[6]** *baseball* season. It was the first inning. He hit a 3–1 pitch **[7]** *that* sailed 400 feet, zooming **[8]** *neatly* over the fence in left center field and driving in the first runs of the 1974 baseball season. Jumping to their feet, Braves fans yelled **[9]** *"Bravo!"* from the packed stands. The **[10]** *horsehide* ball was caught on the first bounce by Clarence Williams, a Cincinnati **[11]** *police officer,* standing **[12]** *behind* the fence. "I couldn't see what was going on," said Williams, **[13]** *one* of Aaron's fans, **[14]** *"but* I knew he was up when I saw 44 on the scoreboard under the 'at bat' sign." While being interviewed by the press after the game, Aaron smiled in his usual gracious **[15]** *way* **[16]** *and* said he was **[17]** *positively* delighted to have tied the Babe's **[18]** *longstanding* record. Later that month, on April 8, Aaron **[19]** *broke* Babe Ruth's record, a feat that **[20]** *many* had thought they would never see.

THE EIGHT PARTS OF SPEECH

noun	verb	conjunction
pronoun	adverb	interjection
adjective	preposition	

The Noun

  A *noun* is a word used to name a person, a place, a thing, or an idea.

PERSONS	architect	travelers	family	Kira Alvarez
PLACES	restaurant	islands	wilderness	Salt Lake City
THINGS	computer	sailboats	insects	Brooklyn Bridge
IDEAS	education	beliefs	ambition	Utopianism

Common and Proper Nouns

A *common noun* names any one of a group of persons, places, or things. A *proper noun* names a particular person, place, or thing. Common nouns are not capitalized; proper nouns are.

COMMON NOUNS	PROPER NOUNS
woman	Sylvia Bryan, Eda Seasongood, Queen of England
nation	Switzerland, Canada, Mexico
event	World Series, Mardi Gras, Fall of Rome
holiday	Memorial Day, Thanksgiving Day, Fourth of July
language	English, Spanish, Japanese

Concrete and Abstract Nouns

A *concrete noun* names an object that can be perceived by the senses. An *abstract noun* names a quality, a characteristic, or an idea.

CONCRETE NOUNS	fire, garlic, cotton, horses, Liberty Bell
ABSTRACT NOUNS	confidence, strength, charm, ability, Zen

Collective Nouns

A *collective noun* names a group.

COLLECTIVE NOUNS	swarm, team, herd, crew, committee, fleet, family, class, group

Compound Nouns

A *compound noun* consists of two or more words used together as a single noun. Some compound nouns are written as one word, some as separate words, and others as hyphenated words.

ONE WORD	sidewalk, tablecloth, Greenland
SEPARATE WORDS	attorney general, telephone pole, Empire State Building
HYPHENATED WORDS	daughter-in-law, great-grandfather, jack-o'-lantern

NOTE: When you are not sure about the form of a compound noun, look it up in a dictionary.

> **EXERCISE 1** **Classifying Nouns**

Classify each of the following nouns as either *concrete* or *abstract*.

1. tradition
2. flower
3. courage
4. cafeteria
5. dancers
6. honor
7. security
8. lake
9. happiness
10. bench

The Pronoun

17b. A *pronoun* is a word used in place of a noun or of more than one noun.

EXAMPLE **Angelo borrowed a hammer and some nails. He will return them tomorrow.** [The pronoun *he* takes the place of the noun *Angelo*. The pronoun *them* takes the place of the nouns *hammer* and *nails*.]

The word that a pronoun stands for is called the ***antecedent*** of the pronoun. In the preceding example, *Angelo* is the antecedent of *he*, and *hammer* and *nails* are the antecedents of *them*.

A pronoun may also take the place of another pronoun.

> **Several** of the students have entered the essay contest because **they** are extremely interested in the topic. [The pronoun *they* takes the place of the pronoun *several*.]

☞ REFERENCE NOTE: For more information about antecedents, see pages 664–666 and 701–707.

Personal Pronouns

A *personal pronoun* refers to the one speaking (first person), the one spoken to (second person), or the one spoken about (third person).

First person	I, me, my, mine, we, us, our, ours
Second person	you, your, yours
Third person	he, him, his, she, her, hers, it, its, they, them, their, theirs

EXAMPLES   **I** hope that **you** can help **me** with **my** homework.
               He said that **they** would meet **us** outside the theater.

NOTE: This textbook refers to the words *my, your, his, her, its, our,* and *their* as possessive pronouns. However, because they come before nouns and tell *which one* or *whose,* many authorities prefer to call these words adjectives. Follow your teacher's instructions regarding these possessive forms.

Reflexive and Intensive Pronouns

A *reflexive pronoun* refers to the subject of a sentence and directs the action of the verb back to the subject. An *intensive pronoun* emphasizes a noun or another pronoun.

First person	myself, ourselves
Second person	yourself, yourselves
Third person	himself, herself, itself, themselves

EXAMPLES   Kimiko wrote **herself** a note. [reflexive]
               Leonora **herself** organized the school's recycling program. [intensive]

Demonstrative Pronouns

A *demonstrative pronoun* points out a person, a place, a thing, or an idea.

this	that	these	those

EXAMPLES   **This** is our favorite song by Ella Fitzgerald.
               The apples I picked today taste better than **these**.

Interrogative Pronouns

An *interrogative pronoun* introduces a question.

who	whom	which	what	whose

EXAMPLES **What** is the answer to the last algebra problem?
Whose car is parked outside?

Relative Pronouns

A *relative pronoun* introduces a subordinate clause.

that	which	who	whom	whose

EXAMPLES The house **that** you saw is a historical landmark.
She is the woman **who** is running for mayor.

👉 REFERENCE NOTE: For more information about relative pronouns
and subordinate clauses, see pages 631–632.

Indefinite Pronouns

An *indefinite pronoun* refers to a person, place, or thing that is
not specifically named.

all	either	much	other
another	everybody	neither	several
any	everyone	nobody	some
anybody	everything	none	somebody
anyone	few	no one	someone
anything	many	nothing	something
both	more	one	such
each	most		

EXAMPLES I have packed **everything** we will need for the trip.
Has **anyone** seen my binoculars?

GRAMMAR

▶ EXERCISE 2 **Identifying Pronouns**

Identify the pronouns in the following sentences.

EXAMPLE **1.** Someone told me they had moved to Iowa.
1. *Someone; me; they*

1. Deven himself knew everyone who either had a ticket or could get one for him at a low price.
2. Nobody has bought more than one of the records on sale at the discount store.
3. A friend of mine said that you won several of the events at the 4-H competition.
4. Those are photographs of some of the many contemporary politicians who are women.
5. What is the large body of water that borders Ethiopia called?

▶ REVIEW A **Identifying Nouns and Pronouns**

Tell whether each italicized word in the following paragraph is a noun or a pronoun.

EXAMPLE Tessellation is the filling of a plane with shapes so that [1] *each* of the [2] *shapes* touches the others without any space between them.
1. *pronoun*
2. *noun*

For centuries, cultures all over the world have used tessellated [1] *designs* to decorate fabrics, walls, floors, pottery, and many other [2] *things* used in daily life. The [3] *Moors*, for example, were masters at creating intricate tiled walls and floors. Because their religion did not allow [4] *them* to make images of any animals or [5] *people*, they worked with geometric shapes. Notice also that [6] *all* of the Moorish designs shown on the next page are symmetrical. One twentieth-century Dutch artist [7] *who* was inspired by designs like [8] *these* from Moorish buildings was [9] *M. C. Escher*. [10] *Many* of Escher's designs, however, feature birds, lizards, and other natural [11] *forms*. In addition, he often used asymmetrical [12] *shapes* in [13] *his* interlocking designs. Of the Escher designs on the next page, the [14] *first* is the only [15] *one* that uses a symmetrical shape to fill the plane. The [16] *others* all consist of asymmetrical shapes. For example, in the second design, one [17] *kind* of creature interlocks with

[18] *another.* In the third—an amazing [19] *achievement*—a single, complicated shape interlocks in two ways with [20] *itself.*

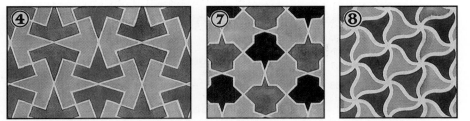

Eight Copies of Space-filling Designs. Ink and watercolor. Number 4 from the Alhambra in Granada, 5 x 7 3/4 inches. Numbers7 and 8 from the Alhambra in Granada, 5 x 5 inches. ©M.C. Escher/Cordon Art—Baarn—Holland.

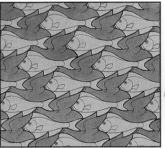

M.C. Escher, Symmetry Work 22: ©M.C. Escher/Cordon Art—Baarn—Holland.

M.C. Escher, Symmetry Work 91: ©M.C. Escher/Cordon Art—Baarn—Holland.

M.C. Escher, Horsemen: ©M.C. Escher/Cordon Art—Baarn—Holland.

GRAMMAR

The Adjective

17c. An *adjective* is a word used to modify a noun or a pronoun.

To modify means "to describe or to make more definite" the meaning of a word. Adjectives modify nouns or pronouns by telling *what kind, which one,* or *how many (how much).*

WHAT KIND?	WHICH ONE?	HOW MANY?	HOW MUCH?
brown shoes	**those** cars	**ten** boxes	**some** water
large animal	**this** street	**several** books	**less** time
narrow road	**first** step	**fewer** mistakes	**more** space
nice person	**last** one	**many** students	**enough** money

Adjectives usually precede the words they modify.

EXAMPLE   The **wild** and **graceful** deer ran through the forest.

For emphasis, however, adjectives are sometimes placed after the words they modify.

EXAMPLE   The deer, **wild** and **graceful,** ran through the forest.

Adjectives may be separated from the words they modify.

EXAMPLES   The casserole was **delicious.**
Luís appeared **ill.**

The adjectives in these two examples are called *predicate adjectives.*

REFERENCE NOTE: For more information about predicate adjectives, see page 595.

Articles

The most frequently used adjectives are *a, an,* and *the.* These words are called *articles.*

A and *an* are *indefinite articles,* which refer to one of a general group. *A* is used before a word beginning with a consonant sound. *An* is used before a word beginning with a vowel sound.

EXAMPLES   Jorge drew pictures of **a** pelican and **an** albatross.
For **an** hour I rode through the park in **a** horsedrawn carriage.

Notice in the second example above that *an* is used before a noun beginning with the consonant *h,* because the *h* in *hour* is not pronounced. *Hour* is pronounced as if it began with a vowel (like *our*).

The is the *definite article.* It indicates someone or something in particular and can precede any word, regardless of the initial sound.

EXAMPLES   **The** lion is often called **the** "king of **the** beasts."

Adjective or Pronoun?

A word may be used as one part of speech in one context and as a different part of speech in another context. For example, the following words may be used as *adjectives* or *pronouns.*

all	each	more	one	that	what
another	either	most	other	these	which
any	few	much	several	this	whose
both	many	neither	some	those	

Remember that an adjective *modifies* a noun and that a pronoun *takes the place* of a noun.

ADJECTIVE **Which** museum did you visit? [*Which* modifies the noun *museum.*]

PRONOUN **Which** did you visit? [*Which* takes the place of the noun *museum.*]

ADJECTIVE Leslie Marmon Silko wrote **these** stories. [*These* modifies *stories.*]

PRONOUN Leslie Marmon Silko wrote **these**. [*These* takes the place of the noun *stories.*]

☞ REFERENCE NOTE: Possessive pronouns may also be classified as adjectives. See the note on page 683.

Nouns Used as Adjectives

Sometimes nouns are used as adjectives.

NOUNS	NOUNS USED AS ADJECTIVES
business	business letter
saxophone	saxophone player
tuna fish	tuna fish salad
United States	United States government

NOTE: Some pairs or groups of nouns are considered *compound nouns* (see pages 554–555).

EXAMPLES road map, blood bank, soap opera, country club, United States of America

By checking an up-to-date dictionary, you can avoid confusing a noun that is used as an adjective with a noun that is part of a compound noun.

GRAMMAR

▶ EXERCISE 3   **Identifying Adjectives and the Words They Modify**

Identify the adjectives and the words they modify in each of the following sentences. [Note: Do not include the articles *a*, *an*, and *the*.]

EXAMPLE   **1.** Put those aluminum cans in that empty box in the hall closet.
1. *those, aluminum—cans; that, empty—box; hall—closet*

1. John lives on this street.
2. You need four cups of flour for this recipe.
3. Your new apartment, so spacious and sunny, certainly seems ideal for you.
4. The image of the eagle is quite powerful in many Native American cultures.
5. Which bookstore did you go to today?
6. All of the books on these shelves were written by Mark Twain.
7. Neither film was enjoyable.
8. The local stores open at 9:00 A.M.
9. Speaking of the space program, which astronaut do you admire more—Colonel Bluford or Dr. Jemison?
10. Tomás bought a new tie for the dance.

▶ REVIEW B   **Identifying Nouns, Pronouns, and Adjectives**

Identify each italicized word in the following sentences as a *noun*, a *pronoun*, or an *adjective*. If the word is an adjective, give the word it modifies.

EXAMPLE   **1.** *Most* people do not realize the *tremendous* number of books the library has available for *them.*
1. *Most—adjective—people; tremendous—adjective—number; them—pronoun*

1. Many *shop* owners decided to close *their* shops early on Halloween.
2. *What* are the *other* choices on the menu?
3. The manuscript for Andrew García's autobiography was found packed in dynamite *boxes* under his bed five years after *he* had died.

4. We had a *family* reunion at my grandparent's house *last* summer.
5. As people encounter different *ways* of life, *they* gradually alter their *speech* patterns.
6. Thanks to the development of *digital* recording, symphony *performances* can now be recorded with higher fidelity.
7. *Oboe* players carry *extra* reeds with *them* because of the *possibility* that a reed might split during a performance.
8. *Alonzo* had never bought *that* brand before.
9. *Some* of the players felt nervous about the *athletic* contests.
10. *They* were penalized *fifteen* yards for holding.

WRITING APPLICATION

Using Specific Adjectives to Make Descriptions Vivid

When you want to describe something—for example, a concert, a painting, or a sports car—the more precisely you choose your words, the more successful you'll be. In choosing your words, try to avoid inexact adjectives such as *great, awesome, amazing, gross, terrible,* and *awful.* These words tell only that your response was positive or negative. Instead, make your description compelling by saying exactly what you like or dislike about your subject.

| TIRESOME | The concert was totally great! The band was excellent. |
| INTERESTING | The **wild, insistent** beat kept us rocking in our seats. The lead singer's **intense** gaze and **husky** voice sent **personal** messages to each of us. |

Which description would be more likely to make you want to buy concert tickets?

WRITING ACTIVITY

Your class is having *Share the Music* week. Each person will bring in a tape of a favorite piece of music and a paragraph describing it. The paragraphs will be displayed, and the tapes will be placed nearby with tape players and headphones. Write a paragraph describing any piece of music that you like. (You don't have to own the tape.) You can choose from rap, rock, country, classical, or another type of music. In your paragraph, use at least ten adjectives. Make each adjective as specific as you can.

 Prewriting Write down the names of five pieces of music that you enjoy. Then decide which piece will make the most interesting topic for your paragraph. (Be sure to get your teacher's approval of your selection.) Listen to your selection several times. Sit quietly with your eyes closed, and think about how the piece sounds and makes you feel. While you are thinking, jot down any adjectives that occur to you.

Writing As you write your first draft, include the adjectives that you jotted down. Try to give a clear description of the music. At the same time, imagine what specific details might persuade your classmates to listen to this piece of music. Think of your paragraph as an advertisement for the music.

Evaluating and Revising Reread your paragraph, replacing vague, inexact adjectives with words that are more descriptive. Ask yourself, *What exactly makes this music great* or *awesome* or *amazing?* Be sure you have included at least ten adjectives.

Proofreading and Publishing Check your spelling, especially of compound nouns. Use a dictionary to find out whether a compound noun is spelled as one word, as separate words, or as a hyphenated word. (See pages 554–555 for more about compound nouns.) You might wish to gather the class's music descriptions and arrange them on a bulletin board titled *Share the Music!* You could also take a survey to find out which three pieces of music sound the most interesting from the descriptions. Then, with your teacher's approval, you might borrow a tape player from the school library and obtain tapes of those pieces to play in class.

The Verb

17d. A *verb* is a word used to express action or a state of being.

Action Verbs

An *action verb* expresses physical or mental activity.

PHYSICAL	write	sit	arise	describe	receive
MENTAL	remember	think	believe	consider	understand

(1) A *transitive verb* is an action verb that takes an *object*— a word that tells who or what receives the action.

EXAMPLES   Everyone in the school **cheered** the football team.
[*Team* receives the action of *cheered.*]
Nikki Giovanni **writes** poetry. [*Poetry* receives the action of *writes.*]

(2) An *intransitive verb* is an action verb that does not take an object.

EXAMPLES   The gorilla **smiled.**
Suddenly, the child next to the door **screamed.**

A verb can be transitive in one sentence and intransitive in another.

EXAMPLES   We **ate** our lunch quickly. [transitive]
We **ate** quickly. [intransitive]

Ms. Marino **measured** the boards carefully. [transitive]
Ms. Marino **measured** carefully. [intransitive]

☞ REFERENCE NOTE: For more on objects of verbs, see pages 592–593.

Linking Verbs

A *linking verb* connects the subject with a word that identifies or describes it. Linking verbs are sometimes called *state-of-being*

GRAMMAR

verbs because they help describe the condition or state of being of a person or thing.

EXAMPLES Patience **is** the best remedy for many troubles. [*Remedy* identifies the subject *Patience*.]

Edmonia Lewis **became** a highly respected sculptor in America. [*Sculptor* identifies the subject *Edmonia Lewis*.]

The dessert **looks** delicious. [*Delicious* describes the subject *dessert*.]

COMMONLY USED LINKING VERBS			
Forms of *Be*			
am	be	will be	had been
is	can be	could be	shall have been
are	may be	should be	will have been
was	might be	would be	could have been
were	must be	has been	should have been
being	shall be	have been	would have been
Others			
appear	grow	seem	stay
become	look	smell	taste
feel	remain	sound	turn

Some linking verbs may be used as action verbs.

LINKING The soup **tasted** spicy.
ACTION We **tasted** the soup.

LINKING She **felt** good about her presentation.
ACTION The explorers **felt** rain on their faces.

NOTE: To determine whether a verb in a sentence is a linking verb, substitute a form of the verb *be*. If the sentence makes sense, the verb is probably a linking verb.

LINKING The milk **smelled** sour. [The verb *was* can replace *smelled: The milk was sour.*]
ACTION I **smelled** the milk to see whether it was fresh. [The verb *was* cannot sensibly replace *smelled.*]

The forms of the verb *be* are not always used as linking verbs. They may be followed by words that tell *where* or *when*.

EXAMPLE   **My relatives from Ohio will be here tomorrow.** [The verb *will be* is followed by *here,* which tells *where,* and *tomorrow,* which tells *when.*]

The Verb Phrase

A *verb phrase* consists of a main verb and at least one *helping verb* (also called an *auxiliary verb*). Notice in these examples that as many as three helping verbs may precede the main verb.

EXAMPLES   **has** spoken   **will be** arriving   **should have been** told

COMMONLY USED HELPING VERBS			
Forms of *Be*	am were	is be	are being	was been
Forms of *Have*	has	have	having	had
Forms of *Do*	do	does	doing	did
Others	may might must	can shall will	could should would

The helping verb may be separated from the main verb by another word.

EXAMPLES   **Should** we **leave** immediately?
I **have** not **read** Alice Walker's latest novel.

☞ REFERENCE NOTE: The word *not* and its contraction, *–n't,* are never part of a verb phrase. Instead, they are adverbs telling *to what extent.* For more information about adverbs, see pages 568–569.

▶ EXERCISE 4   **Identifying and Classifying Verbs**

Identify the verbs and verb phrases in the following sentences. Then classify each verb or verb phrase as *transitive, intransitive,* or *linking.* Be prepared to give the object(s) of each transitive verb and the complement(s) of each linking verb.

1. Throughout its history English has borrowed many words from other languages.
2. Because a newly borrowed word often sounds unfamiliar, people sometimes do not hear it correctly.
3. They will pronounce the word and will spell it as if it had come from other, more familiar English words.
4. The wrong spelling hides the true origin of the word and gives the false impression that its source is contemporary English.
5. The word *woodchuck,* for example, might have come from two English words, *wood* and *chuck.*
6. Actually, *woodchuck* came from the Cree *otchek.*
7. Another word of Native American origin is the Algonquian word *musquash.*
8. When English-speaking settlers adopted the word, it became *muskrat.*
9. In a similar way, the Dutch word for cabbage salad, *koolsla,* became the English word *coleslaw,* and the French word for a kind of cart, *cariole,* is now the English word *carryall.*
10. Linguists generally call this kind of word history "folk etymology."

The Adverb

17e. An *adverb* is a word used to modify a verb, an adjective, or another adverb.

Adverbs modify by telling *how, when, where,* or *to what extent* (*how much* or *how often*).

Adverbs Modifying Verbs

EXAMPLES   Marian Anderson sang **magnificently.** [*how*]
Marian Anderson sang **earlier.** [*when*]
Marian Anderson sang **there.** [*where*]
Marian Anderson sang **frequently.** [*to what extent*]

Adverbs Modifying Adjectives

EXAMPLES   The players are **exceptionally** skillful. [The adverb *exceptionally* modifies the adjective *skillful*, telling *to what extent*.]
The documentary about global warming was **quite interesting**. [The adverb *quite* modifies the adjective *interesting*, telling *to what extent*.]

Adverbs Modifying Other Adverbs

EXAMPLES   Cheetahs can run **extremely** fast. [The adverb *extremely* modifies the adverb *fast*, telling *to what extent*.]
André reacted to the news **rather** calmly. [The adverb *rather* modifies the adverb *calmly*, telling *to what extent*.]

Nouns Used as Adverbs

Some nouns may be used as adverbs.

EXAMPLES   They were happy to return **home.**
The teacher reviewed what had been covered **yesterday.**

In identifying parts of speech, label nouns used in this way as adverbs.

▶ EXERCISE 5   **Identifying Adverbs and the Words They Modify**

Identify the adverbs and the words they modify in the following sentences. Be prepared to state whether the adverb tells *how, when, where,* or *to what extent*.

1. Her calm, friendly manner always inspired confidence.
2. I understand now what he was saying.
3. The index lists all the book's topics alphabetically.
4. The guests have already left.
5. They thought that the decorations would be too expensive.
6. Maurice and Gregory Hines tap-danced professionally when they were very young children.

7. The messenger said that she felt rather uncertain about the quickest route.
8. "Are you quite sure that this is the person you saw?" the detective asked.
9. The teacher told the students, "Take your essays home for revision and return them to me tomorrow."
10. Visitors to China often bring back small figures that are delicately carved from solid blocks of jade.

▶ REVIEW C   **Identifying Parts of Speech**

Identify the part of speech of each italicized word in the following sentences. If the word is an adjective or an adverb, give the word or words it modifies.

1. He *announced* the names of *everybody* who had contributed *time* or money.
2. Jesse Owens *won* four gold medals in the 1936 *Olympics*.
3. In *ancient* Rome the new year began on March 1, and September *was* the *seventh* month of the year.
4. In 6000 B.C. the *usual* transportation for long distance was the *camel* caravan, *which* averaged *eight* miles per hour.
5. The *play* received *generally* excellent reviews, but *several* critics were disappointed with the *rather dull* costumes.
6. As *we* approached Santorini, I saw sparkling *white* houses along the *steep* hillsides.
7. The teacher *posted* a list of students *who* would give *reports* about Sacagawea.
8. *Many* readers complained *angrily* about the editorial *that* appeared in yesterday's newspaper, but *others* found *it* amusing.
9. *Silently,* the drifting *snow blanketed* the *narrow* road.
10. I recall *vividly* that small town in the *southern part* of Texas.

▶ REVIEW D   **Identifying Parts of Speech**

Identify the part of speech of each italicized word in the following paragraph. If the word is an adjective or an adverb, give the word or words it modifies.

My Aunt Laurette is just about the nicest [1] *grown-up* [2] *that* I know. I do [3] *not* get to see her [4] *very* often because she [5] *works* in Chicago, but when she comes [6] *home* to visit, I'm in heaven. [7] *What* do I like about her? For one thing, we share [8] *many* of the same interests—both of us play the piano, [9] *sew* our own clothes, and love to make [10] *puns*. She is also a sympathetic listener and lets me tell about [11] *myself* without interrupting or criticizing me. Laurette shares [12] *her* own [13] *career* stories with me, and sometimes she even asks me for [14] *some* advice. A day with Laurette [15] *is* sometimes silly and sometimes [16] *serious*, but it's always a delight. As you can see in [17] *this* picture of the two of us at the park, I always feel relaxed with Laurette. She's living proof that a person [18] *can* go through adolescence and [19] *still* emerge as a happy, [20] *highly* competent adult!

The Preposition

17f. A *preposition* is a word used to show the relationship of a noun or pronoun to some other word in the sentence.

Notice how the prepositions in the following examples show different relationships between the words *ran* and *me*.

EXAMPLES The playful puppy ran **beside** me.
The playful puppy ran **toward** me.
The playful puppy ran **around** me.
The playful puppy ran **past** me.
The playful puppy ran **after** me.
The playful puppy ran **behind** me.
The playful puppy ran **in front of** me.

A preposition always introduces a phrase. The noun or pronoun that ends a prepositional phrase is called the *object of the preposition*. In each of the preceding examples, the object of the preposition is *me*.

☞ REFERENCE NOTE: For more information about prepositional phrases, see pages 605–607.

Commonly Used Prepositions

about	beneath	in	through
above	beside	inside	throughout
across	besides	into	to
after	between	like	toward
against	beyond	near	under
along	but (meaning	of	underneath
amid	"except")	off	until
among	by	on	unto
around	down	out	up
at	during	outside	upon
before	except	over	with
behind	for	past	within
below	from	since	without

NOTE: Some words in this list may also be used as adverbs. Remember that an adverb is a modifier and does not take an object.

PREPOSITION   We drove **around** the parking lot. [*Parking lot* is the object of *around*.]

ADVERB   We drove **around** for a while. [*Around* modifies *drove*.]

A preposition that consists of more than one word is called a *compound preposition*.

Commonly Used Compound Prepositions

according to	because of	in spite of
along with	by means of	instead of
apart from	in addition to	next to
aside from	in front of	on account of
as of	in place of	out of

EXAMPLES   The young sculptor made a scale model of Mount
                       Rushmore **out of** clay.
                       She placed a photograph of Mount Rushmore **next to**
                       her clay model.

▶ EXERCISE 6   **Writing Sentences Using Prepositions
                           and Compound Prepositions**

The celebrities shown below are noted for the energy and
excitement they bring to their work. Imagine that you are
watching one of them perform, and write five sentences about
the experience. Use at least ten different prepositions in your
sentences, including at least three compound prepositions.
Underline the prepositions you use. Be prepared to identify the
object of each preposition.

EXAMPLE   **1.** *As Robin Williams walked* <u>out of</u> *the wings and* <u>onto</u>
                       the stage, everyone <u>in</u> *the audience began to laugh
                       and applaud.*

The Conjunction

 17g. A *conjunction* is a word used to join words or groups of words.

Coordinating Conjunctions

A *coordinating conjunction* connects words or groups of words used in the same way.

Coordinating Conjunctions

and   but   for   nor   or   so   yet

EXAMPLES   We found a bat **and** a glove. [connects two words]
Will Rogers said, "My folks didn't come over on the *Mayflower,* **but** they were there to meet the boat." [connects two clauses]

Correlative Conjunctions

Correlative conjunctions are pairs of conjunctions that connect words or groups of words used in the same way.

Correlative Conjunctions

both. . .and	not only. . .but (also)
either. . .or	whether. . .or
neither. . .nor	

EXAMPLES   **Both** athletes **and** singers must train for long hours. [connects two words]
Either your fuel line is clogged, **or** your carburetor needs adjusting. [connects two clauses]

Subordinating Conjunctions

A *subordinating conjunction* begins a subordinate clause and connects it to an independent clause.

Commonly Used Subordinating Conjunctions			
after	because	since	when
although	before	so that	whenever
as	even though	than	where
as if	how	that	wherever
as much as	if	though	whether
as though	in order that	unless	while
as well as	provided	until	why

EXAMPLES   We arrived late **because** our train was delayed.
            Sherlock Holmes listened quietly **while** Dr. Watson
            explained his theory.

A subordinating conjunction does not always come between the groups of words it joins. It may come at the beginning of a sentence.

EXAMPLE   **While** Dr. Watson explained his theory, Sherlock
           Holmes listened quietly.

☞ REFERENCE NOTE: For more information about subordinate
clauses, see pages 629–637.

▶ REVIEW E   **Identifying Prepositions and
              Conjunctions; Classifying Conjunctions**

For each of the following sentences, identify every word or word group that is the part of speech indicated in parentheses. Classify each conjunction as *coordinating, correlative,* or *subordinating.*

EXAMPLE   **1.** Seeds were removed from cotton bolls by hand until
           Eli Whitney invented the cotton gin. (*conjunction*)
           1. *until—subordinating*

1. Eli Whitney invented not only the cotton gin but also the interchangeable part. (*conjunction*)
2. Nowadays we take the idea of interchangeable parts for granted, but it was a revolutionary concept at that time. (*conjunction*)
3. For example, when a rifle is constructed with interchangeable parts, a defective part can be replaced quickly and easily with an identically made piece. (*preposition*)

4. Before Eli Whitney introduced the idea of interchangeable parts, manufacturers had to employ many skilled workers. (*preposition*)
5. Although the new technology benefited manufacturers, it cost many workers their jobs, and this has been the case with most technological advances. (*conjunction*)

The Interjection

17h. An *interjection* is a word used to express emotion. It has no grammatical relation to other words in the sentence.

EXAMPLES Ah   Hey   Ouch   Whew
Gosh Oh   Well   Wow

An interjection is set off from the rest of the sentence by an exclamation point or a comma. An exclamation point indicates strong emotion. A comma indicates mild emotion.

EXAMPLES **Ouch!** That hurts!
Well, I think you should apologize to her.

Determining Parts of Speech

17i. The part of speech of a word is determined by the way the word is used in a sentence.

EXAMPLES The coach decided that the team needed more **practice.** [noun]
The girls **practice** every Saturday afternoon. [verb]
They will have a **practice** session after school on Wednesday. [adjective]

Winston-Salem, North Carolina, is the **home** of the talented writer Maya Angelou. [noun]
The last **home** game will be played tomorrow night. [adjective]
We decided to stay **home.** [adverb]

Celine has won the citizenship award **before.** [adverb]
The two candidates debated each other **before** the election. [preposition]
Read the directions **before** you begin answering the questions. [conjunction]

▶ REVIEW F   **Identifying the Parts of Speech**

Identify the part of speech of each italicized word or word group in the following paragraphs.

Suddenly the radio announcer broke in on the [1] *musical* selection. "A [2] *funnel* cloud [3] *has been sighted.* [4] *All* people should take immediate [5] *precautions!*" [6] *Those* were the [7] *last* words Denise Moore heard [8] *before* the electricity went off and the [9] *terrible* roar came closer. [10] *She* and her two children [11] *ran* to the basement [12] *quickly*.

When they [13] *emerged* forty-five minutes later, [14] *they* weren't sure what they might see. [15] *Oh*, the terrible wind had [16] *truly* performed freakish tricks! It had driven a fork [17] *into* a brick up to the handle. It had sucked the [18] *wallpaper* from a living room wall [19] *but* had left the picture hanging [20] *there* intact. It [21] *had driven* a blade of grass into the [22] *back* of Denise Moore's neighbor. Nevertheless, the citizens of the [23] *town* considered [24] *themselves* lucky because [25] *no one* had been killed.

PICTURE THIS

You're backpacking through a Florida forest. In a stand of huge live-oak trees, you sit down to rest and enjoy the scenery. After a short time, you glance up and see the magnificent Florida panther shown on the next page. As you watch, it strides along a tree limb—not twenty yards from where you are sitting!—then the big cat leaps easily to another tree and travels on without noticing you. Thrilled at seeing the big cat, you realize that it's one of only about fifty of these endangered creatures left in the wild. When you get home, you write a one-paragraph article for your school newspaper. Tell what it was like to see the panther and what you learned from the experience. Use at least three interjections to express how you felt. Punctuate the interjections correctly.

Subject: seeing a Florida panther in the wild
Audience: students at your school
Purpose: to inform

Review: Posttest 1

Identifying Parts of Speech

For each sentence in the following paragraph, write each underlined item and identify its part of speech.

EXAMPLE   **[1]** In the past <u>few</u> years, African American film
directors have <u>suddenly</u> begun to flourish.
1. *few—adjective; suddenly—adverb*

[1] <u>Hey</u>, <u>nobody</u> who goes to the movies <u>fairly</u> often can fail to notice <u>this</u> exciting trend! **[2]** In 1991 alone, nineteen <u>feature</u> films <u>directed</u> by African Americans <u>were</u> released. **[3]** <u>Whether</u> you know it <u>or</u> not, that's more <u>than</u> there were in the <u>whole</u> previous decade. **[4]** The success <u>of</u> Spike Lee's films, <u>which</u> include the blockbuster *Do the Right Thing*, inspired <u>other</u> young black directors to create <u>their</u> own movies <u>about</u> the black experience. **[5]** The <u>absorbing</u> stories and real-life settings of these films <u>attract</u> many <u>thousands</u> of moviegoers, not just African Americans. **[6]** <u>Who</u> are some of <u>the</u> black directors building their careers in <u>Hollywood</u> <u>nowadays</u>? **[7]** Rising <u>stars</u> include Charles Lane, Mario Van Peebles, John Singleton, Bill <u>Duke</u>, and <u>Matty Rich</u>. **[8]** Their success helps create <u>job</u> opportunities for <u>all</u> types of black film workers, including <u>hairdress-ers</u>, <u>actors</u>, stuntpersons, <u>cinematographers</u>, and sound technicians. **[9]** For example, the crew <u>that worked</u> <u>along with</u> John Singleton on his 1991 hit film *Boyz N the Hood* was 90 percent black! **[10]** After you've read these facts, maybe you'll <u>watch</u> the <u>movie</u> listings in your <u>local</u> newspaper for <u>some</u> upcoming films from young black directors.

Review: Posttest 2

Writing Sentences with Words Used as Specific Parts of Speech

Write twenty sentences according to the following guidelines.

1. Use *ride* as a verb.
2. Use *hammer* as a noun.
3. Use *sink* as a transitive verb.
4. Use *whose* as an adjective.
5. Use *some* as a pronoun.
6. Use *fast* as an adverb.
7. Use *paper* as an adjective.
8. Use *inside* as a preposition.
9. Use *well* as an interjection.
10. Use *yet* as a conjunction.
11. Use *country* as an adjective.
12. Use *that* as a demonstrative pronoun.
13. Use *which* as an interrogative pronoun.
14. Use *both . . . and* as a correlative conjunction.
15. Use *smell* as a noun.
16. Use *have* as a helping verb.
17. Use *tomorrow* as a noun.
18. Use *down* as an adverb.
19. Use *before* as a subordinating conjunction.
20. Use *as* as a subordinating conjunction.

SUMMARY OF PARTS OF SPEECH

Rule	Part of Speech	Use	Examples
17a	noun	names	**Shane** is playing **soccer** in the **park**.
17b	pronoun	takes the place of a noun	**She herself** said **that all** of **us** have been invited.
17c	adjective	modifies a noun or a pronoun	**This rare** coin is **a valuable** one.
17d	verb	shows action or a state of being	Shelby **is** the candidate who I **believe will win**.
17e	adverb	modifies a verb, an adjective, or another adverb	I jogged **nearly** five miles **today**, but I think I ran **too fast**.
17f	preposition	relates a noun or a pronoun to another word	Some **of** the streets will be closed **on** Friday afternoon **because of** the homecoming parade.
17g	conjunction	joins words or groups of words	**Either** Brandon **or** I will meet you **and** Darla at the airport **so that** you won't have to take a taxi.
17h	interjection	shows emotion	**Hooray!** We're home! **Well,** we'll see.

18 THE SENTENCE

Subjects, Predicates, Complements

Diagnostic Test

A. Identifying Subjects, Verbs, and Complements

Identify the italicized word or word group in each of the following sentences as a *subject*, a *verb*, a *direct object*, an *indirect object*, a *predicate nominative*, or a *predicate adjective*.

EXAMPLE   **1.** Computers *have provided* work and play in today's world.
          1. *verb*

1. Frances Perkins, the first woman in the history of the United States to hold a Cabinet post, was *Secretary of Labor* during Franklin Roosevelt's administration.
2. Thanks to my "green thumb," these squash *plants* are spreading vines and fruits all over the garden!
3. Did Kimi write *you* a letter about her trip to Norway?
4. Since the ballots have not yet been counted, the names of next year's class representatives are not *available* yet.
5. At the end of World War I, the United States signed separate peace *treaties* with Germany, Austria, and Hungary.

6. Please bring *me* the hacksaw and two pipe wrenches from the garage.
7. Edward MacDowell's orchestral work based on Iroquois, Dakota, Chippewa, and Kiowa melodies *was performed* for the first time in 1895.
8. Martin Luther King, Jr., a nonviolent activist and civil rights leader, was a *recipient* of the Nobel Prize for peace.
9. Do *you* know that the difference between wasps and bees is that wasps have long, narrow bodies and slim waists?
10. How stirringly *Sidney Poitier* portrayed Justice Thurgood Marshall!

B. Classifying Sentences

Classify each sentence in Part A as *declarative, interrogative, imperative,* or *exclamatory.*

EXAMPLE   **1.** Computers have provided work and play in today's world.
           1. *declarative*

Sentence or Fragment?

18a.   A *sentence* is a group of words that expresses a complete thought.

A thought is complete when it makes sense by itself.

EXAMPLES   The weary executive had left her briefcase on the commuter train.
         For how many years was Winston Churchill the prime minister of England?
         What extraordinary courage the early settlers must have had!

As you can see, a sentence begins with a capital letter and ends with a period, a question mark, or an exclamation point. Do not be misled, however, by a group of words that looks like a sentence but does not make sense by itself. Such a word group is called a *sentence fragment.*

SENTENCE FRAGMENT	Athletes representing 160 nations.
SENTENCE	Athletes representing 160 nations will compete in the Summer Olympics.
SENTENCE FRAGMENT	The offices designed for high efficiency.
SENTENCE	The offices have been designed for high efficiency.
SENTENCE FRAGMENT	Plans every month for future growth.
SENTENCE	The board of directors plans every month for future growth.

👉 **REFERENCE NOTE:** For more about sentence fragments, see pages 515–519.

GRAMMAR

▶ EXERCISE 1

Writing Complete Sentences from Notes

When making notes, writers often jot down information rapidly, using sentence fragments. Later, when drawing on their notes to write reports or articles, these writers expand the fragments into complete sentences. Read the set of notes below and look at the picture. Then write a paragraph using the information given. Your paragraph should have at least ten complete sentences.

Nat Love
("Deadwood Dick")

fifteen-year-old Tennessee
   sharecropper in 1869
   won raffle--prize was horse
   sold horse, split money with mother
   took his share, headed west to become a cowboy
got to Dodge City, Kansas
   already knew how to train horses (was hired for this)
   fast learner--soon could herd, brand, use gun
   good all-around cowboy, scout, range boss, rodeo rider
Deadwood, South Dakota, 1876
   big Fourth of July celebration
   Love--twenty-two years old
   won marksmanship matches: rifle, handgun
   set records: roping, bronco-riding
   "Deadwood Dick" (nicknamed by admiring townspeople)

The Subject and the Predicate

18b. A sentence consists of two parts: a *subject* and a *predicate*. A *subject* tells *whom* or *what* the sentence is about. A *predicate* tells something about the subject.

Subject Predicate
Lightning | struck.

Subject Predicate
Everyone | enjoyed reading *The Piano Lesson*.

Subject Predicate
All of the seeds | sprouted.

Predicate Subject
Into the sky soared | the young eagle.

Predicate Subject Predicate
Where did | your family | go on vacation?

As you can see, a subject or a predicate may consist of one word or more than one word. In these examples, all the words labeled subject make up the *complete subject,* and all the words labeled predicate make up the *complete predicate.*

The Simple Subject

18c. A *simple subject* is the main word or group of words that tells *whom* or *what* the sentence is about.

EXAMPLES Who was the **coach** of the hockey team in 1988? [The complete subject is *the coach of the hockey team.*]
Supported by grants, **scientists** constantly search for a cure for cancer. [The complete subject is *Supported by grants, scientists.*]
The **scenes** that you see in these tapestries show the beauty of Pennsylvania in the 1700s. [The complete subject is *The scenes that you see in these tapestries.*]
The **Corn Palace** in Mitchell, South Dakota, is quite a popular tourist attraction. [The complete subject is *The Corn Palace in Mitchell, South Dakota.*]

REFERENCE NOTE: A compound noun, such as *Corn Palace,* is considered one noun and may therefore be used as a simple subject. For more about compound nouns, see pages 554–555.

NOTE: In this book, the term *subject* refers to the simple subject unless otherwise indicated.

The Simple Predicate

18d. A *simple predicate* is a verb or verb phrase that tells something about the subject.

EXAMPLES   Catalina **ran** swiftly and gracefully. [The complete predicate is *ran swiftly and gracefully.*]
The puppy **chased** its tail frantically. [The complete predicate is *chased its tail frantically.*]
Another space probe **was** successfully **launched** today. [The complete predicate is *was successfully launched today.*]
Did Ethan ever **find** his history book? [The complete predicate is *did ever find his history book.*]

NOTE: In this book, the term *verb* refers to the simple predicate (a one-word verb or a verb phrase) unless otherwise indicated.

The Compound Subject and the Compound Verb

18e. A *compound subject* consists of two or more subjects that are joined by a conjunction and have the same verb.

Compound subjects are usually joined by the conjunction *and* or *or.*

EXAMPLES   The **ship** and its **cargo** had been lost.
Marva or **Antonio** will drive us to the track meet.
Athens, Delphi, and **Nauplia** are on the mainland of Greece.

18f. A *compound verb* consists of two or more verbs that are joined by a conjunction and have the same subject.

Compound verbs are usually joined by the conjunction *and, but,* or *or.*

EXAMPLES We **chose** a seat near the door and quietly **sat** down.

Kendra **recognized** the song but **could** not **remember** its title.

For exercise I **swim** or **play** racquetball nearly every day.

Truth **enlightens** the mind, **frees** the spirit, and **strengthens** the soul.

How to Find the Subject of a Sentence

A simple way to find the subject of a sentence is to ask *Who?* or *What?* before the verb.

EXAMPLES The **crew** of the whaling ship had worked hard. [Who worked? Crew worked.]

On the quarterdeck stood **Captain Ahab**. [Who stood? Captain Ahab stood.]

Swimming fast toward the ship was the great white **whale**. [What was swimming? Whale was swimming.]

Remembering the following guidelines will also help you locate the subject of a sentence.

(1) The subject of a sentence expressing a command or a request is always understood to be *you,* although *you* may not appear in the sentence.

COMMAND Turn left at the next intersection. [Who is being told to turn? *You* is understood.]

REQUEST Please tell me the story again. [Who is being asked to tell? *You* is understood.]

The subject of a command or a request is *you* even when the sentence contains a ***noun of direct address***—a word naming the one or ones spoken to.

EXAMPLE Jordan, (you) close the window.

(2) The subject of a sentence is never in a prepositional phrase.

EXAMPLES A **group** of students gathered near the library. [Who gathered? Group gathered. *Students* is the object of the preposition *of.*]

GRAMMAR

> **One** of the paintings by Vincent van Gogh sold for $82.5 million. [What sold? One sold. *Paintings* is the object of the preposition *of. Vincent van Gogh* is the object of the preposition *by.*]
> Out of the stillness came the loud **sound** of laughter. [What came? Sound came. *Stillness* is the object of the preposition *out of. Laughter* is the object of the preposition *of.*]

☞ REFERENCE NOTE: For a discussion of prepositional phrases, see pages 619–620 and 652–655.

(3) The subject of a sentence expressing a question usually follows the verb or a part of the verb phrase.

EXAMPLES   Is the **dog** in the house? [What is in the house? Dog is.]
When was **Katherine Ortega** appointed the Treasurer of the United States? [Who was appointed? Katherine Ortega was appointed.]

Turning the question into a statement will often help you find the subject.

QUESTION   Have you read Ernesto Galarza's *Barrio Boy?*
STATEMENT   **You** have read Ernesto Galarza's *Barrio Boy.* [Who has read? You have read.]

QUESTION   Were Shakespeare's plays popular during his own lifetime?
STATEMENT   Shakespeare's **plays** were popular during his own lifetime. [What were popular? Plays were popular.]

(4) The word *there* or *here* is never the subject of a sentence.

EXAMPLES   There is the famous ***Mona Lisa.*** [What is there? *Mona Lisa* is there.]
Here are your **gloves.** [What are here? Gloves are here.]

In these two examples, the words *there* and *here* are used as adverbs telling *where.* The word *there* may also be used as an *expletive*—a word that fills out the structure of a sentence but does not add to the meaning. In the following example, *there* does not tell *where* but serves only to make the structure of the sentence complete.

EXAMPLE   **There** is a soccer game after school this Friday. [What is? Game is. The subject is *game.*]

GRAMMAR

> ▶ EXERCISE 2 **Identifying Subjects and Verbs**

For each of the following sentences, identify the simple subject and the verb. Be sure to include all parts of a compound subject or a compound verb and all words in a verb phrase.

EXAMPLE **1.** In ancient Japan, the fierce-looking **samurai** shown below and **others** like him **ruled** society with an iron hand.
 1. *samurai, others—subject; ruled—verb*

1. The men, women, and children of the peasant class lived in terror of these landlord-warriors.
2. A samurai's powerful position gave him the right to kill any disobedient or disrespectful peasant.
3. Did anyone in Japan refuse to serve the samurai?
4. There was one dedicated group of rebels, called ninja, meaning "stealers in."
5. Off to the barren mountain regions of Iga and Koga fled the ninja people with their families.
6. There they could train their children in the martial arts of ninjutsu.
7. Lessons in camouflage, escape, and evasion were taught to children as young as one or two years of age.
8. Childhood games also provided practice in both armed and unarmed combat.
9. The ninja sneaked down into the settled areas and struck at the samurai in any way possible.
10. In time, the ninja warriors gained a reputation all over Japan and were feared by the mighty samurai.

WRITING APPLICATION

Using Compound Subjects and Compound Verbs to Combine Sentences

Writing is like planning a menu. Just as chefs choose foods to create a meal, writers choose words and sentences to create compositions. Like a good meal, an effective piece of writing has variety. Writers achieve such variety in several ways. They may vary the placement or the kinds of phrases and clauses they use, or they may invert the subject and predicate of a sentence. Another excellent way to add variety to writing is to use a mix of longer and shorter sentences. Often, writers combine short sentences into longer ones by using compound subjects and compound verbs.

TWO SENTENCES	After school yesterday, Suzanne showed me how to rotate the tires on my car. Ron showed me how to rotate the tires, too.
ONE SENTENCE WITH A COMPOUND SUBJECT	After school yesterday, **Suzanne** and **Ron** showed me how to rotate the tires on my car.
THREE SENTENCES	Later that afternoon, I checked the fluid levels. Then I vacuumed the carpeting and the seats. Finally, I washed the car.
ONE SENTENCE WITH A COMPOUND VERB	Later that afternoon, I **checked** the fluid levels, **vacuumed** the carpeting and the seats, and finally **washed** the car.

▶ WRITING ACTIVITY

You've just won the new car of your choice! All you need to do now is to decide what model and options you want. The car will be shipped to your local dealership. Write a letter to the sponsor of the contest thanking them for the prize and telling them what kind of car you want. Name six or more options that you've chosen for your car. Money is no object! For ideas, consult the list of options on the next page. You may also request other options that are not listed. In your letter, use at least three sentences with compound subjects and two sentences with compound verbs.

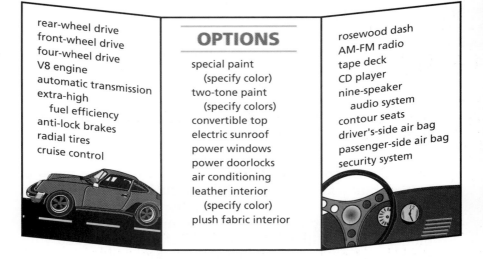

rear-wheel drive
front-wheel drive
four-wheel drive
V8 engine
automatic transmission
extra-high
  fuel efficiency
anti-lock brakes
radial tires
cruise control

OPTIONS

special paint
  (specify color)
two-tone paint
  (specify colors)
convertible top
electric sunroof
power windows
power doorlocks
air conditioning
leather interior
  (specify color)
plush fabric interior

rosewood dash
AM-FM radio
tape deck
CD player
nine-speaker
  audio system
contour seats
driver's-side air bag
passenger-side air bag
security system

Prewriting First, you'll need to decide what kind of car you'd like to have. List the options that interest you the most. Choose as many options as you like. Choose wisely, though—don't pick options that you really wouldn't use.

Writing As you write your draft, use one of the business-letter forms shown on pages 994–1001. Address your letter to an imaginary contest sponsor. Begin by thanking the sponsor for your prize. Then describe your "dream" car as clearly and specifically as possible. Include your telephone number so that the person ordering your car can call you with any questions about your choices.

Evaluating and Revising As you evaluate and revise your letter, you may think of more options you'd like to include. Check to see that your letter includes at least three sentences with compound subjects and two sentences with compound verbs. If it doesn't, you'll need to combine or rewrite some sentences in the letter. (See pages 526–538 for more on combining sentences.)

Proofreading Check over the grammar, spelling, and punctuation of your letter. Be sure that your letter follows one of the standard business-letter forms.

Complements

18g. A *complement* is a word or a group of words that completes the meaning of a verb.

A sentence may contain only a subject and a verb. The subject may be expressed or understood.

                  S   V

EXAMPLES   Everyone participated.

                  V

                  Stop! [The subject *you* is understood.]

Often, however, a sentence also includes at least one complement. Without the complement or complements in the sentence, the subject and the verb may not express a complete thought.

                     S   V

INCOMPLETE   José Canseco caught

                    S   V   C

COMPLETE   José Canseco caught the **ball**.

                    S   V

INCOMPLETE   They sent

                    S   V C   C

COMPLETE   They sent **us** an **invitation**.

                    S   V

INCOMPLETE   The judges named

                    S   V   C   C

COMPLETE   The judges named **Consuelo** the **winner**.

                      S   V

INCOMPLETE   The ancient Picts dyed

                      S   V   C C

COMPLETE   The ancient Picts dyed their **skin blue**.

                    S   V

INCOMPLETE   Denzel Washington became

                    S   V   C

COMPLETE   Denzel Washington became a versatile **actor**.

                    S   V

INCOMPLETE   The players seem

                    S   V   C

COMPLETE   The players seem **weary**.

As you can see in the examples on the previous page, a complement may be a noun, a pronoun, or an adjective. Do not mistake an adverb for a complement.

ADVERB	**Janna writes well.** [The adverb *well* tells *how* Janna writes.]
COMPLEMENT	**Janna writes adventure stories.** [The noun *stories* completes the meaning of *writes*.]

Also, do not confuse a word in a prepositional phrase with a complement.

PREPOSITIONAL PHRASE	**Janna also writes for the school newspaper.** [The noun *newspaper* is the object of the preposition *for*.]

☞ **REFERENCE NOTE:** For more about prepositional phrases, see pages 605–607.

The Direct Object and the Indirect Object

18h. A *direct object* is a word or word group that receives the action of a verb or shows the result of the action. A direct object tells *whom* or *what* after a transitive verb.

EXAMPLES	**Drought destroyed the crops.** [Destroyed what? Crops.] **The journalist interviewed the astronauts** before and after their flight. [Interviewed whom? Astronauts.] **Kerry called me** at noon. [Called whom? Me.]

A direct object may be compound.

EXAMPLES	The dog chased **Eli** and **me** through the park. Beethoven composed **sonatas** and **symphonies.**

NOTE: For emphasis, the direct object may come before the subject and the verb.

EXAMPLE	What a compelling **speech** the senator gave! [Gave what? Speech.]

18i. An *indirect object* is a word or word group that comes between a transitive verb and a direct object and tells to *whom* or to *what* or *for whom* or *for what* the action of the verb is done.

EXAMPLES Ms. Cruz showed our **class** a video about Moorish architecture. [Showed to whom? Class.]
The animal trainer fed the **bears** fish. [Fed to what? Bears.]
Their artistic skill won **them** many honors. [Won for whom? them.]

Do not confuse an indirect object with an object of the preposition *to* or *for*.

INDIRECT OBJECT The principal gave **her** the award.
OBJECT OF THE The principal gave the award to **her**. [*Her* is the
PREPOSITION object of the preposition *to*.]

An indirect object may be compound.

EXAMPLES The architect showed **Mom** and **Dad** the plans for the new family room.
Uncle Eugene built my **cousin** and **me** a tent in the back yard.

The Objective Complement

18j. An *objective complement* is a word or word group that helps complete the meaning of a transitive verb by identifying or modifying the direct object.

An objective complement may be a noun or an adjective.

EXAMPLES The members elected Carlotta **secretary.** [The noun *secretary* identifies the direct object *Carlotta*.]
Everyone considered her **dependable.** [The adjective *dependable* modifies the direct object *her*.]

Only a few verbs take an objective complement: *consider, make,* and verbs that can be replaced by *consider* or *make,* such as *appoint, call, choose, elect, name, cut, paint,* and *sweep*.

EXAMPLES Many literary historians call Shakespeare the greatest **dramatist** of all time. [or *consider* Shakespeare the greatest dramatist]
The flood had swept the valley **clean.** [or *had made* the valley clean]

An objective complement may be compound.

EXAMPLES The Gibsons named their two cats **Bruno** and **Waldo.**
Charlena painted her old bicycle **black** and **silver.**

EXERCISE 3

Identifying Direct Objects, Indirect Objects, and Objective Complements

Identify each complement in the following sentences as a *direct object*, an *indirect object*, or an *objective complement*.

1. Candles have tremendous appeal as decorative, religious, and utilitarian objects.
2. Every year the United States consumes approximately forty million pounds of paraffin for candle making.
3. Tutankhamen's tomb contained a candleholder.
4. Before the invention of electricity, many people lit their homes with candles.
5. Candles on the dinner table can make even an average meal special.
6. Many of the colonists made their own candles at home.
7. Nowadays, candle making offers hobbyists a relaxing and rewarding pastime.
8. These pictures show you the steps in candle making.
9. Incense mixed into the melted wax will give your candles a pleasant scent.
10. You can also dye candle wax various colors.

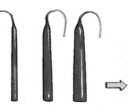

Melt wax in a double boiler or something similar.

Dip wick into wax, remove, and let cool.

Repeat this procedure until the candle is the thickness you want.

Finished product

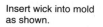

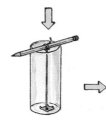

Insert wick into mold as shown.

Carefully pour wax into mold and let cool.

Run mold under hot water, turn upside down, and tap on bottom to remove candle.

Finished product

The Subject Complement

A *subject complement* is a word or word group that completes the meaning of a linking verb and identifies or modifies the subject.

☞ **REFERENCE NOTE:** For a list of linking verbs, see page 566.

There are two kinds of subject complements: the *predicate nominative* and the *predicate adjective.*

18k. A *predicate nominative* is the word or group of words that follows a linking verb and refers to the same person or thing as the subject of the verb.

EXAMPLES   Adela Rogers St. Johns was a famous **journalist.** [The noun *journalist* refers to the subject *Adela Rogers St. Johns.*]
The white bird with the long, slender neck is a **heron.** [The noun *heron* refers to the subject *bird.*]
Of the three applicants, Carlos is the most competent **one.** [The pronoun *one* refers to the subject *Carlos.*]

A predicate nominative may be compound.

EXAMPLES   The two candidates for class treasurer are **Marco** and **I.**
South Dakota's chief crops are **corn, wheat,** and **oats.**

18l. A *predicate adjective* is an adjective that follows a linking verb and modifies the subject of the verb.

EXAMPLES   The ocean is **calm.** [The adjective *calm* modifies the subject *ocean.*]
Does that orange taste **bitter?** [The adjective *bitter* modifies the subject *orange.*]
All of the astronauts look **confident.** [The adjective *confident* modifies the subject *All.*]

A predicate adjective may be compound.

EXAMPLES   Illuminated manuscripts are **rare** and **valuable.**
Eben Flood felt **old, lonely,** and **sad.**

NOTE: For emphasis, the subject complement may come before the subject and the verb.

PREDICATE   What an outstanding basketball **player** Michael
NOMINATIVE   Jordan is! [The noun *player* refers to the subject *Michael Jordan.*]

EXERCISE 4 **Identifying Linking Verbs and Subject Complements**

Identify the linking verb and the subject complement in each of the following sentences. Indicate whether the complement is a *predicate nominative* or a *predicate adjective*.

1. The most common deer in India is a species of axis deer.
2. Icy is the stare of the glacier.
3. Was Jane Austen the author of *Pride and Prejudice*?
4. Wilhelm Roentgen was the discoverer of the X-ray.
5. The violin solo sounded beautiful.
6. The animals grew restless at the sound of the crackling flames.
7. Harriet Tubman was active in the Underground Railroad.
8. Many people feel concerned about the spread of AIDS not just in the United States but throughout the world.
9. Why does the spaghetti sauce taste too spicy?
10. A massive work of carved stone is the Great Sphinx.

REVIEW **Identifying the Parts of Sentences**

For each of the following sentences, identify the sentence part or parts indicated in parentheses. Be sure to include all parts of a compound subject or a compound verb.

EXAMPLE 1. (*complete subject*) The people of New Orleans are famous for their creativity with food as well as with music.
1. *The people of New Orleans*

1. (*simple subject*) Both Creole cooking and Cajun cooking flourish in the kitchens of the city's French Quarter.
2. (*complete predicate*) Some visitors to New Orleans have trouble telling the difference between these two similar styles of food preparation.
3. (*indirect object, direct object*) My aunt, a restaurant critic, showed me the differences between Creole cooking and Cajun cooking.
4. (*verb, direct object*) The French founders of New Orleans developed the savory Creole style of cooking.
5. (*predicate nominative*) The *beignet* (a square doughnut) and *boudin* (a spicy, savory sausage) are tasty local favorites from French cuisine.

6. (*simple subject*) In Creole dishes, there are also tangy traces of Spanish, African, and Caribbean cooking.
7. (*verb*) Cajun cooking is Creole's peppery country cousin and was born in the rural bayou areas surrounding New Orleans.
8. (*predicate adjective*) My aunt's favorite Cajun treat, alligator gumbo, is wonderfully thick and spicy.
9. (*subject, direct object*) Don't the little red shellfish on this platter resemble tiny lobsters?
10. (*objective complement*) They're New Orleans crawfish, and I declare them the tastiest morsels I've ever eaten!

GRAMMAR

Classification of Sentences

18m.   Sentences may be classified according to purpose.

(1) A ***declarative sentence*** makes a statement. It is followed by a period.

EXAMPLES   The lock on the front door is broken.
Jorge Farragut led naval forces against the British in both the Revolutionary War and the War of 1812.

(2) An ***interrogative sentence*** asks a question. It is followed by a question mark.

EXAMPLES   Have you seen a sculpture by Augusta Savage?
Is Santa Fe the capital of New Mexico?

(3) An *imperative sentence* makes a request or gives a command. It is usually followed by a period. A very strong command, however, is followed by an exclamation point.

EXAMPLES   **Please give me the dates for the class meetings.** [request]
Call this number in case of an emergency. [mild command]
Help me! [strong command]

(4) An *exclamatory sentence* expresses strong feeling or shows excitement. It is followed by an exclamation point.

EXAMPLES   **What a noble leader he was!**
Ah, you have discovered the secret!

▶ EXERCISE 5   **Identifying the Four Kinds of Sentences**

Identify each of the following sentences as *declarative, interrogative, imperative,* or *exclamatory.* Also supply the appropriate end mark after the last word in the sentence.

1. Anyone with a little free time and a generous heart can help make the world of books available to people with visual impairments
2. For example, have you ever wondered how Braille schoolbooks for sight-impaired students are created
3. Imagine dozens and dozens of volunteers, all with their fingers flying across the keys of machines that look much like miniature typewriters
4. Different combinations of six keys on the machines make the raised-dot patterns that represent letters and numbers in Braille
5. First, Braille typists take a course to learn how to use the machines
6. Once you learn how, typing in Braille isn't difficult at all
7. If I participate, can I work at home in my spare time
8. What rewarding volunteer work this is
9. When I considered how much time I waste every week, I decided to use that time constructively by volunteering to help create Braille textbooks
10. If you know someone who might be interested in participating, help him or her find out how to get in touch with the Braille Association in your community

PICTURE THIS

What makes people want to run in a long, grueling marathon like this one? As a newspaper reporter covering the marathon, it's your job to find out. You are conducting brief interviews with runners at the finish line. Jot down notes on one of the interviews, writing down at least four of your questions or comments along with the interviewee's responses. In your notes, use at least one of each of the four kinds of sentences— declarative, interrogative, imperative, and exclamatory.

Subject: a marathon
Audience: yourself; readers of your article
Purpose: to record information; to inform

Review: Posttest 1

A. Identifying Subjects, Verbs, and Complements in the Sentences of a Paragraph

Identify the italicized word or word group in each sentence in the following paragraph as a *subject*, a *verb*, or a *complement*. If it is a complement, identify it as a *direct object*, an *indirect object*, a *predicate nominative*, a *predicate adjective*, or an *objective complement*.

EXAMPLE [1] The National Science Foundation (NSF) is undergoing a great *surge* of growth.
1. *complement (direct object)*

[1] The NSF is relatively *small* compared with other government agencies like the National Institutes of Health and the National Aeronautics and Space Administration. [2] Recently, however, it *has accepted* more and more challenges. [3] In 1991, with funding of only $2.3 billion, the *foundation* participated heavily in several big government programs. [4] *One* of these important programs investigates global climate change. [5] There is another *program* for which the NSF is developing sophisticated computer technology. [6] In a third project, the foundation boosts science and mathematics *education* and *literacy*. [7] How important this project *must be* to the foundation's dynamic new director, physicist Walter E. Massey! [8] Throughout his career, Dr. Massey has shown *hundreds* of students the excitement of physics, chemistry, biology, and the other sciences. [9] Dr. Massey is especially sensitive to the needs of minority students because he is an *African American* himself. [10] Perhaps through the programs of the National Science Foundation, many more students will now make themselves *candidates* for rewarding careers in science.

B. Classifying Sentences

Classify each of the following sentences as *declarative, interrogative, imperative,* or *exclamatory.* Then supply the appropriate end mark after the last word in the sentence.

EXAMPLE **1.** The school is five blocks from here
            1. *declarative—here.*

11. The umpire called a strike
12. The pear tree grew well in our back yard
13. His hard work earned him a promotion
14. Anita ran errands during most of the day
15. Why did Earl leave the party so early
16. Debbie Allen is a choreographer
17. What a wonderful day we had yesterday
18. Please hold my umbrella for a minute
19. Where did you park the car
20. Leave your classrooms quickly and quietly

Review: Posttest 2

Writing Sentences

Write your own sentences according to the following guidelines. In your sentences, underline the words that indicate the italicized sentence parts. Also, use a variety of subjects, verbs, and complements in your sentences.

1. a declarative sentence with a *compound subject*
2. an interrogative sentence with a *compound verb*
3. an exclamatory sentence with a *direct object*
4. an imperative sentence with a *compound direct object*
5. a declarative sentence with an *indirect object*
6. a declarative sentence with a *predicate nominative*
7. an interrogative sentence with a *compound predicate adjective*
8. a declarative sentence with an *objective complement*
9. an imperative sentence with an *indirect object*
10. a declarative sentence with a *predicate adjective*

SUMMARY OF COMMON SENTENCE PATTERNS

Together the subject and the verb produce the most basic sentence pattern. All other sentence patterns are combinations of the subject, the verb, and various complements.

   S   V
Emilia sang.

   S   V   D.O.
Emilia sang a solo.

     S   V I.O.   D.O.
The audience gave Emilia a standing ovation.

         S   V D.O.   O.C. (N)
Some people called her an inspired performer.

     S   V   D.O.   O.C. (Adj)
Everyone considered her performance outstanding.

   S   V   P.N.
Emilia was the star of the show.

     S   V   P.A.
Her performance was flawless.

19 THE PHRASE

Kinds of Phrases and Their Functions

Diagnostic Test

A. Identifying Phrases

In each of the following sentences, identify the italicized phrase as a *prepositional phrase*, a *gerund phrase*, a *participial phrase*, an *infinitive phrase*, or an *appositive phrase*. Do not separately identify a prepositional phrase that is part of a larger phrase.

EXAMPLE   **1.** *Smiling warmly*, they greeted us on our arrival.
            1. *participial phrase*

1. In Israel, farmers use innovative agricultural methods to meet the difficulties of *growing food in a desert country.*
2. Harriet Beecher Stowe wrote that famous novel *to awaken the country's consciousness to the evils of slavery.*
3. Woodrow Wilson, *the U.S. President during World War I,* tried with his Fourteen Points to prevent another world war.
4. *In the Roaring Twenties* the Teapot Dome scandal contributed to American dissatisfaction with the presidency of Warren Harding.
5. During our vacation in Hawaii, we saw Mauna Loa, a volcano *rising six miles from the floor of the ocean.*

6. Thomas Nast, *a nineteenth-century illustrator and political cartoonist,* is famous for his numerous drawings of Santa Claus.
7. Withdrawing from the race, the candidate cited personal reasons for her unexpected decision *to return to private life.*
8. To conserve water, farmers water only the roots of plants, using a series *of underground irrigation pipes.*
9. In a speech *delivered to the graduating class,* the principal encouraged the graduates to improve the quality of life in our world.
10. *Using an opponent's strength against himself or herself* is the basis of the martial art jujitsu.

B. Identifying Phrases

Identify each italicized phrase in the following paragraph as a *prepositional phrase,* a *gerund phrase,* a *participial phrase,* an *infinitive phrase,* or an *appositive phrase.* Do not separately identify a prepositional phrase that is part of the larger phrase.

EXAMPLE   **[1]** Have you heard of Susan Butcher, *the four-time winner of the grueling Iditarod Sled Dog Race*?
      1. *appositive phrase*

   [11] *A woman of rare determination,* Butcher raises her own dogs. **[12]** *Tucked away in the Alaskan wilderness not far from the Arctic Circle,* her kennel is a four-hour drive from the nearest grocery store. **[13]** Butcher believes that only when she is this isolated from society can she concentrate on *creating a tight bond with her 150 dogs.* **[14]** *For more than ten years,* she has raised huskies in her own unique way. **[15]** From the moment each puppy is born, she spends plenty of time with it *to get it used to her voice and her touch.* **[16]** She handles and talks *to the newborn puppy* frequently, breathing on it so that it can also learn her scent. **[17]** *Growing closer and closer to Butcher,* the puppy is personally fed, trained, and even sung to and massaged by her. **[18]** When the puppy is four and one-half months old, Butcher allows it *to begin training in harness.* **[19]** By *showing the dogs her love for them,* Butcher gains the devotion needed to create championship teams. **[20]** The Iditarod, *1,130 miles of mountains, frozen seas, and snowy wilderness between Anchorage and Nome,* is the ultimate test of a dog team's devotion.

19a. A *phrase* is a group of related words that is used as a single part of speech and does not contain a verb and its subject.

VERB PHRASE **has been canceled** [no subject]
PREPOSITIONAL PHRASE **before the party** [no subject or verb]

 REFERENCE NOTE: A group of words that has a subject and a verb is called a *clause.* For more about independent and subordinate clauses, see pages 628–637.

The Prepositional Phrase

19b. A *prepositional phrase* begins with a preposition and ends with a noun or a pronoun, called the *object of the preposition.*

EXAMPLES   The tall building **with the red roof** is our new library. [The noun *roof* is the object of the preposition *with.*] **Next to it** is the old library, which is now being used **for storage.** [The pronoun *it* is the object of the compound preposition *Next to.* The noun *storage* is the object of the preposition *for.*]

An object of a preposition may be compound.

EXAMPLE   *Brian's Song* is an inspiring story **about friendship and courage.** [Both *friendship* and *courage* are objects of the preposition *about.*]

 REFERENCE NOTE: For lists of prepositions, see page 572.

The Adjective Phrase

19c. An *adjective phrase* is a prepositional phrase that modifies a noun or a pronoun.

An adjective phrase tells *what kind* or *which one.*

EXAMPLES   Cassie Soldierwolf made a batch **of fry bread,** using a recipe very similar to that **of her ancestors.** [*Of fry bread* modifies the noun *batch,* telling *what kind. Of her ancestors* modifies the pronoun *that,* telling *which one.*]

GRAMMAR

An adjective phrase always follows the word it modifies. That word may be the object of another preposition.

EXAMPLE **Sarah Kemble Knight kept a journal of her trip to New York.** [*Of her trip* modifies the direct object *journal*. *To New York* modifies *trip*, which serves as the object of the preposition *of.*]

More than one adjective phrase may modify the same word.

EXAMPLE **Sarah Knight's journey on horseback from Boston to New York was long and difficult.** [The three phrases *on horseback*, *from Boston*, and *to New York* modify the noun *journey*.]

▶ EXERCISE 1 **Identifying Adjective Phrases and the Words They Modify**

The following sentences contain ten adjective phrases. Identify each adjective phrase and the word it modifies.

1. The instinct for self-preservation is a basic drive in nearly all living things.
2. Yet these small Scandinavian animals, called lemmings, occasionally follow a pattern of self-destruction.
3. Ordinarily, lemmings lead peaceful, quiet lives, eating a diet of moss and roots.
4. Every few years, however, their population exceeds their food supply, and they ford streams and lakes, devouring everything in their path and leaving no trace of vegetation.

5. When they reach the cliffs along the sea, they leap into the water and swim until they drown.
6. Explanations of their rush to the sea are only guesses, and the lemming remains a mystery to those who study animal behavior.

The Adverb Phrase

19d. An *adverb phrase* is a prepositional phrase that modifies a verb, an adjective, or an adverb.

An adverb phrase tells *how, when, where, why,* or *to what extent* (*how long* or *how far*).

An adverb phrase may modify a verb.

EXAMPLE **During the Civil War,** Louisa May Alcott worked **in a hospital as a nurse for six months.** [Each phrase modifies the verb *worked. During the Civil War* tells *when, in a hospital* tells *where, as a nurse* tells *how,* and *for six months* tells *how long.*]

As you can see in this example, more than one adverb phrase can modify the same word. The example also shows that an adverb phrase, unlike an adjective phrase, can precede the word it modifies.

An adverb phrase may modify an adjective.

EXAMPLE Louisa May Alcott wrote *Little Women,* a novel rich **in New England traditions.** [*In New England traditions* modifies the adjective *rich,* telling *how* rich.]

An adverb phrase may modify an adverb.

EXAMPLE Later **in her life,** Louisa May Alcott worked to gain voting rights for women. [*In her life* modifies the adverb *later.*]

▶ EXERCISE 2 **Identifying Adverb Phrases and the Words They Modify**

The following sentences contain ten adverb phrases. Identify each adverb phrase and the word or words it modifies.

1. Duncan is sitting in his chair, eating a bowl of oatmeal.
2. A great part of our life is spent in sleep.

3. In the classic Japanese movie *The Seven Samurai,* fierce professional warriors save a village from bandits.
4. Every rumor in the world has been started by somebody.
5. They were assembled on benches for the presentation.
6. Especially for the children, the mariachi band played "The Mexican Hat Dance."
7. Fear sometimes springs from ignorance.
8. In winter we wear warm clothes.

WRITING APPLICATION

Using Prepositional Phrases to Add Information to Sentences

If you heard that a friend was "modifying" her stereo, you'd probably assume she was adding features or components to improve its sound. Just as an extra set of speakers can make a stereo sound better, a modifying phrase can make a sentence sound clearer and more interesting. Like all modifiers, prepositional phrases help you include more information when you express your ideas. For example, compare the following two sentences. What does the second sentence tell you that the first one doesn't? Without prepositional phrases, could you express the complete idea as clearly or as simply?

> Sean Harrigan hopes to have his own riding stable.
> Sean Harrigan hopes to have his own riding stable with the name Harrigan's Happy Trails in huge letters over the entrance.

▶ WRITING ACTIVITY

There's going to be a special Careers issue of your school newspaper. For a feature page, the editor has invited students to name and describe businesses they'd like to own ten years from now. You've decided to contribute a description of your business-to-be. Think of your business, invent a name for it, and write a paragraph describing it. Use at least five prepositional phrases in your sentences.

Prewriting Brainstorm ideas for three or four kinds of businesses you'd enjoy owning and running ten years from now. List several catchy names for each one. Choose the business and name you like best. Then jot down details about your product or service, your location, your equipment, and your customers.

Writing As you write your first draft, think about the students who will be your audience. What details about your business would interest your readers? Make sure that you include plenty of these specific details in your paragraph. You may choose to use formal or informal language in your paragraph, and your tone may be either humorous or serious.

Evaluating and Revising Ask a friend to read your paragraph before you revise it. Can your friend clearly imagine your business? If not, add, cut, or rearrange details to make your paragraph clearer and more interesting. Then reread your paragraph for sentence style. If your sentences sound choppy, combine them into longer, smoother sentences. (For more about sentence combining, see pages 526–538.) Be sure that you've used at least five prepositional phrases in your paragraph.

Proofreading and Publishing Check over the grammar, spelling, and punctuation of your paragraph. Mentally identify the subject and verb of each sentence to make sure all your sentences are complete. (See the discussion of sentence fragments on pages 515–519.) You and your classmates may want to gather your paragraphs into a booklet to include in a class time capsule. At the tenth reunion of your class, you can open the time capsule to see how your career goals have (or haven't) changed.

REVIEW A **Identifying Prepositional Phrases**

For each sentence in the following paragraph, list all the prepositional phrases. Be sure to include any prepositional phrase that modifies the object of another preposition. Then tell whether each prepositional phrase is an *adjective phrase* or an *adverb phrase.* Be prepared to give the word each prepositional phrase modifies and to identify the word as a *noun,* a *pronoun,* a *verb,* an *adjective,* or an *adverb.*

EXAMPLE [1] From what part of the world do these strange-looking items come?

    1. *from what part—adverb phrase; of the world—adjective phrase*

[1] They come from Africa, and they are from the family of musical instruments called *mbira.* [2] About the size of a paperback book, these small *mbiras,* called *kalimbas,* are boxes made from smooth, warm-colored wood. [3] You pluck the steel keys with your thumbs to play melodies, which explains why the instrument is called a thumb box by some people. [4] Below the keys, there is a sound hole like the one on a guitar. [5] When one or more keys are plucked, the notes resonate inside the box. [6] The *kalimba* sounds like a cross between a small xylophone, a music box, and a set of wind chimes. [7] Small in size, it's portable enough to carry in a pocket or backpack, and it is easy to play. [8] Nearly everybody enjoys the soft, light sound, even if you hit a wrong note with both thumbs! [9] Instruments similar to the *kalimba* were noted by Portuguese explorers in the sixteenth century along the East African coast. [10] In 1586, Father Dos Santos, a Portuguese traveler, wrote that native *mbira* players pluck the keys lightly, "as a good player strikes those of a harpsichord," producing "a sweet and gentle harmony of accordant sounds."

Verbals and Verbal Phrases

A *verbal* is a form of a verb used as a noun, an adjective, or an adverb. The three kinds of verbals are the *participle*, the *gerund*, and the *infinitive*.

A *verbal phrase* consists of a verbal and its modifiers and complements. The three kinds of verbal phrases are the *participial phrase*, the *gerund phrase*, and the *infinitive phrase*.

The Participle

19e. A *participle* is a verb form that is used as an adjective.

There are two kinds of participles—the *present participle* and the *past participle*.

Present participles end in *-ing*.

EXAMPLES   Esperanza has taken **singing** lessons for several years. [*Singing*, a form of the verb *sing*, modifies the noun *lessons*.]
Waving, the campers boarded the bus. [*Waving*, a form of the verb *wave*, modifies the noun *campers*.]
We could hear something **moving** in the underbrush. [*Moving*, a form of the verb *move*, modifies the pronoun *something*.]

Most past participles end in *–d* or *–ed*. Others are irregularly formed.

EXAMPLES   The **baked** chicken with yellow rice tasted delicious. [*Baked*, a form of the verb *bake*, modifies the noun chicken.]
In your own words, define each term **given** in the first column. [*Given*, a form of the verb *give*, modifies the noun *term*.]
Confused and **frightened,** they fled into the jungle. [*Confused*, a form of the verb *confuse*, and *frightened*, a form of the verb *frighten*, modify the pronoun *they*.]

The perfect tense of a participle is formed with the helping verb *having*, as in *having worked* and *having been washed*.

EXAMPLES   **Having worked** all day, Abe was ready for a rest.
Having been washed, the car gleamed in the sun.

Do not confuse a participle used as an adjective with a participle used as part of a verb phrase.

ADJECTIVE	The Vietnam Veterans Memorial, **designed** by Maya Ying Lin, was completed in 1982.
VERB PHRASE	The Vietnam Veterans Memorial, which **had been designed** by Maya Ying Lin, was completed in 1982.

The Participial Phrase

19f. A *participial phrase* consists of a participle and all of the words related to the participle.

Participles may be modified by adverbs and may also have complements.

EXAMPLES *Speaking eloquently,* Barbara Jordan enthralled the audience. [The participial phrase modifies the noun *Barbara Jordan.* The adverb *eloquently* modifies the present participle *speaking.*]

Nodding his head, the defendant admitted his guilt. [The participial phrase modifies the noun *defendant.* The noun *head* is the direct object of the present participle *nodding.*]

Encouraged by his family, he submitted his book of poems for publication. [The participial phrase modifies the pronoun *he.* The adverb phrase *by his family* modifies the past participle *Encouraged.*]

Florence Griffith Joyner, **often called Flo Jo,** holds the U.S. national record for the women's 100-meter dash. [The participial phrase modifies the noun *Florence Griffith Joyner.* The adverb *often* modifies the past participle *called.* The noun *Flo Jo* is the direct object of *called.*]

When writing a sentence with a participial phrase, be sure to place the phrase as close as possible to the word it modifies.

MISPLACED	**Singing in the trees,** the explorers heard the birds **walking along the path.**
IMPROVED	**Walking along the path,** the explorers heard the birds **singing in the trees.**

☞ REFERENCE NOTE: For more information about misplaced participial phrases, see pages 782–786.

▶ EXERCISE 3
Identifying Participial Phrases and the Words They Modify

Each of the following sentences contains at least one participial phrase. Identify each participial phrase and the word or words it modifies.

1. Known as Johnny Appleseed, John Chapman distributed apple seeds and saplings to families headed West.
2. Needing a sustained wind for flight, the albatross rarely crosses the equator.
3. Forty adders coiled together can prevent heat loss.
4. The salmon, deriving its pink color from its diet, feeds on shrimp-like crustaceans.
5. Having been aided by good weather and clear skies, the sailors rejoiced as they sailed into port.
6. Smiling broadly, our champion entered the hall.
7. Searching through old clothes in a trunk, John found a map showing the location of a treasure buried on the shore.
8. Sparta and Athens, putting aside their own rivalry, joined forces to fight the Persians.
9. Trained on an overhead trellis, a white rosebush growing in Tombstone, Arizona, covers some 8,000 square feet of aerial space.
10. I would love to see it bursting into bloom in the spring; it must be quite a sight!

▶ REVIEW B
Identifying Prepositional and Participial Phrases and the Words They Modify

Identify each italicized phrase in the following sentences as a *prepositional phrase* or a *participial phrase*. Then give the word or words each phrase modifies. Do not separately identify a prepositional phrase that is part of a participial phrase.

EXAMPLE   1. *Delighted by the play*, the critic applauded *with great enthusiasm.*
   1. *Delighted by the play—participial phrase—critic; with great enthusiasm—prepositional phrase—applauded*

1. Mahalia Jackson, *called the greatest potential blues singer since Bessie Smith*, would sing only religious songs.
2. Her version of "Silent Night" was one *of the all-time best-selling records* in Denmark.

3. *Setting out in a thirty-one-foot ketch,* Sharon Sites Adams, a woman *from California,* sailed *across the Pacific* alone.
4. *Having been rejected by six publishers,* the story *of Peter Rabbit* was finally published privately *by Beatrix Potter.*
5. *Known for his imaginative style,* architect Minoru Yamasaki designed the World Trade Center, *located in New York City.*
6. *In 1932,* Amelia Earhart, *trying for a new record,* began her solo flight *over the Atlantic.*
7. Maria Tallchief, an Osage Indian, was the prima ballerina *of the New York Ballet Company.*
8. *Dancing to unanimous acclaim in both the United States and Europe,* she was known *for her brilliant interpretation* of Stravinsky's *Firebird.*
9. *Continuing her research on radium after her husband's death,* Marie Curie received the Nobel Prize *in chemistry.*
10. *First elected to the House of Representatives in 1958,* Shirley Chisholm was the first black female member *of Congress.*

The Gerund

19g. A *gerund* is a verb form ending in *−ing* that is used as a noun.

SUBJECT	**Swimming** is excellent exercise.
PREDICATE NOMINATIVE	Janetta's hobby is **knitting.**
DIRECT OBJECT	She has always loved **dancing.**
INDIRECT OBJECT	He gave **studying** all his attention.
OBJECT OF PREPOSITION	In **cooking,** use salt sparingly.

Do not confuse a gerund with a present participle used as an adjective or as part of a verb phrase.

GERUND	I enjoy **reading** late at night. [direct object of the verb *enjoy*]
PRESENT PARTICIPLE	I sometimes fall asleep **reading** late at night. [adjective modifying the pronoun *I*]
PRESENT PARTICIPLE	Sometimes, I listen to classical music while I am **reading** late at night. [part of the verb phrase *am reading*]

NOTE: When writing a noun or a pronoun directly before a gerund, use the possessive form of the noun or pronoun.

EXAMPLES **Rodrigo's** winning the contest surprised no one.
Mom was upset about **our** being late.

▶ EXERCISE 4   **Identifying Gerunds and Their Functions**

Find the gerunds in the following sentences. Then identify each gerund as a *subject*, a *direct object*, an *indirect object*, a *predicate nominative*, or an *object of a preposition*.

EXAMPLE   **1.** By reading the newspaper daily, you will become an informed citizen.
       1. *reading—object of a preposition*

  1. Judging is an exercise in objectivity.
  2. Do you enjoy skiing?
  3. I sometimes dream about flying.
  4. My Navajo grandmother thinks that weaving would be a good hobby for me.
  5. I have given camping a fair try, but I still do not like it.
  6. Some of my friends earn extra money by baby-sitting.
  7. My exercise schedule includes jogging.
  8. Snorkeling gives me hours of pleasure.
  9. Typing is a useful skill.
10. Have you ever wished for a career in acting?

The Gerund Phrase

19h.   A *gerund phrase* consists of a gerund and all of the words related to the gerund.

Like participles, gerunds may have modifiers and complements.

EXAMPLES   **Exercising regularly** is important to your health. [The gerund phrase is the subject of the verb *is*. The adverb *regularly* modifies the gerund *Exercising*.]
My brother likes **working at the travel agency.** [The gerund phrase is the direct object of the verb *likes*. The adverb phrase *at the travel agency* modifies the gerund *working*.]
Walter Mitty daydreamed of **being a courageous pilot.** [The gerund phrase is the object of the preposition *of*. The noun *pilot* is a predicate nominative completing the meaning of the gerund *being*.]
An excellent way to build your vocabulary is **reading good literature.** [The gerund phrase is a predicate nominative explaining the subject *way*. The noun *literature* is the direct object of the gerund *reading*.]

▶ REVIEW C **Identifying Participial Phrases and Gerund Phrases**

Identify the verbal phrase in each of the following sentences as a *participial phrase* or a *gerund phrase*.

1. Mary Shelley wrote *Frankenstein* after having a nightmare about a scientist and his strange experiments.
2. Dr. Mae Jennison became an astronaut by placing among the best fifteen candidates out of two thousand applicants.
3. Beginning with *Pippi Longstocking*, Astrid Lindgren has written a whole series of stories for children.
4. Marian Anderson was the first African American employed as a member of the Metropolitan Opera.
5. Fighting for women's suffrage was Carrie Chapman Catt's mission in life.
6. Appointed principal of the Mason City Iowa High School in 1881, Catt became the city's first female superintendent.
7. The Nineteenth Amendment of the Constitution, adopted in 1920, was largely the result of Catt's efforts.
8. Mildred "Babe" Didrikson, entering the 1932 Olympics as a relatively obscure athlete, won gold and silver medals.
9. Working for *Life* throughout her long career, Margaret Bourke-White was the first female war photographer.
10. Phyllis McGinley, a famous writer of light verse, began publishing her work while she was still in college.

The Infinitive

19i. An *infinitive* is a verb form that can be used as a noun, an adjective, or an adverb. An infinitive usually begins with *to*.

INFINITIVES	
USED AS	EXAMPLES
Nouns	**To fly** was an ambition of humans for many centuries. [subject of *was*] Some fishes must swim constantly, or they start **to sink.** [direct object of *start*] Darius Freeman's dream is **to act.** [predicate nominative identifying the subject *dream*]

INFINITIVES *(continued)*	
USED AS	**EXAMPLES**
Adjectives	His attempt **to fly** was a failure. [adjective modifying the noun *attempt*] The one **to ask** is your guidance counselor. [adjective modifying the pronoun *one*]
Adverbs	With his dog Wolf, Rip van Winkle went into the woods **to hunt**. [adverb modifying the verb *went*] Everyone in the neighborhood was willing **to help**. [adverb modifying the adjective *willing*]

GRAMMAR

NOTE: Do not confuse an infinitive with a prepositional phrase that begins with *to*. An infinitive is a verb form. A prepositional phrase begins with *to* and ends with a noun or a pronoun.

INFINITIVES	to write	to forgive	to visit
PREPOSITIONAL PHRASES	to the game	to someone	to them

The word *to*, the sign of the infinitive, is sometimes omitted.

EXAMPLES   Let us [to] **sit** down.
Please make him [to] **stop** that noise.
We wouldn't dare [to] **disobey.**
Will you help me [to] **finish**?

► EXERCISE 5   **Identifying Infinitives and Their Functions**

Identify the infinitive in each of the following sentences. Then tell whether it is used as a *noun,* an *adjective,* or an *adverb.* If the infinitive is used as a noun, indicate whether it is a *subject,* a *direct object,* or *a predicate nominative.* If the infinitive is used as a modifier, give the word it modifies.

EXAMPLE   **1.** Swans and geese are fascinating to watch.
    1. *to watch—adverb—fascinating*

1. To land on the moon became the national goal of the United States during the 1960s.
2. For me, one of the worst chores is to clean my room.
3. Karl "The Mailman" Malone slam-dunked the ball with one second to go in the game!

4. Since I have taken up track in addition to my other extra-curricular activities, it seems I haven't a moment to spare.
5. Did you find that book difficult to understand?
6. According to our judicial system, the state makes the decision to prosecute the defendant in criminal cases.
7. Mom made me finish the dishes before I could go to the movies.
8. Anita's job was to interview all qualified applicants who had applied for the position.
9. I did not have the time to watch the football game on television.
10. In my spare time I like to read stories by Laurence Yep.

▶ REVIEW D **Identifying Participles, Gerunds, and Infinitives**

Identify the participles, gerunds, and infinitives in the sentences in the following paragraph. For each participle, give the word it modifies. For each gerund, tell what part of a sentence it is used as. For each infinitive, indicate what part of speech it is used as.

EXAMPLE   [1] In Chinese communities all over the world, parading a huge paper dragon is an exciting part of the New Year celebration.
1. *parading—gerund (subject); exciting—participle—modifies* part

[1] Dragons are an honored symbol of happiness to many Chinese people. [2] According to ancient Chinese mythology, dragons are responsible for watching over people and bringing rain to make the crops grow. [3] There are five different types of dragons, but it is the imperial dragon that is chosen to dance through the streets in traditional New Year celebrations. [4] The dragon's role is to chase away bad luck and to bring good fortune for the new year. [5] Holding a stick with a white ball on the top, one dancer runs ahead of the charging dragon figure. [6] The ball symbolizes the highly valued pearl of wisdom, which the dragon chases. [7] The dragon's dance is accompanied by the beating of drums and gongs, the clashing of cymbals, and the popping of firecrackers. [8] The amazing dragon in the photograph on the next page, the largest dragon figure in the world, is three meters tall and nearly 100 meters long. [9] Its

covering is decorated with 84,000 hand-cut mirrors and 6,000 multicolored silk "scales." [10] Because of its great weight and size, this dragon takes two hundred people, working in shifts, to carry it.

The Infinitive Phrase

19j. An *infinitive phrase* consists of an infinitive and all of the words related to the infinitive.

Like other verbals, infinitives may have modifiers and complements.

EXAMPLES   **To finish early** is our plan. [The infinitive phrase is the subject of the verb *is*. The adverb *early* modifies the infinitive *to finish*.]

Julia wants **to go to the beach with us on Saturday.** [The infinitive phrase is the direct object of the verb *wants*. The adverb phrases *to the beach, with us,* and *on Saturday* modify the infinitive *to go*.]

Napoleon's plan **to conquer the world** failed. [The infinitive phrase modifies the noun *plan*. The noun *world* is the direct object of the infinitive *to conquer*.]

Because of his sprained ankle, Chico was unable **to play in the football game.** [The infinitive phrase modifies the adjective *unable*. The adverb phrase *in the football game* modifies the infinitive *to play*.]

GRAMMAR

NOTE: Unlike other verbals, an infinitive may have a subject. Such a construction is called an *infinitive clause.* Notice in the second example below that the subject in the infinitive clause *(them)* is in the objective case.

EXAMPLES The director has asked **Rebecca to star in the play.**
[*Rebecca* is the subject of the infinitive *to star.* The entire infinitive clause is the direct object of the verb *has asked.*]
The sergeant commanded **them to march faster.**
[*Them* is the subject of the infinitive *to march.* The entire infinitive clause is the direct object of the verb *commanded.*]

☞ REFERENCE NOTE: For more information about clauses, see pages 628–637.

 REVIEW E

Identifying Prepositional, Participial, Gerund, and Infinitive Phrases

Identify each italicized phrase in the following sentences as a *prepositional phrase,* a *participial phrase,* a *gerund phrase,* or an *infinitive phrase.* Do not separately identify a prepositional phrase that is part of a larger phrase.

EXAMPLE **1.** *Celebrating the strength of the human spirit,* Christy Brown's book My Left Foot tells the story *of his life.*
1. *Celebrating the strength of the human spirit—* participial phrase; *of his life*—prepositional phrase

1. Christy Brown, *born with cerebral palsy,* was unable *to speak a single word.*
2. Everyone *including his family* assumed he had very little intelligence, because he could not express himself *to them.*
3. Christy's left foot was the only limb he could control, and one day he succeeded in *grabbing a piece of chalk with it* and began *to write the word MOTHER on the wooden floor.*
4. Christy's family, *amazed at this remarkable achievement,* suddenly realized that *his leading a full, rewarding life* was not an impossible dream.
5. *Typing the entire manuscript with his left foot,* Christy Brown was eventually able *to tell his story in this inspiring book about his life.*

Appositives and Appositive Phrases

19k. An *appositive* is a noun or a pronoun placed beside another noun or pronoun to identify or explain it.

An appositive usually follows the word it identifies or explains.

EXAMPLES   We went to the Navajo Gallery in Taos, New Mexico, to see R. C. Gorman's painting *Freeform Lady.* [The noun *Freeform Lady* identifies the noun *painting.*]
Did Dan Namhinga complete *Red Desert,* **one** of his colorful acrylic paintings, in 1980? [The pronoun *one* refers to the noun *Red Desert.*]
Namhinga, a Hopi-Tewa **artist,** often paints abstract images of Hopi pueblos. [The noun *artist* explains the noun *Namhinga.*]

For emphasis, however, an appositive may come at the beginning of a sentence.

EXAMPLE   A younger **painter,** Jaune Quick-to-See Smith shows a deep awareness of her French, Cree, and Shoshone heritage. [The noun *painter* refers to the noun *Jaune Quick-to-See Smith.*]

19l. An *appositive phrase* consists of an appositive and its modifiers.

EXAMPLES   We visited Boston Harbor, **the site of the Boston Tea Party.** [The adjective *the* and the adjective phrase *of the Boston Tea Party* modify the appositive *site.*]
The Kenai Peninsula is the home of the Alaska moose, **the largest deer in the world.** [The adjectives *the* and *largest* and the adjective phrase *in the world* modify the appositive *deer.*]
Our graduating class is planning to hold a reunion on Monday, January 1, 2001, **the first day of the twenty-first century.** [The adjectives *the* and *first* and the adjective phrase *of the twenty-first century* all modify the appositive *day.*]

REVIEW F

Identifying Prepositional, Verbal, and Appositive Phrases

Identify each italicized phrase in the following paragraph as a *prepositional phrase*, a *participial phrase*, a *gerund phrase*, an *infinitive phrase*, or an *appositive phrase*. Do not separately identify a prepositional phrase that is part of a larger phrase.

Each year, thousands of Americans travel [1] *to hundreds of vacation spots in the United States and other countries.* [2] *Anticipating all kinds of weather and activities,* many eager travelers pack far too much clothing and equipment. The most effective way to pack is [3] *to set out clothes for the trip* and then to put half of them back [4] *in the closet.* Of course, travelers should give particularly careful thought to walking shoes, [5] *the most important item of apparel on any sightseeing trip.* Experienced travelers pack only two or three changes of casual clothing, even if they plan [6] *to be away for some time.* [7] *Taking out the smallest piece of luggage they own,* they study its capacity carefully. It is possible [8] *to pack enough clothes for three weeks* in a small duffel bag or shoulder bag. Passengers can easily carry this kind of bag onto an airliner and avoid [9] *waiting at the baggage claim area.* For most people, a bit of hand laundry every few days is preferable to spending their vacation [10] *burdened with heavy suitcases.*

PICTURE THIS

You always knew you'd find a way to travel around the world and satisfy your longing for adventure. As a successful travel writer, you've managed to make your dreams come true. This month you're traveling aboard this schooner along the Great Barrier Reef off the coast of Australia, where fantastic sights like the ones on the next page give you plenty to write about. Write one or two paragraphs to include in your next article. Use at least three verbal phrases and two appositive phrases to add vivid detail to your writing.

Subject: sailing along the northwestern coast of Australia
Audience: readers of a travel magazine
Purpose: to record events of your journey; to describe exotic sights for your readers

Review: Posttest 1

A. Identifying Phrases

Identify the italicized phrase in each of the following sentences as a *prepositional phrase*, a *participial phrase*, a *gerund phrase*, an *infinitive phrase*, or an *appositive phrase*. Do not separately identify a prepositional phrase that is part of a larger phrase.

EXAMPLE **1.** *Talking after the bell rings* is strictly forbidden.
1. *gerund phrase*

1. *Working on the school newspaper* has taught me responsibility.
2. *Delayed by the snowstorm*, the flight from Chicago to Seattle was finally cleared for takeoff.

3. Today's crossword puzzle is difficult *to complete correctly*.
4. If you want *to go to the concert tonight*, give me a call after school.
5. At the beginning of class today, we sang "La Marseillaise," *the French national anthem*.
6. Preserving rare and valuable books and documents is one of the challenges *facing the Library of Congress*.
7. The emu, *a flightless bird from Australia*, is similar to the ostrich.
8. Franklin's history report was on Booker T. Washington, founder *of Tuskegee Institute*.
9. Refreshed by the cool breeze, I didn't object to *going back to work*.
10. The United States, a true "melting pot," has been greatly enriched *by many diverse cultures*.

B. Identifying Phrases

Identify each italicized phrase in the following paragraph as a *prepositional phrase*, a *participial phrase*, a *gerund phrase*, an *infinitive phrase*, or an *appositive phrase*. Do not separately identify a prepositional phrase that is part of a larger phrase.

By **[11]** *being elected to the Baseball Hall of Fame in 1953*, Charles Albert Bender became a symbol of pride for all Native Americans. Bender, **[12]** *born in 1884 in Crow Wing County, Minnesota*, was half Chippewa. "Chief," **[13]** *the nickname given to him by his teammates*, stuck with him throughout his career. **[14]** *Pitching for the Philadelphia Athletics* was his first job in baseball. Although he never played **[15]** *on a minor league team*, he pitched a four-hit victory in his first game. He won twenty-three games and lost only five during the 1910 season, **[16]** *the best season of his career*. **[17]** *During that same year*, he had an earned-run average of 1.58. If it was crucial **[18]** *to win a game*, Connie Mack, the Athletics' manager, would always send Bender to the mound. **[19]** *Finishing with a lifetime total of 212 wins and only 128 losses*, Bender led the American League three times in winning percentage. His last full active year as a pitcher was 1917, but he returned to the mound **[20]** *to pitch one inning for the White Sox in 1925*.

Review: Posttest 2

Writing Sentences with Phrases

Write ten sentences according to the following guidelines. In each of your sentences, underline the italicized phrase given, and tell what kind of phrase it is.

1. Use *whistling softly* as a participial phrase.
2. Use *to go* as an infinitive used as a modifier.
3. Use *with the green shirt* as an adjective phrase.
4. Use *with kindness* as an adverb phrase modifying an adjective.
5. Use *for me* as an adverb phrase modifying a verb.
6. Use *of fruits and vegetables* as an adjective phrase.
7. Use *buying a gift for Jane* as a participial phrase.
8. Use *diving into the pool* as a gerund phrase.
9. Use *to be happy* as an infinitive phrase used as a noun.
10. Use *a city in Mexico* as an appositive phrase.

20 THE CLAUSE

Adjective, Noun, Adverb Clauses

Diagnostic Test

A. Identifying Independent and Subordinate Clauses

Identify the italicized word group in each of the following sentences as an *independent clause* or a *subordinate clause*. Then classify each italicized subordinate clause as an *adjective clause*, an *adverb clause*, or a *noun clause*.

EXAMPLE **1.** This novel, *which is the latest best-seller,* will be the perfect birthday gift for my mother.
  1. *subordinate clause; adjective clause*

  1. *If there is an increase in the amount of carbon dioxide present in the atmosphere,* plant growth also will increase.
  2. *Many Americans believed in and voted for the New Deal,* which was the political philosophy of Franklin D. Roosevelt.
  3. *When you travel abroad,* you gain greater perspective on being American.

GRAMMAR

4. Amy thought *that "The Rockpile" was the best short story in our Literature book,* and she asked the librarian to help her find other stories by James Baldwin.
5. *Since both of Len's parents are short,* Len doesn't expect to be tall.
6. The governor had to answer several questions about the budget *after he addressed the legislature.*
7. Please turn down that stereo *so that I can do my homework.*
8. In 1981 Sandra Day O'Connor, *who had been an Arizona judge,* became the first female Supreme Court Justice.
9. Scientists are carefully monitoring *how much carbon dioxide is present in the atmosphere.*
10. *The Civil War, often called the War Between the States, resulted in the deaths of more than 600,000 Americans;* it devastated the nation socially, politically, and economically.

B. Classifying Sentences According to Structure

Classify each of the following sentences as *simple, compound, complex,* or *compound-complex.*

11. A familiar proverb states that the longest journey begins with a single step; another tells us that little strokes fell great oaks.
12. Many people have heard these wise sayings but haven't applied them to their own lives.
13. For example, suppose you are required to read a 400-page novel before a test at the end of the school year.
14. If you don't start reading the book until the last possible weekend, you will probably not read it well; furthermore, you may not have time to finish the book, and you will almost certainly not enjoy it!
15. Instead, if you start now and read just ten pages a day, you'll be finished within six weeks.
16. The championship golfer Chi Chi Rodriguez knows this technique for completing a large project in small sections.
17. When Rodriguez was a child in Puerto Rico, he learned this approach from his father, who wanted to plant corn in a small field that was thickly overgrown with bamboo.
18. Mr. Rodriguez could not afford to take several weeks off from his job to clear the whole field, so every evening after work, he would cut down a single bamboo plant.

19. Gradually, the field was cleared, and by the following spring, the Rodriguez family was eating corn for dinner.
20. Today, Chi Chi Rodriguez and his dedicated staff at the Chi Chi Rodriguez Youth Foundation help hundreds and hundreds of disadvantaged youngsters—one child at a time.

20a. A *clause* is a group of words that contains a verb and its subject and is used as part of a sentence.

Every clause has a subject and a verb. Not every clause, however, expresses a complete thought.

SENTENCE Lichens are small plants that are composed of both fungi and algae.
CLAUSE Lichens are small plants. [complete thought]
CLAUSE that are composed of both fungi and algae [incomplete thought]

There are two kinds of clauses: the *independent clause* and the *subordinate clause*. When an independent clause stands alone, it is generally called a simple sentence. Like a word or a phrase, a subordinate clause functions as a single part of speech in a sentence.

The Independent Clause

20b. An *independent* (or *main*) *clause* expresses a complete thought and can stand by itself as a sentence.

EXAMPLES **Ms. Martin explained the binary number system.** [one independent clause]

In the binary system, each number is expressed in powers of two, and only the digits *0* and *1* are used. [two independent clauses joined by *and*]

                             S   V
The binary number system is important to know

           S   V
because it is used by computers. [an independent
clause combined with a subordinate clause]

The Subordinate Clause

20c. A *subordinate* (or *dependent*) *clause* does not
express a complete thought and cannot stand
alone as a sentence.

EXAMPLES   that we collected
            what Hui Su named her pet beagle
            when Rudy proofread his essay

The thought expressed by a subordinate clause becomes
complete when the clause is combined with an independent
clause.

EXAMPLES   Mr. Platero took the aluminum cans **that we collected**
            to the recycling center.
            Do you know **what Hui Su named her pet beagle**?
            When Rudy proofread his essay, he found several
            typographical errors.

EXERCISE 1   **Identifying Independent and
              Subordinate Clauses**

Identify each italicized word group in the following paragraph
as an *independent clause* or a *subordinate clause*.

EXAMPLE   [1] The photographs on the next page show *how eggs
           are processed in a large processing plant.*
           1. *subordinate clause*

[1] Large plants like the one in the photographs are *where
most eggs are processed today.* [2] After an egg is laid, *it gently rolls
along the slanted floor of the cage to a narrow conveyor belt.* [3] These
narrow conveyor belts converge into one wide belt *that runs
directly into the processing plant.* [4] *As soon as the eggs reach the processing plant,* they are automatically sprayed with detergent and

water. [5] The eggs then pass through a specially lit inspection area, *where defective eggs can be detected and removed.* [6] After the eggs are weighed, *they are separated by weight into groups.* [7] Each group of eggs goes onto a separate conveyor belt, *which leads to a forklike lifting device.* [8] This device lifts six eggs at a time *while the empty egg cartons wait two feet below it.* [9] *The eggs are gently lowered into the cartons,* which are then shipped to grocery stores and supermarkets. [10] *What is truly amazing* is that no human hands ever touch the eggs during the entire process.

The Adjective Clause

20d. An *adjective clause* is a subordinate clause that modifies a noun or a pronoun.

An adjective clause always follows the word or words that it modifies.

EXAMPLES
In the 1930s, Dr. Charles Richter devised a scale **that is used to measure the magnitude of earthquakes.** [The adjective clause modifies the noun *scale.*]

Ferdinand Magellan, **who was the commander of the first expedition around the world,** was killed before the end of the journey. [The adjective clause modifies the noun *Ferdinand Magellan.*]

Didn't John Kieran once say, "I am a part of all **that I have read"**? [The adjective clause modifies the pronoun *all.*]

GRAMMAR

Relative Pronouns

Usually, an adjective clause begins with a *relative pronoun*—a word that not only relates an adjective clause to the word or words the clause modifies but also serves a function within the clause.

Relative Pronouns				
that	which	who	whom	whose

EXAMPLES   I have read nearly every novel **that Shirley Ann Grau has written.** [The relative pronoun *that* relates the adjective clause to the noun *novel* and serves as the direct object of the verb *has written.*]

The treasure **for which they are searching** belonged to the Aztec emperor Montezuma II. [The relative pronoun *which* relates the adjective clause to the noun *treasure* and serves as the object of the preposition *for.*]

Grandma Moses, **who began painting at the age of seventy-six,** became famous for her primitive style of art. [The relative pronoun *who* relates the adjective clause to the noun *Grandma Moses* and also serves as the subject of the verb *began.*]

An adjective clause may begin with a relative adverb, such as *when* or *where*.

EXAMPLES   Uncle Chim told Lori and me about the time **when he backpacked across the island of Luzon.** [The adjective clause modifies the noun *time.*]
From 1914 to 1931, Isak Dinesen lived in Kenya, **where she operated a coffee plantation.** [The adjective clause modifies the noun *Kenya.*]

Sometimes the relative pronoun or relative adverb is not expressed, but its meaning is understood.

EXAMPLES   The book [that] I am reading is a biography of Harriet Tubman.
We will never forget the wonderful summer [when] we stayed with our grandparents in Mayaguez, Puerto Rico.

Depending on how it is used, an adjective clause is either essential or nonessential. An *essential clause* provides information that is necessary to the meaning of a sentence. A *nonessential clause* provides additional information that can be omitted without changing the meaning of a sentence. A nonessential clause is always set off by commas.

ESSENTIAL	Students **who are going to the track meet** can take the bus at 7:45 A.M. [Omitting the adjective clause would change the meaning of the sentence.]
NONESSENTIAL	Nancy Stevens, **whose father is a pediatrician,** plans to study medicine. [The adjective clause gives extra information. Omitting the clause would not affect the meaning of the sentence.]

☞ REFERENCE NOTE: For more about punctuating nonessential clauses, see pages 851–852.

EXERCISE 2

Identifying Adjective Clauses and the Words They Modify

Identify the adjective clause in each of the following sentences, and give the noun or pronoun that it modifies. Then tell whether the relative pronoun is used as the *subject, direct object,* or *object of a preposition* in the adjective clause.

EXAMPLE **1.** Theo, who is the editor of the school newspaper, wrote an article about the inhumane treatment of laboratory animals.
   1. *who is the editor of the school newspaper; Theo; subject*

1. Some of us have read *Native Son,* which was written by Richard Wright.
2. The book to which he referred was ordered yesterday.
3. In March many countries have festivals that can be traced back to ancient celebrations of spring.
4. The fish that I caught yesterday weighed three pounds.
5. The nominee was a statesman whom everyone admired.
6. It's not easy to understand someone who mumbles.
7. They finally found my briefcase, which had been missing for weeks.
8. Please indicate the people to whom we should go for help.
9. The guide advised those who enjoy Native American art to visit the new exhibit of Hopi weaving and pottery.
10. Everyone cheered for the player that had the better serve.

GRAMMAR

PICTURE THIS

You've been fascinated by archaeology ever since you saw *Raiders of the Lost Ark*. This summer, you're working as a volunteer on this large excavation in Mexico. After a day of digging in the hot sun, you realize that archaeology isn't nearly as glamorous as it looks in the movies. But you're learning many things, and you've experienced the excitement of finding your first artifact—a large shard of Mayan pottery. After the day's work is done, you head back to your tent and begin writing in your journal. Write a journal entry telling about your first day at the excavation site. Tell how you feel about making your first archaeological find. In your journal entry, use at least five adjective clauses to add descriptive details to your sentences.

Subject: archaeological dig in Mexico
Audience: yourself
Purpose: to record the day's events and to express your
           feelings about them

The Noun Clause

20e. A *noun clause* is a subordinate clause used as a noun.

A noun clause may be used as a subject, a predicate nominative, a direct object, an indirect object, or an object of a preposition.

Subject	**That Ntozake Shange is a talented writer** is an understatement.
Predicate Nominative	A catchy slogan is **what we need for this campaign.**
Direct Object	The Greek astonomer Ptolemy believed **that the sun orbited the earth.**
Indirect Object	The choreographer will give **whoever can dance the best** the role of Snow Princess.
Object of a Preposition	Grandmother Gutiérrez has a kind word for **whomever she meets.**

Common Introductory Words for Noun Clauses				
what	whatever	whichever	whoever	whomever
that	which	who	whom	whose
how	whether	when	where	why

The word that introduces a noun clause may or may not have another function in the clause.

EXAMPLES   Do you know **who painted *Washington Crossing the Delaware?*** [The word *who* introduces the noun clause and serves as the subject of the verb *painted.*]
Ms. Picard, an environmentalist, will explain **what the greenhouse effect is.** [The word *what* introduces the noun clause and serves as the predicate nominative to complete the meaning of the verb *is.*]
She said **that she would be late.** [The word *that* introduces the noun clause but does not have any function within the noun clause.]

EXERCISE 3   Identifying Noun Clauses

Identify the noun clause in each of the following sentences. Tell whether the noun clause is a *subject*, a *direct object*, an *indirect object*, a *predicate nominative*, or an *object of a preposition*.

EXAMPLES **1.** Please address your letter to whoever manages the store.
1. *whoever manages the store; object of a preposition*

2. Do you know where the new municipal center is?
2. *where the new municipal center is; direct object*

1. Would you please tell me what the past tense of the verb *swing* is?
2. I will listen carefully to whatever you say.
3. Whatever you decide will be fine with me.
4. Give whoever wants one a free pass.
5. That Jill was worried seemed obvious to us all.
6. Do you know why Eduardo missed the Cinco de Mayo celebration?
7. The teacher said we could leave now.
8. In biology class we learned how hornets build their nests.
9. You can appoint whomever you like.
10. A remote desert island was where the pirates buried their treasure.

▶ REVIEW A **Distinguishing Between Adjective and Noun Clauses**

Identify the subordinate clause in each of the following sentences. Tell whether the subordinate clause is used as an *adjective* or a *noun*. Then give the word that each adjective clause modifies, and state whether each noun clause is used as a *subject*, a *direct object*, an *object of a preposition*, or a *predicate nominative*.

EXAMPLE **1.** Until recently, most scientists believed that the giant sequoias of California were the oldest living trees on earth.
1. *that the giant sequoias of California were the oldest living trees on earth—noun; direct object*

1. Now, however, that honor is given to the bristlecone pine, a small, gnarled tree that few people have ever heard of.
2. Botanists estimate that some bristlecone pines are more than six thousand years old.
3. The oldest sequoias are only 2,200 years old, according to those who know.
4. Whoever respects hardiness has to respect the bristlecone.
5. The high altitude of the Rocky Mountains, the bristlecone's natural habitat, is what makes the tree grow so slowly.

6. Do you think the bristlecone
   pine will win any beauty contests?
7. Judge by what you can see in
   this photograph.

8. The bristlecone's needles last on the branches for twelve to
   fifteen years, a length of time that is extraordinary.
9. Botanists tell us that the bristlecone is a member of the
   foxtail family.
10. Like all members of this family, the bristlecone has needle
    clusters that resemble a fox's tail.

The Adverb Clause

20f. An *adverb clause* is a subordinate clause that
modifies a verb, an adjective, or an adverb.

An adverb clause tells *how, when, where, why, to what extent,* or
under what condition.

EXAMPLES   The pitcher felt **as though all eyes were on her.** [The
            adverb clause modifies the verb *felt,* telling *how* the
            pitcher felt.]
            Frédéric Chopin made his debut as a concert pianist
            when he was eight years old. [The adverb clause
            modifies the verb *made,* telling *when* Chopin made
            his debut.]
            Ariel takes his new camera **wherever he goes.** [The
            adverb clause modifies the verb *takes,* telling *where*
            Ariel takes his new camera.]

At first, communicating with my deaf friend was difficult **because I did not know how to sign.** [The adverb clause modifies the adjective *difficult,* telling *why* communicating was difficult.]

Zoe can explain the theory of relativity to you better **than I can.** [The adverb clause modifies the adverb **better,** telling *to what extent* Zoe can better explain the theory of relativity.]

If we leave now, we will avoid the rush-hour traffic. [The adverb clause modifies the verb *will avoid,* telling *under what condition* we will avoid the traffic.]

Subordinating Conjunctions

An adverb clause is introduced by a *subordinating conjunction*—a word or word group that relates the adverb clause to the word or words the clause modifies.

Common Subordinating Conjunctions			
after	as though	provided that	until
although	as well as	since	when
as	because	so that	whenever
as if	before	than	where
as long as	if	through	wherever
as soon as	in order that	unless	while

☞ **REFERENCE NOTE:** The words *after, as, before, since,* and *until* may also be used as prepositions. See pages 571–572.

The Elliptical Clause

20g. Part of a clause may be left out when the meaning can be understood from the context of the sentence. Such a clause is called an *elliptical clause.*

Most elliptical clauses are adverb clauses. In each of the adverb clauses in the following examples, the part given in brackets may be omitted because its meaning is clearly understood.

EXAMPLES   Roger knew the rules better **than Elgin** [did].
   While [he was] **painting,** Rembrandt concentrated completely on his work.

▶ EXERCISE 4 **Identifying Adverb Clauses and the Words They Modify**

Identify the adverb clause in each of the following sentences, and give the word or words that the clause modifies. Then state whether the clause tells *how, when, where, why, to what extent,* or *under what condition*. [Note: If a clause is elliptical, be prepared to supply the omitted word or words.]

EXAMPLE **1.** If we stop by the mall, we might be late for the movie.
1. *If we stop by the mall; might be; under what condition*

1. When our school has a fire drill, everyone must go outside.
2. Your trip to New York will not be complete unless you see the Alvin Ailey Dance Theater.
3. She walked until she was too tired to take another step.
4. Because he was late so often, he bought a watch.
5. Gazelles need to be able to run fast so that they can escape their enemies.
6. Return this revolutionary, new sonic potato peeler for a full refund if not completely satisfied.
7. As soon as you're ready, we'll leave.
8. You can help by setting the table while I prepare the salad.
9. I visited the collection of Aztec artifacts because I wanted to see the religious and solar calendars.
10. You understand the situation much better than I.

▶ REVIEW B **Identifying Independent and Subordinate Clauses**

In the following paragraph, identify each italicized clause as *independent* or *subordinate*. If the italicized clause is subordinate, tell whether it is used as an *adverb*, an *adjective*, or a *noun*.

EXAMPLE [1] *When thinking of Native Americans,* many people immediately picture the Dakota Sioux.
1. *subordinate—adverb*

Do you know [1] *why the Dakota spring to mind?* I think it is [2] *because they are known for their impressive eagle-feather head-dresses.* Until recently, [3] *if an artist painted or drew Native Americans of any region,* the people were usually shown wearing

Dakota headdresses, fringed buckskin shirts, and elaborately beaded moccasins. Even paintings of the Pemaquid people receiving the Pilgrims [4] *as they landed on Cape Cod* show the Pemaquid dressed in the style of the Dakota, [5] *who lived far away in the northern plains region.* Artists apparently did not recognize [6] *that there are many different groups of Native Americans.* Each group has its own traditional clothing, and [7] *the variety of Native American dress is truly amazing.* For example, [8] *compare the turbans and bearclaw necklaces of these Fox men with the headband and turquoise jewelry of this Navajo boy.* [9] *While these images may not be familiar to you,* they are just as authentic as the image of the Dakota. To see other colorful and unique styles of dress, you might want to research the clothing worn by Native Americans [10] *that live in different regions of the United States.*

Charles Milton Bell (1890)/From the Collection of Kurt Koegler

Carl Moon (1905)/From the Collection of Kurt Koegler

Sentences Classified According to Structure

20h. According to their structure, sentences are classified as *simple, compound, complex,* and *compound-complex.*

(1) A *simple sentence* has one independent clause and no subordinate clauses.

EXAMPLES Uncle Alan taught me how to play the mandolin.
The spotted owl is an endangered species.
Covered with dust and cobwebs, the old bicycle looked terrible but worked just fine.

(2) A *compound sentence* has two or more independent clauses but no subordinate clauses.

Independent clauses may be joined together by a comma and a coordinating conjunction (*and, but, for, nor, or, so,* or *yet*); by a semicolon; or by a semicolon and a conjunctive adverb or a transitional expression.

EXAMPLES Lorenzo's story sounded incredible, but it was true. [two independent clauses joined by a comma and the coordinating conjunction *but*]

Agatha Christie was a prolific writer; she wrote more than eighty books in sixty years. [two independent clauses joined by a semicolon]

The defeat of Napoleon at Waterloo was a victory for England; however, it brought to an end an era of French grandeur. [two independent clauses joined by a semicolon and the conjunctive adverb *however*]

Common Conjunctive Adverbs		
also	however	nevertheless
anyway	instead	otherwise
besides	likewise	still
consequently	meanwhile	then
furthermore	moreover	therefore

Common Transitional Expressions		
as a result	for example	in other words
at any rate	in addition	on the contrary
by the way	in fact	on the other hand

NOTE: Do not confuse a simple sentence that has a compound subject or a compound predicate with a compound sentence.

EXAMPLES The archaeological discovery was made in the fall and was widely acclaimed the following spring. [simple sentence with compound predicate]
The archaeological discovery was made in the fall, and it was widely acclaimed the following spring. [compound sentence]

(3) A *complex sentence* has one independent clause and at least one subordinate clause.

EXAMPLES Thurgood Marshall, who served on the United States Supreme Court for twenty-four years, retired in 1991. [The independent clause is *Thurgood Marshall retired in 1991.* The subordinate clause is *who served on the United States Supreme Court for twenty-four years.*]

While we were on our vacation in Washington, D.C., we visited the Folger Shakespeare Library. [The independent clause is *we visited the Folger Shakespeare Library.* The subordinate clause is *While we were on vacation in Washington, D.C.*]

(4) A *compound-complex sentence* has two or more independent clauses and at least one subordinate clause.

EXAMPLES The two eyewitnesses told the police officer what they saw, but their accounts of the accident were quite different. [The two independent clauses are *The two eyewitnesses told the police officer* and *their accounts of the accident were quite different.* The subordinate clause is *what they saw.*]

Chelsea is only seven years old, but she can already play the violin better than her tutor can. [The two independent clauses are *Chelsea is only seven years old* and *she can already play the violin better.* The subordinate clause is *than her tutor can.*]

EXERCISE 5 Classifying Sentences According to Structure

Classify each of the following sentences as *simple, compound, complex,* or *compound-complex.*

EXAMPLE **1.** Using the pith of the papyrus plant, ancient Egyptians made the first paper.
1. *simple*

1. Charles Drew did research on blood plasma and helped develop blood banks.
2. Supposedly, if the month of March comes in like a lion, it goes out like a lamb.
3. The Malayans believe that sickness will follow the eating of stolen foods.
4. When World War I ended in 1918, many people thought that there would be no more wars; but twenty-one years later, World War II began.
5. In his letter to Mrs. Bixby, Abraham Lincoln consoled her for the loss of several sons and hoped that time would ease her sorrow.
6. After the announcement of the final score, all of us fans cheered the team and clapped enthusiastically.
7. In England and Wales, salmon was once king, yet few salmon rivers remain.
8. The English philosopher Thomas Hobbes once aspired to be a mathematician, but he never fulfilled this ambition.
9. As an older woman, Queen Elizabeth I always wore a dark-red wig, so no one knew whether her own hair had grayed or not.
10. Zina Garrison is considered by many to be one of the best tennis players in America.

WRITING APPLICATION

Using a Variety of Sentence Structures

Style and sense go hand in hand in writing. You may have the most interesting topic in the world, but if your writing style isn't smooth and appealing, you may not hold your reader's interest. One of the best ways to improve your style is to vary the length and structure of your sentences.

As you read the following passage, notice how the writer has used a variety of sentence structures to create an engaging style.

> It was a popular exhibit, and sometimes, when there were too many children about, the entrance had to be roped off, as the children loved to race up and down the blood vessels and match their cries to the heart's beating. I could see that the heart had already been punished for the day—the floor of the blood vessel was worn and dusty, the chamber walls were covered with marks, and the notice "You Are Now Taking the Path of a Blood Cell Through the Human Heart" hung askew. I wanted to see more of the Franklin Institute and the Natural Science Museum across the street, but a journey through the human heart would be fascinating. Did I have time?
>
> Janet Frame, "You Are Now Entering the Human Heart"

▶ WRITING ACTIVITY

The student council has asked your class to write a guide book, describing popular attractions in your area. The purpose of the guide book is to inform new students and their families about the area. Write an entry for the guide book, telling about a local attraction that people might enjoy visiting. Use a variety of sentence structures to add variety and interest to your writing.

Prewriting If you were a newcomer to your area, what exhibits, landmarks, historical sites, and other attractions would you find interesting? Brainstorm a list of points of interest in your city or area. Then choose one attraction that you are familiar with. If possible, visit the attraction and take notes for your description. Be sure to note down specific details, such as when the place is open to the public, how much admission is, and why it's worth a visit.

Writing Begin your guide book entry by identifying the name, location, and significance of the attraction. Then capture your reader's interest with a clear, vivid description of the place. Since your paragraph will appear in a guide book, be sure to use formal English. (For more about formal English, see pages 484–485.)

 Evaluating and Revising Ask a friend to read your paragraph. Does your description give a clear, accurate picture of the attraction? Does it convince your reader that the attraction is worth visiting? Does it give exact information about how to get there and when to go? If not, add, cut, and rearrange details to include all important information. After you've revised the content of your paragraph, read it with an eye for style. Use sentence-combining techniques to vary the structure of your sentences. (For more about sentence combining, see pages 526–538.

Proofreading and Publishing Proofread your paragraph for any errors in grammar, usage, or mechanics. Watch out for subordinate clauses punctuated as if they were complete sentences. (For more about sentence fragments, see pages 515–519.) Your class may want to compile a guide book for your area. Double-check all the information included in your paragraphs. Then type the paragraphs neatly and collect them in a binder. Place your guide book in a central location in your school so that anyone can read it, or make photocopies to give to new students.

Review: Posttest 1

A. Identifying Independent and Subordinate Clauses

Identify the italicized clause in each of the following sentences as *independent* or *subordinate*. If the italicized clause is subordinate, tell whether it is used as an *adverb,* an *adjective,* or a *noun.*

EXAMPLE **1.** Miguel and Bette, *who were visiting us over the weekend,* have returned to Rhode Island.
　　　　1. *subordinate; adjective*

1. *Whenever Jorge practices the clarinet,* his neighbor's beagle howls.
2. Advertisements encourage people to want products, and *many people cannot distinguish between their wants and their needs.*
3. In science class we learned *that chalk is made up mostly of calcium carbonate.*
4. Liliuokalani, *who was the last queen of Hawaii,* was an accomplished songwriter.
5. Does each of you know *how you can protect yourself* if a tornado strikes?
6. *If there is a tornado warning,* go quickly to the lowest level in your house, cover your head with your hands, and lie flat or crouch low until the danger is past.
7. The Native Americans *who inhabited the area of Connecticut around the Naugatuck River* were called the Pequots.
8. *When you enter the school,* the principal's office is the third room on your right.
9. *That the girls' volleyball team was well coached* was clearly demonstrated last night when the team won the state championship.
10. *American music has been enriched by Ella Fitzgerald, Leslie Uggams, and Lena Horne,* who are all contemporary black vocalists.

B. Classifying Sentences According to Structure

Classify each sentence in the following paragraph as *simple, compound, complex,* or *compound-complex.*

[11] Just who is Phoebe Jeter from Sharon, South Carolina? [12] Phoebe Jeter, officially known as Lieutenant Jeter, led an army platoon during the Persian Gulf Conflict in 1991. [13] Jeter will always remember the tense January night when she heard the words "Scud alert!" [14] On her orders, thirteen Patriot missiles were fired, and at least two Scud missiles were destroyed. [15] When the Conflict was over, Jeter was the only woman who had shot down a Scud! [16] That 40 percent of the women who served in the Gulf were African Americans may be an understatement. [17] Figures have not been released by the Pentagon, but some say the actual number may have been closer to 50 percent. [18] The Persian Gulf Conflict tested the mettle of all

female military personnel; throughout the conflict, women shared hazardous assignments, primitive living conditions, and various battle responsibilities with men. **[19]** Their professionalism and courage earned the women who served in the Gulf considerable respect. **[20]** Perhaps now, because of soldiers like Phoebe Jeter, people will think differently about the role of women in the United States armed forces.

Review: Posttest 2

Writing a Variety of Sentence Structures

Write ten sentences according to the following guidelines:

1. a simple sentence with a compound subject
2. a compound sentence with the conjunction *but*
3. a complex sentence with an adverb clause modifying an adverb
4. a complex sentence with an adverb clause modifying an adjective
5. a complex sentence with an adjective clause introduced by the relative pronoun *who*
6. a complex sentence with an adjective clause introduced by the relative pronoun *that*
7. a complex sentence with a noun clause used as the subject of the sentence
8. a complex sentence with a noun clause used as the direct object of the sentence
9. a complex sentence with an elliptical adverb clause
10. a compound-complex sentence

21 AGREEMENT

Subject and Verb, Pronoun and Antecedent

Diagnostic Test

A. Choosing Correct Forms for Subject-Verb and Pronoun-Antecedent Agreement

For each of the following sentences, choose the word in parentheses that completes the sentence correctly.

EXAMPLE   **1.** Both Arapaho and Cheyenne (*is, are*) part of the Algonquian language group of Native Americans.
     1. *are*

1. When I begin cutting out this skirt pattern, I know I'll discover that my scissors (*need, needs*) sharpening.
2. British sailors are frequently called "limeys" because the British navy (*was, were*) responsible for first using limes to prevent scurvy during long sea voyages.
3. Either Dad or my brother (*go, goes*) down to the store to buy a newspaper each morning.
4. In the San Ildefonso Village, two days (*is, are*) not considered a long time to spend polishing one piece of black pottery.

5. A small number of adults (*is, are*) coming along on our trip to Washington, D.C.
6. When Suzanne and Anita arrive, would you please help (*her, them*) find some good seats?
7. (*Here's, Here are*) those extra two tickets for tonight's rap concert at the arena.
8. Exactly one third of the students in my American history class (*is, are*) African American.
9. In-line skates (*is, are*) the fastest way of getting to my best friend's house.
10. *The Borrowers,* a fantasy story about some tiny people, (*was, were*) my favorite book when I was ten years old.

B. Choosing Correct Forms for Subject-Verb and Pronoun-Antecedent Agreement

For each sentence in the following paragraph, choose the word in parentheses that will complete the sentence correctly.

EXAMPLE   Kenny Walker is the only player in the NFL who
[1] (*has, have*) a hearing impairment.
1. *has*

The Denver Broncos, my favorite team, **[11]** (*was, were*) smart to choose Walker in the 1990 football draft. Walker certainly **[12]** (*don't, doesn't*) let his deafness keep him from being a great linebacker. Passed over by many a coach because **[13]** (*he, they*) thought a player who was deaf would be a problem, Walker was finally picked 228th by Denver. Even today, not everyone **[14]** (*know, knows*) that spinal meningitis cost Kenny Walker his hearing when he was two years old. Sign language and lip reading **[15]** (*was, were*) taught to him at a special school, beginning when he was four. Because of his hearing impairment, most of the neighborhood boys **[16]** (*was, were*) unwilling to choose Walker to be on a team. But after they saw him play, everyone wanted him on **[17]** (*their, his*) team! Now that Walker is a professional football player, neither he nor his coaches **[18]** (*has, have*) much difficulty with his deafness. One of the accommodations the Broncos made **[19]** (*was, were*) to hire a full-time interpreter to sign plays to Walker. Although he can't hear a sound, Walker feels the vibrations in his shoulder pads when the crowd **[20]** (*cheers, cheer*) him.

Number

Number is the form of a word that indicates whether the word is singular or plural.

 21a. A word that refers to one person or thing is *singular* in number. A word that refers to more than one is *plural* in number.

SINGULAR	computer	brush	story	woman	this	it
PLURAL	computers	brushes	stories	women	these	they

Agreement of Subject and Verb

21b. A verb should agree with its subject in number.

(1) Singular subjects take singular verbs.

EXAMPLES   My **grandfather trains** dogs.
The **senator is** in favor of the bill.
She owns and **operates** a video store.

(2) Plural subjects take plural verbs.

EXAMPLES   My **grandparents train** dogs.
Many **senators are** in favor of the bill.
They own and **operate** a video store.

Like the one-word verb in each of the preceding examples, a verb phrase must also agree in number with its subject. The number of a verb phrase is indicated by the form of its first auxiliary (helping) verb.

EXAMPLES   This **song was performed** by Bonnie Raitt. [singular subject and verb phrase]
These **songs were performed** by Bonnie Raitt. [plural subject and verb phrase]

The dancer **has been rehearsing** since noon. [singular subject and verb phrase]
The dancers **have been rehearsing** since noon. [plural subject and verb phrase]

Intervening Phrases and Clauses

21c. The number of the subject is not changed by a phrase or a clause following the subject.

EXAMPLES This **tape is** by the Boston Pops Orchestra.
This **tape** of songs **is** by the Boston Pops Orchestra.
[The prepositional phrase *of songs* does not affect the number of the subject *tape.*]

The **characters represent** abstract ideas.
The **characters** in an allegory **represent** abstract ideas.
[The prepositional phrase *in an allegory* does not affect the number of the subject *characters.*]

Langston Hughes was a major influence in the Harlem Renaissance.
Langston Hughes, who wrote *The Weary Blues* and other books of poems, **was** a major influence in the Harlem Renaissance. [The adjective clause *who wrote The Weary Blues and other books of poems* does not affect the number of the subject *Langston Hughes.*]

The number of the subject is also not affected when the subject is followed by a phrase that begins with an expression such as *along with, as well as, in addition to,* and *together with.*

EXAMPLES The history **teacher,** as well as her students, **was fascinated** by the exhibit of artifacts at the DuSable Museum of African American History. [singular subject and verb]
The history **students,** as well as their teacher, **were fascinated** by the exhibit of artifacts at the DuSable Museum of African American History. [plural subject and verb]

EXERCISE 1 **Identifying Subjects and Verbs That Agree in Number**

For each of the following sentences, identify the subject of the verb in parentheses. Then choose the verb form that agrees in number with the subject.

EXAMPLE **1.** The many varieties of American quilts (*reflect, reflects*) the spirit of the people who developed them.
1. *varieties—reflect*

1. During the Colonial Period, only women of means made quilts; however, by the mid-nineteenth century, women throughout the United States (*was making, were making*) quilts.
2. The abilities that someone needs to make a quilt (*include, includes*) patience, coordination, and a good sense of color and design.
3. A scrap-bag full of colorful bits of cotton and wool fabrics (*was put, were put*) to good use in a quilt.
4. Usable fabric from worn-out shirts, as well as from other articles of clothing, (*was cut, were cut*) into pieces of various shapes and sizes.
5. The Amish people, known for their beautiful quilting, (*live, lives*) very simply.
6. Amish quilts, which are often brightly colored, (*seem, seems*) to convey the joyous spirits of their makers.
7. Several quilters, gathering at one person's home for a quilting bee, often (*work, works*) on a quilt together.
8. Quilts designed by the Amish usually (*include, includes*) only solid-color fabrics, not patterned ones.
9. This quilt, which features colors typical to Amish quilts, (*glow, glows*) with red, purple, blue, pink, and green.
10. In contrast, the clothing worn by Amish women (*is, are*) more subdued in color.

USAGE

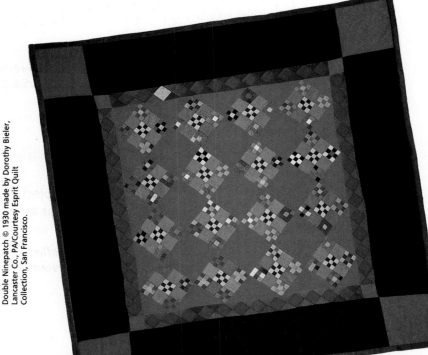

Double Ninepatch © 1930 made by Dorothy Bieler, Lancaster Co., PA/Courtesy Esprit Quilt Collection, San Francisco.

Indefinite Pronouns

21d. The following indefinite pronouns are singular:
one, anybody, anyone, each, either, everybody, everyone, neither, nobody, no one, somebody, and *someone.*

EXAMPLES **Neither** of the books **contains** any illustrations.
Everyone in the Pep Club **is wearing** the school colors.
One of the most beautiful places in North Carolina **is** the Joyce Kilmer Memorial Forest.

21e. The following indefinite pronouns are plural:
both, few, many, and *several.*

EXAMPLES **Both** of the poems **were written** by Claude McKay.
Many of our words **are derived** from Latin.
Several of the juniors **have volunteered.**

21f. The following indefinite pronouns may be singular or plural: *all, any, most, none,* and *some.*

These pronouns are singular when they refer to singular words and are plural when they refer to plural words.

EXAMPLES **Some** of her artwork **is** beautiful. [*Some* refers to the singular noun *artwork.*]
Some of her paintings **are** beautiful. [*Some* refers to the plural noun *paintings.*]

None of the equipment **was damaged.** [*None* refers to the singular noun *equipment.*]
None of the machines **were damaged.** [*None* refers to the plural noun *machines.*]

Most of the food **has been eaten.** [*Most* refers to the singular noun *food.*]
Most of the sandwiches **have been eaten.** [*Most* refers to the plural noun *sandwiches.*]

NOTE: The word *none* is singular when it means "not one" and plural when it means "not any."

EXAMPLES **None** of the hats **fits.** [*Not one* fits.]
None of the hats **fit.** [*Not any* fit.]

▶ EXERCISE 2   **Identifying Subjects and Verbs That Agree in Number**

For each of the following sentences, identify the subject of the verb in parentheses. Then choose the verb form that agrees in number with the subject.

EXAMPLE   **1.** Not one of the pears (*look, looks*) ripe.
            1. *one—looks*

1. Many of the recipes in this cookbook (*is, are*) adaptable to microwave cooking.
2. Neither of my parents (*has, have*) any trouble using the metric system.
3. I know that all the workers (*is, are*) proud to help restore the Statue of Liberty.
4. Most of the English classes in my school (*stresses, stress*) composition skills.
5. Few of the students (*was, were*) able to spell *bureaucracy* correctly.
6. (*Do, Does*) each of you know what you're supposed to bring tomorrow?
7. No written language from the Inca civilization (*remain, remains*), but scholars have learned about these people through oral communication.
8. Some of the word-processing software for our computer (*has, have*) arrived late.
9. Both of the paintings (*shows, show*) the influence of the work of Emilio Sánchez.
10. Others besides you and me (*advocates, advocate*) a town cleanup day.

Compound Subjects

A *compound subject* is two or more subjects that have the same verb.

21g.   Subjects joined by *and* usually take a plural verb.

EXAMPLES   **Basil** and **thyme are** plants of the mint family.
            Following Julius Caesar's death, **Antony, Octavian, and Lepidus become** the rulers of Rome.

A compound subject may name a single person or thing. Such a compound subject takes a singular verb.

EXAMPLES   **The secretary** and **treasurer is** Gretchen. [one person]
Grilled chicken and **rice is** the restaurant's specialty. [one dish]

21h. Singular subjects joined by *or* or *nor* take a singular verb.

EXAMPLES   **Neither Juan nor Jeff wants** to see the movie.
Either Felita or Terry plans to report on Laotzu.
Has your **mother or** your **father met** your teacher?

21i. When a singular subject and a plural subject are joined by *or* or *nor,* the verb agrees with the subject nearer the verb.

EXAMPLES   Neither the **performers** nor the **director was** eager to rehearse the scene again. [The singular subject *director* is nearer the verb.]
Neither the **director** nor the **performers were** eager to rehearse the scene again. [The plural subject *performers* is nearer the verb.]

NOTE: Whenever possible, avoid this awkward construction.

EXAMPLE   The **director was** not eager to rehearse the scene again, and neither **were** the **performers.**

▶ EXERCISE 3 **Correcting Errors in Subject-Verb Agreement**

Most of the following sentences contain verbs that do not agree with their subjects. If the verb does not agree, give the correct form of the verb. If the verb agrees with its subject, write *C*.

EXAMPLE **1.** Each of the issues were resolved.
       1. *was*

1. Emily Dickinson's imagery and verse structure have been analyzed and praised by many critics.
2. One or both of the Shakespearean plays about Henry IV are likely to be performed this summer.
3. The effective date of the new regulations for nuclear power plants have not yet been determined.

4. Each of the region's environmental groups have already presented its recommendations to the governor.
5. My hero, Spike Lee, has made a great contribution to the film industry.
6. The fact that compact discs do not wear out and do not have to be flipped over make them attractive.
7. The sales representative, with the help of her assistant, are making plans to expand her territory.
8. Not one of the speakers in the debate on South America were eager to suggest a solution to the problem.
9. Neither the proposals of the air traffic controllers nor the report of the FAA's committee have been heeded.
10. James Baldwin, along with Richard Wright and Ralph Ellison, rank as one of the major African American writers of the twentieth century.

Special Problems in Subject-Verb Agreement

21j. The verb agrees with its subject, even when the verb precedes the subject.

The verb usually comes before its subject in sentences beginning with *Here* or *There* and in questions.

EXAMPLES   Here **is** a **copy** of my report.
Here **are** two **copies** of my report.

There **was** a **message** on her answering machine.
There **were** no **messages** on her answering machine.

Where **is Arsenio**?
Where **are Arsenio** and his **brother**?

NOTE: Contractions such as *here's, there's,* and *where's* contain the verb *is* (*here is, there is,* and *where is*). Use these contractions only with subjects that are singular in meaning.

NONSTANDARD	Here's your keys.
STANDARD	Here **are** your **keys.**
STANDARD	Here's your **set** of keys.

NONSTANDARD	Where's the islands located?
STANDARD	Where **are** the **islands** located?
STANDARD	Where's **each** of the islands located?

USAGE

21k. Collective nouns may be either singular or plural.

A *collective noun* is singular in form but names a group of persons or things.

Common Collective Nouns			
army	club	family	squadron
assembly	crowd	group	swarm
audience	fleet	herd	team
class	flock	public	troop

A collective noun takes a singular verb when the noun refers to the group as a unit and takes a plural verb when the noun refers to the parts or members of the group.

SINGULAR   The **band practices** every day. [The band practices as a unit.]

PLURAL   The **band buy** their own uniforms. [The members of the band buy separate uniforms.]

SINGULAR   The tour **group is** on the bus. [The group as a unit is on the bus.]

PLURAL   The tour **group are talking** about what they expect to see. [The members of the group are talking to one another.]

SINGULAR   A **flock** of geese **is** flying over. [The flock is flying as a unit.]

PLURAL   The **flock** of geese **are** joining together in a V-shaped formation. [The members of the flock are joining together.]

21l. An expression of an amount may be singular or plural.

An expression of an amount is singular when the amount is thought of as a unit and is plural when the amount is thought of as many parts.

EXAMPLES   **Five thousand bricks is** a heavy load for this truck. [The bricks are thought of as a unit.]
Five thousand bricks are what we need. [The bricks are thought of separately.]

> **Two days is** the amount of time we will spend visiting each college campus. [one unit]
> **Two days** of this month **are** school holidays. [separate days]

A fraction or a percentage is singular when it refers to a singular word and is plural when it refers to a plural word.

EXAMPLES   **One fourth** of the student body **is employed** part-time after school. [The fraction refers to the singular noun *student body.*]
One fourth of the students **are employed** after school. [The fraction refers to the plural noun *students.*]

Seventy-five percent of the junior class **is** sixteen years old. [The percentage refers to the singular noun *class.*]
Seventy-five percent of the juniors **are** sixteen years old. [The percentage refers to the plural noun *juniors.*]

Expressions of measurement (length, weight, capacity, area) are usually singular.

EXAMPLES   **Four and seven-tenths inches is** the diameter of a CD.
Eight fluid ounces equals one cup.
Two hundred kilometers was the distance we flew in the hot-air balloon.

NOTE: In the expression *number of*, the word *number* is singular when preceded by *the* and is plural when preceded by *a*.

EXAMPLES   The **number** of students taking computer courses **has increased.**
A **number** of students taking computer courses **belong** to the Computer Club.

▶ EXERCISE 4   **Selecting Verbs That Agree with Their Subjects**

For each of the following sentences, identify the subject of each verb in parentheses. Then choose the verb form that agrees in number with the subject.

EXAMPLE   **1.** The band (*is, are*) tuning their instruments.
1. *band—are*

1. The gigantic Colossus of Rhodes (*was, were*) one of the Seven Wonders of the Ancient World.
2. The stage crew (*has, have*) just made a rapid scene change for Rita Moreno's entrance.

3. Alertness, as well as stamina and strength, (*is, are*) important to rescue workers.
4. I think that the best thing about calculators (*is, are*) their speed in arriving at accurate answers.
5. The Hispanic population (*is, are*) now the fastest growing segment in American society.
6. On our block alone, over two hundred dollars (*was, were*) collected for the American Cancer Society.
7. Of the world's petroleum, approximately one third (*is, are*) produced by the United States.
8. Red beans and rice (*is, are*) often served as a side dish at Cajun meals.
9. Either brisk walks or jogging (*serves, serve*) as a healthful way to get daily exercise.
10. One sixth of the budget (*is, are*) allocated to health care.

21m. The title of a creative work (such as a book, song, film, or painting) or the name of a country (even if it is plural in form) takes a singular verb.

EXAMPLES   ***Those Who Ride the Night Winds* was written** by the poet Nikki Giovanni.
***Tales from the Vienna Woods* is** only one of Johann Strauss's most popular waltzes.
The **United States calls** its flag "Old Glory."
The **Philippines comprises** more than 7,000 islands.

21n. The name of an organization, though plural in form, usually takes a singular verb.

EXAMPLES   The **United Nations was formed** in 1945.
Avalon Textiles is located on King Street.

The names of some organizations, however, may take singular or plural verbs. When the name refers to the organization as a unit, it takes a singular verb. When the name refers to the members of the organization, it takes a plural verb.

EXAMPLES   The **New York Yankees has won** the World Series **twenty-two times.** [The New York Yankees has won as a unit.]
The **New York Yankees are signing** autographs. [The players are signing autographs.]

21o. Many nouns that are plural in form are singular in meaning.

(1) The following nouns always take singular verbs.

civics	genetics	mumps
economics	mathematics	news
electronics	measles	physics

EXAMPLES **Measles is** a contagious disease.
The **news was** disappointing.

(2) The following nouns always take plural verbs.

binoculars	pliers	shears
eyeglasses	scissors	trousers

EXAMPLES The **scissors are** in the sewing basket.
The first modern **Olympics were held** in Athens.

NOTE: Many nouns ending in *–ics,* such as *acoustics, athletics, ethics, politics, statistics,* and *tactics,* may be singular or plural.

EXAMPLES **Statistics is** a collection of mathematical data.
The **statistics are** misleading.

If you do not know whether a noun that is plural in form is singular or plural in meaning, look in a dictionary.

21p. A verb agrees with its subject, not with its predicate nominative.

EXAMPLES Sore **muscles are** one symptom of flu.
One **symptom** of flu **is** sore muscles.

Perhaps the greatest **contribution** of ancient African scholars **was** many of the concepts used in higher mathematics.
Many of the concepts used in higher mathematics **were** perhaps the greatest contribution of ancient African scholars.

21q. Subjects preceded by *every* or *many a* take singular verbs.

EXAMPLES **Every sophomore** and **junior is participating.**
Many a person supports the cause.

21r. *Doesn't*, not *don't*, is used with singular subjects except *I* and *you*.

Remembering that *doesn't* is the contraction for *does not* and that *don't* is the contraction for *do not* may help you avoid using *don't* incorrectly.

NONSTANDARD	**She don't** [do not] know what the word means.
STANDARD	**She doesn't** [does not] know what the word means.

NONSTANDARD	**It don't** [do not] belong to me.
STANDARD	**It doesn't** [does not] belong to me.

NONSTANDARD	**Don't** [do not] that **boy** understand the rules?
STANDARD	**Doesn't** [does not] that **boy** understand the rules?

 EXERCISE 5 **Selecting the Correct Verb**

For each of the following sentences, choose the correct verb form in parentheses.

1. The Girl Guides (*is, are*) a scouting organization in Great Britain.
2. (*Does, Do*) every boy and girl in the city schools vote in the student council elections?
3. Two teaspoonfuls of cornstarch combined with a small amount of cold water (*makes, make*) an ideal thickener for many sauces.
4. One indication of African Americans' influence on our culture (*is, are*) the use of many black-originated slang expressions by people of other ethnic backgrounds.
5. "Seventeen Syllables" (*recounts, recount*) the story of a Japanese American family.
6. This (*doesn't, don't*) make sense to me.
7. Microelectronics, the area of electronics dealing with the design and application of microcircuits, (*has, have*) made possible many of the tremendous advances in computers and robotics in recent years.
8. There (*is, are*) many a slip between the cup and the lip, as my grandpa says.
9. When she is doing needlepoint, Aunt Ching's scissors always (*hang, hangs*) around her neck on a red ribbon.
10. The majority of high school juniors (*think, thinks*) that computer literacy is important.

USAGE

EXERCISE 6   Choosing the Correct Verb

For each of the following sentences, choose the correct verb form in parentheses.

EXAMPLE   **1.** How many of the foods shown below (*is, are*) native to Central America and North America?
1. *are*

1. Almost every one of the following sentences (*give, gives*) you a clue to the answer.
2. Peanuts, as well as popcorn, (*was, were*) introduced to European settlers by Native Americans.
3. No one in Europe (*was, were*) familiar with the taste of pumpkins, blueberries, or maple syrup until explorers brought these foods back from the Americas.
4. One American food that helped reduce famine in Europe (*was, were*) potatoes.
5. A field planted in potatoes (*produce, produces*) almost twice as much food in about half as much growing time as the same field planted in wheat.
6. News of tomatoes, sweet peppers, beans, and zucchini (*was, were*) received warmly in Europe, and now these foods are the heart and soul of southern Italian cooking.
7. At our school, the Original American Chefs (*is, are*) a club that prepares and serves such Native American foods as baked sweet potatoes and steamed corn pudding.
8. Statistics (*shows, show*) that three fifths of all crops now in cultivation originated in the Americas.
9. (*Doesn't, Don't*) it seem obvious by now that every one of the foods shown here was first eaten by Native Americans?
10. *Indian Givers* (*is, are*) a wonderful book about all kinds of contributions that Native Americans have made to the world.

USAGE

21s. When a relative pronoun (*that, which,* or *who*) is the subject of an adjective clause, the verb in the clause agrees with the word to which the relative pronoun refers.

EXAMPLES Titan, **which is** one of Saturn's satellites, is the largest satellite in our solar system. [*Which* refers to the singular noun *Titan.*]
I have neighbors **who raise** tropical fish. [*Who* refers to the plural noun *neighbors.*]

NOTE: When preceded by *one of [plural word]*, the relative pronoun takes a plural verb. When preceded by *the only one of [plural word]*, the relative pronoun takes a singular verb.

EXAMPLES The dodo is **one of the birds that are** extinct.
Pluto is **the only one of the planets that crosses** the orbit of another planet.

ORAL PRACTICE **Using Subject-Verb Agreement**

Read each of the following sentences aloud, stressing the italicized words.

1. *Has either* of the essays been graded?
2. *Both* green beans and broccoli *are* nourishing vegetables.
3. Here *are* the *minutes* I took at the meeting.
4. The *salary is* the minimum wage.
5. Not *one* of the driver's education students *forgets* to fasten the seat belt.
6. Where *are* her *mother and father?*
7. The *coach doesn't* want us to eat sweets.
8. *Several* of the research papers *were* read aloud.

REVIEW A **Selecting Verbs That Agree with Their Subjects**

For each of the following sentences, identify the subject of the verb in parentheses. Then choose the verb form that agrees in number with the subject.

EXAMPLE 1. Both of the brothers (*play, plays*) in the zydeco band at the Cajun Cafe.
1. *Both—play*

1. Neither the Litchfield nor the Torrington exit (*is, are*) the one you should take.
2. The president, after meeting with several of his advisers, (*has, have*) promised to veto the proposed tax bill.
3. A medical study of World War II veterans (*has, have*) concluded that the veterans have the same health prospects as nonveterans.
4. The list of the greatest baseball players of all time (*is, are*) dominated by outfielders.
5. Babe Ruth, Hank Aaron, Willie Mays, and Joe DiMaggio (*is, are*) all outfielders on the list.
6. The Mariana Trench, located in the Pacific Ocean near the Mariana Islands, (*is, are*) the deepest ocean area in the world.
7. Styles in clothing (*seems, seem*) to change as often as the weather.
8. (*Do, Does*) the New York City Triborough Bridge and Tunnel Authority, which oversees the collection of bridge tolls, have a major problem with a small Mexican coin?
9. Yes, the Mexican peso, worth a fraction of a cent, (*is, are*) easily accepted by the present toll machines.
10. These vegetables (*doesn't, don't*) look fresh.

USAGE

PICTURE THIS

In your daydreams, you've pictured this event a thousand times—delivering a speech in front of the assembled delegates to the U.S. House of Representatives. Write out the speech that you would deliver. It can be on any topic that's important to you and can be humorous or serious. Your speech will be printed in the *Congressional Record,* the daily publication of the proceedings of Congress, so be sure to check your writing carefully for subject-verb agreement.

Subject: an issue that's important to you
Audience: U.S. House of Representatives
Purpose: to inform the other delegates about an issue

USAGE

Agreement of Pronoun and Antecedent

A pronoun usually refers to a noun or another pronoun. The word to which a pronoun refers is called its ***antecedent.***

☞ REFERENCE NOTE: For more on antecedents, see pages 555, 664–666, and 701–702.

21t. A pronoun agrees with its antecedent in number and in gender.

(1) Singular pronouns refer to singular antecedents. Plural pronouns refer to plural antecedents.

EXAMPLES **Sammy Davis, Jr.,** made **his** movie debut in 1931.
The **joggers** took **their** canteens with **them.**

(2) A few singular pronouns indicate gender (*masculine, feminine, neuter*). The singular pronouns *he, him, his,* and *himself* refer to masculine antecedents. The singular pronouns *she, her, hers,* and *herself* refer to feminine antecedents. The singular pronouns *it, its,* and *itself* refer to antecedents that are neuter (neither masculine nor feminine).

EXAMPLES **Shay** has more credits than **he** needs.
Maria has misplaced **her** class ring.
A **snake** swallows **its** prey whole.

21u. Singular pronouns are used to refer to the following antecedents: *anybody, anyone, each, either, everybody, everyone, neither, nobody, no one, one, somebody,* and *someone.*

These words do not indicate gender. To determine their gender, look in phrases following them.

EXAMPLES   **Each** of the **girls** has already memorized **her** part.
One of the **boys** left **his** helmet on the bus.

If the antecedent may be either masculine or feminine, use both the masculine and feminine pronouns to refer to it.

EXAMPLES   **Anyone** who is going on the field trip needs to bring **his or her** lunch.
Any qualified **person** may submit **his or her** application.

You can often avoid the awkward *his or her* construction by substituting an article (*a, an,* or *the*) for the construction or by rephrasing the sentence, using the plural forms of both the pronoun and its antecedent.

EXAMPLES   Any interested **person** may submit **an** application.
All interested **persons** may submit **their** applications.

NOTE: In conversation, plural pronouns are often used to refer to singular antecedents that can be either masculine or feminine.

EXAMPLES   **Everybody** wanted Ms. Hirakawa to sign **their** yearbooks.
Each of the employees will receive **their** new ID cards tomorrow.

This usage is becoming increasingly popular in writing. In fact, using a singular pronoun to refer to a singular antecedent that is clearly plural in meaning may be misleading.

MISLEADING   **Nobody** left the prom early, because **he or she** was enjoying **himself or herself**. [Since *nobody* is clearly plural in meaning, the singular pronouns *he or she* and *himself or herself*, though grammatically correct, are confusing.]

IMPROVED   **Nobody** left the prom early, because **they** were enjoying **themselves**.

MISLEADING   **Everyone** in the audience had enjoyed the performance so much that **he or she** called for an encore.

IMPROVED   **Everyone** in the audience had enjoyed the performance so much that **they** called for an encore.

USAGE

21v. A plural pronoun is used to refer to two or more singular antecedents joined by *and.*

EXAMPLES   If **Jerry and Francesca** call, tell **them** that I will not be home until this evening.
Pilar, Kimberly, and Laura have donated **their** time to the hospital.

21w. A singular pronoun is used to refer to two or more singular antecedents joined by *or* or *nor.*

EXAMPLES   **Either Rinaldo or Philip** always finishes **his** geometry homework in class.
Neither Cindy nor Carla thinks **she** is ready to write the final draft.

NOTE: Revise awkward constructions caused by antecedents of different genders.

AWKWARD   Either Leo or Rose will give her report.
REVISED   Either **Leo** will give **his** report, or **Rose** will give **hers**.

 EXERCISE 7   **Supplying Pronouns That Agree with Their Antecedents**

Complete each of the following sentences by supplying at least one pronoun that agrees with its antecedent. Use standard formal English.

EXAMPLE   **1.** Each of the girls took _____ turn at bat.
1. *her*

1. Each student prepares _____ own outline.
2. One of the birds built _____ nest in our chimney.
3. Both Jane and Ruth wrote _____ essays about ecology.
4. If anyone else wants to drive, _____ should tell Mrs. Cruz.
5. Many of the students in our class have turned in _____ reports on the Frida Kahlo exhibit.
6. Not one of the students typed _____ research paper.
7. Neither Angela nor Carrie has given _____ dues to me.
8. Either Mark or David must hand in a slip to take _____ car on the field trip.
9. Each of the visitors filled _____ own plate with tacos, fajitas, and guacamole at the cookout.
10. Everyone in the class has paid _____ lab fees.

USAGE

WRITING APPLICATION

Using Pronoun-Antecedent Agreement for Clear Meaning

Like many rules in English, the rules of pronoun-antecedent agreement have some exceptions. Checking for agreement can be tricky when an antecedent is an indefinite pronoun like *anyone*, *either*, *neither*, *everyone*, *neither*, *nobody*, or *somebody*. In formal writing, a singular pronoun is generally used to refer to one of these antecedents. However, a plural pronoun should be used if a singular one would be awkward or misleading. How might the following sentence cause confusion?

> Everyone believes that he or she will cut back on spending during this recession.

▶ **WRITING ACTIVITY**

For your term project in history class, you've decided to poll people about what current events they think will be the most important events of the decade. Take a poll of at least ten people and write a brief report discussing your findings. Wherever appropriate, use pronouns to avoid repeating nouns. Be sure that the pronouns you use agree with their antecedents.

Prewriting First, write down several specific questions that you will ask in your poll. Group your questions in categories, such as political events, environmental issues, sports, medicine, and entertainment. Your poll can cover global events or events just in the United States or in your local community. Be sure to ask "open-ended" questions, which prompt people to explain their answers. Next, make a list of people to poll. You can include friends, relatives, and neighbors. Then, poll your subjects, either tape-recording or noting down their answers. If you are using a tape recorder, get your respondent's permission before you begin recording. Be sure to record the answers clearly and accurately and to identify each source by his or her full name. After you take your poll, compile lists of the responses. Finally, note the answers given most often to each question and the reasons why people consider these events the most important.

Writing As you write your report, identify the answers people gave most frequently to each of your questions. Clearly identify your sources as well as the events you're discussing. For each event, sum up the reasons people gave for their choices. You might wrap up your report with a paragraph telling what conclusions you've drawn from the results of the poll.

Evaluating and Revising Check the organization of your report. Make sure your discussion follows a clear, logical order. Also be sure you've accurately represented the responses to your poll. If you find that you've repeated the names of people and events too often, use pronouns for variety. Check for pronoun-antecedent agreement, paying special attention to antecedents that are singular indefinite pronouns. You may need to reword some sentences to avoid awkward or unclear constructions.

Proofreading Proofread your paper for any errors in grammar, spelling, or punctuation. Check again for errors in agreement of pronouns and antecedents.

▶ REVIEW B   **Proofreading a Paragraph for Subject-Verb and Pronoun-Antecedent Agreement**

Most of the sentences in the following paragraph contain errors in agreement. If the sentence contains an error in agreement, identify the incorrect verb or pronoun, and supply the correct form. If the sentence is correct, write *C*.

EXAMPLE   [1] Don't the concept of child prodigies fascinate you?
            1. *Don't—Doesn't*

[1] Prodigies, people who have immense talent, is born very infrequently. [2] One of the most interesting child prodigies of

this century are young Wang Yani of China. [3] Two and a half years were the age at which Wang began painting. [4] How old do you think she was when this wonderful painting of frolicking monkeys were completed? [5] Neither of us were able to guess correctly that she was only nine. [6] It shouldn't surprise you to learn that *Little Monkeys and Mummy* are the painting's title. [7] The people of China has recognized Wang as a prodigy since she was four years old. [8] By the time she was six, she had already painted four thousand pictures. [9] As you can see, wet ink and paint is freely mixed in Wang's pictures, producing interesting puddles and fuzzy edges. [10] Honored at home and abroad, Wang Yani is the youngest painter ever to have their works displayed in a one-person show at the Smithsonian Institution.

USAGE

Review: Posttest

A. Proofreading Sentences for Subject-Verb and Pronoun-Antecedent Agreement

Most of the following sentences contain errors in agreement. If the sentence is correct, write *C*. If it contains an error in agreement, identify the incorrect verb or pronoun, and supply the correct form.

EXAMPLE **1.** Each of the members of the school board are hoping to be reelected this fall.
1. *are hoping—is hoping*

1. Half the members of my history class this year is in the National Honor Society.
2. Over one thousand miles of tunnels travels through El Teniente, the largest copper mine in the world.
3. If she already has needle-nose pliers, she can exchange them for something else at the hardware store.
4. The etchings of Mary Cassatt, one of America's leading impressionist painters, was definitely influenced by the style used in Japanese prints.
5. Either drizzle or heavy rainfall is supposed to be headed this way.
6. If you see either Veronica or Sabrena in the cafeteria, will you please tell them that I won't be able to go with them after school today?
7. Neither Adrianne nor Lillian expect to make the varsity softball team this year; nevertheless, both girls are trying out for it.
8. To learn more about our municipal government, our civics class is planning to invite a number of guest speakers to school.
9. Unfortunately, neither Mayor Ella Hanson nor Mrs. Mary Ann Powell, the assistant mayor, have responded to our invitations yet.
10. *Blue Highways* by William Least Heat-Moon tell about the fascinating people he met on a trip through small-town America.

B. Proofreading a Paragraph for Subject-Verb and Pronoun-Antecedent Agreement

Most of the sentences in the following paragraph contain errors in agreement. If a sentence contains an error in agreement, identify the incorrect verb or pronoun, and supply the correct form. If a sentence is correct, write *C*.

EXAMPLE   **[1]** My friends and I have stopped buying records in favor of its more modern competitor, the compact disc.

    1. *its—their*

[11] Do you know what the differences between records and compact discs is? **[12]** One of the differences are that the music is encoded onto a compact disc by a computer, not pressed into the disc mechanically. **[13]** Another difference is that a CD recording is played back with a laser beam instead of a needle. **[14]** There's several built-in advantages to this technology; for example, because a needle never touches the disc's surface, a CD never wears out. **[15]** And although a CD is usually more expensive than a record album or cassette tape, they can hold over seventy minutes of music on each side. **[16]** You may ask, "Doesn't a record and a compact disc yield the same high-fidelity sound?" **[17]** Yes, both kinds of technology does play the same music, but the compact disc also offers total freedom from unwanted noise and distortion. **[18]** My aunt recently told me that a CD of mine has a brighter treble and a truer bass than their record of the same album. **[19]** This great sound quality is obvious even when you play a compact disc on one of the tiny, inexpensive portable players. **[20]** Because virtually all CD players offers the same excellent performance, you should choose the lowest-priced player that has the features you want.

USAGE

22 CORRECT PRONOUN USAGE

Case Forms of Pronouns

Diagnostic Test

A. Selecting Correct Forms of Pronouns

For each of the following sentences, choose the correct form of the pronoun in parentheses.

EXAMPLE **1.** Since (*he, him*) and I now have our licenses, Aunt Arabella allowed us to drive her car to the lake.
1. *he*

1. This afternoon the talent committee will audition Tina and (*myself, me*).
2. As I waited for the elevator, I heard the receptionist say, "(*Who, Whom*) shall I say is calling?"
3. The best tennis players in school are my cousin Adele and (*he, him*).
4. I helped Two Bear and (*she, her*) take down the tepee and load it onto the travois.
5. (*Who, Whom*) did you talk to at the information desk?

6. Because Alberto and (*they, them*) have taken dancing lessons, they were chosen to be in the chorus line.
7. My math teacher objects to (*me, my*) yelling out answers before I have been called on.
8. I learned about life in post-World War II Cuba from the great-grandmother and (*he, him*).
9. Between you and (*I, me*), I'm glad it's almost lunchtime.
10. When we were small, Ellie always got into more trouble than (*I, me*).

B. Selecting Correct Forms of Pronouns

For each sentence in the following paragraph, choose the correct form of the pronoun in parentheses.

EXAMPLE   [1] As teenagers, my mother and my uncle decided between (*them, themselves*) to enlist in the Army.
    1. *themselves*

[11] Years later, in 1991, Mom served in the Persian Gulf Conflict; in fact, both Uncle Tony and (*she, her*) did. [12] When Mom told my brother Pete and (*me, myself*) that she was going to the Persian Gulf, we were worried. [13] However, Pete and (*I, me*) knew that she was well prepared for the job she had to do. [14] Mom is a fine officer, and the troops she commands respect no one else as much as (*she, her*). [15] Before Mom left for the Gulf, she, Pete, and (*I, myself*) had several interesting discussions about the U.S. military. [16] Mom thought that (*us, our*) knowing some statistics about the fighting forces might make us feel better about her safety. [17] For one thing, (*we, us*) boys learned that the average age of the enlisted troops being sent to the Persian Gulf was twenty-eight years, whereas those who fought in Vietnam had a median age of only twenty-one years. [18] Between you and (*I, me*), both my brother and I were glad to hear that Mom would be serving with older troops who had that extra seven years of maturity and experience. [19] Mom also told Pete and (*I, me*) that, for the first time in U.S. history, a major war was being fought entirely by volunteer troops. [20] I will debate (*anyone, anyone's*) saying that having a volunteer army didn't improve morale.

USAGE

Case

Case is the form that a noun or a pronoun takes to indicate its use in a sentence. In English, there are three cases: *nominative*, *objective*, and *possessive*.

The form of a noun is the same for both the nominative case and the objective case. For example, a noun used as a subject (nominative case) will have the same form if used as an object (objective case).

NOMINATIVE CASE	The **general** explained the strategy. [subject]
OBJECTIVE CASE	The strategy was explained by the **general.** [object of the preposition]

A noun changes its form for the possessive case, usually by adding an apostrophe and an *s* to most singular nouns and only the apostrophe to most plural nouns.

POSSESSIVE CASE	The **general's** explanation was clear and concise. [singular modifier]
	The **generals'** explanations were clear and concise. [plural modifier]

☞ REFERENCE NOTE: For more information about forming possessive nouns, see pages 887–890.

Unlike nouns, most personal pronouns have three forms, one for each case. The form a pronoun takes depends on its function in a sentence.

NOMINATIVE CASE	**We** listened closely to the teacher's directions. [subject]
OBJECTIVE CASE	The teacher gave **us** a vocabulary quiz. [indirect object]
POSSESSIVE CASE	The teacher collected **our** papers. [modifier]

Within each case, the forms of the personal pronouns indicate *number*, *person*, and *gender*.

- *Number* is the form of a pronoun that indicates whether it is *singular* or *plural*.
- *Person* is the form of a pronoun that indicates the one(s) speaking (*first person*), the one(s) spoken to (*second person*), or the one(s) spoken of (*third person*).
- *Gender* is the form of a pronoun that establishes it as *masculine, feminine,* or *neuter* (neither masculine nor feminine).

USAGE

PERSONAL PRONOUNS		
SINGULAR		
	NOMINATIVE CASE	OBJECTIVE CASE	POSSESSIVE CASE
FIRST PERSON	I	me	my, mine
SECOND PERSON	you	you	your, yours
THIRD PERSON	he, she, it	him, her, it	his, her, hers, its
PLURAL		
	NOMINATIVE CASE	OBJECTIVE CASE	POSSESSIVE CASE
FIRST PERSON	we	us	our, ours
SECOND PERSON	you	you	your, yours
THIRD PERSON	they	them	their, theirs

Notice in the chart that *you* and *it* have the same forms for the nominative and the objective cases. All other personal pronouns have different forms for each case. Notice also that only third person singular pronouns indicate gender.

The Nominative Case

Personal pronouns in the nominative case—*I, you, he, she, it, we,* and *they*—are used as subjects of verbs and as predicate nominatives.

 REFERENCE NOTE: Personal pronouns in the nominative case may also be used as appositives. See page 621.

22a. A subject of a verb is in the nominative case.

EXAMPLES **We** ordered the concert tickets. [*We* is the subject of the verb *ordered.*]
Why does **she** think that **they** are too expensive? [*She* is the subject of the verb *does think. They* is the subject of the verb *are.*]

A subject may be compound, with a pronoun appearing in combination with a noun or another pronoun. To help you choose the correct pronoun form in a compound subject, try each form as the simple subject of the verb.

EXAMPLE: **Onawa and (*he, him*) counted the votes.**
CHOICES: *he counted* or *him counted*
ANSWER: **Onawa and he counted the votes.**

EXAMPLE: **(*She, Her*) and (*I, me*) will make the piñata.**
CHOICES: *She will make* or *Her will make*
I will make or *me will make*
ANSWER: **She and I will make the piñata.**

> ORAL
> PRACTICE 1 **Using Pronouns as Subjects**

Read each of the following sentences aloud, stressing the italicized pronoun(s).

1. You and *I* will go to the library this afternoon.
2. *We* and *they* have some research to do on the Kiowa people.
3. Either Terrell or *he* will select a topic about the environment.
4. Neither *they* nor *we* should use periodicals older than three months.
5. Both *she* and *I* will write about modern art.
6. Risa, Irena, and *I* might write about Georgia O'Keeffe.
7. Which playwright did Kaye and *she* select?
8. She said that you and *they* decided to do a production of August Wilson's award-winning play *The Piano Lesson*.

22b. A predicate nominative is in the nominative case.

A ***predicate nominative*** follows a linking verb and explains or identifies the subject of the verb.

A pronoun used as a predicate nominative always follows a form of the verb *be: am, is, are, was, were, be,* or *been*.

EXAMPLES **The chairperson of the prom committee is she.** [*She* follows *is* and identifies the subject *chairperson.*]
The one who made the comment was I. [*I* follows *was* and identifies the subject *one.*]
The lucky winners may have been they. [*They* follows *may have been* and identifies the subject *winners.*]

As you can see, the predicate nominative and the subject of the verb indicate the same individual(s). To help you choose the correct pronoun form to use as a predicate nominative, try each form as the subject of the verb.

EXAMPLE: **The only applicant for the job was (he, him).**
CHOICES: *he was* or *him was*
ANSWER: **The only applicant for the job was he.**

Like a subject, a predicate nominative may be compound.

EXAMPLES **The only students who auditioned for the part of King Arthur were he and Carlos.** [*He* and *Carlos* identify the subject *students*.]
The two debaters are she and I. [*She* and *I* identify the subject *debaters*.]

NOTE: Expressions such as *It's me, This is her,* and *It was them* are examples of informal usage. Though acceptable in everyday situations, such expressions should be avoided in formal speaking and writing.

☞ REFERENCE NOTE: For more about predicate nominatives, see page 595.

USAGE

▶ EXERCISE 1   **Using Pronouns in the Nominative Case**

Complete the following sentences by supplying personal pronouns in the nominative case. For each pronoun you add, tell whether it is used as a *subject* or a *predicate nominative*. Use a variety of pronouns, but do not use *you* or *it*.

EXAMPLE   **1. When the man shown on the next page, Charles L. Blockson, was a child, _____ was eager to learn about African American heroes.**
           1. he—subject

1. When he told his teachers of his interest, it was _____ who said that there had been very few black heroes.
2. Sure that _____ must be wrong, Blockson started looking for African Americans in the history books.
3. He began to collect books, and _____ showed him plenty of heroic black Americans.
4. Blacks had not been inactive in shaping American history, he learned; and in fact, _____ had played important roles in most of its key events!
5. When Blockson's great-grandfather was a teenager, _____ and many other slaves had escaped with the help of the Underground Railroad.

6. It was ——— who inspired Blockson's lifelong study of the Underground Railroad.
7. It may have been my friends Latisha and ——— who read about Blockson's studies in a magazine article and then gave a report in history class.
8. Using Blockson's map as a source, ——— and ——— made this simplified map of the main Underground Railroad routes to freedom.

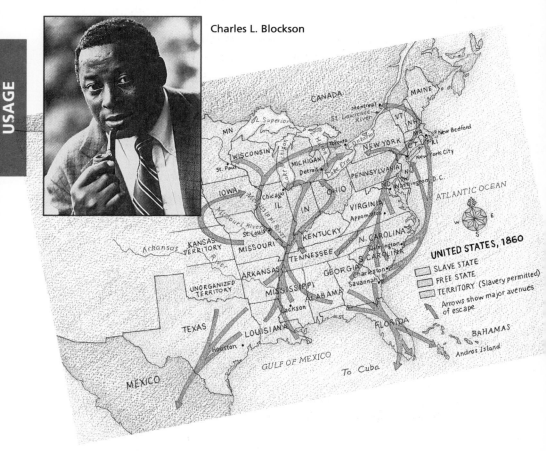

Charles L. Blockson

9. My ancestors escaped from slavery in Kentucky; therefore as you can see, ——— must have followed one of the main routes to arrive in Detroit.
10. Latisha's great-great-great-grandmother traveled with her younger brother on the Underground Railroad from Virginia to Toronto, and later both ——— and ——— moved here to Detroit to find work.

The Objective Case

Personal pronouns in the objective case—*me, you, him, her, it, us,* and *them*—are used as objects of verbs and as objects of prepositions.

☞ REFERENCE NOTE: Personal pronouns in the objective case may also be used as appositives. See page 621.

22c. An object of a verb is in the objective case.

The object of a verb may be a *direct object* or an *indirect object*. A *direct object* follows an action verb and tells *whom* or *what.*

EXAMPLES My pen pal from Manila visited **me** last summer.
The car stalled, and we couldn't restart **it**.

An *indirect object* comes between an action verb and a direct object and tells *to whom or what* or *for whom or what.*

EXAMPLES The coach awarded **her** a varsity letter.
We gathered the chickens and gave **them** some feed.

An object of a verb may be compound. To help you choose the correct pronoun form in a compound object, try each form as the object of the verb.

EXAMPLE: The new student asked Kelly and (*I, me*) for directions.
CHOICES: *asked I* or *asked me*
ANSWER: The new student asked Kelly and **me** for directions.

EXAMPLE: The editor in chief gave (*he, him*) and (*she, her*) an interesting assignment.
CHOICES: *gave he* or *gave him* and *gave she* or *gave her*
ANSWER: The editor in chief gave **him** and **her** an interesting assignment.

☞ REFERENCE NOTE: For more information about objects of verbs, see pages 592–593.

▶ ORAL PRACTICE 2 **Using Pronouns in the Objective Case**

Read each of the following sentences aloud, stressing the italicized words.

1. The judges chose Carmen and *me.*
2. Do you think that they *will provide us* with what we need?

USAGE

3. *Call* either *her* or Rhea about the yearbook deadline.
4. *Him* I *like*, but don't *ask me* about the others.
5. These instructions *confuse* my brother and *me*.
6. *Give* the other girls and *her* the chemistry assignment.
7. *Were* they *accusing them* or *us*?
8. The success of the carwash *surprised* Mr. Kahn and *him*.

▶ EXERCISE 2 **Using Pronouns in the Objective Case**

Complete the following sentences by using personal pronouns in the objective case. For each pronoun you add, tell whether it is used as a *direct object* or an *indirect object*. Use a variety of pronouns, but do not use *you* or *it*.

EXAMPLE **1.** Marcia drove ____ to the civic center.
            1. *us—direct object*

1. Have you given Nick and ____ the outside reading list?
2. Did Bob show ____ his autographed copy of Amy Tan's latest book?
3. With a smile Mrs. Martin handed Lena, Chris, and ____ their notebooks.
4. Our teacher has already graded Latoya and ____ on our oral reports to the class.
5. Ms. Gutiérrez has invited both ____ and ____ the Diez y Seis Festival.
6. Would you please lend ____ and her the manual for the fax machine?
7. During practice today, the coach taught Patricia and ____ the proper form for the inward dive.
8. The play gave ____ some ideas for a skit.
9. My mother is picking up both you and ____.
10. Please tell ____ the plans for the prom.

22d. An object of a preposition is in the objective case.

An *object of a preposition* comes at the end of a phrase that begins with a preposition.

EXAMPLES   for **me**   after **her**   next to **them**
            with **us**   beside **him**   between **you** and **me**

☞ REFERENCE NOTE: For lists of common prepositions, see page 572. For more discussion of prepositional phrases, see pages 605–607.

An object of a preposition may be compound, such as in the phrase *between you and me*. To help you determine which pronoun form to use, read each form separately with the preposition.

EXAMPLE: Esteban wants to go camping with you and (*I, me*).
CHOICES: *with I* or *with me*
ANSWER: Esteban wants to go camping with you and **me**.

EXAMPLE: Please return these videotapes to Ms. Chang and (*he, him*).
CHOICES: *to he* or *to him*
ANSWER: Please return these videotapes to Ms. Chang and **him**.

USAGE

▶ EXERCISE 3   **Selecting Pronouns Used as Objects of Prepositions**

For each of the following sentences, choose the correct form of the pronoun in parentheses.

EXAMPLE   **1.** The Irish terrier belongs to (*she, her*).
          1. *her*

1. Would you like to play baseball with Eugenio and (*I, me*)?
2. These photographs were taken by Dwight and (*she, her*).
3. We can rely on Theresa and (*he, him*) for their help.
4. Would you like to sit next to Elaine and (*I, me*)?
5. There has been much cooperation between the Hispanic Chamber of Commerce and (*we, us*).
6. Teammates like Dave and (*he, him*) can almost read each other's minds on the basketball court.
7. The closing lines of the play will be spoken by you and (*she, her*).
8. We have been studying the early settlers from England and how the Native American people helped (*they, them*) survive in the New World.
9. Most of the credit belongs to (*we, us*).
10. The captain tried to steer the ship between the lighthouse and (*they, them*).

▶ REVIEW A   **Selecting Correct Forms of Personal Pronouns**

For each sentence in the following paragraph, choose the correct form of the pronoun in parentheses. Then identify its use in the sentence—as a *subject*, a *predicate nominative*, a *direct object*, an *indirect object*, or an *object of a preposition*.

EXAMPLE   During our vacation in Mexico, my grandmother, her
            brother Luís, and [1] (*I, me*) visited the Oaxaca Valley.
            1. *I—subject*

The state of Oaxaca is where [1] (*they, them*) and their two older brothers were born. As we drove through Arrazola, their village, Uncle Luís was amazed to find well-built brick homes where all of [2] (*we, us*) had expected to see bamboo houses. Turning to Grandma, [3] (*he, him*) exclaimed, "Something good has happened here, Nita!" After visiting Arrazola, my relatives and [4] (*I, me*) drove to the city of Oaxaca, which is the state capital, and strolled along its main street. I pointed out some painted woodcarvings to Grandma and showed [5] (*she, her*) and Uncle Luís the ones I liked best. I took this picture of a pair of dancing chickens and decided it would be either [6] (*they, them*), this alligator playing a horn, or the striped cat on the right that I'd buy for a souvenir. While I was making up my mind, Uncle Luís spoke to the shopkeeper, asking questions of [7] (*he, him*) and his wife. It seems that not long before, a local man named Manuel Jiménez had started making colorful wooden figures and selling [8] (*they, them*) to American visitors. Seeing his success, others in the Oaxaca Valley soon began carving too, and within a few years [9] (*they, them*) and their fanciful woodcarvings had become famous. These people's imagination, skill, and hard work have rapidly brought [10] (*they, them*) and their communities out of poverty.

The Possessive Case

The personal pronouns in the possessive case—*my, mine, your, yours, his, her, hers, its, our, ours, their, theirs*—are used to show ownership or relationship.

> **NOTE:** Many authorities prefer to call these words adjectives. Follow your teacher's instructions regarding these possessive forms.

22e. The possessive pronouns *mine, yours, his, hers, its, ours,* and *theirs* are used in the same ways that the pronouns in the nominative and the objective cases are used.

SUBJECT	Your car and **mine** need a tune up.
PREDICATE NOMINATIVE	This yearbook is **hers.**
DIRECT OBJECT	We ordered **ours** yesterday.
INDIRECT OBJECT	Ms. Kwan gave **theirs** a quick look.
OBJECT OF PREPOSITION	Next to **yours,** my Siamese cat looks puny.

22f. The possessive pronouns *my, your, his, her, its, our,* and *their* are used as adjectives before nouns.

EXAMPLES   **My** watch is broken.
His first public performance as a concert pianist was in 1968.
Do you know **their** address?

22g. A noun or a pronoun preceding a gerund is in the possessive case.

A *gerund* is a verb form that ends in *–ing* and functions as a noun. Since a gerund acts as a noun, the noun or pronoun that comes before it must be in the possessive case in order to modify the gerund.

EXAMPLES   We were all thrilled by **Joetta's** scoring in the top 5 percent. [*Joetta's* modifies the gerund *scoring.* Whose scoring? Joetta's scoring.]
His parents objected to **his** working late on school nights. [*His* modifies the gerund *working.* Whose working? His working.]

Do not confuse a gerund with a present participle, which is also a verb form that ends in *–ing.* A gerund acts as a noun,

USAGE

whereas a present participle serves as an adjective. A noun or pronoun that is modified by a present participle should not be in the possessive case.

EXAMPLES   She nearly stepped on the **puppy** frolicking around her. [*Puppy* is modified by the participial phrase *frolicking around her.*]
We found **him** sitting on a bench in the park. [*Him* is modified by the participial phrase *sitting on a bench in the park.*]

The form of a noun or pronoun before an *–ing* word often depends on the meaning you want to express. If you want to emphasize the *–ing* word, use the possessive form. If you want to emphasize the noun or pronoun preceding the *–ing* word, avoid the possessive form. Notice the difference in meaning between the two sentences in each of the following pairs.

EXAMPLES   Can you imagine **my** driving in the desert? [emphasis on the gerund *driving*]
Can you imagine **me** driving in the desert? [emphasis on *me,* not on the participial phrase *driving in the desert*]

The **Glee Club's** singing of "Hail, Columbia!" got the most applause. [emphasis on the gerund *singing*]
The **Glee Club** singing "Hail, Columbia!" got the most applause. [emphasis on *Glee Club,* not on the participial phrase *singing "Hail, Columbia!"*]

EXERCISE 4   **Using Pronouns with Gerunds and Present Participles**

For each of the following sentences, identify the *–ing* word as either a *gerund* or a *present participle,* and then choose the correct noun or pronoun in parentheses. Be prepared to explain your choices. [Note: A sentence may be correctly completed in more than one way.]

EXAMPLE   **1.** Jody saw (*us, our*) standing on the corner and waved.
1. *present participle—us*

1. Hao didn't see the huge green wave until she felt (*it, its*) crashing over her shoulders.
2. I like my stepfather, but I just can't get used to (*him, his*) cooking.

3. The baby reached out to touch the shiny (*ribbons, ribbon's*) decorating the gift.
4. (*Him, His*) being sarcastic has ruined our chance to win the debate.
5. Did you mind (*me, my*) telling Denzel that you entered the essay contest?

PICTURE THIS

Along with these other volunteers, you and some friends have spent the weekend gathering up the trash that had been spoiling the beauty of this lake. You worked hard, and you feel good knowing you've helped clean up your community. Now, you want to persuade other people to take part in the clean-up effort. Write a letter to your local newspaper, telling how your group of volunteers cleaned up the shoreline and describing the results of your work. Convince your readers that volunteer "trash detail" is well worth the effort for a cleaner community. In your letter, use at least ten pronouns. Be able to tell whether each pronoun you use is in the nominative, objective, or possessive case.

Subject: cleaning up trash in your community
Audience: readers of the local newspaper
Purpose: to persuade readers to volunteer their time

USAGE

Special Pronoun Problems

Appositives

An *appositive* is a noun or a pronoun placed next to another noun or pronoun to explain or identify it.

☞ **REFERENCE NOTE:** For more information about appositives, see page 691.

22h. An appositive is in the same case as the noun or pronoun to which it refers.

EXAMPLES   My best friends, **Raúl** and **she,** have been nominated for class treasurer. [*Raúl* and *she* are in apposition with the subject *friends.* Since a subject is always in the nominative case, an appositive to a subject is in the nominative case.]
My grandfather paid the two boys, **Mario** and **him,** for raking leaves. [*Mario* and *him* are in apposition with the direct object *boys.* Since a direct object is always in the objective case, an appositive to a direct object is in the objective case.]

To help you choose which pronoun form to use as an appositive, try each form in the position of the word it refers to.

EXAMPLE: Two juniors, Erin and (*she, her*), conducted the survey.
CHOICES: *she conducted* or *her conducted*
ANSWER: Two juniors, Erin and **she,** conducted the survey.

EXAMPLE: The survey was conducted by two juniors, Erin and (*she, her*).
CHOICES: *by she* or *by her*
ANSWER: The survey was conducted by two juniors, Erin and **her.**

NOTE: Sometimes the pronoun *we* or *us* is followed by a noun appositive. To determine which pronoun form to use, try each form without the noun appositive.

EXAMPLE: On our field trip to the planetarium, (*we, us*) students learned many interesting facts about our solar system.
CHOICES: *we learned* or *us learned*
ANSWER: On our field trip to the planetarium, **we** students learned many interesting facts about our solar system.

EXAMPLE: The guidance counselor talked to (*we, us*) students
about the requirements for graduation.
CHOICES: *to we* or *to us*
ANSWER: The guidance counselor talked to **us** students about
the requirements for graduation.

EXERCISE 5   **Using Appositives in Sentences**

Supply an appropriate pronoun for each blank in the following groups of words. Then write a sentence using each group of words in the way specified in parentheses.

EXAMPLE   **1.** my neighbors, _____ and Steven (*indirect object*)
1. *We gave my neighbors, her and Steven, a ride to the basketball game.*

1. the two star players, _____ and Kelly (*direct object*)
2. _____ and _____, the loudest fans (*subject*)
3. _____ Tigers boosters (*object of a preposition*)
4. _____ juniors (*predicate nominative*)
5. the world's best coaches, _____ and Mr. Gresham (*indirect object*)

Pronouns in Elliptical Constructions

An *elliptical construction* is a phrase or a clause from which words have been omitted. The word *than* or *as* often begins an elliptical construction.

22i.   A pronoun following *than* or *as* in an elliptical construction is in the same case as it would be if the construction were completed.

ELLIPTICAL   Keiko was more frustrated by the assignment
than he.
COMPLETED   Keiko was more frustrated by the assignment **than he was frustrated.**

ELLIPTICAL   The assignment frustrated me as much **as him.**
COMPLETED   The assignment frustrated me as much **as it frustrated him.**

The pronoun form in an elliptical construction determines the meaning of the elliptical phrase or clause. Be sure to use the

USAGE

pronoun form that expresses the meaning you intend. Notice how the meaning of each of the following sentences depends on the pronoun form in the elliptical construction.

EXAMPLES   I have known Leigh longer **than she.** [I have known Leigh longer *than she has known Leigh.*]
I have known Leigh longer **than her.** [I have known Leigh longer *than I have known her.*]

Did Mr. Matsuda pay you as much **as I?** [Did Mr. Matsuda pay you as much *as I paid you?*]
Did Mr. Matsuda pay you as much **as me?** [Did Mr. Matsuda pay you as much *as he paid me?*]

> EXERCISE 6   **Selecting Pronouns for Incomplete Constructions**

For each of the following sentences, add words to complete the elliptical clause. Include in the clause the appropriate pronoun form. Then tell whether the pronoun is a *subject* or an *object*. [Note: Some of the elliptical clauses may be corrected in more than one way; you need to give only one correction.]

EXAMPLE   **1.** Jo works longer hours than (*I, me*).
1. *than I work—subject*

1. No one else in my class is as shy as (*I, me*).
2. Judges in the salsa dance contest presented Estella with a larger trophy than (*I, me*).
3. Can you whistle as loudly as (*he, him*)?
4. If you want to sell more raffle tickets than Bradley, you should call on more people than (*he, him*).
5. My coach told me that I had more agility than (*he, him*).
6. We were all more eager than (*he, him*).
7. I am more interested in Spike Lee's films than (*she, her*).
8. The editors of our newspaper have written as much as (*they, them*).
9. They sent Lois as many get-well cards as (*I, me*).
10. No one gave as much time to good causes as (*she, her*).

Reflexive and Intensive Pronouns

Reflexive and intensive pronouns (sometimes called *compound personal pronouns*) have the same forms.

REFLEXIVE AND INTENSIVE PRONOUNS		
	SINGULAR	PLURAL
FIRST PERSON	myself	ourselves
SECOND PERSON	yourself	yourselves
THIRD PERSON	himself, herself, itself	themselves

A *reflexive pronoun* refers to another word that indicates the same individual(s) or thing(s).

EXAMPLES   I hurt **myself.** [*Myself* refers to *I.*]
These computers can repair **themselves.** [*Themselves* refers to *computers.*]

An *intensive pronoun* emphasizes another word that indicates the same individual(s) or thing(s).

EXAMPLES   My grandfather and I restored the car **ourselves.** [*Ourselves* emphasizes *grandfather* and *I.*]
The weather **itself** seemed to be our enemy. [*Itself* emphasizes *weather.*]

NOTE: Unlike a reflexive pronoun, an intensive pronoun can be omitted from a sentence without changing its meaning.

EXAMPLE   The children decorated the gym themselves.
The children decorated the gym.

22j.   A pronoun ending in *–self* or *–selves* should not be used in place of a simple personal pronoun.

NONSTANDARD   Lupe and **myself** went to the ballet.
STANDARD   Lupe and **I** went to the ballet.

NONSTANDARD   Did Rosa make lunch for herself and **yourself**?
STANDARD   Did Rosa make lunch for herself and **you**?

▶ EXERCISE 7   **Using Reflexive and Intensive Pronouns Correctly**

For each of the following sentences, identify the italicized pronoun as *intensive* or *reflexive.* Then, give the word or words that the pronoun refers to or emphasizes. [Note: If the sentence is imperative, the word may be understood.]

EXAMPLE **1.** To get the special beads she wanted for her bead work, Ruthie taught *herself* how to make them.
1. *reflexive—Ruthie*

1. Long before the tiny glass "seed beads" and the larger china "pony beads" were brought from Europe, Native Americans made different kinds of beads *themselves.*
2. Imagine *yourself* laboriously using a hand drill to bore a tiny hole through the center of hundreds of small cylinders of bone, shell, or stone!
3. All by *itself,* an individual bead doesn't look particularly impressive, does it?
4. I asked Ruthie to give me some beads so that I can make *myself* a necklace.
5. The librarian found the address of a bead distributor for us, but Ruthie and I had to order the materials *ourselves.*

Who and *Whom*

Like most personal pronouns, the pronoun *who* (*whoever*) has three case forms.

NOMINATIVE CASE	who	whoever
OBJECTIVE CASE	whom	whomever
POSSESSIVE CASE	whose	whosever

These pronouns may be used in two ways: to form questions and to introduce subordinate clauses. When they are used to form questions, they are called ***interrogative pronouns.*** When they are used to introduce subordinate clauses, they are called ***relative pronouns.***

22k. The form an interrogative pronoun takes depends on its use in the question.

Who is used as a subject or as a predicate nominative. *Whom* is used as an object of a verb or as an object of a preposition.

NOMINATIVE **Who played this role on Broadway?** [*Who* is the subject of the verb *played.*]
Who could it have been? [*Who* is the predicate nominative identifying the subject *it.*]

OBJECTIVE   **Whom** did the president recommend? [*Whom* is the direct object of the verb *did recommend.*]
With whom did Moss Hart write the play? [*Whom* is the object of the preposition *with.*]

NOTE: In spoken English, the use of *whom* is gradually disappearing. Nowadays it's acceptable to begin a spoken question with *who* regardless of whether the nominative or objective form is grammatically correct. In writing, though, it's still important to distinguish between *who* and *whom*.

22l.   The form a relative pronoun takes depends on its use in the subordinate clause.

When choosing between *who* and *whom* in a subordinate clause, follow these steps:

STEP 1:   Find the subordinate clause.
STEP 2:   Decide how the relative pronoun is used in the clause— *subject, predicate nominative, direct object, indirect object,* or *object of a preposition.*
STEP 3:   Determine the case for this use of the relative pronoun.
STEP 4:   Select the correct case form of the relative pronoun.

EXAMPLE: **Ms. Gonzalez, (who, whom) I greatly admire, operates a shelter for homeless people in our community.**
STEP 1:   The subordinate clause is *(who, whom) I greatly admire.*
STEP 2:   The relative pronoun serves as the direct object of the verb *admire.*
STEP 3:   A direct object is in the objective case.
STEP 4:   The objective form of the relative pronoun is *whom.*
ANSWER: **Ms. Gonzalez, whom I greatly admire, operates a shelter for homeless people in our community.**

The case of the relative pronoun in a subordinate clause is not affected by any word outside the subordinate clause.

EXAMPLE: **The prize goes to (whoever, whomever) is the first to solve the riddles.**
STEP 1:   The subordinate clause is *(whoever, whomever) is the first to solve the riddles.*
STEP 2:   The relative pronoun serves as the subject of the verb *is,* not the object of the preposition *to.* (The entire clause is the object of the preposition *to.*)
STEP 3:   A subject of a verb is in the nominative case.
STEP 4:   The nominative form of the relative pronoun is *whoever.*
ANSWER: **The prize goes to whoever is the first to solve the riddles.**

USAGE

NOTE: When choosing between *who* and *whom* to begin a question or a subordinate clause, do not be misled by a parenthetical expression consisting of a subject and a verb, such as *I think, do you suppose, he feels,* or *they believe.* Select the pronoun form you would use if the expression were not in the clause.

EXAMPLES **Who** do you think will win the Super Bowl? [*Who* is the subject of the verb *will win.*]

She is the one **who** we believe was named Teacher of the Year. [*Who* is the subject of the verb *was named.*]

☞ REFERENCE NOTE: For more information about parenthetical expressions, see pages 872–874.

▶ EXERCISE 8 **Using *Who* and *Whom* Correctly**

For each of the following sentences, choose the correct form of the pronoun in parentheses. Then identify its use in the sentence—as a *subject,* a *predicate nominative,* a *direct object,* an *indirect object,* or an *object of the preposition.*

EXAMPLE **1. Here are the names of some of the authors (*who, whom*) we will study this semester.**
1. whom—direct object

1. Betty Smith, the author of *A Tree Grows in Brooklyn,* was an obscure writer (*who, whom*) became a celebrity overnight.
2. Her novel is an American classic about a young girl (*who, whom*) she called Francie Nolan.
3. Francie, (*who, whom*) we follow through girlhood to adulthood, had only one tree in her city back yard.
4. Carson McCullers, (*who, whom*) critics describe as a major American writer, also wrote a novel about a young girl's coming of age.
5. (*Who, Whom*) could not be moved by *The Member of the Wedding*?
6. Do you know (*who, whom*) it was that played Frankie in the Broadway production of *The Member of the Wedding*?
7. Pearl Buck is a novelist (*who, whom*) most Americans are familiar with.
8. Pulitzer Prizes are awarded to (*whoever, whomever*) is selected by the panel of judges.
9. Gwendolyn Brooks, (*who, whom*) you told me won the Pulitzer Prize for poetry, also wrote a book called *Maud Martha.*
10. Guess (*who, whom*) Maud Martha really is.

▶ REVIEW B   **Selecting Correct Forms of Pronouns**

For each sentence in the following paragraph, choose the correct form of the pronoun in parentheses.

Jordan and [1] (*I, me*) had thought of Impressionism as a French style of painting, and for the most part, we are right. But every artist is exposed to other artists' ideas, and often it is [2] (*they, them*) that inspire changes of style. If you have heard of Edgar Degas, you might know that both [3] (*he, him*) and the American Impressionist Mary Cassatt were very much influenced by exhibitions of Japanese prints that came to Paris. At first glance, Impressionist paintings don't appear very Japanese, but just look at [4] (*they, them*) and Japanese prints placed side by side, and you can see strong parallels. This morning, Ms. Kent pointed out some of those stylistic similarities to Jordan and [5] (*me, myself*), using the paintings shown here. Neither of [6] (*we, us*) two art lovers could possibly mistake the resemblance. "Just between you and [7] (*I, me*)," said

Henri Toulouse-Lautrec, "Jane Avril" (color lithograph), 1893. Albi, Musee Toulouse-Lautrec/ Giraudon/Art Resource, New York

Andro Hiroshige, "Branch of a Flowering Apple Tree (color woodcut)". Paris, Galerie Janette Ostier/ Giraudon/ Art Resource, New York (PEC5667/ AR5018)

Mary Cassatt (1845–1926), "The Letter". Drypoint, soft-ground etching and aquatint, printed in color Third state. From a series of ten. H 13 5/8" W 8 15/16" /The Metropolitan Museum of Art, Gift of Paul J. Sachs, 1916 (16.2.9)

Japanese woodcut of a woman/ Art Resource, New York

Ms. Kent, "almost all of the Impressionists openly copied ideas from the Japanese." One of my favorite painters is Toulouse-Lautrec, [8] (*who, whom*) often used the Japanese technique of including a large object in the extreme foreground to lend a

feeling of depth to a picture. Both Mary Cassatt and [9] (*he, him*) learned from the Japanese the principle of cutting figures at the edge of the canvas to achieve a snapshot-like quality. As you can see, the Japanese technique of juxtaposing different patterned fabrics appealed to Mary Cassatt, and this technique was used by Pierre Bonnard as well as by [10] (*she, her*).

REVIEW C
Proofreading Sentences for Correct Pronoun Forms

For each of the following sentences that contains an incorrect pronoun form, identify the error, and then give the correct form. If a sentence is correct, write *C*.

EXAMPLE **1.** Neither Karl nor myself could find the book.
1. *myself—I*

1. Many farm workers voted for Cesar Chavez, who they believed would fight for their rights.
2. Both her father and herself have artistic talent.
3. I can't understand his dropping out of the band during his senior year.
4. The new exchange students, Michelle and her, already speak some English.
5. Robert's parents have no objection to him trying to get a job after school.
6. I thought that Beth and her would make the best officers.
7. They have many more cassette tapes than us.
8. The title of salutatorian goes to whomever has the second highest academic average.
9. Who is supposed to sit in this empty seat between Lauren and I?
10. Who do you suppose won the traditional dance contest at the powwow?

REVIEW D
Selecting Correct Forms of Pronouns

Choose the correct form of each pronoun in parentheses in the following paragraph. Be prepared to explain your choices.

EXAMPLE You have the same features in almost exactly the same positions as [1] (*I, me*), yet nearly anyone can easily tell our faces apart.
1. *I*

[1] (*Who, Whom*) do you think the picture on the left is a portrait of? Reuben thought it was a woman, and I told him I couldn't believe [2] (*him, his*) not recognizing [3] (*who, whom*) it was! You should give [4] (*you, yourself*) a round of applause if you guessed George Washington. Both of these pictures were created when a scientist named Leon D. Harmon asked [5] (*him, himself*) how much information people actually needed to recognize a face. [6] (*He, Him*) and his colleagues took photographs of famous portraits, divided each photo into squares, and then averaged the color and brightness inside each square into a single tone. The computer-generated image gives you and [7] (*I, me*) very little information—there are no features and no outlines, only a pattern of colored blocks. Even though we can't see the eyes, nose, and mouth, the chances of [8] (*us, our*) recognizing a particular human face are very high. For the picture on the right, Reuben was a better guesser than [9] (*I, me*), especially when he held the page a few feet away from his eyes. Suddenly, he saw the [10] (*Mona Lisa, Mona Lisa's*) looking back at him!

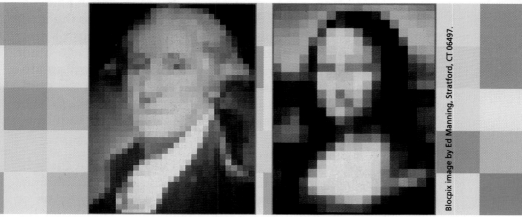

Blocpix image by Ed Manning, Stratford, CT 06497.

USAGE

WRITING APPLICATION

Using *Who* and *Whom* Correctly in Formal English

Distinctions between *who* and *whom* are more important in formal English than in informal English. In a casual conversation or a note to a friend, it's usually acceptable to use *who* rather than *whom*. But in an essay, a business letter, or a formal speech, you should be sure to use the correct case form of the pronoun.

INFORMAL The character who I like best in "The First Seven Years" is Sobel.

FORMAL The character **whom** I like best in "The First Seven Years" is Sobel.

INFORMAL Who did you nominate?
FORMAL **Whom** did you nominate?

▶ WRITING ACTIVITY

Your school's newspaper is planning a special feature on outstanding students and is looking for some suggestions. Write a letter to the editor, describing a student at your school and explaining what makes him or her outstanding. In your letter, use *who* (or *whoever*) three times and *whom* (or *whomever*) twice.

Prewriting Being an outstanding student doesn't necessarily mean getting the best grades or belonging to the most clubs. You may know people who are outstanding for their integrity, their humor or wit, or their helpfulness to other people. Decide who you think is the most outstanding student at your school. Then jot down some notes on the qualities and achievements that make this person special. Note a few specific examples of that person's behavior that illustrate these qualities.

Writing Remember that your goal is to persuade the editors of the newspaper that your classmate is outstanding. Begin by naming the person and telling briefly why he or she should be featured in the newspaper. Then give the examples you listed in your notes. Or, you may want to tell an anecdote about the person that shows his or her special qualities.

Evaluating and Revising Ask a friend to read your paragraph and pretend he or she is the editor of the newspaper. Is your letter clear and convincing? If not, you'll need to revise your examples or replace them with more engaging ones. Be sure each of your examples works to support your description of the person. Does your letter follow one of the correct forms for a business letter? (See pages 994–1001 for more about business correspondence.) Check that you've used the pronoun *who* and *whom* (or *whoever* and *whomever*) correctly.

Proofreading and Publishing Remember that errors in grammar, usage, or mechanics may distract your readers from your message. Proofread your paragraph carefully. Take extra care with pronouns, making sure they're in the correct case. You and your classmates may want to create your own "Wall of Fame." Collect your letters and, perhaps, some photographs of the outstanding students you've written about and arrange the letters and photos in a bulletin-board display.

Review: Posttest

A. Proofreading Sentences for Correct Pronoun Forms

For each of the following sentences that contains an incorrect pronoun form, identify the error and then give the correct form. If a sentence is correct, write *C*.

EXAMPLE **1.** Manuel and him are on the soccer team.
 1. *him—he*

1. Garvin thinks that Debbie is planning a surprise party for Marita and I.
2. Please send Anna and me a copy of the rough draft that you and she wrote.
3. You and I should probably ask Mr. Beauvais because no one else speaks French better than him.
4. Tamisha hopes it will be her and Pete who are appointed to the student council.
5. But seriously, whom did you expect would win the blue ribbon?
6. Who did Justin give that autographed picture of Maria Tallchief to?

USAGE

7. Danielle and I had our Bat Mitzvahs in the same month, and her and I both did very well reading from the Torah.
8. Mrs. Kitts says that our knowing facts is less important than our knowing where to find them.
9. I really appreciated you picking me up after school today.
10. All of us students, especially myself, feel much more confident about repairing autos after taking this course.

B. Proofreading a Paragraph for Correct Pronoun Forms

Identify each incorrect pronoun form in the following sentences, and then give the correct form. [Note: There may be more than one error in a sentence.] If a sentence is correct, write *C*.

EXAMPLE   [1] Meriwether Lewis hired me when him and William Clark set out to explore the Louisiana Purchase.
        1. *him—he*

[11] My cousin John and me were proud to be included in the group that went along with Lewis and Clark. [12] Us cousins were jacks-of-all-trades; both of us did everything from loading pack animals to building campfires. [13] For John and I, one of the best things about the trip was getting to know the other members of the group. [14] Someone who we became good friends with was York, a strong, friendly African American. [15] Everyone, including myself, found York to be one of the most valuable members of the expedition. [16] Many people know that Sacagawea, a Shoshone woman, was an interpreter on the expedition, but York was just as valuable an interpreter as her. [17] In fact, communicating with Native Americans would have been practically impossible without both Sacagawea and himself. [18] Whenever the expedition met with Native Americans, Sacagawea would tell her French husband Charbonneau what was said between her and them. [19] Charbonneau would then repeat the message in French to York, who would translate the French into English for Lewis, Clark, and the rest of we expedition members. [20] When we needed food and horses, York himself did much of the trading with Native Americans because him and them got along very well.

23 CLEAR REFERENCE

Pronouns and Antecedents

Diagnostic Test

A. Revising Sentences by Correcting Unclear References

Most of the following sentences contain pronouns without clear antecedents. Revise each sentence to correct any unclear pronoun references. [Note: Although sentences can be corrected in more than one way, you need to give only one revision.] If a sentence is correct, write *C*.

EXAMPLE **1.** Aaron had not yet seen the new aerobics video, so he had a difficult time doing any of them.
  1. *Aaron had not yet seen the new aerobics video, so he had a difficult time doing any of the exercises.*

  1. In the magazine article, they explain how microprocessors are used in the electrical stimulation of paralyzed muscles.
  2. Lucia wrote to Sara every week while she was visiting her aunt and uncle in Guadalajara, Mexico.

3. The star of the play was sick, two other actors had not memorized their lines, and the stage manager was out of town. This caused the director to cancel rehearsals.

4. Zack likes to browse in music stores but seldom buys any of them.

5. In many families today, you will find that parents have opened savings accounts or have bought stock for their children's college education.

6. The architect discussed with the contractor the changes she had just made on the blueprint.

7. We couldn't ride the mules to Phantom Ranch at the bottom of the Grand Canyon, which was disappointing.

8. It is raining again, but the state highway department crew is working to repair the bridge.

9. When the glass bowl landed on the floor, it shattered.

10. He told many of his own original jokes, one of which was about a penguin on its first visit to Times Square.

B. Revising Sentences by Correcting Unclear References

Most of the following sentences contain pronouns without clear antecedents. Revise each sentence to correct any unclear pronoun references. [Note: Although sentences can be corrected in more than one way, you need to give only one revision.] If a sentence is correct, write C.

EXAMPLE 1. Ferris studied the Chinese poet T'ao Ch'ien in his world literature class last semester.
        1. *In his world literature class last semester, Ferris studied the Chinese poet T'ao Ch'ien.*

11. T'ao Ch'ien loved to work in his garden, which is evident in his poetry.

12. T'ao Ch'ien's topics came from his own simple life. One of these was worrying about his five sons.

13. In our literature book it states that the Chinese consider Tu Fu to be their greatest poet.

14. Many people admire poetry, but most people don't think they can be used for medicinal purposes.

15. In this book, you will find a story about Tu Fu's suggesting that his poetry could cure malarial fever.

16. That more than a thousand of Tu Fu's poems survive is amazing.

17. The poet Li Po liked to travel and to enjoy nature. This gave him many poetry subjects but no family life.
18. Ms. Johnson explained to Alicia the meaning of the Li Po poem she had just read.
19. John Jay liked Po Chu-i's poetry, and he wanted to copy one of the poems.
20. Darnell took almost the whole class period to describe the tragic love story related in Po Chu-i's narrative poem *The Song of Everlasting Regret*. It went by very quickly.

A pronoun has no definite meaning in itself. Its meaning is clear only when the reader knows what word it stands for. This word is called the ***antecedent*** of the pronoun.

23a. A pronoun should always refer clearly to its antecedent.

In the following examples, arrows point from the pronouns to their antecedents.

EXAMPLES   The Pope asked **Leonardo** to do the sculpture, but **he** refused.

The math teacher gave **us** a problem that **we** couldn't solve.

After trying on the long blue **dress**, Mary said, **"This** fits perfectly."

Ambiguous Reference

23b. Avoid an *ambiguous reference,* which occurs when a pronoun refers to either of two antecedents.

AMBIGUOUS   Colleen called Alicia while she was doing her homework. [The antecedent of *she* and *her* is unclear. Who was doing her homework, Colleen or Alicia?]

CLEAR   While Colleen was doing her homework, she called Alicia.

CLEAR   While Alicia was doing her homework, Colleen called her.

AMBIGUOUS   The ship's officer explained to the passenger the meaning of the regulation he had just read. [The antecedent of *he* is unclear. Who had just read the regulation?]

CLEAR   After the ship's officer read the regulation, he explained its meaning to the passenger.

CLEAR   After reading the regulation, the ship's officer explained its meaning to the passenger.

CLEAR   After the passenger read the regulation, the ship's officer explained its meaning to him.

USAGE

▶ EXERCISE 1   **Revising Sentences by Correcting Ambiguous References**

Revise each of the following sentences, correcting the ambiguous pronoun references. [Note: Although sentences can be corrected in more than one way, you need to give only one revision.]

EXAMPLE   **1.** When the ship struck the dock, it burst into flames.
   1. *When it struck the dock, the ship burst into flames.*
   or
   The dock burst into flames when the ship struck it.

1. The loyal forces fought the guerrillas until they were almost entirely destroyed.
2. The police officer told the sergeant that she lost a button from her uniform.
3. The guide explained to the tourist the value of the stone she had found.
4. Leon told Carlos that his report would be better if he were to add more details about César Chávez.
5. When Anna brought Lena to the conference, we asked her for her credentials.
6. Since the show was scheduled for the same night as the intramural playoff game, it had to be postponed.
7. The manager told the dishwasher that he would have to replace all broken dishes.
8. When the ambassador emerged from a long conference with the foreign minister, reporters thought he looked confident.
9. When the truck hit the wall, it was hardly damaged.
10. A copy of the Black History Month schedule was posted on the board, but somebody took it.

General Reference

23c. Avoid a *general reference,* which occurs when a pronoun refers to a general idea rather than to a specific noun.

The pronouns commonly used in making general references are *it, this, that, which,* and *such.*

GENERAL   The wind rose, and dark clouds rolled in from the distant hills. This prompted the campers to seek shelter. [*This* has no specific antecedent.]

CLEAR   The wind rose, and dark clouds began rolling in from the distant hills. These ominous conditions prompted the campers to seek shelter.

CLEAR   As the wind rose and dark clouds began rolling in from the distant hills, the campers sought shelter.

GENERAL   More than 20 percent of those who enter college fail to graduate, which is a shame. [*Which* has no specific antecedent.]

CLEAR   That more than 20 percent of those who enter college fail to graduate is a shame.

▶ EXERCISE 2   **Revising Sentences by Correcting General References**

Revise each of the following sentences, correcting the general pronoun reference. [Note: Although these sentences can be corrected in more than one way, you need to give only one revision.]

EXAMPLE   **1.** England invaded France in 1337. It began a series of wars known as the Hundred Years' War.
1. *England's invasion of France in 1337 began a series of wars known as the Hundred Years' War.*
or
When England invaded France in 1337, a series of wars known as the Hundred Years' War began.

1. On California's San Miguel Island we had a guided tour by a ranger, which made the visit especially interesting.

2. A great many young people have already left Hastings Corners to work in the city, which is unfortunate for this town.

3. The guidance counselor asked me whether I wanted to take German, French, or Spanish, which was difficult to decide.

4. My parents bought a new carpet and new curtains, and they hired someone to paint the walls and ceiling. That certainly improved the appearance of the room.

5. 'After the storm last weekend, the trail to the top of the mountain was washed out in some spots and was blocked in many places with fallen branches. It made the ascent nerve-racking.

6. The first part of the test will be on chemistry, the second on mathematics, the third on physics. This will make it very difficult.

7. Several of the eyewitnesses described the man as short, others said he was tall, and yet others said he was "about average." It confused the police investigators.

8. The principal said that the play will have to be given in the old auditorium unless by some miracle the new auditorium can be completed ahead of schedule, which will be a blow to the Maude Adams Drama Club.

9. We hiked all morning and then went skiing at Gates of the Arctic National Park and Preserve, which made us all extremely tired.

10. I received a notice that three of my library books were overdue, which was a complete surprise.

> REVIEW A

Revising Sentences by Correcting Ambiguous and General References

Most of the following sentences contain ambiguous or general pronoun references. Revise each faulty sentence. [Note: Although these sentences can be corrected in more than one way, you need to give only one revision.] If a sentence is correct, write *C*.

EXAMPLE **1.** Some people still haven't heard about the Civil Rights Memorial, which is unfortunate.

1. *That some people still haven't heard about the Civil Rights Memorial is unfortunate.*

1. Tonya sent a postcard to Alice after she saw the Civil Rights Memorial at the Southern Poverty Law Center in Montgomery, Alabama.

2. Morris S. Dees, cofounder of the Law Center, and other center officials wanted to find a top architect to create a special memorial. This led them to Maya Lin.
3. My mother remembers reading about Lin at the time she was chosen to design the Vietnam Veterans Memorial in Washington, D.C.
4. Before she made up her mind, Lin researched the history of the civil rights movement. That convinced her to accept the project.
5. As you can see here, the granite memorial consists of two distinct parts: a wall with an engraved quotation and a round tabletop. This makes a simple but striking effect.

...UNTIL JUSTICE ROLLS DOWN LIKE WATERS AND RIGHTEOUSNESS LIKE A MIGHTY STREAM

MARTIN LUTHER KING JR.

6. Engraving the events and names associated with the civil rights movement on the tabletop was an inspired idea.
7. Water flows down the wall and over the tabletop of the memorial, which adds a sense of calm and continuity.
8. Mrs. Bledsoe told Tamisha about some of the fifty-three entries she had just read on the tabletop.
9. When the Law Center dedicated the memorial in 1989, it became a popular tourist stop.
10. Nowadays, many people come to Montgomery especially to see the Civil Rights Memorial, which, of course, benefits the city.

Weak Reference

23d. Avoid a *weak reference,* which occurs when a pronoun refers to an antecedent that has not been expressed.

WEAK	Every time a circus came to town, my sister Erin wanted to become one of them. [The antecedent of *them* is not expressed.]
CLEAR	Every time a circus came to town, my sister Erin wanted to become one of the troupe.
WEAK	He was a very superstitious person. One of these was that walking under a ladder would bring bad luck. [The antecedent of *these* is not expressed.]
CLEAR	He was a very superstitious person. One of his superstitions was that walking under a ladder would bring bad luck.
CLEAR	He believed in many superstitions. One of these was that walking under a ladder would bring bad luck.
CLEAR	He believed in many superstitions, one of which was that walking under a ladder would bring bad luck.

EXERCISE 3 **Revising Sentences by Correcting Weak References**

Revise each of the following sentences, correcting the weak pronoun reference. [Note: Although some of these sentences can be corrected in more than one way, you need to give only one revision.]

EXAMPLE **1.** Mom is very interested in psychiatry, but she does not believe they know all the answers.
1. *Mom is very interested in psychiatry, but she does not believe that psychiatrists know all the answers.*

1. Sir Arthur Conan Doyle began his career as a doctor, and it explains his interest in careful observation.
2. She is a careful gardener, watering them whenever the soil gets dry.
3. They planned to eat dinner outdoors by candlelight, but a strong wind kept blowing them out.
4. For years after seeing the Alvin Ailey American Dance Theater perform, Leah dreamed of joining them.

5. Even though it rained on the night of the concert, Eric went because his favorite ones were scheduled to be played.
6. My brother has an anthology of Japanese literature for his college course, but he hasn't read any of them yet.
7. Although Bradley enjoys reading poetry, he has never written one.
8. Sarah's uncle has a huge vegetable garden, and he keeps them supplied with fresh vegetables all summer long.
9. He spent more than an hour at the clothing store but did not try any on.
10. Deep-sea fishing isn't very enjoyable to me unless I catch at least one.

Indefinite Reference

23e. In formal writing, avoid the indefinite use of the pronouns *it, they,* and *you.*

An *indefinite reference* occurs when a pronoun refers to no particular person or thing. Such a pronoun is unnecessary to the meaning of the sentence.

INDEFINITE In the newspaper it reported that a volcano had erupted in the Indian Ocean. [*It* is not necessary to the meaning of the sentence.]

CLEAR The newspaper reported that a volcano had erupted in the Indian Ocean.

INDEFINITE In this history book, they refer to the American Civil War as the War Between the States. [*They* does not refer to any specific persons.]

CLEAR This history book refers to the American Civil War as the War Between the States.

INDEFINITE In some nineteenth-century novels, you will find the vocabulary quite difficult. [*You* has no clear antecedent in the sentence.]

CLEAR In some nineteenth-century novels, the vocabulary is quite difficult.

NOTE: The indefinite use of *it* in familiar expressions such as *it is snowing, it is early,* and *it seems* is acceptable.

USAGE

You are the art critic for the local newspaper, and you're reviewing a new exhibit of modern sculpture. You discover this work by H. C. Westermann to be as surprising and intriguing as its title: *Memorial to the Idea of Man If He Was an Idea.* Write a paragraph about the sculpture to include in your review. In your paragraph, describe the sculpture and give your opinion of it. Should your readers go to see the sculpture for themselves? Tell why or why not. In your review, use clear pronoun references so that your readers aren't confused.

Subject: a modern sculpture
Audience: readers of the local newspaper
Purpose: to inform; to evaluate a sculpture in an exhibit

H.C. Westerman, "Memorial to the Idea of Man If He Was an Idea." Collection of Susan and Lewis Manilow.

EXERCISE 4 — **Revising Sentences by Correcting Indefinite Pronoun References**

Revise each of the following sentences, correcting the indefinite use of *it, they,* or *you*. [Note: Although these sentences can be corrected in more than one way, you need to give only one revision.]

EXAMPLE **1.** In Japan they have the world's tallest roller coaster.
1. *Japan has the world's tallest roller coaster.*
or
The world's tallest roller coaster is in Japan.

1. In *The Diary of Anne Frank* it shows a young Jewish girl's courage during two years of hiding from the Nazis.
2. Everyone is excited about graduation because you have worked so hard for it.
3. In some parts of Africa, they mine diamonds and sell them to jewelers to be cut.
4. In the sports sections of the daily newspapers, it tells all about the day's events in sports.
5. When Grandpa was a child, you were supposed to be absolutely silent at the table.
6. In the movie guide, it states that *The Long Walk Home* is almost a documentary about civil rights.
7. On the book jacket, they say that the authors themselves experienced these thrilling adventures.
8. They had whirled so fast it made them dizzy.
9. One of the attractions of the tour was that they listed free admissions to all places of interest.
10. When the Neville Brothers come to town next week, it will be a sold-out show.

> **REVIEW B** **Revising Sentences by Correcting Weak and Indefinite References**

Most of the following sentences contain weak and indefinite pronoun references. Revise each faulty sentence. [Note: Although sentences can be corrected in more than one way, you need to give only one revision.] If a sentence is correct, write *C*.

EXAMPLE **1.** In the newspaper they ran an article about English actor Jeremy Brett as the detective Sherlock Holmes.
   1. *The newspaper ran an article about English actor Jeremy Brett as the detective Sherlock Holmes.*

1. Every time I see Sherlock Holmes on public television's *Mystery!* series, I want to read some more of them.
2. In the article, they talk about Brett's authentic Holmes wardrobe, an example of which you can see in the picture on the next page.
3. In some old movies, you will find Holmes wearing a deerstalker hat, but he never does in the stories by Sir Arthur Conan Doyle.
4. Holmes is a very theatrical person. One of these is using disguises, such as that of a priest in "Final Problem."

5. In the *Mystery!* series, Brett was given the opportunity to play Holmes as Conan Doyle created the character.
6. Throughout Conan Doyle's stories they present Holmes as confident, fair, and dramatic but also as restless, temperamental, and moody.
7. When we heard that Brett starred as Sherlock Holmes on the London stage, we wanted to see it.
8. In the reviews of *Mystery!* they state that Brett is widely considered the best Sherlock Holmes ever.
9. I joined the local chapter of the Baker Street Irregulars, which is a kind of Sherlock Holmes fan club.
10. From 1887 to 1927, Conan Doyle chronicled the life of Holmes, writing more than fifty of them.

Review: Posttest

A. Revising Sentences by Correcting Faulty Pronoun References

The following sentences contain examples of ambiguous, general, weak, and indefinite references. Revise each sentence, correcting the faulty pronoun reference. [Note: Although sentences can be corrected in more than one way, you need to give only one revision.]

EXAMPLE   **1.** My grandparents walk five miles every day. It is one of the best forms of exercise.

1. *My grandparents walk five miles every day. Walking is one of the best forms of exercise.*

1. I heard the owl hoot from a tree nearby, but I couldn't see it.
2. In small print on the insurance policy, it said that they were not responsible for damage caused by floods.
3. We hiked almost fourteen miles to the campsite, pitched our tents, arranged our sleeping bags, and then made our supper. This so exhausted us that we immediately went to sleep.
4. Many of our presidents began their political careers as minor public officials, which is a good thing.
5. Isaac Bashevis Singer was one of the best-known Jewish novelists of the twentieth century, and I always enjoy them very much.
6. In *Mama's Bank Account,* it describes how a Norwegian American family lives in San Francisco.
7. When we saw the flock of geese, they told us that they had flown all the way from northern Canada.
8. Jan liked the Wynton Marsalis tape but was disappointed that it didn't include her favorite one.
9. The shipwrecked men paddled their raft with their hands day after day, but this brought them no closer to land.
10. Out in the country, far away from city lights, they say you can frequently see the aurora borealis.

USAGE

B. Revising Sentences by Correcting Faulty Pronoun References

Most of the following sentences contain ambiguous, general, weak, or indefinite references. Revise each faulty sentence. If a sentence is correct, write *C.* [Note: Although sentences can be corrected in more than one way, you need to give only one revision.]

EXAMPLE **1.** Carl Sagan praised Stephen W. Hawking after he wrote *A Brief History of Time.*
1. *Carl Sagan praised Stephen W. Hawking after Hawking wrote* A Brief History of Time.

11. In the review of the book, it calls Hawking one of the twentieth-century's greatest physicists.
12. Hawking's 1988 book about physics and the universe became a best-seller, which was surprising.

13. Jamie told Rick that he should have read Hawking's chapter about black holes in space before writing his report.
14. Whenever Francine reads a good book about science she always wants to become one of them.
15. According to Hawking, Galileo was a talented science writer. One of these was the work *Two New Sciences*, the basis of modern physics.
16. In Hawking's book, you will find concepts about quantum mechanics, which can be difficult for nonscientists to understand.
17. In this magazine article on Hawking, they tell about his personal battle with motor neuron disease.
18. Because the disease affects his speech and movement, Hawking wrote his book by using a voice synthesizer and a personal computer on his wheelchair.
19. Even though Hawking carefully explains his theories on the thermodynamic and cosmological arrows of time, it still confuses some readers.
20. That Hawking apparently understands the applications of Einstein's theories to time and the universe does not seem astonishing.

24 CORRECT VERB USAGE

Principal Parts; Tense, Voice, Mood

Diagnostic Test

A. Choosing the Correct Verb Forms

For each of the following sentences, choose the correct form of the verb in parentheses.

EXAMPLE **1.** (*Sit, Set*) this pitcher of juice on the table, please.
    1. *Set*

1. A beautiful oak banister (*rises, raises*) along the staircase.
2. If you (*would have, had*) visited Mexico City, you would have seen the great pyramids at Tenochtitlán.
3. Tammie says that yesterday she should have (*went, gone*) to the beach.

4. Edward said that he wanted (*to go, to have gone*) to the Diez y Seis party, where his friends were celebrating Mexico's independence from Spain.
5. One of the statues has (*fell, fallen*) off its base.
6. How long did it (*lie, lay*) on the floor?
7. Since last September I (*missed, have missed*) only one day of school.
8. The U.S. Census Bureau has predicted that by the year 2000 the Hispanic population in the United States (*will grow, will have grown*) to more than 31 million.
9. Fortunately, I have never been (*stinged, stung*) by a bee.
10. The unusual pattern in this wool material was (*weaved, woven*) by Seamus MacMhuiris, an artist who uses bold geometric designs.
11. The house became very quiet after everyone (*left, had left*).
12. I (*began, begun*) this homework assignment an hour ago.
13. My parents' old car has (*broke, broken*) down again.
14. Everyone who (*saw, seen*) Greg Louganis dive in the 1988 Olympics recognized his superior talent.
15. He likes to (*sit, set*) on the porch in his rocking chair.

B. Revising Verb Voice or Mood

Revise the following sentences by correcting verbs that use an awkward passive voice or verbs that are not in the appropriate mood.

16. If I was you, I would not skate on that lake; the ice is too thin.
17. The ball that was thrown by me was caught by the dog.
18. He now wishes that he was on the field trip to the Diego Rivera exhibit.
19. The quilt that was made by me won second prize at the county fair.
20. The half-time show was enjoyed by the crowd.

☞ REFERENCE NOTE: Depending on their function, verbs may be classified as *action verbs* or *linking verbs* and as *main verbs* or *helping verbs*. For a discussion of these different kinds of verbs, see pages 565–567.

The Principal Parts of Verbs

24a. Every verb has four basic forms called the *principal parts:* the *infinitive*, the *present participle*, the *past*, and the *past participle*. All other forms of a verb are derived from these principal parts.

The following examples include *is* and *have* in parentheses to indicate that helping verbs (forms of *be* and *have*) are used with the present participle and past participle forms of verbs.

INFINITIVE	PRESENT PARTICIPLE	PAST	PAST PARTICIPLE
receive	(is) receiving	received	(have) received
join	(is) joining	joined	(have) joined
bring	(is) bringing	brought	(have) brought
sing	(is) singing	sang	(have) sung
hurt	(is) hurting	hurt	(have) hurt

All verbs form the present participle in the same way: by adding *–ing* to the infinitive form. All verbs, however, do not form the past and past participle in the same way.

Regular Verbs

24b. A *regular verb* is one that forms its past and past participle by adding *–d* or *–ed* to the infinitive form.

INFINITIVE	PRESENT PARTICIPLE	PAST	PAST PARTICIPLE
use	(is) using	used	(have) used
revise	(is) revising	revised	(have) revised
outline	(is) outlining	outlined	(have) outlined
watch	(is) watching	watched	(have) watched
happen	(is) happening	happened	(have) happened
rush	(is) rushing	rushed	(have) rushed

A few regular verbs have alternative past and past participle forms ending in *–t*.

INFINITIVE	PRESENT PARTICIPLE	PAST	PAST PARTICIPLE
burn	(is) burning	burned *or* burnt	(have) burned *or* burnt
dream	(is) dreaming	dreamed *or* dreamt	(have) dreamed *or* dreamt
leap	(is) leaping	leaped *or* leapt	(have) leaped *or* leapt

NOTE: The regular verbs *deal* and *mean* always form the past and past participle by adding *–t: dealt, (have) dealt; meant, (have) meant.*

When forming the past and past participle of regular verbs, avoid omitting the *–d* or *–ed* ending. Pay particular attention to the forms of the verbs *ask, attack, drown, prejudice, risk, suppose,* and *use.*

NONSTANDARD   The firefighter risk his life to save the valuable artifacts.
STANDARD   The firefighter **risked** his life to save the valuable artifacts.

NONSTANDARD   We should have ask for directions.
STANDARD   We should have **asked** for directions.

☞ REFERENCE NOTE: For a discussion of standard and nonstandard English, see page 478.

Irregular Verbs

24c.   An *irregular verb* forms the past and the past participle in some other way than by adding *–d* or *–ed* to the infinitive form.

The best way to learn the principal parts of irregular verbs is to memorize them. No single usage rule applies to the different ways that these verbs form their past and past participle forms.

However, there are some general guidelines that you can use. Irregular verbs form the past and past participle by

- changing vowels *or* consonants
- changing vowels *and* consonants
- making no change

INFINITIVE	PRESENT PARTICIPLE	PAST	PAST PARTICIPLE
swim	(is) swimming	swam	(have) swum
bend	(is) bending	bent	(have) bent
teach	(is) teaching	taught	(have) taught
burst	(is) bursting	burst	(have) burst

USAGE

When forming the past and the past participle of irregular verbs, avoid these common errors:

(1) using the past form with a helping verb

NONSTANDARD   I have never swam in this lake before.
STANDARD   I **have** never **swum** in this lake before.

(2) using the past participle form without a helping verb

NONSTANDARD   She swum to shore to get help.
STANDARD   She **swam** to shore to get help.

(3) adding *–d, –ed,* or *–t* to the infinitive form

NONSTANDARD   We bursted into laughter as soon as we saw the comedian.
STANDARD   We **burst** into laughter as soon as we saw the comedian.

NOTE: If you are not sure about the principal parts of a verb, look in a dictionary. Entries for irregular verbs give the principal parts.

The alphabetical lists on pages 718–724 contain the principal parts of many common irregular verbs. You may use these lists as a reference; however, keep in mind that the lists do not include every irregular verb.

The irregular verbs in the first list, Group 1, form their past and past participle in a similar way.

COMMON IRREGULAR VERBS

GROUP I: Each of these irregular verbs has the same form for its past and past participle.

INFINITIVE	PRESENT PARTICIPLE	PAST	PAST PARTICIPLE
bind	(is) binding	bound	(have) bound
bring	(is) bringing	brought	(have) brought
build	(is) building	built	(have) built
buy	(is) buying	bought	(have) bought
catch	(is) catching	caught	(have) caught
creep	(is) creeping	crept	(have) crept
feel	(is) feeling	felt	(have) felt
fight	(is) fighting	fought	(have) fought
find	(is) finding	found	(have) found
fling	(is) flinging	flung	(have) flung
have	(is) having	had	(have) had
hold	(is) holding	held	(have) held
keep	(is) keeping	kept	(have) kept
lay	(is) laying	laid	(have) laid
lead	(is) leading	led	(have) led
leave	(is) leaving	left	(have) left
lend	(is) lending	lent	(have) lent
lose	(is) losing	lost	(have) lost
make	(is) making	made	(have) made
meet	(is) meeting	met	(have) met
pay	(is) paying	paid	(have) paid
say	(is) saying	said	(have) said
seek	(is) seeking	sought	(have) sought
sell	(is) selling	sold	(have) sold
send	(is) sending	sent	(have) sent
sit	(is) sitting	sat	(have) sat
spend	(is) spending	spent	(have) spent
spin	(is) spinning	spun	(have) spun
stand	(is) standing	stood	(have) stood
sting	(is) stinging	stung	(have) stung
swing	(is) swinging	swung	(have) swung

(continued)

COMMON IRREGULAR VERBS *(continued)*			
GROUP I			
INFINITIVE	**PRESENT PARTICIPLE**	**PAST**	**PAST PARTICIPLE**
teach	(is) teaching	taught	(have) taught
tell	(is) telling	told	(have) told
think	(is) thinking	thought	(have) thought
win	(is) winning	won	(have) won

▶ EXERCISE 1   **Using the Past and Past Participle Forms of Verbs**

For each of the following sentences, give the correct form (past or past participle) of the verb in parentheses.

EXAMPLE   **1.** Bob and Terri have (*lead*) our class in math scores for two years.
       1. *led*

1. The movie monster (*swing*) around and lunged into the woods.
2. Have you (*teach*) your little brother Bobby how to throw a curve ball yet?
3. Mrs. Torres (*tell*) us yesterday that Mexican ballads are called *corridos.*
4. Ever since we met last year, Kitty and I have (*sit*) together in assembly.
5. When we got to the new video store at the mall, you had just (*leave*).
6. Unfortunately, I have already (*spend*) most of my weekly allowance.
7. In an earlier scene, Tarzan had (*catch*) hold of a vine and used it to swing through the trees.
8. Those two paintings by Horace Pippin really (*hold*) our interest.
9. Not only had he juggled six oranges, but he had (*spin*) two plates on sticks.
10. The tiger-striped cat (*creep*) down the hallway and into the dark room.

USAGE

EXERCISE 2   **Using the Past and Past Participle Forms of Irregular Verbs**

Many people like to play with the English language. Some enjoy word games. Others, like the author of the following silly poem, break the rules of standard usage just for fun. Each couplet in the poem contains an incorrect past or past participle form of an irregular verb. For each incorrect form shown in italics, provide the correct form. [Note: The poem will no longer rhyme.]

EXAMPLE   Bake, baked; make, [1] *maked?* Hold it—not so fast!
Verbs that rhyme in the present form may not rhyme
in the past!
1. *made*

Today we fling the same old ball that yesterday we flung;
Today we bring the same good news that yesterday we
[1] *brung*.

And we still mind our parents, the folks we've always
minded;
And I may find a dime, just like the dime you [2] *finded*.

I smell the crimson rose, the very rose you smelled;
I tell a silly joke today, the same joke you once [3] *telled*.

You grin to hear me tell it now, just as last week you grinned;
You win our game of checkers, just as last week you [4] *winned*.

I peek into your closet now, and yesterday I peeked;
I seek my birthday present, as every year I've [5] *seeked*.

You reach to take my hand in yours; it was not I who reached;
You teach me to be friendly, as always you have [6] *teached*.

I beep my horn to warn you; I'm sure my horn just beeped;
I keep all my appointments, the ones I should have [7] *keeped*.

I scream all day, I yell all night, I've screamed and I have
yelled
To sell all my newspapers, and today's batch I [8] *selled*.

I wink my eye at you today, as yesterday I winked;
I think I like you very much, as yesterday I [9] *thinked*.

I lose my train of thought sometimes; my train of thought
I've [10] *losed*.
But I can use my verbs with care; just see the ones I've used!

COMMON IRREGULAR VERBS

GROUP II: Each of these irregular verbs has a different form for its past and past participle.

INFINITIVE	PRESENT PARTICIPLE	PAST	PAST PARTICIPLE
arise	(is) arising	arose	(have) arisen
be	(is) being	was, were	(have) been
bear	(is) bearing	bore	(have) borne
beat	(is) beating	beat	(have) beaten *or* beat
become	(is) becoming	became	(have) become
begin	(is) beginning	began	(have) begun
bite	(is) biting	bit	(have) bitten
blow	(is) blowing	blew	(have) blown
break	(is) breaking	broke	(have) broken
choose	(is) choosing	chose	(have) chosen
come	(is) coming	came	(have) come
dive	(is) diving	dove *or* dived	(have) dived
do	(is) doing	did	(have) done
draw	(is) drawing	drew	(have) drawn
drink	(is) drinking	drank	(have) drunk
drive	(is) driving	drove	(have) driven
eat	(is) eating	ate	(have) eaten
fall	(is) falling	fell	(have) fallen
fly	(is) flying	flew	(have) flown
forbid	(is) forbidding	forbade *or* forbad	(have) forbidden
forget	(is) forgetting	forgot	(have) forgotten *or* forgot
forsake	(is) forsaking	forsook	(have) forsaken
freeze	(is) freezing	froze	(have) frozen
get	(is) getting	got	(have) gotten *or* got
give	(is) giving	gave	(have) given
go	(is) going	went	(have) gone
grow	(is) growing	grew	(have) grown
hide	(is) hiding	hid	(have) hidden

(continued)

USAGE

COMMON IRREGULAR VERBS *(continued)*

GROUP II

INFINITIVE	PRESENT PARTICIPLE	PAST	PAST PARTICIPLE
know	(is) knowing	knew	(have) known
lie	(is) lying	lay	(have) lain
ride	(is) riding	rode	(have) ridden
ring	(is) ringing	rang	(have) rung
rise	(is) rising	rose	(have) risen
run	(is) running	ran	(have) run
see	(is) seeing	saw	(have) seen
shake	(is) shaking	shook	(have) shaken
shine	(is) shining	shone *or* shined	(have) shone *or* shined
shrink	(is) shrinking	shrank *or* shrunk	(have) shrunk
sing	(is) singing	sang	(have) sung
sink	(is) sinking	sank	(have) sunk
slay	(is) slaying	slew	(have) slain
speak	(is) speaking	spoke	(have) spoken
spring	(is) springing	sprang *or* sprung	(have) sprung
steal	(is) stealing	stole	(have) stolen
strike	(is) striking	struck	(have) struck *or* stricken
strive	(is) striving	strove *or* strived	(have) striven *or* strived
swear	(is) swearing	swore	(have) sworn
swim	(is) swimming	swam	(have) swum
take	(is) taking	took	(have) taken
tear	(is) tearing	tore	(have) torn
throw	(is) throwing	threw	(have) thrown
wake	(is) waking	woke	(have) woke, waked, *or* wakened
wear	(is) wearing	wore	(have) worn
weave	(is) weaving	wove	(have) woven
write	(is) writing	wrote	(have) written

EXERCISE 3 **Using Past and Past Participle Forms of Verbs**

For each of the following sentences, give the correct form (past or past participle) of the verb in parentheses.

EXAMPLE **1.** Aunt Barbara (*freeze*) fourteen pints of corn.
        1. *froze*

1. Your friends have (*come*) to see you.
2. He (*do*) his best on the PSAT last Saturday.
3. Elizabeth has finally (*begin*) to understand the value of proofreading.
4. One of the poems I submitted to the contest was (*choose*) to receive a prize.
5. The tour group had (*come*) far into the desert to see the ancient Pueblo dwellings.
6. Strong winds (*blow*) the Dutch galleon off its course.
7. The silence was (*break*) by a sudden clap of thunder.
8. West Side High's team easily (*beat*) its opponents.
9. Miguel (*blow*) up balloons and made decorations for his sister's *quinceañera* party, the celebration of her fifteenth birthday.
10. When I soaked my new jeans in hot water, they (*shrink*) a little.

REVIEW A **Using Past and Past Participle Forms of Verbs Correctly**

In the following paragraph, decide whether each italicized verb is correct. If it is not, give the correct verb form. If a verb is correct, write *C*.

If you have [1] *seen* the maturity and intensity of performances by the young woman shown on the next page, you know firsthand that she has [2] *stealed* the hearts of many music lovers. Excited fans have [3] *brung* down the house with applause and have [4] *threw* bouquets of roses at her feet. Barely out of her teens, Midori has [5] *knew* the joys and struggles of being a professional concert violinist ever since she was a small girl. Whenever she has [6] *spoke* to the press, Midori has [7] *showed* an outgoing and unaffected personality. Her violin teacher at the Juilliard School, Dorothy DeLay, had also [8] *taught* such stars as Itzhak Perlman and Joshua Bell. When

USAGE

Midori was eleven, the famous conductor Zubin Mehta [9] *brung* her onstage as a surprise guest soloist with the New York Philharmonic. Ever since, Midori has [10] *finded* the concert hall a wonderful place; in fact, she says that she loves "the feeling of standing on a stage, whether there is an audience present or not."

COMMON IRREGULAR VERBS

GROUP III:	Each of these irregular verbs has the same form for its infinitive, past, and past participle.		
INFINITIVE	**PRESENT PARTICIPLE**	**PAST**	**PAST PARTICIPLE**
burst	(is) bursting	burst	(have) burst
cost	(is) costing	cost	(have) cost
cut	(is) cutting	cut	(have) cut
hit	(is) hitting	hit	(have) hit
hurt	(is) hurting	hurt	(have) hurt
let	(is) letting	let	(have) let
put	(is) putting	put	(have) put
read	(is) reading	read	(have) read
set	(is) setting	set	(have) set
spread	(is) spreading	spread	(have) spread

USAGE

> **EXERCISE 4**

Using the Past and the Past Participle Forms of Verbs

Most of the following sentences contain an incorrect verb form. If a verb form is incorrect, give the correct form. If a sentence is correct, write *C*.

1. The crowded roots of the plant had bursted the flowerpot.
2. Nancy set the antipasto salad in the center of the dining table.
3. After we've cut the grass, we'll weed the garden.
4. The angry hornet stung me right on the end of my nose, and it hurted all afternoon.
5. Hussein spreaded his pita bread with a thick layer of tasty hummus.
6. Where have I putted my notebook?
7. You must have read the assignment too quickly.
8. As soon as the robin was well, we letted it go free.
9. Skateboards costed less last year.
10. Both Felina and Fernanda hitted home runs in last week's softball game.

> **REVIEW B**

Proofreading Sentences for Correct Verb Forms

For the following sentences, give the correct form for each incorrect verb form. If a sentence is correct, write *C*.

EXAMPLE **1.** When my art class went to the museum of African American art, I seen some collages that Romare Bearden had maked.
1. *saw; made*

1. Seeing the unusual medium of collage has letted me think about art in a new way.
2. Bearden growed up in North Carolina and then spended time studying in New York, Pittsburgh, and Paris.
3. Since the 1930s, when his art career begun, he has gotten a reputation as a leading abstract artist.
4. Instead of specializing in painting or drawing, Bearden finded his niche in the somewhat unusual medium of collage.
5. He fashions his artworks out of pieces of colored paper that have been cutted or teared into small shapes.

6. Often, he has gave his collages more variety by using pieces from black-and-white or color photographs.
7. If you examine his *Blue Interior, Morning* (shown below), you can see that Bearden has built this composition around a family eating breakfast.
8. The materials that he assembled were chose for their textural harmony and for their ability to be wove into the blue color scheme.
9. In his work, Bearden has often depicted universal human figures whose composite nature is clearly showed by their different-colored fingers or legs.
10. I could have swore it was impossible to create a pleasing composition with all the figures way down in one corner, but Bearden has certainly succeeded.

Romare Bearden, "Blue Interior, Morning", 1968. Collage on board, 44 × 56". Collection of The Chase Manhattan Bank, N.A./Courtesy the Estate of Romare Bearden.

▶ REVIEW C

Using the Past and Past Participle Forms of Verbs

For each of the following sentences, give the correct form (past or past participle) of the verb in parentheses.

EXAMPLE   **1.** The pitcher (*strike*) out eleven batters in a row.
        1. *struck*

1. Have you ever (*read*) anything by Gwendolyn Brooks, the lifetime poet laureate of Illinois?
2. We (*drink*) tomato juice with last night's dinner.
3. How many of you (*see*) Fernando Valenzuela pitch?

4. I thought my skates had been (*steal*), but then I finally found them.
5. He had (*write*) a play about his experience in Vietnam.
6. Garrett's dad has (*sing*) in a barbershop quartet for years.
7. We would have bought those Detroit Pistons tickets no matter how much they had (*cost*).
8. Female rap groups like Salt-N-Pepa have (*become*) quite popular lately.
9. Don't you think that the dough for the bread has (*rise*) enough to bake?
10. LaToya says she has never (*ride*) on a roller coaster.
11. Have you ever (*fly*) a Japanese dragon kite?
12. I shivered and (*shake*) after I dented the front fender of Mom's car.
13. When Mrs. Isayama called my name, I (*swing*) around.
14. My father has (*forbid*) my younger sister to use his power tools without supervision.
15. Wanda (*burst*) into the room to greet her friends.
16. Yesterday, Nguyen and I each (*hit*) about two hundred tennis balls.
17. Darius had (*fall*) when he went in for the layup.
18. The government class has (*go*) to observe the city council in session.
19. I was not aware that the telephone had (*ring*).
20. Have you (*have*) a taste of that delicious tabbouleh salad from North Africa yet?

▶ REVIEW D **Using the Past and Past Participle Forms of Verbs**

The following paragraph contains ten numbered blanks. For each blank, choose an appropriate verb from the box below and give its correct past or past participle form.

bring	find	spread	see
become	creep	seek	begin
make	spin	let	think

EXAMPLE   Suppose you were a farmer, and one morning you went out to your fields and [1] _____ a 300-foot-long pattern like the ones shown on the next page!
1. *found*

USAGE

Many circular flattened areas like these [1]_____ to appear in fields across southern England in the late 1970s. The phenomenon soon [2]_____ one of the most popular mysteries the world had ever known. People calling themselves "cereologists" insisted that no human being could have [3]_____ these unusual patterns. The idea quickly [4]_____ that the circles were the landing spots of UFOs that had [5]_____ visitors from space. Respected scientists [6]_____ that the weird designs resulted from ball lightning, whirling columns of air, or other strange weather conditions. When it was reported that circle researchers had [7]_____ public funding, two British landscape painters came forward with the truth. David Chorley and Douglas Bower confessed that they had [8]_____ into the fields at night with a ball of string and a wooden plank and had [9]_____ the plank in a circle to create the flattened areas of grain. Before Chorley and Bower spoke up, millions of people had [10]_____ themselves believe that the crop circles were formed by extraterrestrials—and even now, thousands of diehards still do.

▶ REVIEW E

Using the Past and Past Participle Forms Correctly

For each of the following sentences, decide whether the italicized verb is correct. If it is not, give the correct verb form. If a sentence is correct, write C.

1. American shoppers have certainly *grew* accustomed to the convenience of paper grocery bags.

2. In recent years, many Americans have *went* right on using them—at the rate of forty billion bags a year!
3. Have you ever *thinked* about the history of the standard flat-bottomed grocery bag with pleated sides?
4. Someone must have *cutted* out and pasted together the first flat-bottomed paper bag.
5. Actually, I have *read* that the inventor of these bags was a man named Charles Stilwell.
6. After he had *fighted* in the Civil War, he returned home and began to tinker with inventions.
7. He created a machine to fold and glue brown paper into bags, a job that had previously been *did* by hand.
8. Earlier bags had V-shaped bottoms, which meant that they had not *standed* up by themselves.
9. I have certainly *putted* Charles Stilwell's bags to use in my after-school supermarket job.
10. Many other everyday items that we have always *took* for granted, such as safety pins and eyeglasses, have interesting histories, too.

▶ REVIEW F **Proofreading a Paragraph for the Correct Use of Irregular Verbs**

Most of the sentences in the following paragraph contain an error in the use of irregular verbs. If a verb is incorrect, supply the correct form. If a sentence is correct, write *C*.

[1] Pioneers on their way to California had always losed much time when they hit the rugged Sierra Nevada. [2] Wagon trains had turned and drived many miles out of their way, searching for a trail their oxen and horses could take through these mountains. [3] Then James Beckwourth, an African American frontiersman and explorer, discovered an important route between the forbidding peaks. [4] Have you finded Beckwourth Pass on the map on the next page? [5] Other routes, including Donner Pass, had already been discovered, but soon wagonmasters seen that Beckwourth Pass was the lowest in elevation and, therefore, the easiest to cross. [6] James Beckwourth was a versatile man; he been a trapper, trader, explorer, and mountain man. [7] He even fighted in the Second Seminole War as an army scout. [8] During the Gold Rush, he caught gold fever and spended some time prospecting in California. [9] Beckwourth always gotten along quite well with Native

Americans—especially the Crow people, who adopted him. [10] By the end of his life, he had became such a good friend to the Crow that they gave him the chance to be a chief!

Six Troublesome Verbs

Lie and *Lay*

The verb *lie* means "to rest" or "to stay, to recline, or to remain in a certain state or position." *Lie* never takes an object.

The verb *lay* means "to put [something] in a place." *Lay* usually takes an object.

INFINITIVE	PRESENT PARTICIPLE	PAST	PAST PARTICIPLE
lie (to rest)	(is) lying	lay	(have) lain
lay (to put)	(is) laying	laid	(have) laid

EXAMPLES   The printout **is lying** there next to the computer.
[no object]
The secretary **is laying** a copy of the report on
everyone's desk. [*Copy* is the object of *is laying*.]

The explorers saw that a vast wilderness **lay** before
them. [no object]
She carefully **laid** the holiday decorations in the box.
[*Decorations* is the object of *laid*.]

My basset hound **has lain** in front of the fireplace
since early this morning. [no object]
Tranh **has** already **laid** the fishing gear in the boat.
[*Gear* is the object of *has laid*.]

USAGE

EXERCISE 5   **Choosing the Forms of *Lie* and *Lay***

For each of the following sentences, choose the correct verb
form in parentheses. Be prepared to explain your choices.

EXAMPLE   **1.** The construction workers are (*laying, lying*) the
foundation now.
1. *laying*

1. The old stereoscope had (*lain, laid*) in my grandmother's
attic for years.
2. The interstate (*lays, lies*) north of town.
3. The rake is (*laying, lying*) in a pile of leaves.
4. When was that tile in the foyer (*laid, lain*)?
5. Judy and Adrian (*lay, laid*) their books on the table.
6. She read the paper as she (*laid, lay*) in the recliner.
7. The key to success (*lays, lies*) in determination.
8. (*Lie, Lay*) here and relax before going on.
9. Ms. Collins (*laid, lay*) the study guides on the table.
10. Jack stole the hen that (*lay, laid*) golden eggs.

EXERCISE 6   **Writing Sentences Using the Forms of
Lie and *Lay***

For each numbered item at the top of the next page, use the
subject and verb form given to write a correct sentence. Be sure
to add an object to forms of *lay*. For participle forms, you will
need to supply helping verbs. When two forms are spelled the
same, the information in parentheses tells you which meaning
or form to use.

EXAMPLE   SUBJECT   VERB FORM
    1. package   lying
    1. *The package was lying on the doormat when we got home.*

SUBJECT	VERB FORM
1. detectives	lay (to put)
2. sparrow	laid (past)
3. father	laying
4. dog	lain
5. children	lie
6. butler	laid (past participle)
7. Mr. Hill	lay (to rest)
8. books	lying
9. Miami	lies
10. mechanic	lays

Sit and *Set*

The verb *sit* means "to rest in an upright seated position." *Sit* seldom takes an object.

The verb *set* means "to put [something] in a place." *Set* usually takes an object.

INFINITIVE	PRESENT PARTICIPLE	PAST	PAST PARTICIPLE
sit (to rest)	(is) sitting	sat	(have) sat
set (to put)	(is) setting	set	(have) set

EXAMPLES   **May I sit here?** [no object]
    May I set the chair here? [*Chair* is the object of *May set*.]

    We **sat** in the theater for an hour, waiting for the play to begin. [no object]
    Kishi **set** the candles on the piano. [*Candles* is the object of *set*.]

EXERCISE 7   **Using the Forms of *Sit* and *Set***

Complete each of the following sentences by supplying the correct form of *sit* or *set*.

EXAMPLE   **1.** Carrie is _____ in the rocking chair, reading the newspaper.
      1. *sitting*

1. I _____ in the doctor's waiting room for an hour yesterday morning.
2. We _____ in the front row at the Gloria Estefan concert.
3. _____ the carton down near the door.
4. We were _____ so high up in the theater that the stage looked no bigger than a postage stamp.
5. If we had _____ any longer, we would have been late for class.
6. Let's _____ that pot of hot-and-sour soup on the buffet.
7. Jonathan is _____ aside five dollars each week so that he can buy a CD player.
8. You shouldn't _____ on the damp ground.
9. I hope that Trish and Brandon haven't _____ those plants too close to the radiator.
10. We all _____ around the campfire last night.

USAGE

Rise and *Raise*

The verb *rise* means "to go up" or "to get up." *Rise* never takes an object.

The verb *raise* means "to cause [something] to rise" or "to lift up." *Raise* usually takes an object.

INFINITIVE	PRESENT PARTICIPLE	PAST	PAST PARTICIPLE
rise (to go up)	(is) rising	rose	(have) risen
raise (to lift up)	(is) raising	raised	(have) raised

EXAMPLES   She **rose** from the wheelchair and walked toward the door. [no object]
Willis **raised** the window blinds to brighten the room. [*Window blinds* is the object of *raised.*]

The prices of fresh fruit and vegetables **have risen** considerably because of the drought. [no object]
Salim **has** already **raised** the flag. [*Flag* is the object of *has raised.*]

▶ EXERCISE 8 **Using *Rise* and *Raise* Correctly**

For each of the following sentences, decide whether the italicized verb is correct. If it is not, give the correct verb form. If a sentence is correct, write C.

EXAMPLE **1.** Everyone *raised* for the pledge of allegiance.
1. *rose*

1. The cost of a ticket to see a Kentucky Headhunters concert *has raised*.
2. The student council president *will raise* the flag.
3. The Bunsen burner flame *has raised* too high.
4. While fishing with my uncle Thibeaux in Louisiana, I saw an alligator slowly *raise* out of the mud.
5. The curling smoke *rose* from the pile of leaves.
6. The sun *was rising* behind Pikes Peak.
7. The woman who *is rising* now to address the audience has been nominated for vice-president.
8. How much *has* the price of gasoline *raised* since the end of the Persian Gulf Conflict?
9. The cost of a dozen eggs *has been raised*, but you can use this coupon.
10. *Has* the popularity of video games *risen*?

▶ EXERCISE 9 **Choosing the Forms of *Lie-Lay*, *Sit-Set*, and *Rise-Raise***

For each of the following sentences, choose the correct verb form in parentheses. Be prepared to explain your choices.

EXAMPLE **1.** I think I will (*lay, lie*) here and rest awhile.
1. *lie*

1. They (*sit, set*) the yearbooks in Mr. Cohen's office.
2. The thermostat should have kept the temperature from (*rising, raising*).
3. Where was Emily (*sitting, setting*) at the end of *Our Town*?
4. Is the number of traffic fatalities still (*raising, rising*)?
5. San Francisco (*lays, lies*) southwest of Sacramento.
6. Let's (*set, sit*) down and talk about the problem.
7. The price of citrus fruit (*rises, raises*) after a freeze.
8. Hours of driving (*lay, laid*) ahead of us.
9. A replica of *The Thinker* is (*setting, sitting*) there.
10. The helium-filled balloon (*rose, raised*) into the air.

EXERCISE 10

Choosing the Forms of *Lie-Lay*, *Sit-Set*, and *Rise-Raise*

Many familiar expressions and sayings include forms of *lie*, *lay*, *sit*, *set*, *rise*, or *raise*. Complete each expression below by choosing the correct form from the pair given.

1. Let sleeping dogs ____. (*lie, lay*)
2. ____ down your burden. (*Lie, Lay*)
3. Those who would deceive the fox must ____ early in the morning. (*rise, raise*)
4. I'm ____ on top of the world. (*setting, sitting*)
5. If you can't ____ the bridge, lower the river. (*rise, raise*)
6. He who ____ down with dogs gets up with fleas. (*lies, lays*)
7. Cream always ____ to the top. (*rises, raises*)
8. ____ down—you're rocking the boat! (*Set, Sit*)
9. Whenever possible, ____ to the occasion. (*rise, raise*)
10. ____ high standards. (*Set, Sit*)

REVIEW G

Proofreading a Paragraph for Correct Verb Usage

Most of the sentences in the following paragraph have one or more errors in verb usage. For each error, write the correct form of the verb. If a sentence is correct, write *C*. Be prepared to explain your answers.

EXAMPLE   [1] **As a child, Frida Kahlo had often thinked she would become an explorer.**
  1. *thought*

[1] You have probably saw pictures of murals painted by Diego Rivera, the famous Mexican painter. [2] But you may never have came across the paintings of Frida Kahlo, his wife. [3] Kahlo shined in her own right as a powerful painter, although she often standed in the shadow of her more renowned husband. [4] She taked up painting during her recovery from a streetcar accident in which she had broke several bones. [5] Other medical problems arised from time to time throughout her life, and though sometimes she had to paint from her wheelchair, Kahlo always painted straight from her heart. [6] In fact, she gave this image literal expression in one of her paintings in which she portrays herself using a heart as her palette. [7] Kahlo never forgetted her childhood dream of

USAGE

Frida Kahlo (1907–54), "Self Portrait as a Tehuana (Diego on my Mind)". Oil on canvas. 29⅞″ × 24″ (76 × 61 cm). Private collection, Mexico City. Photograph courtesy of The Metropolitan Museum of Art.

exploration and, instead of seas and mountains, explored the territory of the human spirit. [8] Frida Kahlo striked everyone who met her as an elegant, intense, and talented woman. [9] Although she sometimes found life painful, she was full of fun, high spirits, and love. [10] Kahlo is especially noted for her self-portraits, in which she sometimes choosed to paint herself with a tiny portrait of Rivera on her forehead, as in the painting shown here.

Tense

 The *tense* of a verb indicates the time of the action or state of being expressed by the verb.

Every verb has six tenses: *present, past, future, present perfect, past perfect,* and *future perfect*. These tenses are formed from the four principal parts of a verb.

The Forms of Verbs According to Tense

Listing all of the forms of a verb according to tense is called ***conjugating*** a verb.

CONJUGATION OF THE VERB *SEE*			
PRINCIPAL PARTS			
INFINITIVE	**PRESENT PARTICIPLE**	**PAST**	**PAST PARTICIPLE**
see	seeing	saw	seen

CONJUGATION OF THE VERB *SEE* (continued)

PRESENT TENSE

SINGULAR	PLURAL
I see	we see
you see	you see
he, she, it sees	they see

PAST TENSE

SINGULAR	PLURAL
I saw	we saw
you saw	you saw
he, she, it saw	they saw

FUTURE TENSE
(*will* or *shall* + infinitive)

SINGULAR	PLURAL
I will (shall) see	we will (shall) see
you will see	you will see
he, she, it will see	they will see

PRESENT PERFECT TENSE
(*have* or *has* + past participle)

SINGULAR	PLURAL
I have seen	we have seen
you have seen	you have seen
he, she, it has seen	they have seen

PAST PERFECT TENSE
(*had* + past participle)

SINGULAR	PLURAL
I had seen	we had seen
you had seen	you had seen
he, she, it had seen	they had seen

FUTURE PERFECT TENSE
(*will have* or *shall have* + past participle)

SINGULAR	PLURAL
I will (shall) have seen	we will (shall) have seen
you will have seen	you will have seen
he, she, it will have seen	they will have seen

Each tense also has a ***progressive form,*** which expresses continuing action or state of being. The progressive form consists of the appropriate tense of *be* plus the present participle.

Present Progressive	am, is, are seeing
Past Progressive	was, were seeing
Future Progressive	will (shall) be seeing
Present Perfect Progressive	has been, have been seeing
Past Perfect Progressive	had been seeing
Future Perfect Progressive	will (shall) have been seeing

Only the present and the past tenses have another form called the ***emphatic form,*** which shows emphasis. In the present tense, the emphatic form of a verb consists of *do* or *does* plus the infinitive. In the past tense, the emphatic form consists of *did* plus the infinitive.

Present Emphatic	do, does see
Past Emphatic	did see

The conjugation of the verb *be* differs from that of other verbs. Only the present and past tenses of *be* have the progressive form and none of the tenses has the emphatic form.

CONJUGATION OF THE VERB *BE*

PRINCIPAL PARTS

INFINITIVE	PRESENT PARTICIPLE	PAST	PAST PARTICIPLE
be	being	was, were	been

PRESENT TENSE

SINGULAR	**PLURAL**
I am	we are
you are	you are
he, she, it is	they are

Present Progressive: am, are, is being

PAST TENSE

SINGULAR	**PLURAL**
I was	we were
you were	you were
he, she, it was	they were

Past Progressive: was, were being

(continued)

CONJUGATION OF THE VERB *BE* (continued)

FUTURE TENSE
(*will* or *shall* + infinitive)

SINGULAR	PLURAL
I will (shall) be	we will (shall) be
you will be	you will be
he, she, it will be	they will be

PRESENT PERFECT TENSE
(*have* or *has* + past participle)

SINGULAR	PLURAL
I have been	we have been
you have been	you have been
he, she, it has been	they have been

PAST PERFECT TENSE
(*had* + past participle)

SINGULAR	PLURAL
I had been	we had been
you had been	you had been
he, she, it had been	they had been

FUTURE PERFECT TENSE
(*will have* or *shall have* + past participle)

SINGULAR	PLURAL
I will (shall) have been	we will (shall) have been
you will have been	you will have been
he, she, it will have been	they will have been

The Uses of the Tenses

24e.   Each of the six tenses has its own special uses.

(1) The *present tense* is used mainly to express an action (or a state of being) that is occurring now.

EXAMPLES   Martina **races** down the court and **shoots** the ball. [present]
The fans **are cheering** wildly. [present progressive]
Martina and her teammates **do look** confident. [present emphatic]

The present tense is also used

- to show a customary or habitual action or state of being
- to convey a general truth—something that is always true
- to make a historical event seem current (such use is called the *historical present*)
- to summarize the plot or subject matter of a literary work (such use is called the *literary present*)
- to express future time

EXAMPLES For breakfast I usually **eat** some cereal and **drink** orange juice. [customary action]
The earth **revolves** around the sun, which **is** the central star in our solar system. [general truth]
In a surprise move, the Greeks **construct** a huge wooden horse and **leave** it outside the walls of Troy. [historical present]
The Dark Child **tells** the story of a boy growing up in an African village. [literary present]
The workshop that **begins** tomorrow **continues** for two weeks. [future time]

(2) The *past tense* is used to express an action (or a state of being) that occurred in the past but did not continue into the present.

EXAMPLES In the last lap the runner **fell** and **injured** his knee. [past]
He **was trying** to break the record for that event. [past progressive]
The injury **did prevent** him from competing in the relay race. [past emphatic]

NOTE: A past action or state of being may also be shown in another way.

EXAMPLE I **used to hate** spicy food.

(3) The *future tense* is used to express an action (or a state of being) that will occur. The future tense is formed with *will* or *shall* and the infinitive.

EXAMPLES The president **will** not **return** to Washington today. [future]
The president **will be holding** a press conference at noon. [future progressive]

A future action or state of being may also be expressed by using

- the present tense of *be* followed by *going to* and the infinitive form of a verb
- the present tense of *be* followed by *about to* and the infinitive form of a verb
- the present tense of a verb with a word or phrase that expresses future time.

EXAMPLES   My cousins **are going to visit** Japan in July.
Ms. Scheirer **is about to announce** the winners.
The boxer **defends** his title **next Friday night.**

(4) The present perfect tense is used mainly to express an action (or a state of being) that occurred at some indefinite time in the past. The present perfect tense always includes the helping verb *have* or *has.*

EXAMPLES   Miguel already **has entered** the information into the computer. [present perfect]
Who **has been using** this computer? [present perfect progressive]

NOTE: Avoid the use of the present perfect tense to express a *specific* time in the past. Instead, use the past tense.

NONSTANDARD   They have bought a computer last week. [*Last week* indicates a specific time in the past.]
STANDARD   They **bought** a computer last week. [past tense]

The present perfect tense is also used to express an action (or a state of being) that began in the past and continues into the present.

EXAMPLES   Mr. Steele **has taught** school for twenty-one years. [present perfect]
He **has been coaching** soccer since 1986. [present perfect progressive]

(5) The *past perfect tense* is used to express an action (or a state of being) that was completed in the past before some other past occurrence. The past perfect tense always includes the helping verb *had.*

EXAMPLES   Paul **had traveled** several miles before he realized his mistake. [past perfect]
He discovered that he **had been misreading** the road map. [past perfect progressive]

USAGE

(6) The *future perfect tense* is used to express an action (or a state of being) that will be completed in the future before some other future occurrence. The future perfect tense always includes the helping verbs *will have* or *shall have.*

EXAMPLES   By the time school begins in August, you **will have saved** enough money to buy the car. [future perfect]
By then, you **will have been working** here a year.
[future perfect progressive]

▶ EXERCISE 11   **Understanding the Uses of the Six Tenses**

Identify the tenses of the verbs in each of the following pairs of sentences. Be prepared to explain how these differences in tense alter the meanings of the sentences.

1. **a.** Channel 5 News has reported on how successfully Asians have adjusted to life in America.
    b. Channel 5 News had reported on how successfully Asians have adjusted to life in America.
2. **a.** I took piano lessons for three years.
    b. I have taken piano lessons for three years.
3. **a.** We will do our research on Friday.
    b. We will have done our research on Friday.
4. **a.** Jane has reported on recent fossil discoveries.
    b. Jane had reported on recent fossil discoveries.
5. **a.** Do you know that the secret ballot method of voting originated in Australia?
    b. Did you know that the secret ballot method of voting originated in Australia?
6. **a.** We have sent out invitations.
    b. We had sent out invitations.
7. **a.** I will make a time line of the Middle Ages before this weekend.
    b. I will have made a time line of the Middle Ages before this weekend.
8. **a.** I think that I have seen her somewhere before.
    b. I thought that I had seen her somewhere before.
9. **a.** Did the jury reach a verdict?
    b. Has the jury reached a verdict?
10. **a.** Ms. Wong was the club sponsor for five years.
     b. Ms. Wong has been the club sponsor for five years.

EXERCISE 12 **Writing Sentences in the Present Perfect, Past Perfect, and Future Perfect Tenses**

Write ten original sentences according to the following directions.

1. Using different verbs in the *present perfect tense*, write three sentences about a story you have read.
2. Using different verbs in the *past perfect tense*, write three sentences about a movie you have seen.
3. Using different verbs in the *future perfect tense*, write four sentences about a place you would like to visit.

USAGE

PICTURE THIS

Your friend's science project went berserk! Yesterday she took home her new plant fertilizer and tested it on an ordinary rose-bush. Overnight, the little plant produced this enormous rose bloom. You're the star reporter for your school's newspaper, and your friend has agreed to let you interview her. Think of at least five questions to ask your friend about her experiment and about her plans for her amazing discovery. Then use your imagination to record your friend's answers and comments. Be sure to use the correct tenses of verbs in your questions and in your friend's responses.

Subject: your friend's science experiment
Audience: readers of the school newspaper
Purpose: to record an important discovery; to inform

René Magritte, Le Tombeau des Lutteurs, ©1960 c. Herscovici/Art Resource, New York.

Special Problems in the Use of Tenses

Sequence of Tenses

24f. Use tense forms carefully to show the correct relationship between verbs in a sentence.

(1) When describing events that occur at the same time, use verbs in the same tense.

EXAMPLES The coach **blows** the whistle, and the swimmers **dive** into the pool. [present tense]

The coach **blew** the whistle, and the swimmers **dived** into the pool. [past tense]

(2) When describing events that occur at different times, use verbs in different tenses to show the order of events.

EXAMPLES She now **works** for *The New York Times,* but she **worked** for the *Wall Street Journal* earlier this year. [Because her work for *The New York Times* is occurring now, the present tense form *works* is the correct form. Her work for the *Wall Street Journal* occurred at a specific time in the past and preceded her work at the *Times;* therefore, the past tense form *worked* is the correct form.]

Since the new band director **took** over, our band **has won** all of its contests. [Because the new director took over at a specific time in the past, the use of the past tense is correct. The winning has taken place over a period of time and continues into the present; therefore, the present perfect tense is used.]

The tense you use depends on the meaning that you want to express.

EXAMPLES I **think** I **have** a B average in math. [Both verbs are in the present tense to indicate that both actions are occurring now.]

I **think** I **had** a B average in math. [The change to the past tense in the second verb implies that I no longer have a B average in math.]

Lia **said** that she **lived** near the park. [Both verbs are in the past tense to indicate that both actions no longer occur.]

Lia **said** that she **will live** near the park. [The change in the second verb implies that Lia did not live near the park at the time she made the statement but that she planned to live there.]

24g. Avoid the use of *would have* in "if clauses" that express the earlier of two past actions. Use the past perfect tense.

NONSTANDARD   If she would have handed in her application, she would have gotten the job.

STANDARD   If she **had handed** in her application, she would have gotten the job.

NONSTANDARD   If Felita would have asked her parents, she probably could have gone with us.

STANDARD   If Felita **had asked** her parents, she probably could have gone with us.

EXERCISE 13   **Using Tenses Correctly**

Each of the following sentences contains an error in the use of tenses. Identify the error, and then give the correct form of the verb.

EXAMPLE   **1.** The holidays will begin by the time we arrive in Miami.
   1. *will begin—will have begun*

1. Francesca promised to bring the Papago basket that she bought in Arizona.
2. Who found that the earth revolved around the sun?
3. By the time we get to the picnic area, the rain will stop.
4. In July my parents will be married for twenty-five years.
5. If the books have been cataloged last week, why haven't they been placed on the shelves?
6. I would have agreed if you would have asked me sooner.
7. Val claims that cats made the best pets.
8. We studied *Macbeth* after we learned about the English Renaissance and the Globe Theatre.
9. The graduation valedictory will be delivered by then.
10. As a witness to the accident, Pam told what happened.

The Present Infinitive and the Present Perfect Infinitive

Infinitives have present and present perfect tenses.

PRESENT INFINITIVE	to see	to be	to change
PRESENT PERFECT INFINITIVE	to have seen	to have been	to have changed

24h. The *present infinitive* is used to express an action (or a state of being) that follows another action (or state of being).

EXAMPLES   Latrice hopes **to attend** the Super Bowl. [The action expressed by *to attend* follows the action expressed by *hopes.*]
Latrice had planned **to go** to the game with her brother. [The action expressed by *to go* follows the action expressed by *had planned.*]

24i. The *present perfect infinitive* is used to express an action (or a state of being) that precedes another action (or state of being).

EXAMPLES   The divers claim **to have located** an ancient sailing vessel. [The action expressed by *to have located* precedes the action expressed by *claim.*]
They claimed **to have spent** three weeks exploring the ship. [The action expressed by *to have spent* precedes the action expressed by *claimed.*]

The Present Participle and the Present Perfect Participle

Participles have present and present perfect tenses.

PRESENT PARTICIPLE	seeing	being	changing
PRESENT PERFECT PARTICIPLE	having seen	having been	having changed

24j. The *present participle* is used to express an action (or a state of being) that occurs at the same time as another action (or state of being).

EXAMPLES **Gazing** through the telescope, I saw the rings around Saturn. [The action expressed by *Gazing* occurs at the same time as the action expressed by *saw*.]
Studying the night sky, I identified some celestial objects without the use of a telescope. [The action expressed by *Studying* occurs at the same time as the action expressed by *identified*.]

24k. The *present perfect participle* is used to express an action (or a state of being) that precedes another action (or state of being).

EXAMPLES **Having completed** her outline, Kate wrote the first draft of her research paper. [The action expressed by *Having completed* precedes the action expressed by *wrote*.]
Having proofread her research paper, Kate typed the final draft. [The action expressed by *Having proofread* precedes the action expressed by *typed*.]

▶ REVIEW H **Using Tenses Correctly**

Each of the following sentences contains an error in the use of verbs. Identify the error and then give the correct form of the verb.

EXAMPLE **1.** I would have taken more money on my trip to Japan if I would have known what the exchange rate was.
1. *would have known—had known*

1. When you charge the battery in the car, be sure to have protected your eyes and hands from the sulfuric acid in the battery.
2. Deciding to attend the concert at Boyer Hall, we bought four tickets for Saturday night.
3. Before Friday is over, we will hear some great music.
4. If I would have known about the free offer, I would have sent in a coupon.
5. My old skates lay in my closet for the past two years.
6. I would have liked to have gone swimming yesterday.

7. After singing the aria, Jessye Norman received a standing ovation.
8. If I had the address, I would have been able to deliver the package myself.
9. Dave should have went to the dentist three months ago when his tooth began to hurt.
10. I'll just set here for a while until Dr. López returns.

Active Voice and Passive Voice

Voice is the form a transitive verb takes to indicate whether the subject of the verb performs or receives the action.

☞ REFERENCE NOTE: For more discussion of transitive verbs, see page 565.

When the subject of a verb performs the action, the verb is in the *active voice.* When the subject receives the action, the verb is in the *passive voice.*

The verb in a passive construction always includes a form of *be* and the past participle of a transitive verb. Notice in the following conjugation of the verb *see* in the passive voice that the form of *be* determines the tense of the passive verb.

☞ REFERENCE NOTE: The conjugation of *see* in the active voice is on pages 736–737.

As the examples after the following chart show, transitive verbs in the active voice have objects, and verbs in the passive voice do not.

CONJUGATION OF THE VERB *SEE* IN THE PASSIVE VOICE	
PRESENT TENSE	
SINGULAR	*PLURAL*
I am seen	we are seen
you are seen	you are seen
he, she, it is seen	they are seen
Present Progressive: am, are, is being seen	

(continued)

CONJUGATION OF THE VERB *SEE* IN THE PASSIVE VOICE (*continued*)

PAST TENSE

SINGULAR	PLURAL
I was seen	we were seen
you were seen	you were seen
he, she, it was seen	they were seen

Past Progressive: was, were being seen

FUTURE TENSE

SINGULAR	PLURAL
I will be seen	we will be seen
you will be seen	you will be seen
he, she, it will be seen	they will be seen

Future Progressive: will (shall) be being seen

PRESENT PERFECT TENSE

SINGULAR	PLURAL
I have been seen	we have been seen
you have been seen	you have been seen
he, she, it has been seen	they have been seen

PAST PERFECT TENSE

SINGULAR	PLURAL
I had been seen	we had been seen
you had been seen	you had been seen
he, she, it had been seen	they had been seen

FUTURE PERFECT TENSE

SINGULAR	PLURAL
I will (shall) have been seen	we will (shall) have been seen
you will have been seen	you will have been seen
he, she, it will have been seen	they will have been seen

ACTIVE VOICE   Gloria Naylor **wrote** *The Women of Brewster Place.*
[*The Women of Brewster Place* is the direct object.]

PASSIVE VOICE   *The Women of Brewster Place* **was written** by Gloria Naylor.

USAGE

ACTIVE VOICE	The optometrist **adjusted** the eyeglasses.
	[*Eyeglasses* is the direct object.]
PASSIVE VOICE	The eyeglasses **were adjusted** by the optometrist.

ACTIVE VOICE	Carol **has adopted** the two puppies. [*Puppies* is the direct object.]
PASSIVE VOICE	The two puppies **have been adopted** by Carol.
PASSIVE VOICE	The two puppies **have been adopted.**

From these examples, you can see how an active construction can become a passive construction. The verb from the active sentence becomes a past participle preceded by a form of *be.* The object of the verb becomes the subject of the verb in a passive construction. The subject in an active construction becomes the object of the preposition *by* in a passive construction. As the last example shows, this prepositional phrase is not always necessary.

The Retained Object

A transitive verb in the active voice often has an indirect object as well as a direct object. Either object can become the subject or can remain a complement in the passive construction.

```
         S      V      I.O.       D.O.
ACTIVE   Ms. Ribas gave each student a thesaurus.
PASSIVE  Each student was given a thesaurus (by Ms. Ribas).
PASSIVE  A thesaurus was given each student (by Ms. Ribas).
```

As you can see, the indirect object *student* in the active construction becomes the subject in the first passive construction, and the direct object *thesaurus* remains a complement. In the second passive construction, *thesaurus* is the subject, and *student* is the complement. A complement in a passive construction is called a ***retained object,*** not a direct object or an indirect object.

The Uses of the Passive Voice

Choosing between the active voice and the passive voice is a matter of style, not correctness. In general, however, the passive voice is less direct, less forceful, and less concise than the active voice. In fact, the passive voice may produce an awkward effect.

AWKWARD PASSIVE   Last night, the floor **was scrubbed** by my father, and the faucet **was fixed** by my mother.

ACTIVE   Last night, my father **scrubbed** the floor, and my mother **fixed** the faucet.

AWKWARD PASSIVE   The first wristwatch **was created** by a court jeweler when a watch set in a bracelet **was requested** by Empress Josephine.

ACTIVE   When Empress Josephine **requested** a watch set in a bracelet, a court jeweler **created** the first wristwatch.

Notice that the use of the passive voice in a long passage is particularly awkward.

AWKWARD PASSIVE   When my mother **was asked** by the local camera club to give a lecture on modern photography, she **was amazed** by the request. Mom **had** never **been chosen** to do anything like this before. Since I **am considered** by my mother to be the most imaginative member of our family, I **was given** by her the task of choosing the topics that **would be presented** by her. Dad **was asked** by her to select the slides that **would be shown** to the amateur photographers. Within a few days, the lecture **had been prepared** by Mom. On the night of the presentation, everyone in the audience **was impressed** by Mom's knowledge of modern photography.

ACTIVE   When the local camera club **asked** my mother to give a lecture on modern photography, the request **amazed** her. No one **had** ever **chosen** Mom to do anything like this before. Since my mother **considers** me the most imaginative member of our family, she **gave** me the task of choosing the topics that she **would present**. She **asked** Dad to select the slides that she **would show** to the amateur photographers. Within a few days, Mom **had prepared** the lecture. On the night of the presentation, Mom's knowledge of modern photography **impressed** everyone in the audience.

USAGE

24I. The passive voice should be used sparingly. Use the passive voice in the following situations.

(1) When you do not know the performer of the action

EXAMPLES   Asbestos **was used** for making fireproof materials.
An anonymous letter **had been sent** to the police chief.

(2) When you do not want to reveal the performer of the action

EXAMPLES   Many careless errors **were made** in some of these essays.
The missing paintings **have been returned** to the museum.

(3) When you want to emphasize the receiver of the action

EXAMPLES   Penicillin **was discovered** accidentally.
This book **has been translated** into more than one hundred languages.

▶ EXERCISE 14   **Revising Sentences in the Passive Voice**

Revise the following sentences by changing the passive voice to active voice wherever the change is desirable. If the passive is preferable, write C.

EXAMPLE   **1.** A variety of cooking methods and utensils were invented by early humans.
1. *Early humans invented a variety of cooking methods and utensils.*

1. At first, roots and berries were gathered and eaten by these people.
2. The discovery that certain foods can be improved by cooking may have accidentally been made by them.
3. Slaughtered animals or piles of edible roots may have been left near the fire by hunters and gatherers.
4. It was noticed by them that when food was cooked, it tasted better.
5. The first ovens were formed from pits lined with stones and hot coals.

6. It wasn't long before ovens were built above the ground with some kind of chimney to carry away the smoke.
7. Primitive kettles were made by early humans by smearing clay over reed baskets and drying them in the sun.
8. Liquid foods could then be kept in such a basket for short periods without leaking.
9. When a clay-coated basket was placed near the flames by a prehistoric cook to heat its contents, sometimes the clay was baked by the high temperature into a pottery shell.
10. Once the simple physics of making pottery was mastered by early people, they learned to create the pottery shell without the basket.

WRITING APPLICATION

Using Active Voice and Passive Voice Effectively

Most authorities on writing advise people to use the active voice. In general, this advice is sound—active voice verbs do help to make writing direct and lively. They clearly show who or what performed the action of the verb. Passive voice verbs, on the other hand, de-emphasize the identity of the person or thing performing the action. Consequently, the choice between an active or a passive voice verb in a particular sentence is a matter of style. The decision about which voice to use rests on what the writer wants to emphasize. Compare the following sentences.

SENTENCE 1   The rescue team found the trapped miner and quickly cleared away the debris. [active voice]
SENTENCE 2   The trapped miner was found, and the debris was quickly cleared away. [passive voice]

What does each sentence emphasize? Which sentence might you use in a news update on a mining accident? in a story about emergency rescue workers? Explain your choices.

▶ WRITING ACTIVITY

A writer's club is holding a contest for the most exciting opening of an adventure story. The winner of the contest will get to publish his or her completed story in an upcoming issue of a national magazine. To enter the contest, write a two- or three-paragraph opening for an adventure story. Use active voice verbs to make your sentences lively and concise. Use passive voice verbs wherever they are needed for style or for emphasis.

Prewriting A good adventure story centers around a gripping conflict, a life-or-death problem that the hero must overcome. Brainstorm some ideas for an exciting conflict. Then create a brief plot outline for a story based on the conflict you think would lead to the greatest adventure. (For help with developing a short-story plot, see pages 166–167.) Think of a way to begin your story. You may want to begin at an exciting point in the middle of the action, or you may want to tell the story as a flashback. Jot down interesting details that will grab your readers' attention.

Writing Use your prewriting notes to help you write a first draft. Expand on your original ideas, adding details as you think of them.

Evaluating and Revising Ask a friend to read your story opener. Is the opening interesting and exciting? Can your friend predict what will happen next? Note down any revision suggestions. After you've revised the content of your story opener, focus on your writing style. Have you used active voice and passive voice verbs effectively? Use a thesaurus to help you replace any bland verbs with precise, imaginative ones.

Proofreading Remember that writers from all across the country will be entering the contest. Submit your best writing and check carefully for mistakes in grammar, usage, spelling, and punctuation. Be sure that you've used the correct forms of irregular verbs.

Mood

Mood is the form a verb takes to indicate the attitude of the person using the verb. Verbs may be in one of three moods: the *indicative,* the *imperative,* or the *subjunctive.*

24m. The ***indicative mood*** is used to express a fact, an opinion, or a question.

EXAMPLES   Andrei Sakharov **was** the nuclear physicist who **won** the Nobel Prize for peace in 1975.
All of us **think** that baseball team **is** the best one in the state.
Can you **explain** the difference between a meteor and a meteorite?

 REFERENCE NOTE: For examples of all of the tense forms in the indicative mood, see the conjugations on pages 736–737 and 738–739.

24n. The ***imperative mood*** is used to express a direct command or request.

The imperative mood of a verb has only one form. It is the same as the infinitive form of a verb.

EXAMPLES   **Explain** the difference between a meteor and a meteorite.
Please **fasten** your seat belt.

USAGE

24o. The *subjunctive mood* is used to express a suggestion, a necessity, a condition contrary to fact, or a wish.

Only the present and past tenses have distinctive subjunctive forms. The other tense forms in the subjunctive mood are the same as those in the indicative mood.

The following partial conjugation of *be* shows how the present and past tense forms in the subjunctive mood differ from those in the indicative mood. [Note: The use of *that* and *if,* which are shown in parentheses, is explained at the bottom of this page and on the next page.]

PRESENT INDICATIVE		PRESENT SUBJUNCTIVE	
SINGULAR	*PLURAL*	*SINGULAR*	*PLURAL*
I am	we are	(that) I be	(that) we be
you are	you are	(that) you be	(that) you be
he, she, it is	they are	(that) he, she, it be	(that) they be
PAST INDICATIVE		**PAST SUBJUNCTIVE**	
I was	we were	(if) I were	(if) we were
you were	you were	(if) you were	(if) you were
he, she, it was	they were	(if) he, she, it were	(if) they were

Notice in the conjugation that the present subjunctive form of a verb is the same as the infinitive form. For all verbs except *be,* the past subjunctive form is the same as the past form. The verb *be* has two past tense forms. As you can see, however, the past tense form *was* in the indicative mood becomes *were* in the subjunctive mood. Therefore, *were* is the only past subjunctive form of *be.*

(1) The *present subjunctive* is used to express a suggestion or a necessity.

Generally, the verb in a subordinate clause beginning with *that* is in the subjunctive mood when the independent clause contains a word indicating a suggestion (such as *ask, request, suggest,* or *recommend*) or a word indicating a necessity (such as *necessary* or *essential*).

EXAMPLES   Ms. Chávez suggested that he **apply** for the job.
The moderator at the convention requested that the
state delegates **be seated.**
It is necessary that she **attend** the convention.
It is required that you **be** here on time.

(2) The *past subjunctive* is used to express a condition contrary to fact or to express a wish.

In general, a clause beginning with *if, as if,* or *as though* expresses a condition contrary to fact—something that is not true. In such a clause, use the past subjunctive. Remember that *were* is the only past subjunctive form of *be.*

EXAMPLES   If I **were** you, I'd have those tires checked.
If he **were** to proofread his writing, he would make
fewer errors.
Because of the bad telephone connection, Gregory
sounded as though [as if] he **were** ten thousand
miles away.

Similarly, use the past subjunctive to express a wish—a condition that is desirable.

EXAMPLES   I wish I **were** more patient than I am.
Reiko wishes that her best friend **were**n't moving
away.

USAGE

▶ EXERCISE 15   **Identify the Mood of Verbs**

For each of the following sentences, identify the mood of the italicized verb as *indicative, imperative,* or *subjunctive.*

1. Theo, *stand* back a safe distance while I try again to start this lawnmower.
2. Did you know that Tamisha's mother *is* the new manager at the supermarket?
3. Bradley says that if he *were* president, he'd take steps to reduce the federal deficit.
4. I suggest that these young maple trees *be* planted quickly before they wilt.
5. *Were* you and your two brothers excited about visiting your birthplace in Mexico?
6. This Lenni Lenape moccasin *was* found near Matawan, New Jersey.

7. Stay there and *be* a good dog while I go into the bakery, Molly.
8. When my dad saw the dented fender, he looked as if he *were* ready to explode.
9. "I wish that you *were* not moving so far away," muttered my best friend Bao.
10. Mr. Darwin requested that you *be* the bus monitor on our next class trip.

▶ REVIEW I

Proofreading Sentences for Correct Verb Usage

Most of the following sentences contain errors in the use of verbs. If a sentence has a verb error, identify the error, and then give the correct verb form. If a sentence is correct, write *C*.

EXAMPLE 1. After he had passed the jewelry store, he wished he went into it.
1. *went—had gone*

1. The rock group had finished the concert, but the audience called for another set.
2. Do you think that she would have volunteer to help us if she weren't highly qualified?
3. If Sherrie would not have missed the printer's deadline, the yearbook delivery would have been on time.
4. Although I thought I planned my trip down to the last detail, there was one thing I had forgotten.
5. If you would have remembered to bring along something to read, you would not have been so bored.
6. The smell from the paper mill laid over the town like a blanket.
7. Sarah says she enjoyed working on the kibbutz in Israel last summer, but she hardly got a chance to set down the whole time.
8. By the time they had smelled the smoke, the flames had already begun to spread.
9. I am glad to have the opportunity to revise my essay for a higher grade.
10. If Emiliano Zapata would have known the invitation was a trap, he would not have been ambushed at a farm near Cuautla.

> REVIEW J   **Proofreading a Paragraph for Correct Use of Verbs**

Most of the sentences in the following paragraph contain errors in the use of verbs. If a sentence has an error, identify the error and then supply the correct verb form. If a sentence is correct, write *C*.

EXAMPLE   [1] After he had lit the candle, Dad begun to recite the first principle of Kwanzaa.
  1. *begun—began*

[1] Kwanzaa has been being celebrated by African Americans for more than twenty-five years. [2] This holiday has been created in 1966 by Maulanga Karenga, a professor of black studies at California State University. [3] Dr. Karenga wished that there was a nonreligious holiday especially for black Americans. [4] If he has not treasured his own background, we would not have this inspiring celebration to enjoy. [5] Professor Karenga has believed that people's heritage should be celebrated by them. [6] Recently, more and more African Americans have began to reserve the seven-day period immediately following Christmas for Kwanzaa. [7] If you would have joined my family for Kwanzaa last year, you would have heard my grandfather's talk about family values and about African Americans who have fought for freedom and honor. [8] We all wore items of traditional African clothing like these and displayed a red, black, and green flag to symbolize Africa. [9] Mom lay out a wonderful feast each night, and we lit a candle and talked about one of the seven principles of Kwanzaa. [10] I wish I asked you to our house last year for Kwanzaa, and I will definitely invite you this year.

USAGE

Review: Posttest

A. Proofreading Sentences for Correct Verb Usage

Most of the following sentences contain errors in the use of verbs. If a sentence has a verb error, revise the sentence, using the correct verb form. If a sentence is correct, write *C*.

EXAMPLE   **1.** If I would have seen the accident, I would have reported it.

      1. *If I had seen the accident, I would have reported it.*

1. If modern society was an agricultural one, more of us would know about farming and about the difficulties faced by farmers.
2. The last time a count was taken, there have been more than 39,000 Native Americans living in Wisconsin.
3. How many of us possess the skills to have survived on our own without the assistance of store-bought items?
4. If you would have taken the nutrition class, you would have learned how to shop wisely for food.
5. Wacky, my pet hamster, was acting as if she was trying to tell me something.
6. Yesterday, Dad's pickup truck was washed and waxed by my brother.
7. According to this news article, the concert last Saturday night is "a resounding success."
8. Janet Jackson's concerts have broke all attendance records at the City Arena.
9. Because of the excessive amount of rain this spring, the water in the dam has raised to a dangerous level.
10. After spending the entire morning working in the garden, Jim is laying down for a rest.

B. Proofreading Sentences for Correct Verb Usage

Most of the following sentences contain errors in the use of verbs. If a sentence has a verb error, revise the sentence, using the correct verb form. If a sentence is correct, write *C*.

EXAMPLE   **1.** From our studies we had concluded that women had played many critical roles in the history of our nation.
       1. *From our studies we have concluded that women have played many critical roles in the history of our nation.*

11. In Daytona, Florida, Mary McLeod Bethune had founded a tiny school, which become Bethune-Cookman College.

12. Jane Addams founded Hull House in Chicago to educate the poor and to acquaint immigrants with American ways; for her efforts she had received the Nobel Prize for peace in 1931.

13. In 1932, after a flight lasting almost fifteen hours, Amelia Earhart became the first woman to have flown solo across the Atlantic Ocean.

14. Pearl Buck, a recipient of the Nobel Prize for literature in 1938, strived to bring understanding and peace to people all over the world.

15. When the Republican National Convention met in San Francisco in 1964, Margaret Chase Smith, senator from Maine, received twenty-seven delegate votes for the presidential nomination.

16. Lorraine Hansberry wrote the successful play *A Raisin in the Sun*, which had been translated into thirty languages.

17. Have you ever heard of Belva Lockwood, a woman whose accomplishments paved the way for women in politics?

18. In 1879, a short time after Lockwood was admitted to the bar, she became the first woman lawyer to have argued a case before the United States Supreme Court.

19. Although Lockwood is not well-known nowadays, she did receive more than four thousand votes for the presidency in 1884.

20. By the time you leave high school, you will learn many interesting facts about history.

USAGE

25 CORRECT USE OF MODIFIERS

Forms and Uses of Adjectives and Adverbs; Comparison

Diagnostic Test

A. Selecting Modifiers to Complete Sentences

Select the correct modifier in parentheses for each of the following sentences.

EXAMPLE **1.** When you feel (*nervous, nervously*), take a deep breath and concentrate on relaxing images.
1. *nervous*

1. When Rosa and I had the flu, Rosa was (*sicker, sickest*).
2. As a student, Edmonia Lewis watched (*careful, carefully*) when her teacher demonstrated sculpting techniques.
3. As you approach the next intersection, drive (*cautious, cautiously*).
4. This car is roomier than (*any, any other*) car we ever had.
5. The leaders of the Underground Railroad acted (*quick, quickly*) to help runaway slaves.

6. If you look at the two kittens carefully, you will see that the smaller one is (*healthier, healthiest*).
7. It was obvious from his response at the press conference that the candidate had prepared his answers (*well, good*).
8. This must be the (*baddest, worst*) movie ever made.
9. You will drive more (*steady, steadily*) if you keep your eyes on the road.
10. Mr. Yan thinks that Jacinto Quirarte is the (*better, best*) authority on Mexican American and pre-Columbian art.

B. Proofreading a Paragraph for Incorrect Modifiers

Most of the sentences in the following paragraph contain errors in the use of modifiers. Identify each error and give the correct form. If a sentence is correct, write *C*.

EXAMPLE **[1]** The slogan of Chicago's most largest hands-on museum is "We've got fun down to a science."
    1. *most largest—largest*

[11] Malcolm and I went to visit Chicago's interestingest museum, the Museum of Science and Industry. **[12]** Although the museum houses more than two thousand displays, we decided to go slow even if it meant we could see only a few exhibits. **[13]** To see certain special displays, we planned our day careful. **[14]** First, we walked through an incredible model of a beating heart. **[15]** The thumping and swishing of the heart were better than any sound effects we'd ever heard. **[16]** Next, Malcolm went to play computer games while I decided to explore more livelier happenings at the farm exhibit. **[17]** When we met later for lunch, I asked him which computer game was hardest to win, tic tac toe or the money game. **[18]** As we headed for the Omnimax Theater to view the most advanced film projection system in the world, Malcolm admitted that he hadn't done good at either game. **[19]** We spent the rest of the day looking at a submarine, a lunar module, and, the funniest thing of all—ourselves on television! **[20]** We both agreed that the Museum of Science and Industry is better than any museum we've ever visited.

Forms of Modifiers

A *modifier* is a word that limits the meaning of another word. The two kinds of modifiers are the *adjective* and the *adverb*.

An *adjective* limits the meaning of a noun or a pronoun.

EXAMPLES **strong** wind   **an** alligator
a loud voice   **the original** one

An *adverb* limits the meaning of a verb, an adjective, or another adverb.

EXAMPLES drives **carefully**   **suddenly** stopped
extremely important   **rather** quickly

Most modifiers with an *–ly* ending are used as adverbs. In fact, many adverbs are formed by adding *–ly* to adjectives.

ADJECTIVES perfect   clear   quiet   abrupt
ADVERBS perfectly   clearly   quietly   abruptly

However, some modifiers ending in *–ly* may be used as adjectives.

EXAMPLES a **daily** lesson   an **early** breakfast   a **lively** discussion

A few modifiers have the same form whether used as adjectives or as adverbs.

ADJECTIVES	ADVERBS
a **hard** job	works **hard**
a **late** start	started **late**
an **early** arrival	arriving **early**
a **long** pause	to pause **long**

Uses of Modifiers

25a. Use an adjective to modify the subject of a linking verb.

The most common linking verbs are the forms of *be: am, is, are, was, were, be, been,* and *being*. A linking verb is often followed by a *predicate adjective*—a word that modifies the subject.

EXAMPLES   Our new computer system is **efficient.**
The governor's comments on the controversial issue
were **candid.**

☞ REFERENCE NOTE: For more about predicate adjectives, see

25b. Use an adverb to modify an action verb.

Action verbs are often modified by adverbs—words that tell
how, when, where, or *to what extent* an action is performed.

EXAMPLES   Our new computer system is operating **efficiently.**
The governor **candidly** expressed her view on the
controversial issue.

Some verbs may be used as linking verbs or as action verbs.

EXAMPLES   Carmen looked **frantic.** [*Looked* is a linking verb. The
modifier following it is an adjective, *frantic.*]
Carmen looked **frantically** for her class ring. [*Looked*
is an action verb. The modifier following it is an
adverb, *frantically.*]

To help you determine whether a verb is a linking verb or
an action verb, replace the verb with a form of *seem.* If the substitution sounds reasonable, the original verb is a linking verb.
If the substitution sounds absurd, the original verb is an action
verb.

EXAMPLES   Carmen looked **frantic.** [Since *Carmen seemed frantic*
sounds reasonable, *looked* is a linking verb.]
Carmen looked **frantically** for her class ring. [Since
Carmen seemed frantically for her class ring sounds
absurd, *looked* is an action verb.]

☞ REFERENCE NOTE: For more information about linking verbs and
action verbs, see pages 565–567.

Like main verbs, verbals may be modified by adverbs.

EXAMPLES   Barking **loudly,** the dog frightened the burglar. [The
adverb *loudly* modifies the participle *barking.*]
Not fastening the bracket **tightly** will enable you to
adjust it **later.** [The adverbs *not* and *tightly* modify
the gerund *fastening.* The adverb *later* modifies
the infinitive *to adjust.*]

☞ REFERENCE NOTE: For more about verbals, see pages 611–617.

USAGE

USAGE

> ▶ EXERCISE 1

Selecting Modifiers to Complete Sentences

Select the correct modifier in parentheses for each of the following sentences.

EXAMPLE **1.** When you look (*careful, carefully*) at these pots, you can see the tiny figures etched on them.
1. *carefully*

1. The woman in the picture is Rosemary Apple Blossom Lonewolf, an artist whose style remains (*unique, uniquely*) among Native American potters.
2. Lonewolf combines (*traditional, traditionally*) and modern techniques to create her miniature pottery.
3. In crafting her pots, Lonewolf uses dark red clay that is (*ready, readily*) available around the Santa Clara Pueblo in New Mexico, where she lives.

4. These miniatures have a detailed and (*delicate, delicately*) etched surface called sgraffito.
5. Because of the (*extreme, extremely*) intricate detail on its surface, a single pot may take many months to finish.
6. The subjects for most of Lonewolf's pots combine ancient Pueblo myths and traditions with (*current, currently*) ideas or events.

7. One pot called *Half-Breed's Horizon* (*clear, clearly*) depicts a Pueblo corn dancer walking down a city street lined with skyscrapers.

8. Lonewolf uses such images to show that Native Americans can and do adapt (*real, really*) well to new ways.

9. At first known only in the Southwest, Lonewolf's work is now shown throughout the United States because the appeal of her subjects is quite (*broad, broadly*).

10. Rosemary Lonewolf's talented family includes her father, grandfather, and son, who are all (*high, highly*) skilled potters.

Six Troublesome Modifiers

Bad and *Badly*

Bad is an adjective. *Badly* is an adverb. In standard English, only the adjective form should follow a sense verb or other linking verb.

| NONSTANDARD | If the meat smells badly, don't eat it. |
| STANDARD | If the meat smells **bad,** don't eat it. |

NOTE: Although the expression *feel badly* has become acceptable in informal situations, use *feel bad* in formal speaking and writing.

Good and *Well*

Good is an adjective. *Well* may be used as an adjective or as an adverb. Avoid using *good* to modify an action verb. Instead, use *well,* an adverb meaning "capably" or "satisfactorily."

| NONSTANDARD | The school orchestra played good. |
| STANDARD | The school orchestra played **well.** |

| NONSTANDARD | Although she was nervous, Aretha performed quite good. |
| STANDARD | Although she was nervous, Aretha performed quite **well.** |

Used as an adjective, *well* means "in good health" or "satisfactory in appearance or condition."

EXAMPLES	He says that he feels **well.**
	She looks **well** in that band uniform.
	It's midnight, and all is **well.**

USAGE

Slow and *Slowly*

Slow is an adjective. *Slowly* is an adverb. Avoid the common error of using *slow* to modify an action verb.

NONSTANDARD   Do sloths always move that slow?
    STANDARD   Do sloths always move that **slowly**?

NOTE: The expressions *drive slow* and *go slow* have become acceptable in informal situations. In formal speaking and writing, however, use *drive slowly* and *go slowly*.

> ### Determining the Correct Use of
> EXERCISE 2   *Bad* and *Badly*, *Well* and *Good*,
>   and *Slow* and *Slowly*

Each of the following sentences contains an italicized modifier. If the modifier is incorrect, give the correct form. If the modifier is correct, write C.

EXAMPLE   **1.** When I painted the house, I fell off the ladder and hurt my right arm *bad.*
    1. *badly*

1. The renowned conductor Leonard Bernstein led the New York Philharmonic Orchestra *well* for many years.
2. Despite the immense size and tremendous power of this airplane, the engines start up *slow.*
3. I can hit the ball *good* if I keep my eye on it.
4. Before Uncle Chet's hip-replacement surgery, his gait was painful and *slow.*
5. After studying French for the past three years in high school, we were pleased to discover how *good* we spoke and understood it on our trip to Quebec.
6. Some of the experiments that the chemistry class has conducted have made the corridors smell *badly.*
7. During the Han dynasty in China, candidates who did *bad* on civil service tests did not become government officials.
8. Whenever I watch the clock, the time seems to go *slow.*
9. When my parents correct my little sister, they tell her not to behave *bad.*
10. After hearing how her Navajo ancestors overcame many problems, Anaba felt *well.*

USAGE

REVIEW A   **Determining the Correct Use of Modifiers**

Proofread the following paragraph, correcting any errors in the use of modifiers. If a sentence is correct, write *C*.

EXAMPLE   [1] Some volcanoes rest quiet for many years.
            1. *quietly*

[1] More than five hundred active volcanoes exist on land, and thousands more are found in the sea. [2] Eruptions of these volcanoes are often spectacularly violent. [3] Hugely reddish clouds rise from the volcano, while bright rivers of lava pour down the mountainside. [4] Beyond the eerie, beautiful spectacle that the eye sees, however, is the tremendous destructive force of the volcano. [5] A volcano begins as magma, a river of rock melted by the extreme heat inside the earth. [6] The rock melts slow, forming a gas that, together with the magma, causes the volcano to erupt. [7] Lava flows from the eruption site, sometimes quite rapid, destroying everything in its path. [8] After a volcano erupts, observers usually feel badly because the heat and ash created by the eruption can seriously threaten not only the environment but also the lives and property of people living nearby. [9] On the other hand, volcanoes can also have a positive effect on the environment. [10] Lava and volcanic ash gradually mix with the soil to make it wonderful rich in minerals.

USAGE

PICTURE THIS

Just look at all these beautifully wrapped presents! This holiday season you and many other volunteers worked for an organization that distributes gifts to needy children. The most enjoyable part of your job was wrapping these gifts with colorful paper and ribbons. Now you want to remember

this special time as clearly as possible. Write a journal entry describing the work you did. Tell how you felt when the last present was wrapped. In your journal entry, use at least four adjectives with linking verbs.

Subject: holiday volunteer work
Audience: yourself
Purpose: to record events; to express your feelings

Comparison of Modifiers

25c. *Comparison* refers to the change in the form of an adjective or an adverb to show increasing or decreasing degrees in the quality the modifier expresses.

There are three degrees of comparison: *positive, comparative,* and *superlative.*

	POSITIVE	COMPARATIVE	SUPERLATIVE
ADJECTIVES	neat	neater	neatest
	careful	more careful	most careful
	optimistic	less optimistic	least optimistic
	good	better	best
ADVERBS	soon	sooner	soonest
	calmly	more calmly	most calmly
	commonly	less commonly	least commonly
	well	better	best

Regular Comparison

(1) Most one-syllable modifiers form the comparative and superlative degrees by adding *−er* and *−est.*

POSITIVE	COMPARATIVE	SUPERLATIVE
soft	softer	softest
clean	cleaner	cleanest
fast	faster	fastest
long	longer	longest

☞ REFERENCE NOTE: For information on determining the syllables in a word, see page 976.

(2) Some two-syllable modifiers form the comparative and superlative degrees by adding *–er* and *–est.* Other two-syllable modifiers form the comparative and superlative degrees by using *more* and *most.*

POSITIVE	COMPARATIVE	SUPERLATIVE
simple	simpler	simplest
likely	likelier	likeliest
cautious	more cautious	most cautious
freely	more freely	most freely

If you are not sure how a two-syllable modifier is compared, use a dictionary.

☞ REFERENCE NOTE: For guidelines on spelling modifiers with *–er* and *–est,* see pages 906–907.

(3) Modifiers of more than two syllables form the comparative and superlative degrees by using *more* and *most.*

POSITIVE	COMPARATIVE	SUPERLATIVE
efficient	more efficient	most efficient
punctual	more punctual	most punctual
frequently	more frequently	most frequently
skillfully	more skillfully	most skillfully

USAGE

(4) To show a decrease in the qualities they express, all modifiers form the comparative and superlative degrees by using *less* and *least*.

POSITIVE	COMPARATIVE	SUPERLATIVE
proud	less proud	least proud
honest	less honest	least honest
patiently	less patiently	least patiently
reasonably	less reasonably	least reasonably

Irregular Comparison

Some modifiers do not follow the regular methods of forming the comparative and superlative degrees.

POSITIVE	COMPARATIVE	SUPERLATIVE
bad	worse	worst
good	better	best
well	better	best
little	less	least
many	more	most
much	more	most

▶ EXERCISE 3 **Writing the Comparative and Superlative Forms of Modifiers**

Write the comparative and the superlative forms of each of the following modifiers.

EXAMPLE **1.** stubborn
1. *more (less) stubborn; most (least) stubborn*

1. anxious
2. hard
3. cheerful
4. eager
5. quick
6. well
7. cold
8. stealthily
9. expensive
10. enthusiastically

Uses of Comparative and Superlative Forms

25d. Use the comparative degree when comparing two things. Use the superlative degree when comparing more than two.

COMPARATIVE   Although both puppies look cute, the **more active** one seems **healthier.** [comparison of two puppies]
After reading *King Lear* and *A Winter's Tale,* I can understand why *King Lear* is **more widely** praised. [comparison of two plays]

SUPERLATIVE   Of the four plays that we saw, I think *Death of a Salesman* was the **most moving.** [comparison of four plays]
I sat in the front row because it provided the **best** view of the chemistry experiment. [comparison of many views]

NOTE: In informal situations the superlative degree is sometimes used to emphasize the comparison of only two things. Avoid such use of the superlative degree in formal speaking and writing.

INFORMAL   Which was hardest to learn, French or Spanish?
FORMAL   Which was **harder** to learn, French or Spanish?

The superlative degree is also used to compare two things in some idiomatic expressions.

EXAMPLE   Put your best foot forward.

25e. Include the word *other* or *else* when comparing one member of a group with the rest of the group.

NONSTANDARD   Anita has hit more home runs this season than any member of the team. [Anita is a member of the team. Logically, Anita could not have hit more home runs than herself.]
STANDARD   Anita has hit more home runs this season than any **other** member of the team.
NONSTANDARD   I think that Jean-Pierre Rampal plays the flute better than anyone. [The pronoun *anyone* includes Rampal. Logically, Jean-Pierre Rampal cannot play better than himself.]
STANDARD   I think Jean-Pierre Rampal plays the flute better than anyone **else.**

USAGE

25f. Avoid double comparisons.

A *double comparison* is the use of two comparative forms (usually –*er* and *more*) or two superlative forms (usually –*est* and *most*) to modify the same word.

NONSTANDARD   This week's program is more funnier than last week's.

    STANDARD   This week's program is **funnier** than last week's.

NONSTANDARD   In our school, the most farthest you can go in math is Calculus II.

    STANDARD   In our school, the **farthest** you can go in math is Calculus II.

 EXERCISE 4   **Using the Comparative and Superlative Forms of Modifiers**

Revise the following sentences by correcting the errors in the use of the comparative and superlative forms of modifiers.

EXAMPLE   **1.** It seems I spend more time doing my biology homework than anyone in my class.

         1. *It seems I spend more time doing my biology homework than anyone else in my class.*

1. Which is the most famous Russian ballet company, the Kirov or the Bolshoi?
2. When Barbara-Rose Collins served as a state representative in Michigan, she fought harder than anyone for key legislation to help minorities.
3. According to the National Weather Service, Hurricane Carla did more damage than any hurricane in this century.
4. Although both cars appear to be well constructed, I think that the most desirable one is the one that gets better gas mileage.
5. Which of these two hotels is farthest from the airport?
6. I know this shade of blue is a closer match than that one, but we still haven't found the better match.
7. In the dance marathon, Anton and Inez managed to stay awake and keep moving longer than any couple on the dance floor.
8. Of all the women singers of the 1960s and 1970s, Joan Baez participated in more peace rallies than anyone.

9. Lucia has the most uncommonest hobby I've ever heard of—collecting insects.
10. The newscaster said that the pollen count this morning was higher than any count taken in the past ten years.

WRITING APPLICATION

Using Comparisons in Persuasive Writing

From time to time, you've probably tried to persuade other people to see or do things differently. You likely gave specific reasons why they should change their minds. You may even have presented these reasons as comparisons.

EXAMPLE *Return of the Star Warriors* is **more believable** and has **better** special effects than *Space Creeps*.

▶ WRITING ACTIVITY

How can producers of television shows make their programs more appealing to teenagers? You've decided to write to one of the major networks expressing your opinion on the subject. Write a letter pointing out how producers can better address the interests and concerns of teenage viewers. To support your opinion, draw a comparison between two current television shows—one that you and your friends like and one that you don't like. Explain why one show is more appealing to you than the other. In your letter, use at least five comparative forms of modifiers.

Prewriting You may already have a clear idea of the kinds of shows you like to see. If not, you can get started by listing several current TV programs aimed at teenage audiences. Ask a few friends to tell you what they like or dislike about each show. Jot down your friends' responses along with your own opinions. Then narrow down the list to the most-liked and the least-liked shows. Use your notes to help you identify the kinds of characters, situations, and themes that do and do not appeal to teenage viewers.

Writing Begin your draft by explaining the reason for your letter and clearly stating your opinion. Then use your notes to help you give specific examples to support your opinion. Compare the two TV shows you've chosen, telling why one appeals to you and the other doesn't. Give the producers practical suggestions for creating more interesting programs. Maintain a polite, objective tone throughout your letter. Be sure that you use the proper form for business letters. (See pages 994–996.)

Evaluating and Revising Ask an adult friend or relative to help you evaluate your letter. Is your opinion statement clear? Are your reasons specific and convincing? Remember you are writing to a busy executive. Revise your letter to make it as concise and direct as you can. Be sure that you've used at least five comparative forms of modifiers.

Proofreading and Publishing Make sure you've used the appropriate form for business letters. Proofread your letter for any errors in grammar, spelling, or punctuation. Pay special attention to modifiers, and revise any double comparisons. To publish your letter, you can mail it to the television network. First, find out the address of the network and, if possible, the name of the person to whom you should write. Then, retype or recopy the letter neatly. You and your classmates may want to collect your letters and send them all together, along with a cover note.

REVIEW B **Using Modifiers Correctly**

Proofread the following paragraph, correcting any errors in the use of modifiers. If a sentence is correct, write *C*.

EXAMPLE   [1] Of the two forts, this one is the oldest.
    1. *older*

[1] St. Augustine, Florida, is the home of *Castillo de San Marcos,* the most oldest standing fort in the United States. [2] Earlier wood forts had been extremely difficult to defend, but *Castillo*

de San Marcos, as you can see, was built of stone. [3] Before the construction of this fort, Spain had no strong military base that could withstand a real fierce enemy assault. [4] In fact, previous battles with the British had proved that of the two countries, Spain had the least defensible forts. [5] Begun in 1672, the building of *Castillo de San Marcos* went slow, taking several decades to complete. [6] Replacing the existing nine wood forts in St. Augustine, the new stone fort fared good against attacks. [7] Today, no one is sure which fort was easiest to protect, Spain's *Castillo de San Marcos* or the British fort in Charleston, South Carolina. [8] However, *Castillo de San Marcos*, with its 16-foot-thick walls and 40-foot-wide moat, proved to be one of the most strongest forts in the South and was never taken by force. [9] When Florida finally did come under British control, the Spanish felt especially badly about leaving their impressive fort in the hands of their old enemies. [10] *Castillo de San Marcos* is now a National Monument and stands today as a memorial to all those who fought so courageous to guard St. Augustine long ago.

USAGE

Review: Posttest

A. Using Modifiers Correctly

Most of the following sentences contain errors in the use of modifiers. If the sentence is incorrect, revise it to eliminate the error. If it is correct, write *C*.

EXAMPLE   **1.** Steve, who is the most brightest student in the physics class, is also a whiz in chemistry.
   1. *Steve, who is the brightest student in the physics class, is also a whiz in chemistry.*

1. After listening to "The Battle of the Bands," we thought that the jazz band performed even more better than the rock group.
2. When the treasurer presented the annual report, most of the statistics showed that the company had done badder this year than last.
3. Megan shoots foul shots so good that she has made the varsity team.
4. The more even you distribute the work load among the group members, the more satisfied everyone will be.
5. In 1949, Jackie Robinson was voted the Most Valuable Player in the National League.
6. Last night the weather forecaster announced that this has been the most rainy spring season the area has had in the past decade.
7. This is the most tasty piece of sourdough bread I have ever eaten.
8. After receiving a rare coin for my birthday, I began to take coin collecting more seriously.
9. Before taking a computer course, I couldn't program at all, but now I program very good.
10. When she danced at the Paris Opera, American ballet star Maria Tallchief was received enthusiastic by French audiences.

B. Proofreading for the Correct Use of Modifiers

Proofread the following paragraph, correcting any errors in the use of modifiers.

EXAMPLE   **[1]** When in doubt, dress conservative rather than
              stunningly for a job interview.
         1. *conservatively*

[11] No matter whether three or three hundred candidates apply for a job, a smart employer tries to find the more qualified applicant. **[12]** If you heed the following simple guidelines, you will likely create a more favorable impression than any candidate in your job-hunting market. **[13]** First, a well-prepared data sheet, or résumé, always helps to make a better impression before the interview. **[14]** Second, a proper dressed candidate appears neat and well groomed during the interview. **[15]** Your clothes do not have to be more fancier or more expensive than any other candidate's, but they should look just as professional. **[16]** Third, before your interview, you should try to imagine the most common asked questions for your field. **[17]** There is no worst way to make a lasting impression than to provide poorly thought-out answers to an interviewer's questions. **[18]** Finally, learning all you can about a company is one of the effectivest ways to impress a future employer. **[19]** When two well-qualified candidates apply for the same position, often the one with the greatest knowledge of the company is hired. **[20]** If you follow these guidelines and still don't get the job, try not to feel too badly; instead, set your sights on succeeding at your next job interview.

USAGE

26 PLACEMENT OF MODIFIERS

Misplaced and Dangling Modifiers

Diagnostic Test

A. Revising Sentences by Correcting Faulty Modifiers

Most of the following sentences contain errors in the use of modifiers. Revise each faulty sentence so that its meaning is clear. If a sentence is correct, write *C*.

EXAMPLE **1.** Without access to fresh bamboo, the giant panda's proper diet cannot be maintained.
1. *Without access to fresh bamboo, the giant panda cannot maintain its proper diet.*

1. Racing across their screens, computer owners use animation programs to show cartoon characters.
2. Grant and Lee rode to Appomattox Court House to make an agreement on horses that ended the Civil War.
3. To honor inventor Jan Ernst Matzeliger, the U.S. Postal Service issued a new stamp in the Black Heritage Series.
4. Lue Gim Gong developed a type of orange that could resist frost in his laboratory.

5. Attacking at just the right time, Pensacola was captured by Louisiana Governor Bernardo de Galvéz during the Revolutionary War.
6. The detective writer said that he would introduce a new villain on page one.
7. Scientists have planned carefully to ensure that the space station *Freedom* will soon take flight in all departments of Huntsville's Marshall Space Flight Center.
8. When proofreading on a computer, screen format should be checked as well as spelling.
9. The mayoral candidate stated in a full-page newspaper advertisement an apology would be forthcoming.
10. Did you know that Navajo advisers helped to develop a system of codes that the U.S. Army used while fighting World War II in New Mexico?

B. Revising Sentences by Correcting Faulty Modifiers

Most of the following sentences contain errors in the use of modifiers. Revise each faulty sentence so that its meaning is clear. If a sentence is correct, write C.

EXAMPLE **1.** Carrie Green dreamed of touring Virginia's Historic Triangle while reading travel brochures.
1. *While reading travel brochures, Carrie Green dreamed of touring Virginia's Historic Triangle.*

11. The Greens and the Alvarezes decided to visit the historic town of Williamsburg, Virginia, which has been painstakingly restored on the spur of the moment.
12. Decorated in colonial style, the two families registered at a quaint inn.
13. After resting for an hour or so, the Governor's Mansion, the College of William and Mary, the Capitol, and many other sites were visited.
14. Joel Green quickly snapped a great shot of a candlemaker focusing his camera.
15. A tour guide in the DeWitt Wallace Decorative Arts Center explained how eighteenth-century costumes were sewn.
16. The tour guide said when the families asked she would be happy to go into greater detail.

17. Dressed in colonial garb, a woman at the Raleigh Tavern asked the families to imagine how eighteenth-century residents may have spread news.
18. Having seen enough for the day, a quiet dinner at the inn was enjoyed by all of them.
19. Kevin dipped his spoon into a bowl of peanut butter soup filled with great apprehension.
20. With fond memories and many photographs, the trip to Williamsburg will not soon be forgotten.

Misplaced Modifiers

A modifying phrase or clause that sounds awkward because it modifies the wrong word or group of words is called a *misplaced modifier.*

26a. Avoid using a misplaced modifier.

To correct a misplaced modifier, place the phrase or clause as close as possible to the word or words you intend it to modify.

MISPLACED	Uncle Bill saw a dog gnawing a bone on his way to work. [Was the dog on his way to work?]
CLEAR	**On his way to work,** Uncle Bill saw a dog gnawing a bone.
MISPLACED	They were delighted to see a field of daffodils climbing up the hill.
CLEAR	**Climbing up the hill,** they were delighted to see a field of daffodils.
MISPLACED	The anxious hunter watched the raging lion come charging at him while readying a bow and arrow.
CLEAR	**While readying a bow and arrow,** the anxious hunter watched the raging lion come charging at him.

Two-Way Modifiers

Avoid placing a phrase or clause so that it seems to modify either of two words. Such a misplaced modifier is often called a *two-way,* or *squinting, modifier.*

MISPLACED   The prime minister said in the press interview her
             opponent spoke honestly. [Did the prime minister
             speak in the press interview, or did her opponent?]
CLEAR   **In the press interview,** the prime minister said her
             opponent spoke honestly.
CLEAR   The prime minister said her opponent spoke honestly
             in the press interview.

MISPLACED   The mayor said when the city council met he would
             discuss the proposed budget.
CLEAR   **When the city council met,** the mayor said he would
             discuss the proposed budget.
CLEAR   The mayor said he would discuss the proposed budget
             when the city council met.

MISPLACED   The manager told the two rookies after the game to
             report to the dugout.
CLEAR   **After the game,** the manager told the two rookies to
             report to the dugout.
CLEAR   The manager told the two rookies to report to the
             dugout **after the game.**

▶ EXERCISE 1   **Revising Sentences by Correcting
                Misplaced Modifiers**

The following sentences contain misplaced modifiers. Revise
each sentence so that its meaning is clear and correct.

EXAMPLE   **1.** We listened eagerly to the stories told by
               Scheherazade in *The Arabian Nights,* munching
               peanuts and crackers.
           1. *Munching peanuts and crackers, we listened eagerly
               to the stories told by Scheherazade in* The Arabian
               Nights.

   1. Louise projected the photographs on a large screen that
       she had taken at the zoo.
   2. Mr. Martínez promised in the morning he would tell a
       Native American trickster tale.
   3. I pointed to the fish tank and showed my friends my
       new puffer, swelling with pride.
   4. Ralph Ellison said during an interview Richard Wright
       gave him inspiration to become a writer.
   5. I talked about the problem I had in writing my first draft
       with Megan, and she said she had the same problem.

6. My aunt had finally mastered the art of making stuffed cabbage, filled with a sense of accomplishment.
7. I like to walk along the beach at low tide, digging for clams without a care in the world.
8. Mrs. Jennings sang some folk songs about working on the railroad in the Lincoln School auditorium.
9. There is a bracelet in the museum that is four thousand years old.
10. I found a good book about Virginia Woolf written by her husband at a garage sale.

USAGE

PICTURE THIS

You've heard the saying many times: A picture is worth a thousand words. As the photo editor for a current-events magazine, you take this proverb to heart. You know that incredible photographs like the ones below help make news stories come alive.

However, a photograph doesn't mean much if your readers don't know its *context*. Write a concise, two- or three-line caption for each photograph above. Tell where and when the photograph was taken, and try to sum up its significance. In your captions, use a total of five modifying phrases and clauses. Be sure that each modifier is placed correctly.

Subject: photographs of current events
Audience: magazine readers
Purpose: to inform

Dangling Modifiers

A modifying phrase or clause that does not sensibly modify any word or words in a sentence is called a *dangling modifier.*

26b.   Avoid using a dangling modifier.

You may correct a dangling modifier by adding a word or words that the phrase or clause can sensibly refer to or by adding a word or words to the phrase or clause.

DANGLING	Having selected a college, a trip to the campus was planned. [Who selected a college?]
CLEAR	**Having selected a college,** my friend and I planned a trip to the campus.
CLEAR	**After we selected a college,** my friend and I planned a trip to the campus.
DANGLING	After winning the Pulitzer Prize for poetry, the novel *Maud Martha* was written.
CLEAR	**After winning the Pulitzer Prize for poetry,** Gwendolyn Brooks wrote the novel *Maud Martha.*
CLEAR	**After Gwendolyn Brooks won the Pulitzer Prize for poetry,** she wrote the novel *Maud Martha.*
DANGLING	While correcting papers, the message came from the principal.
CLEAR	**While correcting papers,** the teacher received the message from the principal.
CLEAR	**While the teacher was correcting papers,** the message came from the principal.

NOTE: A few dangling modifiers have become standard in idiomatic expressions.

EXAMPLES   **Generally speaking,** Americans now have a longer life expectancy than ever before.
To be honest, the party was rather boring.

☞ REFERENCE NOTE: For more information about idiomatic expressions, see pages 486–487. For information about using a comma after introductory words, phrases, and clauses, see pages 853–854.

EXERCISE 2   ## Revising Sentences by Correcting Dangling Modifiers

The following sentences contain dangling modifiers. Revise each sentence so that its meaning is clear and correct.

EXAMPLE   1. Waiting at the bus stop, my older brother drove by in his new car.
1. *While I was waiting at the bus stop, my older brother drove by in his new car.*

1. Frightened by our presence, the rabbit's ears perked up and its nose twitched.
2. To interpret this poem, a knowledge of mythology is helpful.
3. All bundled up in a blanket, the baby's first outing was a brief one.
4. When performing onstage, the microphone should not be placed too near the speaker cones.
5. To be a good opera singer, clear enunciation is extremely important.
6. To help colonial soldiers during the Revolutionary War, Haym Solomon's efforts raised money to buy food and clothing.
7. Before moving to Sacramento, Pittsburgh had been their home for ten years.
8. While reaching into his pocket for change, the car rolled into the side of the tollbooth.
9. To work efficiently without sticking, be sure to use the proper solvent and lubricant.
10. When discussing colonial American writers, the contributions of the African American poet Phillis Wheatley should not be forgotten.

> REVIEW

Revising Sentences by Correcting Faulty Modifiers

Most of the following sentences contain errors in the use of modifiers. Revise each faulty sentence so that its meaning is clear and correct. If a sentence is correct, write *C*.

EXAMPLE   **1.** I described my trip to Hawaii to my friends who had never been there when I got back.
      1. *When I got back, I described my trip to Hawaii to my friends, who had never been there.*

1. Visitors soon learn how important one man can be on vacation in Hawaii.
2. Born in the mid-1700s, the Hawaiian people were united under one government by Kamehameha the Great.
3. After capturing Maui, Molokai, and Lanai, Oahu was soon another of Kamehameha's conquests.
4. Kamehameha assured the Hawaiian people when he became the ruler of the entire island they would see peace.
5. By 1810, Kamehameha was certain his conquest would be successful.
6. Having won Kauai and Niihau, Kamehameha's dream of a united country was realized.
7. A hero to his people, Kamehameha's government ruled Hawaii for many years.
8. A statue to honor the great ruler was crafted by Thomas Gould.
9. While being transported by sea, the Hawaiian people lost their beloved statue.
10. Though still at the bottom of the ocean, the sculptor made the duplicate shown here.

Review: Posttest

A. Revising Sentences by Correcting Faulty Modifiers

The following sentences contain errors in the use of modifiers. Revise each sentence so that its meaning is clear and correct.

EXAMPLE   **1.** Attached to my application, you will find a transcript of my grades.
   1. *You will find a transcript of my grades attached to my application.*

1. Having eaten the remains of the zebra, we watched the lion lick its chops.
2. To honor his guests, almost all of the possessions of the Northwest Native American host were given away at an elaborate party called a potlatch.
3. The girls counted thirteen shooting stars sitting on the porch last night.
4. To do well on examinations, good study habits should be developed.
5. When touring the South, a visit to the new Civil Rights Memorial in Montgomery, Alabama, should be planned.
6. The leader of the photo safari promised in the morning we would see a herd of eland.
7. While running for the bus, my wallet must have dropped out of my pocket.
8. Catching the pop fly with her usual skill, the crowd rose to their feet and cheered.
9. She traveled to Paris especially to see the *Venus de Milo* on the train.
10. After crumbling for a hundred years, we found the castle quite dilapidated.

B. Using Modifiers Correctly

Most of the following sentences contain errors in the use of modifiers. Revise each faulty sentence so that its meaning is clear and correct. If a sentence is correct, write C.

EXAMPLE **1.** Before they had computers, all newspaper layout work was done by hand.

1. *Before they had computers, newspaper editors did all layout work by hand.*

11. Computer whiz Kim Montgomery said in the computer resource center anyone can learn to master basic desktop publishing.
12. To prove her point, the editor of the school newspaper was asked to give desktop publishing a try.
13. Kim led Terri, a novice computer user, to an unoccupied terminal with an encouraging smile.
14. In a short tutorial session, Kim emphasized the need to practice adding, deleting, and moving paragraphs.
15. While looking over her shoulder, Terri hit various keys to call up menus on the computer screen.
16. Terri sometimes stared blankly at the computer screen, not knowing what to do next.
17. In need of more information, the tutor was asked many questions by the pupil.
18. "To prepare professional-quality illustrations, a graphics package is what you need," Kim said.
19. Kim said when the computer sounded an error warning she would be happy to offer assistance.
20. Kim was pleased to see Terri confidently keyboarding information as she went to help another student.

USAGE

27 A GLOSSARY OF USAGE

Common Usage Problems

Diagnostic Test

A. Identifying Correct Usage

Choose the correct word or words in parentheses in each of the following sentences. [Note: A sentence may contain more than one choice.]

EXAMPLE **1.** When my math teacher announced the rules for the year, she said she would not (*except, accept*) any papers written in ink.
1. *accept*

1. All of the members of Congress (*except, accept*), I believe, Representative Carpenter voted to retain the present tax structure for another year.
2. My grandparents have (*affected, effected*) all of us with their generosity, hope, and faith in the future.

3. I (*couldn't, could*) hardly believe my eyes when I saw a 90 on my geometry test; I must (*of, have*) remembered the formulas better than I thought I would.
4. (*This, This here*) plane was designed by the world-famous paper-airplane expert Dr. Yasuaki Ninomiya.
5. Does this poem make an (*allusion, illusion*) to the *Iliad*?
6. (*Being that, Because*) Jennifer had never learned to swim, she was afraid to go on the boat ride.
7. At the end of the nineteenth century, two of my great-grandparents (*emigrated, immigrated*) from Ireland to the United States.
8. When Trini Lopez recorded the hit folk song "If I Had a Hammer," he (*had no, didn't have no*) way of knowing that it would sell $4.5 million worth of records.
9. (*Can't none, Can't any*) of the people in town see that the mayor is appointing political cronies to patronage jobs?
10. The (*Gallaghers they, Gallaghers*) have worked for years to increase voter registration in (*this, this here*) town.

USAGE

B. Identifying Correct Usage

For each sentence in the following paragraph, choose the correct item from the pair given in parentheses.

EXAMPLE   Whenever I walk into Montsho Books, I can't help
[1] (*feeling, but feel*) proud to be black.
1. *feeling*

Do you want to know where this bookstore **[11]** (*is, is at*)? I should **[12]** (*of, have*) mentioned that it's in Orlando, Florida, just a short **[13]** (*way, ways*) from the Orlando Arena. Ms. Perkins, **[14]** (*which, who*) runs the store, told me **[15]** (*where, that*) *montsho* means "black" in Tswana, an African language. When Ms. Perkins was a school teacher, she noticed that there **[16]** (*were, weren't*) hardly any children's books that featured African Americans. At first, she thought that she would write children's books about the black experience, but then Ms. Perkins decided she **[17]** (*had ought, ought*) to open a store that sold books exclusively by and about blacks. **[18]** (*Beside, Besides*) poetry and fiction by African Americans, the shop offers all kinds of nonfiction selections including books on philosophy, history, health, humor, and cooking. Montsho Books is quite an unusual **[19]** (*kind of, kind of a*) bookstore; it has become a true cultural center for Orlando's black community. The shop even sponsors the Montsho Sphinxes, a Brain Bowl Black History team of seventh- through twelfth-graders, which looks **[20]** (*like, as if*) it might win the state grand prize some year soon!

A *glossary* is an alphabetical list of special terms or expressions with definitions, explanations, and examples. On the following pages is a short glossary of English usage.

You'll notice that some examples in this glossary are labeled *standard, nonstandard, formal,* or *informal.* The label **standard** or **formal** identifies usage that is appropriate in serious writing and speaking (such as in compositions for school and speeches). The label **informal** indicates standard English that is generally used in conversation and in everyday writing such as personal letters. The label **nonstandard** identifies usage that does not follow the guidelines of standard English usage.

☞ REFERENCE NOTE: For more about standard English, see page 478.

a, an These *indefinite articles* refer to one of the members of a general group. *A* is used before words beginning with a consonant sound. *An* is used before words beginning with a vowel sound.

EXAMPLES "New African" is **a** heartwarming story about **a** young African American girl growing up in Philadelphia during the early 1960s.

The teacher read from the novel **an** excerpt that describes the grandfather as **an** honorable man. [Notice that the *h* in *honorable* is silent; therefore, the word begins with a vowel sound.]

accept, except *Accept* is a verb meaning "to receive." *Except* may be either a verb or a preposition. As a verb, *except* means "to leave out." As a preposition, *except* means "excluding."

EXAMPLES I will **accept** another yearbook assignment.
Should the military services **except** women from combat duty? [verb]
She typed everything **except** the bibliography. [preposition]

affect, effect *Affect* is a verb meaning "to influence." *Effect* may be used as a verb or a noun. As a verb, *effect* means "to bring about [a desired result]," or "to accomplish." As a noun, *effect* means "the result [of an action]."

EXAMPLES   Decisions of the United States Supreme Court **affect** the lives of many people.
Some of the decisions **effect** great social change. [verb]
In history class, did you learn what far-reaching **effects** the *Brown v. Board of Education of Topeka, Kansas* decision had? [noun]

all the farther, all the faster Avoid these expressions by using *as far as* and *as fast as,* respectively.

NONSTANDARD   The first act was all the farther we had read in *A Raisin in the Sun.*
STANDARD   The first act was **as far as** we had read in *A Raisin in the Sun.*

allusion, illusion An *allusion* is an indirect reference to something. An *illusion* is a mistaken idea or a misleading appearance.

EXAMPLES   Flannery O'Connor makes numerous biblical **allusions** in her stories.
Illusions of success haunted Willy Loman.
Makeup can be used to create an **illusion.**

alumni, alumnae *Alumni* (pronounced ə lum' nī) is the plural of *alumnus* (a male graduate). *Alumnae* (pronounced ə lum' nē) is the plural of *alumna* (a female graduate). Considered as a single group, the graduates of a coeducational school are referred to as *alumni.*

EXAMPLES   Each year the **alumni** have provided two athletic scholarships.
Did the administration ask the **alumnae** how they felt about admitting men to the school?
Men and women from the first graduating class attended the **alumni** reunion.

NOTE: In informal usage the graduates from a women's college may be called *alumni.* In formal situations, however, the plural *alumnae* should be used.

among See **between, among.**

USAGE

USAGE

amount, number Use *amount* to refer to a singular word. Use *number* to refer to a plural word.

EXAMPLES   A large **amount** of work is done in the library.
[*Amount* refers to the singular word *work*.]
A large **number** of books have been checked out of our library. [*Number* refers to the plural word *books*.]

and etc. *Etc.* is an abbreviation of the Latin words *et cetera,* meaning "and others" or "and so forth." Since *and* is included in the definition of *etc.,* using *and* with *etc.* is unnecessary.

EXAMPLE   We are studying twentieth-century American novelists: Ernest Hemingway, Margaret Walker, Jean Toomer, Pearl Buck, **etc.** [not *and etc.*]

anyways, anywheres Omit the final *s* in these words and in similar words such as *everywheres* and *nowheres.*

EXAMPLES   I couldn't take both band and art **anyway** [not *anyways*].
Are your grandparents going camping **anywhere** [not *anywheres*] this summer?

as See **like, as.**

as if See **like, as if.**

at Avoid using *at* after a construction beginning with *where.*

NONSTANDARD   Where is the Crow Canyon Archaeological Center located at?
STANDARD   Where is the Crow Canyon Archaeological Center located?

▶ EXERCISE 1   **Identifying Correct Usage**

Choose the correct word or words in parentheses in each sentence in the following paragraph.

EXAMPLE   [1] My mother and Ms. Wang, both (*alumnae, alumni*) of Pratt Institute, went there to see an exhibition of paintings.
    1. *alumnae*

[1] In 1988, the artist Chuck Close suffered spinal-artery collapse, and even though he never fully recovered, he kept painting (*anyway, anyways*). [2] Partially paralyzed, he learned to

work from a wheelchair, with (*a, an*) handy arrangement of straps to hold his brush in place. [3] As he had done before his illness, Close still painted large frontal portraits of friends, fellow artists, (*and etc., etc.*) [4] The picture on the left is an example of how Close often painted before 1988, dividing a photo of a person into a large (*amount, number*) of tiny squares. [5] He would first rule the canvas or paper into a grid, and then he would copy the photo's colors, bit by bit, into the small squares to create the type of (*allusion, illusion*) you see here. [6] A single painting might contain (*anywhere, anywheres*) from a few hundred to several thousand squares. [7] The overall effect is much like a certain kind of computer graphic, (*accept, except*) that the painting is not quite as mechanical. [8] The photograph on the right shows Close in 1991 working on a self-portrait that has a similar (*affect, effect*), but his style is bolder and more colorful. [9] At first glance, you may be surprised by his newer paintings and wonder where that computerlike quality (*is, is at*)! [10] But you soon realize that Close had never gone (*all the farther, as far as*) he could with his grid technique and that his recent paintings are simply a logical extension of his earlier style.

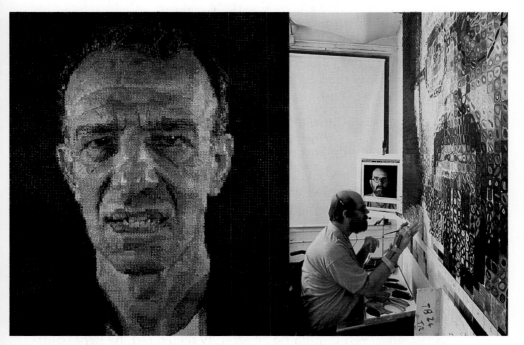

Chuck Close, "Alex" 1987. Oil on Canvas, 100 × 84" John Back/ Photograph courtesy of The Pace Gallery.

Chuck Close, *Self-Portrait*, 1991. Oil on canvas, 100 × 84" (work in progress), Bill Jacobson Studio/Photograph courtesy of The Pace Gallery.

USAGE

bad, badly   See page 767.

because   In formal situations, do not use the construction *reason . . . because*. Instead, use *reason . . . that*.

    INFORMAL   The reason for the eclipse is because the moon has come between the earth and the sun.

    FORMAL   The **reason** for the eclipse is **that** the moon has come between the earth and the sun.

being as, being that   Avoid using either of these expressions for *because* or *since*.

    EXAMPLE   **Because** [not *Being as*] Ms. Ribas is a gemologist, she may know the value of these gemstones.

beside, besides   *Beside* is a preposition meaning "by the side of." *Besides* may be used as a preposition or an adverb. As a preposition, *besides* means "in addition to." As an adverb, it means "moreover."

    EXAMPLES   He set the plate of sandwiches **beside** the bowl of fruit punch.
            Besides fringe benefits, the job offered a high salary. [preposition]
            I am not in the mood to go shopping; **besides,** I have an English test tomorrow. [adverb]

between, among   Use *between* when referring to only two items or to more than two when each item is being compared to each other item.

    EXAMPLES   The money from the sale of the property was divided **between** Sasha and Antonio.
            Do you know the difference **between** a simile, a metaphor, and an analogy?

Use *among* when you are referring to more than two items and are not considering each item in relation to each of the others.

    EXAMPLE   The money from the sale of the property was divided **among** the four relatives.

bring, take   *Bring* means "to come carrying something." *Take* means "to go carrying something."

    EXAMPLES   I will **bring** my Wynton Marsalis tapes when I come over.

Please **take** the model of the Globe Theater to the library.
You may **take** my softball glove to school today, but please **bring** it home this afternoon.

bust, busted Avoid using these words as verbs. Use a form of *break* or *burst,* depending on the meaning you intend.

EXAMPLES One of the headlights on the van is **broken** [not *busted*].
A pipe in the apartment above ours **burst** [not *busted*].

but, only See **The Double Negative,** pages 811–812.

can't hardly, can't scarcely See **The Double Negative,** pages 811–812.

could of See **of.**

done *Done* is the past participle of *do.* Avoid using *done* for *did,* which is the past form of *do* and does not require an auxiliary verb.

NONSTANDARD He done all of his homework over the weekend.
STANDARD He **did** all of his homework over the weekend.
STANDARD He **had done** all of his homework over the weekend.

don't, doesn't *Don't* is the contraction of *do not. Doesn't* is the contraction of *does not.* Use *doesn't,* not *don't,* with singular subjects except *I* and *you.*

EXAMPLES She **doesn't** [not *don't*] like seafood.
The bookstore **doesn't** [not *don't*] have any copies of Faith Ringgold's *Tar Beach* in stock.

PICTURE THIS

The year is 1820. After experimenting for months, you have built the wonderful hot-air balloon shown on the next page. To introduce your fellow townspeople to this new form of transportation, you're going to sell balloon rides at the County Fair. Create a flyer advertising your incredible flying balloon. In your flyer, describe the amazing sensations of a balloon ride, and convince potential customers that the balloon is safe. Use at least five of the following words and expressions correctly.

as far as	don't
as fast as	doesn't
as if	effect
bring	affect
take	beside

Subject: a hot-air balloon
Audience: potential customers
Purpose: to persuade

effect See **affect, effect.**

emigrate, immigrate Emigrate is a verb meaning "to leave a country or region to settle elsewhere." *Immigrate* is a verb meaning "to come into a country or region to settle there."

EXAMPLES   Thousands of people **emigrated** from Germany during the 1870s.
Most of the German refugees **immigrated** to the United States.

NOTE: The nouns that correspond to *emigrate* and *immigrate* are *emigrant* (one who goes away from a country or region) and *immigrant* (one who comes into a country or region).

etc. See **and etc.**

everywheres See **anyways, anywheres.**

except See **accept, except.**

fewer, less Use *fewer,* which tells "how many," to modify a plural noun. Use *less,* which tells "how much," to modify a singular noun.

EXAMPLES **Fewer** students are going out for football this year.
I find that I have a lot more fun now that I spend **less** time watching TV.

good, well See page 767.

▶ EXERCISE 2 **Identifying Correct Usage**

Choose the correct word or words in parentheses in each of the following sentences.

1. There isn't one state that (*doesn't, don't*) have numerous place names derived from Native American words.
2. Your mistakes will be (*fewer, less*) if you proofread your paper.
3. The assignments on Greek philosophers were divided (*among, between*) the juniors in the humanities class.
4. Marcus did (*good, well*) on his driver's exam.
5. Will you (*bring, take*) these books to our study session tomorrow night?
6. (*Being that, Since*) she has passed all the tests, she should be a likely candidate for the military academy.
7. The junkyard just outside the city limits certainly looked (*bad, badly*), didn't it?
8. Chen Rong was a famous Chinese artist who (*did, done*) many beautiful paintings of dragons.
9. (*Beside, Besides*) *The Scarlet Letter* and *The Red Badge of Courage,* we read *The Joy-Luck Club* and *Tortuga.*
10. During the nineteenth century, many people (*emigrated, immigrated*) from Asia to the United States.

USAGE

REVIEW A **Completing Sentences with Correct Usage**

Choose an item from the colored box to complete each of the following sentences correctly. [Note: Be careful! Some of the items in the box are nonstandard usages.]

except	accept	held at	number
being as	busted	is that	is because
immigrate	alumni	alumnae	took
anywheres	held	amount	anywhere
brought	emigrate	since	broke

EXAMPLE **1.** Two years ago, my Uncle Koichi decided to _____ to this country from Japan.
1. *immigrate*

1. Fortunately, he _____ along his marvelous kite-making skills and his keen business sense.
2. At first it was hard for Uncle Koichi to _____ the fact that kite-flying isn't as popular here as it is in Japan.
3. I did some research for him and found out where the big kite festivals are _____.
4. He decided to settle right here in Southern California, _____ plenty of kite enthusiasts live here all year round.

5. First, Uncle Koichi built a small _____ of beautiful kites, and then he started giving kite-flying lessons.
6. All three of my older brothers are enthusiastic _____ of Koichi's Kite Kollege.
7. The reason that Uncle Koichi's shop is successful _____ he loves his work and is very good at it.
8. My first kite _____ into pieces when I crashed it into a tree, but Uncle Koichi built me another one.
9. I took these photographs of his magnificent dragon kite, which takes _____ from three to five people to launch, depending on wind conditions.
10. My uncle's customers and friends all hope that he will never _____ from the United States and take his glorious kites back to Japan.

▶ EXERCISE 3 **Correcting Errors in Usage**

Most of the following sentences contain errors in usage. If a sentence contains an error, revise the sentence. If a sentence is correct, write *C*.

EXAMPLE **1.** The five starting players have twenty fouls between them.
        1. *The five starting players have twenty fouls among them.*

1. It don't look as if the rain will stop this afternoon.
2. Sometimes I can get so absorbed in a movie that I forget where I'm at.
3. Would you bring your guitar when you come to visit us?
4. The drought seriously effected the lettuce crop.
5. You must learn to except criticism if you want to improve.
6. Being as the Black History Month essay contest ends next week, we need to submit our entries soon.
7. The reason that many Irish people moved to France and Argentina after the unsuccessful Irish rebellion in 1798 is because they refused to live under English rule.
8. Although I did badly on the quiz, I did very well on the exam.
9. The title of James Baldwin's *Notes of a Native Son* is an illusion to Richard Wright's famous novel *Native Son*.
10. Beside you and me, who else is going on the hike?

▶ REVIEW B

Proofreading a Paragraph for Correct Usage

For each sentence in the following paragraph, identify the incorrect word or phrase. Then write the correct form. If a sentence is correct, write *C*.

EXAMPLE   [1] If you think you can jump rope as good as these girls, find out if there's a branch of the American Double Dutch League near you.
1. *good—well*

[1] Double Dutch is a fast-action rope-jumping style that's been popular on U.S. playgrounds for anywheres from fifty to a hundred years. [2] In double Dutch, turners twirl two ropes alternately in opposite directions, creating an eggbeater effect. [3] Being that the two ropes are going so fast, jumpers have to jump double-fast. [4] Their feet fly at over three hundred steps a minute—about half that number is all the faster I can go! [5] To make things even more interesting, two jumpers often perform together to rhymes or music, doing flips, twists, cartwheels, and etc. [6] Besides competing in local meets, jumpers can participate in competitions organized by the American Double Dutch League, the sport's official governing body. [7] In competition, all teams must perform the same amount of tests, including the speed test, the compulsory-tricks test, and the freestyle test. [8] This photo isn't an optical allusion—the two jumpers are twins as well as being a double Dutch doubles team! [9] Not only did these girls win their divisional title in the American Double Dutch League World Championships, but also they were chosen to bring their sport to the Moscow International Folk Festival. [10] Olympic athlete Florence "Flo Jo" Joyner enthusiastically supports Double Dutch, and it don't surprise me at all that she likes to jump double Dutch herself!

had of See **of.**

had ought, hadn't ought Do not use *had* or *hadn't* with *ought.*

NONSTANDARD His test scores had ought to be back by now.
STANDARD His test scores **ought** to be back by now.

NONSTANDARD She hadn't ought to have turned here.
STANDARD She **ought not** to have turned here.

hardly See **The Double Negative,** pages 811–812.

he, she, it, they Avoid using a pronoun along with its antecedent as the subject of a verb. Such an error is sometimes called a *double subject.*

NONSTANDARD The computer system it is down today.
STANDARD The **computer system is** down today.

NONSTANDARD Fay Stanley and Diane Stanley they wrote a biography of the Hawaiian princess Ka'iulani.
STANDARD **Fay Stanley and Diane Stanley wrote** a biography of the Hawaiian princess Ka'iulani.

illusion See **allusion, illusion.**

immigrate See **emigrate, immigrate.**

imply, infer *Imply* means "to suggest." *Infer* means "to interpret" or "to draw as a conclusion."

EXAMPLES The governor **implied** in her speech that she would support a statewide testing program.
I **inferred** from the governor's speech that she would support a statewide testing program.

in, into *In* means "within." *Into* means "from the outside to the inside." In formal situations, avoid using *in* for *into.*

INFORMAL He threw the scraps of paper in the litter basket.
FORMAL He threw the scraps of paper **into** the litter basket.

it See **he, she, it, they.**

kind(s), sort(s), type(s) With the singular form of each of these nouns, use *this* or *that.* With the plural form, use *these* or *those.*

EXAMPLES **This kind** of gas is dangerous; **those kinds** are harmless.
These types of reading assignments are always challenging.

kind of, sort of In formal situations, avoid using *kind of* for the adverb *somewhat* or *rather*.

INFORMAL   Jackie was kind of disappointed when she did not make the basketball team.

FORMAL   Jackie was **somewhat** [or *rather*] disappointed when she did not make the basketball team.

kind of a, sort of a In formal situations, omit the *a*.

INFORMAL   What kind of a car do you drive?

FORMAL   What **kind of** car do you drive?

leave, let *Leave* means "to go away." *Let* means "to permit" or "to allow." Avoid using *leave* for *let*.

EXAMPLES   **Let** [not *leave*] them stay where they are.
They **let** [not *left*] Jaime out early for a dentist appointment.

less See **fewer, less.**

lie, lay See pages 730–731.

like, as *Like* is a preposition. In formal situations, do not use *like* for the conjunction *as* to introduce a subordinate clause.

INFORMAL   Plácido Domingo sings like Caruso once did.

FORMAL   Plácido Domingo sings **as** Caruso once did.

☞ REFERENCE NOTE: For more information about subordinate clauses, see pages 629–637.

like, as if In formal situations, avoid using the preposition *like* for the conjunction *as if* or *as though* to introduce a subordinate clause.

INFORMAL   The singers sounded like they had not rehearsed.

FORMAL   The singers sounded **as if** [or *as though*] they had not rehearsed.

might of, must of See **of.**

▶ EXERCISE 4   **Identifying Correct Usage**

Choose the correct word or words in parentheses in each of the following sentences.

1. (*These, This*) kinds of questions require more thought than (*this, these*) kind.
2. I (*had ought, ought*) to check out a good library book.

USAGE

3. It looks (*like, as if*) we'll be able to attend the powwow.
4. Will the coach (*leave, let*) you skip soccer practice today?
5. He serves the ball exactly (*as, like*) the coach showed him.
6. I (*implied, inferred*) from Dad's remark about "slovenliness" that my sister and I had forgotten to clean our room.
7. When Jay Gatsby walked (*in, into*) the room, everyone stared at him.
8. (*Leave, Let*) Rosetta explain the trigonometry problem.
9. Did Mr. Stokes (*imply, infer*) that he was pleased with my research paper on Mexican American authors?
10. What sort (*of, of a*) culture did the Phoenicians have?

▶ REVIEW C   **Identifying Correct Usage**

Each sentence in the following paragraphs contains at least one pair of italicized items. Choose the correct item from each pair to complete the sentence.

EXAMPLE   [1] While we were driving through the Appalachian Mountains, (*my father, my father he*) suddenly started chuckling and pulled over to the side of the road.
  1. *my father*

[1] Dad said that we really (*had ought, ought*) to get out of the car and see the amazing mailbox that somebody had built. [2] Neither Ivy nor I was especially interested in mailboxes, but when we saw the fanciful metal figure that Dad was pointing to, we both smiled just (*as, like*) he had. [3] We jumped out to take the middle photo shown on the next page, and while we were standing (*beside, besides*) the road, a man came out of the house. [4] He introduced himself as Charlie Lucas and said he had built the mailbox man by welding together scraps from (*broken, busted*) machinery. [5] We started chatting with him, and the next thing we knew, he had invited us (*in, into*) the house to see more of his figures. [6] The house was (*kind of, rather*) like an art museum: there were dinosaurs made from colorful twisted wire, a fiddle-player with a head made from a shovel, and an alligator whose body (*might have, might of*) once been a crankshaft.

[7] "Dad, are these figures art?" Ivy whispered, and Dad's answer (*inferred, implied*) that they were. [8] He said that art (*don't, doesn't*) always have to be stuffy and serious or made

USAGE

from bronze or marble and that true artists aren't always (*alumnae, alumni*) of famous art schools. [9] (*Mr. Lucas he, Mr. Lucas*) agreed with Dad that (*these kind, these kinds*) of sculptures and all other kinds of folk art are of great value to human beings. [10] Folk art comes straight from the heart; it often recycles cast-off materials that most people (*would have, would of*) considered junk; it offers a different perspective on life; and it makes people smile!

Charlie Lucas, *Old Buddy*.

Charlie Lucas, Twisted Wire Dinosaur.

USAGE

no, none, nothing   See **The Double Negative,** pages 811–812.

nor   See **or, nor.**

nowheres   See **anyways, anywheres.**

number   See **amount, number.**

of   *Of* is a preposition. Do not use *of* in place of *have* after verbs such as *could, should, would, might,* and *must.*

NONSTANDARD   He could of had a summer job if he had applied earlier.

STANDARD   He **could have** had a summer job if he had applied earlier.

NONSTANDARD   You ought to of taken a foreign language.
    STANDARD   You **ought to have** taken a foreign language.

Also do not use *of* after *had*.

NONSTANDARD   If I had of known the word *raze*, I would have made a perfect score.
    STANDARD   If I **had** known the word *raze*, I would have made a perfect score.

Avoid using *of* after other prepositions such as *inside, off,* and *outside*.

    EXAMPLE   Chian-Chiu dived **off** [not *off of*] the side of the pool into the water.

off, off of   Do not use *off* or *off of* in place of *from*.

NONSTANDARD   You can get a program off of the usher.
    STANDARD   You can get a program **from** the usher.

or, nor   Use *or* with *either;* use *nor* with *neither*.

    EXAMPLES   On Tuesdays the school cafeteria offers a choice for lunch of **either** a taco salad **or** a pizza.
        I wonder why **neither** Ralph Ellison **nor** Robert Frost was given the Nobel Prize for literature.

ought to of   See **of.**

raise, rise   See page 733.

reason . . . is because   See **because.**

scarcely   See **The Double Negative,** pages 811–812.

she   See **he, she, it, they.**

should of   See **of.**

sit, set   See page 732.

slow, slowly   See page 768.

some, somewhat   In formal situations, avoid using *some* to mean "to some extent." Use *somewhat*.

    INFORMAL   My grades have improved some during the past month.
    FORMAL   My grades have improved **somewhat** during the past month.

somewheres   See **anyways, anywheres.**

sort(s)   See **kind(s), sort(s), type(s)** and **kind of a, sort of a.**

sort of See **kind of, sort of.**

take See **bring, take.**

than, then *Than* is a conjunction used in comparisons. *Then* is an adverb telling when.

EXAMPLES He is a better cook **than** I am.
Let the sauce simmer for ten minutes, and **then** stir in two cups of cooked mixed vegetables.

that See **who, which, that.**

them Do not use *them* as an adjective. Use *those.*

EXAMPLE All of **those** [not *them*] paintings are by Carmen Lomas Garza.

they See **he, she, it, they.**

this here, that there Avoid using *here* or *there* after *this* or *that.*

EXAMPLE **This** [not *This here*] story tells about the Hmong people of Laos.

this, that, these, those See **kind(s), sort(s), types(s).**

type(s) See **kind(s), sort(s), type(s).**

type, type of Avoid using *type* as an adjective. Add *of* after *type.*

NONSTANDARD I prefer this type shirt.
STANDARD I prefer this **type of** shirt.

ways Use *way*, not *ways*, in referring to distance.

INFORMAL My home, in Wichita, is a long ways from Tokyo, where my pen pal lives.
FORMAL My home, in Wichita, is a long **way** from Tokyo, where my pen pal lives.

well, good See page 767.

when, where Do not use *when* or *where* to begin a definition.

NONSTANDARD A spoonerism is when you switch the beginning sounds of two words.
STANDARD A spoonerism is **a slip of the tongue in which the beginning sounds of two words are switched.**
NONSTANDARD A thesaurus is where you can find synonyms and antonyms of words.
STANDARD A thesaurus is **a book in which you can find synonyms and antonyms of words.**

where Do not use *where* for *that*.

> EXAMPLE I read **that** [not *where*] Demosthenes learned to enunciate clearly by practicing with pebbles in his mouth.

where . . . at See **at**.

who, which, that *Who* refers to persons only. *Which* refers to things only. *That* may refer to either persons or things.

> EXAMPLES Wasn't Beethoven the composer **who** [or *that*] continued to write music after he had become deaf?
> First editions of Poe's first book, **which** was titled *Tamerlane*, are worth thousands of dollars.
> Is Emily Dickinson the poet **that** [or *who*] wrote on scraps of paper?
> Is this the only essay **that** James Baldwin wrote?

who, whom See pages 690–692.

would of See **of**.

EXERCISE 5 **Identifying Correct Usage**

Choose the correct word or words in parentheses in each of the following sentences.

1. I read in a newspaper article (*that, where*) dogs are being trained to help people with hearing impairments.
2. The earliest feminist author in United States literature was neither Eudora Welty (*or, nor*) Flannery O'Connor; she was Kate Chopin.
3. Jack London must (*of, have*) led an adventurous life.
4. Our teacher assigned us (*this, this here*) chapter to read.
5. Joe had the flu last week, but he's feeling (*some, somewhat*) better today.
6. As we passed Shreveport and crossed the Texas line, El Paso seemed a long (*way, ways*) away.
7. For advice, I go to Ms. Sanchez, (*which, who*) is a very understanding guidance counselor.
8. This (*type, type of*) short story has appealed to readers for many years.
9. Pass me (*them, those*) notes on the experiment, please.
10. He did a flip turn and pushed (*off, off of*) the pool wall.

▶ REVIEW D **Identifying Correct Usage**

Each sentence in the following paragraph has a pair of italicized items. Choose the correct item from each pair to complete the sentence.

EXAMPLE [1] Have you read (*where, that*) Vietnamese refugees are working hard to succeed in the United States?
1. *that*

[1] When Vietnamese immigrants stepped (*off, off of*) the planes that had brought them from refugee camps all over Asia, they didn't know what to expect in America. [2] However, like previous immigrants, they were people (*which, who*) managed to succeed against all odds. [3] The boat people neither spoke English (*or, nor*) understood much about life in the United States. [4] Grateful just to be alive, they could (*have, of*) contented themselves with simple survival. [5] Instead, many of (*them, those*) Vietnamese families have encouraged their children to achieve academic excellence. [6] According to one study, half of the refugee children earn a B average overall and half also receive A's in math; (*that, that there*) study also places these students near the national average in English. [7] One reason Vietnamese students do so well is (*because, that*) they believe that success comes from hard work, not from luck or natural aptitude. [8] Consequently, rather (*than, then*) watch television or go to the mall, families like the one shown here spend weeknights doing homework together. [9] Even parents who do not speak English (*good, well*) help by not assigning chores during study time. [10] Younger brothers and sisters get extra instruction (*from, off of*) older ones, and all this effort is helping the Vietnamese become one of the most successful immigrant groups in the United States.

The Double Negative

A *double negative* is a construction in which two negative words are used where one is enough. Although acceptable until Shakespeare's time, double negatives are now considered nonstandard.

NONSTANDARD	She has not read none of Nadine Gordimer's books.
STANDARD	She has **not** read **any** of Nadine Gordimer's books.
STANDARD	She has read **none** of Nadine Gordimer's books.
NONSTANDARD	I do not know nothing about the Peloponnesian War.
STANDARD	I do **not** know **anything** about the Peloponnesian War.
STANDARD	I know **nothing** about the Peloponnesian War.
NONSTANDARD	Grandma said that she hadn't never seen another pumpkin that was as large as this one.
STANDARD	Grandma said that she **hadn't ever** seen another pumpkin that was as large as this one.
STANDARD	Grandma said that she had **never** seen another pumpkin that was as large as this one.

Common Negative Words

barely	never	not (n't)
but (meaning "only")	no	nothing
hardly	nobody	nowhere
neither	none	only
	no one	scarcely

NOTE: Avoid the common error of using *n't*, the contraction of *not*, with another negative word, especially *barely, hardly,* or *scarcely.*

NONSTANDARD	I can't hardly take another step in these new boots.
STANDARD	I can **hardly** take another step in these new boots.
NONSTANDARD	The film is so long that we couldn't scarcely see it in one class period.
STANDARD	The film is so long that we could **scarcely** see it in one class period.

The words *but* and *only* are considered negative words when they are used as adverbs meaning "no more than." In such cases, the use of another negative word with *but* or *only* is considered informal.

INFORMAL   Whenever I see you, I can't help but smile.
FORMAL   Whenever I see you, I can't help smiling.

EXERCISE 6   **Revising Sentences to Eliminate Double Negatives**

Revise each of the following sentences to eliminate the double negative. Although the following sentences can be corrected in more than one way, you need to give only one revision.

EXAMPLE   **1.** He hadn't no pencils on his desk.
   1. *He had no pencils on his desk.*
or
He hadn't any pencils on his desk.

1. Tom didn't have no time to buy the books.
2. Haven't none of you seen the dog?
3. Isn't nobody else interested in going to visit the pueblo at Tesuque this morning?
4. We haven't but one day to visit the fair.
5. She didn't contribute nothing to the project.
6. The lights were so dim that we couldn't barely see.
7. They said that they didn't think they'd have no time to go to the post office.
8. In the mountains you can't help but feel calm.
9. Can't none of them come to the party?
10. José Martí was sentenced to six years in prison, and he hadn't done nothing but write a letter that the Spanish government didn't like.

"CONFOUNDED DOUBLE NEGATIVES."

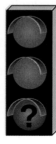  

▶ REVIEW E   **Correcting Errors in Usage**

Most of the following sentences contain errors in usage. If a sentence contains an error or errors, revise the sentence. If a sentence is correct, write C.

EXAMPLE   **1.** Can't none of the staff sort the yearbook pictures?
           1. *Can't any of the staff sort the yearbook pictures?*

1. A New Year's Eve Watch is when African Americans join together to welcome the new year by singing, chanting, and shouting.
2. She didn't do too bad on the quiz.
3. We should of paid closer attention to the instructions.
4. I wonder how many Americans realize the importance of the Minutemen, which were true champions of freedom during the American Revolution.
5. Being as my parents prefer tapes, they don't hardly ever play their records.
6. A large amount of people contributed to the charity drive.
7. Swimming is the type of sport that requires daily training.
8. Did Mr. Jackson mean to infer that we might have a pop quiz tomorrow, or was he just joking?
9. I don't think he knows where he's at.
10. Some speakers make illusions to the "good old days."
11. Remind me to bring my beaded doeskin shirt to the dry cleaner's so that it will be ready in time for the powwow on Saturday.
12. I don't know whether to except his invitation or not.
13. The reason we left the party early is because we had to catch the six o'clock train the next morning.
14. I can't help but think of *The Sound of Music* when I hear the song "Edelweiss."
15. There weren't none of us who were finished with our final copy.
16. I think these kind of stereo speakers give a better sound.
17. I couldn't hardly remember the names of all the states.
18. I infer from your research paper that Gutenberg had a great affect on the way books were printed.
19. My Chinese name, Wan Ju, means "someone who never lets nothing stand in the way of her success."
20. Miguel Castañeda has played ice hockey for Mexico besides being the first competitive speed skater to represent that country.

USAGE

Using Standard English in Writing a Local History

Variety is the spice of life—and of language. In casual conversation you hear many usages that don't follow the rules and guidelines of standard formal English. Often, these usages are part of a *dialect*—a variety of English unique to the speaker's geographical region or cultural group. (For more about dialects, see pages 475–476.) Dialects make conversational English lively and expressive. In writing, they help capture the particular flavor of a speaker's words. When paraphrasing, however, it's best to use standard English.

QUOTATION Great-aunt Celia said, "Don't you pay him no mind."

PARAPHRASE Great-aunt Celia said that I shouldn't pay any attention to him.

▶ WRITING ACTIVITY

Dr. Yolanda Washington, a professor at the nearby community college, is compiling an informal history of your area. She has invited students in American history classes at local high schools to submit historical accounts of local people, places, and events to be included in this project. Write a letter to Dr. Washington, telling a true story about your block, your neighborhood, or your town. You may use dialect in direct quotations, but be sure to use standard English in the rest of your letter. Use the **Glossary of Usage** to check any words or phrases you're not sure about.

Prewriting First, think of some of the stories you may have heard about your community. Maybe the story of how a particular geographical feature got its name springs to mind. Or you might choose to tell about your parents', grandparents', or great-grandparents' arrival in the area. Some local stories might even have taken place during larger historical events such as the Civil War. If you don't know any stories about your community's history, ask an older family member, a friend, or a neighbor to tell you some. Then choose the best story to send to Dr. Washington. Jot down as many concrete details as you can. Record a few good quotations and paraphrases that capture the local flavor of the story.

Writing   Follow the standard form for business letters (pages 994–1002). Begin your draft by greeting Dr. Washington and explaining that you'd like to contribute to her local history project. Then set the scene for your story by indicating the time period and setting. Write down the events of the story in a clear, straightforward order. Include as many details as you can.

Evaluating and Revising   Check with someone who knows the story to be sure you've recorded the facts accurately. Ask for additional details that may make the story more interesting and informative. As you revise, check words and expressions in the **Glossary of Usage** to make sure they're formal standard English. Avoid nonstandard usages in paraphrases. If you've included quotations, check them for correct punctuation. (For more about punctuating quotations, see pages 878–881.)

Proofreading and Publishing   Proofread your letter carefully for errors in grammar, usage, or mechanics. Be sure you've used the correct form for business letters. You and other members of your class may want to compile an informal history of your community. You can publish your stories by collecting them in a booklet and giving copies of the booklet to a local historical society, a tourist information center, school and public libraries, or any other people or organizations that might enjoy them.

Review: Posttest

A. Correcting Errors in Usage

Most of the following sentences contain errors in usage. If a sentence contains an error, revise the sentence. If a sentence is correct, write *C*.

EXAMPLE **1.** Many of us felt badly when our class trip was canceled.
1. *Many of us felt bad when our class trip was canceled.*

1. Do sloths always move that slow?
2. I inferred from what Julio said that he has excepted my apology.
3. Over eighty years ago my great-grandfather immigrated from Mexico.
4. He talked persuasively for an hour, but his words had no affect.
5. The Seminoles of Florida piece together colorful fabrics to create striking dresses, shirts, skirts, and etc.
6. The sizable amount of hours I have spent studying has really helped my grades.
7. Are you implying that you noticed nothing unusual in the cafeteria today?
8. When La Toya, Tamisha, and I ate at the new Ethiopian restaurant, the food was served in communal bowls, and we divided it between ourselves.
9. The reason the book was so difficult to understand was because the writing was unclear.
10. If you kept less fish in your tank, they would live longer.

B. Correcting Errors in Usage

Most of the sentences in the following paragraph contain errors in usage. Identify the error or errors in each incorrect sentence and write the correct form. If a sentence is correct, write *C*.

EXAMPLE **[1]** In-line skates provide such a smooth, fast ride that they give the allusion that you're ice-skating.
1. *allusion—illusion*

[11] Almost no one could of predicted the rollerskating revolution that's taken place in the last few years! [12] Actually, the very first in-line rollerskates were invented somewheres in the Netherlands in the 1700s. [13] I read in the newspaper where, in 1769, a London instrument maker and mechanic wore in-line skates with metal wheels to a party. [14] Playing a violin, he came gliding in the room on the skates, but he made a crash landing because he didn't have no idea how to stop. [15] Maybe

that's why nobody really excepted the newfangled skates in them days. **[16]** Later, an American inventor devised the four-wheeled skate, which became popular, and it looked like in-line skates weren't never going to succeed. **[17]** Finally, in 1980, two Minneapolis brothers noticed that hockey players hated being off of the ice during the summer. **[18]** Thinking that in-line skates would be a perfect cross-training tool to keep hockey players in shape all year, the brothers started building the new skates in their basement. **[19]** The idea might of stopped right there if other people hadn't found out that beside being a good training tool, in-line skating is just plain fun. **[20]** In-line skating offers a great low-impact aerobic workout, and it's safe—as long as skaters wear the right type protective gear and learn how to stop!

USAGE

28 CAPITALIZATION

Rules of Standard Usage

Diagnostic Test

A. Recognizing Correctly Capitalized Sentences

For each of the following sentences, write the words that should be capitalized. If a sentence is correct, write *C*.

EXAMPLE **1.** After Dan finishes shopping, he'll meet us in front of Calvert's grocery.
1. *Grocery*

1. In the fall, aunt Lisa's play will be staged by the Captain Philip Weston theater.
2. We were surprised to find that the film was in spanish, although english subtitles were provided.
3. Was Artemis the Greek goddess who ruled the hunt?
4. Pablo's favorite board game is *Trivial pursuit* because he always wins.
5. Have you seen *A raisin in the sun* yet?
6. Leon stood at the card counter for a full hour, trying to choose just the right card for Valentine's day.

7. The opening speech will be given by ex-Senator Preston.
8. Alnaba's new brother was delivered at Memorial hospital just before dawn.
9. Come to see our fantastic selection of top-quality stereo equipment at our new location just south of interstate 4 and River Road!
10. Can you name four countries located on the continent of Africa?

B. Proofreading for Correct Capitalization

Proofread the following paragraph for errors in capitalization. In each sentence, change lowercase letters to capitals or capital letters to lowercase as necessary. If a sentence is correct, write *C*.

EXAMPLE   **[1]** As humanity has developed more and more of the Earth's wilderness areas, many animal species have become extinct or endangered.
   1. *earth's*

[11] Last year, in a special Ecology course at Charlotte High School, I found out about some endangered North American animals. **[12]** I learned that conservationists here in the south are particularly concerned about the fate of the Florida panther. **[13]** All of that classroom discussion didn't have much impact on me, however, until early one Saturday morning last Spring, when I was lucky enough to sight one of these beautiful creatures. **[14]** My Uncle and I were driving to Big Bass Lake for some fishing, and I saw what looked like a large dog crossing the road some distance ahead of us. **[15]** Suddenly, Uncle Billy stopped his old ford truck and reached for the field glasses in the glove compartment. **[16]** As he handed them to me, he said, "look closely, Chris. You probably won't see a panther again any time soon." **[17]** Standing in the middle of Collingswood avenue, the cat turned and looked straight at us. **[18]** When those brown eyes met mine, I knew I had the title for my term paper—"Hello And Goodbye." **[19]** Then the big cat leisurely turned and crossed the road and loped off into the woods east of Sunshine Mall. **[20]** As the panther disappeared back into the wilds of Charlotte county, Uncle Billy said, "May god go with you, pal."

MECHANICS

In your reading, you'll notice variations in the use of capitalization. Most writers, however, follow the rules presented in this chapter. In your own writing, following these rules will help you communicate clearly with the widest possible audience.

28a. Capitalize the first word in every sentence.

EXAMPLES   **A**uthor Leslie Marmon Silko was born in Albuquerque, New Mexico, and grew up on the Laguna Pueblo Reservation.

When he missed the bus, my brother asked, "**W**ill you drive me to school?"

Traditionally, the first word of a line of poetry is capitalized.

EXAMPLE   **J**oy may be shy, unique,
Friendly to a few,
Sorrow never scorned to speak
To any who
Were false or true.

Countee Cullen, "Any Human to Another"

NOTE: Some modern writers, for reasons of style, do not follow this rule. When you quote from a writer's work, always use capital letters exactly as the writer uses them.

 REFERENCE NOTE: See page 878 for more information about using capital letters in quotations.

28b. Capitalize the interjection *O* and the pronoun *I*.

The interjection *O* is usually used only for invocations and is followed by the name of the person or thing being addressed. Don't confuse it with the common interjection *oh*, which is capitalized only when it appears at the beginning of a sentence and is always followed by punctuation.

EXAMPLES   Walt Whitman's tribute to Abraham Lincoln begins, "**O** Captain! my Captain!"
What **I** meant was—**oh,** never mind.

28c. Capitalize *proper nouns* and *proper adjectives.*

A *common noun* names one member of a group of people, places, or things. A *proper noun* names a particular person, place, or thing. *Proper adjectives* are formed from proper nouns.

☞ **REFERENCE NOTE:** For more information about proper nouns and common nouns, see pages 553–554. See page 561 for a discussion of proper adjectives.

Common nouns are capitalized only if they

- begin a sentence (also, in most cases, a line of poetry)
  or
- begin a direct quotation
  or
- are part of a title

COMMON NOUNS	PROPER NOUNS	PROPER ADJECTIVES
a writer	Dickens	Dickensian characters
a country	Brazil	Brazilian coastline
a president	Jefferson	Jeffersonian ideals
an island	Hawaii	Hawaiian climate

In proper nouns made up of two or more words, all articles, coordinating conjunctions, and short prepositions (those with fewer than five letters) are not capitalized.

EXAMPLES **Queen of Spain**
American Society for the Prevention of Cruelty to Animals

The parts of a compound word are capitalized as if each part stood alone.

EXAMPLES **African American**   **Chinese checkers**
Central American nations   **English-speaking tourists**

NOTE: Proper nouns and proper adjectives may lose their capitals after long usage.

EXAMPLES **madras   sandwich   watt   puritan**

When you're not sure whether to capitalize a word, check a dictionary.

(1) Capitalize the names of persons.

GIVEN NAMES **Patricia   Brian   Toshio   Aretha**
SURNAMES **Sánchez   Goldblum   Williams   Ozawa**

MECHANICS

NOTE: Some names contain more than one capital letter. Usage varies in the capitalization of *van, von, du, de la,* and other parts of many multiword names. Always verify the spelling of a name with the person, or check the name in a reference source.

EXAMPLES **La Fontaine   McEwen   O'Connor   Van Doren**
Yellow Thunder   Ibn Ezra   Villa-Lobos   van Gogh

Abbreviations such as *Ms., Mr., Dr., Gen., Jr. (junior),* and *Sr. (senior)* should always be capitalized.

EXAMPLES **Ms.** Gloria Steinem   **Dr.** Antonia Novello
Gordon Parks, **Jr.**   Martin Luther King, **Sr.**

☞ REFERENCE NOTE: For more about punctuating abbreviations, see pages 844–845.

(2) Capitalize geographical names.

TYPE OF NAME	EXAMPLES	
Towns, Cities	Boston Tokyo	South Bend Rio de Janeiro
Counties, Townships	Marion County Lawrence Township	Lafayette Parish Nottinghamshire
States	Wisconsin New Hampshire	Oklahoma North Carolina
Regions	the East the Southwest	Northern Hemisphere New England

NOTE: Words such as *north, western,* and *southeast* are not capitalized when they indicate direction.

EXAMPLES   east of the river   driving south   western Iowa

☞ REFERENCE NOTE: The abbreviations of names of states are always capitalized. For more about using and punctuating such abbreviations, see page 845.

TYPE OF NAME	EXAMPLES	
Countries	Mozambique Costa Rica	United States of America

(continued)

MECHANICS

TYPE OF NAME	EXAMPLES	
Continents	North America Africa	Asia Europe
Islands	Catalina Island Greater Antilles	Isle of Pines Florida Keys
Mountains	Blue Ridge Mountains Sierra Nevada	Mount McKinley Humphrey's Peak
Other Land Forms and Features	Cape Cod Mojave Desert Mississippi Valley	Isthmus of Panama Horse Cave Point Sur
Bodies of Water	Pacific Ocean Strait of Hormuz	Great Lakes Saint Lawrence Seaway
Parks	Point Reyes National Seashore	Gates of the Arctic National Park
Roads, Highways, Streets	Route 30 Interstate 55 Pennsylvania Turnpike	Michigan Avenue North Tenth Street Morningside Drive

MECHANICS

☞ **REFERENCE NOTE:** In addresses, abbreviations such as *St., Ave., Dr.,* and *Blvd.* are capitalized. For more about abbreviations, see pages 844–845.

NOTE: The second word in a hyphenated number begins with a small letter.

EXAMPLE   Forty-**second** Street

Words such as *city, island, street,* and *park* are capitalized only when they are part of a name.

PROPER NOUNS	COMMON NOUNS
a rodeo in **Carson City**	a rodeo in a nearby city
a ferry to **Block Island**	a ferry to a resort island
swimming in **Clear Lake**	swimming in the lake
along **Canal Street**	along a neighborhood street

▶ EXERCISE 1 **Capitalizing Words and Names Correctly**

If a word or words in the following phrases should be capitalized, write the entire phrase correctly. If a phrase is correct, write C.

1. the far west
2. a city north of louisville
3. the utah salt flats
4. the cape of good hope
5. chris o'malley
6. hoover dam
7. southern illinois
8. lock the door!
9. the kalahari desert
10. the northeast
11. gulf of Alaska
12. mary mcleod bethune
13. a mountain people
14. tom delaney, jr.
15. hawaiian volcanoes state park
16. a north american actor
17. san francisco bay
18. skiing on the lake
19. turned west at the corner
20. a tibetan yak
21. mexican gold
22. the delaware
23. east indian curry
24. decatur street north
25. fifty-sixth street

MECHANICS

PICTURE THIS

What a story! It's 1932, and this pilot, Amelia Earhart, has just completed a record-setting flight. She is the first woman to successfully fly solo across the Atlantic Ocean. However, due to mechanical problems and bad weather, she did not land at her intended destination, Paris. As the map on the next page shows, she has landed instead near Londonderry, Ireland. You are a newspaper reporter covering this exciting story, and Miss Earhart has granted you a brief interview. Write down some questions to ask her, and use your imagination to record her answers. In your interview, include at least five proper nouns. Be sure to capitalize each proper noun you use.

Subject: Amelia Earhart's solo transatlantic flight
Audience: newspaper readers
Purpose: to inform

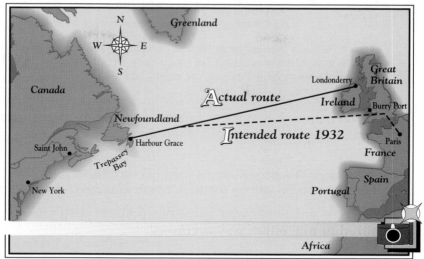

(3) Capitalize the names of organizations, teams, business firms, institutions, buildings, and government bodies.

TYPE OF NAME	EXAMPLES	
Organizations	American Dental Association Future Farmers of America National Science Foundation	
Teams	Detroit Pistons San Diego Padres	Miami Dolphins Cedar Hill Hawks

Business Firms	Roth's Optical
	Diesel Engine
	    Specialists
		Hip-Hop Music, Inc.
		American Broadcasting
		    Corporation

Institutions, Buildings	Duke University Century Center Rialto Theater	Mayo Clinic Meadowlawn High School

Government Bodies	Department of State
	Atomic Energy
	    Commission
		Congress
		House of
		    Representatives

MECHANICS

MECHANICS

☞ REFERENCE NOTE: The names of organizations, businesses, and government bodies are often abbreviated to a series of capital letters.

EXAMPLES Parent-Teacher Association **PTA**
International Business Machines **IBM**
Federal Bureau of Investigation **FBI**

Usually the letters in such abbreviations are not followed by periods, but always check an up-to-date dictionary to be sure. For more about abbreviations, see pages 844–845.

Do not capitalize words such as *democratic, republican,* and *socialist* when they refer to principles or forms of government. Capitalize such words only when they refer to a specific political party.

EXAMPLES The citizens demanded **d**emocratic reforms.
Who will be the **R**epublican nominee for governor?

The word *party* in the name of a political party may be capitalized or not; either way is correct.

EXAMPLE **D**emocratic **p**arty
or
Democratic **P**arty

☞ REFERENCE NOTE: Do not capitalize words such as *building, hospital, theater, high school, university,* and *post office* unless they are part of a proper noun. For more on the differences between common nouns and proper nouns, see pages 553–554 and 820–821.

(4) Capitalize the names of historical events and periods, special events, and holidays and other calendar items.

TYPE OF NAME	EXAMPLES	
Historical Events and Periods	Boston Tea Party Battle of Saratoga Reign of Terror	Middle Ages French Revolution Mesozoic Era
Special Events	Olympics New York Marathon	Ohio State Fair Pan-American Games
Holidays and Other Calendar Items	Wednesday September Kwanzaa	Fourth of July Memorial Day Mother's Day

NOTE: Do not capitalize the name of a season unless the season is being personified or unless it is used in a proper noun.

EXAMPLES The **winter** was unusually warm.
Overnight, **Winter** crept in, trailing her snowy veil.
We plan to attend the school's **Winter Carnival.**

(5) Capitalize the names of nationalities, races, and peoples.

EXAMPLES **Lithuanian Haitian Jewish Asian**
Caucasian Hispanic Bantu Zuni

(6) Capitalize the brand names of business products.

EXAMPLES **Borden milk Colonial bread Zenith television**

Notice that the noun that may follow a brand name is not capitalized: a **Xerox m**achine.

(7) Capitalize the names of ships, monuments, awards, planets, and any other particular places, things, or events.

TYPE OF NAME	EXAMPLES	
Ships, Trains	*Monitor*	*Zephyr*
Aircraft and Spacecraft	*Air Force One* **Minuteman**	*Columbia* *Enola Gay*
Monuments, Memorials, Awards	**Navaho National Monument** **Mount Rushmore National Memorial** **Congressional Medal of Honor**	
Planets, Stars, Constellations	**Jupiter** **Ursa Minor**	**Rigel** **Little Dipper**

MECHANICS

NOTE: Do not capitalize the words *sun* and *moon.* Do not capitalize the word *earth* unless it is used along with the names of other heavenly bodies that are capitalized.

EXAMPLES The **moon** reflects light from the **sun.**
This orchid grows wild in only one place on **earth.**
Venus is closer to the sun than **Earth** is.

28d. Do *not* capitalize the names of school subjects, except for names of languages and course names followed by a number.

EXAMPLES **history   art   physics   geometry**
Spanish   Latin   Algebra I   Chemistry II

NOTE: Do not capitalize the class names *senior, junior, sophomore,* and *freshman* unless they are part of a proper noun.

EXAMPLES   The juniors are planning a surprise for **Senior Day.**
The **Freshman Follies** was a big success.

EXERCISE 2   **Capitalizing Words and Names Correctly**

Write the following words and phrases, using capital letters where they are needed. If a word or phrase is correct, write C.

1. the science department
2. north atlantic treaty organization
3. st. patrick's cathedral
4. *city of new orleans* (train)
5. the federal reserve bank
6. the normandy invasion
7. classes in auto mechanics
8. the world cup
9. chinese cuisine
10. cherokee history
11. midtown traffic
12. jones and drake, inc.
13. spaceflight to mars
14. on labor day
15. *ariadne* (boat)
16. at holiday inn
17. the louisiana world exposition
18. early summer
19. gold medal flour
20. an american history class

REVIEW A   **Proofreading a Paragraph for Correct Capitalization**

For each sentence in the following paragraph, write the word or words that should be capitalized. If a word is improperly capitalized, write the word correctly.

EXAMPLE   [1] Even if you don't know much about horses, you can likely appreciate the beauty of the arabian horses shown on the next page.
1. *Arabian*

[1] Perhaps no other breed of horses can conjure up such images of romance as these beautiful animals from Northern

Africa. [2] Their distinctive and colorful trappings bring to mind the nomadic lives of wandering tribes and the exciting exploits of their bedouin chieftains. [3] Smaller and lighter than many breeds, with proportionally large hooves, these horses are perfectly suited to the hot sands of the Sahara or the Arabian desert. [4] Some evidence suggests that north African peoples may have been breeding these horses as long ago as seven thousand years. [5] Arabians characteristically have elegant heads and necks as well as large, lustrous eyes, features that have been prized by breeders all over the Earth. [6] These horses have played their part in many historical events far from the Continent of Africa. [7] During the Revolutionary war, for instance, George Washington rode a gray said to be the offspring of a famous Arabian stallion. [8] America's love affair with the Arabian horse has continued from the early days of our nation right through to the Present. [9] Today, the Arabian Horse club has thousands of names on its roster. [10] Some of the newer importers include W. R. Brown of Berlin, New Hampshire, and Spencer Bade of Fall river, Massachusetts.

Arabian **Thoroughbred**

Arabian horses in action.

28e. Capitalize titles.

(1) Capitalize a title belonging to a particular person when it comes before the person's name.

EXAMPLES   **General Davis   Dr. Ramírez   President Kennedy**

In general, do not capitalize a title used alone or following a name. Some titles, however, are by tradition capitalized. If you are unsure of whether or not to capitalize a title, check in a dictionary.

EXAMPLES   Who is the **g**overnor of Kansas?
Sherian Grace Cadoria, a **b**rigadier **g**eneral, is the highest-ranking African American woman in the U.S. Armed Forces.
The **S**peaker of the **H**ouse rose to greet the **Q**ueen of England.

A title is usually capitalized when it is used alone in direct address.

EXAMPLES   Have you reached your decision, **G**overnor?
We're honored to welcome you, **M**s. **M**ayor.
Please come in, **S**ir [or sir].

NOTE: For special emphasis or clarity, writers sometimes capitalize a title used alone or following a person's name.

EXAMPLES   The **G**overnor was in the last car in the parade.
Did the **P**resident veto the bill?

Do not capitalize *ex–, –elect, former,* or *late* when they are used with a title.

EXAMPLES   **ex**-Governor Walsh   the president-**e**lect

(2) Capitalize words showing family relationships when used with a person's name but *not* when preceded by a possessive.

EXAMPLES   **Aunt Amy   Uncle Hector   Grandmother Guttman**
my **s**ister   your **c**ousin   Thelma's **n**ephew

(3) Capitalize the first and last words and all important words in titles of books, periodicals, poems, stories, plays, historical documents, movies, radio and television programs, works of art, and musical compositions.

Unimportant words in a title include

- articles: *a, an, the*
- short prepositions (fewer than five letters): *of, to, in, for, from, with*
- coordinating conjunctions: *and, but, for, nor, or, so, yet*

TYPE OF TITLE	EXAMPLES
Books	*The Call of the Wild* *The Way to Rainy Mountain* *One Hundred Years of Solitude*
Periodicals	*Car and Driver* *Louisville Courier-Journal*
Poems	"Tonight I Can Write" "Most Satisfied by Snow"
Stories	"In Another Country" "The Catch in the Shadow of the Sunrise"
Plays	*Song of Sheba* *Watch on the Rhine* *The Importance of Being Earnest*
Historical Documents	Declaration of Independence Mayflower Compact Treaty of Versailles
Movies	*Children of a Lesser God* *No Place to Be Somebody* *Come See the Paradise*
Radio and Television Programs	"Adventures in Good Music" *In Living Color* *WKRP in Cincinnati*
Works of Art	*Woman Before a Mirror* *Prelude to Farewell*
Musical Compositions	"Lift Every Voice and Sing" *Into the Light* *Three Places in New England*

MECHANICS

NOTE: The article *the* is often written before a title but is not capitalized unless it is the first word of the title.

EXAMPLES   the *Austin American-Statesman*
The *Atlantic*

REFERENCE NOTE: For information about which titles should be italicized and which should be enclosed in quotation marks, see pages 875–876 and 882–883.

(4) Capitalize the names of religions and their followers, holy days and celebrations, holy writings, and specific deities.

TYPE OF NAME	EXAMPLES	
Religions and Followers	Christianity Hinduism Judaism	Buddhist Muslim Presbyterian
Holy Days and Celebrations	Epiphany Ramadan Rosh Hashanah	Easter Passover Potlatch
Holy Writings	the Bible the Koran the Talmud	Rig-Veda Genesis the Pentateuch
Specific Deities	Allah Brahma	God the Holy Spirit

The words *god* and *goddess* are not capitalized when they refer to the deities of ancient mythology. The names of specific mythological deities are capitalized, however.

EXAMPLE   The Greek **god** of the sea was **Poseidon.**

NOTE: Some writers capitalize all pronouns that refer to a deity. Others capitalize such pronouns only if necessary to prevent confusion.

EXAMPLE   Through Moses, God commanded the pharaoh to let **His** people go.

MECHANICS

EXERCISE 3   Capitalizing Names and Titles Correctly

Write the following items, using capital letters where they are needed. If an item is correct, write *C*.

1. the *washington post*
2. ex-senator Margaret Chase Smith
3. *soul train* (TV program)
4. captain of the fencing team
5. emancipation proclamation
6. the first chapter in *the grapes of wrath*
7. the teachings of islam
8. the late Bessie Smith
9. "Come with me, dad."
10. the old testament

REVIEW B   Using Capital Letters in a Press Release

You and your classmates have written and produced a play about the plight of homeless people in America. The money that you raise from the sale of tickets will be donated to a local homeless shelter and job-training program. Because you are eager to raise as much money as possible, you have decided to issue a press release to local newspapers and radio stations to announce your class's theatrical debut. Write a short paragraph that includes the following information:

Title of the play
Date(s) and time(s) of the performance(s)
Where the performance will take place
Name(s) of the lead player(s)
The name of the organization that will receive the profits from the play

REVIEW C   Proofreading a Paragraph for Correct Capitalization

For each sentence in the following paragraphs, change lowercase letters to capitals and capital letters to lowercase as necessary. If a sentence is correct, write *C*.

[1] Among the many unusual scenes that captain Christopher Columbus witnessed in the New World was that of native Hispaniolans playing games with balls made of latex, the white liquid that oozes from plants like the rubber tree, guayule, milkweed, and dandelion. [2] Latex balls were also used by the mayas, but unlike the ball games that you may have played

with your Brother or Sister, Mayan games were sacred rituals. [3] According to the *Book Of counsel*, an ancient Mayan document, the games reenacted the story of twins who became immortal. [4] Ball games were so important to the Mayan culture that, along with stately masks of their gods, Mayan artists rendered statues of ball players, and builders erected large stone stadiums for playing. [5] Although columbus did not note his encounters with latex, other explorers did, and one recorded the fascinating use of Latex shown here—the Mayan practice of coating their feet with a protective layer of the milky liquid.

[6] Latex does not hold up well in extreme temperatures, and it was used in europe only for rubbing out pencil marks (hence the term *rubber*), until Charles Goodyear became fascinated with the substance and declared that "elastic gum" glorified god. [7] Goodyear's discovery of vulcanization enabled the successful commercial production of rubber and earned him the public admiration of emperor Napoleon III. [8] In the next decades Brazil increased its rubber production thousands of times over, as Eric R. Wolf points out in *Europe And The People Without History*. [9] Indeed, rubber became such an essential part of our lives that the U.S. army once asked a young Major named Eisenhower to study the matter. [10] Wisely, the Late President Eisenhower advised the military to maintain its own source of this valuable commodity.

WRITING APPLICATION

Using Capitalization in a Letter

Why does one person eat with a knife and fork, another with chopsticks, and still another with his or her hands? Each one is following the social conventions of his or her culture. Like conventions of social behavior, conventions of language are practices that have become standardized over time. For example, the conventions of capitalization taught in this chapter are important because readers of English everywhere expect capital letters to be used in certain ways. Nonstandard capitalization may confuse readers by suggesting a meaning that wasn't intended. Compare the following sentences. How does the use of capital letters and lowercase letters affect the meaning of each?

EXAMPLES   Mom and I spend each New Year's Day watching the rose bowl with our relatives in west Virginia.
Mom and I spend each New Year's Day watching the Rose Bowl with our relatives in West Virginia.

MECHANICS

WRITING ACTIVITY

You've just started corresponding with a teenager in Japan. You and your pen pal are eager to learn more about each other's cultures, including customs, holidays, food, schools, and recreational activities. Write a letter to your pen pal describing some custom or practice that is unique to American culture or special to your family. In your letter, follow the rules of capitalization given in this chapter.

Prewriting List some typically American holidays, customs, and practices that you think might interest your pen pal. For each item on your list, brainstorm as many descriptive details as you can. For example, if you're describing the Fourth of July, you'll want to give specific details about how you celebrate the holiday—what you eat, whether you watch fireworks, how your town decorates for the holiday, and so forth. Choose one item from your list to write about. You may want to use an encyclopedia to look up any historical information you're not sure about.

Writing As you write your draft, organize your information clearly. Add facts, examples, and details as you think of them. Use clear, straightforward language, and try to avoid colloquialisms and idioms that your friend may not recognize. (For more about colloquialisms and idioms, see pages 486–487.) Be sure to capitalize proper nouns, including the names of geographical areas, historical events, and holidays.

Evaluating and Revising Put yourself in the place of your pen pal, who may not be familiar with the custom you're describing. Be sure you've included enough information to help your pen pal understand the meaning behind the holiday or other special event. Also add descriptive, sensory details to help your reader vividly picture the celebration or custom.

Proofreading Proofread your letter for any errors in grammar, usage, and mechanics. Take special care with capitalization of proper nouns. Be sure that you have followed the guidelines on page 1004 for writing personal letters.

Review: Posttest

Capitalizing Words and Phrases Correctly

For each of the following sentences, write the words that should be capitalized. If a sentence is correct, write *C*.

EXAMPLE **1.** The rotary club has invited representative William Bashone to speak at tonight's annual banquet.
1. *Rotary Club; Representative*

1. According to Zack Johnson, the company's representative, you shouldn't buy just any car; you should buy a saturn.
2. One of the earliest cars made by Henry Ford was called the Model T; it had a four-cylinder, twenty-horsepower engine.
3. On our vacation we toured several states in the south.

4. Johnson's bake shop and deli is just north of state street on highway 143.
5. Before you can take this computer course, you must pass algebra II.
6. Aren't they planning a parade to celebrate Martin Luther King, jr., day?
7. Because we cheered so loudly at the special olympics, ms. Andrews made Bill and me honorary cheerleaders for her special education class.
8. In a nationally televised press conference, the president warned that he would veto any tax increase.
9. The british poet Ted Hughes was married to Sylvia Plath, who was an american writer.
10. The only man in American history who was not elected to be vice-president or president, yet held both positions, is ex-president Gerald Ford.
11. My mother asked me to walk to the supermarket and buy a quart container of farmingbury milk and two pounds of pinto beans.
12. When we toured eastern Tennessee, we visited the Oak Ridge Laboratory, where atomic research was carried out during World War II.
13. The Spanish-american Club has planned a festival for late summer; it will be held at the north end of the city.
14. If you are looking for the best apples in the state, follow route 14 until you see the signs for Peacock's Orchard.
15. In a controversial debate on the Panama canal, the United States voted to relinquish its control of the canal to the Panamanian government.
16. When my Aunt Janice visited England last summer, she toured buckingham palace and tried to catch a glimpse of queen Elizabeth.
17. Mayor-elect Sabrena Willis will speak to the public about her proposals to upgrade the city's bilingual education program.
18. Earl and Jamie were lucky to get tickets to see the Indigo girls at the Erwin center.
19. When spring arrives, I know it's time to start thinking about where to look for a summer job.
20. Although the east room of the White house is now used for press conferences, it was once a place where Abigail Adams aired the president's laundry.

MECHANICS

SUMMARY STYLE REVIEW

Names of Persons

Mrs. Martin A. LaForge, Sr.	a neighbor
Louise Brown	a girl in my class
Mr. Peter Echohawk	a math teacher

Geographical Names

Sioux City	a city in Iowa
Orange County	a county in Florida
Staten Island	an island in New York Harbor
Allegheny Mountains	a mountain range
Pacific Ocean	across the ocean
Forty-third Street	a one-way street
Sequoia National Park	a national park
in the East, North, Midwest	heading east, north, south

Organizations, Business Firms, Institutions, Government Bodies

New York Philharmonic	a symphony orchestra
Something from the Oven	a bakery
Madison High School	a large high school
Supreme Court	a district court
Department of the Interior	a department of government

Historical Events and Periods, Special Events, Calendar Items

the Korean War	a veteran of the war
the Stone Age	a prehistoric age
the Super Bowl	a championship game
Father's Day	a national holiday
April, July, October, January	spring, summer, autumn, winter

Nationalities, Races, Religions

Cambodian	a nationality
Caucasian	a race
Judaism	a religion
God	myths about the Roman gods

Brand Names

Stutz Bearcat	an antique automobile
Pac-Man	a video game

(continued)

SUMMARY STYLE REVIEW *(continued)*

Other Particular Places, Things, Events, Awards

Niña	a ship
Metroliner	a train
Galileo	a spacecraft
Springarn Medal	an award
the **Milky Way**	a galaxy
Earth, Venus, Saturn	from the earth
the **Coronado Memorial**	a memorial in **Arizona**
Senior Prom	a senior in high school
Silver Star	a medal for heroism

Specific Courses, Languages

Bookkeeping I	after bookkeeping class
Spanish	a foreign language
Geometry II	a geometry test

Titles

Mayor Dixon	a mayor
President of the United States	president of the club
the **Duke of Edinburgh**	a duke's title
Aunt Rosa	my aunt
The Piano Lesson	a play
the *Oakland Tribune*	a daily newspaper
Holy Bible	a religious book

MECHANICS

29 PUNCTUATION

End Marks and Commas

Diagnostic Test

A. Correcting Sentences by Adding or Deleting End Marks and Commas

Add or delete end marks or commas to correct each of the following sentences.

EXAMPLE **1.** Do you think that it will rain today Brian.
    1. *Do you think that it will rain today, Brian?*

1. Gov Jameston, a well-known Democrat does not plan to run for another term.
2. This year I am taking courses in English, Spanish algebra and history

3. When I joined the staff of the newspaper I was taught to write short powerful headlines

4. The essay, that Ms. Hughes assigned yesterday, is due next Monday.

5. Would you send me a postcard from Hawaii while you're there on vacation

6. Bravo, what a great solo.

7. Geometry which I took last year was not an easy subject for me.

8. Peg asked, "Have you read for example *Animal Farm* by George Orwell"?

9. Please send this package to Mrs Rose Sanchez 116 East Elm Street Allentown P.A. 18001.

10. The letter was dated June 16 1993 and was mailed from Washington D.C..

B. Proofreading a Paragraph for Correct Comma Usage

Add or delete commas to correct each sentence in the following paragraph.

[11] One of the most dangerous assignments for a pilot is to fly over the cold barren stretches of snow and ice north of the Arctic Circle. [12] Ellen Paneok, an Inupiat pilot should know. [13] Even before she learned to drive a car Paneok was flying over the tundra far from her hometown of Kotzebue, in Alaska. [14] Traveling in the Arctic a bush pilot must be alert to the dangers of fatigue vertigo, and the northern lights. [15] Caught in dense fog or a snowstorm a pilot can easily lose his or her bearings and become a victim of vertigo. [16] Furthermore, the pilot, who stares at the northern lights too long, can wind up buried in a snowbank. [17] Paneok therefore keeps a sharp lookout for objects on the ground. [18] A glimpse of a caribou, a patch of brush, a jutting ice dome etc. will help her regain her sense of direction and will also break the boredom. [19] Soaring over the tundra she provides many rural people with produce, and transportation. [20] Paneok loves to fly; for the beauty of Alaska, and the needs of her fellow Alaskans make the risk worthwhile.

MECHANICS

In speaking, the tone and pitch of your voice, the pauses in your speech, and the gestures and expressions you use all help to make your meaning clear. In writing, marks of punctuation such as end marks and commas tell readers where these verbal and nonverbal cues occur. However, if the meaning of a sentence is unclear in the first place, punctuation will not usually clarify it. Whenever you find yourself struggling to punctuate a sentence correctly, take a closer look at your arrangement of phrases or your choice of words. Often you can eliminate the punctuation problem by recasting the sentence.

End Marks

29a. A statement (or declarative sentence) is followed by a period.

EXAMPLE   October is Hispanic Heritage Month in the United States.

29b. A question (or interrogative sentence) is followed by a question mark.

EXAMPLES   Did you get the leading role?
Did you get the leading role?
When is your first performance?

(1) Do not use a question mark after a declarative sentence containing an indirect question.

EXAMPLE   Katie wondered who would win the award.

(2) Orders and requests are often put in question form even when they aren't actually questions. In that case, they may be followed by either a period or a question mark.

EXAMPLES   Will you please complete this brief questionnaire?
or
Will you please complete this brief questionnaire.

(3) A question mark should be placed inside the closing quotation marks when the quotation itself is a question. Otherwise, a question mark should be placed outside the closing quotation marks.

MECHANICS

EXAMPLES   To avoid answering a personal question, simply reply,
"Why do you ask?" [The quotation is a question.]
Did Mr. Shields actually say, "Your reports are due in
three days"? [The quotation is not a question, but
the sentence as a whole is.]

29c.   An imperative sentence is followed by either a
period or an exclamation point.

EXAMPLES   Turn the music down, please.
Turn the music down!

An imperative sentence may be stated as a question. However, since its purpose is to give a command or make a request,
it should be followed by a period or an exclamation point.

EXAMPLES   May we get through, please.
Will you let us through!

29d.   An exclamation is followed by an exclamation
point.

EXAMPLES   I can't believe that!
Don't cross that line!

An exclamation mark should be placed inside the closing
quotation marks when the quotation itself is an exclamation.
Otherwise, it should be placed outside the quotation marks.

EXAMPLES   "Down in front!" yelled the crowd.
Ms. Chen couldn't have said, "No homework"!

☞ REFERENCE NOTE: For information on how sentences are classified
according to purpose, see rule 18m on pages 597–598. For more
discussion on the placement of end marks with closing quotation
marks, see rule 30m (4) on pages 879–880.

An interjection at the beginning of a sentence is usually followed by a comma.

USUAL   Hey, don't do that!
INFREQUENT   Hey! Don't do that!

Notice in the examples above that an exclamation point
may be used after a single word as well as after a sentence.

NOTE: Do not overuse exclamation points. Use an exclamation mark
only when a statement is obviously emphatic.

MECHANICS

EXERCISE 1   Correcting Sentences by Adding End Marks

Write each word that should be followed by an end mark in the following sentences; then add the appropriate end mark. If quotation marks should precede or follow the end mark, write them in the proper place.

EXAMPLES   **1.** Mom asked, "When did you receive the letter
         1. *letter?"*

         2. Terrific What a throw
         2. *Terrific! throw!*

1. When do you want to take your vacation
2. I did have enough money to go to the movies
3. Wow Did you see that liftoff
4. Willie, are you ready to give your report on Thurgood Marshall
5. Carefully set the Ming vase on the display stand
6. Mom wants to know why you did not buy a newspaper
7. What a downpour
8. Leave the theater immediately
9. He yelled across the field, "Hurry
10. Didn't you hear her say "I'm not ready yet

29e.   An abbreviation is usually followed by a period.

TYPES OF ABBREVIATIONS	EXAMPLES		
Personal Names	Susan B. Anthony		
	S. I. Hayakawa		
Organizations and Companies	Assn.	Corp.	Ltd.
	Co.	Inc.	
Titles Used with Names	Dr.	Mr.	Ms.
	Jr.	Mrs.	Ph. D.
Units of Measure	ft.	oz.	mi.
	in.	qt.	yd.
Time of Day	A.M. *(or* a.m.*)*		P.M. *(or* p.m.*)*
Years	B.C. *(written after the date)*		
	A.D. *(written before the date)*		
Addresses	Ave.	Dr.	Rd.
	Blvd.	Pkwy.	St.
States	Ark.	Fla.	S. Car.
	Calif.	Penn.	N. Mex.

NOTE: Two-letter state codes are used only when the ZIP code is included. The state codes are not followed by periods.

EXAMPLE   Springfield, MA 01101

When an abbreviation that ends with a period is the last word in a statement, do not add another period as an end mark. *Do* add a question mark or an exclamation point if one is needed.

EXAMPLES   Mr. Rodríguez lives in Fargo, N. Dak.
Isn't he originally from Dover, Del.?

Some common abbreviations are written without periods.

EXAMPLES   AC, CORE, FBI, GI, IOU, MTV, OK, PC, ROTC, SOS
cc, db, ft, l, lb, kw, ml, psi, rpm

NOTE: As a rule, an abbreviation is capitalized only if the words that it stands for are capitalized. If you're not sure whether to use periods with an abbreviation or whether to capitalize it, check a dictionary.

MECHANICS

PICTURE THIS

You're a cartoonist developing a comic strip for the funny papers. You've drawn these cartoon frames; now you need to add the dialogue in word balloons. Write at least one line of dialogue for each frame. In your comic strip, correctly punctuate at least one of each of the four types of sentences—declarative, interrogative, imperative, and exclamatory. Also, begin at least one sentence with an interjection.

Subject: a cartoon
Audience: readers of the funny papers
Purpose: to entertain

Commas

Items in a Series

29f.   Use commas to separate items in a series.

EXAMPLES   The basketball coach recommended that she practice dribbling, shooting, weaving, and passing. [words]
We can meet before English class, during lunch, or after school. [phrases]
After school I must make sure that my room is clean, that my little brother is home from his piano lesson, and that the garbage has been emptied. [clauses]

(1) When *and, or,* or *nor* joins the last two items in a series, you may omit the comma before the conjunction. Never omit the final comma, however, if such an omission would make the sentence unclear.

UNCLEAR	**Phyllis, Ken and Matt formed a rock band.** [It looks as though Phyllis is being addressed.]
CLEAR	**Phyllis, Ken, and Matt formed a rock band.** [Phyllis is clearly a member of the band.]

Some writers prefer always to use the comma before the *and* in a series. Follow your teacher's instructions on this point.

NOTE: Some words—such as *bread and butter* and *law and order*—are paired so often that they may be considered a single item.

EXAMPLE   For lunch we had soup, salad, bread and butter, and milk.

(2) If all the items in a series are linked by *and, or,* or *nor,* do not use commas to separate them.

EXAMPLES   **Tyrone and Earlene and Lily won awards for their sculptures.**
Should we walk or ride our bikes or take the bus?

(3) Do not place a comma before or after a series.

INCORRECT	**I enjoy, gymnastics, basketball, and wrestling.**
CORRECT	**I enjoy gymnastics, basketball, and wrestling.**

NOTE: The abbreviation *etc.* (meaning "and so forth") at the end of a series is always followed by a comma unless it falls at the end of a sentence.

EXAMPLES   **Randy bought hamburger, buns, onions, etc., for the cookout.**
For the cookout Randy bought hamburger, buns, onions, etc.

29g. Use a comma to separate two or more adjectives preceding a noun.

EXAMPLE   **Lucia is an intelligent, thoughtful, responsible student.**

When the last adjective before the noun is thought of as part of the noun, the comma before the adjective is omitted.

EXAMPLES   **Let's play this new video game.**
I've finally found a decent, affordable used car.

MECHANICS

Compound nouns such as *video game* and *used car* are considered single units rather than two separate words. You can use two tests to determine whether an adjective and a noun form a unit.

TEST 1: Insert the word *and* between the adjectives. If *and* fits sensibly between the adjectives, use a comma. In the first example above, *and* cannot be logically inserted: *new and video game*. In the second sentence, *and* sounds sensible between the first two adjectives (*decent and affordable*) but not between the second and third (*affordable and used*).

TEST 2: Change the order of the adjectives. If the order of the adjectives can be reversed sensibly, use a comma. *Affordable, decent used car* makes sense, but *used decent car* and *video new game* do not.

Independent Clauses

29h. Use a comma before *and, but, or, nor, for, so,* and *yet* when they join independent clauses.

EXAMPLES   I read a review of David Henry Hwang's *M. Butterfly*, and now I want to see the play.
Amy followed the recipe carefully, for she had never made paella before.

NOTE: Always use a comma before *yet, so,* or *for* joining independent clauses. The comma may be omitted before *and, but, or,* and *nor* if the independent clauses are very short and if the sentence is not confusing or unclear without it.

EXAMPLES   The phone rang and I answered it.
We can go in the morning or we can leave now.

The teacher called on Maria and John began to answer. [awkward without comma]
The teacher called on Maria, and John began to answer. [clear with comma]

Don't confuse a compound sentence with a simple sentence that has a compound verb.

SIMPLE SENTENCE   My sister had been accepted at Howard University but then decided to attend Grambling University instead. [one independent clause with a compound verb]

MECHANICS

COMPOUND SENTENCE   **My sister had been accepted at Howard University, but then she decided to attend Grambling University instead.** [two independent clauses]

Also, keep in mind that compound subjects and compound objects are not separated by commas.

EXAMPLES   **What he is saying today and what he said yesterday are two different things.** [two subordinate clauses serving as a compound subject]
Television crews covered the Daytona 500 and the Indianapolis 500. [compound object]

 REFERENCE NOTE: **For more about compound subjects and compound verbs, see pages 585–586.**

▶ EXERCISE 2   **Correcting Sentences by Adding Commas**

Write each word in the following sentences that should be followed by a comma, and add the comma. If a sentence is correct, write *C*.

1. The photograph showed a happy mischievous little boy.
2. Barbara will bring potato salad to the picnic and Marc will bring the cold cuts.
3. Alain LeRoy Locke was a Rhodes scholar taught philosophy created one of the foremost collections of African art and mentored many black writers.
4. We studied the following authors in English class this semester: F. Scott Fitzgerald Lorraine Hansberry and Rudolfo Anaya.
5. The introduction of the hardy sweet potato helped the Chinese to alleviate the famines that plagued them.
6. The committee has suggested that the cafeteria serve a different selection daily that classes not be interrupted by announcements and that pep rallies always be held during sixth period.
7. Students will receive paper pencils rulers etc. at the beginning of the test.
8. April liked the ballet but Jenny thought it was boring.
9. Last winter was abnormally cold icy and snowy.
10. The concert consisted of African American music and featured jazz rhythm and blues spirituals and several gospel songs.

REVIEW A   **Proofreading for the Correct Use of End Marks and Commas**

Add or delete end marks and commas to correct each sentence in the following paragraph.

[1] Known as Stonehenge, the great circle of stones shown here is located in England, and remains one of the most mysterious structures of the ancient world. [2] Much of the riddle of Stonehenge concerns the transport of the awesome massive blue stones that stand in the monument's inner circle. [3] These rocks are indigenous to Wales and many people have asked, "How did these huge stones travel two hundred miles to England" [4] Do you remember Merlin from the stories of King Arthur's legendary court [5] This wily, and powerful sorcerer is said to have moved the stones by magic. [6] The story of Merlin may be fascinating but modern astronomers anthropologists, and other scientists are searching for a more rational explanation. [7] Some theorists believe that many of the gigantic blue Welsh monoliths were shipped by raft through dangerous tidal waters, but other scientists scoff and say, "That's impossible"! [8] Still other theorists wonder if glaciers may have lifted moved, and deposited the stones so far from their home? [9] Visitors to Stonehenge are no longer allowed within the monument and venturing inside the protected area will draw a polite but authoritative, "Will you please step back" [10] So far, Stonehenge has not yielded a solution to the mystery of the blue stones yet a section of the site remains unexplored and may contain clues as to how they got there.

Nonessential Clauses and Phrases

29i. Use commas to set off nonessential clauses and nonessential participial phrases.

A *nonessential* (or *nonrestrictive*) clause or participial phrase is one containing information that isn't needed to understand the main idea of the sentence.

NONESSENTIAL CLAUSES	Lydia Cabrera, **who was born in Cuba,** wrote many books about African Cuban culture.
	Did the Senate hearings, **which were televised,** attract a large audience?
NONESSENTIAL PHRASES	Lee, **noticing my confusion,** rephrased her question.
	Willie Herenton, **defeating the incumbent in 1991,** became the first African American mayor of Memphis.

Each nonessential clause or phrase in the examples above can be left out without changing the main idea of the sentence.

EXAMPLES	Lydia Cabrera wrote many books about African Cuban culture.
	Did the Senate hearings attract a large audience?
	Lee rephrased her question.
	Willie Herenton became the first African American mayor of Memphis.

An *essential* (or *restrictive*) clause or phrase is one that can't be left out without changing the meaning of the sentence. Essential clauses and phrases are *not* set off by commas. Notice how leaving out the essential clause or phrase would change the meaning of each of the following sentences.

ESSENTIAL CLAUSES	The juniors **who were selected for Boys State and Girls State** were named.
	Material **that is quoted verbatim** should be placed in quotation marks.
ESSENTIAL PHRASES	Those **participating in the food drive** should bring their donations by Friday.
	The election **won by Willie Herenton** took place in October 1991.

NOTE: Adjective clauses beginning with *that,* like the one in the second example above, are nearly always essential.

Some clauses and participial phrases may be either essential or nonessential. The presence or absence of commas tells the reader how the clause or phrase relates to the main idea of the sentence.

NONESSENTIAL CLAUSE   Una's cousin**, who wants to be an astro-naut,** attended a space camp in Huntsville, Alabama, last summer. [Una has only one cousin. Her only cousin attended the space camp.]

ESSENTIAL CLAUSE   Una's cousin **who wants to be an astro-naut** attended a space camp in Huntsville, Alabama, last summer. [Una has more than one cousin. The one who wants to be an astronaut attended the space camp.]

NONESSENTIAL PHRASE   Your cat**, draped along the back of the couch,** seems contented. [You have only one cat. It seems contented.]

ESSENTIAL PHRASE   Your cat **draped along the back of the couch** seems contented. [You have more than one cat. The one on the back of the couch seems contented.]

☞ REFERENCE NOTE: See pages 628–637 for more information on clauses and page 612 for more information on participial phrases.

▶ EXERCISE 3   **Correcting Sentences by Adding Commas**

For each of the following sentences, write each word that should be followed by a comma, and add the comma. If a sentence is correct, write C.

1. All students going on the trip tomorrow will meet in the auditorium after school today.
2. The White River Bridge which closed today for resurfacing will not be open for traffic until mid-October.
3. The symphony that Beethoven called the *Eroica* was composed to celebrate the memory of a great man.
4. From the composer's letters, we learn that this "great man" whom he had in mind was Napoleon Bonaparte.
5. Natalie Curtis always interested in the music of Native Americans was an early recorder of their songs.

6. The driver who caused the wreck was going too fast.
7. The musician who founded the annual music festival in Puerto Rico was Pablo Casals.
8. Semantics which is concerned with the meanings of words is an interesting subject of study for high school students.
9. My car which is seven years old simply refuses to start on cold mornings.
10. All contestants submitting photographs for the contest must sign a release form.

Introductory Elements

29j. Use a comma after certain introductory elements.

(1) Use commas to set off interjections such as *well, oh, why,* and *hey.* Other introductory words such as *yes* and *no* are also followed by commas.

EXAMPLES   Well, I guess so.
Yikes, are we late!
Yes, I heard your question.

(2) Use a comma after an introductory participial phrase.

EXAMPLES   Looking poised and calm, Jill walked to the podium.
Exhausted after the five-mile hike, the scouts took a break.

NOTE: Don't confuse a gerund phrase used as the subject of a sentence with an introductory participial phrase.

EXAMPLES   **Following directions** can sometimes be difficult.
[The gerund phrase *Following directions* is the subject of the sentence.]
Following directions, I began to assemble the bike.
[*Following directions* is an introductory participial phrase modifying *I.*]

(3) Use a comma after two or more introductory prepositional phrases.

EXAMPLE   In the first round of the golf tournament, I played one of the best golfers in the state.

MECHANICS

A single introductory prepositional phrase does not require a comma unless the sentence is awkward to read without one or unless the phrase is parenthetical.

EXAMPLES   At the track meet our school's team placed first.
At the track, meet me in front of the snack bar. [The comma is needed to avoid reading "track meet."]
By the way, I need to borrow a quarter. [The comma is needed because *By the way* is parenthetical.]

☞ REFERENCE NOTE: See rule 29k (3) for more information on using commas with parenthetical elements.

(4) Use a comma after an introductory adverb clause.

An introductory adverb clause may appear at the beginning of a sentence or before any independent clause in the sentence.

EXAMPLES   After I had locked the car door, I remembered that the keys were still in the ignition.
Fortunately, I had a spare set of keys with me; if I hadn't, I would have had to walk home.

NOTE: An adverb clause that follows an independent clause is usually not set off by a comma.

EXAMPLE   Thousands of homes in the Philippines were destroyed **when Mt. Pinatubo erupted in 1991.**

▶ REVIEW B   **Using Commas in a Paragraph**

For each sentence in the following paragraph, write each word that should be followed by a comma, and add the comma. If a sentence is correct, write *C*.

[1] Have you ever had a dream that seemed absolutely real, but, as you awoke you realized how outlandish it had been? [2] An artist painting a surrealistic picture can sometimes generate that same dreamlike feeling in an audience. [3] For example this painting which is one of many surreal landscapes by Salvador Dali conveys the strange experience of a dream. [4] In a dream time has a different meaning, and the bizarre can seem ordinary. [5] While only five minutes may actually have passed events requiring hours or days may have taken place in a dream. [6] Dali's clocks drooping as limply as a sleeper show that the rigid march of time can relax in a dream. [7] In the liquid time and unearthly space of dreams not even solid reality can

be certain. [8] Objects far more fantastic and incredible than the creature who reclines on the sand can seem in dreams to be as familiar as your own face. [9] Sleeping peacefully Dali's strange creature does not seem to realize that it is saddled with the burden of time. [10] Well until the alarm clock wakes you from your own dreams you probably don't realize it either.

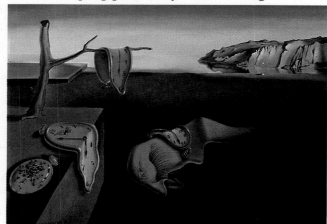

Salvador Dali, The Persistence of Memory (Persistance de la memoire), 1931. Oil on canvas, 9 1/2 × 13" (24.1 × 33 cm). Collection, The Museum of Modern Art, New York. Given Anonymously.

Interrupters

29k. Use commas to set off elements that interrupt a sentence.

(1) Appositives and appositive phrases are usually set off by commas.

An *appositive* is a noun or pronoun that follows another noun or a pronoun to identify or explain it. An *appositive phrase* consists of an appositive and its modifiers.

EXAMPLES   My favorite book by Claude McKay, *Banjo,* was first published in 1929.
Is that he, the one with the red hair?

Sometimes an appositive is so closely related to the word preceding it that it should not be set off by commas. Such an appositive is called a *restrictive appositive.*

EXAMPLES   my nephew Jim
the young American gymnast Lanna Apisukh
the saying "Haste makes waste"

☞ REFERENCE NOTE: See page 621 for more information on appositives and appositive phrases.

MECHANICS

(2) Words used in direct address are set off by commas.

EXAMPLES   Mom, have you called Mrs. Johnson yet?
            Your essay, Theo, was well organized.
            Will you answer the question, Monica?

(3) Parenthetical expressions are set off by commas.

Parenthetical expressions are remarks that add incidental information or relate ideas to each other.

Commonly Used Parenthetical Expressions		
after all	I believe (hope, etc.)	naturally
at any rate	incidentally	nevertheless
by the way	in fact	of course
consequently	in general	on the contrary
for example	in the first place	on the other hand
for instance	meanwhile	that is
however	moreover	therefore

EXAMPLES   Incidentally, I won't be home for supper.
            Simón Bolívar liberated much of South America from
              Spanish rule, and, moreover, he became the most
              powerful man on the continent.
            It's too late to call now, I believe.

☞ REFERENCE NOTE: Parentheses and dashes are sometimes used to
set off parenthetical expressions. See pages 872–874.

Some of these expressions do not have to be used paren-
thetically. When they are not, don't set them off with commas.

EXAMPLES   **By the way,** she is in my vocal music class. [parentheti-
            cal, meaning "incidentally"]
            You can tell **by the way** she sings that she enjoys the
            class. [not parenthetical, meaning "by the manner in
            which"]

NOTE: A contrasting expression introduced by *not* is parenthetical and
        must be set off by commas.

        EXAMPLE   Margaret Walker, **not Alice Walker,** wrote the novel
                   Jubilee.

MECHANICS

> **EXERCISE 4**   **Correcting Sentences by Adding Commas**

For each of the following sentences, write each word that should be followed by a comma, and add the comma. If a sentence is correct, write C.

1. As a matter of fact your lateness is your own fault since you knew what time the bus would be leaving.
2. Have you seen Mr. Welch our new accounting teacher?
3. Zimbabwe's stone ruins once a stronghold for an ancient empire attest to the skill of those early stonemasons.
4. Please listen class while Jim makes an announcement.
5. Texans have a right to be proud of men such as Sergeants José Mendoza López and Macario García who earned the Congressional Medal of Honor.
6. Our neighbor Mrs. Kirby gets our mail when we are away.
7. The expressive brushstrokes of Chinese calligraphy make it not only beautiful but also complex perhaps the most complex of all written languages.
8. Mr. Beck the yearbook photographer always tries I think to place each person in the most flattering pose.
9. It is the pressure of getting work in on time not the work itself that gets on my nerves.
10. It's the phone that's ringing Suzanne not the doorbell.

Conventional Uses

291.   Use a comma in certain conventional situations.

(1) Use a comma to separate items in dates and addresses.

EXAMPLES   On Friday, October 23, 1991, my niece Leslie was born.
Please address all inquiries to 92 Keystone Crossings, Indianapolis, IN 46240.

Notice that no comma separates the month from the day, the house number from the street name, or the ZIP code from the two-letter state code.

If the day is given before the month or only the month and the year are given, no comma is used.

EXAMPLES   On 15 June 1924 Congress approved a law making all Native Americans U.S. citizens.
Will our new school be open by August 1996?

> NOTE: No comma is needed when items in an address or a date are joined by a preposition.
>
> EXAMPLE   The play is at the Melrose Theater **on** Broad Avenue **in** Midland Heights.

(2) Use a comma after the salutation of a friendly letter and after the closing of any letter.

EXAMPLES   **Dear Rosa,**   **Sincerely yours,**

(3) Use a comma after a name followed by an abbreviation such as *Jr., Sr.,* or *M.D.* and also after the abbreviation when the name and abbreviation are used together in a sentence.

EXAMPLES   **Coretta Jones, M.D.**
Is Juan Fuentes, Jr., your cousin?

Unnecessary Commas

29m.   Do not use unnecessary commas.

Using too many commas can be confusing. Use a comma only if a rule requires one or if the meaning is unclear without one.

INCORRECT   **The teacher in the room across the hall, is Cam's aunt.**
[*Teacher* is the subject; it must not be separated by a comma from the verb *is.*]
CORRECT   **The teacher in the room across the hall is Cam's aunt.**

REVIEW C   **Correcting Sentences by Adding End Marks and Commas**

Write each of the following sentences, adding end marks and commas where they are needed.

1. Wow Little Bear who taught you to draw a bow like that
2. First performed on March 11 1959 on Broadway in New York City Lorraine Hansberry's play *A Raisin in the Sun* which was later made into a movie was awarded the New York Drama Critics Circle Award
3. Although the house was a mess Mom said that if we all helped put away toys and books picked up all the clothes lying around dusted the furniture and vacuumed the rug it would look presentable by the time Grandma arrived

MECHANICS

4. After all you could look at the map to see if there is an exit off of Interstate 70 to a state road that will take us south to Greenville Illinois instead of just complaining because I don't know the way

5. On her way to work each morning she saw young people on their paper routes children waiting for school buses mail carriers beginning their deliveries and the inevitable joggers puffing along on their morning workouts

6. City buses can be a pleasant way to travel but why do they run so infrequently and when they do arrive why are they in bunches of three or four or more

7. Gen Benjamin O Davis Sr the first African American who was promoted to the rank of general in the U.S. Army was the grandson of a slave.

8. If you are going to paint window frames cover the panes of glass with masking tape which will protect the glass from being spattered.

9. On a beautiful fall day in New England it is wise to go for a walk play a game outdoors or go for a drive; for it won't be long until everything is bleak cold and dreary

10. If I had my way I would live in a climate where it would be warm not hot in the daytime and cool in the evening all year round

WRITING APPLICATION

Using Interrupters Correctly

Sometimes you feel as though you just have to interrupt. In conversation, you listen for a pause—a chance to slip in a comment at just the right moment. Interruptions in writing have to be carefully placed, too. Avoid awkward phrasing by reading a sentence aloud and listening for the most natural place to insert an interrupter.

AWKWARD Bob enjoys fishing, so he decided to write, naturally, about Santiago in *The Old Man and the Sea.*

BETTER Bob enjoys fishing, so, **naturally,** he decided to write about Santiago in *The Old Man and the Sea.*

Always use commas to set off interrupters. Commas signal a shift in thought and help avoid confusion.

CONFUSING   Because I like comic strips, I'm going to write my
                      essay I believe on Calvin of *Calvin and Hobbes.*
                      [Does the writer intend to write on Calvin?]
        CLEAR   Because I like comic strips, I'm going to write my
                      essay, I believe, on Calvin of *Calvin and Hobbes.*

WRITING ACTIVITY

Next Friday, your English class will celebrate Literary Heroes Day. Your teacher has asked you to write a brief essay (two or three paragraphs long) about your favorite fictional character. Describe the character and explain why the character is your hero. In your essay use at least two appositives and three parenthetical expressions. Be sure to use commas correctly with each interrupter.

 Prewriting   First, you'll need to decide on a character to write about. If one doesn't come to mind right away, think back on the novels, stories, and poems that you've read or heard. Next, jot down the names of the three characters you remember most clearly. Then, from your list, choose the character that impressed or entertained you the most. You may then want to skim the work that the character appears in to find passages that give important information about the character. In your notes, be sure to include the character's strongest and most interesting traits.

Writing   Use your notes to help you write your first draft. Begin by describing the character and noting some of the most important traits that make this person your hero. Illustrate these traits by giving at least two examples of things the character does or says. Wherever appropriate, use appositives and parenthetical expressions to add information to your sentences.

Evaluating and Revising   Ask a friend or relative to read your essay. Does your description give a vivid picture of the character? Is it clear why this character is your hero? If not, add or revise details to help make your point more clearly. Be sure that you've used at least two appositives and three parenthetical expressions.

Proofreading and Publishing Proofread your essay for any errors in grammar, usage, or mechanics. Pay special attention to commas before and after parenthetical expressions. You and your classmates may want to celebrate Literary Heroes Day by creating a bulletin board display. Place a typed or neatly written copy of each essay on the bulletin board along with illustrations of the different characters.

Review: Posttest

A. Correcting Sentences by Adding or Deleting End Marks and Commas

Write the following sentences, adding or deleting end marks and commas as necessary. If a sentence is correct, write C.

EXAMPLE **1.** Sally asked, "Where do you want to go after the recital"?

1. *Sally asked, "Where do you want to go after the recital?"*

1. Who was it who said, "I only regret that I have but one life to give for my country?"
2. Startled, we heard a high-pitched, whining, noise just outside the window.
3. Any student, who has not signed up for the contest by three o'clock, will not be eligible to participate.
4. My friend Esteban, running up the stairs two at a time, yelled out the good news.
5. "Why does the telephone always ring just as soon as I sit down to work," she asked?
6. My parents are trading in their car a two-door model with a sunroof bucket seats and air conditioning.
7. I have drilled practiced trained and exercised for weeks and now I am too tired to compete.
8. "Well Coach I can promise you that I'll be ready for the game next week," Kit said.

9. James King an Iroquois guide used to conduct tours of the Somers Mountain Indian Museum in Somers Connecticut.
10. "Where should the question mark be placed in a quoted sentence," Yolanda inquired?

B. Proofreading a Letter for the Correct Use of End Marks and Commas

Add or delete end marks or commas to correct each sentence in the following letter.

EXAMPLE [1] Dear Toni
          1. *Dear Toni,*

[11] As she promised our friend, Takara, and her family were waiting for us at the Osaka airport on Monday June 16. [12] I'm so glad that you introduced us and that I could come to visit such a kind generous, and friendly family [13] Wow I love their house; it's totally different from any home that I've ever seen before and my favorite part of it is the garden [14] In the middle of the house and down one step a large rectangular courtyard lies open to the sun and air; the garden is in the courtyard. [15] Rocks not plants and trees dominate the space, and clean white sand instead of grass covers the ground [16] I wonder who carefully rakes the sand every day leaving small rows of lines covering the ground? [17] Takara told me that the sand represents the ocean the lines are like waves, and the rocks stand for islands. [18] Sitting in the garden I believe she is right for the garden is as peaceful as any deserted beach.

[19] My flight by the way will be arriving in Portland in ten short days; if you're free would you please meet me at the airport.

[20] Sincerely yours.

Ramona

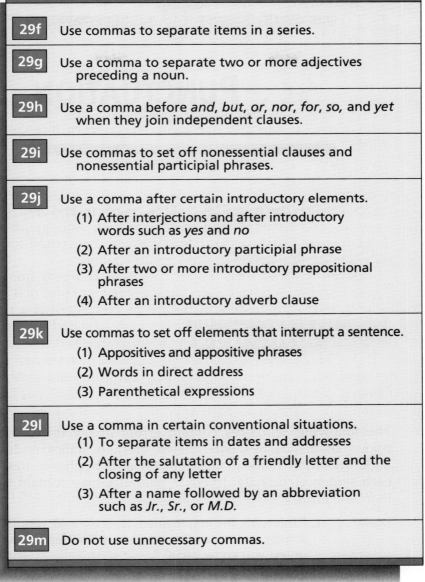

SUMMARY OF COMMA USES

29f Use commas to separate items in a series.

29g Use a comma to separate two or more adjectives preceding a noun.

29h Use a comma before *and, but, or, nor, for, so,* and *yet* when they join independent clauses.

29i Use commas to set off nonessential clauses and nonessential participial phrases.

29j Use a comma after certain introductory elements.

(1) After interjections and after introductory words such as *yes* and *no*

(2) After an introductory participial phrase

(3) After two or more introductory prepositional phrases

(4) After an introductory adverb clause

29k Use commas to set off elements that interrupt a sentence.

(1) Appositives and appositive phrases

(2) Words in direct address

(3) Parenthetical expressions

29l Use a comma in certain conventional situations.

(1) To separate items in dates and addresses

(2) After the salutation of a friendly letter and the closing of any letter

(3) After a name followed by an abbreviation such as *Jr., Sr.,* or *M.D.*

29m Do not use unnecessary commas.

MECHANICS

30 PUNCTUATION

Other Marks of Punctuation

Diagnostic Test

A. Proofreading Sentences for Correct Punctuation

The following sentences contain errors in the use of semicolons, colons, dashes, parentheses, brackets, italics (underlining), quotation marks, apostrophes, and hyphens. Rewrite each sentence correctly. [Note: A sentence may contain more than one error.]

EXAMPLE   **1.** "This job", the employment director said, requires some experience with computers, dont apply for it unless you know BASIC.".

             1. *"This job," the employment director said, "requires some experience with computers; don't apply for it unless you know BASIC."*

1. She learned the word daube from working the crossword puzzle in the New York Times.
2. I like everything about my new car it's design, color, and smooth ride," Cari said.

3. Our school has had exchange students from: Denmark, Liberia, Korea, Uruguay, and France.
4. Our flight will land in Rio de Janeiro by 8 00 P.M. more over, our hotel reservations have already been confirmed.
5. The presidency of Franklin Delano Roosevelt 1933–1945 was the longest one in American history.
6. Did you hear about the student councils decision that the class song must be chosen by a three fourths majority?
7. Last year The Dance do you know that song? was chosen overwhelmingly.
8. The guide added, "Rosa Bonheur a French artist painted Buffalo Bill on his favorite horse.
9. Nancy asked, "Can you remember whether there are two cs or two s's in occasion"?
10. Mr. Elliott's favorite books are Atlas Shrugged, by Ayn Rand, East of Eden, by John Steinbeck, and Beloved, by Toni Morrison.

B. Proofreading Paragraphs for Correct Punctuation

The following paragraphs of conversation contain errors in the use of semicolons, colons, dashes, parentheses, italics (underlining), quotation marks, apostrophes, and hyphens. Rewrite each paragraph, correcting the errors.

EXAMPLE   **[1]** "The Renaissance Festival will open at 10 30 in the morning, therefore, we should be in line for tickets by 9 30, Janice said.

     1. *"The Renaissance Festival will open at 10:30 in the morning; therefore, we should be in line for tickets by 9:30," Janice said.*

[11] What in the world please dont think me too uninformed is a Renaissance festival"? Leroy asked.

[12] "Its a fair that celebrates Europes Renaissance, which lasted from about A.D. 1300 to around A.D. 1600," Janice said.

[13] "Well, I'm ready to go, I know what to expect because Ive seen the movies Camelot and The Princess Bride," Leroy said.

[14] "Even so, youll be amazed Janice said, because youll see people dressed up as: kings and queens, jesters, peasants, knights and ladies, wizards, and even dragons."

[15] "I suppose Id better mind my ps and qs with wizards and dragons around"! Leroy exclaimed.

[16] "Oh, all the wizards's manners are good and the fierce looking dragons actually are friendly," Janice said.

[17] "And there are many other sights to see, too jousts, mazes, elephants and camels, games of strength, music, and all kinds of crafts".

[18] Leroy asked: "Isnt there any Renaissance food?

[19] "Plenty!" Janice said. "My favorites are: bagels, which are sold from traveling carts, soup served in bread bowls, which are freshly baked, and apple and pineapple fritters."

[20] "I've been to several Renaissance fairs, including big ones in Texas and Missouri, but, of course, I think theyre all great," Janice added.

Semicolons

MECHANICS

30a. Use a semicolon between independent clauses that are closely related in thought and are not joined by *and, but, for, nor, or, so,* or *yet.*

EXAMPLES   The rain had finally stopped; a few rays of sunshine were pushing their way through breaks in the clouds.

"Tart words make no friends; a spoonful of honey will catch more flies than a gallon of vinegar."
Benjamin Franklin, *Poor Richard's Almanack*

Do not join independent clauses unless there is a close relationship between the main ideas of the clauses.

NONSTANDARD   For Ramón, oil painting is a difficult medium to master; when he was younger, he had enjoyed taking photographs.

STANDARD   For Ramón, oil painting is a difficult medium to master. When he was younger, he had enjoyed taking photographs.

30b. Use a semicolon between independent clauses joined by a conjunctive adverb or a transitional expression.

A *conjunctive adverb* or a *transitional expression* indicates the relationship of the independent clauses that it joins.

EXAMPLES   The snowfall made traveling difficult**;** **nevertheless,** we arrived home safely.
Denisa plays baseball well**;** **in fact,** she would like to try out for a major-league team.

Commonly Used Conjunctive Adverbs		
accordingly	however	moreover
besides	indeed	nevertheless
consequently	instead	otherwise
furthermore	meanwhile	therefore

Commonly Used Transitional Expressions		
as a result	for instance	in other words
for example	in fact	that is

NOTE: When a conjunctive adverb or a transitional expression is used *between* independent clauses, it is preceded by a semicolon and followed by a comma. When used *within* a clause, a conjunctive adverb or a transitional expression is set off by commas.

EXAMPLES   Most members of Congress favor the new tax bill**;** **however,** the president does not support it.
Most members of Congress favor the new tax bill; the president**,** **however,** does not support it.

☞ REFERENCE NOTE: For more information about conjunctive adverbs and transitional expressions, see pages 640–641.

30c.   Use a semicolon (rather than a comma) before a coordinating conjunction to join independent clauses that contain commas.

EXAMPLE   During the seventeenth century—the era of such distinguished prose writers as Sir Thomas Browne**,** John Donne**,** and Jeremy Taylor—the balanced compound sentence using commas and semicolons reached a high degree of perfection and popularity**;** but the tendency today is to use a fast-moving style with shorter sentences and fewer commas and semicolons. [commas within the first clause]

MECHANICS

30d. Use a semicolon between items in a series if the items contain commas.

EXAMPLES   The president of the club has appointed the following to chair the standing committees: Richard Stokes, planning; Rebecca Hartley, membership; Salvador Berrios, financial; and Ann Jeng, legal.

The summer reading list includes *Behind the Trail of Broken Treaties,* by Vine Deloria; *House Made of Dawn,* by N. Scott Momaday; and *Blue Highways: A Journey into America,* by William Least Heat-Moon.

EXERCISE 1   **Using Semicolons Correctly**

Add semicolons where they are needed in the following sentences.

EXAMPLE   **1.** The great American humorist Will Rogers was proud of his Cherokee heritage he often referred to it in his talks and writings.

1. *The great American humorist Will Rogers was proud of his Cherokee heritage; he often referred to it in his talks and writings.*

1. William Penn Adair Rogers was born in 1879 in Oologah, Indian Territory, which is now Oklahoma, and he spent his childhood on his father's ranch, a prosperous holding of about sixty thousand acres.

2. As a youth, Will Rogers liked to learn and practice rope tricks he often could be found roping instead of attending to his chores.

3. Rogers was captivated by professional roping performers at the Chicago World's Fair in 1893 in fact, that experience probably marked the start of his interest in show business.

4. He went on to do some roping and humorous speaking at fairs and other public gatherings however, his actual show business debut came in 1902.

5. That year Rogers joined Texas Jack's Wild West Show as a "fancy lasso artist" he also rode horses and performed in various western scenes during the show.

6. Notice how confident the young Rogers appears in the publicity photo on the next page his expression, stance, and costume suggest an accomplished performer.

7. Rogers greatly enjoyed earning his living by doing what he most loved—roping consequently, he decided to take his act to New York City's vaudeville theaters.

8. Rogers' stage shows, combining his roping with humorous comments, were popular they led to starring roles in musicals, the legendary Ziegfeld Follies, and movies.

9. In Hollywood, Rogers made such films as *The Ropin' Fool*, in which he performed fifty-three rope tricks, *Steamboat 'Round the Bend*, directed by John Ford, and *A Connecticut Yankee in King Arthur's Court*, based on the Mark Twain novel.

10. Beginning in 1922 and continuing until his death in 1935, Rogers wrote a syndicated newspaper column that Sunday column featured his humorous insights into national and world news.

Colons

30e. Use a colon to mean "note what follows."

(1) Use a colon before a list of items, especially after expressions such as *as follows* and *the following*.

EXAMPLES The Iroquois Confederation consisted of five Native American nations**:** Mohawk, Oneida, Onondago, Cayuga, and Seneca.

The magazine article profiles the following famous women of nineteenth-century America**:** Mary Baker Eddy, Clara Barton, Maria Mitchell, Mary Church Terrell, Susan B. Anthony, and Sarah Winnemucca.

NOTE: Do not use a colon before a list that directly follows a verb or a preposition.

EXAMPLES   The emergency kit included safety flares, jumper cables, and a flashlight. [The list directly follows the verb *included*.]
Each student taking the math test was provided with two sharpened pencils, paper, and a ruler. [The list directly follows the preposition *with*.]

(2) Use a colon before a long, formal statement or quotation.

EXAMPLE   Patrick Henry concluded his revolutionary speech before the Virginia House of Burgesses with these ringing words: "Is life so dear, or peace so sweet as to be purchased at the price of chains and slavery? Forbid it, Almighty God! I know not what course others may take, but as for me, give me liberty or give me death!"

☞ REFERENCE NOTE: For more information about using long quotations, see page 880.

(3) Use a colon between independent clauses when the second clause explains or restates the idea of the first.

EXAMPLES   Lois felt that she had done something worthwhile: she had designed and sewn her first quilt.
Thomas Jefferson had many talents: he was a writer, a politician, an architect, and an inventor.

▶ EXERCISE 2   **Writing Sentences Using Colons**

For your American history class, you're writing a report on the women's suffrage movement in the United States during the early 1900s. In the process of researching your topic, you have collected the pictures shown on the next page and have made the accompanying preliminary notes. Use the pictures and notes to write five sentences for your report. Include a colon in each sentence; give at least one example of each of the three uses of colons presented in this chapter so far.

EXAMPLE   **1.** *Major leaders in the women's suffrage movement included the following: Carrie Lane Chapman Catt, Susan B. Anthony, Lucretia Mott, and Elizabeth Cady Stanton.*

NOTES

Marches—such demonstrations common, helped influence people. Describe marchers?

Wyoming, Utah, Colorado, Idaho—granted full voting rights to women by 1900. Seven more states did so by 1914.

The women who did get to vote organized demonstrations, organized marches, pressured Congress, formed associations (state and national), participated in World War I efforts

Some other early feminist leaders—Susan B. Anthony, Lucretia Mott, Elizabeth Cady Stanton

Carrie Lane Chapman Catt—president of National American Women's Suffrage Association, 1900–1904. Also a founder and honorary chair of National League of Women Voters. Had been a school superintendent in Mason City, Iowa. Intelligent and informed. Active in women's rights in Iowa in 1880s. Spoke throughout U.S. and world.

Nineteenth Amendment to the U.S. Constitution (ratified Aug. 26, 1920):
   "The right of citizens of the United States to vote shall not be denied
      or abridged by the United States or by any State on account of
      sex.
   "Congress shall have power to enforce this article by appropriate
      legislation."

MECHANICS

30f.   Use a colon in certain conventional situations.

(1) Use a colon between the hour and the minute.

EXAMPLES   5**:**20 P.M.   8**:**45 in the morning

(2) Use a colon between chapter and verse in referring to passages from the Bible.

EXAMPLES   Proverbs 10**:**1   Deuteronomy 5**:**6–21

(3) Use a colon between a title and subtitle.

EXAMPLES   *Another View**:** To Be Black in America* [book]
*Superman IV**:** The Quest for Peace* [movie]
*Impression**:** Sunrise* [painting]

(4) Use a colon after the salutation of a business letter.

EXAMPLES   **Dear Mrs. Rodríguez:**   **To Whom It May Concern:**
Dear Sir or Madam: **Dear Service Manager:**

NOTE: Use a comma after the salutation of a friendly letter.

EXAMPLE   **Dear Mom and Dad,**

Dashes

30g.   Use a dash to indicate an abrupt break in thought.

EXAMPLES   The poor condition of this road—it really needs to be
paved—makes this route unpopular.
The real villain turns out to be—but I don't want to
spoil the ending for those of you who have not yet
seen the movie.

30h.   Use a dash to mean *namely, in other words, that is,* and similar expressions that come before an explanation.

EXAMPLES   Amanda joined the chorus for only one reason—she
loves to sing.
Very few people in this class—three, to be exact—
have completed their projects.

Parentheses

 30i. Use parentheses to enclose informative or explanatory material of minor importance.

EXAMPLES Harriet Tubman **(***ca.* 1820–1913**)** is remembered for her work in the Underground Railroad.
A *roman à clef* **(**literally, "novel with a key"**)** is a novel about real people to whom the novelist has assigned fictitious names.

Be sure that the material enclosed in parentheses can be omitted without losing important information or changing the basic meaning and construction of the sentence.

IMPROPER USE
OF PARENTHESES George Eliot (whose real name was Mary Ann Evans) was one of many women in nineteenth-century England who wrote under a masculine pseudonym. [The information in parentheses clarifies that George Eliot was a woman. Each parenthesis should be replaced by a comma.]

Follow these guidelines for capitalizing and punctuating parenthetical sentences.

(1) A parenthetical sentence that falls within another sentence

- should not begin with a capital letter unless it begins with a word that should always be capitalized
- should not end with a period but may end with a question mark or an exclamation point

EXAMPLES The Malay Archipelago **(see the map on page 350)** includes the Philippines.
Legendary jazz musician Louis "Satchmo" Armstrong **(have you heard of him?)** was born in Louisiana.

(2) A parenthetical sentence that stands by itself

- should begin with a capital letter
- should end with a period, a question mark, or an exclamation point before the closing parenthesis

EXAMPLES The Malay Archipelago includes the Philippines. **(See the map on page 350.)**
Legendary jazz musician Louis "Satchmo" Armstrong was born in Louisiana. **(That's a coincidence! My hero Harry Connick, Jr., was born there, too.)**

MECHANICS

When parenthetical material falls within a sentence, punctuation should never come before the opening parenthesis but may follow the closing parenthesis.

INCORRECT   The first professional baseball team, the Cincinnati Red Stockings, (the Reds), was formed in 1869.

CORRECT   The first professional baseball team, the Cincinnati Red Stockings (the Reds), was formed in 1869.

Brackets

30j. Use brackets to enclose an explanation within quoted or parenthetical material.

EXAMPLES   The newspaper article stated that "at the time of that Democratic National Convention [in Chicago in 1968] there were many protest groups operating in the United States."

I think that Hilda Doolittle (more commonly known as H.D. [1886–1961]) is best remembered for her Imagist poetry.

PICTURE THIS

What a great day for people watching! It's a warm Saturday morning, and you're taking a leisurely walk through the park in this photograph. As you pass each person, you can't help but wonder what he or she is thinking and feeling. The scene gives you an idea for a *stream-of-consciousness* story, a story that records the natural, continuous flow of a character's thoughts and feelings.

Write the first paragraph or two of a story about one of the people in the park. Record whatever you imagine is going through the person's mind. In your story, use at least two pairs of dashes, two pairs of parentheses, and one pair of brackets to help express the many levels of your character's thoughts and feelings.

Subject: a character's thoughts and feelings
Audience: readers of a fictional story
Purpose: to reveal the character's thoughts; to entertain

Italics

Italics are printed characters that slant to the right. To indicate italics in handwritten or typewritten work, use underlining.

PRINTED   *The Heart Is a Lonely Hunter* was written by Carson McCullers.

HANDWRITTEN   *The Heart Is a Lonely Hunter was written by Carson McCullers.*

NOTE: If you use a personal computer, you may be able to set words in italics. Most word processing software and many printers are capable of producing italic type.

30k. Use italics (underlining) for titles of books, plays, periodicals, newspapers, works of art, films, television programs, long musical compositions, trains, ships, aircraft, and spacecraft.

TYPE OF NAME	EXAMPLES	
Books	*The Scarlet Letter* *Invisible Man*	*Fifth Chinese Daughter*
Plays	*The Crucible*	*West Side Story*
Periodicals	*Reader's Digest*	*Newsweek*

(continued)

MECHANICS

TYPE OF NAME	EXAMPLES	
Newspapers	*Dallas Morning News*	*San Francisco*
	Philadelphia Inquirer	*Examiner*
Works of Art	*The Kiss*	*Starry Night*
Films	*Rain Man*	*Stand and Deliver*
	It's a Wonderful Life	*Out of Africa*
TV Programs	*Jeopardy!*	*Star Trek: The Next*
	American Playhouse	*Generation*
Long Musical Compositions	*Liverpool Oratorio*	*Hiawatha's Wedding*
	The Planets	*Feast*
Trains, Ships	*Century Limited*	*Queen Mary*
Aircraft, Spacecraft	*Solar Challenger*	*Apollo 11*
	Graf Zeppelin	*Landsat-1*

NOTE: The article *the* before the title of a newspaper is neither italicized nor capitalized when written within a sentence.

EXAMPLE   I found this information in the *New York Times.*

☞ REFERENCE NOTE: For examples of titles that are not italicized but are enclosed in quotation marks, see pages 882–883.

30l. Use italics (underlining) for words, letters, and symbols referred to as such and for foreign words.

EXAMPLES   Should the use of *their* for *there* be considered a
spelling error or a usage error?
The teacher couldn't tell whether I had written a
script *S* or an *&*.
Some U.S. coins were stamped with the inscription
E pluribus unum.

 EXERCISE 3 **Revising Sentences by Adding Semicolons, Colons, Dashes, Parentheses, Brackets, and Italics (Underlining)**

Revise the following sentences by adding semicolons, colons, dashes, parentheses, brackets, and italics (underlining) where they are needed.

MECHANICS

EXAMPLE   **1.** Did you watch World of Discovery last night?
   1. *Did you watch <u>World of Discovery</u> last night?*

1. Les Brown be sure to watch his show is a tremendous motivational speaker who encourages people to make positive changes in their lives.
2. First aid for a snake bite is as follows keep the victim still if the bite is in an arm or a leg, place the limb below the level of the heart if a hospital is less than thirty minutes away, take the victim there immediately.
3. Providing visuals pictures, charts, maps, or graphs can often help an audience understand technical information more easily.
4. The citizen who spoke before the Nuclear Regulatory Commission stated, "If you permit this project the new Marblehead nuclear plant to be completed, you will be creating another Three Mile Island."
5. *The Little Foxes,* a play by Lillian Hellman its title, by the way, is taken from the Song of Solomon 2 15 had a truly remarkable effect upon Maxine last year it may have been the reading of this play that helped her decide to major in drama in college.
6. Engineers' quests for the ideal high-fidelity speaker *ideal* means the ability to reproduce exactly whatever recorded signals are fed to a speaker have led to many innovative designs for instance, electrostatic panels and truncated pyramids have been offered as alternatives to the traditional box-shaped enclosure.
7. We're looking forward to spending tomorrow at the Alabama-Coushatta Indian Reservation in East Texas however, we won't arrive until around 10 30.
8. While reading a history book called The Rise and Fall of Nazi Germany, I used my dictionary to look up the definitions of the following terms Anschluss, Luftwaffe, and Wehrmacht.
9. When you talk in front of an audience, remember these four principles speak loudly and clearly, refrain from nervous habits and gestures, look directly at your audience, and above all, have something to say.
10. There was an article in Omni about Arthur C. Clarke's 2001: A Space Odyssey and the similarities to our own space flights; the article also reviewed Clarke's 2010: Odyssey Two.

MECHANICS

Quotation Marks

30m. Use quotation marks to enclose a *direct quotation*—a person's exact words.

Be sure to place quotation marks both before and after a person's exact words.

EXAMPLES   Chief Joseph said, after his surrender in 1877, **"**The earth is the mother of all people, and all people should have equal rights upon it.**"**
"The track meet is canceled because of the unusually cold weather,**"** announced Coach Griffey.

Do not use quotation marks to enclose an *indirect quotation*—a rewording of a direct quotation.

DIRECT QUOTATION   Aaron said, **"**I can type ninety-five words a minute.**"**
INDIRECT QUOTATION   Aaron said that he can type ninety-five words a minute.

(1) A direct quotation begins with a capital letter.

EXAMPLE   The poet Emily Dickinson wrote in a letter to Thomas Wentworth Higginson, her literary advisor, "If I feel physically as if the top of my head were taken off, I know *that* is poetry."

However, when the quotation is only a part of a sentence, do not begin it with a capital letter.

EXAMPLE   In her essay "On the Mall," Joan Didion describes shopping malls as "toy gardens in which no one lives."

(2) When the expression identifying the speaker divides a quoted sentence, the second part begins with a small letter.

EXAMPLE   "I really have to leave now," said Gwen, "so that I will be on time." [Notice that each part of a divided quotation is enclosed in quotation marks.]

When the second part of a divided quotation is a sentence, it begins with a capital letter.

EXAMPLE   "Teddy Roosevelt was the first U.S. President who was concerned about the depletion of the nation's natural resources," explained Mr. Fuentes. "He established a conservation program that expanded the national park system and created many wildlife sanctuaries."

NOTE: When a direct quotation of two or more sentences is not divided, only one set of quotation marks is used.

EXAMPLE   "Teddy Roosevelt was the first U.S. President who was concerned about the depletion of the nation's natural resources. He established a conservation program that expanded the national park system and created many wildlife sanctuaries," explained Mr. Fuentes.

(3) A direct quotation is set off from the rest of the sentence by a comma, a question mark, or an exclamation point, but not by a period.

EXAMPLES   "I nominate Pilar for class president," said Erin.
"What is the capital of Thailand?" asked Mr. Klein.
"This chili is too spicy!" exclaimed Brian.

NOTE: If the quotation is only a word or a phrase, do not set it off with commas.

EXAMPLE   When Clara tried to keep the crystal vase from falling off the shelf and knocked over the china plates in the process, she knew what "clumsy as an ox" meant.

(4) When used with quotation marks, the other marks of punctuation are placed according to the following rules:

■ **Commas and periods are always placed inside the closing quotation marks.**

EXAMPLE   "On the other hand," he said, "your decision may be correct."

■ **Semicolons and colons are always placed outside the closing quotation marks.**

EXAMPLES   My neighbor said, "Of course I'll buy a magazine subscription"; it was lucky that I asked her on payday.
Edna St. Vincent Millay uses these devices in her poem "Spring": alliteration, slant rhyme, and personification.

MECHANICS

■ Question marks and exclamation points are placed inside the closing quotation marks if the quotation itself is a question or an exclamation. Otherwise, they are placed outside.

EXAMPLES   "Dad, will you please call the doctor tomorrow morning?" I asked.

"Move those golf clubs right now!" yelled my mother.

Did Langston Hughes write the line "My soul has grown deep like rivers"?

I'm sick of hearing "This is so boring"!

Notice in the last two examples given above that the end mark belonging with each quotation has been omitted. In a question or an exclamation that ends with a quotation, only the question mark or exclamation point is necessary, and it is placed outside the closing quotation marks.

(5) When quoting a passage that consists of more than one paragraph, put quotation marks at the beginning of each paragraph and at the end of only the last paragraph in the passage.

EXAMPLE   "The water was thick and heavy and the color of a mirror in a dark room. Minnows broke the surface right under the wharf. I jumped. I couldn't help it.

"And I got to thinking that something might come out of the water. It didn't have a name or a shape. But it was there."

Shirley Ann Grau, *The Land and the Water*

NOTE: A long passage quoted from a printed source is often set off from the rest of the text. The entire passage may be indented or set in smaller type. The passage is sometimes single-spaced instead of double-spaced, though Modern Language Association guidelines call for double-spacing. When a quotation is set off in any of these ways, no quotation marks are necessary.

(6) Use single quotation marks to enclose a quotation within a quotation.

EXAMPLES   The teacher requested, "Jorge, please explain what Emerson meant when he said, 'To be great is to be misunderstood.' " [Notice that the period is placed inside the single quotation mark.]

The teacher asked, "Jorge, do you understand what Emerson meant when he said, 'To be great is to be misunderstood'?" [The question mark is placed inside the double quotation marks, not the single quotation mark, because the entire quotation of the teacher's words is a question.]

(7) When writing *dialogue* (a conversation), begin a new paragraph every time the speaker changes, and enclose the speaker's words in quotation marks.

EXAMPLE   "But what kind of authentic and valuable information do you require?" asked Klapaucius.

"All kinds, as long as it's true," replied the pirate. "You never can tell what facts may come in handy. I already have a few hundred wells and cellars full of them, but there's room for twice again as much. So out with it; tell me everything you know, and I'll jot it down. But make it snappy!"

"A fine state of affairs," Klapaucius whispered in Trurl's ear. "He could keep us here for an eon or two before we tell him everything we know. Our knowledge is colossal!!"

"Wait," whispered Trurl, "I have an idea."

Stanislaw Lem, from "The Sixth Sally"

EXERCISE 4   Using Quotation Marks with Other Marks of Punctuation

Add quotation marks and other punctuation marks where they are needed in the following dialogue. Also correct any errors in the use of capitalization, and begin a new paragraph each time the speaker changes.

EXAMPLE   [1] You can tell from this picture Lloyd said that people have a lot of fun during the Juneteenth holiday. [2] But I don't get it

[1] *"You can tell from this picture," Lloyd said, "that people have a lot of fun during the Juneteenth holiday.* [2] *But I don't get it."*

[1] Do you mean Janelle asked that you don't understand having fun or you don't understand Juneteenth [2] Lloyd, who didn't like being misunderstood, quickly replied stop joking around [3] Janelle said I'll be glad to tell you what Juneteenth is;

MECHANICS

she hadn't meant to upset Lloyd. [4] Juneteenth is celebrated every year on June 19 she continued to mark the day in 1865 when a Union general proclaimed the slaves in Texas to be free. [5] It's celebrated not only in Texas but also throughout the South [6] Lloyd interrupted why were the Texas slaves proclaimed free so long after Lincoln's Emancipation Proclamation [7] Remember that Lincoln gave his proclamation in 1863, but the Civil War continued until April 9, 1865 Janelle replied and then it took a while for news to spread [8] Janelle thought that her explanations had satisfied Lloyd, but then he asked So how is Juneteenth celebrated [9] Now that's a question you don't need to ask she replied Because you go to the Juneteenth parade every year. [10] It's celebrated much the same everywhere she added With families enjoying picnics, parades, games, and music.

30n. Use quotation marks to enclose titles of short works, such as short stories, poems, essays, articles, songs, episodes of television series, and chapters and other parts of books.

TYPE OF NAME	EXAMPLES	
Short Stories	"The Open Boat"	"The Tell-Tale Heart"
Poems	"Guitarreros"	"Thanatopsis"
Essays	"On the Mall"	"The Creative Process"
Articles	"Old Poetry and Modern Music" "How to Improve Your Grades"	

(continued)

TYPE OF NAME	EXAMPLES
Songs	"On Top of Old Smoky" "Wind Beneath My Wings"
TV Episodes	"The Flight of the Condor" "Tony's Surprise Party"
Chapters and Parts of Books	"The World Was New" "The Colonies' Struggle for Freedom"

☞ REFERENCE NOTE: For examples of titles that are italicized, see pages 875–876.

30o. Use quotation marks to enclose slang words, invented words, technical terms, and dictionary definitions of words.

EXAMPLES Chloe reached for a high note and hit a "clinker."
The newspaper reporter described the Halloween festival as "spooktacular."
Although I am not familiar with computer language, I do know that to "boot" a disk does not mean to kick it.
The verb *recapitulate* means "to repeat briefly" or "to summarize."

NOTE: Avoid using slang words in formal speaking and writing. When using technical terms, be sure to explain their meanings. If you are not sure whether a word is appropriate or its meaning is clear, consult an up-to-date dictionary.

Correcting Sentences by Adding Quotation Marks, Other Punctuation Marks, and Capitalization

▶ EXERCISE 5

Revise the following sentences by adding quotation marks, other marks of punctuation, and capitalization.

EXAMPLE **1.** In one of his books, Mark Twain wrote It is easier to stay out than get out
1. *In one of his books, Mark Twain wrote, "It is easier to stay out than get out."*

1. The section called People in the News in this book has some interesting facts about celebrities.

MECHANICS

2. Are you going to the Greek Festival asked Mr. Doney or didn't you know that it's scheduled for this weekend

3. Our teacher quoted Willa Cather's words there are only two or three human stories, and they go on repeating themselves as fiercely as if they had never happened before.

4. How do I find out who wrote the poem Dream Deferred Jill asked her English teacher

5. The phrase frosting on the cake has nothing to do with dessert it refers to something additional that is a pleasant surprise.

6. I'm still hungry complained Donna after finishing a plate of stew that baked apple looks tempting

7. When faced with a frightening situation, I often recite Psalm 23 4, which starts Yea, though I walk through the valley of the shadow of death, I will fear no evil.

8. Perhaps the finest memorial to Abraham Lincoln is the poem When Lilacs Last in the Dooryard Bloom'd in Walt Whitman's book Sequel to Drum-Taps.

9. Are you saying I don't know the answer or I don't understand the question

10. Ms. Hammer warned us that the movie was, to use her words, a parody of the novel furthermore she advised us not to waste our money and time by seeing it.

▶ REVIEW A

Proofreading a Dialogue for Correct Punctuation

In the following dialogue, correct any errors in the use of quotation marks and other marks of punctuation. Also correct any errors in the use of capitalization, and regroup sentences to form a new paragraph each time the speaker changes.

EXAMPLE [1] I think The Weeping Woman would be a good title for my new song Tomás told Jim. can you guess what it's about

1. *"I think 'The Weeping Woman' would be a good title for my new song," Tomás told Jim. "Can you guess what it's about?"*

[1] Well, I once read a magazine article titled La Llorona the Weeping Woman about a popular Mexican American legend, Jim replied. [2] That's the legend I'm talking about Tomás

exclaimed I first heard it when I was a little boy growing up in southern California.

[3] I think Jim commented, People in the music business would call the song a tear-jerker because it tells a sad story.

[4] I'll say it's sad Tomás replied it's about a poor, wronged woman who goes crazy, drowns her children, and kills herself; then she returns as a ghost to look for them forever.

[5] It's frightening to hear when you're young because La Llorona is usually described as a headless woman dressed all in white.

[6] Isn't she usually seen around water Jim asked. [7] Yes, Tomás said but you didn't mention one of the scariest things: her fingernails look like knives

[8] Didn't your mother ever say, Don't believe those horrible stories, son asked Jim

[9] Oh, sure Tomás replied. to tell the truth, I never did really believe them. But they are great stories.

[10] Well, maybe, but give me a humorous story like The Catbird Seat any day Jim said.

Ellipsis Points

30p. Use ellipsis points (. . .) to mark omissions from quoted material and pauses in a written passage.

Omissions from Quoted Material

ORIGINAL Sitting here tonight, many years later, with more time than money, I think about those faces that pass before my eyes like it was yesterday. They remind me of the chances and temptations to become an outlaw. I sure came through a tough mill. I see those men as they stood in those old days of the Golden West— some of them in the springtime of their manhood, so beautiful and strong that it makes you wonder, because their hearts are as black as night, and they are cruel, treacherous and merciless as a man-eating tiger of the jungle.

Andrew García, from *Tough Trip Through Paradise*

(1) If the quoted material that comes before the ellipsis points is not a complete sentence, use three ellipsis points with a space before the first point.

EXAMPLE In his autobiography, *Tough Trip Through Paradise,* Andrew García reflects, "Sitting here tonight, . . . I think about those faces that pass before my eyes like it was yesterday."

(2) If the quoted material that comes before or after the ellipsis points is a complete sentence, use an end mark before the ellipsis points.

EXAMPLE García observes, "I see those men as they stood in those old days of the Golden West—some of them in the springtime of their manhood. . . ." [The period is placed before the ellipsis points.]

(3) If one sentence or more is omitted, ellipsis points follow the end mark that precedes the omitted material.

EXAMPLE Recalling his youth, Andrew García writes, "Sitting here tonight, many years later, with more time than money, I think about those faces that pass before my eyes like it was yesterday. . . . I sure came through a tough mill." [The period precedes the ellipsis points.]

To show that a full line or more of poetry has been omitted, use an entire line of spaced periods.

EXAMPLE A single flow'r he sent me, since we met.
All tenderly his messenger he chose;
. . . .
Why is it no one ever sent me yet
One perfect limousine, do you suppose?

Dorothy Parker, from "One Perfect Rose"

Pauses in Written Passages

(4) To indicate a pause in a written passage, use three ellipsis points with a space before the first point.

EXAMPLE "Well . . . I can't really say," hedged the company's representative.

▶ EXERCISE 6 **Using Ellipsis Points Correctly**

Omit the italicized parts of the following passages. Use ellipsis points to punctuate each omission correctly.

1. Yet El Hoyo is not an outpost of a few families against the world. *It fights for no cause except those which soothe its immediate angers.* It laughs and cries with the same amount of passion in times of plenty and of want.

   Mario Suárez, from "Tucson, Arizona: El Hoyo"

2. Yellowstone, it seemed to me, was the top of the world, *a region of deep lakes and dark timber, canyons and waterfalls.* But beautiful as it is, one might have the sense of confinement there.

   N. Scott Momaday, from the Introduction to *The Way to Rainy Mountain*

3. A cloud, *the exact color of the boy's hat and shaped like a turnip,* had descended over the sun, and another, worse looking, crouched behind the car.

   Flannery O'Connor, from "The Life You Save May Be Your Own"

4. I am silver and exact. I have no preconceptions.
   Whatever I see I swallow immediately
   Just as it is, unmisted by love or dislike.
   I am not cruel, only truthful—

   Sylvia Plath, from "Mirror"

5. What would happen to me here? *Would I survive?* My expectations were modest. I wanted only a job.

   Richard Wright, from *American Hunger*

Apostrophes

Possessive Case

The *possessive case* of a noun or a pronoun shows ownership or relationship.

OWNERSHIP	the **performers'** costumes	**Ellen Zwilich's** music
	Grandmother's recipe	**your** responsibility
RELATIONSHIP	the **team's** coach	ten **dollars'** worth
	my best **friend's** sister	**our** cousins

MECHANICS

30q. Use an apostrophe in forming the possessive of nouns and indefinite pronouns.

(1) To form the possessive of a singular noun, add an apostrophe and an *s*.

EXAMPLES   **a bird's** nest   **Ross's** opinion
                the **principal's** office   **everyone's** responsibility

NOTE: When forming the possessive of a singular noun ending in an *s* sound, add only an apostrophe if the noun has two or more syllables and if the addition of *'s* will make the noun awkward to pronounce. Otherwise, add *'s*.

      EXAMPLES   for **conscience'** sake   Ms. **Schwartz's** car
                     Hercules' strength   the **witness's** testimony

(2) To form the possessive of a plural noun ending in *s*, add only the apostrophe.

EXAMPLES   the **girls'** gym   the **Joneses'** house
                the **players'** uniforms   the **volunteers'** efforts

    The few plural nouns that do not end in *s* form the possessive by adding an apostrophe and an *s*.

EXAMPLES   **men's** fashions   **children's** toys

NOTE: Do not use an apostrophe to form the plural of a noun. Remember that an apostrophe indicates ownership or relationship, not number.

      INCORRECT   Carl Lewis has won six Olympic gold medal's.
      CORRECT   Carl Lewis has won six Olympic gold **medals.**

MECHANICS

(3) Do not use an apostrophe with possessive personal pronouns or with the possessive pronoun *whose*.

Possessive Personal Pronouns	
my, mine	our, ours
your, yours	their, theirs
his, her, hers, its	

INCORRECT	The books were her's.
CORRECT	The books were **hers.**

INCORRECT	The leopard can't change it's spots.
CORRECT	The leopard can't change **its** spots.

INCORRECT	Marjorie is the girl who's mother I met.
CORRECT	Marjorie is the girl **whose** mother I met.

☞ REFERENCE NOTE: Do not confuse the possessive pronouns *its, your, their, theirs,* and *whose* with the contractions *it's, you're, they're, there's,* and *who's.* See pages 919, 925, 924, and 892. For more about possessive pronouns, see pages 674–675 and 683–684.

(4) To form the possessive of an indefinite pronoun, add an apostrophe and an *s*.

EXAMPLES   Each **one's** time is recorded separately.
He seems to need **everybody's** attention.

Indefinite Pronouns in the Possessive Case			
another's	everybody's	no one's	somebody's
anybody's	everyone's	one's	someone's
anyone's	nobody's	other's	

NOTE: In such forms as *anyone else* and *somebody else,* the correct possessives are *anyone else's* and *somebody else's.*

▶ EXERCISE 7   **Proofreading for Correct Possessive Forms**

Most of the following items contain an incorrect possessive form. For each error, give the correct form of the word. If an item is correct, write *C*.

MECHANICS

EXAMPLE   **1.** Chris' tapes
           1. *Chris's tapes*

1. It is her's.
2. womens' department
3. that boys' radio
4. Who's is it?
5. fly's wings
6. scissors' blades
7. mice's tails
8. childrens' program
9. no ones' fault
10. the Harlem Globetrotters's game

11. San Jose's industries
12. a Buddhist's beliefs
13. leaves' color
14. It is somebody's else.
15. soldiers' rations
16. it's shiny surface
17. That is their's.
18. churches' spire
19. the Siouxs' land
20. a horses' hooves

(5) Form the possessive of only the last word in a compound word, in the name of an organization or business firm, or in a word group showing joint possession.

EXAMPLES   father-in-**law's** gloves
            Taylor, Sanders, and **Weissman's** law office
            Roz and **Denise's** idea

☞ REFERENCE NOTE: For more information about compound nouns, see pages 554–555.

When a possessive pronoun is part of a word group showing joint possession, each noun in the word group is also possessive.

EXAMPLE   Chen's, Ramona's, and **my** project

(6) Form the possessive of each noun in a word group showing individual possession of similar items.

EXAMPLES   **Baldwin's** and **Ellison's** writings
            the **doctor's** and **dentist's** fees

(7) When used in the possessive form, words indicating time, such as *minute, hour, day, week, month,* and *year,* and words indicating amounts in cents or dollars require apostrophes.

EXAMPLES   a **week's** vacation   four **weeks'** vacation
            a **dollar's** worth   five **dollars'** worth

EXERCISE 8   **Forming Possessive Nouns
and Pronouns**

Each of the following phrases expresses a possessive relationship. Revise each word group so that a possessive noun or
pronoun expresses the same relationship.

EXAMPLE   **1.** promise of my sister-in-law
           1. *my sister-in-law's promise*

1. party of Juan and Geraldo
2. clothes of babies
3. jobs of my brothers-in-law
4. village of Inuits
5. pay of two weeks
6. restaurant of Charlie and Barney
7. worth of one dollar
8. coats of the gentlemen
9. singing of the birds
10. plans of the school board
11. victory of the players
12. languages of Sumer and Egypt
13. delay of six months
14. testimonies of the clerk and the customer
15. streets of West Baden
16. name of it
17. flooding of the Guadalupe River
18. hope of everyone else
19. opinions of the people
20. route of our mail carrier

Contractions

30r. Use an apostrophe to show where letters, words,
or numbers have been omitted in a contraction.

A *contraction* is a shortened form of a word, word group, or
figure in which an apostrophe takes the place of all the letters,
words, or numbers that are omitted.

EXAMPLES
I am	**I'm**	they had............	**they'd**
let us	**let's**	where is	**where's**
of the clock.....	**o'clock**	we are	**we're**
she would	**she'd**	you will	**you'll**
1992	**'92**	Pat is...............	**Pat's**

The word *not* can be shortened to *n't* and added to a verb,
usually without any change in the spelling of the verb.

EXAMPLES
is not.............	**isn't**	has not	**hasn't**
do not...........	**don't**	should not	**shouldn't**
does not.......	**doesn't**	were not........	**weren't**
EXCEPTIONS will not.........	**won't**	can not	**can't**

MECHANICS

Do not confuse contractions with possessive pronouns.

CONTRACTIONS	POSSESSIVE PRONOUNS
It's [*It is*] late. **It's** [*It has*] been an exciting week.	**Its** wing is broken.
Who's [*Who is*] in charge? **Who's** [*Who has*] been keeping score?	**Whose** ticket is this?
You're [*You are*] a good student.	**Your** shoe is untied.
They're [*They are*] in the library. **There's** [*There is*] no one at home.	**Their** house is for sale. Those dogs are **theirs**.

WRITING APPLICATION

Using Contractions in Informal Dialogue

MECHANICS

In casual conversation, people often take shortcuts. For example, how many times have you heard "how's it going" for *how is it going* and "there're" for *there are?* Writers use apostrophes to help show these shortened forms, called *contractions*, in written dialogue. Using contractions makes a written work sound more like natural speech. In the following passage, notice how the contractions help make the conversation between two friends, Jean and Berenger, more believable.

> BERENGER: [*admiringly*] You always look so immaculate.
> JEAN: [*continuing his inspection of* BERENGER] Your clothes are all crumpled, they're a disgrace! Your shirt is downright filthy, and your shoes . . . [BERENGER *tries to hide his feet under the table.*] Your shoes haven't been touched. What a mess you're in! And look at your shoulders . . .
> BERENGER: What's the matter with my shoulders?
> JEAN: Turn round! Come on, turn round! You've been leaning against some wall. [BERENGER *holds his hand*

> *out docilely to* JEAN.] No, I haven't got a brush with me;
> it would make my pockets bulge. [*Still docile,* BERENGER
> *flicks his shoulders to get rid of the white dust;* JEAN *averts his
> head.*] Heavens! Where did you get all that from?
>
> Eugène Ionesco, from *Rhinoceros*

Although contractions are a natural part of speech, they are inappropriate in formal writing such as research papers, business letters, and reports. (For more about the differences between formal and informal English, see pages 484–488.)

▶ WRITING ACTIVITY

For your final project in drama class, you've decided to write and produce a short play. You've already drafted a scene-by-scene outline of the play. In one scene, the two main characters will have a heated discussion about something that's important to them. Write the dialogue for your scene. Use contractions to make the characters' speech sound natural and realistic.

Prewriting First, brainstorm some ideas for your main characters. Are they two teenagers? an older and a younger brother or sister? a parent and a child? Once you decide who your characters are, think about the sort of discussion they might have. You can make their argument silly, humorous, serious, dramatic, or whatever you wish. Jot down some notes for the dialogue. Decide how the characters will resolve their argument at the end of the scene. Before you begin your draft, you may want to look at the **Writing Workshop** on pages 193–196 for help with writing dialogue for plays.

Writing Follow the form for presenting dialogue in a play (pages 193–196). In your first draft, concentrate on getting down the basic content of your characters' conversation. You can polish the dialogue later as you evaluate and revise. Be sure that your dialogue focuses on a specific topic or issue and that you maintain a consistent tone throughout.

Evaluating and Revising To help you evaluate the dialogue, you might ask two friends to read the parts of the characters. As you listen, ask yourself these questions. Does each line of dialogue sound natural? Does your dialogue have the tone you want? Do the characters resolve their argument in a realistic way? If not, add, cut, or revise words, phrases, or entire lines to achieve the effect you want. Use contractions to help make your dialogue sound like an actual discussion between two people.

Proofreading and Publishing Because they're small, apostrophes and other punctuation marks are easy to miss. Proofread your dialogue carefully for correct punctuation. Make sure you've begun a new paragraph each time the speaker changes. With your teacher's permission, you may want to produce your scene for the class. Cast two volunteer actors for the roles, and work with them to get the dialogue just right. Decide what actions and gestures should accompany the dialogue. Use simple props to help make the scene realistic.

Plurals

30s. Use an apostrophe and an *s* to form the plurals of all lowercase letters, some uppercase letters, and some words referred to as words.

EXAMPLES   There are two *r*'s and two *s*'s in *embarrassed.*
Try not to use so many *I*'s in your cover letter. [Without the apostrophe, the plural of the pronoun *I* would spell *Is.*]
After the happy couple said their *I do's,* everyone cheered.

You may add only an *s* to form the plurals of such items—except lowercase letters—if the plural forms will not cause misreading.

EXAMPLE   Compact discs **(CDs)** were introduced more than ten years ago.

NOTE: Use apostrophes consistently.

EXAMPLE   On her report card were three **A's** and three **B's.**
[Without the apostrophe, the plural of *A* would spell
As. The apostrophe in the plural of *B* is unnecessary
but is included for consistency.]

☞ **REFERENCE NOTE:** For more about forming these kinds of plurals
and the plurals of numbers, see page 912.

▶ EXERCISE 9   ## Proofreading for Errors in Contractions and Plurals

Add or delete apostrophes as needed in the following sentences.
[Note: You may need to change the spelling of some words.]

EXAMPLE   **1.** Lets try to find a modern puzzle maze that wont be
too difficult for us to explore.
1. *Let's; won't*

1. Your lucky if youve ever been through an old-fashioned
hedge maze such as the one pictured below.
2. Its like a maze from an English castle; in fact, we cant help
being reminded of the maze at Hampton Court Palace.
3. From above, some of the bushes look like *hs, ts,* and other
letters.
4. Dont you wonder if these people will find they're way out
by dusk or even ten o clock?
5. Ive read that mazes like this one became popular in Europe
during the 1500s and 1600s; however, my uncle said that hes
read about mazes that were built two thousand years ago.

MECHANICS

Hyphens

30t. Use a hyphen to divide a word at the end of a line.

When dividing a word at the end of a line, remember the following rules:

- Do not divide a one-syllable word.

INCORRECT	The treaty that ended the war was sign-ed in Paris in 1783.
CORRECT	The treaty that ended the war was signed in Paris in 1783.

- Divide a word only between syllables.

INCORRECT	Shashona wrote a story about the enda-ngered gray wolf.
CORRECT	Shashona wrote a story about the endan-gered gray wolf.

NOTE: When you are not sure about the division of a word, look in a dictionary.

- Divide an already hyphenated word at the hyphen.

INCORRECT	Among Elena's drawings were two self-por-traits.
CORRECT	Among Elena's drawings were two self-portraits.

- Do not divide a word so that one letter stands alone.

INCORRECT	Most of the buildings there are made of a-dobe.
CORRECT	Most of the buildings there are made of adobe.

30u. Use a hyphen with compound numbers from *twenty-one* to *ninety-nine* and with fractions used as modifiers.

EXAMPLES   six hundred **twenty-five**
a **three-fourths** quorum [*Three-fourths* is an adjective modifying *quorum.*]
three fourths of the audience [*Three fourths* is not a modifier. *Fourths* is a noun modified by the adjective *three.*]

30v. Use a hyphen with the prefixes *ex–*, *self–*, and *all–*, with the suffix *–elect*, and with all prefixes before a proper noun or proper adjective.

EXAMPLES   **ex-**mayor   **pre-**Civil War
                self-improvement   **mid-**Atlantic
                governor**-elect**   **trans-**Siberian
                all-star   **pro-**American

 REFERENCE NOTE: For more guidelines on adding prefixes and suffixes to words, see pages 905–907.

30w. Hyphenate a compound adjective when it precedes the noun it modifies.

EXAMPLES   a **well-designed** engine   an engine that is **well designed**

               a **world-famous** skier   a skier who is **world famous**

Do not use a hyphen if one of the modifiers is an adverb ending in *–ly*.

EXAMPLE   a **partly finished** research paper

NOTE: Some compound adjectives are always hyphenated, whether they precede or follow the words they modify.

        EXAMPLES   an **up-to-date** dictionary   a dictionary that is **up-to-date**

                     a **well-informed** debater   a debater who is **well-informed**

If you are unsure about whether a compound adjective is hyphenated, look up the word in a dictionary.

30x. Use a hyphen to prevent awkwardness or confusion.

EXAMPLES   **de-**emphasize [prevents awkwardness of two identical vowels]
                anti-inflammatory [prevents awkwardness of two identical vowels]
                re-cover a chair [prevents confusion with *recover*]
                a **re-**creation of the event [prevents confusion with *recreation*]

MECHANICS

▶ EXERCISE 10   **Writing Sentences Using Hyphens**

Write five sentences according to the following guidelines. In your sentences, use a variety of subjects and verbs.

1. Write a sentence with a compound number.
2. Write a sentence with a fraction used as an adjective.
3. Write a sentence containing a word with the prefix *ex–*.
4. Write a sentence with a compound adjective preceding the word it modifies.
5. Write a sentence in which you break a word at the end of a line.

▶ REVIEW B   **Using Apostrophes and Hyphens**

Revise the following groups of words by adding apostrophes and hyphens where needed. If a word group is correct, write C.

EXAMPLE   **1.** post World War II Europe
          1. *post-World War II Europe*

1. my sister in laws new pickup truck
2. transAlaskan
3. Achilles heel
4. Youre from Peru, arent you?
5. one third of the class
6. Isnt soda bread Irish?
7. Who are all of these *you's* and *theys*?
8. three quarter length sleeves
9. There are three *as* in *alphabetical*.
10. Its theirs, not ours.
11. remark the boundary lines
12. politics in the 1960s
13. dotted all of your *is*
14. Didnt Anthony make your piñata?
15. self appointed critic
16. Its after five oclock.
17. part time job
18. Why didn't someone an swer the phone?
19. That's all there is to know.
20. Wheres the Shaker box you bought?

▶ REVIEW C   **Proofreading a Paragraph for Correct Punctuation and Capitalization**

Most of the sentences in the following paragraph contain errors in the use of punctuation and capitalization. Rewrite each incorrect sentence, adding the necessary punctuation and capitalization. If a sentence is correct, write *C*.

EXAMPLE [1] Can we be sure sports historians arent that Abner Doubleday invented baseball, that Princeton and Rutgers played the first football game, or that golf originated in China in the second century B.C.?

1. *Can we be sure (sports historians aren't) that Abner Doubleday invented baseball, that Princeton and Rutgers played the first football game, or that golf originated in China in the second century B.C.?*

[1] The origins of most sports are unknown try as we may, we cannot say exactly when or where or how such games as baseball, football, and golf were first played. [2] There is, however, one exception to this rule the game of basketball. [3] Historians of sports know precisely where basketball began, they know precisely when it began, and perhaps the most interesting fact of all they know the name of the man who invented it Dr James Naismith. [4] In the winter of 1891–1892, Naismith who was then an instructor at the YMCA Training College now called Springfield College in Springfield Massachusetts had a problem on his hands. [5] The football season was over the baseball season had not yet begun. [6] His students needed indoor exercise at a competitive sport however no such sport existed. [7] Working with the materials at hand, Naismith set himself the task of creating a new indoor sport. [8] He fastened two peach baskets to the walls at opposite ends of his gymnasium and using a soccer ball, he devised the game that we call basketball today. [9] He started with eighteen available players, and the first rule he wrote read as follows there shall be nine players on each side. [10] Imagine eighteen players set loose on a modern basketball court!

MECHANICS

Review: Posttest

A. Proofreading Sentences for Correct Punctuation

The following sentences contain errors in the use of semicolons, colons, dashes, parentheses, brackets, italics (underlining), quotation marks, apostrophes, and hyphens. Rewrite the sentences correcting the errors. [Note: There may be more than one error in a sentence. You may have to add punctuation where it is needed, or you may have to delete punctuation that is incorrectly used.]

EXAMPLE   **1.** Did you say "that you want to join us"?
             1. Did you say that you want to join us?

1. Ed and Jim's essays were both titled Kwanzaa: A Special Time for African Americans.
2. "Among the writers in America today, he Galway Kinnell has earned his reputation as an outstanding poet," noted the critic in Newsweek.
3. The circus audience applauded and cheered as the acro bats performed the perfectly-timed stunt.
4. Paula said in a desperate tone, "I know Sue's directions stated, "Turn right when you get to the gas station; "but, unfortunately, I'm not sure which gas station she meant.
5. William Butler Yeats 1865–1939, an Irish poet who won the Nobel Prize for literature, was once a member of the Irish parliament.
6. I couldn't get along in school without the following; a college dictionary, a thesaurus, and a pocket calculator.
7. My driver's license wo'nt expire for another two weeks.
8. "Well, I dont know," Lauren said. "Where do you think all this soot comes from?"
9. Several people I respect think Raintree County by Ross Lockridge, Jr. is the greatest American novel, I plan to read it soon.
10. Heres my telephone number, call me if you decide to go to the movie.

B. Proofreading Paragraphs for Correct Punctuation

The following paragraphs of conversation contain errors in the uses of semicolons, colons, dashes, parentheses, italics (underlining), quotation marks, apostrophes, and hyphens. Rewrite each paragraph, correcting the errors.

EXAMPLE   **[1]** "You may like mystery, comedy, and science fiction movies, but my favorite movies are those about real peoples lives, Ben said."

1. *"You may like mystery, comedy, and science fiction movies; but my favorite movies are those about real people's lives," Ben said.*

[11] Tell me we've got time some of your all time favorites, then," Tani said.

[12] "I recently saw Mountains of the Moon for the first time I really learned a lot about the life of Sir Richard Burton from it," Ben replied.

[13] Whats his claim to fame"? Tani asked.

[14] "Sir Richard Burton was a man of many talents he was an explorer, an author, a scholar, a linguist, and a diplomat."

[15] "Did the movie try to show all those talents?" Tani asked. That would seem difficult to do."

[16] "The movie is mostly an African adventure its about Burtons search for the source of the Nile River," Ben said.

[17] "Some of my other favorites include: Gandhi, about the Indian independence leader, Amadeus, about Mozart's life, and *The Spirit of St. Louis*, a really old film about Charles Lindbergh."

[18] "I'll bet three-fourths of our friends have never heard of most of the movies youve seen," Tani said.

[19] "The downtown video store the one owned by Ross' brother has them all," Ben said.

[20] "Biographical movies well researched ones, anyway are a good way to learn about famous people," Tani said.

MECHANICS

31 SPELLING

Improving Your Spelling

Good Spelling Habits

Using the following techniques will improve your spelling:

1. **Pronounce words carefully.**

   EXAMPLES   ath • lete [not *ath • e • lete*]
   ac • ci • den • tal • ly [not *ac • ci • dent • ly*]
   can • di • date [not *can • i • date*]

2. **Spell by syllables.** A *syllable* is a word part that can be pronounced by itself.

   EXAMPLES   per • ma • nent [three syllables]
   op • ti • mis • tic [four syllables]
   oc • ca • sion • al • ly [five syllables]

3. **Use a dictionary.** By using a dictionary, you will become familiar with the correct pronunciations and divisions of words. In fact, using a dictionary to check the spelling of one word may help you spell other words. For example, checking the spelling of *democracy* may help you spell other words ending in *–cracy*, such as *theocracy*, *autocracy*, and *aristocracy*.

4. **Proofread for careless spelling errors.** Always reread what you have written so that you can eliminate careless spelling errors, such as typos (*thier* for *their*), missing letters (*familar* for *familiar*), and the misuse of similar-sounding words (*affect* for *effect*).

5. **Keep a spelling notebook.** Divide each page into four columns.

COLUMN 1   Write correctly any word you find troublesome.
COLUMN 2   Write the word again, dividing it into syllables and marking the stressed syllable(s). (You will likely need to use a dictionary.)
COLUMN 3   Write the word again, circling the part(s) that cause you trouble.
COLUMN 4   Jot down any comments that will help you remember the correct spelling.

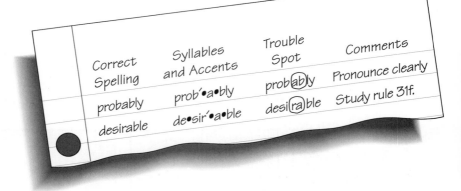

Correct Spelling	Syllables and Accents	Trouble Spot	Comments
probably	prob′•a•bly	prob(ab)ly	Pronounce clearly
desirable	de•sir′•a•ble	desi(ra)ble	Study rule 31f.

▶ EXERCISE 1   **Dividing Words into Syllables**

Write the syllables of each of the following words, using hyphens between the syllables. Do not look up the words in a dictionary. Be sure that the division of each word includes all of the letters of the word. When you have finished, use a dictionary to check your work.

EXAMPLE   **1.** accommodate
          1. *ac-com-mo-date*

1. adversary
2. alias
3. barbarous
4. chimney
5. costume
6. deficit
7. genuine
8. incidentally
9. procrastinate
10. temperature

Spelling Rules

ie and *ei*

31a. Write *ie* when the sound is long *e*, except after *c*.

EXAMPLES   bel**ie**ve   f**ie**ld   conc**ei**t   c**ei**ling   rec**ei**ve   n**ie**ce
EXCEPTIONS   **either**   **leisure**   **neither**   **seize**   **weird**

31b. Write *ei* when the sound is not long *e*.

EXAMPLES   forf**ei**t   fr**ei**ght   **ei**ght   n**ei**ghbor   w**ei**gh
EXCEPTIONS   **ancient**   **view**   **friend**   **mischief**   **conscience**

▶ EXERCISE 2   **Spelling *ie* and *ei* Words**

1. gr. . .f
2. th. . .r
3. v. . .l
4. h. . .r
5. bel. . .f
6. counterf. . .t
7. dec. . .ve
8. ch. . .ftain
9. perc. . .ve
10. rec. . .pt
11. p. . .rce
12. l. . .sure
13. th. . .f
14. sl. . .gh
15. bes. . .ge
16. shr. . .k
17. f. . .rce
18. . . .ght
19. cash. . .r
20. y. . .ld

BORN LOSER reprinted by permission of NEA, Inc.

−cede, *−ceed*, and *−sede*

31c. The only English word ending in *−sede* is *supersede*. The only words ending in *−ceed* are *exceed*, *proceed*, and *succeed*. All other words with this sound end in *−cede*.

EXAMPLES   ac**cede**   con**cede**   inter**cede**   pre**cede**   re**cede**   se**cede**

Adding Prefixes

A *prefix* is a letter or group of letters added to the beginning of a word to create a new word with a different meaning.

EXAMPLES   il + legible = **il**legible   pre + historic = **pre**historic
in + correct = **in**correct   un + certain = **un**certain

31d.   When adding a prefix, do not change the spelling of the original word.

EXAMPLES   dis + satisfy = **dis**satisfy   im + mature = **im**mature
mis + spell = **mis**spell   re + adjust = **re**adjust

REFERENCE NOTE: For a listing of prefixes, see pages 984–986.

Adding Suffixes

A *suffix* is a letter or group of letters added to the end of a word to create a new word with a different meaning.

EXAMPLES   help + less = help**less**   work + ed = work**ed**
move + ment = move**ment**   hope + ful = hope**ful**

31e.   When adding the suffix *–ness* or *–ly*, do not change the spelling of the original word.

EXAMPLES   plain + ness = plain**ness**   casual + ly = casual**ly**
gentle + ness = gentle**ness**   final + ly = final**ly**

EXCEPTION   For most words ending in *y*, change the *y* to *i* before adding *–ness* or *–ly*.

empty + ness = empt**iness**   busy + ly = bus**ily**
heavy + ness = heav**iness**   ready + ly = read**ily**

NOTE: One-syllable adjectives ending in *y* generally follow rule 31e.

EXAMPLES   dry + ness = dry**ness**   shy + ly = shy**ly**

REFERENCE NOTE: For a listing of suffixes, see pages 986–987.

EXERCISE 3   **Spelling Words with Prefixes and Suffixes**

Spell each of the following words, adding the prefix or suffix given.

1. mis + inform
2. habitual + ly
3. il + legal
4. happy + ness
5. stubborn + ness

6. crafty + ly
7. in + animate
8. im + movable
9. dis + appear
10. dis + similar

31f. Drop the final silent *e* before a suffix beginning with a vowel.

EXAMPLES   care + ing = car**ing**   dose + age = dos**age**
love + able = lov**able**   simple + er = simpl**er**

EXCEPTIONS   **Keep the final silent *e***
- in a word ending in *ce* or *ge* before a suffix beginning with *a* or *o:* peac**eable;** courag**eous**
- in *dye* before *–ing:* dy**eing**
- in *mile* before *–age:* mil**eage**

31g. Keep the final silent *e* before a suffix beginning with a consonant.

EXAMPLES   hope + ful = hop**eful**   love + ly = lov**ely**
care + less = car**eless**   place + ment = plac**ement**

EXCEPTIONS   awe + ful = aw**ful**   whole + ly = who**lly**
argue + ment = argu**ment**   nine + th = nin**th**
judge + ment = judg**ment**   true + ly = tru**ly**
acknowledge + ment = acknowledg**ment** *or*
acknowledg**ement**

31h. For words ending in *y* preceded by a consonant, change the *y* to *i* before any suffix that does not begin with *i.*

EXAMPLES   thirsty + est = thirst**iest**
plenty + ful = plent**iful**
modify + ing = modif**ying**
accompany + ment = accompan**iment**

31i. For words ending in *y* preceded by a vowel, keep the *y* when adding a suffix.

EXAMPLES   gray + est = gray**est**   obey + ing = obey**ing**
play + ed = play**ed**   enjoy + ment = enjoy**ment**
EXCEPTIONS   day—da**ily**   lay—la**id**   pay—pa**id**   say—sa**id**

EXERCISE 4 **Spelling Words with Suffixes**

Spell each of the following words, adding the suffix given.

1. employ + ment
2. thrifty + ness
3. beauty + fy
4. modify + cation
5. sure + ly
6. lively + er
7. share + ing
8. glide + ed
9. loose + est
10. play + ful

31j. Double the final consonant before a suffix that begins with a vowel if the word *both* (1) has only one syllable or has the accent on the last syllable *and* (2) ends in a single consonant preceded by a single vowel.

EXAMPLES thin + est = thi**nn**est   occur + ence = occu**rr**ence
rap + ing = ra**pp**ing   refer + ed = refe**rr**ed

Do not double the final consonant unless the word satisfies both of the conditions.

EXAMPLES prevent + ing = preven**t**ing [has accent on the last syllable but does not end in a single consonant preceded by a single vowel]
mellow + er = mellow**er** [ends in a single consonant preceded by a single vowel but does not have accent on the last syllable]
refer + ence = reference [satisfies both conditions but addition of suffix causes shift in accent]

NOTE: The final consonant of some words may or may not be doubled. Either spelling is acceptable.

EXAMPLES cancel + ed = cance**led** *or* cance**lled**
travel + er = trave**ler** *or* trave**ller**

If you are not sure whether you should double the final consonant, follow rule 31j, or consult a dictionary.

REVIEW A **Spelling Words with Suffixes**

Spell each of the following words, adding the suffix given.

1. plan + ed
2. prefer + ence
3. friendly + er
4. achieve + ment
5. propel + er
6. seize + ure
7. definite + ly
8. joy + ful
9. argue + ment
10. prepare + ed

MECHANICS

 REVIEW B

Proofreading a Paragraph for Spelling Errors

Proofread the following paragraph and correct each misspelled word.

[1] The sceintist Granville T. Woods (below, center) was quite an inventor. [2] After leaveing school at the age of ten, Woods worked on the railroads in Missouri. [3] However, his love of electrical and mechanical devices led him to study engineering and later to open a factory where his managment skills and knowledge served him well. [4] Later, Woods succeded in devising a telegraph that allowed stationmasters to communicate with engineers on moving trains. [5] With this device, speeding trains could be notifyed of any problems along the track, and train engineers could quickly alert stations to dangerous situations. [6] His successes permited Woods to relocate to New York City, and there he learned that the method theaters used for diming lights was responsible for many fires. [7] Woods revaluated the design and devised a new system. [8] This new lighting system operated safly and was, at the same time, 40 percent more efficient than the old one. [9] Not surprisingly, companies like American Bell Telephone and General Electric payed generous sums for Woods' inventions. [10] In all, Woods recieved over 150 patents for his inventions, and many of them, such as the electrified rail for New York City's subway, are still in use.

MECHANICS

Forming the Plurals of Nouns

31k. Remembering the following rules will help you spell the plural forms of nouns.

(1) For most nouns, add –s.

SINGULAR	player	beagle	ship	island	senator	Jefferson
PLURAL	players	beagles	ships	islands	senators	Jeffersons

(2) For nouns ending in s, x, z, ch, or sh, add –es.

SINGULAR	class	tax	waltz	match	brush	Chávez
PLURAL	classes	taxes	waltzes	matches	brushes	Chávezes

(3) For nouns ending in y preceded by a vowel, add –s.

SINGULAR	monkey	journey	alloy	decoy	tray	McKay
PLURAL	monkeys	journeys	alloys	decoys	trays	McKays

(4) For nouns ending in y preceded by a consonant, change the y to i and add –es.

SINGULAR	fly	country	comedy	trophy	cavity	theory
PLURAL	flies	countries	comedies	trophies	cavities	theories

EXCEPTION **For proper nouns, add –s.**
Kennedy—Kennedys   Gregory—Gregorys

(5) For some nouns ending in f or fe, add –s. For others, change the f or fe to v and add –es.

SINGULAR	gulf	roof	belief	leaf	shelf	knife
PLURAL	gulfs	roofs	beliefs	leaves	shelves	knives

NOTE: If you are not sure how to spell the plural of a word ending in *f* or *fe*, look in a dictionary.

(6) For nouns ending in o preceded by a vowel, add –s.

SINGULAR	studio	radio	cameo	stereo	igloo	Ignacio
PLURAL	studios	radios	cameos	stereos	igloos	Ignacios

(7) For nouns ending in o preceded by a consonant, add –es.

SINGULAR	torpedo	tomato	hero	veto	potato
PLURAL	torpedoes	tomatoes	heroes	vetoes	potatoes

MECHANICS

For some common nouns ending in *o* preceded by a consonant, especially those referring to music, and for proper nouns, add only an *−s*.

SINGULAR	taco	photo	piano	solo	alto	Ibo	Suro
PLURAL	tacos	photos	pianos	solos	altos	Ibos	Suros

NOTE: For some nouns ending in *o* preceded by a consonant, you may add either *−s* or *−es*.

SINGULAR	motto	tornado	mosquito	zero	banjo
PLURAL	mottos	tornados	mosquitos	zeros	banjos
	or	*or*	*or*	*or*	*or*
	mottoes	tornadoes	mosquitoes	zeroes	banjoes

If you are ever in doubt about the plural form of a noun ending in *o* preceded by a consonant, check the spelling in a dictionary.

(8) The plural of a few nouns is formed in irregular ways.

SINGULAR	tooth	goose	woman	mouse	foot	child
PLURAL	teeth	geese	women	mice	feet	children

(9) For a few nouns, the singular and the plural forms are the same.

SINGULAR AND PLURAL	sheep	deer	trout	salmon
	moose	species	Japanese	Sioux

(10) For most compound nouns, form the plural of only the last word of the compound.

SINGULAR	notebook	bookshelf	baby sitter	ten-year-old
PLURAL	notebooks	bookshelves	baby sitters	ten-year-olds

(11) For compound nouns in which one of the words is modified by the other word or words, form the plural of the noun modified.

SINGULAR	sister-in-law	runner-up	mountain goat
PLURAL	sisters-in-law	runners-up	mountain goats

NOTE: Some compound nouns have two acceptable plural forms.

SINGULAR	attorney general	court-martial	notary public
PLURAL	attorney generals	court-martials	notary publics
	or	*or*	*or*
	attorneys general	courts-martial	notaries public

NOTE: Check an up-to-date dictionary whenever you are in doubt about the plural form of a compound noun.

(12) For some nouns borrowed from other languages, the plural is formed as in the original languages.

SINGULAR	alumnus [male]	alumna [female]	phenomenon
PLURAL	alumni [male]	alumnae [female]	phenomena

A few nouns borrowed from other languages have two plural forms. For each of the following nouns, the plural form preferred in English is given first.

SINGULAR	index	appendix	formula	cactus
PLURAL	index**es**	appendix**es**	formula**s**	cactu**ses**
	or	*or*	*or*	*or*
	ind**ices**	append**ices**	formul**ae**	cac**ti**

NOTE: Whenever you are in doubt about which spelling to use, remember that a dictionary lists the most frequently used spelling first.

Drawing by Lorenz; © 1970 The New Yorker Magazine, Inc.

FOUNTAN OF YOOTH

"I don't know, Harry. This has the ring of authenticity."

MECHANICS

(13) To form the plural of figures, most uppercase letters, signs, and words used as words, add an *–s* or both an apostrophe and an *–s.*

SINGULAR	*8*	1990	*C*	*&*	*and*
PLURAL	*8*s	1990s	*C*s	*&*s	*and*s
	or	*or*	*or*	*or*	*or*
	8's	1990's	*C*'s	*&*'s	*and*'s

To prevent confusion, add both an apostrophe and an *–s* to form the plural of all lowercase letters, certain uppercase letters, and some words used as words.

EXAMPLES   The word *Mississippi* contains four *s*'s and four *i*'s. [Without an apostrophe, the plural of *s* would look awkward, and the plural of *i* could be confused with *is.*]
Sebastian usually makes straight A's. [Without an apostrophe, the plural of *A* could be confused with *As.*]
Because I mistakenly thought Evelyn Waugh was a woman, I used *her*'s instead of *his*'s in my paragraph. [Without an apostrophe, the plural of *her* would look like the possessive pronoun *hers* and the plural of *his* would look like the word *hiss.*]

☞ REFERENCE NOTE: For more information about forming these kinds of plurals, see pages 894–895.

▶ EXERCISE 5   **Spelling the Plural Forms of Nouns**

Spell the plural form of each of the following nouns.

1. gulf	6. soprano	11. valley	16. elk
2. penny	7. life	12. try	17. *o*
3. father-in-law	8. larva	13. corps	18. politics
4. right of way	9. bunch	14. half	19. niece
5. 1700	10. Murphy	15. echo	20. turkey

▶ REVIEW C   **Understanding the Spelling Rules**

By referring to the rules on the previous pages, explain the spelling of each of the following words.

1. senators-elect	6. obligation	11. wharves	16. secede
2. parentheses	7. conceive	12. iciness	17. wheels
3. teaspoonfuls	8. immature	13. illegible	18. *c*'s
4. data	9. changeable	14. proceed	19. rodeos
5. handkerchief	10. liberally	15. biggest	20. lovely

MECHANICS

Writing Numbers

31l. Spell out a *cardinal number*—a number that shows how many—that can be expressed in one or two words. Otherwise, use numerals.

EXAMPLES   **seven** juniors   **fifty-one** votes   **one thousand** miles
203 juniors   **421** votes   **1,242** miles

 REFERENCE NOTE: For information about hyphenating numbers, see page 896.

NOTE: Do not spell out some numbers and use numerals for others in the same context. Be consistent by using numerals to express all of the numbers.

INCONSISTENT   William Shakespeare wrote thirty-seven plays and 154 sonnets.

CONSISTENT   William Shakespeare wrote **37** plays and **154** sonnets.

However, to distinguish between numbers appearing beside each other, spell out one number, and use numerals for the other.

EXAMPLES   I need to buy **ten 29**-cent stamps.
Corey sold **135 five**-dollar tickets.

31m. Spell out a number that begins a sentence.

EXAMPLES   **Eighty-eight** senators voted in favor of the bill.
Three hundred thirty-two tickets were sold.

If the number appears awkward when spelled out, revise the sentence so that it does not begin with the number.

AWKWARD   Two thousand five hundred sixty-four pounds is the combined weight of those seven sumo wrestlers.
IMPROVED   The combined weight of those seven sumo wrestlers is **2,564** pounds.

31n. Always spell out an *ordinal number*—a number that expresses order.

EXAMPLES   Thurgood Marshall was the **first** [not *1st*] African American to serve on the U.S. Supreme Court.
The Rio Grande is the **twenty-second** [not *22nd*] longest river in the world.

31o. Use numerals to express numbers in conventional situations.

TYPES OF NUMBERS	EXAMPLES		
Identification Numbers	Chapter **26**	pages **41–54**	Act **5**
	Interstate **20**	lines **10–14**	Channel **8**
Measurements/ Statistics	**98.6** degrees	**42** years old	**8** percent
	14.6 ounces	ratio of **5** to **1**	**4½** feet
Addresses	**512** Willow Drive		
	Arrowhead, DE **34322–0422**		
Dates	July **7, 1993**	**44** B.C.	A.D. **145**
Times of Day	**6:20** P.M. (*or* p.m.)	**8:00** A.M. (*or* a.m.)	

NOTE: Spell out a number used with *o'clock*.

EXAMPLE   **nine** o'clock

REVIEW D **Proofreading a Paragraph for Spelling Errors**

Proofread the following paragraph and correct each misspelled word.

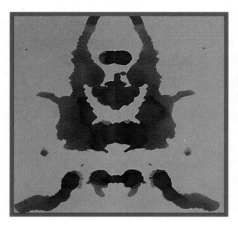

[1] Does this inkblot remind you of monkies? [2] Maybe you see two Eskimos in igloos perched on the back of a polar bear fishing for salmon in a trout stream full of flys. [3] Then again, may-be four geese chasing a dozen mice down Interstate Four is the image that comes to your mind as you gaze at the dark shapes and white spaces. [4] To psychiatrists and psychologists who

have taken special class's, the pictures you imagine are really images of your own mind. [5] 1 of ten standard inkblots, this design is part of a special psychological test devised by Hermann Rorschach. [6] Although Rorschach was not the 1st to study inkblots and the imagination, his inkblots are one of the most famous methods of gaining insights into people's minds. [7] As you might suspect, a group of five-years-olds will see very different images in these inkblots than a group of adults would. [8] By having a person describe what he or she saw in each inkblot, Rorschach was able to infer a great deal about that person's fears, beliefes, desires, and hopes. [9] For example, what does it mean if you see seven tacos playing banjos made of white potatos, waltzing with two walruses on loaves of bread? [10] Maybe you're hungry, or maybe you feel like dancing, and it's time to put your tap shoe's on.

Words Often Confused

all ready	*all prepared* Are you *all ready* for the exam?
already	*previously* We have *already* studied that chapter.
all together	*everyone in the same place* My family will be *all together* during this Thanksgiving holiday.
altogether	*entirely* The president is *altogether* opposed to the bill.
altar	[noun] *a table or stand at which religious rites are performed* This is the *altar* used in the Communion service.
alter	[verb] *to change* Do not *alter* your plans on my account.

ascent	[noun] *a rise; a climb* The climbers' *ascent* was a slow one.
assent	[verb] *to agree;* [noun] *consent* Will they *assent* to our proposal? Our last proposal won their *assent*.

born	*given life* Ynes Mexia was *born* in Washington, D.C.
borne	*carried; endured* They have *borne* their troubles better than we thought they would.

brake	[verb] *to stop or slow down;* [noun] *a device for* *stopping or slowing down* He *braked* the car and swerved to avoid hitting the child. An automobile *brake* will overheat if used too often.
break	[verb] *to cause to come apart; to shatter;* [noun] *a fracture* If you're not careful, you'll *break* the mirror. The *break* in the bone will heal in six weeks.

capital	[noun] *a city that is the seat of government of a* *country or state; money or property;* [adjective] *punishable by death; uppercase; of major* *importance* Manila is the *capital* of the Philippines. The company has *capital* of $100,000. *Capital* punishment was the subject of the debate. A proper noun begins with a *capital* letter. That is a *capital* suggestion.
capitol	[noun] *building in which a legislature meets* [capitalized when it refers to the building where the U.S. Congress meets] The *capitol* in Austin is a popular tourist attraction. Our Senate and House of Representatives meet in the *Capitol* in Washington.

clothes	*wearing apparel*
	I'd like to buy some summer *clothes.*
cloths	*pieces of fabric*
	Use these *cloths* to clean the car.

► EXERCISE 6 **Distinguishing Between Words Often Confused**

From the choices in parentheses, select the correct word or words for each of the following sentences.

1. The governor said that the roof of the (*capital, capitol*) needs to be repaired.
2. We have finished packing and are (*all ready, already*) to go.
3. Saying nothing, the major gave a nod of (*ascent, assent*).
4. At night, Tokyo, the (*capital, capitol*) of Japan, is filled with vivid neon lights advertising all sorts of shops, clubs, and products.
5. You called us after we had (*all ready, already*) left.
6. Please keep your foot on the (*brake, break*).
7. The expenditures will be (*born, borne*) by the taxpayers.
8. Seminole jackets are made from long, narrow strips of different colored (*cloths, clothes*) carefully sewn together to make one garment.
9. The new dam will (*altar, alter*) the course of the river.
10. Your arguments are not (*all together, altogether*) convincing.

MECHANICS

coarse	[adjective] *rough; crude*
	The driveway was covered with *coarse* sand.
	His *coarse* language and manners prevented him from getting the job.
course	[noun] *path of action; passage or way; study or group of studies; part of a meal;* [also used with *of* to mean *naturally* or *certainly*]
	What *course* do you think I should follow?
	Geraldo's parents go to the golf *course* every Saturday.
	The *course* in world history lasts a full year.
	My favorite main *course* is bolichi.
	Of *course*, you may go with us.

complement	[noun] *something that makes whole or complete;* [verb] *to make whole or complete* The diagram shows that the angle *WXY* is the *complement* of the angle *YXZ*. A good shortstop would *complement* the team.
compliment	[noun] *praise; respect;* [verb] *to express praise or respect* The performer was pleased and flattered by the critic's *compliments*. Did the critics *compliment* all of the other performers, too?
consul	[noun] *a person appointed by a government to serve its citizens in a foreign country* The Israeli *consul* held a press conference to pledge his support for the peace talks.
council	[noun] *a group assembled for conferences or legislation* The student *council* meets this afternoon.
councilor	[noun] *a member of a council* The queen's *councilors* met together for several hours but could not agree.
counsel	[noun] *advice;* [verb] *to advise* Shandra sought *counsel* from Mr. Nakai. Mr. Nakai *counseled* her to apply for the scholarship.
counselor	[noun] *one who gives advice* Shandra's guidance *counselor* helped her complete the application.
des´ert	[noun] *a dry region* Irrigation has brought new life to the *desert*.
desert´	[verb] *to leave or abandon* A good soldier never *deserts* his or her post.
dessert´	[noun] *the final course of a meal* My favorite *dessert* is frozen yogurt with strawberries on top.

formally	*in a strict or dignified manner* Mayor Pérez will *formally* open the new recreation center on Wednesday.
formerly	*previously* Mrs. Ling was *formerly* the head of the math department at Leland High School.

ingenious	*clever; resourceful; skillful* Carla has an *ingenious* plan to earn some money this summer.
ingenuous	*innocent; trusting; frank* Ian is as *ingenuous* as a five-year-old child.

its	[possessive form of *it*] Our city must increase *its* water supply.
it's	[contraction of *it is* or *it has*] *It's* almost time for the bell to ring. *It's* been nice talking to you.

later	[adjective] *more late;* [adverb] *at a subsequent time* I wasn't on time, but you were even *later*. I'll see you *later*.
latter	[adjective] *the second of two* (as opposed to *former*) Dr. Edwards can see you in the morning or the afternoon, but the *latter* time is more convenient for her.

lead	[verb, pronounced "leed"] *to go first; to guide* Who will *lead* the discussion group?
led	[verb, past tense of *lead*] Elaine *led* the band onto the field.
lead	[noun, pronounced "led"] *a heavy metal; graphite in a pencil* The mechanic used small weights made of *lead* to balance the wheel. My pencil *lead* broke during the test.

MECHANICS

MECHANICS

▶ EXERCISE 7   **Distinguishing Between Words Often Confused**

In the following sentences, select the correct word from each pair in parentheses.

1. Court is (*formally, formerly*) opened with a bailiff's cry of "Oyez, Oyez!"
2. When her painting was purchased by the museum, the artist received many (*complements, compliments*).
3. One of my father's favorite sayings is "What's next—(*desert, dessert*) or (*desert, dessert*) the table?"
4. The discovery and development of synthetic fibers must have required an (*ingenious, ingenuous*) mind.
5. I enjoy both chicken and steak but prefer the (*later, latter*).
6. One of the guidance (*councilor's, counselor's*) jobs is to (*lead, led*) students to take the proper (*coarse, course*) of study.
7. Have you tried out the new public golf (*coarse, course*)?
8. Ebenezer D. Basset, the first African American diplomat, was appointed minister to Haiti by President Grant; Basset later served as Haiti's (*Consul, Council*) General.
9. Do you know the song "(*Its, It's*) Later Than You Think"?
10. The stark simplicity of the sand painting forms a perfect (*complement, compliment*) to its complex spiritual meaning.

loose	[adjective, pronounced "loos"] *not firmly fastened; not tight* The front wheel on your bike is *loose.* Clothes with a *loose* fit are stylish now.
lose	[verb, pronounced "looz"] *to suffer loss* The trees will *lose* their leaves soon.
miner	[noun] *a worker in a mine* American *miners* lead the world in the production of coal.
minor	[noun] *a person under legal age;* [adjective] *of small importance* (as opposed to *major*) Normally, a *minor* is not permitted to sign a legal paper. Let's not list any of the *minor* objections to the plan.

moral	[adjective] *good; virtuous;* [noun] *a lesson of conduct derived from a story or event* Good conduct is based upon *moral* principles. The *moral* of this old folk tale is "Be true to yourself."
morale	[noun] *spirit; mental condition* Teamwork is impossible without good *morale*.
peace	*calmness* (as opposed to *strife* or *war*) Disarmament is an important step toward *peace*.
piece	*a part of something* Four *pieces* of the puzzle are missing.
personal	[adjective] *individual; private* My *personal* opinion has nothing to do with the case. Do you feel that details of the candidates' *personal* lives should be made public?
personnel	[noun] *a group of people employed in the same work or service* Most large companies prefer to recruit their executive *personnel* from among college graduates.
plain	[adjective] *not fancy; undecorated; clear;* [noun] *a large area of flat land* Although the new uniforms are *plain*, they are quite attractive. Does my explanation make things *plain* to you? Many Western movies are set on the Great *Plains*.
plane	[noun] *a flat surface; a woodworking tool; an airplane* Some problems in physics deal with the mechanical advantage of an inclined *plane*. Use this *plane* to make the wood smooth. We watched the *plane* circle for its landing.

MECHANICS

principal	[noun] *the head of a school;* [adjective] *main; most important* The *principal* will address the entire student body tomorrow. Florida and California are our *principal* citrus-growing states.
principle	[noun] *a rule of conduct; a fact or a general truth* The *principle* of the Golden Rule is found in many religions. This machine operates on a new *principle*.
quiet	[adjective] *still; silent* The library is usually a *quiet* place to study.
quite	[adverb] *completely; rather; very* Are you *quite* finished? We are *quite* proud of Angel's achievements.
rout	[noun] *a disorderly flight;* [verb] *to put to flight; to defeat overwhelmingly* What began as an orderly retreat ended as a *rout*. The coach predicts that his Bears will *rout* the Wildcats in the playoffs.
route	*a road; a way to go* This highway is the shortest *route* to the mountains.

MECHANICS

▶ EXERCISE 8   ### Distinguishing Between Words Often Confused

In the following sentences, select the correct word from each pair in parentheses.

1. As Surgeon General of the United States, the (*principal, principle*) duty of Dr. Antonia Novello is to safeguard the health of Americans.
2. Automated methods of extracting ore have put thousands of (*miners, minors*) out of work.
3. Coral has a sign that she puts on her desk in the library; it reads: "(*Quiet, Quite*) please. Genius at work."

4. When Kurt's (*plain, plane*) failed to return, the (*moral, morale*) of his squadron sank to zero.
5. The accident that completely demolished the car was caused by a (*loose, lose*) cotter pin worth ten cents.
6. Follow the marked (*rout, route*), or you will surely (*loose, lose*) your way.
7. The (*principal, principle*) that underlies that company's choice of (*personal, personnel*) is "An educated person is usually willing to learn more."
8. The columnist described the game as a (*rout, route*) for our team.
9. To prevent infection, always apply first aid to (*miner, minor*) cuts.
10. For his contribution in bringing an end to the first Arab-Israeli war, Dr. Ralph J. Bunche was awarded the Nobel Prize for (*piece, peace*) in 1950.

stationary	[adjective] *in a fixed position* The new state power plant contains large *stationary* engines.
stationery	[noun] *writing paper* I always save my best *stationery* for important letters.
straight	[adjective] *not crooked or curved; direct* Draw a *straight* line that connects points A and B.
strait	[noun] *channel connecting two large bodies of water;* [usually plural] *difficulty; distress* The *Strait* of Gibraltar links the Atlantic Ocean and the Mediterranean Sea. His family always helped him when he was in bad *straits*.
than	[conjunction, used for comparisons] Loretta is taller *than* I.
then	[adverb] *at that time; next* We lived on Garden Street until last year; *then* we moved to our new house.

MECHANICS

(continued)

their	[possessive form of *they*] The performers are studying *their* lines.
there	[adverb] *at that place;* [expletive, used to fill out the meaning of a sentence] I will be *there* after rehearsal. *There* will be four performances of the play.
they're	[contraction of *they are*] *They're* performing a play by Sonia Sánchez.
to	[preposition; part of the infinitive form of a verb] Let's go *to* the movies. After the rain, the birds began *to* sing.
too	[adverb] *more than enough; also* Is it *too* far to walk? You, *too*, are invited to the sports banquet.
two	[adjective] *one plus one;* [noun] *the number between one and three; a pair* They serve *two* flavors: vanilla and chocolate. *Two* of my favorite writers are Nadine Gordimer and Ntozake Shange.
waist	*the midsection of the body* These slacks are too tight at the *waist*.
waste	[noun] *useless spending; unused or useless material;* [verb] *to use foolishly* The movie was simply a *waste* of time. Don't *waste* your money on movies like that.
weather	[noun] *atmospheric conditions* We had good *weather* for the picnic.
whether	[conjunction, used to express an alternative] I don't know *whether* Denzel will help us or not.
who's	[contraction of *who is* or *who has*] *Who's* going to portray the Navajo detective in the play? *Who's* been using my typewriter?
whose	[possessive form of *who*] *Whose* artwork is this?

> **your** [possessive form of *you*]
> Is this *your* book?
> **you're** [contraction of *you are*]
> I hope *you're* able to come to my graduation.

▶ EXERCISE 9 **Distinguishing Between Words Often Confused**

In the following sentences, select the correct word or words from the choices given in parentheses.

1. (*Their, There*) Great Dane is taller and heavier (*than, then*) (*your, you're*) Irish wolfhound.
2. Since the roof of the stadium is not (*stationary, stationery*), we can put it up or take it down as needed.
3. If the (*weather, whether*) isn't (*to, too, two*) awful, we will go (*to, too, two*) the game.
4. The Mexican women over (*there, their, they're*) are wearing *rebozos*, versatile shawls worn over the head, around the shoulders, or about the (*waist, waste*).
5. (*Who's, Whose*) planning to write a term paper about Ida Tarbell?
6. If that is not (*your, you're*) car, then (*who's, whose*) is it— (*there's, theirs*)?
7. Half of India's population could be fed on the food that is (*waisted, wasted*) every year in the United States.
8. What did (*your, you're*) family say when you told them about the scholarship (*your, you're*) going to get?
9. What styles of (*stationary, stationery*) did you order for the class project?
10. Deep in the jungles of Cambodia lies a maze of (*straight, strait*) roads and canals that were part of the ancient Khmer capital of Angkor Thom.

▶ REVIEW E **Proofreading Paragraphs for Spelling Errors**

Proofread the following paragraphs and correct each misspelled word.

[1] Last winter, as we flew over the Nazca Planes of Peru, I took photographs of the eighteen famous bird images that

MECHANICS

have puzzled archaeologists for years. [2] Excitement rippled through the aircraft as the dessert seemed to come alive with mysterious images like this one. [3] Although the group of fig-

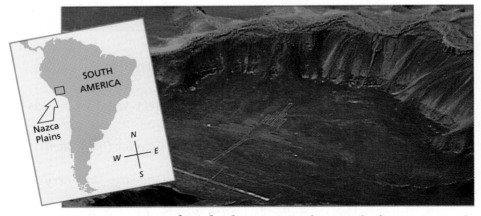

ures covers two hundred square miles, each figure is made only of lose mounds of rocks and pebbles. [4] The dry whether in the region has preserved these fragile messages for more than fifteen hundred years.

[5] Because many of the designs cannot be perceived from the ground, some people believe that the Nazca had aircraft, perhaps balloons or huge kites, capable of an assent to a thousand feet or more. [6] To test this hypothesis, one group of investigators actually constructed a crude hot-air balloon made of course vegetable fiber. [7] A violent gust threw the balloon and it's passengers to the ground before carrying them some three miles away.

[8] One of the more astounding theories about the designs is that the strait lines were landing strips for spaceships. [9] Other theorists wonder if the flight routs of the birds represented by the patterns helped warn the Nazca of cold winds and rain. [10] Maria Reiche, an astronomer and mathematician who has studied the area, believes that the lines form an ingenuous calendar. [11] However, a computer analysis of lunar and solar patterns has lead astronomers to doubt this theory.

[12] As our plane landed, we tourists were already for a closer look at these weird figures. [13] Early the next day, we met our tour guide in front of the hotel and boarded a small bus; than we headed for the Nazca lines.

[14] Our guide told us that parts of the fragile figures have all ready been ruined by car and foot traffic. [15] Following the

consul of Maria Reiche, the Peruvian government no longer allows tourists to walk or drive over the area. [16] Consequently, we could view the figures only from an observation tower that had been built close too them. [17] Nevertheless, we were quiet impressed by the amount of planning and work that must have been required to create these fascinating lines.

[18] When our guide signaled us back to the bus, I picked up a stone and, for a moment, held a peace of history in my hand; then I carefully put the stone back where I found it. [19] Latter, I sat in my hotel room and thought about the Nazca and the unusual images they'd made. [20] Who, I wondered, were these ancient people who's achievements continue to baffle modern science?

300 Spelling Words

The following list contains three hundred commonly misspelled words. The words are grouped so that you can study them ten at a time. To master any words that give you difficulty, follow the five-step procedure given at the beginning of this chapter (see pages 902–903).

accidentally	arctic	benefited
accommodate	argument	bicycle
accurate	arrangement	biscuit
acknowledgment	assassinate	bookkeeper
acquaintance	association	bracelet
across	athletics	breathe
aerial	atomic	bruise
aisle	attach	bulletin
all right	attention	bureau
always	attitude	business
amateur	auxiliary	calendar
analyze	awful	campaign
announce	awkward	candidate
anonymous	bachelor	catastrophe
apologize	background	cellophane
appearance	banana	cemetery
appreciate	bargain	ceremony
approaching	beggar	challenge
appropriate	beginning	chaperon
approval	believe	classroom

college
colonel
colossal
column
commission
committee
comparatively
compel
competition
completely

complexion
concentrate
conscience
conscientious
contemptible
convenience
copies
cordially
corps
correspondence

corroborate
courageous
courteous
criticism
criticize
cylinder
decide
decision
defense
definitely

dependent
descendant
descent
description
desirable
develop
dictionary
different
dining
dinosaur

disappear
disappoint
discipline
discuss
disease
dissatisfied
divided
doesn't
economical
efficient

eighth
elementary
eligible
embarrass
emphasize
endeavor
environment
equipment
especially
etiquette

exaggerate
excellent
excitement
exercise
exhausted
existence
expense
experienced
extraordinary
familiar

fascinating
fatigue
February
feminine
fiéry
financial
foreign
forfeit
fourth
fragile

generally
genius
government
governor
grammar
grateful
guarantee
guard
gymnasium
handkerchief

happened
harass
haven't
height
heroes
hindrance
hoping
horizon
hospital
humorous

imitation
immediately
incident
inconvenience
indispensable
inevitable
influence
initial
interpreted
interrupted

irrelevant
irresistible
jewelry
laboratory
leisure
license
lightning
likelihood
literacy
loneliness

losing
luxurious
maintenance
maneuver
marriage
matinee
meant
medicine
medieval
mentioned

microphone
minimum
mischievous
missile
misspelled
movable
municipal
necessary
neighbors
nickel

ninety
ninth
nonsense
noticeable
nuclear
nuisance
occasionally
occur
occurred
omitted

opinion
opportunity
optimistic
pamphlet
parallel
parliament
particularly
pastime
permanent
permissible

perseverance
personally
personnel
perspiration
persuade
playwright
pleasant
pneumonia
possess
possibility

potato
practice
preference
prejudice
privilege
probably
procedure
professor
pronunciation
propaganda

propeller
prophecy
psychology
pursue
questionnaire
realize
receive
recognize
recommend
referral

rehearse
reign
relief
repetition
representative
restaurant
rhythm
satisfactorily
schedule
scissors

seize
semester
separate
sergeant
shiny
siege
similar
sincerely
souvenir
straight

strategy
subtle
successful
sufficient
suppress
surprised
suspension
syllable
sympathy
synonym

tariff
television
temperament
temperature
thoroughly
tomorrow
tournament
traffic
tragedy
transferred

twelfth
tyranny
undoubtedly
unforgettable
unfortunately
unnecessary
vacuum
valuable
villain
weird

MECHANICS

PART THREE

RESOURCES

32 FORMAL SPEAKING AND DEBATE

Skills and Strategies

A formal speech is one that takes place at a specified time and location. You will use this type of public speaking in many different settings on many different occasions, but whenever you make a formal speech, you will usually have time to prepare the exact message you want to deliver at the appointed time.

Becoming an Effective Speaker

For every type of formal speaking, there are specific techniques and strategies you can use to help you effectively communicate your intended message to your audience and to evaluate and respond to a speech effectively when you are a member of an audience.

The more you prepare, plan, and practice for a speech, the more likely you are to be successful in accomplishing your purpose for speaking. Several important factors that you should consider in planning your speech include

- your purpose for speaking
- the topic you are speaking about
- the occasion for your speech and the audience you will be speaking to

Preparing a Speech

A good speech doesn't just happen. You have to analyze the situation to decide what will be appropriate, then make your plans and prepare your speech. The first step in preparing your speech is to identify your purpose for speaking. Some of the most common purposes are to inform, to persuade, or to entertain your audience.

PURPOSE	DESCRIPTION OF SPEECH	EXAMPLES OF SPEECH TITLES
To inform	gives facts *or* explains how to do something	New Ideas in Computer Technology How to Publish Your First Novel
To persuade	attempts to change an opinion *or* attempts to get listeners to act	Why Beagles Make Good Pets Why We Should Live Without Television
To entertain	relates to an amusing story or incident	The Dinner Date Disaster

Selecting a Topic

Sometimes your speech topic will be assigned, but often you will be able to choose your own topic. If so, remember to focus on something you're interested in. If you're not interested in your subject, your audience will also lose interest. In selecting your topic, you will probably consider the answers to the following questions.

- *What is your overall purpose in speaking?* Do you want to inform, persuade, or entertain your listeners?
- *What is the occasion for the speech?* Will the topic you have chosen fit the occasion?
- *How much time will you have?* Have you limited your speech topic to a manageable length?

Analyzing Your Audience

In planning your speech and focusing your topic, you will also need to consider your audience's needs and interests.

AUDIENCE CONSIDERATIONS		
QUESTIONS ABOUT AUDIENCE	EVALUATION	YOUR SPEECH WILL NEED
What does the audience already know about this subject?	very little	to provide background or details to better inform your listeners
	a little	to include some background details
	a lot	to focus on interesting aspects or issues
How interested will the audience be in this subject?	very interested	to maintain their interest
	somewhat interested	to focus on aspects that most interest them
	uninterested	to focus on persuading your listeners that this topic is important

Organizing Speech Notes and Materials

Once you have identified and focused the topic for your speech so that it suits your overall purpose, you will need to gather and organize the information you plan to present.

☞ REFERENCE NOTE: For more details about researching information, see pages 412–417 and 959–966.

The most common type of speech, the one most often used by experienced public speakers, is an ***extemporaneous speech*** that is prepared but not memorized. When you organize your materials for an extemporaneous speech, you first write out a complete outline of your speech. Then you prepare note cards that you can refer to when you are presenting your speech.

GUIDELINES FOR SPEECH NOTE CARDS

1. Put only one key idea, possibly accompanied by a brief example or detail, on each card.
2. Make a special note card for material that you plan to read word for word, such as a quotation, a series of dates, or a list of statistics.
3. Make a special note card to indicate when you should pause to show a visual, such as a chart, diagram, graph, picture, or model.
4. Number your completed cards to keep them in order.

Practicing Your Speech

Once you have written your outline and made your speech notes, you're ready to practice delivering your speech. To give a successful speech, you'll need to rehearse your presentation. Remember that there are only three aspects of your speech that your audience can judge by, and that you can improve all of these with practice: your ideas, your body, and your voice.

Your Ideas.   These are expressed in your written speech outline and transferred onto your speech notes. Practice until you are comfortable and familiar with what you plan to say. Try to use expressive words that help your listeners visualize clearly what you want them to understand.

Your Body.   Your speech will be more effective if you use "body language" that reinforces the impression you intend to make.
- *Stand confidently.* Look alert and interested in what you're saying.
- *Use natural gestures.* Use relaxed, normal gestures as you speak.

■ *Make direct eye contact with your audience.* When you look at various people in your audience, it makes them feel that you are speaking *with* them rather than speaking *at* them.

Your Voice.   Speak clearly and loudly enough so everyone in the audience can hear. Use a normal variety of vocal patterns so that your voice is interesting to listen to.

■ *Volume.* You always need to be loud enough to be heard, but you can also raise and lower your volume for emphasis as you speak.

■ *Pitch.* Use the natural rise and fall of your voice to emphasize various ideas and avoid a monotone.

■ *Stress.* Emphasize important words or phrases.

■ *Rate.* Generally, you should speak at a comfortable, relaxed pace, although you can vary your rate or pause briefly where it's effective for emphasis.

Delivering a Speech

There are several methods that you can use to present a speech. The speaking occasion usually determines the type of method that you should choose when you present a speech.

METHODS OF DELIVERING A SPEECH		
TYPE OF SPEECH	ADVANTAGES	DISADVANTAGES
Manuscript speech (read to audience word for word from a prepared script)	provides exact words you wish to say; less chance of errors or omissions	doesn't permit audience feedback; tends to be dull
Memorized speech (memorized word for word from a script and recited to the audience)	gives speaker freedom to move around and look at audience	may not sound natural; requires much practice and memorization; risk of forgetting speech

(continued)

METHODS OF DELIVERING A SPEECH *(continued)*		
TYPE OF SPEECH	ADVANTAGES	DISADVANTAGES
Extemporaneous speech (outlined and carefully prepared, but not memorized; speech notes often used)	sounds natural; allows speaker to respond to audience in a natural manner	requires practice and preparation
Impromptu speech (given on the spur of the moment, without preparation or notes)	sounds very natural	can sound disorganized, not suited for formal speech

Speeches given on radio or television often use the manuscript method in order to stay within rigid time limits. Speeches given in contests or for formal programs are often memorized. Impromptu speeches are given whenever an unexpected short speech is required.

However, for a prepared speech delivered to a live audience, the extemporaneous method is usually the most effective. Audiences respond best to extemporaneous speeches because they sound natural and provide more opportunities for interaction between the speaker and the audience.

Speaking Effectively

It's normal to feel nervous before you give your speech. But it's important not to allow nervousness to distract you or affect your speaking. Here are some suggestions that can help.

1. *Be prepared.* Avoid excessive nervousness by organizing and being familiar with your speech notes and visuals.
2. *Practice your speech.* Rehearse as if you're giving your actual presentation.
3. *Focus on your purpose for speaking.* Think about what you want your listeners to do, believe, or feel as a result of your speech.

RESOURCES

Active Listening

Hearing is a passive process, but listening requires you to think as well as hear. There are some specific procedures that you can follow to help you listen effectively to a speaker and evaluate what you hear.

Listening Politely

When you listen to a speaker, you need to be sure that you have given the speaker a fair opportunity to express his or her message. The speaker responds to you as a listener, depending on how well it appears you are paying attention.

Here's how to be a courteous and encouraging listener.

1. *Respect the speaker.* Be tolerant of individual differences. Show respect for the speaker's cultural background, such as customs, race, or religion.
2. *Don't interrupt.* Wait until the speaker finishes.
3. *Pay attention.* Don't distract others.
4. *Keep an open mind.* Try to understand the speaker's point of view. Also, be aware of how your own point of view affects the way you evaluate the opinions and values of others.
5. *Don't judge too soon.* Wait to hear the speaker's whole message before you make judgments about the speech.

Using the LQ2R Method

The LQ2R study method is especially helpful when you are listening to a speaker who is giving information.

L   *Listen* carefully to material as it is being presented. Focus your attention on the speaker.

Q   *Question* yourself as you listen. Make a list, mentally or by taking notes, of questions that occur to you.

R   *Recite* in your own words the information as it is being presented. Summarize information in your mind or jot down notes as you listen.

R   *Re-listen* as the speaker concludes the presentation. Major points may be reemphasized.

RESOURCES

Listening Critically

When you listen in order to evaluate a speech, you are listening critically. Critical listening is important whenever a speaker is presenting information that is new to you or when a speaker is trying to persuade you to accept his or her opinions about an issue.

To sway their listeners, speakers may use *propaganda devices*. **Propaganda devices** are statements, often based on invalid arguments, that attempt to convince listeners to believe in something or to take some action. The mass media, such as television, radio, and newspapers, often feature paid advertisements that use propaganda or persuasive devices to influence you. If you learn to recognize propaganda devices, you will be able to weigh the evidence of a speaker's arguments without being swayed by misleading appeals. (See pages 288–292 for more about persuasive methods.)

When you listen to a speech, you can't possibly remember every word the speaker says. However, if you listen critically, you'll be able to find the parts of the speaker's message that are most important.

GUIDELINES FOR LISTENING CRITICALLY

Find main ideas.	What are the most important points? Listen for clue words a speaker might use, such as *major, main, most important,* or similar words.
Identify significant details.	What dates, names, or facts does the speaker use to support the main points of the speech? What kinds of examples or explanations are used to support the main ideas?
Distinguish between facts and opinions.	A fact is a statement that can be proved to be true. An opinion is a belief or a judgment about something; it cannot be proved to be true.

RESOURCES

GUIDELINES FOR LISTENING CRITICALLY *(continued)*	
Identify the order of organization.	What kind of order does the speaker use to arrange the presentation—time sequence, spatial order, order of importance?
Note comparisons and contrasts.	What details are compared or contrasted with others?
Understand cause and effect.	What events are related to or affect others?
Predict outcomes and draw conclusions.	What reasonable conclusions can you make from the facts and evidence from the speech?

☞ REFERENCE NOTE: For help with interpreting and analyzing information, see pages 1010–1012.

Debating

A formal debate involves two groups, or teams, who publicly discuss a controversial topic in a systematic way. The topic under discussion is called the *proposition.* One team, the *affirmative team,* argues that the proposition should be accepted or adopted. The other side, the *negative team,* argues that the proposition should be rejected. To win the debate, the affirmative side must present enough proof to establish its case.

Stating a Debate Proposition

The central issue in a debate is stated as a proposition that is phrased as a resolution and limited to a specific idea. The proposition should be an issue that is actually debatable, and should offer each side an equal chance to build a reasonable case. The proposition should be clearly stated in language that is understandable to the debaters and to the audience.

DEBATE PROPOSITIONS		
TYPE	**DEFINITION**	**EXAMPLE**
Proposition of fact	determines what is true or false	*Resolved:* That the ozone layer is depleted by synthetic products.
Proposition of value	states the value of a person, place, or thing	*Resolved:* That American students can compete with foreign students in all areas of study.
Proposition of policy	determines what action should be taken	*Resolved:* That the United States should adopt national health insurance for all citizens.

Preparing a Debate Brief

To be an effective debater you must prepare thoroughly: you must research the proposition and plan a strategy for the debate.

1. *Research the proposition.* Consult reference books to obtain information. Record facts and evidence on note cards.
2. *Identify specific issues.* The **issues** in a debate are the main differences between the affirmative and the negative positions. Every debatable proposition rests on several issues. To prove your proposition, list all the arguments you have for supporting your side of the proposition. To refute your opposition, list all the reasons you think your opponents will give for disagreeing with your views.
3. *Support your arguments.* Based on the information gathered during your research, identify evidence that supports your arguments—examples, quotations, statistics, expert opinions, analogies, and logic. Also, find evidence that will refute arguments your opponents are likely to use.

4. *Build a brief.* A *brief* is an outline for debate. It contains a logical arrangement of all the arguments needed to prove or disprove a proposition, as well as the evidence you have gathered to support your arguments.

EXCERPT OF A BRIEF—OPPOSING ARGUMENTS

Resolved: That the U.S. jury system should be significantly changed.

Affirmative

I. Jury trials in civil cases cause unfair delay and clog the courts.
    A.   Only a few jury cases can be heard at a time; others must await trial. A survey by the Institute of Judicial Administration showed an average delay of 13.3 months.
    B.   Delay only helps wrongdoers.
        1. The memory and the availability of witnesses diminishes.
        2. Delays may cause wronged parties to give up their cases.
    C.   Delays force the innocent to wait before clearing themselves.

II. Jury trials waste time and money.
    A.   They take the time of courts, participants, and jurors.
    B.   They add to court costs, including juror payment.
    C.   In New York city alone, jury service each year is equal to 50,000 people taken from their jobs for ten days--a huge loss of time and money to jurors' businesses.

III. Juries should be composed of fewer than twelve members.
    A.   There is no specific reason for having twelve jurors.
    B.   States that use smaller juries--with eight or even six jurors-- report no reduction in the administration of justice.
    C.   If juries were smaller, fewer jury members would need to be challenged: costs would be cut and verdicts reached sooner.

Negative

I. Court congestion is not caused by jury trial alone but by
    A.   Increasing population
    B.   Government failure to provide enough judges and courts.

II. The jury system does not waste time, money, or human energy.
    A.   It costs little compared to other government expenditures.
    B.   Jury expense represents only 1/170 of 1% of total costs in Federal courts, or only $1 for each $17,000 spent.
    C.   In a University of Chicago survey of jurors, 94% said they'd serve again, 3% were very willing, and only 3% were unwilling.

III. The proposal to reduce the size of juries hides many dangers.
    A.   It might represent a first step in eliminating juries entirely.
    B.   Ethnically diverse citizens are less likely to be represented.

Refuting the Opposing Arguments

In addition to building a strong case for or against the proposition, each of the teams in a debate must argue against its opponents' case. To refute, or attack, your opponents' arguments, you should

- state clearly the arguments you are going to refute
- tell the audience how you plan to refute the argument
- present proof to refute the argument by using facts, statistics, quotations, and other supporting data or evidence
- explain how the proof you have presented effectively refutes your opponents' arguments

Building a Rebuttal

The rebuttal should attempt to rebuild your case. This part of the debate allows each of the opposing sides a chance to repair the arguments that have been attacked by their opponents during the refutation. An effective rebuttal should

- restate your original arguments
- state your position on the issues your opponents have already attacked
- present proof that supports your arguments
- point out any weaknesses in your opponents' arguments
- summarize your original arguments and present any additional evidence you have gathered that supports your position

Participating in a Debate

Good debaters are courteous. Ridicule, sarcasm, or personal attacks are not acceptable. Do not deliberately misquote your opponents or attempt to distract or disturb them. A debate should be won or lost only on the basis of reasoned argument and convincing delivery.

It is customary to refer to participants in a debate by using, instead of names, polite terms such as "The first affirmative speaker," "My worthy opponents," "My colleagues," or "My teammates."

Speaking Order for a Debate

Most debates are divided into two parts. During the first part, both teams make *constructive speeches,* attempting to "build" their cases by presenting their arguments for or against the proposition, and attempting to refute, or disprove, the points they believe will be raised by the opposing team. After an intermission, the second part of the debate begins, and both teams make *rebuttal speeches,* trying to reply to damaging arguments raised by the opposing team in their closing speeches. Specific time limits are assigned for each speech, although these limits vary, depending on the type of debate.

ORDER OF SPEAKING FOR A STANDARD DEBATE

1. CONSTRUCTIVE SPEECHES	2. REBUTTAL SPEECHES
a. First affirmative	a. First negative
b. First negative	b. First affirmative
c. Second affirmative	c. Second negative
d. Second negative	d. Second affirmative

Cross-Examination Debate Format.   Opposing teams, in a cross-examination debate, have the opportunity to question the opponents' major points immediately after each constructive speech. This style of debate tests a debater's ability to think critically and respond quickly.

ORDER OF SPEAKING FOR A CROSS-EXAMINATION DEBATE

1. CONSTRUCTIVE SPEECHES
   a. First affirmative constructive
   b. Cross-examination by second negative
   c. First negative constructive
   d. Cross-examination by first affirmative
   e. Second affirmative constructive
   f. Cross-examination by first negative
   g. Second negative constructive
   h. Cross-examination by second affirmative

(continued)

> **ORDER OF SPEAKING FOR
> A CROSS-EXAMINATION DEBATE** *(continued)*
>
> 2. REBUTTAL SPEECHES
>   a. First negative rebuttal
>   b. First affirmative rebuttal
>   c. Second negative rebuttal
>   d. Second affirmative rebuttal

Lincoln-Douglas Debate. A Lincoln-Douglas debate has only one speaker on each team. Also, propositions in this type of debate are always propositions of value rather than propositions of fact or policy.

This one-on-one debate format is often used when opposing candidates for political office debate in the presence of voters. The name commemorates the sensational series of debates between rival political candidates, Abraham Lincoln and Stephen Douglas.

> **ORDER OF SPEAKING FOR
> A LINCOLN-DOUGLAS DEBATE**
>
> 1. CONSTRUCTIVE SPEECH
>   a. Affirmative constructive
>   b. Cross-examination by negative
>   c. Negative constructive
>   d. Cross-examination by affirmative
> 2. REBUTTAL SPEECHES
>   a. Affirmative rebuttal
>   b. Negative rebuttal
>   c. Affirmative rebuttal

RESOURCES

Conducting and Judging a Debate

A chairperson often presides during the debate. A speaker may appeal to the chairperson if he or she believes that any debating procedures or time limits have been violated by the opposing team.

The most common method of determining the winner of a debate is by decision of three appointed judges. The judges are expected to base their decision on the merits of the debate and not on their own views of the proposition. Occasionally, an audience may vote to determine the winning team.

▶ EXERCISE 1 **Preparing and Giving a Speech**

Choose a topic for a three- to five-minute speech to present to your English class, considering the occasion and the interests of your listeners when selecting a topic. Identify your purpose for speaking. Gather material, make an outline, and prepare note cards. Include at least one visual. Then deliver your speech, using effective speaking techniques.

▶ EXERCISE 2 **Listening Critically**

Listen to a short speech presented by a classmate, by your teacher, or on television or radio. Take brief notes. Then answer the following questions about the speech.

1. Identify the purpose of the speech.
2. What are the main ideas expressed in the speech?
3. What details support or explain the key ideas in the speech?
4. In what ways did the speaker's body language and voice contribute to the message of the speech?
5. Did the speaker achieve the purpose he or she intended? Explain why or why not.

▶ EXERCISE 3 **Preparing a Debate Brief**

Divide the class into groups of four or six members. Each group will either select one of the following general topics or choose their own. Then the group will write a specific debate proposition. Each group will then divide into affirmative and negative teams, research the topic, and prepare written debate briefs, using the example on page 942 as a model.

1. Animal rights
2. Lie detector tests
3. Equal rights amendment
4. Year-round school year
5. Crime and law enforcement
6. Censorship of music
7. Raising the driving age
8. Energy conservation
9. Compulsory military service
10. Mass transit

▶ EXERCISE 4   **Conducting a Debate**

Stage a debate, using the affirmative and negative teams, the debate proposition, and the briefs developed for Exercise 3. Select one of the debate formats discussed on pages 944–946 for conducting a debate and assign specific time limits for each stage of the procedure. Appoint a chairperson to preside over the debate. Either select judges or create a ballot for use by the whole class when deciding the outcome of the debate.

33 COMMUNICATION SKILLS

Types and Techniques

Communicating requires skill in both speaking and listening. You might think that communicating simply means talking. However, communication is complex. It occurs in many different settings and under a variety of circumstances, but its purpose is always the same: to share information or ideas. To improve your ability to communicate, you can practice your speaking skills.

The Communication Cycle

Communication is a two-way process. A speaker expresses feelings or ideas, and the listener (or listeners) responds to the speaker's message. This response is called *feedback.* Listener feedback may be in the form of a verbal response (words) or a nonverbal response (gestures, facial expressions, body language, or nonword sounds such as sighs or giggles).

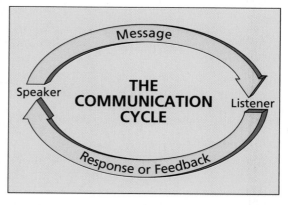

Message

Speaker

THE COMMUNICATION CYCLE

Listener

Response or Feedback

Giving and Receiving Information

In some of the simplest communication situations, the purpose is to transmit specific items of information. For situations of this type, successful communication takes place whenever the speaker is clear and precise and whenever the listener clearly understands the information that the speaker is attempting to convey. This type of communication exchange includes occasions when someone is giving or receiving instructions or directions and giving or receiving telephone messages. The following chart contains suggestions for improving your effectiveness in situations of this type whether you are the speaker or the listener.

GIVING AND RECEIVING DIRECTIONS	
Giving	**Receiving**
Make each step as simple and easy to understand as possible. Explain the steps in an order that makes sense.	Listen to each step. Look for transitional words that tell you when each step of the process ends and the next one begins, such as *first, second, next, then, last,* and *finally*.
Remember to include every step or all the necessary information.	Listen carefully so that you can keep track of the number of steps and their order. In your mind, picture yourself doing each step. Take notes if necessary.
Repeat all directions or instructions so that the other person can remember them.	Make sure you have all the necessary information and that you understand the directions. Ask questions if you are unclear about any steps.

RESOURCES

Here are suggestions for improving your effectiveness when you are giving or receiving telephone messages.

GIVING AND RECEIVING TELEPHONE MESSAGES	
Making Calls	**Receiving Calls**
If you reach the wrong number, tell the person who answers that you are sorry for the disturbance.	Be understanding if someone dials your number in error. Everyone makes mistakes.
Avoid calling early in the morning, late at night, or at mealtimes.	If someone calls at an inconvenient time, ask if you may return the call later.
Say who you are as soon as the person answers. If the person you're calling is not there, leave your name and number and a short message.	Say hello when you answer. Take a message if the call is for someone who is out. Repeat the message to make sure you wrote it correctly.
Don't stay on the phone too long. If you place the call, it's your responsibility to end it.	If you need to end the call, say politely that you need to go. You might offer to call back at another time.

Interviewing

An *interview* is a communication situation in which the object is to exchange ideas or information. You might take part in an interview to gather information, apply for a job, or apply for admission to a college.

Conducting an Interview

At times when you are preparing a research paper, a class report, a speech, or a newspaper article, you may need to interview certain people for firsthand information. Some suggestions about how you can be an effective interviewer follow.

Preparing for the Interview

- Make arrangements well in advance. Set up a time that is convenient for the other person to meet with you.
- Make a list of questions to ask. Make sure the questions are arranged in a logical order and require more than yes or no answers.

Participating in the Interview

- Arrive on time and be polite and patient.
- Ask the other person's permission if you plan to take notes or use a tape recorder.
- Avoid argument. Be tactful and courteous. Remember, the interview was granted at your request.
- Listen carefully and ask follow-up questions if you do not understand an answer or if you think you need more information.

Following up on the Interview

- Review your notes to refresh your memory, and then make a summary of the material you have gathered.
- Send a note expressing your appreciation for the interview.

Interviewing for a Position

When you apply for a position such as a job, an employer will usually require an interview with you before agreeing to hire you. Other situations for which you may be interviewed for a position require the same general preparations.

HOW TO INTERVIEW FOR A POSITION

1. *Arrange an appointment.* Write a business letter of application in which you request an interview for the job. If you are granted an interview, be prompt for your appointment.
2. *Bring a résumé.* If you haven't already submitted a résumé, take your résumé to the interview and give it to the interviewer.

(continued)

RESOURCES

> **HOW TO INTERVIEW FOR A POSITION** *(continued)*
>
> 3. *Be neat and well-groomed.* It's important to look your best when you are interviewing to apply for any type of job.
> 4. *Answer questions clearly and honestly.* Answer the questions the interviewer asks, adding any additional information that might inform the employer that you are the right person for the job.
> 5. *Ask questions.* Questions that job applicants usually ask include requests for information about work hours, salary, or chances for advancement. By your questions, show that you know something about the company or business.
> 6. *Be prepared to be tested.* The employer may require you to take tests that demonstrate your skills, intelligence, or personality.
> 7. *Follow up the interview.* After the interview, write a short thank-you note. Tell the interviewer that you appreciated the opportunity for the interview and that you look forward to hearing from the company in the near future.

☞ REFERENCE NOTE: For more about writing a letter of application and preparing a résumé, see pages 999–1001.

Group Discussions

Groups of every kind—cooperative learning groups, school clubs, city councils, parent and teacher groups, community organizations, labor unions, legislative assemblies—communicate through group discussions.

There are many types of group discussions. However, each group discussion has a specific purpose. Some of the most common purposes for group discussions are

- to share ideas
- to suggest solutions for solving a problem
- to make an evaluation, decision, or recommendation

RESOURCES

When a group is establishing the purpose to be accomplished by its discussion, one important factor to be considered is the time available. If there is a specific limit on the time for discussion, the group will need to set a goal that can be accomplished in the time allowed.

Informal Group Discussions

An informal group discussion is one that usually takes place between members of a group small enough to allow everyone to participate without using parliamentary procedures.

Effective group discussions require that each participant play a role. In a discussion each role has specific responsibilities. For example, a chairperson may be elected (or appointed) whose task is to keep the discussion moving smoothly. Another group member may serve as secretary, or reporter, taking notes during the discussion.

In its discussion, a group may follow a prepared outline, or *agenda,* of topics in the order they will be discussed. In some groups, the chairperson sets the agenda; in others, the agenda is established by a preliminary discussion and is agreed upon by the members.

Here are some of the responsibilities of members of a group discussion.

A Chairperson's Responsibilities

1. Announce the topic and explain the agenda.
2. Follow the agenda, keeping the discussion on the topics to be considered.
3. Encourage participation by each member.
4. Avoid disagreements by being objective and settling conflicts or confusions fairly.

A Secretary's or Reporter's Responsibilities

1. Make notes of significant information or actions.
2. Prepare a final report.

A Participant's Responsibilities

1. Take part in the discussion
2. Cooperate with other members, being fair and considerate of others' opinions and suggestions.

RESOURCES

Formal Group Discussions

Clubs, organizations, and other groups often meet on a regular basis to discuss issues of importance to the entire group. To conduct effective meetings, formal groups often follow an established set of rules known as *parliamentary procedure.* The single most authoritative source is a book called *Robert's Rules of Order, Revised* by Henry Robert.

The basic principles of parliamentary procedure as found in *Robert's Rules of Order* protect the rights of individual members of the group while providing a systematic means for dealing with issues that come before the group for a decision.

Here are some of the basic principles of parliamentary procedure:

- The majority decides.
- The minority has the right to be heard.
- Decisions are made by voting.

The benefit of parliamentary procedure is that it allows a group of individuals to deal in an orderly, organized way with issues that are raised and decisions that the group needs to make about those issues. This system of organized procedures provides the following advantages:

- Only one issue is decided at a time.
- Everyone is assured of the chance to be heard, everyone has the right to vote, and all votes are counted as equal.
- All sides of an issue are debated in open discussion.

RESOURCES

ORDER OF BUSINESS

A formal group meeting usually follows the standard order of business suggested in *Robert's Rules of Order:*

1. *Call to order:* The chairperson says, "The meeting will come to order."
2. *Reading and approval of the minutes:* The chairperson says, "The secretary (or recorder) will read the minutes from our last meeting." The secretary reads these minutes, and the chairperson inquires, "Are there any additions or corrections to the minutes?" The minutes are then approved, or they are corrected and then approved.

(continued)

ORDER OF BUSINESS *(continued)*

3. *Officers' reports:* The chairperson calls for a report from other officers who need to report, as by saying, "Will the treasurer please give us a report?"
4. *Committee reports:* The chairperson may ask the presiding officer of standing committees and then of special committees to make reports to the group.
5. *Old business:* Any issues that have not been fully resolved at the last meeting may now be discussed. The chairperson may ask the group, "Is there any old business to be discussed?"
6. *New business:* Any new issues that have not previously been discussed may now be addressed.
7. *Announcements:* The chairperson may ask the members, "Are there any announcements?"
8. *Adjournment:* The chairperson ends the meeting, saying, "The meeting is now adjourned."

PROCEDURES FOR DISCUSSION OF BUSINESS

The meeting follows specific procedures for discussion of business.

1. Anyone who wishes to speak must be recognized by the chairperson.
2. A participant may introduce a motion, or proposal, for discussion, by beginning "I move that . . . "
3. To support the motion, another member must second it, saying "I second the motion." A motion that is not seconded is dropped.
4. A motion that has been seconded may be discussed by the group.
5. Other motions made by members may amend the motion under consideration; may postpone, limit, or extend debate or discussion; or may refer the motion to a committee for further research.
6. After discussion, the group votes on the motion. The chairperson usually votes only in the case of a tie.

RESOURCES

Oral Interpretation

Oral interpretation involves the presentation of a work of literature to a group of listeners in order to express the meaning contained in the literary work. You might use acting as well as speaking skills—vocal techniques, facial expression, body language, and gestures—to express the overall meaning of the literary work.

Adapting Material

When you are adapting material for an oral interpretation, you usually have a specific purpose and audience in mind. Every occasion has its own requirements. Be sure you have thought about factors such as the length of time that will be allowed for your presentation and your audience's interests. As a general rule, no props or costumes are provided for oral interpretations; instead, performers usually rely on the imagination of the audience to provide the scenery and other dramatic enhancements.

For your oral interpretation, you will need to make an abbreviated version, or *cutting,* of a work of fiction or nonfiction, a long poem, or a play.

HOW TO MAKE A CUTTING

1. Follow the story line of the literary work in time order.
2. Delete dialogue tags such as *she replied sadly*. Instead, use these clues to tell you how to interpret the character's words as you express them.
3. Delete passages that don't contribute to the overall effect or impression you intend to create with your oral interpretation.

Presenting an Oral Interpretation

For your interpretation you may need to write an introduction that sets the scene, tells something about the author, or gives some necessary details about what has already taken place in the story.

The common practice, when presenting an oral interpretation, is to prepare a *reading script*. A reading script is usually typed (double-spaced) and can be marked to assist you in your interpretive reading. For example, you might underline words to remind you to use special emphasis, or mark a slash (/) to indicate where you'd like a dramatic pause.

Once you have developed a reading script, rehearse several different interpretations until you are satisfied that you have chosen the most effective manner of expressing the meaning of the selection.

Use your voice in a manner that suits your presentation. Pronounce words carefully. You can use your body and your voice to show that you are portraying different characters. Use body language and gestures to emphasize the meaning or to reveal traits of the major characters in the story as you narrate and act out what they say and do.

Review

EXERCISE 1 **Planning an Interview**

Select a topic that requires firsthand information from an individual. Design a checklist that includes setting up the interview, doing research, and preparing questions to ask the person being interviewed. Make sure that your questions are organized, and clear, and that they require thoughtful responses.

EXERCISE 2 **Preparing for a Job Interview**

Check the classified section of a local newspaper and find a job that you might like and for which you are qualified. List the questions that you would expect an interviewer to ask you and the answers you would provide. Also, make a list of questions you would ask the interviewer about the job or position.

EXERCISE 3 **Practicing a College Interview**

Working with a partner, make a list of questions you would likely be asked by a college admissions officer. Then make a list of questions you might ask this representative of the college you might attend. Have one person act as the interviewer and the other as the person being interviewed. Present the interview in class and respond to the feedback from your classmate.

▶ EXERCISE 4 **Presenting a Group Discussion**

Your class is to select one of the following broad subjects and narrow the focus to a specific topic. The purpose of this discussion should be to share ideas and suggest solutions to a problem. Work in groups small enough to allow thorough discusion of the topic. Select a reporter to convey your group's findings to the class.

1. Choosing a career
2. Professional vs. amateur sports
3. Vandalism
4. Prejudice
5. American foreign policy

▶ EXERCISE 5 **Presenting an Oral Interpretation**

Select a portion of a literary work suitable for an oral presentation and adapt the material for a short presentation to your class. First, prepare a reading script. Second, write an introduction that tells the author and title of the selection and that provides enough background information so that your audience can understand the meaning of the scene. Then, present your material in class.

34 THE LIBRARY/ MEDIA CENTER

Finding and Using Information

For centuries, libraries have been storehouses for information recorded in manuscripts, books, newspapers, and other written forms. In the past few decades, information has also become increasingly available in other forms, such as audio and video recordings and computer programs. With the addition of these nonprint forms, the library is now often called a media center or media resource center.

The Librarian

To find books in the library, you need to know how they're classified and arranged. If you need help finding specific information, don't hesitate to ask your librarian. Librarians are professionals trained to track down information; they can show you how to use the library's resources effectively. Also, a librarian may be able to find information for you by borrowing sources from other libraries.

Finding Books in the Library

The Call Number

In most libraries, books are assigned *call numbers* to identify each book and indicate where it's shelved. Call numbers are assigned according to one of two classification systems: the *Dewey decimal system* or the *Library of Congress system*.

The Dewey Decimal System

Nonfiction.   In the Dewey decimal system, nonfiction books and some works of literature are grouped by subject into ten general subject areas, each assigned a range of numbers. Within this range, subgroups of numbers identify more specific categories.

DEWEY DECIMAL CLASSIFICATION SYSTEM		
NUMBERS	SUBJECT AREAS	EXAMPLES OF SUBDIVISIONS
000–099	General Works	encyclopedias, periodicals, bibliographies
100–199	Philosophy	psychology, ethics, personality
200–299	Religion	theology, bibles, mythology
300–399	Social Science	economics, education, government, law
400–499	Philology or Language	grammar, dictionaries, foreign languages
500–599	Science	biology, chemistry, geology, mathematics
600–699	Technology	agriculture, engineering, health, medical science, environment
700–799	The Arts	motion pictures, music, painting, photography, sports
800–899	Literature	criticism, drama, essays, poetry
900–999	History	archaeology, geography, travel, collective biographies

NOTE: Some libraries use the letter *R* before the call numbers of reference books in any of these categories.

Fiction. The Dewey decimal system groups books of fiction together in alphabetical order according to the authors' last names. Works of fiction by the same author are arranged alphabetically by the first important word of the title (excluding *A*, *An*, and *The*). Collections of short stories may be grouped separately from novels.

NOTE: Authors' names that begin with *Mc* are alphabetized as *Mac*. Names beginning with *St.* are alphabetized as *Saint*.

The Library of Congress System

The Library of Congress system uses code letters to identify subject categories. The first letter of a book's call number tells the general category. The second letter tells the subcategory. The librarian can provide you with a complete list of letter codes for Library of Congress categories and subcategories.

LIBRARY OF CONGRESS CLASSIFICATION SYSTEM	
GENERAL CATEGORIES	
A General Works	M Music
B Philosophy, Psychology, Religion	N Fine Arts
	P Language and Literature
C–F History	Q Science
G Geography, Anthropology, Recreation	R Medicine
	S Agriculture
H Social Science	T Technology
J Political Science	U Military Science
K Law	V Naval Science
L Education	Z Bibliography and Library Science

RESOURCES

The Card Catalog

The *card catalog* is a cabinet of drawers filled with alphabetically arranged cards: *title cards*, *author cards*, and *subject cards*. You may also find cross-reference cards that advise you where to look for additional information. Catalog cards may give publication facts, list the number of pages, and tell whether the book contains illustrations or diagrams.

INFORMATION IN THE CARD CATALOG

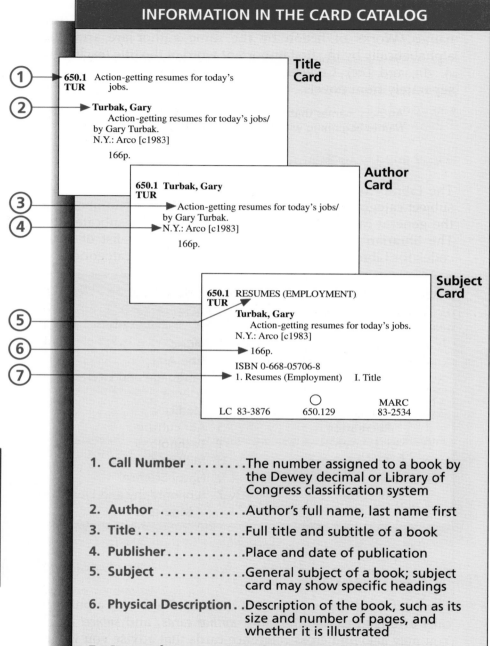

Title Card

(1) → 650.1 Action-getting resumes for today's
     TUR   jobs.

(2) → **Turbak, Gary**
         Action-getting resumes for today's jobs/
     by Gary Turbak.
     N.Y.: Arco [c1983]
         166p.

Author Card

650.1 **Turbak, Gary**
TUR
(3) → Action-getting resumes for today's jobs/
     by Gary Turbak.
(4) → N.Y.: Arco [c1983]
         166p.

Subject Card

650.1 RESUMES (EMPLOYMENT)
TUR
         Turbak, Gary
             Action-getting resumes for today's jobs.
         N.Y.: Arco [c1983]
(6) →   166p.
         ISBN 0-668-05706-8
(7) →   1. Resumes (Employment)   I. Title
                         ○
     LC 83-3876   650.129   MARC
                                 83-2534

1. **Call Number** . . . . .The number assigned to a book by the Dewey decimal or Library of Congress classification system

2. **Author** . . . . .Author's full name, last name first

3. **Title**. . . . . .Full title and subtitle of a book

4. **Publisher**. . . . . .Place and date of publication

5. **Subject** . . . . .General subject of a book; subject card may show specific headings

6. **Physical Description**. .Description of the book, such as its size and number of pages, and whether it is illustrated

7. **Cross-references** . . . .Refers to other headings or related topics where you can look for other books

The On-line Catalog

The *on-line catalog* is a computerized version of the card catalog. To view a catalog listing on a library's computer, you type in an author's name, a title, or a subject on the keyboard. The computer then displays on the screen the information that you'd find if you looked under this heading in the card catalog. The on-line catalog can locate information quickly and may tell you if a book you are looking for is checked out or if it is available at another library.

Using Reference Materials

The *Readers' Guide*

When you need to find a magazine article, use the *Readers' Guide to Periodical Literature*. It indexes articles, poems, and stories from more than one hundred magazines. As you can see in the following excerpt, the *Readers' Guide* gives a great amount of information in a very compact space.

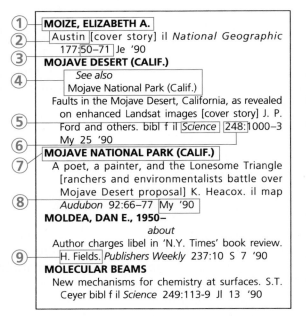

(1) **Author entry**

(2) **Title of article**

(3) **Page reference**

(4) **Subject cross-reference**

(5) **Name of magazine**

(6) **Volume number of magazine**

(7) **Subject entry**

(8) **Date of magazine**

(9) **Author of article**

RESOURCES

Throughout the year, paperback editions of the *Readers' Guide* are published. Each issue lists materials published two to four weeks previously. The paperback issues are then bound into a single, hardcover volume at the end of the year.

As the sample entry on page 963 shows, magazine articles are listed by subject and by author but not by title. The *Readers' Guide* also gives *"see"* and *"see also"* references. A key at the front of the *Readers' Guide* explains the meaning of the abbreviations used in entries.

The Vertical File

The *vertical file* is a file cabinet containing a variety of up-to-date materials. Libraries generally keep current pictures, pamphlets, newspaper clippings, and catalogs in special folders in the vertical file. Organized by subject, these materials often consist of government, business, or educational publications. Ask the librarian to help you use the vertical file to find current materials.

Microforms

To save space, many libraries photographically reduce periodicals and newspapers and store them on *microforms.* The two most common kinds of microforms are *microfilm* (a roll or reel of film) and *microfiche* (a sheet of film). The librarian can tell you if your library stores periodicals on microforms and, if so, where they are kept, and how you can view them.

Computers

Computer systems have become information networks. Large volumes of printed and visual materials can be stored on optical storage devices. In some libraries, you can access reference information on computers. Like the on-line catalog, reference materials are available in *databases*—collections of information that are stored on a computer for easy retrieval. The kinds of information you can find on a computer depend on what database systems the library has or is connected to.

Recorded Materials

Your library may have audiovisual materials that you can use to help you whenever you need to do research. For example, you might find audiocassettes of famous speeches or of well-known poets reading their works. On videotapes, you might find documentaries and other educational programs that relate to your research topic. Ask the librarian what audiovisual materials are available in the library.

Review

▶ EXERCISE 1   **Using the Card Catalog**

Use the card catalog to find the following books. For each book, give its title, author or editor, and call number.

1. a biography of Benjamin Franklin
2. a collection of plays by one of the following authors: Amiri Baraka, Tennessee Williams, or Lillian Hellman
3. a guide to colleges and universities
4. a collection of essays about American history
5. a recent book on movie making

▶ EXERCISE 2   **Using the *Readers' Guide***

In your school or neighborhood library find answers to the following questions about the *Readers' Guide*.

1. Where are the volumes of the *Readers' Guide* kept in this library?
2. What is the date of the most recent monthly issue of the *Readers' Guide* found in this library?
3. In the *Readers' Guide*, find a heading for an article on the subject of recycling. Write the title of the article, the name of the author, the name of the magazine, the date the article was published, and the page numbers listed for this article. In addition, list any *"see"* or *"see also"* references you find for this heading.

RESOURCES

4. Check in the *Readers' Guide* under a subject heading of a career that interests you. Write down the title, author, magazine, date, and page numbers for three articles listed.
5. List the title, author, name of the magazine, date, and page numbers of an entry for a review of a recent television program or movie that interests you.

EXERCISE 3 — Learning the Arrangement of Your Library

Draw a diagram of your school library, labeling the areas where the following resources are found. List, below your diagram, any items that you could not find.

1. the card catalog (or on-line catalog)
2. the fiction section
3. the reference section
4. the *Readers' Guide*
5. current magazines
6. the librarian's desk
7. the vertical file
8. microforms
9. computers
10. the checkout and return desk

RESOURCES

35 REFERENCE WORKS

Principal References and Their Uses

In the library you will find a special, separate section known as the *reference section*. Reference works contain facts and information organized in a way that makes it easier to find whatever information you need. If you are familiar with your library's reference books and other resources, you will have a wealth of information at your disposal.

The Reference Section of the Library

Through its many reference works, your library can give you answers to almost any question you can imagine. Become familiar with the location of the reference section in your library. Learn to be a more resourceful researcher, able to find information from a variety of sources.

Your library may contain references in a variety of forms. The most common type of references are found in books, but your library may also provide reference sources in other forms, such as on a computer database or in the form of microfilm or microfiche. Ask your librarian to tell you about the various types of reference works found in your library.

Common Reference Books

BOOKS OF SYNONYMS	
EXAMPLES	DESCRIPTION
Roget's International Thesaurus	uses a categorized index system of synonyms; words grouped into categories and subcategories
The New Roget's Thesaurus in Dictionary Form *Webster's New Dictionary of Synonyms*	list entries alphabetically, as in a dictionary

ENCYCLOPEDIAS	
EXAMPLES	DESCRIPTION
Collier's Encyclopedia *The Encyclopedia Americana* *The Encyclopaedia Britannica* *The World Book Encyclopedia*	multivolume works; articles arranged alphabetically by subject; may contain an index or an annual supplement
Lincoln Library of Essential Information *The New Columbia Encyclopedia* *The Random House Encyclopedia*	single-volume works; articles are briefer and less comprehensive in coverage than in multivolume encyclopedias

GENERAL BIOGRAPHICAL REFERENCE BOOKS	
EXAMPLE	DESCRIPTION
Biography Index	tells where to find books and periodicals with biographical information about specific, prominent people

OTHER BIOGRAPHICAL REFERENCE BOOKS

EXAMPLES	DESCRIPTION
Current Biography Yearbook	monthly issues, bound at year end; often has photographs
The International Who's Who *Webster's New Biographical Dictionary*	profile of famous people from many nationalities; give details about their birth, careers, and accomplishments
Who's Who in America *Who's Who Among Black Americans*	profiles of famous people, their lives, and their major accomplishments

LITERARY BIOGRAPHIES

EXAMPLES	DESCRIPTION
American Authors 1600–1900 *American Women Writers* (series) Magill's *Cyclopedia of World Authors* *Dictionary of Literary Biography* *Twentieth Century Authors*	profiles of authors; usually have details about dates of authors' birth or death, titles of major works and dates when they were published, awards or honors won

SPECIAL FIELD BIOGRAPHIES

EXAMPLES	DESCRIPTION
American Men and Women of Science *Biographical Dictionary of American Sports* (series) *A Biographical Dictionary of Film* Vasari's *Lives of the Most Eminent Painters, Sculptors, and Architects*	profiles of individuals who are famous for their distinctions or accomplishments in a specific field or career

RESOURCES

ATLASES

EXAMPLES	DESCRIPTION
Goode's World Atlas *Hammond Medallion World Atlas* *National Geographic Atlas of the World* *The New York Times Atlas of the World*	primarily, provide maps; may also give statistics about industries, raw materials, exports and imports, or climate of various countries or regions of the world

HISTORICAL ATLASES

EXAMPLES	DESCRIPTION
The American Heritage Pictorial Atlas of United States History *Atlas of World Cultures* Heyden's *Atlas of the Classical World* *Rand McNally Atlas of World History*	give graphic representations of significant historical changes, such as the rise and fall of empires, movement of peoples, and spread of cultures

ALMANACS AND YEARBOOKS

EXAMPLES	CONTENTS
The World Almanac and Book of Facts	summary of year's notable events; index in front
Information Please Almanac, Atlas and Yearbook	less formal and complete than *World Almanac;* articles may be more comprehensive
The International Year Book and Statesmen's Who's Who	facts about international organizations, nations of the world, and sketches of world leaders
Statistical Abstract of the United States	statistics on many topics, such as population, health and nutrition, education

INDEXES AND BIOGRAPHIES

EXAMPLES	DESCRIPTION
Art Index *Biography Index* *General Sciences Index* *The National Geographic* *Magazine Cumulative Index* *The New York Times Index* *Social Sciences Index*	provide information as a guide to articles found in periodicals or other information sources

A Biographical Guide to the
  Study of Western American
  Literature
Three Centuries of English
  and American Plays:
  A Checklist
World Historical Fiction Guide
	lists of books or articles; grouped by subject, author, or time period; annotated bibliographies include descriptions and notes

BOOKS OF QUOTATIONS

EXAMPLES	DESCRIPTION

Bartlett's *Familiar Quotations*
Flesch's *The New Book of*
  Unusual Quotations
The Oxford Dictionary of
  Quotations
	famous quotations; usually indexed by subject; some are arranged by author or time period; often tell author, date, and source of quotation

REFERENCES TO LITERATURE

EXAMPLES	DESCRIPTION
Granger's Index to Poetry	tells where to find specific poems; entries indexed by subject, by title, and by first line
Subject Index to Literature	tells where to find short stories and poems in collections or anthologies; entries indexed by subject

OTHER LITERATURE REFERENCE GUIDES

EXAMPLES	DESCRIPTION
Benét's Reader's Encyclopedia	contains information about works of literature, such as plots, main characters; also gives summaries of poems, descriptions of operas
Book Review Digest *Book Review Index* *Brewer's Dictionary of Phrase and Fable* *Essay and General Literature Index* *An Index to One-Act Plays* *Play Index* *Short Story Index*	guides to book reviews, essays, short stories, plays, poems, and other literary works that may be found in periodicals or in collections or anthologies

LITERATURE AND AUTHOR DIRECTORIES

EXAMPLES	DESCRIPTION
The Cambridge History of American Literature *Harper's Dictionary of Classical Literature and Antiquities* *The Oxford Companion to American Literature* *The Oxford Companion to English Literature*	contain information about authors and their major works; may include brief critiques of best-known works by specific authors or plot outlines of selected works; may offer information on literary movements or genres

CURRENT EVENTS RESOURCES

EXAMPLES	DESCRIPTION
Social Issues Resources Series (SIRS) (audiotapes, video-tapes, reprints of news-paper and magazine articles, photographs, letters, and posters)	up-to-date information on a number of important subjects, such as crime or family issues, scientific discoveries, or documents from the National Archives

SPECIAL REFERENCES FOR SPECIFIC SUBJECTS

EXAMPLES	DESCRIPTION
The Encyclopedia of American Facts and Dates *The Encyclopedia of Religion* *The International Encyclopedia of the Social Sciences* *Facts on File* (series of books and yearbooks) *The New Grove Dictionary of Music and Musicians* (series) *McGraw-Hill Encyclopedia of Science & Technology* *The Sports Encyclopedia* *Webster's New Geographical Dictionary*	contain information related to specific topics or of interest to researchers in specific fields; may include short biographies of major figures or evaluations of a person's major contributions to the particular field

COLLEGE REFERENCE BOOKS

EXAMPLES	DESCRIPTION
Barron's Index of College Majors	arranged by state; highlights majors offered at each school
Barron's Profile of American Colleges *Peterson's Guide to Two-Year Colleges* *Peterson's Guide to Four-Year Colleges*	profile most accredited, four-year colleges; include articles on choosing a college, taking entrance exams, preparing applications; give information about student life, application deadlines, and financial aid
The Directory of Educational Institutions	covers business schools that offer programs in secretarial science, business adminis-tration, accounting
Technical, Trade, and Business School Data Handbook	divided into regional volumes; includes community and junior colleges; has index of programs and index of schools

CAREER GUIDES	
EXAMPLES	**DESCRIPTION**
The Encyclopedia of Careers and Vocational Guidance *The Dictionary of Occupational Titles* *Occupational Outlook Handbook* *Career Opportunities Series* *Guide to Federal Jobs*	contain information about various industries and occupations, such as job descriptions, projected figures for employment for specific occupations, and job-related education requirements

EXERCISE 1   Selecting Reference Books

Name a reference book you could use to find each of the following items of information.

1. international records in track events
2. the source of the expression "All the world's a stage"
3. a description of the climate of the Falkland Islands
4. a critique of a prominent author's works
5. entrance requirements for Yale, Harvard, and Princeton

EXERCISE 2   Finding Reference Books

Find and list three books in your library from one of the following categories. For each book, give the title, describe the contents and arrangement of the information in the book, and explain when students should use it.

biographical reference books
literature reference books
guides to colleges and universities
reference books on history or science

books about authors
books of quotations
almanacs
reference books on
art or music

RESOURCES

36 THE DICTIONARY

Arrangement and Contents

Dictionaries record how words are used in the English language. A dictionary shows how most English speakers say or spell a word and what the word means to different people under particular circumstances. In a dictionary you will also find information such as word histories and various forms a word can appear in.

Types of Dictionaries

There are many kinds of dictionaries. Each of the different kinds offers a particular range and amount of information about the words it contains. Two of the most common types of dictionaries, the ones most often used as references on word usage by the majority of speakers of the English language, are *unabridged dictionaries* and *abridged* (or *college*) dictionaries. Unabridged dictionaries are large books, usually found in libraries. Abridged dictionaries are more likely to be found in homes or in school classrooms.

Contents of a Dictionary Entry

① ② ③

ob·scure (əb skyoor′, äb-) *adj.* 〚OFr *obscur* < L *obscurus*, lit.,
covered over < *ob-* (see OB-) + IE **skuro-* < base **(s)keu-*, to cover,
conceal > HIDE¹, SKY 〛 **1** lacking light; dim; dark; murky *[the obscure
night]* **2** not easily perceived; specif., *a)* not clear or distinct; faint or
undefined *[an obscure figure or sound] b)* not easily understood;
vague; cryptic; ambiguous *[an obscure explanation] c)* in an incon-
spicuous position; hidden *[an obscure village]* **3** not well-known; not
famous *[an obscure scientist]* **4** *Phonet.* pronounced as (ə) or (i)
because it is not stressed; reduced; neutral: said of a vowel —***vt.***
-scured′, -scur′ing 〚L *obscurare* < the *adj.*〛 **1** to make obscure;
specif., *a)* to darken; make dim *b)* to conceal from view; hide *c)* to
make less conspicuous; overshadow *[a success that obscured earlier
failures] d)* to make less intelligible; confuse *[testimony that
obscures the issue]* **2** *Phonet.* to make (a vowel) obscure —***n.*** [Rare]
OBSCURITY —**ob·scure′ly** *adv.* —**ob·scure′ness** *n.*
SYN.—**obscure** applies to that which is perceived with difficulty either
because it is concealed or veiled or because of obtuseness in the perceiver
[their reasons remain obscure]; **vague** implies such a lack of precision or
exactness as to be indistinct or unclear *[a vague idea]*; **enigmatic** and
cryptic are used of that which baffles or perplexes, the latter word implying
deliberate intention to puzzle *[enigmatic behavior, a cryptic warning]*;
ambiguous applies to that which puzzles because it allows of more than
one interpretation *[an ambiguous title]*; **equivocal** is used of something
ambiguous that is deliberately used to mislead or confuse *[an equivocal*
answer] —***ANT.*** **clear, distinct, obvious**

④ ⑤ ⑥ ⑦ ⑧ ⑨ ⑩

From *Webster's New World Dictionary, Third College Edition.* Copyright © 1988 by Webster's New
World Dictionaries. A division of Simon and Schuster, New York.

1. **Entry word.** The boldfaced entry word shows how the
   word is spelled and how it is divided into syllables. The
   entry word may also show capitalization and provide
   alternate spellings.
2. **Pronunciation.** The pronunciation is shown by the use of
   accent marks and either diacritical marks or phonetic
   respelling. A pronunciation key explains the sounds
   represented by these symbols.
3. **Part-of-speech labels.** These labels (usually in abbreviated
   form) indicate how the entry word should be used in a
   sentence. Some words may be used as more than one
   part of speech. In this case, a part-of-speech label is given
   before each numbered (or lettered) series of definitions.
4. **Etymology.** The etymology is the origin and history of
   a word. It tells how the word (or its parts) came into
   English, tracing the word from its earliest known form
   in the language it came from.
5. **Definitions.** If there is more than one meaning for a
   word, the definitions are numbered or lettered. Most
   dictionaries list definitions in order of frequency of use,

but some order definitions according to the date when the word came to have each meaning. Read your dictionary's introduction to be sure you know how a word's definitions are listed.

6. **Examples.** Phrases or sentences may demonstrate how the defined word is to be used.

7. **Other forms.** Your dictionary may show spellings for other forms of the word. Full or partial spellings of plural forms of nouns, different tenses of verbs, or the comparison forms of adjectives and adverbs may be given.

8. **Special usage labels.** These labels may show that a definition is limited to certain forms of speech (such as [archaic] or [slang]). Or, the labels may indicate that a definition is used only in a certain field, such as *Law, Med.* (medicine), or *Chem.* (chemistry). Your dictionary will have a key for abbreviations used.

9. **Related word forms.** These are various forms of the entry word, usually created by adding suffixes or prefixes.

10. **Synonyms and antonyms.** Synonyms and antonyms may appear at the end of some word entries. You may also find synonyms included within the list of definitions, printed in capital letters.

Information Found in Dictionaries

Unabridged Dictionaries

An *unabridged dictionary* is the most comprehensive source for finding information about a word. Unabridged dictionaries offer more word entries, including words that are relatively rare. In addition, they usually give more information, such as fuller word histories or longer lists of synonyms or antonyms.

The Oxford English Dictionary is the largest unabridged dictionary. The *OED*, as it is often called, attempts to list and define every word in the English language. Consisting of many large volumes, the *OED* gives the approximate date of a word's first appearance in English and shows, in a quotation, how the word was used at that time. The *OED* also traces the changes in spelling or meaning that a word has had over the centuries. Because its entries emphasize a word's history instead of its current meanings, the *OED* is not used like most dictionaries.

Unabridged dictionaries commonly consist of one large volume. One well-known, single-volume unabridged dictionary is *Webster's Third New International Dictionary*. It is called an *international* dictionary because it contains words (with variations in spelling and meaning) that occur in several English-speaking countries. Another widely used unabridged dictionary is the *Random House Dictionary of the English Language*.

Abridged Dictionaries

An *abridged* or *college dictionary* is the most commonly used reference book in America. Abridged dictionaries do not contain as many entries or as much information about entry words as unabridged dictionaries. However, abridged dictionaries are revised frequently, so they give the most up-to-date information on meanings and uses of words. Besides word entries, most abridged dictionaries contain other useful information, such as tables of commonly used abbreviations, selected biographical entries, or tables of signs and symbols.

Specialized Dictionaries

A *specialized dictionary* contains entries that relate to a specific subject or field. For example, there are specialized dictionaries for terms used in art, music, sports, gardening, mythology, and many other subjects.

Specialized dictionaries are useful when you want information about a word or term that might not be included in a general dictionary or that might have a different meaning when the term is used in a particular context. Other dictionaries of special terms include dictionaries for slang words and idioms.

Another type of specialized dictionary contains ordinary words grouped or arranged to suit a particular purpose. For example, there are rhyming dictionaries (often used by poets) that group words according to the sound of their last syllable.

Foreign language dictionaries are specialized dictionaries that contain foreign words and phrases. They may also contain lists of irregular verbs and rules of grammar or punctuation.

Review

▶ EXERCISE 1   **Finding Information in the Dictionary**

Using an unabridged or a college dictionary, find the answers to the following questions.

1. Copy the correct pronunciation of *foliicolous*, including diacritical marks. Be sure that you are able to pronounce the word correctly.
2. How many different meanings are given in your dictionary for the word *gauge*?
3. What is the height of Mount Everest?
4. How did *guinea* get its meaning?
5. From what language is the word *pajamas* derived?

▶ EXERCISE 2   **Finding Information in the Dictionary**

Using an abridged or college dictionary, look up the answers to the following questions.

1. What was Galileo's full name?
2. What is the scientific notation for pyridoxine?
3. What is the meaning of the Latin phrase *mare liberum*?
4. When was the Great Wall of China constructed?
5. From what language is *pest* derived?

▶ EXERCISE 3   **Finding the Etymologies of Words**

Using an abridged or college dictionary, look up the etymologies of the following words. [Note: Refer to the guide at the front of your dictionary for the meanings of abbreviations and symbols.]

1. office
2. velvet
3. cave
4. library
5. oil
6. quick
7. hospitable
8. boral
9. tea
10. tarnish

RESOURCES

37 VOCABULARY

Learning and Using New Words

An effective vocabulary increases the power and persuasiveness of what you write and say. Studies have shown that a large vocabulary is an important indicator of your success in high school, in college, and in your future career. College entrance examinations place great emphasis on vocabulary, and many job tests have sections devoted to word knowledge.

Adding to Your Word Bank

One method of increasing your vocabulary is to make a habit of collecting words. You can expand your knowledge with each addition to your word bank. Whenever you find new words in your reading or in school, write these words in your notebook along with their definitions. Then consult your dictionary to be sure you have understood the meaning of each word.

Using Context Clues

Frequently, you can figure out the meaning of unfamiliar words that are used in conversation or in reading passages by analyzing how these words are used. Determining the meaning of new words in this way is known as using *context clues.* The *context* of a word is made up of the phrases and sentences that surround it. Look at all of the circumstances in which a word is used so that you can find clues to its meaning.

The following chart shows examples of some of the most common types of context clues.

TYPES OF CONTEXT CLUES	
TYPE OF CLUE	**EXPLANATION**
Definitions and Restatements	Look for words that define or restate the meaning of a word. ■ Vonelle studied *ethnology,* that is, the science dealing with the cultures of various people.
Examples	A word may be accompanied by an example that illustrates its meaning. ■ His acts of *benevolence* were well-known, especially his generous donations to children's hospitals.
Synonyms	Look for clues that indicate an unfamiliar word is similar in meaning to a familiar word. ■ Rosita has always been so dependably prompt that she has been given a special award by her employer for her consistent *punctuality.*
Comparisons	Sometimes an unknown word may be compared with a more familiar word. ■ Registration procedures for the *symposium* will be similar to those of other conferences.

(continued)

RESOURCES

TYPES OF CONTEXT CLUES *(continued)*	
TYPE OF CLUE	EXPLANATION
Contrast	An unfamiliar word may sometimes be contrasted with a more familiar word. ■ Everyone from the largest *metropolis* to the smallest village participated in the nationwide peace effort.
Cause and Effect	Look for clues that indicate an unfamiliar word is related to the cause, or is the result of, an action, feeling, or idea. ■ Since the instructions were given in the wrong order, it's not surprising that most of the students looked quite *flummoxed.*

Determining Meanings from the General Context

Sometimes context clues are subtle. You may need to read an entire passage to understand the meaning of an unfamiliar word. In such a case, you must infer the meaning of the unfamiliar word by drawing on your own knowledge of the general topic or by making connections between the unfamiliar word and the other information provided in the material.

Using Word Parts

In general, English words are of two kinds: those that can be divided into smaller parts (*unthinkable, displeased*) and those that cannot (*youth, money*). Words that stand alone and are complete by themselves are **base words.** Words that can be divided are made up of two or more word parts. The three types of word parts are

- roots
- prefixes
- suffixes

Learning the meanings of some of the most commonly used word parts can often help you determine the meanings of unfamiliar words.

Roots

A word's *root* is the part that carries the core meaning of the word. When other word parts are added to a word root, new words are formed.

The English language contains many words formed from Greek and Latin roots. A knowledge of these roots and meanings can help you determine the meanings of many words.

COMMON WORD ROOTS		
ROOT	MEANING	EXAMPLES
GREEK		
–anthrop–	human	anthropology, anthropomorphic
–bio–	life	biography, bionic
–chrom–	color	chromatic, monochrome
–dem–	people	demagogue, democrat
–derm–	skin	dermatology, epidermis
–graph–	write, writing	calligraphy, autograph
–hydr–	water	hydrant, hydroelectric
–log–, –logy–	study, word	logic, theology
–ortho–	straight	orthodox, orthography
–phil–	like, love	philosophy, philanthropy
–zo–	life, animal	zoo, zoology
LATIN		
–audi–	hear	audio, auditorium
–ben–, –bene–	good	benign, beneficial
–cent–	hundred	centennial, century

(continued)

RESOURCES

COMMON WORD ROOTS *(continued)*		
ROOT	MEANING	EXAMPLES
–cogn–	know	cognizant, recognize
–duc–, –duct–	draw, lead	induce, deduct
–loc–	place	locality, locate
–magn–	large, grand	magnify, magnitude
–man–	hand	manicure, manual
–mater–, –matr–	mother	maternal, matriarch
–mor–, –mort–	death	moribund, mortal
–omni–	all	omnipresent, omniscient
–pater–, –patr–	father	paternal, patriarchy
–prim–	early	primeval, primitive
–solv–	loosen, accomplish	dissolve, solvent
–spir–	breath	expire, inspire
–uni–	one	unify, universe
–vid–, –vis–	see	video, vision

Prefixes

A *prefix* is a word part that is added onto the beginning of a word or in front of a word root to form a new word. The new word's meaning reflects the combined meanings of its parts.

COMMON PREFIXES		
PREFIX	MEANING	EXAMPLES
GREEK		
a–	lacking, without	amorphous, atheistic
anti–	against, opposing	antipathy, antithesis
dia–	through, across	diagnose, diameter
hyper–	excessive	hypersensitive, hypertension
hypo–	under, below	hypodermic, hypothermia

COMMON PREFIXES *(continued)*

PREFIX	MEANING	EXAMPLES
mon–, mono–	one	monandry, monotheism
para–	beside, beyond	paradox, paralegal
peri–	around	perimeter, periscope
psych–, psycho–	mind	psychic, psychopath
sym–	with, together	sympathy, symphony
LATIN AND FRENCH		
ab–	from, away	abdicate, abjure
contra–	against	contradict, contravene
de–	away, from, off	deflect, defrost
dif–, dis–	away, not, opposing	differ, disappoint
e–, ef–, ex–	away, from, out	emigrate, effront, extract
in–, im–	in, into, within	infer, insurgent, impression
inter–	among, between	intercede, interrupt
intra–	within	intramural, intrastate
per–	through	perceive, permit
post–	after, following	postpone, postscript
pre–	before	preclude, prevent
pro–	forward, favoring	produce, pronoun
re–	back, backward, again	recur, replant, revoke
retro–	back, backward	retrograde, retrospect
semi–	partly	semiofficial, semiprivate
ultra–	beyond, excessively	ultramodern, ultraviolet

(continued)

COMMON PREFIXES *(continued)*		
PREFIX	**MEANING**	**EXAMPLES**
OLD ENGLISH be– for– mis– over– un–	around, about away, off, from not, badly, wrongly above, excessively not, reverse of	belay, bemoan forgo, forswear miscalculate, mismatch oversee, overdo unhappy, unlock

☞ REFERENCE NOTE: For guidelines on spelling when adding prefixes, see page 905.

Suffixes

A *suffix* is a word part that is added onto the end of a word or after a word root to form a new word. There are two main kinds of suffixes: those that provide a grammatical signal of some kind but do not greatly change the basic meaning of the word (*–s, –ed, –ing*) and those that create new words. The suffixes listed below are primarily those that create new words.

COMMON SUFFIXES		
NOUN SUFFIXES	**MEANING**	**EXAMPLES**

GREEK, LATIN, AND FRENCH
–ance, –ence
 	
–cy
–er, –or
–ism
 	
–tude
–ty, –y
 	
–ure
	
	act, condition
	
	state, condition
	doer, action
	act, doctrine, manner
	
	quality, state
	quality, state, action
	
	act, result, means
		
		acceptance,
		  turbulence
		accuracy, currency
		baker, donor
		barbarism, cubism,
		  patriotism
		aptitude, quietude
		beauty, enmity,
		  inquiry
		culture, signature

(continued)

COMMON SUFFIXES *(continued)*		
NOUN SUFFIXES	**MEANING**	**EXAMPLES**
OLD ENGLISH		
–dom	state, rank, condition	serfdom, wisdom
–hood	state, condition	statehood, womanhood
–ness	quality, state	kindness, shortness
ADJECTIVE SUFFIXES	**MEANING**	**EXAMPLES**
GREEK, LATIN, AND FRENCH		
–able, –ible	able, likely	tolerable, possible
–ate	having, characteristic of	desolate, separate
–esque	in the style of, like	humoresque, picturesque
–fic	making, causing	beatific, terrific
–ous	marked by, given to	religious, riotous
OLD ENGLISH		
–en	like, made of	ashen, wooden
–ful	full of, marked by	thankful, zestful
–less	lacking, without	countless, hopeless
–ly	like, characteristic of	kingly, yearly
–some	apt to, showing	lonesome, tiresome
–ward	in the direction of	downward, outward
VERB SUFFIXES	**MEANING**	**EXAMPLES**
GREEK, LATIN, AND FRENCH		
–ate	become, cause to be	animate, sublimate
–esce	become, grow, continue	acquiesce, obsolesce
–fy	make, cause to have	fortify, glorify
–ize	make, cause to be	criticize, motorize
OLD ENGLISH		
–en	cause to be, become	blacken, weaken

RESOURCES

☞ REFERENCE NOTE: For guidelines on spelling when adding suffixes, see pages 905–907.

Other Ways to Form New Words

New words are constantly added to the English language. The most common way new words are formed is by a process of combination. *Affixes,* prefixes or suffixes, are usually added to a base word or to a word root to make a new word. Sometimes, however, two base words can be combined or put together with a hyphen to make a new word. Here are some of the most common ways new words are made.

PROCESS	DESCRIPTION	EXAMPLES
combining	combining two base words to make a compound or combining a word with an affix	doorway, high-rise unfold, wonderful
shortening	omitting part of an original word to shorten it or to change it to another part of speech	telephone → phone burglar → burgle nuclear → nuke
blending	shortening and combining two words	breakfast + lunch = brunch smoke + fog = smog
shifting	changing the meaning or usage of a word	host (n.) → host (v.) farm (n.) → farm (v.)

Choosing the Appropriate Word

Using the Dictionary

Whether you are writing or speaking, it's very important that the words you choose match your purpose. Most words in the English language have a number of different meanings. Whenever you look in a dictionary for the definition of a word, be sure to scan *all* the definitions given. Keep in mind the context in which you originally encountered the word. Then try the various definitions in the same context until you find the one that fits best.

To help you, dictionaries often provide sample contexts. Compare these sample contexts to the context in which you first heard or read the word to make sure you've found the correct meaning.

Choosing the Right Synonym

Synonyms are words that have the same or nearly the same meaning. However, synonyms often have subtle shades of differences in meaning. Use a dictionary or thesaurus to make sure you understand the exact differences in meanings between synonyms.

Many words have two kinds of meaning: *denotative* and *connotative*. The **denotative** meaning of a word is the meaning given by a dictionary. The **connotative** meaning of a word is the feeling or tone associated with it. For example, the words *smirk* and *grin* both mean "to smile." However, the word *grin* has a more positive connotation than *smirk*, which suggests an affected, insincere, or annoying smile. When you read, listen, or speak, be aware of both the denotative and connotative meanings of words.

REFERENCE NOTE: For more information about denotative and connotative meanings, see page 492.

Analogies

Analogies provide a special type of context in which you are asked to analyze the relationship between one pair of words in order to identify or to supply a second pair of words that has the same relationship.

Analogy questions frequently appear on standardized tests because they measure your command of vocabulary as well as your ability to identify the relationships and patterns among

RESOURCES

words. On standardized tests, analogies are frequently presented in multiple-choice form, as in the following example.

EXAMPLE   **1.** INCH : FOOT : : _____

      A quart: measure
      B weight: peck
      (C) ounce: pound
      D meter: yard

HOW TO ANSWER ANALOGY QUESTIONS	
Analyze the first pair of words.	Identify the relationship between the first two items. In the example given, an *inch* is a measurement, part of a *foot*.
Express the analogy in sentence or question form.	The example given above could be read as "An *inch* has the same relationship to a *foot* as . . . (what other pair of items among the choices given?)."
Find the best available choice to complete the analogy.	■ If multiple choices are given, select the pair of words that has the same type of relationship between them as the first pair given in the question. (In this example, only choice C shows the same relationship, which is that of a part to a whole unit of measurement.) ■ If you are required to fill in the blank to complete the analogy, you are often given one word of the second pair of items, and you are expected to supply the final word.

Although there are many different relationships that can be represented in analogies, a smaller number of specific relationships are fairly common. Examples of these common types are shown in the following chart.

TYPES OF ANALOGY RELATIONSHIPS	
TYPE	**EXAMPLE**
Word to synonym	NEWS : TIDINGS :: adage : proverb
Word to antonym	RECKLESS : CAUTIOUS :: rash : prudent
Cause to effect	VIRUS : FLU :: tension : headache
Part to whole	FLOOR : BUILDING :: step : staircase
Whole to part	WEEK : DAY :: decade : year
Item to category	ALLIGATOR : REPTILE :: mosquito : insect
Time sequence	TUESDAY : THURSDAY :: June : August
Object to function	PEN : WRITING :: chisel : sculpturing
Action to object	CUTTING : KNIFE :: pruning : shears
Action to performer	PAINTING : ARTIST :: paddling : canoeist

Review

▶ EXERCISE 1   **Using Context Clues**

For the italicized word in each of the following sentences, write a short definition based on the clues you find in the context. Check your definitions with the dictionary.

1. Instead of *ameliorating* the skin condition, the treatment seemed to be worsening it.
2. The amount of *arable* land—that is, land that can be cultivated—is very small.
3. Watch for *concomitants* of a severe head cold, such as a feeling of tiredness accompanied by aches and pains in the joints and muscles.

4. Mr. Ryko always seemed so nervous and confused that he irritated co-workers with his tendency to be *distraught.*
5. Since Dixie is *taciturn* by nature, our attempts to get her to join in the conversation were in vain.

▶ EXERCISE 2 ## Using the General Context to Determine Meaning

For each italicized word, write your own definition or synonym. Then check the dictionary's definitions of each word. If you guessed incorrectly, check the context again.

Along with the [1] *proliferation* of fax machines in the United States, there has also been an increase in what is called "junk fax mail." Many businesses commonly use fax machines when they want to [2] *disseminate* their advertisements. However, this practice sometimes [3] *impedes* the everyday business of companies who use the machines to [4] *expedite* business transactions. Important documents can be [5] *dispatched* and returned in a matter of minutes rather than days. Many businesses have found themselves missing [6] *acute* deadlines because their fax machines were tied up with incoming advertisements. For example, it was [7] *imperative* for a Baltimore law firm to fax the news of a concluded deal by exactly 5 P.M. But they missed this critical deadline because their fax machine was receiving a multiple-page fax from a nearby restaurant. State legislatures are attempting the task of [8] *appeasing* two demands that [9] *inevitably* clash. Some states have considered [10] *remedial* measures, such as requiring businesses who fax ads to first consult a list of people who have requested not to receive advertisements on their fax machines.

▶ EXERCISE 3 ## Learning New Words with Latin and Greek Roots

Underline the root or roots in each of the following words. Using your dictionary, write a brief definition of the word.

1. benevolent
2. graphology
3. incognito
4. biosphere
5. misanthrope
6. magnate
7. solvent
8. dermatitis
9. chromophil
10. omnivorous

▶ EXERCISE 4   **Understanding the Meanings of Prefixes**

Give the meaning of each of the following words. Then identify the prefix in each word and its meaning. Be prepared to explain the link between the meaning of the prefix and the meaning of the whole word.

EXAMPLE   **1.** antithesis
             1. *meaning: direct contrast or opposition of ideas*
                prefix: anti– (against, opposing)

1. hyperventilate   **4.** retroactive
2. promotion   **5.** intervene
3. misgiving

▶ EXERCISE 5   **Identifying Suffixes and Defining Words**

For each word, identify the suffix and guess what the whole word means. Use a dictionary to check your answers.

EXAMPLE   **1.** novelty
             1. *–ty; the state or condition of being novel (new or unusual)*

1. forbearance   **4.** constancy
2. conductor   **5.** toilsome
3. collegiate

▶ EXERCISE 6   **Completing Analogies**

In the following items, choose the pair of words whose relationship is most similar to that of the first pair given.

1. SPEAK : COMMUNICATE :: **(a)** swim : sink **(b)** sing : enthrall **(c)** gaze : observe **(d)** walk : move
2. RELEVANT : PERTINENT :: **(a)** wasteful : efficient **(b)** thoughtful : pensive **(c)** implicit : explicit **(d)** quiet : slow
3. ENCOURAGE : PROHIBIT :: **(a)** endorse : approve **(b)** gyrate : maneuver **(c)** bless : redeem **(d)** nurture : reject
4. QUIVER : ARROW :: **(a)** movie : scene **(b)** pitcher : water **(c)** governor : pardon **(d)** scholarship : college
5. ERASER : PENCIL :: **(a)** scabbard : sword **(b)** mountain : ore **(c)** crown : queen **(d)** tree : limb

38 LETTERS AND FORMS

Style and Contents

Letters can be an effective means of communicating for a variety of purposes. You may want to request information, order products, make a complaint, convey your appreciation, or apply for a job. You will also need to write letters of social correspondence. Or, you may need to complete printed forms. Your letters and completed forms will be judged on their content as well as on their appearance.

The Appearance of a Business Letter

Business letters follow certain standards of style and format.

- Use plain paper ($8\frac{1}{2}''$ × 11″).
- Type your letter if possible (single-spaced, leaving an extra line between paragraphs). Otherwise, write legibly, using black or blue ink.
- Center your letter on the page with equal margins, usually one inch, on all sides.
- Use only one side of the paper. If you need a second page, leave a one-inch margin at the bottom of the first page and carry over at least two lines to the second page.
- Avoid markouts, erasures, or other careless marks. Check for typing errors and misspellings.

Writing Business Letters

The Parts of a Business Letter

A business letter contains six parts:

    (1) the heading
    (2) the inside address
    (3) the salutation
    (4) the body
    (5) the closing
    (6) the signature

Block Style

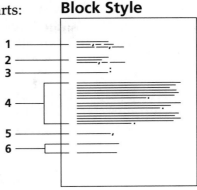

There are two styles used frequently for business letters. With the *block form,* every part of the letter begins at the left-hand margin, and paragraphs are not indented. In the *modified block form,* the heading, the closing, and the signature are aligned along an imaginary line just to the right of the center of the page. The other parts of the letter begin at the left-hand margin. All paragraphs are indented.

Modified Block Style

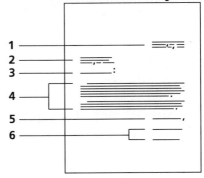

The Heading. The heading usually consists of three lines:

- your street address (or post office box number)
- your city, state, and ZIP code
- the date that you wrote the letter

The Inside Address. The inside address shows the name and address of the person or organization you are writing. If you're writing to a specific person, use a courtesy title (such as *Mr., Ms., Mrs.,* or *Miss*) or a professional title (such as *Dr.* or *Professor*) in front of the person's name. After the person's name, include the person's business or job title (such as *Owner* or *Sales Manager*), followed by the name of the company or organization and the address.

The Salutation. The salutation is your greeting. If you are writing to a specific person, begin with *Dear*, followed by a courtesy title or a professional title and the person's last name. End the salutation with a colon.

If you don't have the name of a specific person, you can use a general salutation, such as *Dear Sir or Madam* or *Ladies and Gentlemen*. You can also use a department or a position title, with or without the word *Dear*.

The Body. The body, or main part, of your letter contains your message. If the body of your letter contains more than one paragraph, leave a space between paragraphs.

The Closing. In closing, you should end your letter in a courteous manner. Closings often used in business letters include *Sincerely, Yours truly, Respectfully yours*, and *Regards*. Capitalize only the first word of the closing.

The Signature. Your signature should be written in ink, directly below the closing. Sign your full name. Do not use a title. If you type your letter, type your name neatly below your signature.

GUIDELINES FOR THE CONTENTS OF A BUSINESS LETTER

Business letters usually follow a few simple guidelines.

- *Use a courteous, positive, and professional tone.* Maintain a respectful, constructive tone—even if you're angry. Rude or insulting letters are counterproductive.
- *Use formal, standard English.* Avoid slang, dialect, contractions, or abbreviations. Business letters are usually formal in tone and use of language.
- *State your purpose clearly and quickly.* Assume that the person reading your letter is busy. Tell why you are writing in the first or second sentence of the letter.
- *Include all necessary information.* Provide all the information your reader needs to understand and respond appropriately to your letter.

Types of Business Letters

Request or Order Letters

Occasionally you may require something that you can obtain by writing a *request letter.* For example, you might write to a college to request a catalog of courses offered, or you might write to a state's tourism agency to request a brochure about a travel destination. An *order letter* is a special kind of request letter that is written to order merchandise by mail, especially when you do not have a printed order form.

Here is the body of a sample request letter. The writer is asking a college to send information and an admission form.

> Please send me a catalog of courses as well as an application form for admission to Stanville College. I am a junior in high school and beginning to consider my choices among colleges.
>
> Along with the catalog and application, please also send a list of the admissions requirements for both the School of Liberal Arts and the School of Engineering.

When you are writing a request or order letter, follow these guidelines.

1. State your request clearly.
2. If you're asking for information, enclose a self-addressed, stamped envelope.
3. If you're asking an individual for a special request, make sure your request is reasonable and that you have allowed enough time for the person to answer you well in advance of the time you must have the information.
4. If you're ordering something, include all important details, such as the size, color, style, and price. You might include information about the magazine or newspaper in which you saw the item advertised. Compute correctly if there are costs involved, including any necessary sales tax or shipping charges.

Complaint or Adjustment Letters

The purpose of a *complaint* or *adjustment letter* is to report a problem and to request a satisfactory resolution of the difficulty. This type of letter calls attention to errors that you feel need to be addressed by the organization responsible.

Here is the body of a sample adjustment letter. The writer is reporting a problem and is telling the company how she believes the problem should be resolved.

> On October 25, I bought a silk button-down shirt at your store for $42.26. The shirt was charged to my mother's account. Since the size I wanted was not in stock, the shirt was later delivered to my home. When the shirt arrived, on October 28, the package had split open and the shirt was stained.
>
> I am returning the shirt and would like the full amount of $42.26 credited to my mother's account. The account is under the name of Sabrina Tallwood. Her account number is 55-432-6591-2.

When you are writing a complaint or adjustment letter, follow these suggestions.

1. Register your complaint as soon as possible after noticing the problem.
2. Explain exactly what is wrong. Necessary information might include
   - what product or service you ordered or that you expected
   - why you are not satisfied (for example: because of damaged goods, incorrect merchandise, or bad service)
   - how you were affected (for example: because you lost time or money)
   - what you want the individual, company, or organization to do about it
3. Keep the tone of your letter calm and courteous. Despite your possible frustration about the mistake or error, you will be much more effective if you are cool-headed and communicate clearly about the problem.

Appreciation or Commendation Letters

An *appreciation* or *commendation letter* is written to compliment or to express appreciation to a person, group, or an organization. For example, you might write to a television network, telling how much you like a particular program and encouraging the network not to cancel it. Or, you might write to a restaurant where you enjoyed a particularly good meal to express your appreciation. Your appreciation or commendation letters are usually most effective when you are very clear about exactly why you are pleased.

Here is the body of a sample appreciation letter. The writer is expressing appreciation for a specific television program.

On Tuesday, June 13, I watched the first show in your series about the problems facing today's teens. I wanted to let you know that I especially appreciate your broadcast of "Teenagers in the 90's."

As a teenager, I considered your portrayal of some of the problems we face very accurate. But instead of focusing only on the dilemmas of modern adolescence, your program gave helpful--and hopeful--suggestions about where teens like me might find information, resources, or support as we deal with these crucial concerns.

Many parents, such as my own, rarely hear about these issues from an unbiased source. I hope your network will continue to broadcast programs such as this one that help to increase people's understanding of one another's concerns. We need more programs like yours that contribute to frank and open talks about serious issues.

RESOURCES

Letters of Application

You write a *letter of application* to provide a selection committee or a possible employer enough information to determine whether you are a good candidate for a position. This position may be a job, membership in an organization, or a scholarship.

On the next page is a sample of a job application letter.

321 Fifth Street
Riverside, MO 64168
May 26, 1992

Personnel Director
Value Insurance Company
41 Bank Street
Riverside, MO 64168

Dear Personnel Director:

Please consider me an applicant for the summer stenographer position advertised in Sunday's Herald.

I am seventeen years old and a junior at Central High School. My course of study has included business classes such as typing, bookkeeping, and business English. I can take dictation at the rate of ninety words a minute and can type either from shorthand notes or recordings at a rate of about fifty words a minute.

Last summer I was employed as a fill-in stenographer for the Superior Trucking Company. I did filing and billing, and performed other tasks as well as regular stenographic work. I feel at home in a business office and enjoy responsibility.

I will gladly supply you with references who can tell you about my qualifications for this position.

I am available for a personal interview at your convenience. My telephone number is 555-7023. I can be reached most evenings after 5:00 p.m.

Very truly yours,

Veronica Harjo

Veronica Harjo

When you are writing a letter of application, remember the following points.

1. Identify the job or position you are applying for. Mention how you heard about it.
2. Depending on the position you are applying for, you might include
   - your age, grade in school, or grade-point average
   - your experience, or your activities, awards, and honors
   - personal qualities or characteristics that make you a good choice for the position
   - the date or times you are available

3. Offer to provide references. Your references should include two or three responsible adults (usually not relatives) who have agreed to recommend you. Be prepared to supply their addresses and telephone numbers.

The Personal Résumé

A *résumé* is a summary of your background and experience. For many job positions, you submit a résumé along with your letter of application. There are many different styles of arranging the information on a résumé. Whatever style you select, be sure your résumé looks neat and businesslike.

<u>JOHN L. ZENO</u>	1632 Garden View Drive Allentown, PA 18103 Telephone: (215) 555-6160
EDUCATION:	Junior, St. Timothy High School Major studies: College preparatory courses in business and foreign languages Grade-point average: 3.0 (B)

WORK EXPERIENCE:	Summer 1991 Camp counselor
	                  Camp Holiday
	                  Beaver Lake, PA
	Summer 1990 Volunteer office worker
	                  YMCA
	                  Allentown, PA

SKILLS:	Shorthand: 120 words a minute
	Typing: 70 words a minute
	Business dictating, calculating, and
	machines: duplicating machines
	
	Languages: Can speak and translate
	               Spanish fluently
	
	Extracurricular Vice President, Future Business
	activities: Leaders of America; member,
	               Spanish Club

REFERENCES:	Dr. Walter A. Smidt, Principal (215) 555-1019 St. Timothy High School Allentown, PA Mary Francis Tate, Teacher (215) 555-1019 St. Timothy High School Allentown, PA Mr. Glen Ramos, Director (215) 555-4593 Camp Holiday Beaver Lake, PA

Addressing an Envelope

A business letter should be sent in a plain business envelope. Write or type your name and address in the upper left-hand corner of the envelope. Write or type the name and address of the person or organization to whom you are writing (the addressee) on the center of the envelope. The addressee's name and address should exactly match the inside address on the letter. Use the two-letter postal service abbreviations for state names, and be sure to include correct ZIP codes.

Completing Printed Forms and Applications

As you enter the work force or begin applying to colleges, you'll be asked to fill out a variety of forms and applications. The person or organization who receives your form or application will be able to help you best if you fill the form out neatly, completely, and legibly.

GUIDELINES FOR COMPLETING FORMS

1. Always read the entire form to make sure you understand exactly what items of information you are being asked to supply.
2. Type neatly or print legibly, using a pen or pencil as directed.
3. Include all information requested. If a question does not apply to you, write *N.A.* or *not applicable* instead of leaving the space blank.
4. Keep the form neat and clean. Avoid smudges or cross-outs.
5. When you have completed the form, proofread it carefully in order to correct any spelling, grammar, punctuation, or factual errors.
6. Submit the form to the correct person or mail it to the correct address.

Application for Employment

Personal Information

1. Social Security Number _____034-38-3151_____ Date _____5/20/94_____
2. Name _____COHEN_____ _____SARAH_____ _____LYNN_____
   Last | First | Middle
3. Present Address _____10226 Zenith Lane_____ _____Omaha_____ _____Nebraska 68154_____
   street | city | state | ZIP
4. Permanent Address _same as above_
5. Phone No. _____(402) 555-3376_____ 6. Date of Birth _____9/19/76_____
7. Height _____5'3"_____ Color of Hair _____Brown_____
   Color of Eyes _____Brown_____
8. If related to anyone in our employ, state name and department.
   _____N/A_____
   Referred by _____Ms. Bernie Schulman_____

Employment Desired

9. Position _Sales Clerk_ Date you can start _6/8/92_ Salary Desired _$5.25/hr_
10. Are you employed now? _____yes_____
    If so, may we inquire of your present employer? _____yes_____
11. Ever applied to this company before? _no_
    Where | When

Education

12. Name and Location of Last School _Lincoln High School_ _Omaha, NE_
    Years Attended _91–present_ Date Graduated _N/A_
    Subjects Studied _Academic_

Former Employers (List below last two employers, beginning with most recent.)

13.	Date Month/Year	Name and Address of Employer	Salary	Position	Reason for leaving
	6/91–	Mrs. Richard Lance 1225 N. Washington, Omaha, NE	$4.25/hr	Yard Work	None
	3/89–7/91	Minneapolis *Tribune* Minneapolis, MN	$2.50/hr	Paper Carrier	Moved to Nebraska

References: List the names of three persons not related to you, whom you have known at least one year.

	Name	Address	Business	Years Aquainted
14.	Dr. Yolanda Torres	208 De Kalb Omaha, NE 61851	Veterinarian	1
15.	Mr. Howard Dannenberg	535 S. Fifth St. Omaha, NE 61854	Nurse (Retired)	1
16.	Mrs. Gretchen Musich	104 York Lane Omaha, NE 61853	Beautician	1

Signature: _Sarah L. Cohen_ **Date:** _5/20/94_

RESOURCES

Writing Informal or Social Letters

Occasionally, the most appropriate way to communicate with people you know personally is through the mail. When you want to thank someone formally, congratulate someone for an accomplishment, send an invitation, or respond to an invitation extended to you, you should write a social letter.

Social letters are much less formal in style than business letters. For example, social letters don't include an inside address and most use the modified block form.

Thank-you Letters. The purpose of a thank-you letter is to express appreciation for a gift or a favor someone gave you. Try to say more than just "thank you": Give details about how the person's gift or efforts were helpful or appreciated.

Invitations. An invitation should contain specific information about a planned event, such as the occasion, the time and place, and any other special details guests might need to know.

Letters of Regret. If you have been invited to a party or function and will be unable to attend, it's polite to send a letter of regret. A written reply is especially appropriate if you were sent a written invitation with the letters *R.S.V.P.* (in French, these letters are an abbreviation for "please reply").

Review

▶ EXERCISE 1 **Writing Business Letters**

Write two of the following business letters. Using either block or modified block form, place the parts of the business letter correctly on the page. Use your own return address and today's date, but make up any other information you need.

1. In a letter, order two tickets (at $8.00 each) for the June 17 performance of *The Piano Lesson* at the Summer Stock Playhouse; P.O. Box 15; Slaughter Beach, Delaware 19963.

2. Write a letter of adjustment or complaint. Inform a store's credit department that items (specify them) you ordered but returned to the store have not been credited to your account; ask that your account balance be adjusted.
3. Write a letter to a local radio station expressing your delight over a new talk show the station has added to its programming. State exactly why you find the program appealing.
4. Write to a local, state, or national elected official explaining your position on a public issue; request a response.
5. Write a letter of application answering a help-wanted advertisement in your local newspaper.

▶ EXERCISE 2 **Writing a Résumé**

Choose a job that interests you. Then write a personal résumé that shows you are qualified for such a position. Include a short letter explaining how you heard about the job and requesting a personal interview.

▶ EXERCISE 3 **Completing Forms**

Choose one of the following activities.

1. Obtain an application form for a driver's license or a learner's permit and complete it correctly.
2. Complete an auto insurance application form, using information about your car or a car owned by a friend or relative.
3. Complete an application form for employment with a company.
4. Locate a mail-order catalog and select several items to order. Complete the mail-order form in the catalog, indicating the items you have chosen.

▶ EXERCISE 4 **Writing Social Letters**

Write a social letter for one of the following situations.

1. Write a thank-you letter expressing appreciation for a gift or favor you have received.
2. Write an invitation letter for an upcoming event you are planning.
3. Write a letter of regret explaining that you will not be able to attend an event to which you have been invited.

RESOURCES

39 STUDYING AND TEST TAKING

Using Skills and Strategies

As you continue your high school studies and prepare for college or a career, you need to develop skills and strategies that will make your studying and test taking more effective. The ability to study efficiently is a skill that you will find valuable no matter what profession you pursue. When you have learned productive study methods, you will have mastered techniques for analyzing, evaluating, and utilizing information that are necessary skills in almost every career.

Following a Study Plan

All studying has two basic purposes. First, you study to acquire information, and then to apply it. Developing good study habits is enormously important. To study effectively

- keep track of your assignments and due dates
- select a time and place to study free from distractions
- break large assignments into smaller steps and then schedule time to complete each step
- allow a reasonable amount of study time to complete each of your assignments

Strengthening Study Skills

Reading and Understanding

To read productively, you need to determine your purpose for reading. Then adjust your reading rate to suit the material and your purpose for reading.

READING RATES ACCORDING TO PURPOSE		
READING RATE	**PURPOSE**	**EXAMPLE**
Scanning	Reading for specific details or points of reference	Searching a short story for the name of the main character's pen pal
Skimming	Reading for main points	Reviewing characteristics of an economic theory to prepare for an essay test
Reading for mastery	Reading to understand and remember	Reading a new chapter in your history book before outlining it

Writing to Learn

Writing contributes many benefits to the learning process. Writing helps you to focus your thoughts, respond to ideas, record your observations, and plan your work. Writing can also help you recall and understand information and provide you with ideas that you might use for future assignments.

TYPE OF WRITING	PURPOSE	EXAMPLE
Freewriting	To help you focus your thoughts	Writing to connect ideas between a class lecture and assigned readings

(continued)

TYPE OF WRITING	PURPOSE	EXAMPLE
Autobiographical Sketches	To help you examine and express the meaning of key events in your life	Writing about your impressions on the day your brother left home to go to college
Diaries	To help you recall your impressions and express your feelings	Writing about a problem you faced and overcame in one of your classes
Journals and Learning Logs	To help you record your observations, descriptions, solutions, and questions	Writing to keep a record of each step in the progress of a team project
	To help you present a problem, analyze it, and propose a solution	Writing about the issues you plan to raise during an upcoming group discussion

Using a Word Processor as a Writing Tool

The word processor makes it easier to produce written work because it eliminates many time-consuming tasks. Although it can't do the job for you, word processing can help you produce your best writing; it offers benefits at each stage of the writing process.

Prewriting. You can freewrite and brainstorm ideas easily on the computer. Then you can fill in notes or outlines without having to type them in again.

Writing First Drafts. After a little practice, you can compose your thoughts quickly on the word processor.

Evaluating. Because changes are easy to make, the word processor is great for analyzing work in progress. You can save a copy of your document and then insert and delete text freely.

If you decide you don't like the changes, you still have your original document saved.

Revising. A word processor is a great time-saver for revisions. You can insert, move, or delete text easily. Then you can print out a clean copy without having to repeat steps.

Proofreading. You can use a spell-checking function on most word processors to find errors. You may also have a search-and-replace function that you can use to correct a specific type of error wherever it occurs throughout your document.

Writing the Final Version. After you have made all your revisions and have proofread and made all corrections, you can print out one or more final copies.

Using the SQ3R Method

One frequently used method of study, called *SQ3R*, was developed by an educational psychologist named Francis Robinson. The SQ3R study method is made up of five simple steps.

S *Survey* the entire study assignment to understand the general scope of the material. Read all titles, headings, subheadings, and terms in boldface and italic type. Also, look over any charts, outlines, and summaries.

Q *Question* yourself. What should you know after completing your reading? Make a list of questions to be answered. Also, look at any questions provided at the end of a reading selection.

R *Read* the material carefully. Think of answers to your questions as you read.

R *Recite* in your own words answers to each question.

R *Review* the material by rereading quickly, looking over the questions, and recalling the answers.

☞ REFERENCE NOTE: For study techniques to help with listening skills, see page 938.

RESOURCES

Interpreting and Analyzing Information

Finding the Main Idea

To understand a passage of reading, you must determine what it means and how the information it contains fits together. An important first step is to determine the main idea of the selection.

Stated Main Idea. The main idea is often stated directly in a thesis statement or can be found in one or two specific sentences in a passage.

Implied Main Idea. The main idea is not always easy to find. Sometimes the main idea of a reading passage may be implied, or suggested, rather than stated directly. To find an implied main idea in a passage, you must analyze all of the supporting details and decide what overall meaning these details combine to express.

HOW TO FIND THE MAIN IDEA

- Identify the overall topic. (What is the passage about?)
- Identify what the passage reveals about the topic. (What's the message of the passage as a whole?)
- Sum up the meaning of the passage in one clear, effective sentence.
- Review the passage. (If you have correctly identified the main idea, all of the other details included in the passage will support it.)

☞ REFERENCE NOTE: For additional information on finding the main idea, whether stated or implied, see pages 64–66.

Recognizing Relationships Among Details

After you have identified the main idea of a reading passage, you will need to identify the details that support the main idea and evaluate how they are related to the main idea and to each other.

FINDING RELATIONSHIPS AMONG DETAILS

Identify specific details.	What details answer specific questions such as *Who? What? When? Where? Why?* and *How?* (*5W-How?* questions)?
Distinguish between fact and opinion.	What information can be proved true or false (facts)? What statements express a personal belief or attitude (opinions)?
Identify similarities and differences.	Are any details shown to be similar to or different from one another?
Understand cause and effect.	Do prior events have an impact on, or affect, later events?
Identify an order of organization.	In what order are the details arranged—chronological order, spatial order, order of importance, or any other ordered pattern?

Reading Passage

When the great Italian conductor Arturo Toscanini heard Marian Anderson sing, he proclaimed that her voice was of a quality that is heard only once in a hundred years. Although she came to be regarded as perhaps the greatest contralto of the twentieth century, Marian Anderson, an African American, struggled against discrimination for many years.

Born to poor parents in Philadelphia in 1902, Marian Anderson first gained notice in a children's church choir. Soon she was performing in a number of churches. Money was scarce, but numerous supporters contributed toward her operatic training. Eventually, she began

Sample Analysis

OPINION: What did Arturo Toscanini think of Marian Anderson's singing?
ANSWER: *He said that a voice like hers was heard only once in a hundred years.*

FACT: Where did Ms. Anderson first receive public recognition?
ANSWER: *She gained recognition in a children's church choir.*

RESOURCES

making concert appearances. However, she continually faced discrimination. Many music schools and concert halls were closed to her. Also, while making concert appearances in the South, Ms. Anderson was forced to endure the indignity of inferior, segregated railroad and hotel accommodations.

Frustrated, Ms. Anderson left the United States in the mid-1930s for study and concert tours in Europe. There she finally received critical and popular success. Ms. Anderson returned to the United States as a triumphant concert star.

Yet even at the height of her success, Marian Anderson continued to face discrimination at home. In one incident in Washington, D.C., the Daughters of the American Revolution (DAR) refused Ms. Anderson permission to perform at Constitution Hall. Many Americans protested this action, and many women, including First Lady Eleanor Roosevelt, resigned their memberships in the DAR.

In a public show of support for Marian Anderson, Secretary of the Interior Harold L. Ickes invited her to sing from the steps of the Lincoln Memorial on Easter Sunday, 1939. Over 75,000 people attended Anderson's brilliant, historic performance.

In 1955, Marian Anderson became the first black soloist ever to sing at the Metropolitan Opera House in New York City. In 1958, she was named to serve as a delegate to the United Nations, and she received the Presidential Medal of Freedom in 1963.

In the course of her operatic career, Marian Anderson's talent and courage helped to remove discriminatory barriers for other African American artists.

CONTRAST: How did Anderson's success in Europe contrast with her earlier career in the United States?
ANSWER: *In Europe, Anderson became very successful.*

CAUSE AND EFFECT: What was the effect of the DAR's refusal to allow Anderson to sing at Constitution Hall?
ANSWER: *Many people protested the DAR's actions, including members who resigned from the organization. Anderson then performed at the Lincoln Memorial.*

DETAIL: How many people attended Anderson's Easter Concert at the Lincoln Memorial?
ANSWER: *Over 75,000 people attended her concert at the Lincoln Memorial.*

ORDER: What honor did Marian Anderson receive eight years after she sang at the Metropolitan Opera?
ANSWER: *She received the Presidential Medal of Freedom.*

Applying Reasoning Skills

You can draw conclusions by evaluating, interpreting, and analyzing the facts and evidence presented in a reading passage. A *valid conclusion* is one that is firmly grounded in facts, evidence, or logic. An *invalid conclusion*, however, is one that is not consistent with the evidence presented. For example, it is invalid to conclude that Marian Anderson achieved success effortlessly. This conclusion conflicts with details in the reading passage, such as Ms. Anderson's early poverty and her having to leave the United States to prove her talent and to escape the discriminatory treatment she had faced here.

HOW TO DRAW CONCLUSIONS OR MAKE INFERENCES	
Gather all the evidence.	What facts or details have you learned about the subject?
Evaluate the evidence.	Do you know enough to make a few observations based on facts or reasonable assumptions?
Make appropriate connections.	What can you reasonably conclude or infer from the evidence you have gathered and evaluated?

Analyzing Graphics and Illustrations

Informational materials frequently include graphics, such as diagrams, maps, and charts. Graphics visually organize bodies of information that might be difficult to understand in written form. For example, the graph on page 1014 shows the relationship between the amounts of several types of waste generated by urban areas of the United States and the projections for the amounts generated in the future.

Suppose you are a city manager trying to find ways to reduce the amount of solid waste being dumped in the city landfill. By looking at the graph, you would see that a major paper recycling campaign could be the single most important factor in slowing the rate of increase in future landfill costs.

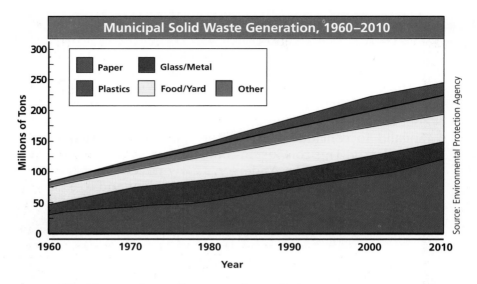

Graphs such as the one above help you make decisions because you can see relationships among items of data.

Applying Study Methods

Various study methods can be used to organize and process information. Among the most common study methods are

- taking notes
- classifying
- organizing information visually
- outlining
- paraphrasing
- summarizing
- writing a précis
- memorizing

Taking Notes

Careful note taking can help you remember what you read or hear in a lecture. Note taking also helps you organize information for studying, taking tests, and writing research papers.

Look at the study notes on pages 1015–1016. These notes cover the reading passage on pages 1011–1012. The main points in the passage are identified and arranged in groups. Then each of these groups is given a heading that indicates the key idea.

HOW TO TAKE STUDY NOTES

Recognize and record main points.	Set off main points as headings in your notes. ■ In a lecture, key words such as *major* or *most important* may indicate main points. ■ In a textbook, chapter headings and subheadings are usually reliable indicators of main ideas.
Summarize.	Don't record every detail. Summarize or abbreviate, using single words or phrases to record key ideas and supporting details.
Note important examples.	A few vivid examples can help you recall the main ideas.

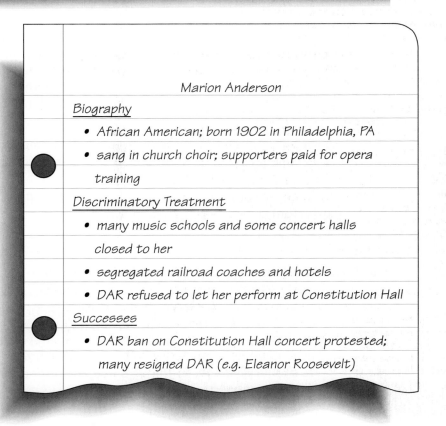

Marion Anderson

Biography

- African American; born 1902 in Philadelphia, PA
- sang in church choir; supporters paid for opera training

Discriminatory Treatment

- many music schools and some concert halls closed to her
- segregated railroad coaches and hotels
- DAR refused to let her perform at Constitution Hall

Successes

- DAR ban on Constitution Hall concert protested; many resigned DAR (e.g. Eleanor Roosevelt)

<u>Successes</u> (cont.)

- in 1930s, studied in Europe; concerts praised
- Cabinet member invited her to sing at Lincoln Memorial on Easter Sunday, 1939; over 75,000 attended
- 1st black soloist at Metropolitan Opera
- conductor Arturo Toscanini said her voice quality heard only every 100 yrs.
- some called her greatest contralto of 20th century
- 1958, delegate to U.N.; 1963, Pres. Medal of Freedom
- career inspired other black artists

Classifying

Classification is a method of organizing by arranging items into categories. For example, you use classification when you make an outline, determining the ideas that fit together under a specific heading. When you group items, you identify relationships among them.

EXAMPLE **What do each of the following have in common? ostriches, rheas, emus, penguins, kiwis**
ANSWER **They are all flightless birds.**

You also classify when you recognize patterns. For example, look at the following sequence of numbers.

What's the next number in the series?
105   111   118   126   135 _____ **?**

ANSWER To the first number (105), *6* is added to produce the second number (111). To the second number, *7* is added to produce the third number (118); *8* is added to the third number, and *9* is added to the fourth (126). So: *10* should be added to the fifth number (135) to produce the answer, which should be *145*.

Organizing Information Visually

You may find it helpful to reorganize information from a reading passage into a chart, map, or diagram. For example, the passage that follows presents facts about early automobile history.

> Inventors from several countries contributed to the development of the automobile. Nicolas Cugnot, a French engineer, built a steam-powered road vehicle in 1769 that crashed on its trial run. In 1801, Richard Trevithick, an Englishman, tested another steam-powered horseless carriage. Unlike Cugnot's invention, however, Trevithick's ran. Shortly after the trial run of Trevithick's steam engine, the American inventor Oliver Evans built a steam-powered machine used to clear sediment from waterways: the amphibious digger. Completed in 1805, it was the first steam-powered vehicle that could travel on land *and* water. Once the internal-combustion engine was developed in France in the middle of the nineteenth century, work on the automobile accelerated. In 1886, Gottlieb Daimler, a German inventor, designed an engine that ran on gasoline. Then, in the 1890s, a French engineer, Émile Levassor, produced a chassis that fit Daimler's engine. The car, the first gasoline-powered vehicle with the engine in front, is considered the forerunner of today's automobile.

By making a table similar to the one below, you would find the information in the paragraph easier to recall.

INVENTOR'S NAME	COUNTRY OF ORIGIN	DATE OF INVENTION	CONTRIBUTION
Nicolas Cugnot	France	1769	steam-powered road vehicle
Richard Trevithick	England	1801	first successful steam auto
Oliver Evans	U.S.A.	1805	amphibious digger
Gottlieb Daimler	Germany	1886	engine that ran on gasoline
Émile Levassor	France	1890s	chassis for Daimler's engine

RESOURCES

Outlining

An outline can help you organize ideas and information. When you write an outline, you identify and record major concepts and supporting details. You also group these ideas in an organized pattern that shows their order and their relationship.

If you are taking lecture notes, however, you might want to use an informal outline form. This method helps you organize information quickly. (See the sample notes on pages 1015–1016.)

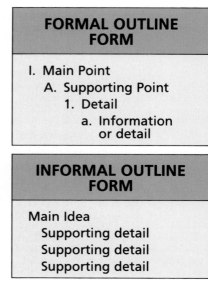

FORMAL OUTLINE FORM

I. Main Point
  A. Supporting Point
    1. Detail
      a. Information or detail

INFORMAL OUTLINE FORM

Main Idea
  Supporting detail
  Supporting detail
  Supporting detail

Paraphrasing

A *paraphrase* is a restatement of someone's ideas in your own words. Paraphrasing helps you understand what you read, especially if the original is written in poetic or elaborate language. A paraphrase is often about the same length as the original, so this technique is rarely used for long passages.

Paraphrasing a Literary Selection.   At times you may write a paraphrase of a poem or a literary passage in order to express in simpler terms the meaning of a complex work.

For example, in language arts classes, you may be asked to paraphrase a poem like the one that follows.

Ozymandias
by Percy Bysshe Shelley

I met a traveler from an antique land
Who said: Two vast and trunkless legs of stone
Stand in the desert . . . Near them, on the sand,
Half sunk, a shattered visage lies, whose frown,
And wrinkled lip, and sneer of cold command,
Tell that its sculptor well those passions read
Which yet survive, stamped on these lifeless things,

> The hand that mocked them, and the heart that fed;
> And on the pedestal these words appear:
> "My name is Ozymandias, king of kings;
> Look on my works, ye Mighty, and despair!"
> Nothing beside remains. Round the decay
> Of that colossal wreck, boundless and bare
> The lone and level sands stretch far away.

As an example, here is a possible paraphrase of this poem.

> The speaker in this poem repeats a traveler's tale about something the traveler saw in a land that had been inhabited by people since ancient times. While in the desert, the traveler came across the legs of what had once been a complete stone statue of a king. Next to the legs, partly covered by sand, lay the broken pieces of the statue's face. The traveler could tell from the harsh and proud expression carved on the face that the artist had skillfully captured the character of the king. However, the king's passions, as well as the heart that held them and the hand that carried them out, were long outlived by the stone that recorded them. The statue's pedestal bore an inscription declaring that the king, Ozymandias, considered himself the greatest of rulers and commanding that other monarchs should observe the kingdom he built and thereupon lose hope of ever equaling its splendor. Of Ozymandias's self-proclaimed accomplishments, there is nothing left. The giant, ruined statue is surrounded by a huge, lonely desert.

Paraphrasing Prose.   At times you may need to paraphrase a portion of an essay, an article, or another type of prose work. For instance, you may need to paraphrase information you find in an essay in order to fit it smoothly into a report.

For example, the following is an excerpt from *Novum Organum*, an essay by Francis Bacon, published in 1620.

> The human understanding is no dry light, but receives an infusion from the will and affections; whence proceed sciences which may be called "sciences as one would." For what a man had rather were true he more readily believes.

> Therefore he rejects difficult things from impatience of research; sober things, because they narrow hope; the deeper things of nature, from superstition; the light of experience, from arrogance and pride, lest his mind should seem to be occupied with things mean and transitory; things not commonly believed, out of deference to the opinion of the vulgar. Numberless in short are the ways, and sometimes imperceptible, in which the affections color and infect the understanding.

Here's how you might paraphrase this passage and incorporate your paraphrase into a report.

> Although modern scientists have available the most advanced technology, the greatest single obstacle to new discoveries is the human tendency to ignore information if it challenges people's preconceived notions. This human limit is as much an obstruction to the advance of science as it was in 1620, when Francis Bacon commented in his *Novum Organum* that no one's knowledge is pure; it is strongly affected by human desires and emotions. Bacon is commented that science could be described as the study of what people wanted to believe. Bacon complained that humans decline things that are hard because they grow impatient or frustrated; things that are serious because they prefer to feel happily hopeful; things that are mysterious because people are superstitious; things that have been gained through experience because of their smug, vain belief that past events are of little importance; and things that are new and different because of fear that others will disagree. Bacon concluded by saying that there are many ways, some of them not easily noticeable, that people's ideas can be influenced by their own beliefs and wishes.

HOW TO PARAPHRASE

1. Read the entire selection to get the overall meaning before you begin writing your paraphrase.
2. Identify the main idea of the selection. Keep it in mind while you write your paraphrase.

(continued)

HOW TO PARAPHRASE *(continued)*

3. Identify the speaker in fictional material. (Is the poet or author speaking, or is it a character?)
4. Write your paraphrase in your own words, using complete sentences and standard paragraph form.
5. Review the selection to be sure that your paraphrase expresses the same ideas as the original.

Summarizing

A *summary* is a restatement in condensed form of main ideas. Summarizing is a useful way to record the basic meaning of a selection you are studying. In addition, writing a summary helps you think critically; you have to analyze the material, identify the most important ideas, and eliminate details that can be left out.

HOW TO SUMMARIZE

1. Review the material carefully, identifying the main ideas and supporting details.
2. Condense the material. Focus only on key ideas, removing unnecessary details, examples, or repetitions. Write a sentence in your own words about each main idea.
3. Use your list of sentences to write your summary in paragraph form. If necessary, add transitional words to show how the ideas are related.
4. Revise your summary. Be sure it covers the most important points, that the information is clearly expressed, and that your words remain faithful to the author's intent.

Here is a sample summary of the article on pages 404–406.

> In 1583, Galileo Galilei, observing an altar lamp, discovered isochronism—the idea that the time it takes a pendulum to swing depends on how long it is, not how widely it swings. Galileo's discovery was part of the new

RESOURCES

science that involved direct observation rather than the study of other people's teachings. Galileo's discovery also led to the precision clock that allowed worldwide synchronization and standardization of time. Since the earth spins on its axis, every point on the planet experiences a 24-hour day, with 15° of spin being an hour of time. The time difference between two points depends on the number of degrees longitude in between.

Writing a Précis

A *précis* is a written summary. When you write a précis, you shorten a piece of writing—a reading passage, a chapter, an article, a report—to its bare essentials. Most of the techniques that you use for writing a précis are the same as summarizing skills. However, there are certain standard practices that you should follow when you are writing a précis.

GUIDELINES FOR WRITING A PRÉCIS

1. *Be brief.* A précis is seldom more than a third as long as the material being summarized, often less.
2. *Don't paraphrase.* If you merely put each sentence of the original version in slightly different words, you will wind up with as much material as the original.
3. *Stick to the central points.* Avoid examples, unnecessary adjectives, and repetitions.
4. *Use your own wording.* Don't just take phrases or sentences from the original.
5. *Be faithful to the author's points and views.* Don't add your own comments, and don't use such expressions as "The author says" or "The paragraph means."

Following is a paragraph from which to write a précis.

Rapidity in reading has an obvious direct bearing on success in college work because of the large amount of reading which must be covered in nearly all college courses. But it is probably also a direct measure of the special kind of aptitude that can be called bookish, because rapidity of reading usually correlates with comprehension and retention. Generally speaking, the more rapidly a reader reads, the more effectively he grasps and retains. The normal reading speed of college freshmen has been found to be around 250 words a minute on ordinary reading matter, and a student who reads more slowly than that will certainly have difficulty in completing his college tasks within reasonable study periods. To be a really good college risk under this criterion, one should readily and habitually cover not fewer than 300 words a minute on ordinary reading matter. [143 words]

The chart below shows errors to be avoided in a précis.

COMMON ERRORS IN PRÉCIS-WRITING	
ERROR	**EXAMPLE FROM FAULTY PRÉCIS**
uses phrases taken directly from original	Reading speed has a <u>direct bearing on success in college</u> since college classes often demand much reading. <u>Rapidity of reading</u> usually means a student has better <u>comprehension and retention</u>.
précis misses the point of the original; emphasizes unimportant points	Great amounts of reading are required in most college courses. It's important to read fast <u>to have success in college</u>. A person who reads slowly won't have enough time to get all the work done.
writer of précis injected own ideas	For college success, reading speed is important since college classes, <u>such as history and English</u>, often demand much reading. <u>Surprisingly</u>, students who read quickly retain and recall material better than slower readers, <u>who may flunk out if they can't keep up with their homework</u>.

The following précis is acceptable; it is an appropriate length, and it is stated in the writer's own words.

For college success, reading speed is important; college classes often demand much reading. Students who read quickly retain and recall material better than slower readers. The average college freshman's speed is 250 words a minute, but higher achievers read faster than 300 words a minute. [45 words]

Memorizing

You are more likely to retain information if you follow these guidelines.

1. *Condense the information.* A chapter, for example, can often be summarized or condensed.
2. *Rehearse the material in several different ways.* Use several different senses to commit the material to memory. Write or copy the material so you can see it and use touch and muscle movements. Say the material out loud so you can hear it.
3. *Use memory games.* Use the first letter of each word in a series to form a new word. Make a rhyme to help you remember dates or facts. Associate information with a vivid mental image.
4. *Repeat the material.* Recite the material frequently in short sessions.

Improving Test-Taking Skills

Preparing for Tests

To improve your performance on all types of tests, you need to prepare carefully and learn various test-taking strategies. For example, one of the most important factors that affect your performance on a test is your attitude. If you think that you can do well and know that you have prepared to the best of your ability, you will be more likely to focus your energies on the test and concentrate on doing well. Most people feel nervous before a big test, but you can learn how to channel that energy into useful effort.

Kinds of Tests

Classroom Tests.   The purpose of the typical classroom test is to measure your ability to use key academic skills or to demonstrate your knowledge of specific academic subjects. Classroom tests often combine several types of test questions. For example, a test might be made up of twenty multiple-choice questions worth four points each and two essay questions worth ten points each. Many different combinations of test questions and scoring methods may be used.

The best way to prepare for classroom tests is to be sure that you are familiar with the material or that you have practiced the skill you must demonstrate at the time of testing. Apply the study skills suggested earlier in this chapter to improve your performance on classroom tests.

Standardized Tests.   A standardized test is one in which your score is evaluated according to a "standard" or "norm" compiled from the scores of other students who have taken the same test. Some standardized tests may be developed by a school district or state. The best-known tests of this type are those given to students across the entire United States.

- the *Preliminary Scholastic Aptitude Test (PSAT)*
- the *National Merit Scholars Qualifying Test (NMSQT)*
- the *Scholastic Aptitude Test (SAT-I Reasoning Test)*
- the *Scholastic Aptitude Test (SAT-II Subject Test)*
- the *American College Testing Program (ACT)*

There are two basic types of standardized tests: those testing aptitude and those testing achievement.

Aptitude (or Reasoning) Tests	■ intended to evaluate basic skills or reasoning abilities needed in various general areas of study ■ often cover material you have learned during many years of study (such as verbal expression skills and critical thinking ability)
Achievement (or Academic Subject) Tests	■ intended to measure knowledge of specific subjects (such as history, literature, sciences, mathematics, or foreign languages)

HOW TO PREPARE FOR STANDARDIZED TESTS

1. *Learn what specific abilities will be tested.* Information booklets may be provided. Practice with these or with published study guides.
2. *Know what materials you will need.* On the day of the test, you may need to bring specific materials, such as your official test registration card, number 2 pencils, or lined paper for writing an essay answer.
3. *Determine how the test is evaluated.* If there is no penalty for wrong answers, make your best guess on all questions possible. However, if wrong answers are penalized, make guesses only if you are fairly sure of the correct answer.

Taking Standardized Tests

One purpose of standardized tests is to give a prediction of how well you may perform in the college environment. They test your ability to identify and correct problems with verbal expression as well as your ability to analyze and interpret the meaning, purpose, and organization of reading passages.

Kinds of Test Questions

Most test questions are either limited-response questions or open-response questions.

Limited-Response Questions. Limited-response questions give you a limited number of choices from which you select the most appropriate answer. Questions of this type include

- multiple-choice questions
- true/false questions
- matching questions

Open-Response Questions. Open-response questions require you to provide a written response to a specific prompt. These responses may vary widely in their length:

- fill-in-the-blank questions
- short-answer questions
- essay questions

Tests of Verbal Expression

Standardized tests often contain limited-response questions that measure your understanding of written expression and expression of meaning clearly and with grammatical correctness.

MATERIAL COVERED ON VERBAL EXPRESSION TESTS	
Grammar Questions	You identify the most correct answer, using standard grammar and usage rules. These test items often cover correct use of ■ subject-verb agreement (649–664) ■ principal parts of verbs (713–730) ■ pronouns (672–698)
Punctuation Questions	You identify use of correct punctuation. These test items often cover correct use of ■ end marks and commas (840–863) ■ dashes, semicolons, and colons (866–872) ■ parentheses and apostrophes (873–883) ■ quotation marks and hyphens (887–898)
Sentence Structure Questions	You demonstrate knowledge of what is (and what is not) a complete sentence. These test items often cover correction of ■ fragments and run-on sentences (515–523) ■ combining sentences (526–540) ■ modifiers (762–779) ■ verb tense (713–754) ■ parallel structure (512–514) ■ transitional words (79–81, 117–118)
Revision-in-Context Questions	You show appropriate revision to a part of or to an entire composition. These test items often cover correct use of ■ composition structure (96–123) ■ unity and coherence (72–81) ■ tone (33–37) ■ arranging ideas (38–42)
Rhetorical Strategies Questions	You show an understanding of strategies used by writers to express ideas and opinions. These test items often cover ■ strategies of development (82–89) ■ sequence of ideas (75–78) ■ style and tone (33–37)

For the best-known national tests, these multiple-choice, verbal expression questions are not asked in isolated form. Instead, they appear in the context of a reading passage. You are given a sample passage, usually a long paragraph, with several words and phrases underlined and numbered. Then you are given a series of test items related to the passage. You are expected to pick the choice that best expresses the meaning, is most grammatically correct, or is more consistent with the style and tone of the passage.

Here is a sample test passage with sample questions.

Sample Verbal Expression Test Passage

In an Age of Science—and among all the periods of history, <u>none of them merits</u> that name better than our own—trained scientists are
1
fortunate people. Their training is a matter of national <u>concern,</u>
2
<u>because</u> our nation badly needs more scientists than it has. They can often advance quickly. They can climb as far in science as their ambitions and talents permit. <u>Most important is that they stand</u> at the
3
very center of the forces that are conquering and remaking the world around us. Their futures are bright. It is small wonder that so many young people dream of entering one of the scientific professions.

SAMPLE VERBAL EXPRESSION QUESTIONS	

1. (A.) NO CHANGE
  B. are meriting
  C. meriting
  D. merit
	[This is a question about grammar; it requires you to know the correct subject-verb agreement.]

2. A. NO CHANGE
  B. concern; because
  C. concern. Because
  (D.) concern because
	[This is a question about punctuation; it requires you to know which mark of punctuation is appropriate here.]

(continued)

SAMPLE VERBAL EXPRESSION
QUESTIONS *(continued)*

3. How should the third and fourth sentences be combined? A. In science, because they can often advance quickly, they can climb as far as their ambitions and talents permit. (B.) They can often advance as fast and as far in science as their ambitions and talents permit. C. They can often advance quickly and far in science, because of their ambitions and talents. D. As quickly and as far in science as their ambitions and talents will permit them, they can advance.	[This is a question about sentence structure; it requires you to know how to combine sentences effectively.]
4. Which is the best revision of the portion of the passage indicated by the number 3? (A.) Most important, they stand B. It is most important that they stand C. It is most important; they stand D. Most importantly that they stand	[This is a revision-in-context question; it requires you to use revision skills to best express the ideas in the passage.]
5. This passage might next discuss A. how our government should provide grants to help scientific research. B. why science is not respected in other nations. (C.) specific occupations for young people in the sciences. D. why there are not enough scientists.	[This is a question about rhetorical strategies; it requires you to use your knowledge of writing strategy, organization, and style in order to draw conclusions and make inferences about the passage.]

RESOURCES

As you can see, there are only two basic types of questions used to test verbal expression on the most current, best-known national tests.

MOST COMMON TYPES OF VERBAL EXPRESSION TEST ITEMS	
"NO CHANGE" Items	■ give list of suggested revisions of under-lined, numbered portions of passage ■ always contain one "NO CHANGE" choice (these words are often printed in capital letters) among list of choices; selected if indicated part is correct as is
Critical Thinking Items	■ ask you to analyze and evaluate the passage as a whole ■ ask you to make inferences about portions of a passage as related to the whole

Tests of Critical Reading

Standardized tests may contain a number of limited-response questions that measure your ability to analyze and interpret a piece of writing. These questions require you to look critically at a particular piece of writing to find the meaning, purpose, and organization of the selection. In addition, these questions require you to evaluate the effectiveness of the passage in conveying the meaning intended by the writer.

Questions used in tests of critical reading and critical analysis cover the following subject matter:

CRITICAL READING
■ organization
■ evaluation
■ interpretation
■ synthesis
■ vocabulary in context
■ style

CRITICAL ANALYSIS
■ analogies
■ logic

MATERIAL COVERED ON CRITICAL READING TESTS

Organization Questions	You identify the organizational techniques used by the writer of a passage. These test items often cover identification of ■ author's use of particular writing strategies (82–89) ■ the main idea of a passage (1010) ■ arrangement of supporting details (64–70) ■ transitional devices that make the passage coherent (79–81) ■ techniques used to conclude the passage (119–121)
Evaluation Questions	You judge the effectiveness of techniques used by the author of a passage. These test items often cover identification of ■ the author's opinion (1011) ■ the author's intended audience (33–37) ■ the author's tone or point of view (33–37) ■ the author's purpose (33–37)
Interpretation Questions	You draw conclusions or make inferences about the meaning of information presented in a passage. These test items often cover identification of ■ ambiguities in information (503–525) ■ conclusions or inferences based on given material (1013) ■ specific conclusions or inferences that can be drawn about the author or the topic of a passage (1013)
Synthesis Questions	You demonstrate knowledge of how parts of a passage fit together into a whole. These test items often cover interpretation of ■ techniques used to unify details (72–74) ■ the cumulative meaning of details in a passage (1010–1012)

(continued)

RESOURCES

MATERIAL COVERED ON CRITICAL READING TESTS *(continued)*	
Vocabulary in Context Questions	You infer the meaning of an unfamiliar word by an analysis of its context. These test items often cover determination of ■ the meaning of a passage to learn the meaning of a word (1010–1012) ■ the meaning of an unfamiliar word, using context clues (1043–1044)
Style Questions	You analyze a passage to evaluate the author's use of style (480–497). These test items often cover identification of ■ the author's style ■ the author's voice and tone ■ the author's intended audience

Here is a sample reading passage with sample questions.

Sample Reading Passage

By the end of 1855, Walt Whitman was seeing his "wonderous and ponderous book," *Leaves of Grass,* through its final stages. He read the typeset pages by candlelight. When the poet Hart Crane began working on *The Bridge* some sixty years later, he worked under an electric light. Before 1920, few major American cities had been electrified. By the 1930s, nearly every American city was illuminated.

Henry Adams saw his first electric generator, or dynamo, in Paris at the Great Exposition of 1900. Because they could produce cheap electricity, these dynamos had commercial use. In time they were used to generate the brilliant arc lights of San Francisco, New York, and Philadelphia, thus replacing gas street lamps that were the hallmark of American cities in the nineteenth century.

Yet arc lights were simply unsuitable for home use because of their intense brightness. Credit for the discovery and promotion of the incandescent light used in household light bulbs must go to Thomas Alva Edison. Financed by a group of wealthy backers, Edison and his team designed an entire system to provide electricity: filaments, wiring, efficient dynamos, safety features, and even the sockets themselves. In 1881, Edison unveiled his famous Pearl Street Station in New York

City. Edison's men laid the wires to the square mile around 257 Pearl Street, and they wired individual households and installed meters to measure electricity use. Edison's stations would eventually supply power to over 400,000 lamps in places such as Chicago and Milan, New Orleans, and Berlin.

At the outset, electricity for the home was an expensive luxury for the elite. In 1907, for example, only 8% of American homes had electricity. However, large-scale generators and greater consumption gradually allowed the costs to drop. By 1920, 34% of American homes had electricity, and by 1941 nearly 80% were supplied with electricity. Today, we simply take electricity for granted.

By candlelight, Whitman handwrote his poetry. By fluorescent light, a modern poet keystrokes poetry into a computer. Electrification, communication, urbanization—all are processes and systems that affect our lives. Only by understanding the history of these technological developments can we truly understand their importance.

SAMPLE CRITICAL READING QUESTIONS

1. According to the passage, in which order (from earliest to latest) did the following events occur?
   I. Eighty percent of American homes have electricity.
   II. Walt Whitman writes *Leaves of Grass*.
   III. Henry Adams sees the dynamo at the Great Exposition.
   IV. Edison begins operation of the Pearl Street Station in New York.

   A. II, IV, III, I
   B. II, III, IV, I
   C. II, I, III, IV
   D. II, IV, I, III

   [This is an organization question; it requires you to identify the time sequence of these events and to arrange them in the correct historical time order.]

2. The word *elite* in the fourth paragraph may be defined as
   A. a variety of type found on a typewriter.
   B. a group of arrogant, stubborn people.
   C. the last people to agree to a new idea.
   D. the wealthiest members of a social group.

   [This is a vocabulary-in-context question; it requires you to examine the context in which the word appears in the passage in order to determine the appropriate definition.]

(continued)

RESOURCES

SAMPLE CRITICAL READING QUESTIONS *(continued)*

3. Imagine that after reading the passage your classmate wrote the following paragraph.

   In the home, women were thought to be the benefactors of electrification. Irons, vacuum cleaners, hot water heaters, clothes washers, and refrigerators—all were hailed as inventions that would make women's lives easier. But they also reinforced the idea that the woman's place was in the home. These gadgets were indeed labor-saving devices, but only if someone remained in the home to use them. Only recently have we questioned whether these so-called technological advances were advantages at all.

   You could assume that your classmate is critical of the idea that technological advances

   A. are often invisible.
   B. are inexpensive.
   C. are beneficial to everyone.
   D. exist independently of each other.

   [This is an evaluation question; it requires you to identify the main points of the original passage and to recognize which of these points your classmate disputed.]

4. The phrase "keystrokes poetry into a computer" is best taken to mean that electrification is a form of progress that

   A. jeopardizes our historical awareness.
   B. influences daily the way we live our lives.
   C. improves our ability to compose poetry.
   D. most affects students.

   [This is an interpretation question; you are asked to examine the context of the word noted in order to explain its meaning in the passage.]

5. It can be inferred from the description of Thomas Alva Edison that he was

   A. a man who represented the nineteenth century.
   B. a man who changed his ideas frequently.
   C. an organized, driven man.
   D. a capitalist concerned only for his own welfare.

   [This is a synthesis question; it requires you to read, in the passage as a whole, about the efforts needed to electrify a small urban area. Then you can infer that Edison, the project director, was a driven man of great organizational powers.]

(continued)

SAMPLE CRITICAL READING QUESTIONS *(continued)*

6. Readers of this passage are likely to describe it as
A. informal.
B. historical.
C. inspirational.
D. biographical.

[This is a question of style; it requires you to analyze the way the passage is written to determine the category or type of writing it represents.]

Tests of Critical Analysis

Standardized tests may contain a number of limited-response questions that measure your ability to recognize specific kinds of relationships.

MATERIAL COVERED ON CRITICAL ANALYSIS TESTS	

Analogy Questions	These ask you to analyze the relationship between a pair of words and to use reasoning skills to identify a second pair of words that have the same relationship (989–991).
	 EXAMPLE: SEW : CUT :: _____
	     A. paint : brush
	     B. willow : tree
	     C. plaster : break
	     D. wind : moan

Logic Questions	These ask you to analyze a sentence or a brief passage to fill in one or more blanks with the most appropriate word or words given.
	 EXAMPLE: Because electrification began to gain _____ at the turn of the century, this era signals an important _____ in American history.
	     A. mediocrity . . . collapse
	     B. momentum . . . juncture
	     C. patents . . . tragedy
	     D. popularity . . . rendezvous

Essay Tests

Essay tests require you to think about and express your understanding of selected material in an organized way. Because essay tests call for critical thinking and writing skills, answers can vary. However, a well-written essay must be complete, organized according to the directions, and supported with sufficient detail.

Essay questions usually ask you to perform specific tasks. Each of these tasks is expressed with a verb. Each task requires a specific response that you can prepare for by becoming familiar with the key terms and the kinds of information called for.

ESSAY TEST QUESTIONS		
KEY VERB	**TASK**	**SAMPLE QUESTION**
analyze	Take something apart to see how each part works.	Analyze the main character in Nathaniel Hawthorne's "The Minister's Black Veil."
argue	Take a viewpoint on an issue and give reasons to support this opinion.	Argue whether or not your school should forbid students to work on weekday evenings.
compare	Point out likenesses.	Compare the British Parliament with the U.S. Congress as law-making bodies.
contrast	Point out differences.	Contrast organic farming methods with traditional procedures.
define	Give specific details that make something unique.	Define the term *osmosis* as it relates to the permeability of membranes.

(continued)

ESSAY TEST QUESTIONS *(continued)*		
KEY VERB	TASK	SAMPLE QUESTION
demonstrate (also illustrate, present, show)	Provide examples to support a point.	Demonstrate that an electrical charge is conducted by metal.
describe	Give a picture in words.	Describe an incident in *Othello* that features Iago.
discuss	Examine in detail.	Discuss the term *Romanticism.*
explain	Give reasons.	Explain why congruent angles are complementary.
identify	Point out specific persons, places, things, or characteristics.	Identify members of the presidential cabinet and their duties.
interpret	Give the meaning or significance of something.	Interpret the importance of the dismantling of the Berlin Wall.
list (also outline, trace)	Give all steps in order or all details about a subject.	List events leading to the Persian Gulf Conflict.
summarize	Give a brief overview of the main points.	Summarize the plot of F. Scott Fitzgerald's *The Great Gatsby.*

Before you start writing on an essay test, scan the questions quickly. Determine how many answers you are expected to write. If you have a choice between several items, decide which of them you can answer best. Then plan how much time to spend on each answer, and stay on this schedule.

Read the essay question carefully. There may be several parts to the question that you need to answer.

Pay attention to important terms in the question. Find the key verbs; these identify tasks you must accomplish in your essay.

Take a moment to use prewriting strategies. On scratch paper, make notes or a simple outline to help you decide what to write.

Evaluate and revise as you write. You will not be able to redraft your whole essay, but you can edit to strengthen specific parts.

QUALITIES OF A GOOD ESSAY ANSWER

- The essay is well organized.
- The main ideas and supporting points are clear.
- The sentences are complete and well written.
- There are no distracting errors in spelling, punctuation, or grammar.

Review

EXERCISE 1   **Using Study Skills**

The following numbered items suggest ways for you to practice using the study skills discussed on pages 1009–1016.

1. In a brief paragraph, identify ways that you use different rates of reading, such as those noted on page 1007, in order to accomplish different purposes.
2. Choose a magazine article or a textbook chapter. Read the selection, using the SQ3R method outlined on page 1009. List at least five questions and write brief answers to each one.
3. Working with a group of two or three classmates, write a list of critical reading questions about Chief Joseph's "An Indian's View of Indian Affairs" (pages 278–280). Use the sample analysis of the reading passage on pages 1011–1012 as a model. Let each group's members ask their questions to test the rest of the class.

4. Find a passage in a textbook, a nonfiction book, a magazine, or a newspaper that gives information that you can express in graphic form. Using the information and example on page 1017 as a model, make a diagram, chart, or other visual arrangement of the most pertinent information from the passage.

5. Select a chapter from one of your textbooks that you have been assigned as homework and take study notes, using the strategies explained on pages 1014–1016.

EXERCISE 2 **Paraphrasing a Poem**

Write a paraphrase of "The New Colossus" by Emma Lazarus (page 11). Follow the guidelines on pages 1018–1021.

EXERCISE 3 **Writing a Précis**

Write a précis of the essay by James West Davidson, "The Frontier Kitchen of the Plains" (pages 256–259). Follow the guidelines on pages 1022–1024.

EXERCISE 4 **Preparing for Tests of Verbal Expression**

Read the passage, then answer the questions that follow, using the guidelines on pages 1027–1030.

Planes of the future may be held together by glue instead of by thousands of rivets or metal bolts. Experiments conducted by American aircraft manufacturers and the Air Force revealed that a glued aircraft would have several advantages over a riveted one. It would weigh 15 percent less. It would also cost 20 percent less to build and maintain. Structural tests on a glued fuselage showed that it could survive 120,000 hours of flight; four times the life of the average riveted aircraft. Furthermore, the glued fuselage proved to be less likely to develop cracks and the glue even retarded the growth of cracks cut into the fuselage deliberately. Encouragement was also found in the results from tests of the plane's resistance to environmental stresses such as salt air, high humidity, and freezing temperatures.

RESOURCES

1. **A.** NO CHANGE
   B. flight, four times
   C. flight. Four times
   D. flight, and four times

2. **A.** NO CHANGE
   B. develop cracks; the glue
   C. develop cracks. And the glue
   D. develop cracks, and the glue

3. How should the third and fourth sentences be combined?
   A. It would weigh and cost 20 percent less for building and maintenance.
   B. In addition to less weight by 15 percent, it would cost 20 percent less as building and maintenance.
   C. It would weigh 15 percent less, and it would cost 20 percent less to build and maintain.
   D. Because it would weigh 15 percent less, it would cost 20 percent less to build it and maintain it.

4. Which of the following is the best revision of the last sentence?
   A. Encouragement was also found in the results from tests of the plane's resistance to environmental stresses such as: salt air; high humidity; and freezing temperatures.
   B. The results from tests of the plane's resistance to environmental stresses such as salt air, high humidity, and freezing temperatures were also encouraging.
   C. The resulting tests of the plane's resistance to environmental stresses such as salt air, high humidity, and freezing temperatures were also encouraged.
   D. Resulting from tests of the plane's resistance to environmental stresses such as salt air, high humidity, and freezing temperatures were also encouraged.

5. In telling about the various tests that the glued plane was subjected to, the writer is
   A. giving concrete examples to prove the plane's durability.
   B. using the extremes of the environmental factors to create a humorous effect.
   C. giving the reader an idea of how frustrating these tests were for the scientists.
   D. using description to make the reader feel a part of the scene.

▶ EXERCISE 5   **Preparing for Tests of Critical Reading Skills**

Using the sample test passage on pages 1032–1033, answer the following questions.

1. What idea does this passage show best?
   A. the conflict between people and technology
   B. the drawbacks of technology
   C. the effect of technological change on American cities
   D. the difficulty in finding financial backing for new inventions

2. The word *electrification* in the final paragraph may be defined as
   A. a shock or jolt.
   B. an increase in excitement.
   C. decay of the cities.
   D. conversion to electric power.

3. The author's predominant attitude about the subject seems to be
   A. criticism of the rate of technological change.
   B. distrust of power companies.
   C. approval of technological change.
   D. interest in how electrification affected Whitman's poetry.

4. Which of the following interpretations is suggested by the second paragraph?
   A. In 1900, Henry Adams saw possibilities for the dynamo.
   B. In 1900, American cities had arc lights but needed cheap electricity to run them.
   C. Gas lamps were not used in Europe.
   D. Gas lamps were less expensive than electric light.

5. This passage most probably has the purpose of
   A. persuading the reader.
   B. giving information to the reader.
   C. expressing the author's creativity.
   D. entertaining the reader.

RESOURCES

Glossary of Terms

A

Action verb Expresses physical or mental activity. (See page 565.)

Active voice The voice a verb is in when it expresses an action done *by* its subject. (See page 748.)

Adjective Modifies a noun or a pronoun. (See page 559.)

Adjective clause A subordinate clause that modifies a noun or a pronoun. (See page 630.)

Adjective phrase A prepositional phrase that modifies a noun or a pronoun. (See page 605.)

Adverb Modifies a verb, an adjective, or another adverb. (See page 568.)

Adverb clause A subordinate clause that modifies a verb, an adjective, or an adverb. (See page 636.)

Adverb phrase A prepositional phrase that modifies a verb, an adjective, or an adverb. (See page 607.)

Agreement The correspondence, or match, between grammatical forms. (See Chapter 21.)

Aim One of the four basic purposes, or reasons, for writing. (See pages 7 and 20.)

Ambiguous reference Occurs when a pronoun refers to either of two antecedents. (See page 701.)

Antecedent The word that a pronoun stands for. (See page 555.)

Appositive A noun or a pronoun placed beside another noun or pronoun to identify or explain it. (See page 621.)

Appositive phrase Consists of an appositive and its modifiers. (See page 621.)

Article *A*, *an*, and *the*, the most frequently used adjectives. (See page 560.)

C

Case The form of a noun or pronoun that shows how it is used in a sentence. (See page 674.)

Cause-and-effect explanation A form of writing in which a writer explains the causes and/or effects of a situation. (See Chapter 7.)

Chronological order A way of arranging ideas in a paragraph or composition according to when events happen. (See pages 39 and 75.)

Classification A strategy of development: looking at a subject as it relates to other subjects in a group. (See page 86.)

Clause A group of words that contains a verb and its subject and is used as part of a sentence. (See page 628.)

Coherence A quality achieved when all the ideas in a paragraph or composition are clearly arranged and connected. (See pages 75 and 117.)

Comparison Refers to the change in the form of an adjective or an adverb to show increasing or decreasing degrees in the quality the modifier expresses. (See page 770.)

Comparison/Contrast essay A form of writing in which a writer discusses similarities or differences (or both) between two subjects. (See Chapter 6.)

Complement A word or group of words that completes the meaning of a verb. (See page 591.)

Complex sentence Has one independent clause and at least one subordinate clause. (See page 641.)

Compound-complex sentence Has two or more independent clauses and at least one subordinate clause. (See page 641.)

Compound sentence Has two or more independent clauses but no subordinate clauses. (See page 640.)

Conjunction Joins words or groups of words. (See page 574.)

Dangling modifier A modifying word, phrase, or clause that does not clearly and sensibly modify a word or a group of words in a sentence. (See page 785.)

Declarative sentence Makes a statement and is followed by a period. (See page 597.)

Description A strategy of development: using sensory details and spatial order to describe individual features of a specific subject. (See page 83.)

Direct object A word or word group that receives the action of the verb or shows the result of the action, telling *whom* or *what* after a transitive verb. (See page 592.)

Direct reference Connects ideas in a paragraph or composition by referring to a noun or pronoun used earlier. (See page 79.)

Double negative The use of two negative words when one is enough. (See page 811.)

Elliptical clause A clause from which words have been omitted. (See page 637.)

Essential clause/Essential phrase Also called **restrictive:** is necessary to the meaning of a sentence; not set off by commas. (See page 851.)

Evaluating A stage in the writing process: making judgments about a composition's strengths and weaknesses in content, organization, and style. (See pages 6 and 45.)

Evaluation A strategy of development: making judgments about a subject in an attempt to determine its value. (See page 89.)

Exclamatory sentence Expresses strong feeling and is followed by an exclamation point. (See page 598.)

Expository writing Aims at being informative, explanatory, or exploratory. (See page 7.)

General reference Occurs when a pronoun refers to a general idea rather than to a specific noun. (See page 703.)

Gerund A verb form ending in *–ing* that is used as a noun. (See page 614.)

Gerund phrase Consists of a gerund and its modifiers and complements. (See page 615.)

Imperative mood Used to express a direct command or request. (See page 755.)

Imperative sentence Gives a command or makes a request and is followed by either a period or an exclamation point. (See page 598.)

Indefinite reference Occurs when a pronoun refers to no particular person or thing. (See page 707.)

Independent clause Also called a **main clause:** expresses a complete thought and can stand by itself as a sentence. (See page 628.)

Indicative mood Used to express a fact, an opinion, or a question. (See page 755.)

Indirect object A word or word group that comes between a transitive verb and object and tells *to whom* or *to what* or *for whom* or *for what* the action of a verb is done. (See page 592.)

Infinitive (1) One of the principal parts of a verb. (See page 715.) **(2)** A verb form usually preceded by *to*, used as a noun, an adjective, or an adverb. (See page 616.)

Infinitive phrase Consists of an infinitive and its modifiers and complements. (See page 619.)

Interjection Expresses emotion and has no grammatical relation to the rest of the sentence. (See page 576.)

Interrogative sentence Asks a question and is followed by a question mark. (See page 597.)

Intransitive verb An action verb that does not take an object. (See page 565.)

Linking verb Connects the subject with a word that identifies or describes it. (See page 565.)

Literary analysis A form of writing in which a writer examines and responds to a piece of literature critically. (See Chapter 10.)

Literary writing Aims at creating imaginative works. (See page 7.)

Logical order A way of arranging details in a paragraph or composition according to what makes logical sense, such as grouping related ideas together. (See pages 39 and 76.)

Misplaced modifier A word, phrase, or clause that makes a sentence awkward because it seems to modify the wrong word or group of words. (See page 782.)

Modifier A word that limits the meaning of another word. (See page 764.)

Mood The form a verb takes to indicate the attitude of the person using the verb. (See page 755.)

Narration A strategy of development: relating events or actions over a period of time, usually using chronological order. (See page 84.)

Nonessential clause/Nonessential phrase Also called **nonrestrictive:** adds information not necessary to the main idea in the sentence and is set off by commas. (See page 851.)

Noun Names a person, place, thing, or idea. (See page 553.)

Noun clause A subordinate clause used as a noun. (See page 634.)

Number The form of a word that indicates whether the word is singular or plural. (See page 649.)

Objective complement A word or word group that helps complete the meaning of a transitive verb by identifying or modifying the direct object. (See page 593.)

Object of a preposition The noun or pronoun that ends a prepositional phrase. (See page 605.)

Order of importance A way of arranging details, in a paragraph or composition, from least to most important or from most to least important. (See pages 39 and 76.)

Participial phrase Consists of a participle and its complements and modifiers. (See page 612.)

Participle A verb form used as an adjective. (See page 611.)

Passive voice The voice a verb is in when it expresses an action done *to* its subject. (See page 748.)

Personal essay A form of writing in which an author explores and shares the meaning of an experience that was especially important to him or her. (See Chapter 4.)

Persuasive essay A form of writing in which a writer supports an opinion and tries to persuade an audience. (See Chapter 8.)

Persuasive writing Aims at convincing people to accept an idea or to take action. (See page 7.)

Phrase A group of related words used as a single part of speech and does not contain a verb and its subject. (See page 605.)

Point of view The vantage point, or position, from which a writer tells a story or describes a subject. (See page 169.)

Predicate The part of a sentence that says something about the subject. (See page 584.)

Predicate adjective An adjective that follows a linking verb and modifies the subject of the verb. (See page 595.)

Predicate nominative A word or word group that follows a linking verb and refers to the same person or thing as the subject of the verb. (See page 595.)

Preposition Shows the relationship of a noun or a pronoun to some other word in a sentence. (See page 571.)

Prepositional phrase A group of words beginning with a preposition and ending with an object (a noun or a pronoun). (See page 605.)

Prewriting The first stage of the writing process: thinking and planning, deciding what to write about, collecting ideas and details, and making a plan for presenting ideas. (See pages 6 and 22.)

Problem-solution essay A form of exploratory writing in which a writer explains a problem and proposes an effective solution. (See Chapter 9.)

Pronoun Is used in place of a noun or more than one noun. (See page 555.)

Proofreading A stage of the writing process: carefully reading a revised draft to correct mistakes in grammar, usage, and mechanics. (See pages 6 and 50.)

Publishing The last stage of the writing process: making a final, clean copy of a paper and sharing it with an audience. (See pages 6 and 50.)

Purpose A reason for writing or speaking. (See pages 7 and 21.)

Research report A form of writing in which a writer presents factual information discovered through exploration and research. (See Chapter 11.)

Revising A stage of the writing process: making changes in a composition's content, organization, and style in order to improve it. (See pages 6 and 45.)

Self-Expressive writing Aims at expressing a writer's feelings and thoughts. (See page 7.)

Sentence A group of words that contains a subject and a verb and expresses a complete thought. (See page 582.)

Simple sentence Has one independent clause and no subordinate clauses. (See page 640.)

Spatial order A way of arranging details in a paragraph or composition according to location. (See pages 39 and 75.)

Style A writer's unique way of adapting language to suit different occasions. (See Chapter 13.)

Subject Tells whom or what a sentence is about. (See page 584.)

Subject complement A word or word group that completes the meaning of a linking verb and identifies or modifies the subject. (See page 595.)

Subjunctive mood Used to express a suggestion, a necessity, a condition contrary to fact, or a wish. (See page 756.)

Subordinate clause Also called a **dependent clause:** does not express a complete thought and cannot stand alone as a sentence. (See page 629.)

Supporting sentences Give specific details or information to support a main idea. (See page 67.)

Tense Indicates the time of an action or state of being expressed by a verb. (See page 736.)

Theme The underlying meaning or message a writer wants to communicate to readers. (See page 172.)

Thesis statement Announces the limited topic of a composition and the main, or unifying, idea about that topic. (See page 102.)

Tone The feeling or attitude a writer conveys about a topic. (See page 34.)

Topic sentence Expresses the main idea of a paragraph. (See page 64.)

Transitional expressions Words and phrases that indicate relationships between ideas in a paragraph or composition. (See page 79.)

Transitive verb An action verb that takes an object. (See page 565.)

Unity A quality achieved when all the sentences or paragraphs in a composition work together as a unit to express or support one main idea. (See pages 72 and 117.)

Verb Expresses an action or a state of being. (See page 565.)

Verbal A form of a verb used as a noun, an adjective, or an adverb. (See page 611.)

Verbal phrase Consists of a verbal and its modifiers and complements. (See page 611.)

Verb phrase Consists of a main verb preceded by at least one helping verb. (See page 611.)

Voice (1) The unique sound and rhythm of a writer's language. (See page 482.) **(2)** The form a transitive verb takes to indicate whether the subject of the verb performs or receives the action. (See page 748.)

Weak reference Occurs when a pronoun refers to an antecedent that has not been expressed. (See page 706.)

Writing A stage of the writing process: putting ideas into words, following a plan that organizes the ideas. (See pages 6 and 43.)

Writing process The series of stages, or steps, that a writer goes through to develop ideas and to communicate them clearly in a piece of writing. (See pages 6 and 21.)

Glossary

This glossary is a short dictionary of words found in the professional writing models in this textbook. The words are defined according to their meanings in the context of the writing models.

Pronunciation Key

Symbol	Key Words	Symbol	Key Words
a	asp, fat, parrot	b	bed, fable, dub, ebb
ā	ape, date, play, break, fail	d	dip, beadle, had, dodder
ä	ah, car, father, cot	f	fall, after, off, phone
e	elf, ten, berry	g	get, haggle, dog
ē	even, meet, money, flea, grieve	h	he, ahead, hotel
		j	joy, agile, badge
i	is, hit, mirror	k	kill, tackle, bake, coat, quick
ī	ice, bite, high, sky	l	let, yellow, ball
ō	open, tone, go, boat	m	met, camel, trim, summer
ô	all, horn, law, oar	n	not, flannel, ton
oo	look, pull, moor, wolf	p	put, apple, tap
ōo	ooze, tool, crew, rule	r	red, port, dear, purr
yōo	use, cute, few	s	sell, castle, pass, nice
yoo	cure, globule	t	top, cattle, hat
oi	oil, point, toy	v	vat, hovel, have
ou	out, crowd, plow	w	will, always, swear, quick
u	up, cut, color, flood	y	yet, onion, yard
ʉr	urn, fur, deter, irk	z	zebra, dazzle, haze, rise
ə	a in ago	ch	chin, catcher, arch, nature
	e in agent	sh	she, cushion, dash, machine
	i in sanity	th	thin, nothing, truth
	o in comply	*th*	then, father, lathe
	u in focus	zh	azure, leisure, beige
ər	perhaps, murder	ŋ	ring, anger, drink

Abbreviation Key

adj.	adjective	*vi.*	intransitive verb
adv.	adverb	*vt.*	transitive verb
n.	noun		

A

a • cute [ə kyōōt'] *adj.* Sharp and quick.

an • nals [an'əlz] *n.* A written history in chronological order.

an • tiq • ui • ty [an tik'wə tē] *n.* The condition of being very old.

ar • ti • fice [ärt'ə fis] *n.* Craft.

B

bluff [bluf] *n.* A high, steep cliff.

bois • ter • ous [boi'tər əs] *adj.* Loud and lively.

C

cir • cum • vent [sur'kəm vent'] *vt.* To get the better of someone by cleverness.

com • pli • ance [kəm plī'əns] *n.* Giving in to a request.

crass [kras] *adj.* Extremely stupid.

D

dec • o • rous [dek'ə rəs] *adj.* Proper.

de • lin • e • ate [di lin' ē āt'] *vt.* To describe in words.

de • rail [dē rāl'] *vt.* To cause to go off course.

Di • vine Prov • i • dence [də vīn'präv' ə dəns] *n.* Guidance from God.

E

en • deav • or [en dev'ər] *n.* A serious effort.

en • dow • ment [en dou'mənt] *n.* Talent.

es • chew [es chōō'] *vt.* To avoid.

F

fa • ce • tious • ly [fə sē' shəs lē] *adv.* Jokingly.

fan • cy [fan' sē] *vt.* To form an idea.

G

grave • ly [grāv' lē] *adv.* Seriously.

H

his • tri • on • ic [his'trē än'ik] *adj.* Overly dramatic.

I

id • i • o • syn • cra • sy [id'ē ō sin' krə sē] *n.* A peculiarity.

im • pe • cu • ni • ous [im'pi kyōō' ne əs] *adj.* Poor.

in • ces • sant [in ses' ənt] *adj.* Seemingly endless.

in • cur • sion [in kur'zhən] *n.* A raid.

M

mal • a • dy [mal'ə dē] *n.* A disease.

mar • tial [mär'shəl] *adj.* Having to do with war.

min • strel [min'strəl] *n.* A performer of the mid-1800s who blackened his face and sang and told jokes.

moor [mōōr] *vt.* To hold in place with ropes or cables.

N

no • mad • ic [nō mad'ik] *adj.* Having no permanent home; moving constantly.

oc • tave [äk′tiv] *n.* Seven tones above or below any given tone on the music scale.

Om • nip • o • tence [äm nip′ə təns] *n.* God.

pen • du • lous [pen′dyoo ləs] *adj.* Hanging and swinging freely.

per • func • to • ri • ly [pər funk′tə rə lē] *adv.* Done out of routine.

per • il [per′əl] *n.* Danger.

plau • si • bly [plô′zə blē] *adv.* In a seemingly true manner.

pneu • mat • ic drill [noo mat′ik dril] *n.* A hole-boring device operated by compressed air.

pri • mal [prī′məl] *adj.* Original.

pro • di • gious [prō dij′ əs] *adj.* Enormous.

rasp [rasp] *vt.* To scrape.

ring • er [rin′ər] *n.* A person substituted for another in a competition.

ru • di • ment [roo′də mənt] *n.* The basic principles of a subject.

scur • vy [skur′vē] *n.* A disease caused by a lack of vitamin C resulting in weakness and bleeding gums.

sheep dip [shēp′ dip′] *n.* A chemical mixture to rid sheep of insects.

slov • en • li • ness [sluv′ən lē nes] *n.* Untidiness.

stand • pipe [stand′pīp′] *n.* A cylinder for storing water supply.

sub • sist • ence [səb sis′təns] *n.* That which provides essential support such as food.

suf • fice [sə fīs′] *vi.* To be good enough.

sur • plus • age [sur′plus′ij] *n.* Unnecessary words.

syn • chro • nize [sin′krə nīz] *vt.* To make to agree in time.

thrum [thrum] *n.* A drumming sound.

tu • to • ri • al [too tôr′ē əl] *adj.* Of or about individualized teaching, especially for helping students overcome learning problems.

ven • er • a • ble [ven′ər ə bəl] *adj.* Honorable because of age.

vi • car • i • ous [vī ker′ē əs] *adj.* Feeling as if one is taking part in something that is actually happening to someone else.

waft [wäft] *vi.* To float.

wane [wān] *vi.* To decrease in amount.

wist • ful [wist′fəl] *adj.* Longing.

Index

F

INDEX

R

W

Acknowledgments

For permission to reprint copyrighted material, grateful acknowledgment is made to the following sources:

Andrews and McMeel, a Universal Press Syndicate Company: From "Star Wars" from *Roger Ebert's Movie Home Companion 1988 Edition* by Roger Ebert. Copyright © 1988 by Roger Ebert. From *The Far Side Gallery* by Gary Larson. Copyright © 1985 by Uiversal Press Syndicate.

Isaac Asimov: "Learning Science" from *The Tyrannosaurus Prescription and 100 Other Essays* by Isaac Asimov. Copyright © 1981 by American Chemical Society.

Atheneum Publishers: From "Beware: Do Not Read This Poem" from *New and Collected Poems* by Ishmael Reed. Copyright © 1968, 1970 by Ishmael Reed.

Augsburg Fortress: From "It's Up to You" from *Straight from the Heart* by Jesse Jackson. Copyright © 1987 by Jesse Jackson.

Bantam Books, a division of Bantam Doubleday Dell Publishing Group, Inc.: From *Yeager: An Autobiography* by General Chuck Yeager and Leo Janos. Copyright © 1985 by Yeager, Inc.

Barron's Educational Series, Inc.: From *The Black Almanac* by Alton Hornsby. Copyright © 1977 by Alton Hornsby.

Beacon Press: From *Thousand Pieces of Gold* by Ruthanne Lum McCunn. Copyright © 1981 by Ruthanne Lum McCunn.

BOA Editions, Ltd., 92 Park Ave., Brockport, NY 14420: "the thirty eighth year" (Retitled: "An Ordinary Woman") from *good woman: poems and a memoir 1969–1980* by Lucille Clifton. Copyright © 1987 by Lucille Clifton.

Georges Borchardt, Inc.: From "Introduction" by John Lahr from *Baby, That Was Rock and Roll* by Robert Palmer. Copyright © 1978 by John Lahr.

The Boston Globe: From "Lax regulation, inadequate laws promote insider-lending abuse" by Mitchell Zuckoff from *The Boston Globe,* vol. 240, no. 68, September 6, 1991. Copyright © 1991 by *The Boston Globe.*

Brandt & Brandt Literary Agency, Inc.: From "You Are Now Entering the Human Heart" by Janet Frame from *The New Yorker.* Copyright © 1969 by The New Yorker Magazine, Inc. From "The Land and the Water" from *The Wind Shifting West* by Shirley Ann Grau. Copyright © 1973 by Shirley Ann Grau.

Clarion Books, an imprint of Houghton Mifflin Company: From *From Top Hats to Baseball Caps, From Bustles to Blue Jeans* by Lila Perl. Text copyright © 1990 by Lila Perl. All rights reserved.

Don Congdon Associates, Inc.: From "The Toynbee Convector" from *The Toynbee Convector* by Ray Bradbury. Copyright © 1988 by Ray Bradbury.

The Crossroad/Continuum Publishing Group: From "The Sixth Sally" from *The Cyberiad: Fables for the Cybernetic Age* by Stanislaw Lem, translated from the Polish by Michael Kandel. Copyright © 1974 by The Seabury Press, Inc.

Darhansoff & Verrill Agency: From "The World in Its Extreme" by William Langewiesche from *The Atlantic,* vol. 268, no. 5, November 1991. Copyright © by William Langewiesche.

Delacorte Press/Seymour Lawrence, a division of Bantam Doubleday Dell Publishing Group, Inc.: From "Tom Edison's Shaggy Dog" from *Welcome to the Monkey House* by Kurt Vonnegut, Jr. Copyright © 1953 by Kurt Vonnegut, Jr. Originally published in *Colliers.*

Doubleday, a division of Bantam Double-day Dell Publishing Group, Inc.: From "Dogs that have known me" from *Please don't eat the daisies* by Jean Kerr. Copyright © 1957 by Jean Kerr. "Once Is Not Enough" from *Magic in the Movies: The Story of Special Effects* by Jane O'Connor and Katy Hall. Copyright © 1980 by Jane O'Connor. From "Animal Senses" from *The Living World* by Tony Seddon and Jill Bailey. Copyright © 1986 by BLA Publishing, Ltd.

Ebony Magazine: From "Black, Blue and Gray: The Other Civil War" from *Ebony*, vol. XLVI, no. 4, February 1991. Copyright © 1991 by Johnson Publishing Company, Inc.

Anita Endrezze: "Sunset at Twin Lake" by Anita Endrezze from *Harper's Anthology of 20th Century Native American Poetry*, edited by Duane Niatum.

Farrar, Straus and Giroux, Inc.: From *The Magic Barrel* by Bernard Malamud. Copyright © 1954, 1958 and copyright renewed © 1986 by Bernard Malamud.

The Feminist Press: From "To Da-Duh in Memoriam" from *Reena and Other Stories* by Paule Marshall. Copyright © 1983 by The Feminist Press at The City University of New York.

The Georgia Review: "The Gift" by Louis Dollarhide. Copyright © 1969 by The University of Georgia. First appeared in *The Georgia Review*.

Gibbs Smith Publisher: From "A Flight of Geese" from *The Girl from Cardigan* by Leslie Norris. Copyright © 1988 by Leslie Norris.

Grove Press, Inc.: From "Rhinoceros" from *Rhinoceros and Other Plays* by Eugéne Ionesco, translated by Derek Prouse. Copyright © 1960 by John Calder (Publishers) Ltd.

Harcourt Brace Jovanovich, Inc.: From "The Life You Save May Be Your Own" from *A Good Man Is Hard to Find and Other Stories* by Flannery O'Connor. Copyright 1953 by Flannery O'Connor; copyright renewed © 1981 by Regina O'Connor. From "The Jilting of Granny Weatherall" from *The Flowering Judas and Other Stories* by Katherine Anne Porter. Copyright 1930 and renewed © 1958 by Katherine Anne Porter.

Harmony Books, a Division of Crown Publishers, Inc.: From *Labyrinth: Solving the Riddle of the Maze* by Adrian Fisher & Georg Gerster. Text copyright © 1990 by Adrian Fisher. Compilation copyright © 1990 by Adrian Fisher and Georg Gerster.

HarperCollins Publishers: From *Pilgrim at Tinker Creek* by Annie Dillard. Copyright © 1974 by Annie Dillard. From *Dust Tracks on a Road* by Zora Neale Hurston. Copyright 1942 by Zora Neale Hurston, renewed copyright © 1970 by John C. Hurston. From *Jonah's Gourd Vine* by Zora Neale Hurston. Copyright 1934 by Zora Neale Hurston; copyright renewed © 1962 by John C. Hurston. From "Mirror" from *The Collected Poems of Sylvia Plath*, edited by Ted Hughes. Copyright © 1963 by Ted Hughes. From *Seven Arrows* by Hyemeyohsts Storm. Copyright © 1972 by Hyemeyohsts Storm. From *American Hunger* by Richard Wright. Copyright 1944 by Richard Wright; copyright renewed © 1977 by Ellen Wright.

Harvard University Press and the Trustees of Amherst College: From "A Narrow Fellow in the Grass" from *The Poems of Emily Dickinson*, edited by Thomas H. Johnson. Copyright 1951, © 1955, 1979, 1983 by the President and Fellows of Harvard College. Published by the Belknap Press of Harvard University Press, Cambridge, MA.

Hendrick-Long Publishing Company: From *Dinosaur Days in Texas* by Tom and Jane D. Allen with Savannah Waring Walker. Copyright © 1989 by Hendrick-Long Publishing Company, Dallas, TX.

Hill and Wang, a division of Farrar, Straus and Giroux, Inc.: From *I Wonder As I Wander* by Langston Hughes. Copyright © 1956 by Langston Hughes. From *What's That Pig Outdoors? A Memoir of Deafness* by Henry Kisor. Copyright © 1990 by Henry Kisor.

The New York Review of Books: From "In Sorrow's Kitchen" by Zora Neale Hurston from *The New York Review of Books*, vol. XXV, no. 20, December 21, 1978. Copyright © 1978 by Nyrev, Inc.

The New York Times Company: Quote by Doris Lessing from *The New York Times*, April 22, 1984. Copyright © 1984 by The New York Times Company. From "On rewriting" by Richard Selzer from *The New York Times*, September 28, 1979. Copyright © 1979 by The New York Times Company. From a review of *Their Eyes Were Watching God* by Zora Neale Hurston from "Books of the Times" by Ralph Thompson from *The New York Times*, October 6, 1937. Copyright 1937 by The New York Times Company. From "Típica Sound of Cuba" by Peter Watrous from *The New York Times*, February 28, 1991. Copyright © 1991 by The New York Times Company.

The New Yorker Magazine, Inc.: From "Notes and Comment" from "The Talk of the Town" from *The New Yorker*, July 15, 1991. Copyright © 1991 by The New Yorker Magazine, Inc. From "Blue Spruce" by David Long from *The New Yorker*, November 12, 1990. Copyright © 1990 by David Long.

Newsweek, Inc.: From "Dances with Garbage" by Mary Hager, Bill Harlan, Michael Mason, and Andrew Murr from *Newsweek*, vol. CXVII, no. 17, p. 36, April 29, 1991. Copyright © 1991 by Newsweek, Inc. All rights reserved. From "The Last Days of Eden" by Spencer Reiss from *Newsweek*, vol. CXVI, no. 23, p. 48, December 3, 1990. Copyright © 1990 by Newsweek, Inc. All rights reserved.

W. W. Norton & Company, Inc.: From "The Making of a Scientist" from *"What do YOU Care What Other People Think?": Further Adventures of a Curious Character* by Richard P. Feynman, as told to Ralph Leighton. Copyright © 1988 by Gweneth Feynman and Ralph Leighton.

Pantheon Books, a division of Random House, Inc.: From "The Moustache" from *Eight Plus One* by Robert Cormier. Copyright © 1975 by Robert Cormier.

Pocket Books, a division of Simon and Schuster, Inc.: From *Life, The Universe and Everything* by Douglas Adams. Copyright © 1982 by Douglas Adams.

Eliot Porter Estate and Life Magazine: From "Eliot Porter" from *Life*, November 1990.

Publishers Weekly: Quote by Gloria Steinem from *Publishers Weekly*, August 12, 1983. Copyright © 1983 by Publishers Weekly.

The Putnam Publishing Group: From "Rules of the Game" from *The Joy Luck Club* by Amy Tan. Copyright © 1989 by Amy Tan. From the back cover from *Riding the Iron Rooster: By Train Through China* by Paul Theroux. Copyright © 1988 by Cape Cod Scriveners Co.

Random House, Inc.: From "Graduation" from *I Know Why the Caged Bird Sings* by Maya Angelou. Copyright © 1969 by Maya Angelou. From "Making Time Portable" from *The Discoverers* by Daniel Boorstin. Copyright © 1983 by Daniel Boorstin. From *A Raisin in the Sun* by Lorraine Hansberry. Copyright © 1958 by Robert Nemiroff, as an unpublished work. Copyright © 1959, 1966, 1984 by Robert Nemiroff. From "New African" from *Sarah Phillips* by Andrea Lee. Copyright © 1983 by Andrea Lee. From "The Wheelbarraow" from *Selected Stories* by V.S. Pritchett. Copyright © 1978 by V. S. Pritchett.

St. Martin's Press, Inc.: "Wheelchair Hell: A Look at Campus Accessibility" from *The Great American Bologna Festival and other student essays* by Elizabeth Rankin. Copyright © 1991 by St. Martin's Press, Inc.

Michael Schumacher: From "Jay McInerney" by Michael Schumacher. Copyright © 1984 by Michael Schumacher.

Charles Scribner's Sons, an imprint of Macmillan Publishing Company: From "In Another Country" from *Men Without Women* by Ernest Hemingway. Copyright 1927 by Charles Scribner's Sons; copyright renewed © 1955 by Ernest Hemingway. From "Becoming a Writer" from *Kaffir Boy in America: An Encounter with Apartheid* by Mark Mathabane. Copyright © 1989 by Mark Mathabane.

Argelia L. L. de Sedillo: From "Gentleman of Rio en Medio: from *We Are Chicanos* by Juan A. A. Sedillo, edited by Philip D. Ortego.

Simon & Schuster, Inc.: From "Visual Displays" from *The Birder's Handbook* by Paul R. Ehrlich, David S. Dobkin, and Darryl Wheye. Copyright © 1988 by Paul R. Ehrlich, David S. Dobkin, and Darryl Wheye. From "Insert Flap 'A' and Throw Away" from *The Most of S. J. Perelman* by S. J. Perelman. Copyright © 1930, 1931, 1932, 1933, 1935, 1936, 1953, 1955, 1956, 1958 by S. J. Perelman; copyright renewed © 1986 by Adam and Abby Perelman.

Smithsonian Institution: "The engaging habits of chameleons suggest mirth more than menace" (Retitled: "Chameleon Comedians") by James Martin from *Smithsonian*, Vol. 21, No. 3, June 1990. Copyright © 1990 by Smithsonian Institution.

The Society of Authors as representative of the Literary Trustees of Walter de la Mare: From "Sam" by Walter de la Mare.

Gary Soto: From "The Jacket" from *Small Faces* by Gary Soto. Copyright © 1986 by Gary Soto.

Mario Suárez: From "Tuscon, Arizona: El Hoyo" by Mario Suárez from *Aztlán: An Anthology of Mexican American Literature*, edited by Luis Valdez and Stan Steiner. Published by Alfred A. Knopf, Inc., 1972.

Universe Publishing: From "An Indian's View of Indian Affairs" by Chief Joseph from *Red & White: Indian Views of the White Man, 1492–1982* by Annette Rosenstiel. Copyright © 1983 by Annette Rosenstiel.

University of Illinois Press: From *Zora Neale Hurston: A Literary Biography* by Robert E. Hemenway. Copyright © 1977 by the Board of Trustees of the University of Illinois.

The University of New Mexico Press: From "The Way to Rainy Mountain" from *The Way to Rainy Mountain* by N. Scott Momaday. Copyright © 1969 by The University of New Mexico Press. Originally published in *The Reporter*, January 26, 1967. From "My Wonder Horse" from *Tierra Amarilla: Stories of New Mexico* by Sabine Ulibarrí. Copyright © 1971 by The University of New Mexico Press.

University of Notre Dame Press: From *Barrio Boy* by Ernesto Galarza. Copyright © 1971 by University of Notre Dame Press.

University Press of New England: From "Leisure" from *The Complete Poems of W. H., Davies.* Copyright © 1963 by Jonathan Cape Limited.

USA Today: "Wyoming dinosaur find may be a fossil first" by Linda Kanamine from *USA Today*, September 26, 1991, p. 3A. Copyright © 1991 by *USA Today*.

Viking Penguin, a division of Penguin Books USA Inc.: From "Pencils" from *Reading The Numbers* by Mary Blocksma. Copyright © 1989 by Mary Blocksma. From *The Floating World* by Cynthia Kadohata. Copyright © 1989 by Cynthia Kadohata. From "From Japlish to Franglais" from *The Story of English* by Robert McCrum, William Cran, and Robert MacNeil. Copyright © 1986 by Robert McCrum, William Cran, and Robert MacNeil. "One Perfect Rose" from *The Portable Dorothy Parker*, Introduction by Brendan Gill. Copyright 1928 and copyright renewed © 1956 by Dorothy Parker. From pp. 63–64 (selection by Mike Montgomery) from *It Was a Dark and Stormy Night: The Best (?) from the Bulwer-Lytton Contest*, edited by Scott Rice. Copyright © 1984 by Scott Rice. From "Flight" from *The*

Long Valley by John Steinbeck. Copyright 1938 and copyright renewed © 1966 by John Steinbeck. From *The Red Pony* by John Steinbeck. Copyright 1933, 1937, 1938 and copyright renewed © 1961, 1965, 1966 by John Steinbeck. From an Interview with E. B. White from *Writers at Work: The Paris Review Interviews*, Eighth Series, edited by George Plimpton, Introduction by Joyce Carol Oates.

José Garcia Villa: From "Be Beautiful, Noble, like the Antique Ant" from *Have Come, Am Here* by José Garcia Villa. Copyright 1941, 1942, © 1970 by José Garcia Villa.

Wallace Literary Agency, Inc.: From "On the Mall" from *The White Album* by Joan Didion. Copyright © 1979 by Joan Didion.

Webster's New World Dictionaries, a Division of Simon & Schuster, New York: From the entry "obscure" from *Webster's New World Dictionary, Third College Edition.* Copyright © 1988 by Simon & Schuster, Inc.

Vicki Williams: From "Keep 'The Star Spangled Banner'" by Vicki Williams from *USA Today*, August 1, 1990, p. 10A. Copyright © 1990 by Vicki Williams.

The H. W. Wilson Company: Entries from "Moisturizers" through "Moldings (Architecture)" from *Readers' Guide to Periodical Literature*, 1990. Copyright © 1990, 1991 by The H. W. Wilson Company.

Workman Publishing Company, Inc.: From "Three Great Homemade Props" from "Get Ready" from *Be A Clown!* by Turk Pipkin. Copyright © 1989 by Turk Pipkin.

PHOTO CREDITS

CHAPTER 5: Page 162, Costa Manos/Magnum; 164(l), Orion/Shooting Star; 164(tr), Shooting Star; 164(br), Shooting Star; 165, HRW Photo by Lisa Davis; 168(l), Allen Russell/ProFiles West; 168(r), Michael J. Howell/ProFiles West; 173, Stuart N. Dee/The Image Bank; 175, R. Llewellyn/SuperStock; 183, 185, 186, Del Valle High School, Del Valle, Texas/HRW Photo by Michelle Bridwell; 192, HRW Photo by Michelle Bridwell; 193, Melanie Carr/Zephyr Pictures; 194, UPI/Bettmann Newsphotos; 196, Nawrocki Stock Photo; 200, The Stock Market; 202(l), HRW Photo Research Library; 202(tc), Everett Collection Inc.; 202(bc), Hackett/Archive Photos; 202(r), Frederick Hill Meserve, Litt D./HRW Photo Research Library.

CHAPTER 6: Page 208, © Robert Foothorap; 211(l), The Bettmann Archive; 211(r), The Bettmann Archive; 212(l), Doc Pele/Stills/Retna Ltd.,; 212(c), SuperStock; 212(r), D. Strohmeyer/Allsport; 215(t), Richard Steedman/The Stock Market; 215(b), Mauritius/SuperStock; 217(l), The Bettmann Archive; 217(r), The Bettmann Archive; 219, Farrar, Straus & Girous, Inc./© John H. White; 221, Jane Brown/Camela Press/Globe Photos; 223(t), Peter Vadnai/The Stock Market; 223(c), Michael Kevin Daly/The Stock Market; 223(cr), Michael Kevin Daly/The Stock Market; 223(b), R. Llewellyn/SuperStock; 225, The Bettmann Archive; 230, Culver Pictures, Inc.; 235, Anthony Edgeworth/The Stock Market; 236(l), P. Barry Levy/ProFiles West; 236(r), Myrleen Ferguson/PhotoEdit; 239(t), Runk/Schoenberger/Grant Heilman Photography; 239(c), 239(b), Custom Medical Stock Photo.

CHAPTER 7: Page 242, UPI/Bettmann; 243(tl), FPG International; 243(c), 243(tr), 243(bl),243(br), UPI/Bettmann; 244, Gary Gershoff/Retna Ltd; 245, Courtesy of Charles Scribner's Sons/MacMillian Publishing Company; 247, Richard Hutchins/InfoEdit; 248, P. Rivera/SuperStock; 253(l), 253(r), HRW Photo by Michelle Bridwell; 254, Zig Leszczynski/Animals, Animals; 259(l), 259(r), Sears & Roebuck Catalogue, 1897 Reprint/HRW Photo By Michelle Bridwell; 261, Alan Oddie/PhotoEdit; 264(l), C. Dallas/SuperStock; 264(r), Chris Jones/The Stock Market; 269, Bob Daemmrich Photography; 271, Everett Collection.

CHAPTER 8: Page 279, Culver Pictures, Inc.; 285(l), H. Alexander/SuperStock; 285(r), Freda Leinwand; 287(r), Joe Sohn/Chronosohn/The Stock Market; 287(l), Barbara Kirk/The Stock Market; 289(l), P. Barry Levy/ProFiles West; 289(cl), Tony Freeman/PhotoEdit; 289(cr), Allen Russell/ProFiles West; 289(r), Tony Freeman/PhotoEdit; 295, George Rose/Gamma Liaison Network; 297, R. King/SuperStock; 299(l), 299(r), HRW Photo by Lisa Davis; 303, The Granger Collection, New York; 304, The Stock Market; 308, Anderson High School/HRW Photo By Michelle Bridwell; 309, HRW Photo by Lisa Davis; 310, Mary Kate Denny/PhotoEdit; 312, Thomas Craig/FPG International.

CHAPTER 9: Page 325(l), © Melanie Carr/Zephyr Pictures; 325(r), HRW Photo by Michelle Bridwell; 326, HRW photo by Michelle Bridwell; 328(l), Rainer Drexel/Bildererg/The Stock Market; 328(r), Bill Strode/Woodfin Camp; 336, HRW Photo by Michael Lyon; 337, David R. Frazier Photolibrary; 339, © Mary Kate Denny/PhotoEdit; 341, M. Richards/PhotoEdit; 343(l), HRW Photo by Michael Lyon; 343(r), HRW Photo By Michael Lyon; 345, Richard Hutchins/Info Edit; 351, Steve Dunwell/The Image Bank; 352, HRW Photo by Michelle Bridwell; 355, 356, The Stock Market; 357, Jim Wright/Zephyr Pictures.

CHAPTER 10: Page 362, The Bettmann Archive; 365, The Bettmann Archive; 370, UPI/Bettmann Photos; 377, The Stock Market; 379, Courtesy of St. Mary's College; 382, PhotoEdit; 385, David R. Frazier Photolibrary; 387, T. Rosenthal/SuperStock; 389(t), HRW Photo By Lisa Davis; 389(b), © Todd Powell/ProFiles West; 396(l), Archive Photos; 396(r), Everett Collection; 398, Schuster/SuperStock; 400, Reprinted by permission of The Putnam Publishing Group from RIDING THE IRON ROOSTER by Paul Theroux Copyright ©1988 by Cape Cod Scriveners Company.

CHAPTER 11: Page 404, The Bettmann Archive; 410, James Weldon Johnson Collection/Yale Collection of American Literature, Beinecke Rare Book & Manuscript Library, Yale University/Courtesy of the Estate of Carl Van Vechten, Joseph Solomon, Executor; 417, David R. Frazier Photolibray; 421, Photographed by Eric Beggs; 423, H. Kanus/SuperStock; 425, The Stock Market; 426(l), James Weldon Johnson Collection/Yale Collection of American Literature, Beinecke Rare Book & Manuscript Library, Yale University/Courtesy of the Estate of Carl Van Vechten, Joseph Solomon, Executor; 426(c), UPI/Bettmann; 426(r), The Bettmann Archive; 427, © George Gerster/© 1989 Comstock, Inc.; 436(l), David R. Frazier Photolibrary; 436(r), David R. Frazier Photolibrary; 438, Archive Photos; 451, © Spencer Grant/New England Stock Photo; 453 (l), 453(r), Photographed by Eric Beggs; 455(t), David Young-Wolff/PhotoEdit; 455(bl), Deborah Davis/PhotoEdit; 455(br), R. Llewellyn/SuperStock; 458, T. Algire/SuperStock; 459, UPI/Bettmann.

CHAPTER 12: Page 463, Charlene Smith/ProFiles West; 477(l), 477(r), ©Mavournea Hay/Michelle Bridwell Photography.

CHAPTER 13: Page 482, HRW Photo By Michelle Bridwell.

CHAPTER 14: Page 504, James Newberry; 509, Archive Photos; 511(l), HRW Photo by © Stan Byers; 511(r), Keystone View Co./Courtesy Museum of New Mexico; 512, HRW Photo by Lisa Davis; 514(l), David Madison/Bruce Coleman; 514(r), Archive Photos; 517(l), Bettmann Archive; 517(c), FPG International; 517(r), Culver Pictures; 520(l), The Bettmann Archive.

CHAPTER 15: Page 528, Patrick Aventurier/ Gamma Liaison; 530, John White/HRW Photo Research Library; 533, Paul Steel/The Stock Market; 534, Nathan Benn/Woodfin Camp Associates; 539, Paul S. Howell/Gamma Liaison.

CHAPTER 16: Page 541, Hillel Burger/Peabody Museum of Archaeology and Ethnology; 546, Camermann International, Ltd; 549, HRW Photo by Lisa Davis.

CHAPTER 17: Page 571, Dan Bosler/Tony Stone Worldwide/Chicago Ltd.; 573(tl), Mel Gigiacomo/The Image Bank; 573(tr), Paul J. Sutton/ Duomo; 573(bl), Harry J. Landon/Shooting Star; 573(br), Archive Photos; 578, James Valentine.

CHAPTER 18: Page 583, The Bettmann Archive; 597, Jon Reis/The Stock Market; 599, Phil Schofield/AllStock.

CHAPTER 19: Page 606(l), 606(r), © B. Lyon / Valan Photos; 606(c), © Albert Kuhnigk/Valan Photos; 610, HRW Photo By Joe Jaworski; 623(c), Copyright 1991, Comstock; 623(bl), Robbi Newman/The Image Bank; 623(bc), © Franklin Viola/ Copyright 1991, Comstock; 623(br), Martha Stradiotto/The Image Bank; 623(tl), Copr. William W. Bacon, III/Allstock; 623(tr), © Kelvin Aitken/Peter Arnold, Inc.

CHAPTER 20: Page 630(tc), 630(tr), 630(bc), Congdon Egg Farm, Lockhart, Texas/Lisa Davis; 630(tl), 630(br), J.C. Allen & Son, Inc.; 633, 633(inset), Colha Pre Classic Project/Courtesy of Dr. Tom Hester, Texas Archeological Research Laboratory. The University of Texas at Austin; 636(l), © Lee Watson/Unicorn Stock Photos; 636(r), Jack S. Grove/PhotoEdit.

CHAPTER 21: Page 663, Wide World Photos; 669(t), Photographs by Zheng Zhensun copyright © 1991/Copyright © 1991 Byron Preiss Visual Publications, Inc. & New China Pictures Company/All rights Reserved. Published by Scholastic Inc.

CHAPTER 22: Page 678, Charles L. Blockson/ Afro American Collection, Sullivan Hall, Temple University, Philadelphia, PA; 682(l), 682(c), 682(r), Vicki Ragan; 685, HRW Photo by Michelle Bridwell.

CHAPTER 23: Page 705(t), 705(b), Courtesy of Martin Luther King Civil Rights Memorial /Photograph by Paul Roberton.; 710, Everett Collection, Inc.

CHAPTER 24: Page 724, Carol Friedman/Maya Panvell, Courtesy Sony Classical Records; 728, Terence Meaden/Sipa Press; 730, Colorado Historical Society; 759(l), 759(c), 759(r), African American Cultural Center, Los Angeles, CA.

CHAPTER 25: Page 766(t), 766 (b), Jerry Jacka Photography; 769, © Bob Daemmrich Photography; 777, A. Hyde Jr. /SuperStock.

CHAPTER 26: Page 784(l), Stephane Compoint/ Sygma.784(c), S. Franklin/Magnum; 784(r), Louise Gubb/JB Pictures; 787, Ron Watts/Westlight.

CHAPTER 27: Page 800(l), 800 (r), Gene Stein/ Westlight; 802(r), Paul J. Sutton/Duomo; 802(l), Daniel R. Westergren/© National Geographic Society; 806(l), 806(c), 806(r), Paul Rocheleau Photographer; 810, Michael Newman/PhotoEdit.

CHAPTER 28: Page 824, Seaver Center for Western History Research, Natural History Museum of Los Angeles County; 829, © Jason Laure, 1980.

CHAPTER 29: Page 850, Copyright © Christian Vioujard/Gamma Liaison.

CHAPTER 30: Page 869, Courtesy Will Rogers Memorial Archives; 871(l), HRW Photo Research Library; 871(r), Culver Pictures, Inc.; 874, R. Llewellyn/SuperStock; 882, Kolvoord/TexaStock; 895, Mark Hess/The Image Bank.

CHAPTER 31: Page 908(l), The Granger Collection, New York; 908(c), 908(r), Culver Pictures, Inc.; 914, Custom Medical Stock Photo; 926, Larry Dale Gordon/The Image Bank.

ILLUSTRATION CREDITS

Linda Blackwell—154, 227, 320, 323, 334, 367, 384, 441, 449, 534

Keith Bowden—475

Stephen Brayfield—xix, 84, 281, 520, 528, 530, 544, 834

Neesa Becker—375, 394

Rondi Collette—594, 829, 888

Chris Ellison—177, 178, 180

Richard Erickson—55, 263, 275, 466, 540

Janice Fried—798

Tom Gianni—xxxii, 44, 113, 146, 148, 153, 230, 509, 606, 777, 869, 882

Tom Herzberg—276–277

Mary Jones—315, 316, 470, 487

Linda Kelen—xvii, 25, 191, 464, 468, 494, 500, 846

Susan Kemnitz—145, 155, 156

Rich Lo—xx, 42, 115, 355, 423, 438, 472, 479, 501, 512, 521, 549, 844, 911

Yoshi Miyake—xxiii, 533, 588

Pamela Paulsrud—313, 408

Precision Graphics—471, 535, 825, 926

Doug Schneider—105, 119, 137, 360, 506, 546, 571, 597, 661, 678, 730

Jack Scott—165, 357

Steve Shock—206, 207, 208, 237, 257, 258, 405, 406

Chuck Solway—226

Troy Thomas—160–161, 162, 320–321

Nancy Tucker—483